THE LIBERAL ARTS COLLEGE

BASED UPON SURVEYS OF THIRTY-FIVE COLLEGES RELATED TO THE METHODIST EPISCOPAL CHURCH

FLOYD W. REEVES
JOHN DALE RUSSELL
H. C. GREGG
A. J. BRUMBAUGH
L. E. BLAUCH

39-215

THE UNIVERSITY OF CHICAGO PRESS
CHICAGO · ILLINOIS

FOREWORD

At the meeting of the Educational Association of the Methodist Episcopal Church—a voluntary organization of school and college presidents—in January, 1927, a paper was read suggesting the need for scientific study of the member institutions. After an extended discussion a representative committee was created and the matter canvassed carefully. The following year there was a unanimous vote on the report of this committee, memorializing the General Conference of the Methodist Episcopal Church to order a survey of all the educational institutions related to the Church. Acting upon this request, the General Conference of 1928 ordered that such a survey be made, and directed the Board of Education to appoint one or more commissions to take charge of the organization of the survey. In the Conference resolution the following purposes of the survey were cited:

"*First.*—To furnish the bases to determine the nature and quality of the service rendered the cause of Christian Education by our Educational Institutions, to appraise their work and suggest improvement of it, to co-operate in formulating a constructive, statesmanlike policy for them, to inform the Church so that it may be inspired to increased confidence and more generous support.

"*Second.*—The findings of the Commission are to be taken into consideration by the Board of Education in making their annual appropriations, and utilized by the institutions as they solicit support."

Pursuant to this order the Board of Education appointed the following Commission on Survey:

THOMAS NICHOLSON, Bishop of the Methodist Episcopal Church
ARLO AYRES BROWN, President of Drew University
FREDERICK C. EISELEN, President of Garrett Biblical Institute
CHARLES H. JUDD, Dean of the School of Education of the University of Chicago
RAYMOND A. KENT, then Dean of the College of Liberal Arts, Northwestern University, now President of the University of Louisville
FRANK E. MOSSMAN, then President of Morningside College, now President of Southwestern College
RALPH E. PECK, Headmaster of Wilbraham Academy
JOHN L. SEATON, President of Albion College

v

Ex-officio:

THE BOARD OF EDUCATION OF THE METHODIST EPISCOPAL CHURCH
WILLIAM S. BOVARD, Corresponding Secretary
JOSEPH P. MACMILLAN, Assistant Secretary, Division of Educational
    Institutions

The Commission met March 27, 1929, and elected the following officers:
THOMAS NICHOLSON, Chairman
JOHN L. SEATON, Vice-Chairman
JOSEPH P. MACMILLAN, Secretary

At the same meeting the general objectives of the survey were outlined, and Professor Floyd W. Reeves was selected to direct it.

The organization of the survey program for the four-year colleges was undertaken early in the autumn of 1929. A meeting of the Commission on Survey on October 3 considered the detailed plans and gave approval to the general outline as presented by the director of the survey.

The Commission on Survey authorized the appointment of the following persons as members of the staff for the survey of the four-year colleges: Floyd W. Reeves, director of the survey, professor of education at the University of Chicago; John Dale Russell, assistant director of the survey, associate professor of education at the University of Kentucky; H. C. Gregg, business manager at Albion College; A. J. Brumbaugh, dean of students in the College and assistant professor of education at the University of Chicago; and L. E. Blauch, professor of education at the North Carolina College for Women. Since the completion of the survey, Mr. Russell has become associate professor of education at the University of Chicago, Mr. Gregg has taken a position on the research staff of the Committee on the Revision of Standards of the Commission on Higher Institutions of the North Central Association of Colleges and Secondary Schools, and Mr. Blauch has become executive secretary of the National Survey of Dental Education.

In studying the libraries of the colleges surveyed, the staff had the assistance of Professor William M. Randall of the Graduate Library School of the University of Chicago. Mr. Randall was engaged during the period of the survey in making a series of inspections of college libraries for the Carnegie Corporation, and was able to combine visits for this purpose with an inspection for the purposes of the survey program in a number of the colleges. In addition to making the actual survey of the libraries in several of the colleges, Mr. Randall assisted in drawing up the schedule form for obtaining data concerning the college libraries; he has also read and criticized the sections of this report (chaps. xv, xvi, xvii, and xviii) that deal with library problems.

The survey staff also had the assistance of Professor Jordan Cavan of Rockford College in analyzing problems of the students' relations to the finances of the colleges studied. Mr. Cavan personally collected data regarding tuition fees, scholarships, loan funds, student employment, etc., in a few of the colleges surveyed; he also prepared many of the tabulations used in chapters lxv–lxxi of this report.

The survey, on which this study is based, included thirty-five colleges, all of which at the time of the visit were offering a four-year program of liberal arts work, and all of which recognize an affiliation with the Methodist Episcopal Church. The colleges included in this study, their locations, and the dates of their survey visits are as follows:

Albion College, Albion, Michigan, October, 1930
Allegheny College, Meadville, Pennsylvania, April, 1930
Baker University, Baldwin City, Kansas, January, 1931
Baldwin-Wallace College, Berea, Ohio, October, 1930
Brothers College of Drew University, Madison, New Jersey, March, 1931
Central Wesleyan College, Warrenton, Missouri, May, 1930
University of Chattanooga, Chattanooga, Tennessee, November, 1929
Cornell College, Mount Vernon, Iowa, December, 1929
Dakota Wesleyan University, Mitchell, South Dakota, July, 1930
DePauw University, Greencastle, Indiana, November, 1930
Dickinson College, Carlisle, Pennsylvania, April, 1930
Evansville College, Evansville, Indiana, March, 1930
Gooding College, Gooding, Idaho, February, 1931
Hamline University, St. Paul, Minnesota, October, 1929
Illinois Wesleyan University, Bloomington, Illinois, January, 1931
Intermountain Union College, Helena, Montana, February, 1931
Iowa Wesleyan College, Mount Pleasant, Iowa, December, 1929
Kansas Wesleyan University, Salina, Kansas, December, 1930
Lawrence College, Appleton, Wisconsin, May, 1930
McKendree College, Lebanon, Illinois, December, 1930
MacMurray College, Jacksonville, Illinois, January, 1931
Morningside College, Sioux City, Iowa, December, 1929
Mount Union College, Alliance, Ohio, October, 1930
Nebraska Wesleyan University, Lincoln, Nebraska, December, 1930
Ohio Northern University, Ada, Ohio, October, 1930
Ohio Wesleyan University, Delaware, Ohio, October, 1930
Oklahoma City University, Oklahoma City, Oklahoma, May, 1930
Ozark Wesleyan College, Carthage, Missouri, May, 1930
College of the Pacific, Stockton, California, February, 1931

College of Puget Sound, Tacoma, Washington, February, 1931
Simpson College, Indianola, Iowa, December, 1929
Southwestern College, Winfield, Kansas, December, 1930
Union College, Barbourville, Kentucky, December, 1929
West Virginia Wesleyan College, Buckhannon, West Virginia, March, 1931
Willamette University, Salem, Oregon, February, 1931

In order to conserve space the institutions will usually be referred to throughout this report by a shortened form of their full title, omitting the designation "College" or "University."

The first step in the procedure of the survey was the drawing-up of an outline of the topics to be included and the drafting of a set of schedules for obtaining the data needed.[1] The outline and the schedules were approved by the Commission on Survey at one of its early meetings. The secretary of the Commission then arranged with the colleges for the date of visitation by the survey staff.

In the case of each institution all the data were collected during personal visits by two or more members of the survey staff, and most of the colleges were visited by from three to five men. During these visits the members of the survey staff not only collected personally the data needed, but also held conferences with the officers of administration, the faculty, representative students, and in almost all cases with some members of the board of trustees. In this manner the survey staff was able to gather not only objective facts concerning the college but also subjective impressions of great value in analyzing the situation within each institution. At the time of the visit the members of the staff also gave considerable personal counsel and advice to officers and faculty members regarding possible improvements in the service of the college.

After the visit of the survey staff to a given college, the data collected were set up in tabular form. As far as possible the tables of data were made in comparative form, so that each college might be shown its relative position with reference to the institutions already surveyed. A survey report was then written for the college, dealing in detail with its problems, analyzing its situation, and making specific recommendations for improvement. The president of the college was then asked to read the report in this preliminary form in order to catch any errors of fact and to criticize in general the attitude taken by the survey staff toward

[1] Sets of the schedules used may be obtained in mimeographed form at a price of $1.00 each from The Board of Education of the Methodist Episcopal Church, 740 Rush St., Chicago, Ill.

the problems of his institution. This reading of the preliminary report also served to give those connected with the college a preview of the findings; in many cases a large number of the recommendations made in the report were thus actually put into effect before the official delivery of the survey. In several cases the report was read in preliminary form not only by the president, but by one or more other officers of the college, generally the business manager and the dean. Particularly important in the procedure is the fact that each institution had the opportunity to check all the factual data included in its report before this document was put into final form.

After necessary corrections were made following the reading of the preliminary report by the officers of the institution, the report was read by a committee of the Commission on Survey, a separate committee being created for each college survey. The secretary of the Commission, Dr. MacMillan, also read each report. When the approval of the committee of the Commission was received, the report was typed in final form and released to the college. Approximately half of the colleges requested a mimeographed edition of their reports, in order that sufficient copies might be available for circulation among board members, the officers of the college, and interested faculty members.

This procedure as outlined above was carried through in each of the thirty-five colleges. Subsequent to the completion of these individual surveys this general summary report has been prepared.

This published report is necessarily based on conditions as they were observed at the time of the visit. It should be pointed out that almost all the colleges are making vigorous efforts toward improvement in their academic programs; these efforts in most colleges antedated the inception of the survey. If it had been possible to bring the data down to the date of publishing this report, a large number of the institutions would show a markedly improved condition. In each of the individual survey reports a number of specific recommendations, usually from forty to ninety, were made. In many of the colleges a majority of these recommendations have already been put into effect. Some of the recommendations had even before the survey visit been recognized as desirable by those connected with the college.

The survey staff desires to acknowledge its indebtedness to the many persons and agencies that have co-operated toward the successful completion of the program. Recognition should be given first of all to the boards of trustees, officers of administration, faculty, and students of the colleges surveyed; the co-operation received from these groups was perfect. The collection of the necessary data imposed no inconsiderable burden upon some of the officers in each of the colleges, particularly the presidents, the deans, the registrars, and the business managers, but in every case the task of gathering the data was cheerfully undertaken and all information necessary for the survey was supplied.

The members of the Commission on Survey have given very generously of their time and counsel to the furtherance of this project. The criticisms of this group on the original plans for the survey and on the texts of the reports to the various colleges have been invaluable. Especially valuable have been the criticisms of the secretary of the Commission, Dr. J. P. MacMillan, who gave unsparingly of his time and energy in co-operating with the survey staff. His knowledge of the general problems of American higher education and his intimate acquaintance with the educational policies of the denomination have been of great benefit to the survey. These acknowledgments to the Commission and its secretary should not be construed, however, as an effort by the survey staff to shift the responsibility for its findings. In every case the survey staff considered criticisms strictly on their own merits, and the staff assumes full responsibility for the findings and recommendations in all the survey reports.

The survey staff also acknowledges with appreciation the many courtesies extended by the staff of The Board of Education of the Methodist Episcopal Church. The Board took general charge of all the financial arrangements for the survey, relieving the staff of the burdensome details of accounting, billing, collecting, purchasing, etc.

Finally, recognition should be given to the faithful service of the members of the survey office staff—particularly to Marjorie Carr, who served as office manager and chief file clerk; to Madge Poore, secretary; to Marion Ueberle, editor and proofreader; to Christian Miller and Ed Wight, statistical assistants.

The program of survey has been carried out with the benefit to the colleges included as the primary concern. At the same time the survey staff has had clearly in mind the possible benefits to higher education in general of an intensive survey of a large group of colleges distributed throughout the United States. The group of institutions included constitutes a fairly representative cross-section of American higher education in four-year colleges. In the preparation of this volume there has been the attempt to generalize the findings obtained from the program of surveys, as far as the number of institutions included makes possible, so as to be of interest and profit to all colleges of liberal arts. For that reason the book has been given the title, *The Liberal Arts College*, rather than a designation which would limit its apparent scope merely to a report of a survey of thirty-five colleges. It is the sincere hope of the survey staff that this report may prove profitable to the program of liberal arts education in this country.

> FLOYD W. REEVES
> JOHN DALE RUSSELL
> H. C. GREGG
> A. J. BRUMBAUGH
> L. E. BLAUCH

CONTENTS

PART I. THE SERVICE AND ADMINISTRATION OF COLLEGES

LIST OF TABLES

LIST OF ILLUSTRATIONS

PART I
THE SERVICE AND ADMINISTRATION OF COLLEGES

CHAPTER I

HISTORICAL SUMMARY

The interest of the Methodist Episcopal Church in higher education dates from the very beginning of the denomination. At the famous "Christmas Conference" of 1784, which marks the formal establishment of the Church, a resolution was passed looking toward the founding of a college. A site was later selected at Abingdon, Maryland, and a building erected at a cost of over forty thousand dollars. Instruction in the new institution, known as Cokesbury College, began in December, 1787. Financial discouragements soon arose. To make matters worse, the college building was destroyed by fire in 1795. The institution was relocated in Baltimore and a building purchased, but within a few months this also was destroyed by fire.

The discouragement of these disasters seems to have led temporarily to the abandonment of hope of further endeavor in the field of higher education on the part of the Methodist Episcopal Church. From 1796 to 1820 there is no mention of education in the General Conference journals, although there were some sporadic efforts at the establishment of institutions by local Annual Conferences. In 1820, however, the General Conference "recommended to all the annual conferences to establish, as soon as practicable, literary institutions, under their own control, in such a way and manner as they may think proper," and the leaders of the Church began a vigorous advocacy of the cause of higher education as a church enterprise.

The establishment of Wesleyan University and of Randolph-Macon College really marks the beginning of the college movement in the Methodist Episcopal Church. The former institution was opened at Middletown, Connecticut, in 1831; Randolph-Macon College, at Boydton, Virginia, was chartered in 1830, but did not begin instruction until 1832. With the division of the Church in 1844, Randolph-Macon College passed under the control of the Methodist Episcopal Church, South.

In 1833, shortly after the establishment of Wesleyan University and Randolph-Macon College, two existing institutions, both originally established by the Presbyterians, were taken over by the Methodists—Dickinson College, established in 1783, and Allegheny College, dating from 1817. Following this, colleges were founded in increasing numbers

3

during the thirties and the forties. There seems to have been a slowing-up of the process of college founding during and immediately following the Civil War, but the 1880's witnessed another rapid increase in the number of Methodist institutions.

In 1892 there was created by the General Conference the organization known as the University Senate, with authority to classify the various colleges and to issue an official list of the institutions of the Church. The creation of this agency appears to have exercised a notable check upon the establishment of new colleges under the auspices of the Methodist Episcopal Church.[1] Of the colleges officially recognized in 1931, only one (Gooding College) has been founded during the forty years of service of the University Senate. Four other colleges which date their beginning during the last forty years represent either offshoots or reorganizations of older institutions.

A number of colleges formerly maintained have ceased to exist as separate institutions under Methodist auspices. The first official list of the University Senate, published in March, 1897, contains the names of thirteen colleges which are no longer existent as Methodist institutions. Eight of these either have merged with some other Methodist college or have been relocated under a different name, continuing their Methodist connection. Two continue to exist although not listed by The Board of Education of the Methodist Episcopal Church. One is now a secondary school. Two have ceased to exist.

It is also interesting to compare the list of colleges as published in 1891, before the University Senate was created, with the 1897 list. Evidently the gathering of statistics and reports in these years constituted a difficult problem, for there are a number of institutions omitted from the 1891 list which were in existence at that time and which were recognized in the 1897 list. Altogether there are twenty colleges listed in the 1891 report that in 1931 do not exist as Methodist colleges. Eight of these either have been relocated under a different name although continuing their Methodist connection or have merged with some other Methodist institution. Two have become secondary schools, and two continue to exist although no longer on the official list of The Board of Education of the Methodist Episcopal Church. Eight have ceased to exist. These data reflect in an interesting manner the mortality of educational institutions.

Figure 1 presents a graphic picture of the dates of founding of the thirty-five colleges included in this study. In this analysis a college is

[1] This should not be taken to imply that it is the principal function of the Senate to check the establishment of new colleges.

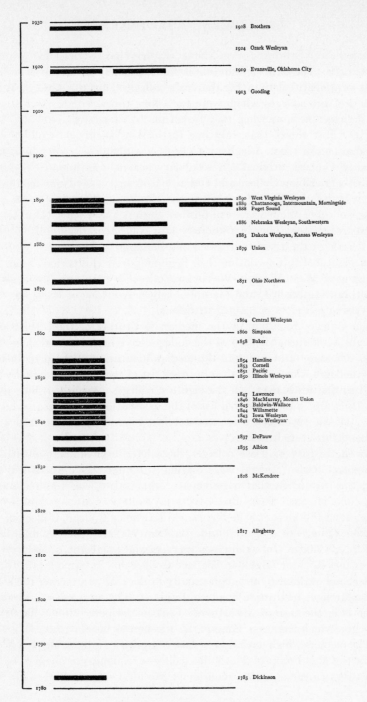

FIG. 1.—Dates of founding of thirty-five colleges

considered as a new institution whenever it has changed both its name and its location. The date of founding is considered as the date of establishment as an institution, rather than as a college. Thus the dates given for several of the colleges which were for a long time secondary schools do not indicate the time when they began to do college work.

This chart shows that only one institution, Dickinson College, was founded before 1800. Allegheny College was founded in 1817, and McKendree College, originally a secondary school, was founded in 1828. Two others, Albion College and DePauw University, were founded during the next decade. The 1840's witnessed the establishment of seven colleges, and five more were established during the 1850's. During the twenty years beginning in 1860 only four colleges were established, but the decade of the 1880's witnessed another spurt in the founding of colleges, eight institutions dating their beginning from this period. Since the founding of West Virginia Wesleyan College in 1890 only five colleges have been established, and, as previously noted, four of these are outgrowths or offshoots of older institutions.

The date of founding of the median institution of these thirty-five colleges is 1860; that is, half of the colleges have been founded since that date. The date of founding of the median institution of the seventeen of these colleges which are on the approved list of the Association of American Universities is 1847. Of the eighteen colleges established since 1860, only three are on the approved list of the Association of American Universities. Of the seventeen colleges established before 1860, fourteen have attained this accreditation.

In the history of these colleges there have been numerous cases of changes of name. Several were originally founded as universities, but with the realization that a university organization was too ambitious, they have changed their official titles to "college." Among those which have taken this step may be mentioned Lawrence College, College of the Pacific, College of Puget Sound, Baldwin-Wallace College, and Iowa Wesleyan College. In some cases mergers and amalgamations have led to changes in name (Baldwin-Wallace College and Intermountain Union College are examples), although usually in the case of a merger the name of the stronger institution has been retained. The most recent change of name is in the case of MacMurray College (formerly Illinois Woman's College), which has been named after a generous benefactor.

The mergers which have taken place comprise an interesting part of the history of this group of Methodist colleges. Among the mergers of the last twenty years may be mentioned Mount Union College with Scio

College in 1911; Baldwin University with German Wallace College in 1913; Morningside College and Charles City College in 1914; Oklahoma City University, an outgrowth of the merger of Epworth University and Fort Worth University, in 1919; Intermountain Union College, formed in 1923 from the consolidation of the College of Montana, a Presbyterian institution, with Montana Wesleyan College; and Baker University with Missouri Wesleyan College in 1930. Doubtless other mergers and amalgamations could be traced in the history of earlier years. In general, these developments have tended to consolidate and conserve the interests of the Church in higher education, and have not led to any lessening of the amount of service rendered.

Twenty-eight of these thirty-five colleges have been related to the Methodist Episcopal Church since the date of their establishment. It has been explained previously that Dickinson College and Allegheny College were originally Presbyterian institutions, but came under Methodist auspices in 1833, fifty years and sixteen years, respectively, after their founding. Ohio Northern University was established and operated for many years as a private enterprise. All the other colleges came under the auspices of the Methodist Episcopal Church either at their founding or within a very few years thereafter.

In general, the conclusion may be drawn that the tendency during the last generation has not been one of expansion in the number of colleges maintained by the Methodist Episcopal Church. Instead there is evident a trend toward actual reduction in the number of separate institutions. The policy of the Church has evidently been looking toward the conservation of the welfare of established institutions rather than toward expansions in the number of colleges maintained.

CHAPTER II

AIMS OF THE INSTITUTIONS

THE NEED FOR A SATISFACTORY STATEMENT OF AIMS

An institution of higher learning exists for certain more or less definite purposes. In some colleges the purposes of the institution have been clearly formulated, but in others there has never been set up any definite statement of aims. It seems self-evident that an educational institution should have a clear and adequate statement of its objectives. This statement should serve at least two functions: (1) it should introduce the ideals of the institution to both the students and the public; (2) it should be the basis of the educational program that the institution provides.

It is recognized that each institution has the inherent right, as well as the duty, to set its own aims and objectives; these aims, however, should fall within the recognized scope of higher education. The statement of aims should not be phrased merely in general terms applicable alike to all institutions of higher education, but should apply specifically to the individual college, differentiating it clearly from other institutions, even those of the same general type. The effectiveness of an institution should then be judged not only by the kind of aims which it has set for itself but also by the efforts it is making to achieve its own objectives.

To be satisfactory a statement of aims should meet the following requirements: (1) it should be set up in terms of an institutional clientèle, taking into account the social groups which the college attempts to serve; (2) it should stress the relationship of the particular aims to the organization of the curriculum offerings; (3) it should include only aims which are understood and shared by the faculty.

The institutional clientèle will be determined on the basis of factors such as the following: (1) the type of community in which the college is located; (2) the geographical location of the college with reference to its constituency; (3) the religious affiliations of students; (4) the occupational distribution of parents; (5) the economic and social background of students; and (6) the scientific and scholarly qualities of the program of offerings.

The adequacy of a college curriculum must be judged on the basis of the established aims of the institution; therefore these aims should be stated with sufficient definiteness and detail to serve as a basis for curricu-

8

lum construction. In case an institution declares as its purpose education for some particular vocation such as teaching, business, journalism, music, medicine, or engineering, it should be expected to provide the curriculum offerings recognized as essential for such special education. In case an institution announces its purpose as that of educating for certain limited fields, it should not be criticized adversely if it does not provide offerings in other fields.

An institution in which the aims as viewed by the faculty differ from those of the administration or the board of trustees is not in a satisfactory situation. Within the scope of the general aims established and announced by a board of trustees the particular statement of educational aims is a function of the faculty. Since such a statement pertains to professional matters, its formulation requires expert skill and knowledge. The faculty only is equipped to prepare this statement. In many of the institutions included in this group it would be desirable if the faculty would engage in redefinition of the institution's purposes. Such activity would do much to give staff members a sympathetic understanding of the purposes of the institution and to revitalize faculty adherence to these purposes.

STATED AIMS OF THE INSTITUTIONS

Of the thirty-five colleges included in this survey, fifteen have published their aims, eighteen have prepared statements of aims which are as yet unpublished, and two were unable at the time the data for this report were assembled to provide the survey staff with any statement concerning their aims and purposes. In all but one of the fifteen institutions having published statements of aims, the statements appear in the catalogues; in three cases the statements are in the by-laws of the board of trustees; there are two cases in which the aims appear in both the catalogues and the by-laws of the boards. In the case of the latter two, the statements appearing in the by-laws of the boards differ in many respects from those which appear in the catalogues. Of the eighteen statements of institutional aims provided by institutions in unpublished form, ten were prepared by the president of the institution at the request of the survey staff, three were obtained from reports made by the president to the board of trustees or to the general public, and five were prepared by deans or faculty committees for use within the institution.

Table 1 shows the aims which appear in these statements and the number of institutions reporting each aim.

This table shows that the aim most frequently mentioned is the development of Christian character. This is to be expected since all these institutions are receiving support from church sources. It is somewhat surprising to note that only twenty-six of the thirty-three institutions report this aim.

Only ten of the institutions mention vocational training as an aim, and only eight mention prevocational training; yet the curriculums of at least

TABLE 1

AIMS REPORTED BY THIRTY-THREE COLLEGES

Aims of the Institution	Number of Institutions Reporting Aim
The development of Christian character	26
The development of scholarly attitudes and habits	19
Vocational training	10
A broad, liberal, and cultural education	9
Preprofessional training	8
Training for citizenship	7
To assist students in acquiring valuable knowledge	6
Physical development and health	5
Preparation for graduate work	5
Training for leadership	4
A liberal education for a selected group of high-grade students	4
Development of an appreciation of the fine arts	3
To provide tools of learning useful for later study	3
Training for the ministry	2
To assist the student in acquiring self-mastery	2
To provide an education for students of limited means	2
To provide a satisfactory educational plant	2
To provide an opportunity for students to secure an education near their homes	1
To raise teaching standards of faculty members	1
To meet the special needs of young women	1
To secure funds	1
To encourage the integration of the intellectual life of the student	1
To maintain superior standards and sound a distinctive note	1

thirty of the thirty-three institutions provide specifically either for vocational or prevocational training, and in most instances provision is made for both. Apparently these institutions should either modify their statements of aims or modify their curriculums to conform to the statements which they have made. As a matter of fact, a number of institutions state definitely that it is not their purpose to provide either vocational or prevocational training; yet in most instances these same institutions actually do provide curriculums for these purposes.

Most of the colleges provide programs of intercollegiate and intramural athletics, and more than half of them have made specific provision for health education; yet only five of the group have seen fit to include physical development and health education as one of their stated aims.

Unsatisfactory statements of aims.—Many of the aims stated by the institutions of this group tell in a general way what the institution is attempting to do but are not presented in sufficient detail to make them useful bases of curriculum construction or to acquaint the students and the public with the work of the institution. The president of one of the institutions in which no aims had been formulated prior to the time of the survey, when asked to prepare a statement of aims, submitted the following:

This section of the country was settled in the early days by men and women from New England. They brought with them the New England tradition of an appreciation of higher learning. Methodism occupied a position of leadership among the religious forces of the pioneers. The founders of ———— University clearly believed in intellectual training accompanied by the development of sound Christian character. The motto of the institution is *Primum vir esto.* "Let him first be a man." The seal indicates the scope of training, for on it are in Greek words: "Spirit, mind, body."

While the training of ministers may have been prominent in the thought of the founders, from the beginning they held much wider interests, for from the first the institution was coeducational.

It is clear that a statement such as that presented above would not serve adequately as a guide in constructing a curriculum, or as a guide to students in selecting an institution in which to secure their undergraduate training.

A second example typical of the unsatisfactory statements prepared at a number of these institutions was furnished by the president of one of the smaller colleges.

To afford an opportunity for ———— College young men and women to obtain a liberal arts education near home in an atmosphere and environment that is safe, homelike, and Christian, and to furnish the basic culture and academic background for those who expect to prepare for special, professional, and technical work.

Although this statement is typical of the aims in many colleges, it also is not sufficiently definite to serve as a basis of an educational program. An almost identical statement would readily fit most of the colleges in the territory in which this institution is situated.

Relatively satisfactory statements of aims.—Among the institutions having relatively satisfactory statements of aims are DePauw University, Hamline University, Evansville College, Baldwin-Wallace College, and Brothers College.

The catalogue of DePauw University contains the following statement of the purposes and aims of the institution:

The purpose of the University is to give its students, through a broad and liberal education, an understanding and appreciation of the cultural and scientific achievements of man, past and present, to inspire them with a love for truth and beauty, and to prepare them to live in society more effectively for themselves and more helpfully for others.

The particular aims of the University are:

1. The conservation and development of the physical health, the moral character and the religious life of its students.

2. To give its students familiarity with such tools of learning as will make further study in college and life more pleasant and effective.

3. To offer its students the opportunity to familiarize themselves with the general content, the achievements and ideals of the several departments of knowledge, and the methods of study therein.

4. To require such intensive training in one department as will give the student a reasonable understanding and mastery of the content and technique in that field of knowledge.

5. To offer its students basic training for those professional and technical studies which may most advantageously be pursued upon a foundation of liberal education.

The consummation of the intellectual aims of the University is to encourage the search for truth, to develop the ability of its students to think clearly, accurately, constructively, and fearlessly on all subjects and to express their thoughts effectively.

To the achievement of these ends, the University will admit only such students as the facilities of the College permit to be taught well and to retain only those students who give promise of satisfactory development under its guidance.

This statement was prepared by the education policy commission of the university and adopted by the faculty in 1928. Quite clearly the purpose and aims set forth are those of a liberal arts college which disavows any intention of vocational or professional training except as liberal arts training is basic to further educational training. Although relatively satisfactory, this statement is not as complete as would be desirable in that it does not cover the work of the institution in teacher-training, the professional aspects of the institution in music, or offerings designated as "business training." Either the statement of aims or the offerings of the university are in need of revision if the two are to be definitely and clearly related.

Hamline University has set up its aims in terms of the purposes of its junior college and its senior college. The catalogue of Hamline University carries the following statement:

Hamline University offers its students a liberal education with the following specific purposes in view:

JUNIOR COLLEGE

A. To bring each student to the best possible state of vigorous health as a basis for successful living
B. To assist the student in acquiring self-mastery
C. To encourage adequate integration of the intellectual life
D. To widen the student's range of interest and appreciation by introduction into the main fields of significant knowledge
E. To enable the student to make proper choice of a field of concentration for the Senior College, and to make necessary preparation therefor

SENIOR COLLEGE

A. To continue in the main the specific purposes of the Junior College, enlarging "E" to the proper choice of life work
B. To require for each student a reasonable degree of concentration in his chosen field of interest
C. To give the student after satisfying requirements wide powers of election, either to do further intensive work in his chosen field of concentration or further widen his range of interests
D. To prepare adequately for graduate work or entry into vocations success in which calls for a high degree of general culture and a relatively small degree of specialization
E. To encourage all students to work up to a level of their ability and to develop power in self-directed study
F. Finally, to permit the student the widest scope for the development and integration of his personality along the lines of his personal needs, his greatest abilities, and his most pronounced interests

It is the purpose of the institution also to encourage in all proper ways the development of Christian character in its students, and to assist them in finding an adequate philosophy of life.

Most of the institutions recognize a distinction between the type of training given in the lower and the upper divisions. It would appear advisable for such institutions to follow the example of Hamline University and prepare separate statements for the aims of these divisions.

In a recent address to the Board of Trustees, the President of Evansville College definitely outlined the major aims of that institution. These aims as stated may be summarized as follows:

First, the educational work of Evansville College must have a definite, vital, and vocational emphasis.

Second, the original purpose for which Evansville College was chartered and the amount of financial support available dictate that it shall be essentially a college of liberal arts.

Third, as a liberal arts college, all the departments of the institution should be of equal standing and any addition or change in the vocational offerings and requirements should be made in the light of the liberal arts program.

Fourth, in recognition of the educational program of this institution, the Bachelor of Arts degree should be given basic emphasis. Highly professionalized courses and degrees should be reduced and modified so as to fit into a program of a liberal arts college.

Fifth, a general self-help program should be established throughout the entire school.

Sixth, Evansville College should increasingly put itself at the service of the City of Evansville in the spirit of a civic institution but should also continue to be the true and loyal servant of the Indiana Conference of the Methodist Episcopal Church, and as such must emphatically and fundamentally stress vital religious principles in its program of instruction, life, and service.

This statement summarizes concisely and clearly the educational emphasis which the present administration desires to give to this institution.

In the report of the President of Baldwin-Wallace College to the Board of Trustees in December, 1928, the college objectives were stated in the following words:

The college program is distinctly confined to the fundamental subjects and courses and does not undertake to go far afield in specialized or vocational study. It is the approved policy of this institution that foundations should be broadly laid in undergraduate studies for whatever further special or professional study students may wish to pursue after graduation, rather than to undertake to furnish exact substitute credits for technical or professional courses.

These are good general statements, but the aims of the college should be set forth in some more definite form if they are to serve fully the two purposes referred to above. A faculty committee has been appointed at Baldwin-Wallace College to draft a statement of objectives. Such a statement was submitted for faculty consideration, but at the time the data for this survey were obtained it had not yet been finally approved. The statement includes the following objectives: (1) physical fitness; (2) discovering and developing interests and aptitudes; (3) appreciation of beauty; (4) the application of ethical ideals in individual and economic relationships; (5) worthy home relationships; (6) proper use of leisure time; (7) understanding and appreciation of racial heritages and the development of world-mindedness; (8) social adjustments; (9) scholarship through, first, the creative, open mind; and, second, grounding in the fundamentals of the different fields of study and a wide and thorough knowledge in some special field of concentration; and (10) a Christian philosophy of life. Although these objectives are not yet formulated with sufficient definiteness to serve as the basis for the educational program, they offer an excellent foundation for the further elaboration of the aims of the college.

In 1928 the Board of Trustees of Brothers College adopted a statement of the purpose of the institution which has been printed in the catalogues of the institution since that time. Recently the faculty revised the statement in the interests of accuracy and definiteness. This new statement, prepared for the catalogue of 1931–32 and submitted to the survey staff, is as follows:

Brothers College of Drew University is in a real sense an adventure in excellence. In an age in which greatness has often come to be identified with bulk or numbers, Brothers College desires to become great rather because of its faculty, its student body, and its standards of scholarship, culture, and conduct.

As an adventure in excellence Brothers College will not attempt to minister to all types of college students or to all the differing and opposing purposes of college students. While fully appreciating the value of technical training it feels that as a College of Liberal Arts its primary emphasis should be cultural rather than commercial or vocational. It would, therefore, prefer not to attract the student whose sole purpose in attending college is to increase his earning capacity. Again, while recognizing that social and extra-curriculum activities have some place in student life, Brothers College sees the more fundamental values threatened by the growing importance attached to these activities in many American colleges. It would, therefore, prefer not to attract the student whose chief purpose in attending college is social enjoyment or competition in intercollegiate sports.

On the other hand, Brothers College does desire to attract the student whose purpose in attending college is to secure a key to the world's libraries and to the minds of men, to acquire a new appreciation of beauty, a finer character, a stronger faith, a deeper knowledge, a broader vision, and a richer culture, in order that he may become a better companion to himself and a more useful member of society.

It expects that through acquaintance with the traditional intellectual disciplines its students will acquire a command of written and spoken English and of scientific method, a knowledge of the great cultures of the world, and a more exact knowledge of some one branch of learning. Brothers College does not believe, however, that true education ends with the rote learning of great masses of unrelated and undigested information. It believes that education is incomplete unless the student knows the significance of what he has learned. It believes that the awakening of intellectual curiosity, the fostering of mental initiative, and the formation of habits of accurate observation, of logical analysis and of critical reflection are quite as important as the acquisition of factual knowledge.

SPECIFIC OBJECTIVES

1. *The achievement of high excellence in scholarship.*—The courses of Brothers College are designed for students of ability whose primary interest is in intellectual excellence. To promote this end instruction will be given in small classes, lectures and discussions will be supplemented by individual conferences, and honors courses will be provided for students in the upper classes.

2. *The encouragement of an experimental point of view.*—Brothers College is in a real sense an adventure in excellence. While it forcefully emphasizes the great traditional disciplines, it does not commit itself to any rigid organization of content or method of presentation; it is itself experimental, and will promote continued experiment in problems of curriculum, instruction, and intellectual culture.

3. *The realization of Christian character.*—Brothers College provides education in an atmosphere sympathetic to Christian ideals and Christian faith. As an integral part of Drew University, it is under the general direction of the Methodist Episcopal Church but is open without discrimination as to religious affiliation and its approach to the problems of religion is in no sense sectarian. It offers specific training in religion, teaching its students the contents and significance of the Old and New Testaments, and helping them to achieve moral and religious standards by an understanding of the central problems of conduct and faith.

4. *Preparation for citizenship.*—Brothers College believes that the political ideal of the educated man should transcend mere nationalistic patriotism. It desires to produce informed and socially minded citizens who will be willing to assume their full responsibilities in the life of the community, the Republic and, in consequence, the world.

5. *The worthy use of leisure.*—Brothers College, in placing cultural training above vocational, implies that leisure, rightfully employed, is priceless opportunity. It will therefore endeavor to teach its students such habits and to acquaint them with such pursuits as will assure the proper and happy use of leisure time.

6. *The acquisition and maintenance of sound health.*—Brothers College has established a system of physical education which requires periodical physical examinations, and which insures supervision over the physical activity of the students. Their natural love of sports is provided for in a program of intramural and intercollegiate competition. Brothers College purposes to establish athletics in its proper position in the life of the college by discouraging professionalism and encouraging the amateur spirit.

7. *The foundation for professional and business training.*—The primary emphasis of the training provided by Brothers College is cultural rather than

commercial or vocational. Its courses do, however, offer to students elementary preparation for business or the following professions: Teaching, ministry, medicine, and law. The number of specialized courses is limited since the purpose of the college is to provide foundations for a broad culture.

In a recent revision of the curriculum made since the foregoing statement was published, definite objectives of the lower-class and upper-class units were adopted, as follows:

The lower-class unit of Brothers College should have for its objective the completion of the student's secondary education: first, the giving of certain basic information; second, training in the ability to use the tools of knowledge and in habits of study; and third, the inculcation of a liberal attitude toward life, philosophy, religion, and the social problems of the day.

The upper-class unit, which corresponds to the present junior and senior years, shall have as its objective the gaining of specialized knowledge in a particular field of learning, coupled with the development of the student's general cultural background.

The statements prepared by the faculty of Brothers College represent one of the best efforts which has been found among any of the institutions to define the purposes of the college.

CRITICISM OF THE PLAN OF STATING AIMS

In the case of a few institutions the administrators and faculty apparently see no value to be secured from the preparation of a statement of aims and purposes. In response to a request for such a statement for use in the survey, the president of one of the colleges furnished the following statement:

It is not an accident, but the result of settled policy that there is no clearcut formulation of the aims of this institution. The college is a living and growing enterprise, changing with the times, and constantly seeking to adapt itself to conditions. It has always seemed to me that there is some danger of giving the *status quo* an undue advantage in any such formulation. . . . . We seek to have a college growing in effectiveness rather than in size, and with as little vocational training as is possible considering environmental and other pressures. We seek to avoid crystallization of immature ambitions, and to promote the development of new ambitions and objectives—to that end postponing as much as possible rigid vocational choices until the student has sufficient maturity to have a social as well as individual outlook. Our purpose is social and ethical, as well as intellectual, the objectives being the development of men and women capable of adaptation to varied social and vocational environments, and with enough religious and moral enthusiasm and conviction to make them significant in civic and church life.

The survey staff is not in agreement with the idea that there is danger of crystallization inherent in an explicitly formulated set of aims for an institution of higher learning. There is obvious need for everyone connected with a college to know exactly what the institution is trying to do, in order that each may bend his own efforts in that general direction. In the absence of such a general understanding there is a strong probability that each department and instructor may adopt, consciously or unconsciously, an individual set of aims. Under such circumstances cross-purposes develop and the program of the institution is likely to suffer from a lack of unification. It may be noted in passing that the statement furnished the survey staff quoted above, although disavowing any faith in aims as such, itself sets up a rather clear formulation of the aims of the typical college of liberal arts.

DEPARTMENTAL AIMS

After the general objectives of an institution have been agreed upon, the several departments should express their departmental aims. Obviously the departmental aims should be in harmony with the larger aims of the college as a whole and the courses should be definitely organized to obtain the stated objectives. In only one or two of the colleges in this group have the departments prepared statements of departmental aims in conformity with the aims set forth for the institution. In several of the colleges a few of the departments have developed excellent statements of aims, which are printed in the respective catalogues. These statements render conspicuous the absence of similar statements for other departments of the college.

REVISION OF AIMS

The fact that a set of aims has been adopted does not mean that these aims or their statement should be considered final. It is desirable that there should be constant study and revision of the goals set forth. The aims of a college cannot be static. New points of view and shifting social needs make it necessary from time to time to study and revise the aims. In fact, the maintenance of constant adjustment between the aims of an institution and the needs of society may well be recognized as one of the important duties of the faculty and administration.

CHAPTER III

ACCREDITATION

There are three distinct levels in the accreditation of American colleges of liberal arts. The first is recognition by the state in which the institution is located. In some cases this type of accreditation is exercised by the state board of education or the state department of public instruction, in other cases it involves recognition by the state university, and in a few cases there is a voluntary association within the state which exercises accrediting powers. This type of accreditation usually involves certification for training teachers for the public schools of the state, and frequently carries with it the acceptance of credits earned in the institution upon transfer to the state university.

The holding of this type of accreditation is practically the *sine qua non* of collegiate existence today. Institutions that are not recognized by the official accrediting agencies of their own states find it very difficult to continue. Each of the thirty-five colleges included in this study held state accreditation at the time of the survey visit; in three institutions, however, the continuation of this recognition was being questioned by the state agency, and there is strong probability that these colleges will be denied accreditation in the future unless their programs are markedly improved.

The second level of accreditation for American colleges is recognition by the regional standardizing associations. There are four such agencies in the United States which accredit colleges: the North Central Association of Colleges and Secondary Schools, the Association of Colleges and Secondary Schools of the Southern States, the Middle States Association of Colleges and Secondary Schools, and the Northwest Association of Secondary and Higher Schools. The regions in which these agencies operate are indicated by their titles. In addition there is the New England Association of Colleges and Preparatory Schools, an organization which has only within the past year or two begun to accredit colleges. California is the only state in the Union which is not now included within the jurisdiction of one of these regional associations. Recently the educational institutions of California have organized themselves into the Southwest Association of Colleges and Secondary Schools. This Association is patterned after the New England Association of a few years ago, and does not have a list of accredited institutions.

The regional associations are voluntary organizations, possessing only the power of admitting institutions to membership. They wield a very potent influence, however, and particularly in areas where there is strong competition among colleges an institution finds it almost impossible to continue today without regional accreditation. Inclusion in the list of member institutions carries two important privileges for the college: (1) its graduates are permitted to teach in the member secondary schools, which usually include the strongest and best-equipped high schools of the region; (2) its graduates are usually accepted without question as matriculants in the better graduate schools of the region.

Of the thirty-five institutions included in the present study, twenty-five held accreditation with their respective regional standardizing associations at the time of the survey visit. One other college is located in California and is thus outside the jurisdiction of any regional association that accredits institutions, but the general standing of this institution would probably entitle it to be considered in this class of accredited colleges. One of the twenty-five colleges holds approval only as a junior college, although it is giving four years of work and offers the Bachelor's degree. One college has received accreditation by the North Central Association, and one has been added to the non-member list of the Southern Association, since the respective survey visits. Two of the colleges have been dropped from the list of the North Central Association since the data for this study were collected. One other college has been reduced to the status of provisional accreditation by the North Central Association, subject to an annual reinspection.

Fourteen of the twenty-five colleges holding regional accreditation have been members of their respective associations ever since the latter were organized. Six of the other colleges achieved membership between 1915 and 1920, and the remaining five have been admitted since 1920.

The third level of accreditation involves national recognition, a place on the approved list of the Association of American Universities. This type of approval is based on membership in a regional accrediting association plus the passing of an inspection with regard to the facilities for preparing students for graduate study. The achievement of this, the highest goal of accreditation for American colleges of liberal arts, guarantees the acceptance of suitably qualified graduates as matriculants at any of the better graduate schools of the country.

In the group of thirty-five colleges included in this study, seventeen are on the approved list of the Association of American Universities. Six of these seventeen were on the first list of this Association, published in 1913. By 1920 there were nine of these colleges on the approved list; the other eight have received this recognition since 1920. Two other colleges had applications pending with the Association of American Universities at the time of the survey visit.[1]

The various levels of accreditation provide a valuable stimulus for improvement in American colleges. Those institutions in this group which have only a state or local recognition are almost without exception making vigorous efforts to attain to membership in their respective regional associations. Those with regional membership are striving for recognition by the Association of American Universities. It is to be hoped, of course, that by the time the college has achieved this final recognition, it will be sufficiently interested in its own excellence to continue the improvement of its program without any direct stimulation in the form of advanced accreditation. Unfortunately this does not seem to be the case in all of the colleges of this group which are on the approved list of the Association of American Universities. There are two or three of these colleges which seem to have taken this recognition as an indication that they need make no further efforts at improvement; as a result they now lag far behind most of the other colleges holding this type of accreditation on many of the significant indices of educational excellence.

The holding of one or another of the various types of accreditation must not be taken too seriously as an absolute index of the educational excellence of any one college. Unquestionably there are a few colleges lacking regional membership which are better than many colleges holding this type of recognition; and there are probably a few colleges on the approved list of the Association of American Universities which are maintaining a poorer program than some colleges which do not have this type of recognition. By and large, however, the various types of accreditation do indicate a significant difference in the levels of educational excellence, and the averages of the groups of colleges holding various types of accreditation show an important gradation.

Since approximately one-half of the colleges of the group being studied are on the approved list of the Association of American Universities, this type of accreditation has been made the basis of differentiation between institutions throughout this study. For many of the tables of data separate averages or medians are computed, showing the central tendencies for all the colleges, for those on the approved list of the Association of American Universities, and for those not holding this type of accreditation.

[1] One of these was placed on the approved list of the Association in November, 1931.

CHAPTER IV

LOCATION AND DENOMINATIONAL CONSTITUENCY

GEOGRAPHICAL LOCATION

The thirty-five colleges included in this study are located in twenty-two different states of the Union. These states are scattered from New Jersey and Pennsylvania on the east to California, Oregon, and Washington on the west; and from Wisconsin, Minnesota, and Montana on the north to Tennessee and Oklahoma on the south. Figure 2 presents an outline map of the United States showing the locations of the thirty-five colleges.

It will be noted from this figure that the majority of the institutions included in this study are located in the Middle West, with a fair representation in the West, with relatively few in the East, and with no colleges in the extreme South. The distribution of the colleges among the states is rather uneven. There are two states (Iowa and Ohio) which have four colleges each; two other states (Kansas and Illinois) have three colleges each; and three states (Indiana, Missouri, and Pennsylvania) have two colleges each. Fifteen of the states represented in this study each have only one college affiliated with the Methodist Episcopal Church.

SIZE OF LOCAL POPULATION

Table 2 presents data showing the population of the city and of the county in which each college is located. The size of the county is given in order to present some idea of the local concentration of population. Counties vary in geographical area, and several of the colleges included in this study are situated so as to draw upon two or more counties as their local constituency. For most of the institutions, however, a fairly accurate idea of the size of the local population group is obtained from the figures for the city and the county in which the college is located.

It will be observed from this table that there is a marked variation among this group of colleges in the size of the local community. A few of the colleges are located in metropolitan centers, while others are in rural villages. The population of the county does not correspond in all cases to the size of the city; several of the colleges are located in small cities or villages near a fairly large center of population. Thus Baldwin-Wallace College is located in Berea, Ohio, a city of 5,697 population, but in the

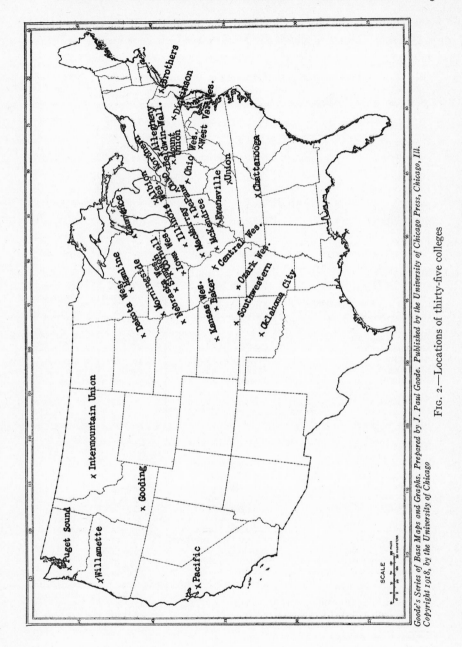

Goode's Series of Base Maps and Graphs. Prepared by J. Paul Goode. Published by the University of Chicago Press, Chicago, Ill. Copyright 1918, by the University of Chicago

FIG. 2.—Locations of thirty-five colleges

same county is the city of Cleveland, the population of the county being in excess of 1,000,000. Similarly, McKendree College is located at Leba-

TABLE 2

POPULATION OF COMMUNITIES IN WHICH THIRTY-FIVE
COLLEGES ARE LOCATED

College	Location	Population of City†	Population of County†
Baldwin-Wallace...............	Berea, Ohio	5,697	1,201,455
*Hamline......................	St. Paul, Minn.	271,606	286,721
*Mount Union.................	Alliance, Ohio	23,047	221,784
Oklahoma City...............	Oklahoma City, Okla.	185,389	221,738
Puget Sound..................	Tacoma, Wash.	106,817	163,842
*Chattanooga..................	Chattanooga, Tenn.	119,798	159,497
McKendree...................	Lebanon, Ill.	1,828	157,775
Evansville....................	Evansville, Ind.	102,249	113,320
Brothers.....................	Madison, N.J.	7,481	110,445
*Pacific......................	Stockton, Calif.	47,963	102,940
*Morningside..................	Sioux City, Iowa	79,183	101,669
Nebraska Wesleyan...........	Lincoln, Neb.	75,933	100,324
*Albion......................	Albion, Mich.	8,324	87,043
*Cornell.....................	Mount Vernon, Iowa	1,441	82,336
Ozark Wesleyan..............	Carthage, Mo.	9,736	73,810
*Illinois Wesleyan.............	Bloomington, Ill.	30,930	73,117
*Dickinson...................	Carlisle, Pa.	12,596	68,236
*Allegheny...................	Meadville, Pa.	16,698	62,980
*Lawrence....................	Appleton, Wis.	25,267	62,790
*Willamette..................	Salem, Ore.	26,266	60,541
Southwestern.................	Winfield, Kan.	9,398	40,903
*MacMurray..................	Jacksonville, Ill.	17,747	34,240
Kansas Wesleyan.............	Salina, Kan.	20,155	29,337
Ohio Northern...............	Ada, Ohio	2,499	27,635
Union.......................	Barbourville, Ky.	2,380	26,266
*Ohio Wesleyan...............	Delaware, Ohio	8,675	26,016
*Baker.......................	Baldwin, Kan.	1,127	25,143
*DePauw.....................	Greencastle, Ind.	4,613	20,448
Intermountain................	Helena, Mont.	11,803	18,224
West Virginia Wesleyan.......	Buckhannon, W.Va.	4,374	17,944
*Simpson.....................	Indianola, Iowa	3,488	17,700
Iowa Wesleyan...............	Mount Pleasant, Iowa	3,743	17,660
Dakota Wesleyan.............	Mitchell, S.D.	10,942	16,821
Central Wesleyan.............	Warrenton, Mo.	1,250	8,082
Gooding.....................	Gooding, Idaho	1,592	7,580
Median, all colleges........	....	10,942	62,980
*Median, A.A.U. colleges....	....	17,747	68,236
Median, non-A.A.U. colleges	....	8,540	35,120

* Institutions on the approved list of the Association of American Universities.
† According to the United States Census of 1930.

non, Illinois, a village of only 1,828 inhabitants; but in the same county are East St. Louis and Belleville and several smaller cities, so that the county has a total population of more than 100,000.

The medians shown in Table 2 indicate that the typical college of this group is located in a city of approximately eleven thousand inhabitants, and in a county having a population slightly in excess of sixty thousand. In general, the colleges holding accreditation from the Association of American Universities tend to be located in larger cities and more populous counties than the colleges which do not hold this type of accreditation.

TABLE 3

DISTRIBUTION OF THIRTY-FIVE COLLEGES ACCORDING TO POPULATION OF
CITY AND OF COUNTY IN WHICH LOCATED, AND ACCORDING
TO TYPE OF ACCREDITATION

POPULATION	NUMBER OF COLLEGES LOCATED IN CITIES OF EACH SIZE			NUMBER OF COLLEGES LOCATED IN COUNTIES OF EACH SIZE		
	A.A.U. Colleges	Non- A.A.U. Colleges	Total	A.A.U. Colleges	Non- A.A.U. Colleges	Total
200,000 or more..........	1	....	1	2	2	4
100,000–199,999..........	1	3	4	3	5	8
40,000– 99,999..........	2	1	3	7	2	9
20,000– 39,999..........	4	1	5	4	3	7
10,000– 19,999..........	3	2	5	1	4	5
5,000– 9,999..........	2	4	6	....	2	2
3,000– 4,999..........	2	2	4	....	....	....
1,000– 2,999..........	2	5	7	....	....	....
Total...............	17	18	35	17	18	35

Table 3 presents data showing the distribution of the thirty-five colleges according to the size of the local community. Separate distributions are shown for the colleges on the approved list of the Association of American Universities and for those not holding this type of accreditation.

It will be observed from this table that the majority of the colleges of this group are located in relatively small cities or villages. Only five of the thirty-five colleges are situated in cities of more than one hundred thousand inhabitants, and 30 per cent of the entire group are located in cities of less than five thousand. On the other hand, it appears that the great majority of these colleges are located in counties which have a fairly good-sized population.

The data for this group of colleges do not indicate any important relationship between the size of the local community and the number of students enrolled. When the colleges are grouped on the basis of the size of the city in which located, there is no significant difference between the average enrolments of colleges located in cities of over fifty thousand population and those located in cities of less than ten thousand. The real relationship between the population of the local community and the size of the student body in this group of colleges appears to be obscured by other factors, such as the age of the institution, its financial resources, and its general reputation. These factors appear, in combination, to have greater weight than the size of the local community in determining the size of the student body of a given college. For example, the two colleges with the largest enrolments of any in this group (DePauw and Ohio Wesleyan) are both located in relatively small communities, but are old, well-established institutions, with very favorable reputations and with relatively large financial resources. On the other hand, Evansville College has as yet a relatively small enrolment, owing to the fact that it is a new institution and has not until recently held satisfactory accreditation, even though it is located in a rather large city. It seems probable that, if there were some way of equalizing these other factors, there would be found a fairly marked relationship between the size of the local community and the enrolment of the college. The present group of institutions does not provide a sufficient number of cases to make a satisfactory analysis of this type.

Besides the present size of the population of the city in which a college is located, the rapidity of growth of the population is also an important factor in judging the excellence of the location. An institution which is located in a rapidly growing center of population has much more favorable prospects than one situated in an area which is static or even decreasing in population. Since there has been a pronounced swing for many decades toward a concentration of population in urban areas, the colleges which are remote from any urban centers have in general less favorable future prospects than those located in or near relatively large cities. This does not necessarily mean that the colleges which are located at considerable distances from centers of population are all doomed to an early extinction; but such colleges must necessarily build up relatively large supporting resources, must put more effort into student recruiting, and must on the whole maintain superior programs, if they are to continue to serve student groups large enough to provide economical operating units.

TRANSPORTATION FACILITIES

Since a large proportion of the students must leave home in order to attend the college of their choice, the adequacy of transportation facilities is an important factor in judging the location of an educational institution. Standards of what constitutes adequate transportation facilities, however, have undergone an important change within the last decade or two. Formerly the essential point was that the college be located on railway lines with good passenger service and with satisfactory connections throughout the constituent territory. While this is still important today, other means of transportation, the automobile and motor bus, have come in and have made location upon all-year-round roads of concrete or other hard-surface material almost indispensable to the college. The well-located college today must have satisfactory transportation facilities both by rail and by motor car.

Almost without exception the colleges included in this study are now located on well-paved roads and are easily accessible by motor car throughout the entire year. Several of them, however, do not have good railway transportation. The coming of hard roads and motor-bus transportation has led many of the railroads to curtail and even to discontinue their passenger service to some of the smaller towns in which these colleges are located.

RESIDENCE OF STUDENTS

Table 4 presents data showing for each of the colleges included in this study the percentage of students coming from various distances.

This table shows that the thirty-five colleges differ considerably in their relative drawing-power, as shown by the proportion of students coming relatively long distances. The figures for the percentages of the student body drawn from within a fifty-mile radius range from 22 per cent in the case of one college to 91 per cent in the case of another.

The accredited status of the college seems to have much to do with the percentage of students drawn from relatively long distances. It will be noted that the medians for the colleges on the approved list of the Association of American Universities exceed those for the colleges not having this type of accreditation, with regard both to the percentage of students coming more than one hundred miles and also to the percentage drawn from the zone between fifty and one hundred miles distant from the college. The colleges holding accreditation from the Association of American Universities typically obtain about two-fifths of their students from within a fifty-mile radius; the colleges which do not have this type of accreditation typically obtain five-eighths of their students from a similar area.

In studying the drawing-power of colleges attention should be given not only to the proportion of students coming from a distance, but also to the actual number. A small college may have a relatively large proportion of its students coming from more than one hundred miles, and

TABLE 4

PERCENTAGE OF REGULAR YEAR FULL-TIME STUDENTS AT THIRTY-FIVE
COLLEGES RESIDING AT VARIOUS DISTANCES FROM THE INSTITUTION

Institution	Year	Over 100 Miles	50–100 Miles	Commuting Distance to 50 Miles	Within Commuting Distance	Total within 50 Miles
*Ohio Wesleyan..............	1930–31	54.3	23.7	15.2	6.8	22.0
Intermountain...............	1930–31	55.4	14.9	1.3	28.4	29.7
*MacMurray.................	1930–31	50.4	19.4	18.9	11.3	30.2
*DePauw...................	1930–31	26.4	40.8	23.5	9.3	32.8
*Cornell...................	1929–30	37.6	28.8	31.6	2.0	33.6
*Albion....................	1929–30	19.7	45.0	16.3	19.0	35.3
*Dickinson.................	1929–30	50.2	14.5	7.6	27.7	35.3
Nebraska Wesleyan.........	1930–31	40.4	24.1	19.8	15.7	35.5
*Allegheny.................	1929–30	32.2	32.1	17.0	18.7	35.7
*Hamline...................	1929–30	39.7	20.0	10.3	30.0	40.3
*Pacific...................	1930–31	29.4	29.6	....	41.0	41.0
*Lawrence.................	1929–30	41.3	17.0	16.4	25.3	41.7
McKendree................	1930–31	33.5	19.5	10.8	36.2	47.0
Brothers..................	1930–31	26.9	25.4	14.9	32.8	47.7
*Illinois Wesleyan...........	1930–31	26.5	25.4	16.9	31.2	48.1
Ohio Northern..............	1930–31	39.7	11.9	17.2	31.2	48.4
*Baker....................	1930–31	28.0	23.4	32.3	16.3	48.6
*Willamette................	1930–31	25.4	24.2	7.7	42.7	50.4
*Morningside...............	1929–30	26.3	23.1	13.1	37.5	50.6
Dakota Wesleyan...........	1929–30	24.6	22.8	24.0	28.6	52.6
Southwestern..............	1930–31	29.2	18.0	19.3	33.5	52.8
Kansas Wesleyan...........	1930–31	25.6	19.7	17.5	37.2	54.7
*Simpson..................	1929–30	18.2	27.1	34.1	20.6	54.7
West Virginia Wesleyan......	1930–31	30.2	9.8	14.3	45.7	60.0
Gooding...................	1930–31	27.2	7.8	32.5	32.5	65.0
Central Wesleyan...........	1929–30	17.8	13.3	10.4	58.5	68.9
Union.....................	1929–30	21.0	8.4	26.1	44.5	70.6
Oklahoma City.............	1929–30	16.4	11.5	5.9	66.2	72.1
Iowa Wesleyan.............	1929–30	6.6	17.3	36.7	39.4	76.1
*Mount Union..............	1930–31	10.8	12.9	24.9	51.4	76.3
*Chattanooga...............	1929–30	15.9	5.9	3.2	75.0	78.2
Ozark Wesleyan............	1929–30	9.6	12.1	23.7	54.6	78.3
Puget Sound...............	1930–31	10.7	5.4	10.9	73.0	83.9
Baldwin-Wallace............	1930–31	9.0	4.8	53.5	32.7	86.2
Evansville.................	1929–30	6.4	2.2	24.1	67.3	91.4
Median, all colleges......	....	26.5	19.4	17.0	32.7	50.4
*Median, A.A.U. colleges..	....	28.0	23.7	16.4	25.3	41.0
Median, non-A.A.U. colleges.................		25.6	12.7	18.4	36.7	62.5

* Institutions on the approved list of the Association of American Universities.

yet the actual number of such students may be much smaller than in the case of a larger institution. For the thirty-five colleges the range in the actual number of students coming from more than one hundred miles is from 20 students in one institution to 989 in another, the median for the entire group being 113. The colleges on the approved list of the Association of American Universities have, on the average, more than two and one-half times as many students from this distance as is the case with the colleges lacking this type of recognition, the respective medians being 186 and 70. It thus appears that the type of accreditation held is a very important factor in determining the number of students which will be drawn from a considerable distance.

TABLE 5

AVERAGE PERCENTAGE OF STUDENTS COMING FROM WITHIN COMMUTING
DISTANCE FOR COLLEGES LOCATED IN COUNTIES OF
VARIOUS POPULATIONS

POPULATION OF COUNTY	COLLEGES ON THE APPROVED LIST OF THE ASSOCIATION OF AMERICAN UNIVERSITIES		COLLEGES NOT ON THE APPROVED LIST OF THE ASSOCIATION OF AMERICAN UNIVERSITIES	
	Number	Average Percentage of Students Coming from within Commuting Distance	Number	Average Percentage of Students Coming from within Commuting Distance
100,000 or more............	5	47.0	7	46.3
40,000–99,999.............	7	23.8	2	44.1
Less than 40,000...........	5	12.9	9	38.4

The size of the local community may reasonably be expected to have an important bearing upon the proportion of students drawn from a distance. Table 5 shows the average percentage of students coming from within commuting distance for colleges located in counties of various sizes. Since it has been shown that the type of accreditation held has an important influence upon the drawing-power of a college, the analyses in this table are presented separately for the colleges on the approved list of the Association of American Universities and for those not holding this type of recognition.

It will be observed from this table that the size of the local community has a very marked relationship to the percentage of students coming from commuting distance in the case of the colleges on the approved list of the Association of American Universities, but that in the case of the colleges not holding this type of accreditation, the relationship between population of the local community and percentage of students coming from within commuting distance is much less marked. Colleges located in relatively large communities tend on the average to have approximately the same percentage of students coming from within commuting distance, regardless of the type of accreditation held. Colleges located in small population centers tend, if approved by the Association of American Universities, to have a relatively small proportion of their total enrolment from the local community; but colleges located in communities of this size, if not holding national accreditation, still tend to have a rather large percentage of their enrolments drawn from the local area, and, it may be added, also have a relatively small total enrolment.

The data which have been presented make possible the drawing of an important generalization regarding the location of institutions of higher learning. A college with resources which permit an excellent educational program, one worthy of recognition by a national accrediting agency, can succeed in attracting students even though it be located in a relatively small community; but a college lacking satisfactory recognition must be located in a comparatively large population center if it is to succeed in attracting a student body of sufficient size to provide an economical operating unit.

CHURCH CONSTITUENCY

All the colleges included in this study were either founded by or, at an early stage of their history, came under the auspices of an Annual Conference of the Methodist Episcopal Church. In the case of some institutions, two or more Annual Conferences have joined in the sponsorship.

There is no strictly defined territorial assignment for each of these colleges, such as is sometimes found in institutions of other communions.[1] Although by mutual consent these colleges have tended to recognize the Conference territory as pre-empted for the institution sponsored by the Conference, the administrators of one or two of the colleges insist that they are not bound to respect such boundaries and carry on rather active student-recruiting within the normal territory of other colleges of the same denomination. Some confusion on this matter is also occasioned by the fact that several Conferences have two colleges and one Conference has three colleges under its auspices. Many of the Conferences, in addition to one or more colleges, have under their auspices a secondary school, a university, or other types of educational or philanthropic enterprises, such as children's homes, aged people's homes, hospitals, etc.

[1] For a discussion of the territorial assignments of the Disciples' institutions see Reeves and Russell, *College Organization and Administration* (Indianapolis: Board of Education, Disciples of Christ), pp. 296–97.

Membership of constituent Conferences.—It is important for the purposes of this study to obtain fairly accurate figures regarding the total membership of the supporting denomination in the constituent territory of each college. Owing to the indefiniteness of the Conference relationships, in a few cases this has proved somewhat difficult. In the great majority of cases accurate figures are obtained by simply taking the total membership of the Conference or Conferences considered as the constituent territory. In cases where one Conference sponsors two (or three) institutions, one-half (or one-third) of the membership has been assigned to each institution. Other philanthropic institutions or educational enterprises sponsored by the various Conferences have been ignored in arriving at these figures. When the data are treated by reasonably broad categories no appreciable error seems to be introduced by the plan used in apportioning membership to the various institutions.

A tabulation of the number of members of the supporting denominations within the constituent territory of each of the colleges reveals a striking variation among these thirty-five institutions. Each of eight of the colleges has in excess of 100,000 members in its territory, while three have fewer than 14,000 members each; the remainder are scattered rather evenly throughout the range indicated. The median college of the group has 58,826 members of the supporting denomination in its constituent territory.

There is a pronounced tendency for the colleges on the approved list of the Association of American Universities to have larger constituent memberships than is the case with the colleges not holding this type of accreditation. The respective medians for these two groups of colleges are 76,509 and 42,710. Of the eight colleges of the entire group having fewer than 30,000 members in the supporting territory, not one is on the approved list of the Association of American Universities. There are only four of the seventeen colleges holding national accreditation which have fewer than 60,000 members in their territory. It seems fairly clear from these data that it is ordinarily necessary for denominational groups of considerable size to join in the support of an educational institution if a college is to be maintained on a satisfactory accreditation basis.

Noffsinger[1] has shown that the accredited denominational colleges of the country have an average constituency of 63,333 church members. An analysis of the data for these Methodist colleges indicates that approximately 60,000 members are needed as a constituency in order that

[1] John Samuel Noffsinger, *A Program for Higher Education in the Church of the Brethren* (New York: Teachers College, Columbia University, 1925), p. 24.

a college may have a reasonable opportunity for a satisfactory educational program. Almost without exception the colleges of this group which have a constituent membership in excess of 60,000 are well established and are reasonably certain of continuance; the only colleges having constituent membership of less than 60,000 concerning which the survey staff does not have strong presentiments of necessary reorganization in some new form or even discontinuance are those located in large population centers or those with relatively large and well-managed endowments.

Relation of constituent membership to size of enrolment.—Data showing the relationship between the membership of the constituent territory and the number of students enrolled in the college are presented in Table 6.

TABLE 6

AVERAGE NUMBER OF STUDENTS IN COLLEGES HAVING CHURCH
CONSTITUENCIES OF VARIOUS SIZES

Number of Church Members in Constituent Conferences	Number of Colleges in Group	Average Number of Students Enrolled	Average Number of Methodist Students Enrolled	Average Number of Non-Methodist Students Enrolled
100,000 or more...........	7	687	365	322
60,000–99,999.............	9	679	385	294
30,000–59,999.............	10	535	280	255
10,000–29,999.............	8	278	145	133

In this table the figures are given separately for the number of Methodist students, number of non-Methodist students, and number of all students.

This table shows that there is on the average no important difference in the size of the student body between colleges having over 100,000 church members in the constituent territory and those having from 60,000 to 100,000. Below the figure of 60,000 members, however, the relationship between the size of the college and the number of members is marked. It is interesting to note that the effect is the same on the size of the non-Methodist student body as it is on the number of Methodist students in attendance. This fact is probably related to the accreditation status of the colleges having the smaller constituencies.

It may be observed that the line of reasoning followed in the foregoing paragraphs assumes that the church membership in the constituent territory is a cause, not an effect. In other words, no evidence has been offered to show that the tendency toward relatively large church memberships in the territory of the better colleges may not be the result of maintaining for several generations a good educational institution. Unfortunately the data give no objective basis for an answer to this question. It seems clear that the resulting effect (if any) of the maintenance of an educational institution upon the number of church members is slow in being felt, while the causal elements in the church-membership situation are felt immediately by the college. It may be pointed out, however, that there are in the Methodist Episcopal Church a few rather strong Conferences that do not maintain a college; clearly the absence of an educational institution of college rank under denominational auspices has not prevented the growth of membership in these Conferences. Finally, it may be pointed out that almost without exception the colleges themselves disclaim any purpose or intent to proselyte; indeed, they insist vigorously that they are open alike to young people of all creeds and beliefs and that their teaching is without sectarian bias. Thus, while a broadly evangelical motive lies behind the maintenance of the colleges, it is not likely to be apparent in important additions to the number of members of the supporting church group.

Plans for maintaining college facilities for small constituencies.—The fact that church groups having a relatively small membership find it difficult, if not impossible, to maintain an educational institution of satisfactory grade suggests that serious consideration needs to be given by some of the Annual Conferences to the wisdom of attempting to continue the maintenance of the college under their auspices. One plan for meeting the needs of constituencies with small memberships is through the joint support of an institution by two or more denominational groups. This plan is working with a fair degree of success at Intermountain Union College, where the Presbyterians have joined with the Methodists in maintaining the institution. Oklahoma City University has also worked out a plan for joint support with the Methodist Episcopal Church, South, although this had not been put into full operation at the time of the survey visit.

A plan of a different type has been working for twenty-five years in North Dakota, where Wesley College has been operating as an "affiliated college" with the University of North Dakota at Grand Forks and with the State Agricultural College at Fargo.[1]

A third method for dealing with constituencies too small to permit the maintenance of a satisfactory four-year college is the Wesley Foundation plan, whereby pastoral care and religious instruction are provided for the students at state educational institutions.

A fourth plan is one which has been used on several occasions in the

[1] Data for Wesley College are not included in the present report. A survey of this institution has been made, however, and is on file in unpublished form in the offices of The Board of Education of the Methodist Episcopal Church, 740 Rush St., Chicago, Ill.

past history of Methodist educational endeavor—the merger of two institutions. Where a small constituency which is unsuccessfully struggling to maintain a college is located adjoining another Conference, a plan can often be worked out for the joint support of a single college on a satisfactory basis.

The data which have been presented regarding the denominational constituencies of these thirty-five colleges indicate that in many cases serious consideration needs to be given to the early adoption of some plan whereby the needs of certain relatively small groups for education under denominational auspices may be adequately met. It must be emphasized that the maintenance of a substandard institution, which does not have hope of attaining rather early accreditation, cannot be considered an adequate educational service. In fact, the maintenance of such an institution is frequently a "disservice" rather than a service to the cause of education. The adoption of any of the four plans outlined above is preferable to the indefinite continuation of a college on a substandard level.

COMPETING INSTITUTIONS

Another factor affecting the location of colleges is the number and grade of similar institutions so located as to serve essentially the same population groups. For the purposes of this study these are called "competing" institutions, and are defined as any educational institution offering work of the same level, for similar vocational or cultural objectives, and so situated as to recruit students from a portion of the area served by the college under consideration.

Eleven of the thirty-five colleges are located where they are subject to strong competition from other neighboring institutions. In almost every one of these eleven cases the competing institution or institutions are within commuting distance of the college. There is another group of nineteen of these thirty-five colleges, each of which has no important local or nearby competition but has one or more relatively strong competitors within a fifty-mile radius. There are five colleges of the entire group which have no important competition within fifty miles.

Junior colleges are beginning to be an important factor in higher education in the territories served by several of the institutions included in this study. During the course of the survey visits the question was frequently raised as to the probable ultimate effect of the junior college movement upon the service of the four-year college of liberal arts. It now seems clear that the strong and well-administered colleges of liberal arts have nothing to fear from the competition of the junior college, although a few of the weaker four-year colleges in this group may ultimately find it desirable to become public or interdenominational junior colleges. While the development of public junior colleges in neighboring centers of population has at some of these colleges resulted in temporary decreases in the enrolments of the freshman and sophomore years, when the situation once becomes established this loss is more than made up by the additional enrolments in the junior and senior years. Thus the final result of the junior college development seems to be an improvement rather than a deterioration in the service of the four-year college. The situation is perhaps best illustrated in California, where the junior college movement has reached its most extensive development. The College of the Pacific, which is located so as to feel the full effect of the junior college competition, finds that it has larger enrolments in the two upper years than in the lower division, and has also a rather large postgraduate student body.

The factor of competition must be considered in connection with the size of the population group served. From this standpoint, and considering also the absence of competition, two of the thirty-five institutions, the University of Chattanooga and Evansville College, clearly lead all the others with respect to desirability of location. The three other colleges which have no competitors within fifty miles (Dakota Wesleyan University, Gooding College, and Intermountain Union College) are located in relatively sparsely populated territory and do not have a large concentration of population or a large church constituency to serve. Next to the University of Chattanooga and Evansville College, three other institutions may be mentioned—College of Puget Sound, College of the Pacific, and Morningside College—as having a large local population group to serve with no important competition from neighboring colleges.

At the opposite end of the scale of desirability of location from the standpoint of competition may be mentioned Hamline University and Nebraska Wesleyan University, each of which, although located in a rather large city, has its state university almost at its very doors. In addition to the University of Minnesota, Hamline University also has competition from four other colleges within the Twin Cities' area. Almost as keen is the competition faced by Baker University and Oklahoma City University, each of which is within easy commuting distance of its state university. Oklahoma City University, however, has the tremendous advantage of location in a large population center. The other colleges of the group surveyed range between the extremes which have been indicated with regard to freedom from competition.

An American humorist has said that "a reasonable amount of fleas is good for a dog"; the remark may well be paraphrased to apply to competition and colleges. A reasonable amount of competition undoubtedly stimulates a college to continued self-analysis, to constant internal improvement, and to unrelenting efforts in adjusting its service to the needs of its constituency. Too much competition, however, means a duplication of effort, the maintenance of uneconomical programs, and, unless the population group served is relatively large, the ultimate extinction of the weaker or weakest institution.

Even within the group of Methodist colleges there is possibly some overlapping of effort and duplication of service. As has been shown above, in the great majority of these colleges there is more or less important competition from other institutions located within a fifty-mile radius. It is undoubtedly true that no grave educational loss would result if a few of these colleges were discontinued, provided only the energies now used in supporting them were diverted to the support of other existing colleges.

DIFFICULTIES FACED BY POORLY LOCATED COLLEGES

The college located so as to serve only a small population group, with a relatively small denominational constituency and with some important competition from other colleges, will find it difficult to survive, if indeed it ought to survive. Such a college must have exceptionally capable leadership and must have ample supporting resources if it is to continue successfully the struggle for existence. On the other hand, a capable administration finds it relatively easy to build up an excellent institution if there is a large local population to be served, if competition with other institutions is not too severe, and if there is a large denominational constituency behind the college.

The question may well be raised as to whether it would be wise to adopt the policy of concentrating educational efforts largely upon institutions which serve relatively large local population groups and denominational constituencies—institutions which even without direct subsidy seem to have an excellent chance for successful continuance; or whether the policy should be to concentrate the resources of the denomination upon the colleges which serve small local and denominational constituencies—institutions which have small chance of successful continuance without relatively large subsidy. There is need for careful and extended consideration of this matter in determining the future educational program of the denomination.

It may be pointed out that the second policy mentioned, namely, the policy of devoting the available resources largely to the support of colleges for constituencies which would otherwise be too small to maintain a college of their own, partakes largely of the character of a "missionary" service, and may be justified on that ground. On the other hand, if the results are measured by the amount of educational opportunity of a satisfactory grade which is made available, the funds of the denomination will go much farther if devoted to the subsidy of institutions so located as to serve relatively large population groups. Under this policy the educational needs of constituencies which are too small to support institutions of their own may be taken care of by one or another of the plans which have been outlined previously, i.e., joint support with other denominations, the Wesley College plan, the Wesley Foundation plan, or mergers with other existing institutions.

SUGGESTIONS FOR REMOVALS

So vital is a satisfactory location to the successful continuance of a college—especially to a weak college—that in the case of several of the institutions surveyed recommendations were made for the consideration of a relocation. This is usually a very difficult matter to consider dispassionately. There are always strong ties to the present location. There are the questions of the sacrifice of the present plant, of the feelings of the local townspeople, of the losses devolving upon faculty members who have invested in homes, and many other problems of this type. On the other hand, the ultimate service of the college should be the paramount issue. If in the long run it seems probable that greater service can be rendered in another location, the authorities of the college should not hesitate to move. Although the decision seems difficult at the time, it must be remembered that colleges have moved in the past, and where wise consideration has been given to the matter, it is rare indeed that the institution has not benefited.

One of the most recent cases of this type in the group of colleges being studied is that of the College of the Pacific, which moved to its new location at Stockton, California, only six or seven years ago. Today no one connected with the institution doubts that the move was wise, and it is clearly evident that the college has entered upon a larger field of service than was ever possible for it before. Several of the colleges of the group being surveyed can well give thought to the possibilities of moving to a new and better location.

CHAPTER V

ENROLMENT TRENDS

TRENDS IN NUMBERS OF STUDENTS ENROLLED

Table 7 presents data showing the enrolments in each of the thirty-five colleges over a period of years. The figures given are for the average number of full-time students enrolled during the two semesters or the three terms of the regular academic year plus the number of part-time students equated to the equivalent full-time basis. The data do not include summer-session students or extension students. Figures are presented for the year 1916–17 for all colleges that could furnish these data. The next year for which the data were collected was the year 1922–23. The third year used in the study was 1928–29. Data were also collected for the year 1929–30 in order to show more specifically the recent trends in enrolments. Enrolments for the year 1930–31 in the colleges visited that year are also presented. The latest enrolment figure shown for each college is the October 15 enrolment of the year indicated. In most of the institutions this figure does not differ materially from the average enrolment of the regular year.

The medians for this table indicate that there was a pronounced upward trend in the enrolments of this group of colleges between 1916–17 and 1922–23. In the six-year period following 1922–23 there was a still further tendency toward an increase, although the rate was not nearly as rapid as in the preceding period. Since 1928–29 enrolments have been practically constant in this group of colleges. The figures for 1930–31 indicate a slight upward trend in the institutions for which data are available. Caution should be used in interpreting this trend, however, because of the fact that data were not collected from all of the colleges for the year 1930–31. Furthermore, a few of the colleges have placed a limitation on their enrolments.

The medians of Table 7 show that the institutions on the approved list of the Association of American Universities tend in general to be larger than those not holding this accreditation. In each of the years studied there are not more than one or two colleges holding the highest accreditation which have an enrolment below the median for the colleges lacking national accreditation. Similarly, in each of the years studied there are only three or four colleges lacking national accreditation which have an

TABLE 7

TREND OF ENROLMENT FROM 1916 TO 1931 IN THIRTY-FIVE COLLEGES

INSTITUTION	REGULAR YEAR FULL-TIME STUDENTS AND PART-TIME STUDENTS EQUATED TO A FULL-TIME BASIS				
	1916–17	1922–23	1928–29	1929–30	1930–31
*Ohio Wesleyan..............	1,119	1,741	1,827	1,785	1,831
*DePauw...................	717	1,141	1,464	1,385	1,442
Ohio Northern..............	732	968	1,056	897	799
Oklahoma City..............	....	443	835	839	....
*Lawrence..................	556	809	781	782	....
*Albion....................	426	562	787	752	....
*Pacific....................	465	411	771	729	673
*Illinois Wesleyan...........	319	496	677	683	668
Nebraska Wesleyan.........	518	597	688	655	573
*Allegheny.................	393	551	595	641	....
*Simpson...................	363	524	651	621	....
Puget Sound...............	188	295	582	616	658
*Morningside...............	368	626	694	599	....
*Dickinson..................	355	491	545	570	....
*Cornell....................	558	669	497	546	....
Southwestern..............	314	722	639	545	536
*Willamette.................	347	451	508	512	557
*Mount Union..............	259	393	467	480	528
*Baker.....................	430	483	447	461	422
Baldwin-Wallace............	263	303	394	440	455
*Hamline...................	473	584	396	435	....
*Chattanooga...............	....	294	381	421	....
Dakota Wesleyan...........	218	382	336	347	....
Evansville..................	....	....	397	324	....
West Virginia Wesleyan......	250	360	353	323	354
Kansas Wesleyan...........	196	420	333	306	267
Iowa Wesleyan.............	333	292	326	303	....
*MacMurray................	165	277	349	297	425
McKendree.................	119	116	224	252	261
Union.....................	....	224	227	204	....
Ozark Wesleyan............	....	....	210	199	....
Intermountain..............	....	143	160	151	162
Central Wesleyan...........	110	135	191	135	....
Gooding...................	....	98	155	128	114
Brothers...................	....	....	12	31	64
Median,† all colleges	355	447	467	480	528
*Median,† A.A.U. colleges	410	524	595	599	613
Median,† non-A.A.U. colleges................	250	303	335	315	354

* Institutions on the approved list of the Association of American Universities.
† Medians are based on the institutions for which data are shown.

enrolment above the median for the colleges on the approved list of the Association of American Universities.

The enrolment trends for the individual institutions are rather irregular, and in most cases do not exactly follow the pattern shown by the medians of the table. There are several colleges which have had constant increases in enrolment over the period studied. There are a few, on the other hand, which have had constant declines, particularly since 1922–23. The majority of the colleges have increased their enrolments over this period but have at some time or another experienced a decline in enrolment.

RATES OF INCREASE OR DECREASE IN ENROLMENT

The enrolment trends may be analyzed by studying the percentage of increase or decrease in enrolments. In making these computations two bases were used: the enrolments of 1916–17 and those of 1922–23. Since only twenty-seven institutions were represented in the enrolment figures for 1916–17, the trends from this date could be analyzed in only this number of institutions. Similarly, there are only thirty-two colleges for which enrolment data were available for the year 1922–23.

Table 8 presents an analysis of the number of colleges having various percentages of increase or decrease in enrolments over the 1916–17 and the 1922–23 bases.

TABLE 8

NUMBER OF COLLEGES HAVING VARIOUS PERCENTAGES OF INCREASE
OR DECREASE IN ENROLMENTS OVER CERTAIN PERIODS

Amount of Increase or Decrease over Enrolment of Earliest Year Shown	1916–17 to 1922–23	1916–17 to 1928–29	1916–17 to 1929–30	1922–23 to 1928–29	1922–23 to 1929–30
More than 200 per cent increase	....	1	1	....	....
Increase of 100–199 per cent...	2	4	2	....	2
Increase of 50–99 per cent.....	8	13	14	5	2
Increase of 25–49 per cent.....	8	5	4	7	5
Increase of 1–24 per cent......	6	1	3	12	12
Decrease of 1–15 per cent.....	3	2	3	5	7
Decrease of more than 15 per cent......................	....	1	....	3	4
Total...................	27	27	27	32	32

This table shows that there is a wide variation in the colleges with respect to the rate of increase in enrolment. When the 1916–17 enrolments are used as a base, very few of the colleges show decreases in enrolment and the majority show increases of 50 per cent or more up to the latest years included in the study. When the 1922–23 data are used as a base, however, a considerable number of the institutions, from one-third to one-fourth of the total, show declines in enrolments; and the number showing increases of more than 50 per cent in this period is not large.

Relation between rate of increase and the size of enrolment.—The trends in enrolment may be analyzed according to the sizes of the colleges. The institutions which now have relatively large enrolments tend to be those which have increased most rapidly over the period covered by this study, while those with relatively small enrolments tend to be those with low or negative rates of increase. Exactly the opposite condition is true if rates of increase in enrolment are studied in relationship to the size of the colleges at the beginning of the period. On this basis the colleges that were small at the beginning of the period tend to show the largest rates of increase. This seems to be due to the fact that a relatively small numerical increase in an institution having a small enrolment results in a rather large percentage increase. The paradox found in this analysis makes it almost impossible to predict future trends in enrolment from the present size of the institutions. The only conclusion that can be reached is that small colleges have an opportunity to increase their enrolments more rapidly than those with relatively large enrolments, but that colleges which have large enrolments tend to increase the actual number of their students more rapidly than is the case with the small colleges.

Relation between trend of enrolment and population of local community.— The trend of enrolment may also be studied in relation to the size of the local community. Tables 9 and 10 show the average percentage of increase in enrolment for various groups of colleges classified according to the population of the county in which they are located. The first of these tables relates to the increase during the period from 1922–23 to 1929–30; the second relates to the period from 1916–17 to 1929–30.

These tables show a general tendency for the colleges located in the larger communities to be those with the more rapid rates of increase. According to Table 9 the average enrolment of the colleges lacking accreditation by the Association of American Universities and located in counties of under 100,000 population actually decreased between 1922–23 and 1929–30. The size of the local community seems to have a less important relationship to the trend of enrolment in the colleges on the approved list of the Association of American Universities than is the case with the colleges not holding national accreditation. In fact, between the years 1916–17 and 1929–30 nationally accredited colleges located in the small communities tended to have somewhat larger increases than those in the larger communities. Two factors probably account for this reversal of the usual relationship. The first is that a few of these colleges holding national accreditation have limited their enrolments or have introduced selective measures in the admission of students. The second factor relates to the growth of public institutions, particularly state universities and teachers colleges, in a few of the larger communities represented in this study.

TABLE 9

AVERAGE PERCENTAGE OF INCREASE IN ENROLMENT BETWEEN 1922–23
AND 1929–30 FOR THIRTY-TWO COLLEGES GROUPED ACCORDING
TO POPULATION OF COUNTY IN WHICH LOCATED

POPULATION OF COUNTY	ALL COLLEGES		A.A.U. COLLEGES		NON-A.A.U. COLLEGES	
	Number	Average Percentage of Increase	Number	Average Percentage of Increase	Number	Average Percentage of Increase
Over 100,000.......	10	48.2	6	20.3	4	90.0
40,000–99,999......	8	9.0	7	13.9	1	−25.0*
Under 40,000.......	14	1.7	5	9.0	9	− 2.3*

* Decrease

TABLE 10

AVERAGE PERCENTAGE OF INCREASE IN ENROLMENT BETWEEN 1916–17
AND 1929–30 FOR TWENTY-SEVEN COLLEGES GROUPED ACCORDING
TO POPULATION OF COUNTY IN WHICH LOCATED

POPULATION OF COUNTY	ALL COLLEGES		A.A.U. COLLEGES		NON-A.A.U. COLLEGES	
	Number	Average Percentage of Increase	Number	Average Percentage of Increase	Number	Average Percentage of Increase
Over 100,000.......	8	78.8	5	44.6	3	135.7
40,000–99,999.......	8	59.5	7	57.4	1	74.0
Under 40,000.......	11	44.7	5	62.2	6	30.2

Relation between trend of enrolment and size of church constituency.—The enrolment trends may also be studied in relation to the size of the church constituency supporting each institution. There seems to be no consistent trend in this relationship except in the case of colleges having a denominational constituency of less than thirty thousand members. On every basis studied the seven colleges of the group having a church constituency below thirty thousand show, on the average, a smaller increase than is the case with the colleges having a larger constituency than this number.

As has already been pointed out, a few of the colleges have set definite limitations on the number of students to be enrolled. Albion College has fixed the size of its enrolment at 800; Willamette University and Mount Union College each limits its enrolment to 500 students. Willamette University has also introduced a further limitation upon the number of students that will be accepted from the local community. Selective admission of students is employed by a considerable number of the colleges without any fixed limitation upon the total number which will be admitted.

Table 11 presents data showing the sex distribution of students in thirty-three of the colleges included in this study. MacMurray College, which admits only women students, and Brothers College, which admits only men students, have been omitted from the table. This table shows for each college the percentage of students that are women. The corresponding percentages of men students may be obtained in each case by subtracting the number given from 100.

The medians of this table indicate that there is a slight trend over the period of years to enrol a decreasing percentage of women students in this group of colleges. The percentage of women students enrolled, as indicated by the medians for all colleges, has declined over the thirteen-year period from 52.0 per cent to 47.3 per cent. This decline is more noticeable in the colleges on the approved list of the Association of American Universities than in the colleges which do not hold national accreditation.

It will be noted from the table that in most of the institutions the sex distribution of students tends to be rather evenly balanced. There is no college of the group in which the women students, during the period studied, have consistently comprised as much as 60 per cent of its total enrolment.[1] In four colleges the women students have rather consistently comprised less than 40 per cent of the total enrolment. At Ohio Northern University the presence of the professional schools of law, pharmacy, and engineering accounts for the relatively small percentage of women students.

In the cases of Dickinson College and Allegheny College there has been a definite limitation with regard to the number of women students to be admitted, which accounts for the unbalanced condition of the distribution. Only one other college has adopted any limitation of its enrolment

[1] Except MacMurray College, which is a woman's college.

with regard to sex. At Albion College it is planned to admit an equal number of men and women, although the number of women applicants is

TABLE 11

PERCENTAGE WHICH WOMEN STUDENTS ARE OF TOTAL FULL-TIME STUDENT ENROLMENT IN THIRTY-THREE COLLEGES

INSTITUTION	PERCENTAGE OF WOMEN STUDENTS			
	1916–17	1922–23	1928–29	1929–30
Gooding..........................	....	50.8	66.0	67.2
Nebraska Wesleyan...............	57.8	57.6	61.1	60.7
Dakota Wesleyan.................	66.0	63.6	57.6	59.3
*Simpson........................	58.7	53.2	58.2	58.5
*Pacific.........................	....	53.8	54.6	56.1
*Ohio Wesleyan..................	51.9	56.9	54.8	55.6
Intermountain...................	....	55.9	53.1	54.1
Oklahoma City...................	....	66.1	60.0	54.0
*Willamette......................	57.8	51.2	50.7	52.7
West Virginia Wesleyan..........	46.1	49.4	51.5	52.5
Southwestern....................	45.4	59.2	56.3	52.0
*Baker..........................	52.0	54.6	48.9	50.8
*Morningside....................	79.6	50.4	49.5	50.7
*Cornell........................	46.9	51.9	50.7	50.7
Union..........................	....	48.6	50.8	50.4
Baldwin-Wallace.................	47.8	41.5	49.7	48.4
*Albion.........................	44.7	42.6	46.9	47.3
*Lawrence.......................	48.5	44.4	46.1	47.0
Iowa Wesleyan..................	55.5	58.5	45.5	46.7
*Chattanooga....................	....	19.2	42.1	46.5
*Illinois Wesleyan...............	....	....	43.7	46.4
Ozark Wesleyan.................	....	....	44.3	45.6
Kansas Wesleyan................	53.2	48.6	45.1	45.5
*Hamline.......................	58.6	41.0	43.3	44.4
Evansville......................	....	....	47.3	43.0
Puget Sound....................	68.0	54.7	42.2	42.1
Central Wesleyan................	42.7	46.6	44.8	41.5
McKendree.....................	45.4	39.7	38.6	40.9
*DePauw........................	52.0	45.4	41.4	40.0
*Mount Union...................	32.3	39.0	41.7	38.7
*Allegheny......................	38.1	39.9	37.0	38.4
Ohio Northern..................	13.4	25.7	25.3	25.8
*Dickinson......................	....	36.4	25.4	25.1
Median,† all colleges..........	51.9	49.9	47.3	47.3
*Median,† A.A.U. colleges......	52.0	45.4	46.5	47.2
Median,† non-A.A.U. colleges..	47.8	50.8	49.7	48.4

* Institutions on the approved list of the Association of American Universities.

† Medians are based on the institutions for which data are presented.

greater than the number of men. Since selective measures are in effect for all students at the three colleges which definitely restrict the proportion of women students, it naturally follows that the selection of women is more rigid than that of men. The wisdom of this policy is open to considerable question. It is probably both educationally and socially unwise for the women students of a college to be a more highly selected and intellectually superior group as compared with the men students.

It would seem that these artificial restrictions with regard to the sex distribution of enrolment serve no valid educational or social purpose. The history of enrolments in these other colleges indicates that a strong coeducational institution has nothing to fear from "overfeminization" of the student body.

CHAPTER VI

CLASSIFICATION AND RETENTION OF STUDENTS

CLASSIFICATION OF STUDENTS

In each of the colleges studied an analysis was made of the percentage of students enrolled at the various class levels over a period of years. A summary of these data is presented in Table 12, showing for each of the institutions the average percentage of students at each class level. In each case the period used is the five years immediately preceding the survey visit. Data are not presented for Brothers College because of the fact that this is a new institution and its enrolments have not yet been built up to the place where an analysis would be significant.

It will be noted from this table that the average distribution of student enrolment among the classes varies markedly in this group of colleges. The standardizing associations have generally set up the principle that a standard college should have at least one-fourth of its students enrolled in the junior and senior years. Many of these colleges exceed this proportion by a considerable percentage although several of the colleges lacking national accreditation do not meet the minimum standards on this point.

There is a general tendency for the colleges on the approved list of the Association of American Universities to have somewhat higher percentages of their students in the upper division than is the case in the colleges not holding this type of accreditation. In Table 12 the institutions are arranged in order of the percentage of students enrolled in the upper division. It will be noted that the first seven colleges on the list are on the approved list of the Association of American Universities and that the six having the lowest percentage of students in the upper division all lack accreditation by the Association of American Universities. It may be pointed out, however, that there are three colleges on the approved list of the Association of American Universities that have barely one-fourth of their student enrolments in the upper division. Every college having less than 25 per cent of its student body in the upper division lacks accreditation by this Association.

Classification figures not an index of retention.—Three or four factors may be mentioned which introduce some difficulty in the interpretation of the figures regarding the classification of students. In the first place, it should be clearly borne in mind that these figures are not an accurate in-

TABLE 12

Average Classification of Students in Thirty-four Colleges for a Five-Year Period

INSTITUTION	Average Percentage of Total Enrolment at the College Level Belonging to Each Class or Division							
	Fresh-man	Sopho-more	Junior	Senior	Gradu-ate	Special	Lower Division	Upper Division
*Baker	29.7	25.0	23.6	20.4	0.7	0.6	54.7	44.7
*Allegheny	34.1	26.0	21.0	18.0	0.6	0.3	60.1	39.6
*Ohio Wesleyan	33.1	25.8	18.9	18.5	2.0	1.7	58.9	39.4
*Dickinson	35.5	25.5	20.4	18.6	......	......	61.0	39.0
*Mount Union	35.9	26.1	19.9	17.6	......	0.5	62.0	37.5
*Pacific	28.3	18.5	15.0	14.6	7.9	15.7	46.8	37.5
*DePauw	38.9	23.8	19.3	16.5	0.1	1.4	62.7	35.9
Southwestern	35.1	26.2	18.1	17.7	......	2.9	61.3	35.8
*Albion	38.8	25.5	18.8	16.2	0.3	0.4	64.3	35.3
Baldwin-Wallace	33.4	24.0	17.6	17.4	0.3	7.3	57.4	35.3
Ohio Northern†	35.1	27.6	19.3	15.4	......	2.6	62.7	34.7
Intermountain	36.9	25.0	19.2	15.4	......	3.5	61.9	34.6
*Cornell	38.7	25.7	16.3	16.8	0.7	1.8	64.4	33.8
*Willamette	35.9	23.2	18.3	14.6	0.9	7.1	59.1	33.8
West Virginia Wesleyan	35.5	27.6	17.0	16.2	0.5	3.2	63.1	33.7
*Hamline	41.1	24.5	17.2	15.1	1.0	1.1	65.6	33.3
*Simpson	38.0	28.1	18.1	14.6	0.3	0.9	66.1	33.0
*Chattanooga	36.4	21.5	17.0	15.1	......	10.0	57.9	32.1
Central Wesleyan	41.9	26.0	14.6	15.1	1.5	0.9	67.9	31.2
Kansas Wesleyan	39.6	24.2	14.4	15.4	......	6.4	63.8	29.8
Iowa Wesleyan	38.7	28.4	16.1	13.2	......	3.6	67.1	29.3
Dakota Wesleyan	40.4	28.5	14.7	14.1	......	2.3	68.9	28.8
*Illinois Wesleyan	41.0	26.8	15.0	13.6	......	3.6	67.8	28.6
McKendree	43.7	23.6	14.6	13.9	......	4.2	67.3	28.5
Nebraska Wesleyan	40.2	30.2	14.3	13.9	0.3	1.1	70.4	28.5
*Lawrence	37.8	21.8	14.4	11.8	0.8	13.4	59.6	27.0
*Morningside	39.3	26.9	14.7	12.0	......	7.1	66.2	26.7
*MacMurray	45.6	23.3	13.7	12.0	......	5.4	68.9	25.7
Puget Sound	44.7	25.2	14.0	10.2	0.5	5.4	69.9	24.7
Evansville	37.7	28.7	15.0	9.3	0.2	9.1	66.4	24.5
Gooding	28.2	18.8	12.5	11.7	......	28.8	47.0	24.2
Oklahoma City	40.6	22.6	13.1	10.8	......	12.9	63.2	23.9
Union	58.0	25.6	8.0	8.4	......	......	83.6	16.4
Ozark Wesleyan	55.6	31.8	8.4	4.2	......	......	87.4	12.6
Median, all colleges	38.4	25.6	16.2	14.9	0.1	3.1	63.5	32.6
*Median, A.A.U. colleges	37.8	25.5	18.1	15.1	0.3	1.7	62.0	33.8
Median, non-A.A.U. colleges	39.6	26.0	14.6	13.9	0.0	3.5	66.4	28.8

* Institutions on the approved list of the Association of American Universities.
† Two-year period, 1929–30 and 1930–31, only.

dex of the retention of students. The number and percentage of students transferring from other institutions during the upper years vary from college to college. The presence of these transfer students tends to increase somewhat the apparent holding-power of the college.

Effect of enrolment trends on classification.—A second factor which must be taken into account is the effect of growth or decline in enrolment on the distribution of students. It is natural to suppose that an increase in enrolment will result temporarily in a higher percentage of students being enrolled at the lower-division level than would be the case if the enrolment were stable. If a college is increasing its enrolment, the increase tends to

TABLE 13

AVERAGE PERCENTAGE OF STUDENTS IN UPPER DIVISION OF COLLEGES,
GROUPED ACCORDING TO TREND OF ENROLMENT FROM
1922–23 TO 1929–30

TREND OF ENROLMENT BETWEEN 1922–23 AND 1929–30	AVERAGE PERCENTAGE OF STUDENTS IN UPPER DIVISIONS OVER A FIVE-YEAR PERIOD					
	All Colleges		A.A.U. Colleges		Non-A.A.U. Colleges	
	Number	Average Percentage	Number	Average Percentage	Number	Average Percentage
Increase of 50 per cent or more..................	4	28.6	1	37.5	3	25.7
Increase of 25 per cent to 49 per cent..............	5	31.1	3	32.0	2	29.8
Increase of less than 25 per cent..................	12	34.0	8	35.5	4	30.9
Decrease................	11	31.3	5	33.1	6	29.9

be manifested first in the freshman class, to be followed in successive years by corresponding increases in the sophomore, junior, and senior classes. Table 13 presents an analysis of the relationship between enrolment trends and the classification of students. In this table the colleges are grouped according to the trend of enrolment, and data showing the average percentage of students in the upper division for each of the groups are presented.

It will be observed from this table that the average percentage of the student body classified in the upper division tends to vary with the rate of increase in enrolment. As has already been suggested, this would be expected from the fact that increases tend to be manifested first in the freshman class. It will also be noted from this table that decreases in enrolment apparently have not been accompanied by any marked change in the classification of students. In other words, when decreases occur, they apparently take place all along the line and affect the enrolments of the four college years almost indiscriminately. The application of this principle to specific institutions varies, of course, with the circumstances. The conclusion drawn concerns only the general trends as shown by the data and does not take into account specific factors in a given institution which may operate to nullify the action of this principle.

Special students.—A third factor which makes the interpretation of data regarding the classification of students somewhat confusing is the large percentage of special students. This term is used by many of the colleges to cover a somewhat miscellaneous category of students. As far as possible the data of Table 12 have been refined to eliminate from the classification of special students such categories as children enrolled for music instruction, graduate students, and part-time students.

In the strict sense of the term, special students are those who are enrolled for college work not leading toward a degree, most of whom have not met the regular entrance requirements. In many of the colleges, however, the term applies to all students who have not yet been classified due to some irregularity of transcript, conditioned entrance, or lack of time on the part of the officers of the college to make the necessary classification. In many of the colleges the term "special" also covers part-time music students who are not enrolled for a degree and who are of doubtful classification so far as their college status is concerned.

A high percentage of special students is generally looked upon with some suspicion by the standardizing agencies. In so far as this may mean a relaxing of admission requirements, it is clear that too large a percentage might endanger the work of the regular students. When regular college students are put in classes containing a considerable number of people who are not of standard college caliber, it is clear that the instructional program is likely to suffer.

The practice of classifying as "special" those students who have merely delayed their formal classification is not a satisfactory method of procedure. Students should be urged in every possible way to regularize their classification at the earliest possible date after matriculation. It should be the policy of the college to keep the number of special and unclassified students at the very lowest possible point. This does not mean that qualified students who do not wish to work for a degree should be prohibited from entering the institution, but the number of such students should always be relatively small. Practically all students classified as "specials" in Table 12 are actually working on either the lower division or the subcollegiate level. Very few of them could classify as upper-division students.

Basis of classification.—A fourth factor affecting the analysis of the classification of students relates to the fact that the basis of classification differs among the various colleges of this group. The qualifications which are necessary to become a sophomore, a junior, or a senior are not uniform. Table 14 presents data showing the credit-hour requirement necessary for classification in each of the three upper classes in this group of colleges.

TABLE 14

NUMBER OF SEMESTER HOURS OF CREDIT NECESSARY FOR CLASSI-
FICATION AS SOPHOMORE, JUNIOR, AND SENIOR IN
THIRTY-FIVE COLLEGES

	Sophomore	Junior	Senior
Largest number of semester hours required for given classification by any of the thirty-five colleges..................	39	69	109
Largest number of semester hours required for given classification by one-fourth of the thirty-five colleges................	26	60	90
Median number of semester hours required for given classification by the thirty-five colleges*............................	24	56	88
Smallest number of semester hours required for given classification by one-fourth of the thirty-five colleges................	24	54	86
Smallest number of semester hours required for given classification by any of the thirty-five colleges..................	20	50	80

* Medians for the A.A.U. colleges, the non-A.A.U. colleges, and all colleges are identical in each case.

This table is read as follows: For classification as a member of the sophomore class one college requires thirty-nine semester hours of credit; 25 per cent of the colleges require twenty-six or more semester hours of credit for sophomore classification; the median amount of credit required for this classification is twenty-four semester hours; and one-fourth of the colleges require twenty-four hours or less for this classification. There is one college which classifies students as sophomores on the basis of the completion of as few as twenty semester hours of work.

It will be noted from this table that there is a rather extreme variation in the credit-hour requirements for classification at the various levels in this group of colleges. The middle 50 per cent, however, have a relatively small range in the credit requirements. Although the minimum and maximum requirements for a given classification differ markedly, this fact probably does not seriously disturb the interpretation of Table 12, since the great majority of students in each institution classified at a given level will have not the minimum amount of credit necessary for classification, but rather the normal fraction of the total amount required for graduation, i.e., thirty, sixty, or ninety semester hours, or the equivalent in term hours.

Besides the credit-hour requirements most of the colleges make some sort of a requirement regarding the quality of the work done. Typically, the quality required for classification in the upper division is somewhat higher than that in the freshman and sophomore classes. For example, a college may require twenty-four credit hours for classification as a sophomore one-half of which must be of grade C or better, but for classification as a junior may require fifty-six semester hours with an average grade of C.

In addition to the credit-hour requirements, many colleges have specific subject-matter requirements. For example, at Illinois Wesleyan University a student must have six hours of credit in rhetoric to be classified as a sophomore. In order to be classified as a junior at this institution a student must have completed, in addition, four hours of religion, four hours in physical education, and one year of a foreign language. At Willamette University no one is classified as a sophomore until all freshman requirements are met. In some colleges a student cannot receive classification higher than freshman until all entrance conditions are met.

Some question may be raised regarding the educational importance of the scheme of classifying students as freshmen, sophomores, juniors, and seniors. The students themselves seem to place considerable importance upon the classification, and the various class groups become the units of organization for many of the student activities. The plan offers a convenient method for students to measure their progress toward a degree. Assuming the classification is of sufficient importance to be continued, it would seem desirable to introduce somewhat greater uniformity with regard to the standards for classification. If institutions are to be judged, for example, upon the percentage of students in the upper division, it is clear that the college with rather strict classification requirements is at a disadvantage compared to the institution which classifies students on a somewhat more liberal basis. It should be possible for some agency or for the colleges acting as a group to determine rather definitely what specific standards should apply to the classification at various levels. This has been accomplished in the case of standards for the Bachelor's degree, but as has been shown in the preceding discussion, there is no uniformity regarding the standards for classification at the various class levels preceding the granting of the degree. Perhaps it would be wise to place less emphasis on the traditional classification of the freshman, sophomore, junior, and senior years and to insist upon a somewhat sharper line of demarcation between the lower and upper divisions, or the junior college and senior college levels.

RETENTION OF STUDENTS

In nineteen of the colleges surveyed careful studies were made of the retention of students. These studies were made by the case method, tracing the complete history of the enrolments of each of the individual students who entered as freshmen in the autumn of three years, 1921, 1923, and 1925. For each student in each of these three classes the history of subsequent enrolments was carefully analyzed and the data were summarized by computing the percentage of the entering group who were enrolled the following year as sophomores, the next year as juniors, the next year as seniors, and who graduated on time with their class at the end of four years. Computation was also made of the percentage of each entering group who had ever graduated from the college up to June, 1929. This last computation permitted an estimate of the degree to which the college finally graduates its entering freshmen, while the other percentages show the extent to which students progress regularly through a consecutive four-year curriculum.

Table 15 presents a summary of the data regarding the retention of students at nineteen colleges. The data of this table are based upon the averages of the three classes included in this study.

This table shows that it is typical for approximately 60 per cent of the entering freshmen to return the following year for the second year's work. Only three-eighths of the entering freshmen are enrolled for the work of the junior year two years after their entrance, and slightly more than one-fourth of the students return for the work of the senior year on time with their class. The medians show that 26.9 per cent of the students who entered as freshmen in this group of colleges graduate at the end of four years. A considerable number, however, who do not graduate on time with their class eventually obtain their degrees, the total number being 35.7 per cent of the entering group of freshmen.

It will be observed that there is a rather wide range in the holding-power of the nineteen institutions included in this study. Two of the colleges eventually graduate almost one-half of their entering group of freshmen; two other colleges graduate less than one-fifth of the entering

TABLE 15

RETENTION OF STUDENTS AT NINETEEN COLLEGES, BASED ON AVERAGE
EXPERIENCE OF THE CLASSES ENTERING IN SEPTEMBER,
1921, 1923, AND 1925

INSTITUTION	AVERAGE PERCENTAGE OF THREE ENTERING CLASSES RETURNING IN CONSECUTIVE YEARS				
	For Sophomore Year	For Junior Year	For Senior Year	Who Were Graduated at End of Four Years	Who Were Graduated by June, 1929
*Allegheny............	72.2	51.8	44.8	43.1	49.2
*Dickinson............	68.1	54.1	49.7	47.0	48.8
*Ohio Wesleyan........	69.7	52.8	47.1	43.0	46.6
*Mount Union†........	63.7	44.4	35.6	35.4	44.2
Central Wesleyan......	51.2	29.6	28.2	26.9	41.6
*DePauw..............	61.2	45.7	39.3	35.3	39.5
Baldwin-Wallace.......	58.7	39.8	34.5	32.4	38.9
*Albion...............	58.3	39.5	31.9	30.5	38.1
Dakota Wesleyan......	64.8	39.6	33.7	33.9	35.7
*Lawrence†...........	53.9	35.1	27.6	26.9	§
*Cornell..............	60.4	36.0	28.5	26.8	33.9
Iowa Wesleyan........	70.2	40.1	30.1	28.3	33.7
*Simpson.............	62.9	37.4	26.8	23.8	29.7
*Hamline.............	51.3	30.9	24.2	22.6	27.0
Ozark Wesleyan‡......	56.3	32.5	21.3	21.3	....
*Morningside..........	50.6	28.0	20.7	20.4	25.8
Evansville............	42.9	25.4	18.8	16.2	21.6
Ohio Northern†.......	60.3	37.6	17.0	16.0	19.0
Oklahoma City........	49.9	18.7	12.0	12.0	16.0
Median, all colleges.	60.3	37.6	28.5	26.9	35.7
*Median, A.A.U. colleges............	61.2	39.5	31.9	30.5	38.8
Median, non-A.A.U. colleges........	57.5	35.5	24.8	24.1	33.7

* Institutions on the approved list of the Association of American Universities.
† Data were not available for the class entering in 1921.
‡ Data were available only for the class entering in 1925.
§ Data not available.

group. The holding-power at various stages of the student's progress also varies among this group of institutions. There is a general tendency for those having superior holding-power, as evidenced by the percentage of entering students who graduate, to have superior holding-power at each of the various stages of progress.

It will be noted, also, that the colleges on the approved list of the Association of American Universities have a better holding-power than those which are not on this list. This condition is to be expected since students frequently transfer from regionally unaccredited colleges to accredited colleges in order that their degrees may be received from a standard institution.

One of the factors affecting the holding-power of liberal arts colleges is the transferring of students to professional schools at the end of the second or third year. Failure to hold such students should not be considered a discredit to the program of the college. There is evidence to indicate that many such students should be encouraged to transfer at the end of the third year or possibly earlier, rather than to take the full four years of liberal arts work before beginning their professional work. One institution reports that its holding-power in the upper division has been increased by the organization of combined degree courses, whereby a student takes three years of work in the college and, upon the satisfactory completion of an additional year in a professional school of his choice, is granted the Bachelor's degree by the college.

The data of Table 15 do not indicate the trend in holding-power since only averages for the three entering groups are presented. A separate analysis on this point in the various colleges included in the study indicates that in general holding-power was improving during the period covered by this study. On the average, a larger percentage of the students who entered in 1925 progressed regularly through the four years of college than was the case with the group entering in 1921.

The type of analysis presented in this study is one not often made by colleges of liberal arts. It will be recognized that this is the only accurate basis for studying holding-power in an institution of higher learning. Conclusions drawn from a simple analysis of the number of students in each of the various classes are likely to be misleading because of the presence of transfer students. By tracing through the individual case histories of a group of entering students it is possible to determine rather accurately the relative holding-power. Data of this type should be a fruitful starting-point for an analysis of the curriculum, the faculty, instructional conditions, the personnel service for students, and other similar factors which may have a bearing on the holding-power of the college. As an ideal, of course, colleges desire the largest possible percentage of entering students to persist through the four-year course. An abnormally high percentage of drop-outs should be a cause for a thorough investigation in an effort to determine any factors within the institution which might be causing such a condition.

CHAPTER VII

OCCUPATIONAL ANALYSIS OF GRADUATES

NUMBER OF GRADUATES IN VARIOUS OCCUPATIONS

In thirty of the institutions included in this study, data were collected regarding the occupational distribution of the graduates. A separate analysis was made of the graduates of each of the last three decades. Table 16 presents data showing for each of the thirty institutions the percentage of the graduates of the last ten-year period engaged in various occupations.

This table shows that almost half of the alumni of these institutions graduating during the past ten years are now engaged in educational pursuits. The colleges are arranged in the table in accordance with the percentage of alumni engaged in educational work. It will be noted that there is a rather wide variation within the group with regard to the percentage who are working in this field. The second most important occupation, from the standpoint of the number of persons involved, is homemaking. Since this occupation is available only to the women graduates, its relative importance among the alumnae is almost twice as large as is indicated by the figures in the table. Commercial and clerical pursuits occupy the third place in importance from the standpoint of the percentage of graduates involved. Religious service is fourth, and the professions are fifth. In almost all of the colleges there is a small group engaged in miscellaneous occupations not classifiable under any of these categories. These are grouped together in the final column of the table with the alumni who are deceased and those whose occupations are unknown.

It will be noted that the colleges on the approved list of the Association of American Universities have, on the average, a larger percentage of their graduates in commercial pursuits, homemaking, and the professions than is the case with the colleges not holding this type of accreditation. On the other hand, the colleges without national accreditation have a larger percentage of their graduates in educational work and religious service. Since the colleges with national accreditation are typically larger than those of the other group, the actual numbers of graduates in the various fields of service cannot be inferred from the percentage figures.

An analysis of the occupational distribution of graduates of the colleges according to the size of the community in which the institution is located

TABLE 16

OCCUPATIONAL DISTRIBUTION OF GRADUATES DURING THE
LAST TEN YEARS FROM THIRTY COLLEGES

INSTITUTION	PERIOD	PERCENTAGE OF GRADUATES OF EACH INSTITUTION REPORTED IN VARIOUS VOCATIONAL GROUPS					
		Education	Home-making	Commercial and Clerical Pursuits	Religious Service	Professions†	Others, Unknown, and Deceased
Union......................	1920–28	72.8	9.6	3.2	4.8	8.0	1.6
Oklahoma City............	1920–29	63.0	12.6	11.3	6.0	3.5	3.6
McKendree...............	1921–30	61.0	10.3	5.8	13.5	8.9	0.5
West Virginia Wesleyan.....	1921–30	60.5	13.5	13.4	8.0	4.6	......
*Hamline.................	1920–29	59.7	12.3	15.1	4.8	2.9	5.2
Kansas Wesleyan..........	1921–30	57.6	18.5	11.2	6.5	4.7	1.5
Iowa Wesleyan............	1920–29	54.4	18.6	12.1	7.7	2.1	5.1
*Pacific....................	1921–30	53.1	21.2	10.5	5.1	4.5	5.6
Gooding..................	1921–30	53.0	17.4	8.7	5.2	3.5	12.2
Evansville.................	1920–29	51.8	9.7	15.8	8.6	11.6	2.5
*Morningside...............	1920–29	51.7	13.1	17.3	10.7	6.1	1.1
Dakota Wesleyan..........	1920–29	50.3	19.1	13.0	10.4	2.3	4.9
Central Wesleyan..........	1920–29	49.6	13.8	9.7	16.4	5.4	5.1
Baldwin-Wallace...........	1921–30	49.0	9.2	14.4	10.8	11.0	5.6
*Simpson..................	1920–29	48.9	19.0	14.3	9.1	7.6	1.1
Puget Sound...............	1921–30	47.7	7.8	6.1	8.5	5.1	24.8
Southwestern..............	1921–30	45.1	22.9	9.3	5.8	6.8	10.1
*Cornell...................	1920–29	44.4	21.2	12.0	6.2	7.6	8.6
Ozark Wesleyan...........	1920–29	42.5	13.1	19.4	10.0	3.7	11.3
*Mount Union..............	1921–30	42.0	14.9	17.8	5.6	17.9	1.8
Nebraska Wesleyan........	1921–30	41.7	19.2	11.9	11.1	6.1	10.0
*Dickinson.................	1920–29	41.5	9.6	15.7	12.0	17.6	3.6
*Baker....................	1921–30	40.2	28.8	16.7	8.9	3.8	1.6
*DePauw..................	1921–30	39.2	14.6	16.9	4.8	11.6	12.9
Intermountain.............	1921–30	39.1	20.7	16.6	10.1	7.7	5.8
*Allegheny.................	1920–29	38.7	13.8	20.1	4.0	13.2	10.2
*Illinois Wesleyan..........	1921–30	38.5	17.7	12.3	7.3	16.6	7.6
*MacMurray...............	1921–30	37.2	48.5	5.8	3.1	1.3	4.1
*Ohio Wesleyan............	1921–30	34.6	32.2	12.7	10.9	6.8	2.8
*Albion...................	1920–29	30.6	18.9	8.3	8.3	5.7	28.2
Median, all colleges.....	....	48.3	16.2	12.5	8.2	6.1	5.1
*Median, A.A.U. colleges.	....	40.9	18.3	14.7	6.8	7.2	4.7
Median, non-A.A.U. colleges.................	....	51.1	13.7	11.6	8.6	5.3	5.1

* Institutions on the approved list of the Association of American Universities.
† Law, medicine, engineering, dentistry, and journalism are included.

indicates no important relationship on this point in the case of any occupational group. A similar analysis, grouping the colleges on the basis of the size of the denominational constituency served, indicates that the institutions serving a relatively large constituency (60,000 members or more) tend to have the higher proportions of their graduates in commercial pursuits and the professions, while the colleges serving smaller constituencies (less than 60,000 members) have the larger percentages of their graduates in education. There seems to be no relationship between the size of the constituency served and the percentage of graduates in homemaking and religious service.

SEX DISTRIBUTION OF ALUMNI OCCUPATIONS

In fifteen of the colleges the data regarding the occupational distribution of alumni were collected separately for each sex. Table 17 shows

TABLE 17

OCCUPATIONAL DISTRIBUTION OF MEN GRADUATES DURING THE
LAST TEN YEARS FROM FOURTEEN COLLEGES

INSTITUTION	PERCENTAGE OF MEN GRADUATES REPORTED IN VARIOUS OCCUPATIONAL GROUPS				
	Education	Commercial and Clerical Pursuits	Religious Service	Professions	Others, Unknown, and Deceased
*Baker...................	36.3	34.5	18.1	8.2	2.9
Baldwin-Wallace...........	34.4	23.6	16.4	17.1	8.5
*DePauw..................	28.1	26.1	7.7	20.7	17.4
*Illinois Wesleyan..........	29.8	21.7	13.2	32.2	3.1
Intermountain.............	33.3	29.0	18.8	13.1	5.8
Kansas Wesleyan..........	56.9	18.8	13.2	7.6	3.5
McKendree...............	57.3	8.4	19.6	14.0	0.7
*Mount Union.............	32.5	26.1	8.9	29.4	3.1
Nebraska Wesleyan........	34.7	22.0	18.7	10.8	13.8
*Ohio Wesleyan...........	26.6	30.5	21.5	16.8	4.6
*Pacific..................	46.4	24.2	11.3	10.2	7.9
Puget Sound..............	33.7	11.2	15.3	9.7	30.1
Southwestern.............	41.0	20.0	11.6	12.9	14.5
West Virginia Wesleyan......	52.1	24.6	14.7	8.6	....
Median, all colleges.....	34.6	23.9	15.0	13.0	5.2
*Median, A.A.U. colleges..	31.2	26.1	12.3	18.8	3.9
Median, non-A.A.U. colleges................	37.9	21.0	15.9	11.9	7.2

* Institutions on the approved list of the Association of American Universities.

the occupational distribution of the men who have graduated during the past ten years from the fourteen coeducational colleges. Table 18 presents similar data for the women graduates of fifteen institutions, one of which is a woman's college.

Table 17 shows that in the typical institution of this group, as indicated by the median, slightly more than one-third of the men have gone into educational work, almost one-fourth have gone into commercial and cleri-

TABLE 18

OCCUPATIONAL DISTRIBUTION OF WOMEN GRADUATES DURING THE
LAST TEN YEARS FROM FIFTEEN COLLEGES

INSTITUTION	PERCENTAGE OF WOMEN GRADUATES REPORTED IN VARIOUS OCCUPATIONAL GROUPS					
	Education	Home-making	Commer-cial and Clerical Pursuits	Religious Service	Profes-sions	Others, Unknown, and Deceased
*Baker..................	43.4	52.9	1.8	1.1	0.2	0.6
Baldwin-Wallace.........	66.0	20.1	3.5	4.2	1.2	5.0
*DePauw.................	50.3	29.2	7.7	1.8	2.4	8.6
*Illinois Wesleyan.........	52.5	38.7	3.8	2.0	2.3	0.7
Intermountain...........	43.0	35.0	8.0	4.0	4.0	6.0
Kansas Wesleyan........	58.0	28.8	7.0	2.7	3.1	0.4
McKendree..............	67.5	28.8	1.3	2.4	....	....
*MacMurray.............	55.4	30.8	5.8	6.1	1.3	0.6
*Mount Union...........	54.3	34.4	7.0	1.3	3.0	....
Nebraska Wesleyan......	48.6	38.2	1.9	3.5	1.4	6.4
*Ohio Wesleyan..........	38.6	48.4	3.8	5.6	1.8	1.8
*Pacific.................	57.3	34.4	1.9	1.2	0.9	4.3
Puget Sound............	60.5	14.9	1.4	2.3	0.9	20.0
Southwestern...........	48.0	39.6	1.6	1.6	2.4	6.8
West Virginia Wesleyan..	70.4	29.6	....	....	....	....
Median, all colleges..	54.3	34.4	3.5	2.3	1.4	1.8
*Median, A.A.U. col-leges.............	52.5	34.4	3.8	1.8	1.8	0.7
Median, non-A.A.U. colleges..........	59.3	29.2	1.8	2.6	1.3	5.5

* Institutions on the approved list of the Association of American Universities.

cal pursuits, a little less than one-sixth have gone into religious service, and approximately one-eighth have gone into the professions. Table 18 shows that a larger percentage of the women have gone into educational work than is true of the men, as shown in Table 17. Education and homemaking together account for almost 90 per cent of the women gradu-ates in the median institution.

These tables confirm the differences in occupational distribution of graduates of unapproved and approved colleges which were observed in Table 16. For both the men and the women graduates the median percentages going into commercial pursuits and the professions are larger in the colleges on the approved list of the Association of American Universities than is the case with the colleges not holding this type of accreditation. The latter group, however, exceed in the percentage going into educational work and religious service. As previously stated, owing to the difference in the size of institutions the actual numbers entering various fields of service cannot be inferred from the percentage figures.

TRENDS IN OCCUPATIONAL DISTRIBUTION OF ALUMNI

The data thus far presented have related only to the graduates of the last ten-year period. Table 19 presents data showing separately the present occupational distribution of the group of alumni graduated during each of the last three decades from twenty-five colleges. In this table data are presented separately for men and for women graduates, as well as for the total of all graduates. The data for men are based upon the totals for fourteen coeducational colleges; data for women are based upon the totals for these same colleges plus one woman's college; data for totals are based upon these same fifteen colleges plus ten others in which the figures were not originally collected according to a sex classification. Five of the colleges included in Table 16 are omitted from Table 19 because their history does not extend back to the year 1901, or because data for some of the earlier periods were not available. The percentages for men and for women are based upon the total number of graduates of the respective sexes for the period indicated. Similarly, the percentages for the total are based upon the grand total number of graduates of the group of twenty-five colleges for the period.

This table shows striking differences in the percentage of graduates of the three periods who are now doing educational work. Educational service now engages twice as great a proportion of the graduates of the decade 1921–30 as of the decade 1901–10. There is little difference in the percentages of the graduates during the three periods who are now engaged in clerical and commercial pursuits. Religious service and the professions both claim a larger percentage of the earlier than of the later alumni. The percentage of alumnae who have become homemakers is also larger for the graduates of 1901–10 than for those of 1921–30.

Caution must be used in interpreting the data of Table 19 because of the fact that the alumni of the latest period in many cases have not yet had time to settle down to their ultimate occupations. Thus it is entirely probable that many of those now engaged in educational service will later become homemakers, and probably a few of those in the educational group will later shift over into the professional occupations. There will not likely be any corresponding shift of any importance from other fields

TABLE 19

NUMBER AND PERCENTAGE* OF TOTAL GRADUATES FROM TWENTY-FIVE
COLLEGES DURING EACH OF THREE DECADES NOW
ENGAGED IN VARIOUS OCCUPATIONS

OCCUPATION AND SEX	1901–10		1911–20		1921–30	
	Number of Graduates	Percentage of Total	Number of Graduates	Percentage of Total	Number of Graduates	Percentage of Total
Education:						
Men†	452	19.8	799	24.0	1,897	34.8
Women†	427	24.3	1,017	28.9	3,437	50.0
Total†	1,601	22.0	3,094	26.9	8,350	43.8
Commercial and clerical pursuits:						
Men	488	21.4	851	25.6	1,344	24.7
Women	58	3.3	88	2.5	281	4.1
Total	1,038	14.3	1,679	14.6	2,585	13.6
Homemaking:						
Women	1,098	62.5	2,050	58.2	2,541	37.0
Total	1,812	24.9	3,347	29.1	3,614	18.9
Religious service:						
Men	523	22.9	742	22.3	760	13.9
Women	49	2.8	123	3.5	205	3.0
Total	1,020	14.0	1,294	11.3	1,522	8.0
Professions:						
Men	637	27.9	654	19.6	927	17.0
Women	36	2.1	69	2.0	121	1.7
Total	1,059	14.6	1,131	9.9	1,598	8.4
Others, unknown, and deceased:						
Men	182	8.0	284	8.5	521	9.6
Women	88	5.0	174	4.9	290	4.2
Total	742	10.2	941	8.2	1,401	7.3

* Percentages are based upon the total number of graduates of the respective sex in the case of data for men and women and upon the total number of graduates in the case of data for totals for each of the three decades.

† Figures for men are based upon totals of fourteen coeducational colleges; those for women are based upon totals for these same fourteen colleges plus one woman's college. Figures for totals are based upon these same fifteen colleges plus ten others in which the original data were not gathered according to a sex classification.

into educational service. This tends to overweight somewhat the field of education. It is, nevertheless, obvious from this table that these colleges of liberal arts are tending more and more to become teacher-training institutions. This fact has important implications for the curriculum organization of the college. Even if teaching is considered by many of the graduates as a relatively temporary occupation, as something to be done immediately upon graduation in order to earn a little money while awaiting the opportunity to shift into some other calling, the college clearly has obligations to do the best possible job of preparing those graduates who go out to teach in the public schools.

Another caution should be observed in interpreting Table 19. The trends should be studied not only from the standpoint of the percentage of graduates but also from that of the actual numbers entering the several fields of work. Thus it will be seen that while the professions and religious service have declined in relative importance, actually there has been no decrease in the number of graduates entering these fields.

CHAPTER VIII

CHARTERS AND BY-LAWS

CHARTER PROVISIONS

All of the colleges included in this study exist by virtue of some form of official authorization from the government of the commonwealths in which they are located. There are two forms of this official authorization: the charter, and the articles of incorporation. The charter may be described, in general, as a specific enactment by the legislature of the state authorizing the establishment of the institution and defining its powers and privileges. The articles of incorporation consist of an agreement by the founders of the institution, drawn up under the provisions of a general statute, and filed with some official of the commonwealth in a manner prescribed by the general statute. The essential difference between the charter and the articles of incorporation lies in the fact that in the case of the former the action of the state legislature is specific, applying to the one institution only, while in the latter case the legislative action is general, the institution merely taking advantage of the provisions which are made for the incorporation of similar institutions.

The question of whether a college will be "chartered" or "incorporated" is, of course, a matter of state policy. While almost all the earlier colleges were separately chartered, many states now provide for the incorporation of educational institutions under a general statute. Of the thirty-five colleges included in this study, sixteen exist by virtue of charters, seventeen are incorporated without specific legislative enactment, and two are both chartered and incorporated. In the case of states which have changed their policy with regard to the chartering of institutions, the colleges that held charters at the time of the change have, of course, been protected in their charter rights; for this reason it has been deemed advantageous by two colleges to retain the charter while incorporating under the new act.

An exhaustive analysis of the policies of all the states of the Union, with reference to the chartering or the incorporating of educational institutions, has not been undertaken in this study. The data at hand indicate that thirteen of the states in which one or more of the colleges being surveyed are located now have the policy of incorporating rather than chartering educational institutions. These states are: California, Idaho, Iowa, Kansas, Kentucky, Missouri, Montana, Nebraska, Ohio, Oklahoma, Oregon,

Washington, and West Virginia. Possibly the same policy now obtains in some other states represented by institutions included in this study, and has been overlooked in this analysis because the colleges have preferred to retain their old charters rather than to take advantage of the new act of incorporation.

In general, the charters tend to be much older documents than the articles of incorporation. Most of the latter have been filed since 1900, while the charters generally date from the beginning of the institution.

Many of the earlier charters grant special privileges, such as perpetual tax-exemption, and for that reason are especially valuable to the institutions. On the other hand, the articles of incorporation are usually more flexible and are easier to amend than the charters, giving this form of official authorization the advantage of being easily adaptable to changing conditions.

There seems to be no common understanding as to what shall be included in the charter or articles of incorporation of an educational institution. All of those available for examination contain some form of an enabling act (in the case of the charters) or declaration of intention (in the case of articles of incorporation). There is usually some statement of the object or purpose of the proposed institution, but this is always broad and general, and not infrequently embraces a wider field of service than the college has any intention of entering upon. Almost all the charters or articles of incorporation specify the way in which the government of the institution is to be exercised, providing for the number of trustees and the method of their selection. There is usually some definite specification of the rights and powers of the institution, and in some of the charters, as before noted, special privileges are granted. Beyond these more or less general matters, the charters and articles of incorporation of the various colleges deal with a miscellaneous assortment of items. Some of them go into considerable detail regarding the internal organization of the institution, a matter which is usually covered in the by-laws of the board. Some specify the number and time of the board meetings, the officers which shall be elected, the duties of the faculty, etc.

BY-LAWS OF THE BOARD

Each of the thirty-five colleges included in this study has a set of by-laws for the government of the institution. In one college there were no by-laws at the time of the survey visit, but a set has since been framed and adopted. In several colleges the by-laws were in process of revision at the time of the survey visit.

As in the case of the charters and articles of incorporation, there is little agreement among these institutions with regard to the items covered in the by-laws. Many topics that are treated in the charters of some colleges are covered in the by-laws of others. In general, the by-laws deal principally with the organization of the board of trustees itself (officers, committees, time and place and frequency of meetings, quorums, order of business, terms of membership, methods of choosing new members), the internal organization of the college (duties of various officers, their relationships to each other and to the board), the fiscal management of the college, the faculty (its constitution, powers, and duties), and the procedures for amending the by-laws.

The by-laws of a college may be likened to the statute laws of a commonwealth, the charter or articles of incorporation corresponding to the constitution of the state. The by-laws should represent the codification of the existing policies of the board, and should therefore be relatively easy to change. The provision is generally made that the by-laws may be amended at any meeting of the board by a two-thirds vote of the members present if the proposed amendment has been previously sent out for study by board members.

It is important that the by-laws be complete, i.e., that they cover every point on which the board has definitely established a policy affecting the government of the institution. If decisions of this sort are recorded only in board minutes, they are likely to become lost and, owing to the limited circulation of the minutes, cannot become generally known. The by-laws, on the other hand, are an open document and should therefore contain every important policy of the board which can conceivably be of interest to persons not having access to the official minutes.

If the by-laws are to be most serviceable, they must be kept constantly revised and up to date, and should be issued in printed or mimeographed form so as to be readily available. Fifteen of the thirty-five colleges surveyed have issued their by-laws in printed form. In most cases a single handbook contains both the by-laws and the charter or the articles of incorporation. In several colleges the by-laws have not been kept up to date by the inclusion of recent revisions and amendments. In others, there has been no recent revision of the by-laws, with the result that many of the provisions are entirely out of date.

CHAPTER IX

BOARDS OF CONTROL

DESIGNATION OF THE CONTROLLING BOARD

The thirty-five colleges studied are all under the direct control of boards, known in every institution but one as the board of trustees. In one college, Dakota Wesleyan University, the controlling agency is known as the board of directors.

Visitors.—Seventeen of the colleges have provision for official visitors from the supporting Annual Conference. Eighteen colleges have no provision for visitors. In most of the colleges having official visitors these persons do not participate directly in the control of the institution but serve rather in an advisory capacity, or as a liaison between the college and the ecclesiastical organization. For the most part it seems to be the function of the visitors to assure the denomination that the policies of the college are in accordance with the desires of the church body. In four of the seventeen cases in which there are official visitors, however, these persons are considered as members of the board of trustees, with the right to sit in meetings, to participate in discussions, and to vote on all questions. In one of these four colleges, Illinois Wesleyan University, the visitors have the sole power to nominate persons for the office of president of the university, and the trustees have the sole power to elect the president, the two groups not being otherwise allocated any distinctive functions in the control of the institution. It may be noted that it seems like splitting hairs to make a distinction between a *trustee* elected by a Conference, and a *visitor* elected by the same Conference with the privilege of sitting in meetings of the board and voting on all questions.

Cornell College has provided for three classes of visitors, of two members each, who function as advisers to the college, but have no vote at board meetings. One class is appointed by the Annual Conference, one by the board of trustees, and one by the faculty. Although this arrangement looks well on paper, there is little evidence that it has functioned effectively in practice.

The whole matter of the place and function of official visitors in the administration of these colleges needs special consideration. In many of the colleges these officials are established by the charter or articles of incorporation. In most of the institutions the visitors function only nomi-

65

nally, if at all. Under present conditions in higher education, there seems to be little need for a board of visitors; and such an agency always affords a potential source of interference with the legally responsible board of trustees in the performance of the functions of general control that are unquestionably the province of the board.

SIZE OF THE BOARD

The number of members on the boards of these colleges ranges from thirteen in Intermountain Union College to fifty-four in Morningside College.[1] The median institution of the thirty-five colleges has thirty-six board members, and the median for the seventeen colleges on the approved list of the Association of American Universities falls at exactly the same point. Only three of the college boards have fewer than twenty members, and twenty-nine of them have thirty or more members. Approximately half of the colleges have between thirty and forty members on the board. Almost one-third of them have forty or more members on their boards, and there are three institutions with boards of fifty or more.

The total number of members on the boards of these colleges seems rather large. Data presented by Reeves and Russell for a group of fifteen colleges of the Disciples of Christ show that only two of the institutions of that group have boards of more than thirty members.[2]

Merely from the standpoint of the effective control of the institution, it seems useless to provide such large boards as are commonly found in these thirty-five colleges. A board of from seven to nine members could easily carry on all the necessary functions of government and could provide a breadth of viewpoint and a diversification of interests sufficient for all the purposes of effective directon of the institution.

It might be pointed out that many of the large state universities have boards no larger than seven or nine members. Most of the large public-school systems of the country are controlled by boards of less than ten members. Of the forty-five land-grant colleges and universities in the United States, only five have boards with a membership of greater than twenty-five, and approximately half of these institutions have boards of less than ten members.[3] In all of the cases cited the responsibilities involved are larger than in the typical institution of the thirty-five colleges

[1] In case the Annual Conference visitors sit in with the board and have a vote, they are considered in these data as board members.

[2] Reeves and Russell, *College Organization and Administration* (Indianapolis: Board of Education, Disciples of Christ, 1929), p. 55.

[3] *Survey of Land-Grant Colleges and Universities,* U.S. Department of the Interior, Office of Education, Bull. 9, I (1930), 54–55.

in the group being studied. The maintenance of large boards for these colleges cannot, therefore, be justified on the basis of the extent of the responsibilities involved or the importance of the office itself.

Not only is a board of seven or nine members fully able to carry all the responsibilities devolving upon a college board of control, but a board of this size also avoids many of the disadvantages which are inherent in the larger board. Four of these disadvantages will be briefly discussed.

The first disadvantage of a large board is that meetings are apt to be attended by only a small proportion of the members. Data have been collected regarding the number of members attending meetings held during the past four years in twenty-eight of the colleges studied. The average attendance in these colleges for the four-year period ranges from 31 to 77 per cent of the board membership, with a median of 57 per cent. This means that in the typical college, with a board of thirty-six members, as a rule not more than twenty will be present at board meetings. Thus, although the sizes of the boards in these institutions are rather large, in actual practice the control is exercised by a group only slightly more than half as large as the entire board. The services of the remainder who are listed on the board are frequently of questionable value to the institution and, in many cases, could be dispensed with without any great loss.

A second disadvantage of a large board is that the individual members tend to take less responsibility and feel less interest in the work of the institution. A board of seven or nine members, all of whom are vitally interested in the college, would undoubtedly be of more service than a group of thirty or forty, many of whom, because of the size of the group, have only a casual interest.

A third disadvantage of a large board is that it tends to disintegrated action by committees. In a large group it becomes practically impossible to bring every question before the entire body. As a result, a committee organization is formed, and matters are referred to standing committees. The board as a whole tends more or less to become a rubber stamp for committee actions. In the interim between board meetings the executive committee, and frequently other committees as well, are typically given rather wide powers and, to all intents and purposes, function as the board of trustees. Although these committees may technically report to the entire board at an annual or semiannual meeting, only in very rare instances are their actions even questioned and almost never are they reversed. In fact, the approval of the actions of committees is frequently *ex post facto*, and the board could not, if it would, in such cases reverse the committee action.

The fourth disadvantage of a large board of trustees is that some more or less private matters pertaining to the institution become common information to a large group, some of whom may be indiscreet in discussing the affairs of the college with outsiders. In order to protect the institution against this disadvantage, some of the colleges refuse to give out information to all members of the board. For example, in one college the board of trustees is expected to pass the annual budget in summary form only, without being given any information as to details, particularly those relating to salaries. In some of the colleges officials have withheld important information from the trustees regarding the financial condition of the institution. In one or two cases objection was made to the inclusion in the survey report[1] of factual material relating to the finances of the institution because of the effect which this information would have on the members of the board of trustees.

The use of the term "board of trustees" in these colleges is inaccurate. The boards as constituted typically do not function as the controlling agents of the colleges. It seems rather that the title "trustee" is generally considered by the majority of those holding the office as an honorary position, giving one the right to have his name printed in the annual catalogue of the college and the right to attend a meeting once or twice a year (if he wishes to do so), but imposing no important responsibilities or obligations. As a matter of current practice, the most important controlling body in most of these colleges is not the entire board but the executive committee. Thus, the thesis that a small board of seven or nine members is sufficient for the effective control of a college seems to be demonstrated in actual practice, even in those institutions which nominally have boards with much larger membership.

It is apparent that, while the boards are nominally very large in the colleges of this group, in practice, the control is placed by two stages in successively smaller groups. First, there is the limited attendance at board meetings, resulting in a reduction of almost one-half in the effective size of the board. Second, there is a delegation of large powers to committees, which further reduces the effective controlling body for specific phases of the management of the college to the proportions of the committees.

The report of the Survey of Land-Grant Colleges and Universities,[2] speaking of the boards in these institutions with membership above thirty, states:

[1] The report to which reference is made is the confidential report made to each institution, dealing with the problems of immediate concern to the college.

[2] *Survey of Land-Grant Colleges and Universities*, U.S. Department of the Interior, Office of Education, Bull. 9, I (1930), 56.

These boards are unwieldy. It is moreover obvious that the entire membership does not function in the actual government of the institutions. Extended study of detailed data concerning attendance at board meetings over a period of years shows conclusively that it is impossible to secure the attendance of a large number either at the regular sessions or at specially called meetings. The result is that only a few actively interested members assume the responsibility of conducting the affairs of the board.

Speaking further of those institutions with boards of from ten to twenty-five members, this report states: ". . . . these governing bodies are also cumbersome and unwieldy, and it is frequently necessary to handle their business largely through committees to which large authority is delegated, rather than through the entire membership." All of the disadvantages of large boards mentioned in the report of the Survey of Land-Grant Colleges are equally apparent in connection with the colleges included in this study.

In spite of the disadvantages of large boards, with their tendencies to turn over the actual control of the institutions to smaller groups, many college administrators think that relatively large boards of trustees are preferable to smaller ones for institutions which are dependent upon financial gifts from churches or individuals. It appears that official connection with an institution as a member of its board of trustees often creates an interest in the program on the part of prominent men whose support might not otherwise be secured. Sometimes those who are selected as members of the board of trustees of an institution become large donors to its funds, or participate actively in the program of financial development.

While this argument has a sound theoretical basis, the actual conditions among the colleges of the group being studied indicate that all too often none of the board members take an active interest in the provision of financial resources for the institution. Even in the colleges which are so fortunate as to have some board members who are generous contributors or who actively seek to promote the financial welfare of the institution, the number of such trustees is in nearly every case relatively small. Typically, not more than one or two members of the board will be found to have made any substantial financial contribution to the college.

Among this group of colleges there are three or four conspicuous exceptions to the general rule that members of the board do not assist in providing financial resources. In these colleges the members of the board have not only been active in giving their own funds to the institution but have provided the financial promotion officers with valuable contacts with other people of means and have themselves solicited the interest of their friends and acquaintances in the college. The institutions which have been fortunate in attracting this type of board member are without exception among the very best colleges of the group, and in these cases there is some justification for relatively large boards. Other institutions, however, would probably be better managed if some reduction were made in the number of members of the board of control.

SELECTION OF BOARD MEMBERS

There are three methods by which members of the boards of these colleges are selected: (1) election by the constituent Annual Conference; (2) election by the board itself; (3) election by the alumni. In addition, there are frequently one or more members ex officio. Combinations of these methods are used in many of the colleges.

Election or confirmation by Annual Conference.—In the majority of these institutions there is technically a relatively large degree of ecclesiastical control in the selection of board members, although in practice the church bodies seem to depend upon advice from those associated with the college in their determination of the membership of the board. In eleven of the thirty-five colleges all the elected board members are chosen by the church body. On the other hand, there are four colleges in which none of the board members are subject either to election or approval by an Annual Conference. The other colleges range between these two extremes, the median institution having 60 per cent of its board members chosen by the church body. The median institution of the seventeen colleges on the approved list of the Association of American Universities has 51 per cent of its board members chosen by the Annual Conference.

There are three distinct ways in which the will of the church group is exercised in the selection of board members. In the majority of cases the members are chosen directly by the Annual Conference (in one case by General Conference) without provision for formal action by the board of trustees itself. In several colleges the board nominates those whom it wishes placed on the board and the Conference confirms the list of nominees. In one or two colleges the Conference nominates and the board elects from the list of nominees. Under the plan whereby the board nominates and the Conference confirms the list of nominees, it is very unusual for a person nominated by the board for membership to fail to be elected by the Conference. Under this arrangement the degree of ecclesiastical control is usually not large.

In practically all cases, irrespective of the method of selection employed, it appears that the wishes of the college authorities are consulted by the Conference in the selection of board members.

Election by the board itself.—The second method of selecting members, election by the board itself, is the essence of a self-perpetuating board. In all but ten of the thirty-five colleges some of the members of the board are elected by the board itself. In the case of three of these ten in which all the board members are elected by the Conference, the board nominates to the Conference those who are to be elected. There is one case in which all the board members are nominated by the Conference, subject to election by the board itself. There are two colleges in which the entire list of board members is chosen by the board itself.

Election by the alumni.—Twenty of the thirty-five colleges have made provision for alumni representation on the board of trustees. The proportion of the board members who represent the alumni in these twenty colleges ranges from 7 to 29 per cent, with a median for the entire group of thirty-five colleges of 8 per cent. The median institution of the seventeen colleges on the approved list of the Association of American Universities has 12 per cent of its board members representing the alumni. In some cases the powers of the alumni are limited to the nomination of members to represent them, the actual election being confirmed by the board or, in one case, by the Annual Conference. In other cases the power of election is vested directly in the alumni body.

The policy of having some members on the board to represent alumni interests seems to be wise. The alumni have a vital concern in the welfare of the college, and it is only fair to allow them a voice in controlling its destinies. In only one college was it found that the alumni representation on the board had led to embarrassment or friction, and in this case the difficulty seemed to lie in the personality of the man chosen to be in charge of alumni interests, rather than with the alumni trustees themselves.

Ecclesiastical control.—Serious question may be raised as to the wisdom of as large a measure of direct ecclesiastical control over the selection of board members as is exercised in many of the colleges of this group. While it is recognized that these are church institutions, and that the church group has a right to be assured that the affairs of the colleges are being managed in accordance with their wishes, it would seem that, at most, the election of a majority of the trustees would be ample to satisfy this requirement.

The provision for election of all board members by the Annual Conference is not generally satisfactory where this method is employed. Occasionally the institution finds itself handicapped in its search for the most capable persons to serve on its board. Sometimes very suitable persons are found who are both interested in the college and able to give it valuable help, but who do not care to go through the formality of an election by an Annual Conference. Sometimes objection is raised to such men by some members of the Conference.

It would, therefore, seem wise to leave a considerable group of trustees subject to nomination and election by the board itself. Some of the colleges having such a provision were found not to be exercising it effectively. They were electing as members exactly the same type of persons as were being chosen by the church groups. This, of course, defeats the purpose of the provision for election of members by the board itself, which is intended to assure the presence of persons on the board who represent varied interests and points of view.

Geographical limitations on board membership.—Some of the colleges have an unfortunate geographical limitation on board membership. Sometimes by charter or by-laws and at other times by custom the membership of the board is limited to persons residing in the state in which the college is located. This is particularly unfortunate if the state has only a relatively small population, as is the case in almost every college where this condition obtains.

A college should be on the alert to guard against any provincialism, and one of the best methods of doing this is to have a breadth of representation on the board of trustees. Frequently wealthy persons living in a distant state can be interested in the college through friends, alumni, or other connections; such persons are very suitable as board members. In some of the colleges where this type of provincialism obtains it was stated that the desire not to trespass on the territory of other institutions of the same denomination had led to the restriction of board membership. This is not a valid argument, since there is no reason why a person should not become interested in an educational institution other than the one sponsored by his local denominational group.

THE PERSONNEL OF THE BOARDS OF TRUSTEES

A complete analysis of the personnel of the boards of trustees was not carried on in all of the colleges studied. The discussion in this section is based upon data collected from some of the institutions and upon first-hand observation by the survey staff in all of them.

Ages of board members.—Although specific data were not collected concerning the ages of board members in this group of colleges, the members of the survey staff in practically every case met with the trustees or with a committee of the board. The impression gained from these meetings is that the boards in this group of colleges are very largely dominated by trustees who are too old to be able to exercise a satisfactory control over a modern educational institution. Many of these trustees have passed the time of life when they can be receptive to new ideas. A college is primarily a service institution for youth; for it to be too largely dominated by the ideas of old age is unwise. A sounder policy would provide for a fairly even representation of all ages on the board, some of the members being relatively young, the majority middle-aged, and only a few in older ages.

None of the colleges of this group has a plan for the retiring of trustees upon reaching the usual age of retirement. One of the large universities of this country has recently provided that members of its board who attain the age of seventy in any calendar year while serving as trustees automatically become honorary members at the end of their terms of office. A plan of this type would be worthy of consideration in all the thirty-five colleges of this group.

Ministers on the board.—In several of the colleges adverse criticism was made because of failure to choose board members from various walks of life. The typical board in this group of colleges contains more ministers than representatives of any other calling. In twenty-five colleges for which data are available, the proportion of ministers on the membership of the boards ranges from 12 per cent in one college to 69 per cent in another, with a median of 31 per cent for all the colleges. The colleges on the approved list of the Association of American Universities have a median of 22.5 per cent of their board members ministers, and only one college of the group having national accreditation has a proportion of ministers on its board higher than the median for the entire group of colleges. Some of the colleges have a charter or by-law provision to the effect that one-half of the board members must be ministers. One college, apparently with an inkling of the disadvantages of ministerial dominance, has the provision that *not* more than one-half of the board members *may* be ministers.

The wisdom of having such a large representation from the ministry on the boards of trustees is open to serious question. Historically the practice has a logical explanation—the colleges were founded as agencies of the church group, and, since the ecclesiastical control was lodged for the most part in the ministry, it was natural to make this the dominant element in the control of the church institution. In the early days, one of the most important functions of the college was the training of those who were later to become ministers and other types of religious workers. Under such conditions it was natural to provide for a strong ministerial element on the boards of control. Furthermore, in the earlier days the clergy represented one of the most important social groups interested in higher education of the liberal arts type.

During the past generation, however, the college, without lessening its function of the preparation of those who are to enter the ministry, has taken on many other functions. There has grown up a generation of laymen, large numbers of whom have had the advantages of a cultural higher education and who carry the same vital interest in its furtherance as was formerly found only in the clergy group. These developments have lessened the need for the dominance of the ministerial element in the control of higher education. The colleges are now training teachers, business men, housekeepers, professional men of all types, musicians, and people engaged in a host of occupations other than the ministry. Logically this would call for representation of these other groups in substantial proportions on the board of trustees. This is a need which it would be well for the colleges and the church bodies to recognize as far as possible in the selection of new board members.

Women on the board.—Another index of the catholicity of the board membership is the proportion of women on the board. In any college admitting women students it would appear advisable to provide representation of this important group of interests on the board of trustees. Fourteen of the thirty-four colleges which admit women students have no women members on the board. Only four of these fourteen are in the group of seventeen colleges on the approved list of the Association of American Universities. There are only three colleges of the entire group of thirty-five in which women comprise 10 per cent or more of the membership of the board. In two colleges women occupy 14 per cent of the places on the board, and in one—a woman's college—33 per cent of the board members are women.

Trustees ex officio.—Twenty-three of the thirty-five colleges have provision for some trustees ex officio. In only seven colleges is there more than one trustee ex officio, although in one college there are ten and in two others there are seven. The persons named as members of the board ex officio most frequently are the president (in twenty colleges) and the resident bishop of the area in which the college is located (in eight colleges). In three colleges the district superintendents of the Annual Conference are ex officio on the board, and in one of these the local Methodist pastor is also a member ex officio. The policy of having members ex officio on the board of trustees is open to serious adverse criticism from the standpoint of administrative principle. Members should be on the board because of their interest in and attachment to the institution, not because of their holding particular offices. It is recognized that the provisions for trustees ex officio are written into many of the charters and cannot be changed now.

Bishops on the board.—It is customary in most of these colleges to have the resident bishop a member of the board, although in ten institutions there is no bishop on the board. It has been noted that in eight colleges the bishop is on the board ex officio. In fourteen other colleges one or more bishops (as many as six in one case) are named on the board as regular members. In one other case the bishop is named as an advisory member, and in two other colleges he is named as an honorary member of the board of trustees.

Honorary trustees.—Although none of the colleges has a regular plan for the retirement of trustees, eight of them have honorary trustees or trustees emeriti on their boards. Four colleges have one such trustee, one has two, two have three, and one has seven honorary members of the board of trustees.

Administrative officers of the college on the board.—In twenty-two of these thirty-five colleges the president is a member of the board of trustees. In ten of the colleges executive officers other than the president hold membership on the board. These are usually the business officers, endowment fund managers, or the officers of financial promotion.

There is a grave question as to whether or not any salaried officer of the college ought to be a member of the board of trustees. It is the function of the board to exercise general supervision over the work of all executive officers, to pass on the satisfactoriness of the services rendered, and upon occasion to discontinue the connection of the college with the person concerned. For an executive officer to hold membership on the board is thus to put him in the position of supervising and judging his own services.

It is clear that the president of the college should be allowed a seat at board meetings and should have the privilege of speaking on all matters, but it does not seem necessary to give him a vote as a board member. If this practice is questionable in the case of the chief executive officer, it is even more so in the case of subordinate officers. In two or three colleges an even worse condition obtains—the president is not a member of the board, although one or more of the financial officers who work under him are board members. The chief executive is thus put in the anomalous position of being administratively responsible to those who are subordinate to him.

Former presidents on the board.—Somewhat similar is the case of six colleges in which former presidents have been named as members of the board. The opportunities for embarrassment which this practice occasions are numerous, and in several of the colleges where this condition obtains some friction and unpleasantness have arisen. It is very difficult for one who has been in active control of a college for many years to be placed in a position where he must look on while another hand guides the destinies of the institution. Under such circumstances it is almost impossible for the former president to refrain from interfering with the administration in a manner that is outside his province as a board member. Some method should be found for holding the interest and good will of a former president other than that of assigning him the doubly difficult rôle of board member.

LENGTH OF TERM OF BOARD MEMBERS

In the case of every one of the thirty-five colleges studied, provision is made for overlapping terms of board membership, in such a way that the majority of board members are always experienced. This is a wise provision and assures continuity and stability in policy. In twenty of the colleges board members are elected for three-year terms; in ten, for four-year terms; in two, for five-year; in two, for six-year; and in one, for twelve-year terms. In many cases it is apparently customary to elect the same person for several successive terms, thus effectually lengthening the term of membership. One or two of the colleges elect one class of members for indefinite terms, the presumption being that these persons will continue to serve as trustees until their death or voluntary resignation.

FUNCTIONS OF THE BOARD

The function[1] of the board of trustees of a college or university is generally described as legislative—that is, this body is the agency for policy determination. In addition to this function, it is recognized that definitive action on many matters, such as the election of faculty members, the choosing of executive officers, the investing of endowment funds, the erection of new buildings, the requirements for admission, degrees, and awards, the scale of tuition charges, the adoption of the financial budget, etc., is within the province of the board. In the third place, the board has

[1] For an analysis of the functions of boards of trustees, see the summary of a paper by D. W. Springer, *Bulletin of the American Association of University Professors*, XVII (May, 1931), 369-71.

an important function in judging the work of its executive officers and in deciding upon their retention or dismissal. In the fourth place, the board must bear the full and complete legal responsibility for the institution as a corporate entity.

Although the board is the supreme authority in the control of the college, there are two important limitations upon its functions. The first is that power is lodged in the trustees only as a group. An individual member of the board of trustees has no legal right to take any action affecting the college or anyone connected with it, unless he has been specifically commissioned for this purpose by the board itself. Even when power is vested in a committee, it is usually definitely limited, so far as final action is concerned. This principle seems to be well observed in this group of colleges, the instances of its violation being rare indeed.

A second important limitation upon the functions of the board is in the sphere of executive or administrative action. It is generally recognized that the board must delegate to its chosen executive officers the work of administering the institution. Although the board properly has a function in the determination of policies, the application of those policies to specific cases is a matter for executive action, not for board control. In general, the boards of trustees in the colleges studied have confined themselves very properly to the sphere of legislative control and have not interfered with the administrative phases of the management of the institutions. The few examples of violation of this principle seem to be sporadic cases, rather than a definite policy in the case of any college.

MEETINGS OF THE BOARD

The practice with regard to the number of regular meetings held each year varies in these thirty-five colleges. Seven of the boards hold only one regular meeting a year; twenty-one hold two meetings yearly; six hold three meetings; and one holds four meetings annually. With the provision for an executive committee to function in the interim between board meetings, it would scarcely seem necessary to hold meetings of the board oftener than twice a year. If the boards were smaller, it would be well to have meetings as often as once a month; but with the present unwieldy boards semiannual meetings seem to be preferable. Under this plan there will be a "mid-year" meeting and a "commencement" meeting. At the mid-year meeting the budget for the coming year can be adopted in tentative form, notices given faculty members who are not to be retained, any necessary revisions in the current year's budget authorized, and the work of the current year carefully studied. At the commencement meeting the degrees can be formally passed upon, last-minute revisions made in the budget for the ensuing year, the reports of officers heard for the year which is just closing, and necessary legislation considered.

In each of the colleges visited the minutes of the board of trustees for the past five or six years were carefully read. Almost without exception they give evidence of having been carefully recorded and faithfully preserved. A few of the colleges follow the practice of mimeographing the minutes of the board and sending them out to all the members. This is an excellent plan. It should enlist the interest of many board members who either neglect or are unable to attend the meetings. Errors in the minutes can be more readily detected when copies are circulated shortly after the date of the meeting. The presence of several duplicate copies of the minutes makes the safeguarding of the official minute-book a much less important matter.

COMMITTEE ORGANIZATION OF BOARDS OF TRUSTEES

It has already been pointed out that the unwieldy size of the boards of trustees in these colleges has led to the creation of an organization of standing committees. Every one of the colleges studied has one or more standing committees of the board, the maximum number being fourteen. The median institution of the group of thirty-five colleges maintains eight standing committees of its board of trustees. Only five of the colleges have fewer than six standing committees, and fourteen have ten or more committees.

Types of committees.—The committees which are maintained may be classified into nine more or less distinct types, on the basis of the kind of matters dealt with. The first is the executive committee, which is present in every college with one exception. In addition to the executive committee, three colleges also have an administration committee. One college has both an executive committee and a local committee, the latter apparently functioning in the way that most of the executive committees do in the other colleges.

The second type is the buildings and grounds committee. This committee is maintained at all of the colleges except five, none of these five having a board committee dealing with any phase of buildings and grounds supervision. In addition to the buildings and grounds committee, four colleges have a committee on dormitories; nine have a committee on library; six have a committee on libraries, laboratories, and equipment; one has a committee on equipment; two have a committee on laboratories; and one has a committee on insurance.

The third type of board committee deals with problems of faculty, instruction, and curriculum. Twenty-four of the colleges have a committee on faculty, six have a committee on instruction, and fifteen have a committee on degrees. There are only four colleges in the group which do not have a committee of the board to deal with one or more of the above matters. Five of the colleges have, in addition, board committees for matters affecting special schools such as music, business administration and commerce, etc.

The fourth type of board committee is one which deals with endowment, investments, and finance. Twenty-two of the colleges have an endowment committee or an investment committee, and twenty-five have a finance committee. There is one college that does not have either a finance committee, an endowment committee, or an investment committee. One college has two endowment committees, each dealing with a specific portion of the fund. One college has two committees to administer special foundations. One college has a securities committee in addition to an endowment committee, and one has a real estate committee in addition to an endowment committee.

The fifth type of committee is the budget committee. This is found in only fourteen of the colleges studied. One of these fourteen colleges has both a budget committee and a bills committee. In several of the colleges the finance committee handles matters that fall within the province of the budget committee in other institutions.

The sixth type of committee is the audit committee. Nineteen of the thirty-five colleges have a standing committee on audit.

The seventh type of committee is one which deals with financial promotion. There are only six colleges which have committees of this type. One of these six also has a committee on publicity and student promotion, and another has a committee on civic relations.

The eighth type of committee is one which deals with the machinery of board operation. Only eighteen of the colleges have board committees dealing with any phase of this question. Thirteen of these eighteen have a committee on nominations, four have a committee on reports, four have a committee on minutes, two have a committee on by-laws, one has a committee on rules and government, one has a committee on resolutions and courtesies, and one has a committee on memorials.

The ninth type of committee is one which deals with student affairs. Only nineteen of the colleges have board committees dealing with any phase of this problem. Nine of these nineteen colleges have a committee on athletics; four have a committee on student activities; three have a committee on religious life; three, on scholarship; two, on student loans; and one each, on fraternities, student appeals, women students, boarding clubs, and alumnae.

It will be observed from the foregoing data that only the first four types of committees are common to practically all the colleges. Almost every institution has an executive committee; a committee on buildings and grounds; a committee on endowment, investments, or finance; and a committee on faculty, instruction, and curriculum.

The executive committees range in size from five members up to eighteen, the median being nine. Two-thirds of the executive committees have either five, seven, or nine members. The finance and investment committees range in size from three to nineteen members, the median being seven. All the other committees mentioned usually do not exceed a membership of seven, and typically are composed of five members.

Disadvantages of the committee plan of board control.—Question has already been raised regarding the wisdom of providing an extensive committee organization in the board of trustees. The creation of these standing committees tends to disintegrate the action of the board, the committees being held more or less finally responsible for decisions in their respective fields, with the board as a whole taking little or no interest in questions within the province of special standing committees.

In the by-laws of some of the colleges the provision has been inserted that each member of the board is to be a member of some standing committee. Thus, it would seem that, when a member is appointed to the board of trustees in such colleges, he is expected to specialize his interests and look after one particular phase of the work of the institution. This is not at all desirable. Ideally the board as a whole should be concerned about all the problems of the institution, and it is a serious mistake to particularize the interests of the various members in such a way that adequate attention is not given to all problems by all the trustees.

A further danger in the committee type of organization is that the members, having been appointed as a committee and seeking some worthwhile function to perform, will begin to step over into the field of administrative activity and will perform functions that should be delegated to properly constituted executive officers. An excellent illustration is found in the case of the committee on buildings and grounds. The definition of the duties of this committee as found in many college by-laws would indicate that the functions of the superintendent of buildings and grounds are to be usurped, the committee being empowered to make a careful inspection of all the buildings and to report to the board the specific needs for repairs and improvements. In actual practice this committee usually does not function in this manner at all, but is used by the administrative officers of the college for advice and counsel on matters pertaining to the physical plant and equipment.

A possible exception to the general rule that committees should not perform executive functions may be made in the case of the investment committee. Frequently this committee will be composed of persons who are experts in the investment field and will be able to administer directly the investing of the college funds.

Needed committees of the board.—There seems to be a place for four standing committees of the board of trustees: the executive committee, the investment committee, the committee on buildings and grounds, and the committee on faculty. The last two should function chiefly in an advisory capacity to the executive officers of the college. It will be observed that these four committees are the only ones which are common to the most of the colleges studied. The abandonment of an extensive organization of standing committees should not preclude the appointment of temporary committees whenever a study of a particular problem is necessary.

CHAPTER X

INTERNAL ADMINISTRATIVE ORGANIZATION

The internal administrative organizations of the colleges will be discussed under six topics: (1) what officers comprise the administrative organizations; (2) what the duties of these officers are; (3) how the various officers are related one to another with regard to lines of responsibility; (4) what salaries are paid the administrative officers; (5) what the arrangements are for academic administration; and (6) how the control of the athletic program is organized.

OFFICERS OF ADMINISTRATION

Table 20 shows the titles of the administrative officers listed in the catalogues of this group of colleges, together with the number of institutions listing each title.

In this table the various offices are classified into groups. Officers combining two types of administrative functions are listed under both groups. For example, the six officers bearing the title "dean-registrar" are listed both under the classification of "dean" and also under the classification of "registrar."

It will be observed that in the case of some of the offices there is a lack of uniformity in the titles assigned those who perform essentially the same function. For example, the chief business officer appears under at least nine different titles.

There is an opportunity for some errors in the number of colleges listing each officer shown in the table, because of variations in the policies with respect to what officers shall be listed. Thus the failure to list a secretary to the president in many of the colleges does not indicate that the president lacks a secretary. On the other hand, the catalogue listing does afford a fairly reliable index as to the officers considered by each institution as essential components of the administrative organization.

Each of the colleges included in this study has a chief executive officer, usually with the title of president, but in one case with the title of chancellor. Only eleven of the colleges have a vice-president. All the colleges but two have a business officer, though this officer may appear under any one of several titles. There is an academic dean in every college except five, and all but one of the institutions have a registrar. The dean of women is

TABLE 20

KINDS OF ADMINISTRATIVE OFFICES AND TITLES OF OFFICERS
LISTED IN THE CATALOGUES OF THIRTY-FIVE COLLEGES

Kinds of Administrative Offices and Titles of Officers	Number of Colleges Listing Such Officers
Chief executive officer:	
President	34
Chancellor	1
Vice-president:	
Vice-president	7
Vice-president and auditor	2
Vice-president and dean	1
Vice-president in charge of finance	1
Executive vice-president	1
Dean (of college of liberal arts):	
Dean	24
Dean-registrar	6
Vice-president and dean	1
Registrar:	
Registrar	24
Assistant registrar	10
Dean-registrar	6
Dean of men and registrar	1
Registrar and examiner	1
Registrar and bursar	1
Associate registrar	1
Deans and directors of schools and divisions:	
Director of school of music	10
Curator of museum	7
Dean of fine arts	6
Dean of school of music	5
Director of summer session	3
Dean of the summer session	2
Dean of the college (or school) of education	2
Dean of summer school and evening college	1
Dean of extension	1
Director of correspondence work	1
Dean of teachers college and director of summer session	1
Director of school of art	1
Director of school of expression	1
Director of little theater	1
Director of school of commerce	1

TABLE 20—*Continued*

Kinds of Administrative Offices and Titles of Officers	Number of Colleges Listing Such Officers
Deans and directors of schools and divisions:—*Continued*	
Director of observatories	1
Director of laboratory schools	1
Dean of college of engineering	1
Dean of college of pharmacy	1
Dean of college of law	1
Secretaries:	
Secretary to president	21
Secretary to faculty	17
Secretary to president, secretary to faculty, and appointment secretary	1
Personnel officers:	
Dean of women	30
Dean of men	9
Assistant to dean of women	2
House director	2
Dietitian	2
House mother	2
Matron	2
Director of residence halls	1
Social director	1
Supervisor of dining-hall	1
Dean of women and matron of hall	1
Dean of men and registrar	1
Dean of men and assistant to president	1
Director of men's halls	1
Preceptor of men's dormitory	1
Director of vocational guidance	1
Adviser of Y.M.C.A.	1
Adviser of Y.W.C.A.	1
Secretary of student loan fund	1
Personnel officer	1
Student secretary	1
Director of student employment	1
Appointment secretary	1
Secretary to president, secretary to faculty, and appointment secretary	1
Alumni and publicity agents:	
Alumni secretary	9
Secretary to president in charge of alumni records	1

TABLE 20—*Continued*

Kinds of Administrative Offices and Titles of Officers	Number of Colleges Listing Such Officers

Alumni and publicity agents:—*Continued*

Assistant alumni secretary	1
Publicity director	1
Director of news service	1
Church-relations secretary	1

Business officers:

Treasurer	12
Assistant treasurer	8
Treasurer and business manager	5
Business manager	4
Business secretary	4
Cashier	4
Comptroller	3
Bursar	2
Assistant bursar	2
Executive secretary	2
Manager of bookstore	2
Vice-president and auditor	2
Secretary	1
Secretary of corporation and business manager	1
Accountant	1
Assistant cashier	1
Vice-president in charge of finance	1
Registrar and bursar	1
Manager of farm properties	1

Financial promotion agents:

Field secretary	3
Director of promotional service	2
Field secretary and treasurer of annuity fund	1
Field agent	1
Financial agent	1
Endowment secretary	1
Special representative	1

Supervisors of buildings and grounds:

Superintendent of buildings and grounds	12
Superintendent of buildings	1
Superintendent of power plant	1
Chief engineer	1
Landscape gardener	1

found in all but two of the thirty-four colleges admitting women students. Other officers appearing less regularly are the dean of men (found in only eleven of the colleges admitting men students), the superintendent of buildings and grounds (in fifteen colleges), and the promotional agent (in seven colleges).

These tabulations show that there is no common pattern of internal administrative organization in this group of thirty-five colleges. The usual administrative staff consists of a president, a dean, a registrar, a business officer, and a dean of women. Beyond these five, there is a fringe of other officers each of which is found in relatively few of the colleges.

DUTIES OF ADMINISTRATIVE OFFICERS

An exhaustive survey of the duties performed by the several administrative officers was not undertaken in the present study, although in each institution a general analysis was made of the distribution of administrative functions. The results of this study indicate the probability that, if enough colleges were visited, the range of duties performed by each of the major officers would be found to include the total scope of administrative responsibilities. In other words, if enough colleges are included, the deans will be found to be doing everything done by any administrative officer; the same will be true for the president, the registrar, and the business manager. For example, in one of the thirty-five colleges included in this study the registrar handles all the business affairs; in another, the chief executive officer cares for all the duties connected with the business office; in still another, the superintendent of buildings and grounds handles a part of the business matters, the remainder being cared for in the office of the president.

Despite this wide variation in the range of duties performed by the several officers, it is possible to pick out for most of them a list of duties that are commonly attached to each office. The following lists show the responsibilities most frequently assigned to the offices of the president, the dean, the registrar, and the business officer.

Duties of the President

1. To act as executive officer of the board of trustees, charged with putting into effect its policies and regulations.
2. To preside over meetings of the faculty.
3. To act as executive officer of the faculty, charged with seeing that its policies and regulations are put into effect.
4. To bear responsibility to the board of trustees for the satisfactory government and administration of the college.

5. To select a competent and harmonious teaching and administrative staff, and to recommend their employment to the board of trustees.
6. To make recommendations to the board of trustees on all matters pertaining to the promotion, demotion, and dismissal of members of the teaching and administrative staff.
7. To represent the institution to its constituency, to the general public, and in educational groups.
8. To prepare and carry out the annual budget for the operation of the college.
9. To make reports to the board of trustees, to the standardizing agencies, and to the constituency of the college.
10. To assist as far as possible in raising funds for the support of the college.
11. To maintain amity and unity of purpose among all members of the teaching and administrative staff, the board of control, the alumni, and the college constituency.

Duties of the Academic Dean

1. To direct the educational activities of the college.
2. To act as chief adviser of the president in matters of college policy, particularly in academic affairs.
3. To formulate educational policies and to present them to the president and faculty for consideration.
4. To direct attention of faculty members to changing educational thought and practice, particularly as they affect higher education.
5. To transmit to the president the budget recommendations for academic activities, after details have been worked out with department heads.
6. To make reports relating to the work of the college.
7. To supervise curriculums, courses, and methods of instruction.
8. To co-operate with heads of departments in the nomination of new members for the teaching staff, and to make suggestions to the president regarding the promotion, demotion, or dismissal of members of the faculty.
9. To assist in the recruiting of students.
10. To classify students and assign them to classes.
11. To study the progress and academic welfare of students.
12. To serve as chief disciplinary officer of the college.
13. To represent the college at meetings of educational associations.

Duties of the Registrar

1. To maintain academic records of all kinds.
2. To handle all matters relating to personnel accounting.
3. To examine and pass upon the qualifications of students for admission to the college.
4. To direct the program of registering students in classes.
5. To prepare and supervise the time- and room-schedules of classes.

6. To check the credentials of all candidates for graduation and for the various honors connected with academic success.
7. To serve as secretary of the faculty and of important faculty committees.
8. To organize materials for statistical use.
9. To prepare material for educational publicity.
10. To edit the college catalogue and other official publications.
11. To prepare reports of various kinds relating to personnel problems of students and faculty.
12. To maintain a bureau of information.

Duties of the Business Officer

1. To collect all income due the college.
2. To keep the financial accounts of the college.
3. To maintain the records necessary for the effective control of the current operating budget.
4. To purchase all supplies.
5. To pay all bills.
6. To assist in supervising the management of the endowment and other trust funds.
7. To administer the program of temporary financial aid to students and the student loan funds, with the advice of a competent representative of the educational interests of the college.
8. To supervise the management of the supplementary business activities maintained by the college.
9. To supply such reports as are required by the president, the board of trustees, or other official agencies.
10. To provide for the safekeeping and safeguarding of all money, securities, and valuable papers belonging to the institution.
11. To supervise the operation and maintenance of the physical plant.
12. To assist in the supervision of new building construction.

A college should not be criticized adversely because it departs from the general pattern in its assignment of administrative duties. Responsibilities should be assigned to the person who can perform them best, regardless of the manner in which this policy may disarrange the usual assignment of administrative functions. Thus administration in a college becomes much more a matter of adaptation to personnel than a matter of adherence to formal principle. It is important, however, that the duties assigned each officer be somewhat related, and that duties which are very similar not be assigned to two different officers.

Although the exact assignment of duties among the various officers is relatively unimportant, it is imperative that each person in the administrative staff should know exactly for what duties he and every other officer of the college are responsible. Failure to define clearly the duties expected of each officer is very likely to lead to confusion and inefficiency. It would be very much worth while for each of the colleges of this group to reduce to writing the list of duties expected of the several administrative officers. In this way undesirable overlappings can be avoided, and assurance can be given that each of the necessary administrative duties is clearly understood to be within the province of some responsible officer.

ORGANIZATION OF THE ADMINISTRATIVE STAFF

The question of administrative organization concerns the relationship of the various officers to one another and to the board of trustees, and the manner in which the lines of responsibility descend from the board to the various subordinate officers. Although the administrative organizations of this group of colleges differ materially each from the other, and although a complete analysis will usually reveal a very complex situation even in a small college, it is possible to classify the organizations into two general types. The basis of this classification is the number of officers responsible directly to the board of trustees. In one kind of organization, known as the "unit" type, there is only one officer of the college responsible directly to the board, all the other officers being responsible to the board through this chief executive officer.

The contrasting organization is known as the "multiple" type, in which two or more officers are independently responsible to the board. In the latter type of organization it is usual to find the president responsible only for academic matters, while the business officer is directly responsible for all financial affairs. Sometimes there is a third independent officer in charge of financial promotion, and occasionally there is an even larger number of persons directly responsible to the board.

Examples of plans of administrative organization typical of institutions of this group are presented in Figures 3, 4, 5, 6, 7, 8, and 9.

Fourteen of the thirty-five colleges included in this study have the unit type of administrative organization. Of the twenty-one having the multiple type, thirteen have two officers directly responsible to the board, six have three co-ordinate officers, one has four, and one has five. The type of accreditation held does not seem to be a factor affecting the administrative organization, the colleges on the approved list of the Association of American Universities being rather evenly distributed among the two kinds of administrative organization.

In every instance where the multiple type of organization is in effect, two of the officers directly responsible to the board are the president and

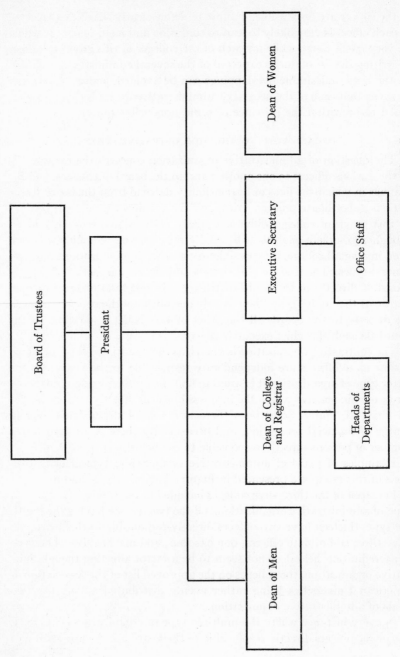

FIG. 3.—A simple example of the unit-type organization in a small institution—Evansville College

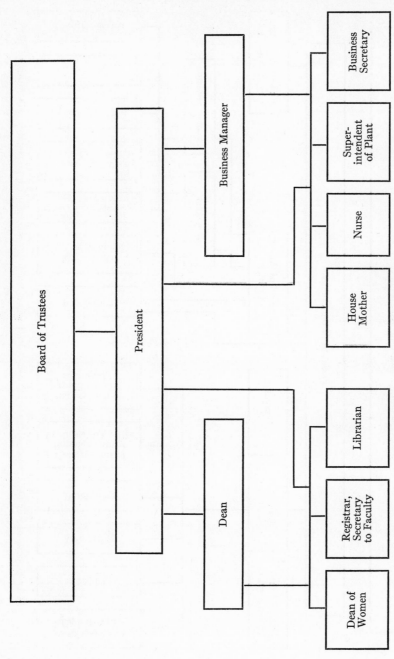

Fig. 4.—An example of a unit type of administrative organization, with both direct and delegated control of subordinate administrative officers from the president's office—Albion College.

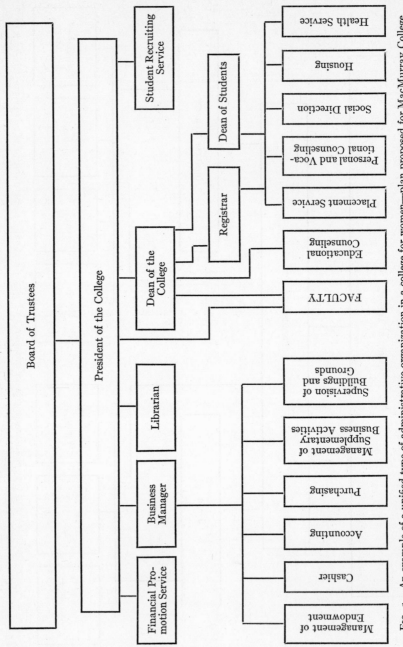

FIG. 5.—An example of a unified type of administrative organization in a college for women—plan proposed for MacMurray College

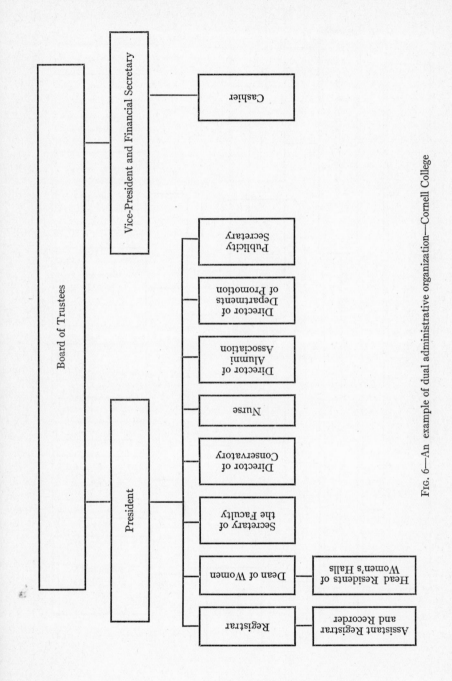

Fig. 6—An example of dual administrative organization—Cornell College

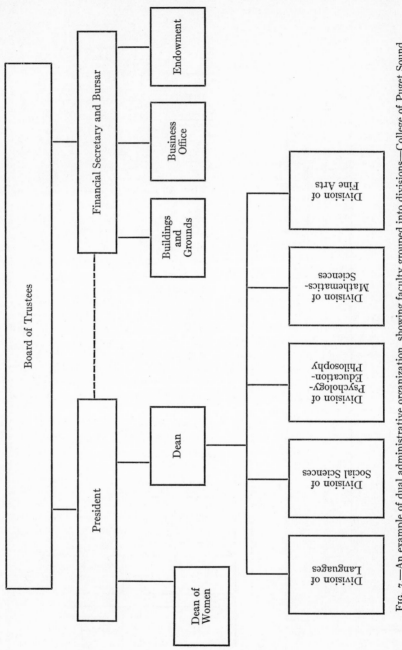

FIG. 7.—An example of dual administrative organization, showing faculty grouped into divisions—College of Puget Sound

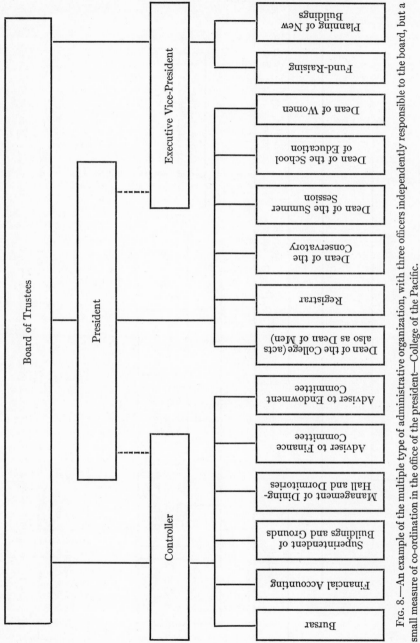

FIG. 8.—An example of the multiple type of administrative organization, with three officers independently responsible to the board, but a small measure of co-ordination in the office of the president—College of the Pacific.

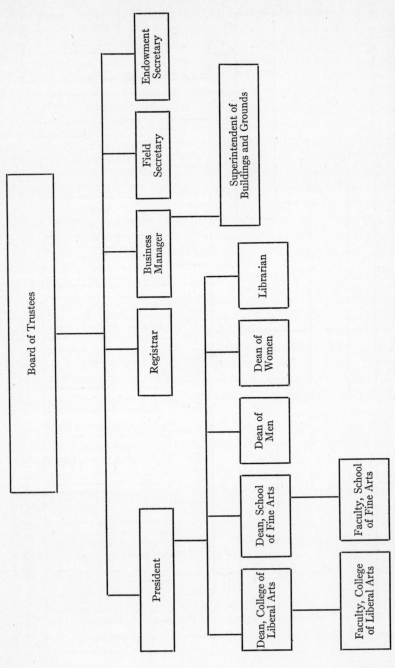

FIG. 9.—An example of the multiple type of administrative organization, with five officers independently responsible to the board—Southwestern College.

the business manager. Other officers independent of the president in some of the multiple organizations are: treasurer, vice-president, field secretary (promotion officer), endowment secretary, and registrar.

The question of the comparative effectiveness of the two types of administrative organization is a difficult one. Each type seems to be working very effectively in some of the institutions visited. The only examples of inefficiency because of friction in the administrative organization were found in colleges having the multiple type. It is obvious that the opportunities for difficulty in the multiple type of organization are much larger than in the unit type. It appears that in the colleges where the multiple type of organization is proving effective it is because of the congenial relationships of the personalities involved, rather than because of any inherent virtues in the system itself.

It must be noted, furthermore, that in many of the colleges which have, according to their by-laws and statutes, a multiple type of organization, the actual practice tends to be that of the unit type. Thus, although the business manager may be co-ordinate with the president and equally responsible to the board, he may confer and consult with the president to such a degree that he really becomes a subordinate officer. Under a strong president this is almost certain to be the case. It is conceivable that with a strong business officer, the multiple type of organization may tend to subordinate the president, the real policies of the institution being determined by the business officer. This situation had actually developed in at least two of the colleges surveyed. The interesting conclusion may, therefore, be drawn that the multiple type of administrative organization tends strongly in practice to become a unit type.

One of the inherent difficulties with the multiple type of administrative organization lies in the impossibility of separating and disentangling the various duties and responsibilities. Separation is commonly attempted along the line of finance and educational activities; but almost every educational policy has its financial implications, and almost every financial policy has its educational bearings. The members of the board are not usually in a position to judge the relative merits of proposals which may be wise financially and unwise educationally, or vice versa. There is need for an administrative officer whose vision embraces both the educational and the financial aspects of every question. It is only such a person who can give sound advice to a board of trustees on matters of policy.

As a rule, the president's financial judgment will be better than the business officer's educational judgment. It thus appears that the unit type of organization, with the president placed in complete charge of all the affairs of the college, both educational and financial, is preferable. Such an organization does not prevent the president from delegating to the business officer all the actual authority in financial matters; but it does prevent the bringing of proposals to the board which have not had adequate consideration from every point of view affecting the service of the institution.

An example of the working of a multiple type of organization may be drawn from one of the colleges included in this study. In this institution the president by his own request is limited strictly to the educational side, and other officers are responsible directly to the board for all the business affairs. This college has run an annual deficit of approximately $75,000 for the past few years. There has been an almost complete failure to add anything to the permanent funds of the institution, and relatively large amounts of undesignated funds have been transferred out of endowment and used for plant purposes and liquidation of indebtedness incurred through operating deficits. In an attempt to separate educational policies from financial matters, instructional salaries are fixed in an inflexible scale according to rank. The president determines the rank to be assigned each faculty member, and opportunities for salary promotion are limited to the occasions when a change is made in academic rank. The curricular offerings in this college are far beyond the resources available for the satisfactory support of the program. A thorough analysis of the situation at this institution made it evident that the fundamental need was for a change in the type of administrative organization, with the provision that the chief executive officer be assigned complete responsibility for all phases of the program, both the educational and the financial policies being coordinated through the single administrative head.

The general conclusions to be drawn from the study of the various types of administrative organization indicate that the unit type generally is the more satisfactory.[1] In actual practice there is a strong tendency for the multiple types of organization to become similar to the unit type. It would be advisable for many of the colleges of this group to revise their by-laws, doing away with the multiple of organization which is therein set forth, and setting up a true unit type of organization which conforms with the actual practice of the institution.

ADMINISTRATIVE SALARIES

Table 21 presents data regarding the salaries of administrative officers in the colleges studied. One institution, Brothers College, is omitted

[1] For a further discussion of this point, see Reeves and Russell, *College Organization and Administration* (Board of Education of Disciples of Christ, 1929), pp. 65–66.

from this tabulation because its officers, with the exception of the dean, serve also as the administrative staff for Drew University. Five of the thirty-four colleges included in this study had no one occupying the office of dean at the time of the survey visit, and for that reason only twenty-nine deans are included. For a similar reason data are presented for only thirty-two business officers, twenty-eight deans of women, and twenty-one secretaries to the president.

TABLE 21

SALARIES OF ADMINISTRATIVE OFFICERS IN THIRTY-FOUR COLLEGES*

ANNUAL SALARY	NUMBER OF COLLEGES PAYING SALARIES WITHIN THE RANGE INDICATED FOR VARIOUS ADMINISTRATIVE OFFICERS				
	President	Dean of the College of Liberal Arts	Business Officer	Dean of Women	Secretary to the President
$10,000 and above.......	2	....	....	....	....
7,500–$9,999..........	6	....	....	....	....
6,500– 7,499..........	4	....	....	....	....
5,500– 6,499..........	12	1	2	....	....
4,500– 5,499..........	6	4	5	....	....
4,000– 4,499..........	2	7	3	2	....
3,500– 3,999..........	1	3	8	....	....
3,000– 3,499..........	....	10	12	4	....
2,500– 2,999..........	1	3	....	8	....
2,000– 2,499..........	....	1	2	9	4
1,800– 1,999..........	....	....	....	2	3
1,600– 1,799..........	....	....	....	....	2
1,400– 1,599..........	....	....	....	....	7
Below $1,400..........	....	....	....	3	5
Total.............	34	29	32	28	21
Median,† all colleges.	$6,000	$3,500	$3,500	$2,450	$1,560

* Brothers College not included, since the president and business officers serve for both Brothers College and the remainder of the Drew University organization.

† Calculated from an ungrouped distribution.

The data of this table show a wide range in the salaries paid for the various administrative officers at these colleges. Two of the presidents receive an annual salary of $10,000 or above, while there is one that receives less than $3,000 (actually $2,500). The figures shown include a fair valuation for house rent and similar perquisites where received as a part of the remuneration for the office. The range in the salaries of deans is also large. One dean receives $5,500 or more annually, while another receives less than $2,500. The range in the salaries of business managers is the same as that of the deans, and the median salaries of these two officers are the same. There are two deans of women who are paid $4,000 or more, while there are three who receive less than \$1,400. There are four secretaries who receive \$2,000 or more, but there are five who receive less than \$1,400.

Relation of administrative salaries to size of enrolment and type of accreditation.—The wide range in the salaries paid the administrative officers in these colleges suggests that it would be well to study the average salaries paid in colleges of various sizes and types. Table 22 presents these data.

TABLE 22

MEDIAN SALARIES PAID CERTAIN ADMINISTRATIVE OFFICERS
IN VARIOUS GROUPS OF COLLEGES

TYPE OF COLLEGE	PRESIDENT		DEAN		BUSINESS OFFICER		DEAN OF WOMEN		SECRETARY TO PRESIDENT	
	Number of Cases	Median Salary	Number of Cases	Median Salary	Number of Cases	Median Salary	Number of Cases	Median Salary	Number of Cases	Median Salary
All colleges..........	34	\$6,000	29	\$3,500	32	\$3,500	28	\$2,450	21	\$1,560
A.A.U. colleges......	17	6,900	13	4,200	17	3,600	14	2,850	13	1,700
Non-A.A.U. colleges..	17	5,500	16	3,200	15	3,200	14	2,025	8	1,470
Colleges with enrolment of 700 or over.	6	7,850	6	4,500	6	4,500	5	3,000	5	1,900
Colleges with enrolment of 400–699...	17	6,000	13	3,800	17	3,600	14	2,550	11	1,560
Colleges with enrolment under 400....	11	5,000	10	3,000	9	3,000	9	2,000	5	1,200

This table shows that in the case of each of the administrative offices for which data are presented there is a marked tendency to pay higher salaries in the colleges on the approved list of the Association of American Universities than in those which do not hold this type of accreditation. There is also a marked relationship between the size of the college and the average salary paid administrative officers. The colleges in the largest-sized group (those with 700 or more students enrolled) have the highest average salary for administrative officers, and those colleges in the smallest-sized group (fewer than 400 students) pay the lowest average salaries, this relationship holding for each of the five administrative officers without a single exception. The medium-sized colleges are in each case approximately halfway between the two extremes.

It will be noted that the ratios between the salary of the president and those of the other administrative officers remain surprisingly constant throughout this grouping. In the six groupings shown in the table, the median salary for deans is never less than 57 per cent nor more than 63

per cent of the salary of the president; the median salary for business officers is always between 52 and 60 per cent of the president's salary; the
medians for the deans of women range between 37 and 42 per cent of the
president's salary; and the medians for the secretaries are from 24 to 27
per cent of the president's salary.

TABLE 23

RATIOS OF SALARIES OF ADMINISTRATIVE OFFICERS TO AVERAGE
FACULTY SALARIES IN THIRTY-FOUR COLLEGES*

RATIOS (QUOTIENT OF ADMINISTRATIVE OFFICERS' SALARIES DIVIDED BY AVERAGE FACULTY SALARIES)	NUMBER OF INSTITUTIONS HAVING EACH INDICATED RATIO OF SALARIES OF ADMINISTRATIVE OFFICERS TO AVERAGE FACULTY SALARIES					
	President		Dean		Business Officer	
	To Average Salary of All Full-Time Faculty Members	To Average Salary of All Full-Time Professors	To Average Salary of All Full-Time Faculty Members	To Average Salary of All Full-Time Professors	To Average Salary of All Full-Time Faculty Members	To Average Salary of All Full-Time Professors
3.50 and above to 1..	2	....	....	....	....	....
3.25–3.49 to 1......	1	1	....	....	....	....
3.00–3.24 to 1......	....	....	....	....	....	....
2.75–2.99 to 1......	3	1	....	....	1	1
2.50–2.74 to 1......	8	2	....	....	....	....
2.25–2.49 to 1......	10	8	....	....	....	....
2.00–2.24 to 1......	5	11	.........,	....	1	....
1.75–1.99 to 1......	2	5	2	....	5	....
1.50–1.74 to 1......	2	3	8	2	5	6
1.25–1.49 to 1......	1	3	11	10	8	8
1.00–1.24 to 1......	....	....	8	17	11	11
0.75–0.99 to 1......	....	....	....	....	1	5
0.50–0.74 to 1......	....	....	....	....	....	1
Total..........	34	34	29	29	32	32
Median,† all colleges........	2.35	2.15	1.42	1.21	1.34	1.24

* Brothers College not included.
† Calculated from an ungrouped distribution.

Ratio of administrative salaries to faculty salaries.—The opinion has been
expressed that the salaries of administrative officers, particularly the
president, should bear a somewhat definite relationship to the faculty
salary scale.[1] Table 23 presents data covering this point for three types
of administrative officers—presidents, deans, and business managers. In
this table, the salary of the administrative officer is expressed as a ratio to

[1] Charles Franklin Thwing, *The College President* (New York: Macmillan Co., 1926),
p. 214.

the average faculty salary at his institution. Thus in a college which pays its president $6,000 and which has an average faculty salary of $2,400, the ratio would be 2.5 to 1 ($6,000 divided by $2,400). A similar ratio is also presented for the average salary of all full-time professors.

This table shows that there is no agreement in this group of colleges in the relationship which the salary of the president bears either to the average salary of all full-time faculty members or to the average salary of all full-time professors. In two colleges the salary of the president is at least three and one-half times the average salary of all faculty members, while in another college it is less than one and one-half times the general faculty average. The range between the extremes of the ratios in the case of the average salary of full-time professors is almost as large. The typical situation, as shown by the median, is for the president to be paid a salary which is approximately two and one-third times the average salary of all full-time faculty members, or two and one-sixth times the average salary of those who hold the rank of professor.

The ratios of the dean's salary to average faculty salaries show a much smaller range than was found in the case of presidential salaries. There are no colleges in this group that pay their dean twice as much as the average faculty salary or more than one and three-fourths as much as the average salary of professors. A considerable number of the group pay their deans less than one and one-fourth as much as the average salary of faculty members, but no college in this group pays its dean less than the average salary of all full-time professors.

The ratios of the salaries of business managers to average faculty salaries show a range almost as wide as was found in the case of the presidential salaries, and much wider than that found in the deans' salaries. There is only one college which pays its business manager less than the average faculty salary, but there are six which pay this officer less than the average salary for professors. The extreme in the other direction is presented by one college which pays its business officer more than two and three-fourths as much as the average faculty salary.

The variations found in the ratios of administrative salaries to average faculty salaries suggest a study of these ratios in colleges of comparable size and type. Table 24 presents these data.

This table shows that in the case of each of these three officers the spread between their salaries and the average for all faculty members is larger in the institutions on the approved list of the Association of American Universities than it is in the colleges which do not hold this type of accreditation. This principle does not hold in the case of the ratios of administrative salaries to the average salaries of those holding the rank of professor, the differences in the average ratios in the two groups of colleges, classified on the basis of accreditation, being small; in the case of deans and business officers, the median ratios are actually slightly larger in the colleges not on the approved list of the Association of American Universities than they are in the colleges that hold national accreditation.

There is a direct relationship between the size of the institution and the size of the ratios of the salaries of presidents and deans to the average of all faculty salaries. The spread between faculty salaries and the salaries of deans and presidents tends to be greater in the larger institutions than in

TABLE 24

MEDIAN RATIO OF SALARIES OF CERTAIN ADMINISTRATIVE OFFICERS TO
AVERAGE FACULTY SALARIES IN VARIOUS GROUPS OF COLLEGES

TYPE OF COLLEGE	PRESIDENT			DEAN			BUSINESS OFFICER		
	Number of Cases	Ratio to Average Salary of All Full-Time Faculty Members	Ratio to Average Salary of All Full-Time Professors	Number of Cases	Ratio to Average Salary of All Full-Time Faculty Members	Ratio to Average Salary of All Full-Time Professors	Number of Cases	Ratio to Average Salary of All Full-Time Faculty Members	Ratio to Average Salary of All Full-Time Professors
All colleges...............	34	2.35	2.15	29	1.42	1.21	32	1.34	1.24
A.A.U. colleges...........	17	2.65	2.16	13	1.51	1.20	17	1.37	1.18
Non-A.A.U. colleges......	17	2.35	2.14	16	1.32	1.24	15	1.31	1.24
Colleges with enrolment over 700...............	6	2.64	2.32	6	1.54	1.32	6	1.34	1.19
Colleges with enrolment of 400–699...............	17	2.50	2.14	13	1.37	1.16	17	1.46	1.29
Colleges with enrolment under 400...............	11	2.26	2.07	10	1.24	1.24	9	1.18	1.18

the smaller ones. This finding holds true for the ratio between the salary of the president and the average salary of professors, but does not hold true for the ratio between the salary of the dean and the average salary of professors.

There does not seem to be any marked relationship between the size of the institution and the size of the ratio of the business manager's salary to the average faculty salaries or professorial salaries. The medium-sized group of colleges is out of line on this point.

ACADEMIC ADMINISTRATION

Academic officers.—The officers specifically charged with the responsibility of academic administration are the dean, the registrar, and the department heads. The duties of deans and registrars have been discussed in a preceding section.

In many of the colleges the dean is one of the older members of the faculty. Appointment to this office, while not exactly a matter of seniority, has tended in such colleges to be limited to teachers long associated with the institution. In a few colleges the choice of a dean has been influenced by teaching loads, the theory being that a teacher with a small load will have more time for the administrative duties of the deanship. The person assigned this office in such colleges will typically be a member of a department which attracts relatively few students. In other colleges there has been an attempt to bring into the deanship someone who is not only an able scholar in his own field but who has also been trained in the professional aspects of education, with special reference to the problems of higher education. This movement offers much promise, particularly as improved training facilities in the field of higher education become available.

In several of the colleges the registrar is a high-grade clerk in the office of the dean. This seems to be a satisfactory and an economical arrangement for institutions which do not have a large enrolment. In other colleges a member of the faculty serves as registrar, giving only a part of his time to the office, most of the routine work being performed by clerks. In two of the colleges the registrar serves as the chief financial officer of the institution. The larger colleges have a full-time registrar who is one of the major officers of administration.

Departmental administration.—Department heads are usually charged with some administrative responsibility for the affairs of their own departments.[1] In many of the colleges the status of department heads is exceedingly vague. One of the larger colleges insists that it has no department heads, every member of the faculty being on an equal status so far as direct responsibility to the president is concerned. On further inquiry, however, it appears that one member in each department is usually considered responsible for such matters as arranging the budget and planning the schedule of classes, so that, in spite of the denial of the presence of departmental headships, some members of the faculty actually serve in this capacity.

In other colleges the vagueness regarding departmental headships seems to arise from the failure to define clearly the status of departments. In such cases the lists of department heads fail to correspond with the lists of departments as published in the catalogues, the general tendency being to list more departments in the catalogue than are recognized in the

---

[1] For a discussion of the administrative functions of departments, see Reeves and Russell, *op. cit.*, pp. 76–81.

list of departmental headships. Undoubtedly the fact that the standards of the regional accrediting associations insist upon higher qualifications for department heads than for other faculty members has something to do with the apparent conservatism in listing department heads.

There is an evident tendency in many of these colleges to swing away from the departmental plan of organization in the direction of a divisional plan. Under this latter plan the subject-matter offerings are grouped into a few divisions—from four to seven is the usual number—and the departments receive considerably less emphasis, or even disappear entirely. The administration of each division is in charge of a chairman, and the division becomes the responsible unit for administrative control. In a few colleges, however, the introduction of the divisional plan has affected only the curriculum organization, and the divisions have not been recognized as a part of the administrative machinery. So long as the standardizing agencies insist upon the maintenance of eight departments as a standard for accreditation, it is necessary to retain, on paper at least, this minimum number of departments, even though the administrative and curricular organization of the college has actually been put upon a divisional basis.

Faculty committees.—In all of the colleges included in this study the faculty is the legislative authority for matters dealing with the general academic affairs of the institution. This means that the determination of policies relating to academic matters is in the hands of the faculty. The duty of applying general policies to specific cases or individuals, commonly known as "administration," is usually assigned to certain executive officers of the institutions, although many colleges depend to some extent upon committees of the faculty for administrative work.

The number of standing committees of the faculty ranges from three in one college to thirty-three in another, the median for the entire group being seventeen standing committees. Figure 10 shows the relationship between the size of the institution, as measured by the number of students enrolled, and the number of standing committees of the faculty. Only thirty-four institutions are included in this tabulation, data not being available for Simpson College.

This figure shows that the average number of standing committees of the faculty varies directly with the size of the college, the larger institutions tending to have a greater number of committees than the smaller ones.

A large number of the committees are maintained for administrative purposes, a plan which may be criticized adversely for several reasons. In the first place, the committee plan of administration tends to make diffi-

cult the fixing of responsibility for actions or for failure to act. In the
second place, committee service if seriously carried out is time-consuming
for faculty members. In the third place, the committee plan frequently

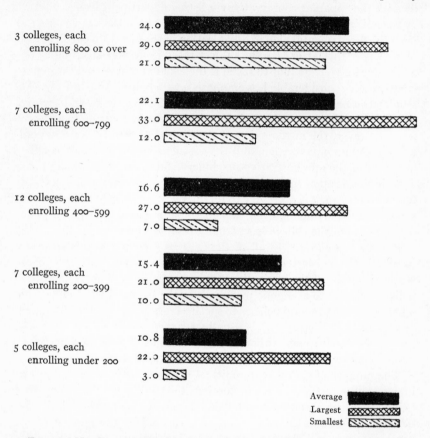

3 colleges, each
    enrolling 800 or over

24.0
29.0
21.0

7 colleges, each
    enrolling 600–799

22.1
33.0
12.0

12 colleges, each
    enrolling 400–599

16.6
27.0
7.0

7 colleges, each
    enrolling 200–399

15.4
21.0
10.0

5 colleges, each
    enrolling under 200

10.8
22.0
3.0

Average
Largest
Smallest

FIG. 10.—Number of standing committees of the faculty in colleges having various
numbers of students enrolled.

tends in actual practice to degenerate into action by one person, the chairman of the committee. In the fourth place, committees appear to be much
more vacillating in their decisions than is the case when administrative
matters are handled by executive officers.

Observations made in this group of colleges lead very definitely to the
conclusion that administrative matters are usually better handled when
specifically assigned to responsible executive officers than when handled

through committees of the faculty. As one college president expressed it, the most effective committee is a committee of one. Faculty members who have a flair for administrative work can well be named to part-time executive posts, where they will be held individually responsible for the duties assigned them.

The counter-argument in favor of the use of faculty committees for administrative purposes has its basis in the supposed democracy of the diffused type of executive control. Some presidents have deliberately built up the plan of administering their institutions largely through faculty committees in order to overcome traditions of autocracy developed in preceding administrations. Although instructors may well object to an autocratic type of control that is arbitrary and unreasoning in its decisions, experience with the teaching staffs of many colleges leads to the conclusion that faculty members, in general, are not interested in assuming the burdens of administrative responsibility implied in the committee plan. Most capable faculty members prefer to confine their activities to the classroom and to scholarly research and writing, leaving to other competent hands the burdensome details of applying policies to specific cases.

These criticisms of faculty committees for administrative purposes do not imply that all faculty committees are subject to the same objection. There is a clear place for committees of the faculty to deal with matters of policy formation. For the most part committees of this sort will be temporary, rather than standing committees, and will be discharged upon the completion of the task assigned. On a few matters, such as curriculum, standing committees to deal with questions of policy may be necessary.

There is one type of administrative committee which seems to be justified—a committee on discipline. In the case of this administrative duty there is a real advantage in a diffusion of responsibility and in the removal of the administration of justice from possible bias on the part of any one person.

ADMINISTRATION OF ATHLETICS

The problem of the administrative control of athletics is a vexing question in many American colleges. If the recently issued report by the Carnegie Foundation[1] is fairly representative of conditions over the country as a whole, it must be concluded that the group of thirty-five colleges included in the present study have, in general, somewhat better than average conditions in their administration of athletics. Although many of the abuses pointed out in the Carnegie report were found in one

[1] Howard J. Savage, *American College Athletics*, Bull. 23 (New York: Carnegie Foundation for the Advancement of Teaching, 1929).

or more of the thirty-five colleges, there are only three or four in the entire group in which the athletic situation at the time of the survey visit was subject to serious adverse criticism. The unsatisfactory conditions found related to such matters as the control of the athletic program by outside agencies, the subsidization of athletes, restriction of the program to intercollegiate competition, undue domination by the athletic coach, unethical recruiting, failure to handle the finances of the athletic program through the regular college officers, failure to maintain an adequate check on the expenditures for athletic purposes, and direct payment of a part of the salary of coaches by persons outside the college group. In most of the colleges to which these criticisms apply, steps have recently been taken to reorganize the administration of athletics, and the unsatisfactory conditions are being removed.

The question of the purity of athletic conditions in colleges is an important one from the standpoint of the future of amateur sport. The Carnegie report, to which attention has already been called, presents an excellent treatment of this topic. The present discussion is more directly concerned with the effect of athletic conditions on the college than with their bearing on the future of amateurism. From the standpoint of the effect of the athletic situation on the college itself two important phases of the problem may be distinguished: (1) the pressures which are brought to bear upon the academic organization by the athletic program; (2) the effect of the athletic program on the general tone of the institution.

The wisdom of assigning responsibility for the control of such a technical matter as college athletics to the faculty and administration of the college is sometimes called into question. Townspeople and alumni frequently get the idea that if they were allowed to manage the athletic affairs of the college—select the coaches and determine their rate of remuneration, schedule the games, collect the gate receipts, and disburse the funds—the teams representing the institution would win more games, the prestige of the college would be greatly increased, and the spectators would have more interesting contests to watch. The motives of those who would make such a suggestion are usually entirely sincere; they consider themselves generous in their offer to take the burden of managing athletics off the shoulders of a college administration which seems to them incompetent to handle such a technical problem.

One of the colleges included in this group had received, shortly before the survey visit, a proposal of this sort from a group of prominent citizens, headed by the mayor of the city and including many warm friends of the college. This group naïvely proposed that they would select the coach for the college, would fix his salary and take the responsibility for raising the funds necessary to pay him, would attend to the scheduling of games, would collect the gate receipts, and would either make up from their own pockets any deficits or, if income was larger than expenditure, pay the net surplus over to the college. The college had not had successful athletic teams for several years, and the group of citizens were entirely unselfish in their proposal to take over the management of athletics in an effort to improve the athletic standing of the institution.

It is axiomatic that the college exists for the giving of education to young people, and that no influence should be allowed to distort the academic program. At the same time it is clear that the athletic program cannot be handled as a thing apart from the academic program. The two are so closely related at innumerable points that almost every policy in one program has an effect of some sort upon the other program. In fact, some would go so far as to say that athletics is an integral part of the academic program. It therefore follows that a divided control is administratively unsound; the same agency should be in charge of both the athletic and the academic program. The outside group usually has no interest in managing the academic program, even if it could be admitted that the academic program might benefit by outside control. The only logical solution is to put the control of both the athletic and the academic programs in the same hands, namely, the faculty and administrative staff of the college.

The argument for faculty control of athletics is thus seen not to be based on any peculiar competence of the faculty for the handling of this problem but rather upon the impossibility of separating athletic policies from academic affairs, granting the absolute necessity for control of academic affairs by the faculty. The cogency of this argument is recognized both by regional standardizing agencies concerned primarily with the academic standing of the colleges and by athletic conferences interested in fair and sportsmanlike competition.

The use of the term "outside control" is not intended to preclude the seeking of advice on any point from persons not directly connected with the college and its administration. The college must, of course, remain sensitive in all its departments to public opinion and general social movements. The only argument here is that outside influence on the athletic program should not be greater than, or of a different kind from, that on academic policies, such as the amount of foreign language required for graduation, the establishment of new departments of instruction, the selection of textbooks to be used in courses, etc. On matters of this kind the opinion of townspeople, alumni, and students may well be accepted for what it is worth, but no one would seriously recommend the delegation of the actual control of purely academic matters to any agency other than the faculty and administrative staff of the college.

If the inadvisability of direct control of athletics by an outside agency be granted, there is still the question of control by indirect means. It should be obvious that this has all the disadvantages of direct outside control, and is even worse in that it is hidden and irresponsible. The only satisfactory solution of this problem is for a complete centralization of the control of athletics in the hands of the regularly constituted college authorities, with no opportunity for any outside influence in the management of athletics other than that which would normally be sought in the case of the academic program. The lodging of the final control of athletic policies in the faculty itself is an important step in obviating the possibilities of indirect pressures from outside sources upon officers of administration. It is difficult for such pressure to make itself felt upon the entire faculty; and administrative officers, upon whom pressure might be effective, thus have the opportunity to respond to self-constituted outside advisers with the unanswerable statement that the faculty as a whole decides all matters of athletic policy.

A second phase of the relationship between athletics and the college administration is the effect of the athletic program upon the tone of the institution. An unsatisfactory athletic situation almost inevitably affects the morale of students and faculty, and the whole institution becomes permeated with an unwholesome influence. However well the college may succeed in concealing its violations of athletic standards from accrediting agencies or athletic conferences, the students and faculty are usually not blind to the truth of the situation. Such an atmosphere is equally as deleterious in its effect upon academic standards as in its effect upon the moral tone of the institution.

From the standpoint of the college, two things are important in the administration of the athletic program: (1) that the control be lodged in the faculty and its administrative staff, with no opportunity for outside influence to affect the policies or their administration unduly in either a direct or an indirect manner; (2) that the conduct of the athletic program be honest and above board, so as not to constitute a source of baneful influence on the general morale and tone of the institution.

PART II
PHYSICAL PLANTS, EQUIPMENT, AND LIBRARIES

CHAPTER XI

BUILDINGS AND GROUNDS

CAMPUS

One of the distinctive features of the physical plant of the American college or university is the campus. The term generally includes both the land and buildings located thereon, and in some connotations has come to represent the very spirit of the institution.

The size of the campus varies among the thirty-five colleges studied. Two institutions have only 7 and 8 acres, respectively, while there are two others each of which have in excess of 100 acres in the campus. The median institution has 35 acres, and three-fourths of the colleges have 25 acres or more. One-third of the colleges have 50 acres or more in the campus.

The campus sizes may be compared on the basis of acreage per student. On this point the institutions also vary widely, one college having only 1 acre for every 100 students, while another has more than one-third of an acre for each student. The median for the thirty-five colleges is 0.07 acre per student, or approximately 1 acre for each 14 students. Three-fourths of the colleges have 0.05 acre or more per student, and one-fourth of them have 0.12 acre per student.

There are no scientifically validated standards of what constitutes a satisfactory size for a college campus. There must be a sufficient amount of room for a satisfactory placing of all the buildings that are needed, and also adequate space for recreational and athletic activities. In the case of a coeducational school, this usually means separate playing fields for men and women. A few of the colleges have added golf courses, thus increasing considerably the acreage necessary.

For a college of five hundred students under present-day conditions a campus of 40 acres seems to be large enough to provide most of the necessary facilities, particularly if a golf course is not included. Almost half of the colleges studied have a campus of this size or larger. The difficulty of foreseeing future needs for expansions makes it imperative for the colleges to hold even more land for campus development than may seem immediately necessary. Many educators believe that the future trends in recreational activities for colleges will demand an even larger campus than has been considered satisfactory in the past. The college which has any expectation of expanding its enrolment should also give thought to the provision of adequate ground space. As a rule, it is much more economical to purchase the necessary land while the institution is relatively small than it is to wait until after the development of the college has resulted in an increase in the value of neighboring property.

Two or three of the colleges having rather limited campuses are located in cities where the acquisition of a large amount of land would result in an almost prohibitive outlay. In some cases expansion of the present campus is almost impossible owing to cost of contiguous property. In one of the colleges surveyed, a new campus is being developed at some distance from the present site in order to carry on the program of expansion which lies ahead. The suggestion was made in one or two other colleges for similar development. Other colleges are buying up contiguous property as opportunity offers, with the idea of ultimately adding it to the campus.

One institution is using its endowment fund to buy income-producing properties situated in the direction of needed campus expansion. There can be no objection to this procedure so long as care is taken to replace in the endowment fund the purchase value of the property whenever it is developed for campus purposes, and so long as the properties produce a satisfactory rate of income. This plan not only provides for future expansion of the campus but also serves, for the present, to protect the college against undesirable neighbors, since the institution itself is the renting agency for the properties held in the endowment fund.

TYPES OF BUILDINGS

The thirty-five colleges studied have a total of 345 buildings of all kinds. Slightly less than half of these buildings are used for academic purposes, the remainder consisting of dormitories,[1] dining-halls, gymnasiums, heating plants, residences, etc. Approximately one-fifth of the academic buildings are of stone construction, three-fourths are of brick construction, and the remaining 5 per cent are of frame construction. Buildings of fireproof construction are conspicuously rare. Even among the more recently erected buildings, there are relatively few that are of fire-resistive construction. The development of fireproof construction is one of the notable achievements in educational architecture during the twentieth century. It is unfortunate that greater advantage has not been taken of this type of construction in some of the newer buildings in the colleges studied.

[1] A dormitory with some classrooms is considered an academic building in this tabulation.

DATES OF ERECTION OF BUILDINGS

An attempt was made in each college to obtain information regarding the dates of the erection of the various buildings. This information was available for more than two-thirds of the buildings in the colleges studied. There is one building in the group that was constructed prior to 1800, and there is one that was constructed in the period between 1800 and 1824. Three buildings still in use were constructed between 1825 and 1849. The quarter of a century between 1850 and 1875 witnessed the construction of twenty-two buildings which are still in use in these colleges, and approximately the same number were erected in the fifteen-year period between 1875 and 1889. More than two-thirds (69 per cent) of the buildings for which data are available have been constructed since 1900. The five-year period from 1920 to 1925 witnessed the construction of more buildings now in use than any ten-year period in previous history. Since 1925 there has apparently been a slackening in the rate of new building construction.

The fact that such a large proportion of buildings have been erected since the beginning of the twentieth century indicates in general a relatively satisfactory building situation. Unfortunately, in planning many of the buildings constructed during this period utilization has not been made of the latest information on educational architecture available at the time of construction. As a result, many of these buildings which are less than thirty years old are similar in design and construction to the type of architecture which prevailed in colleges a half-century ago.

For the most part the recently erected buildings are either gymnasiums or dormitories. A number of the colleges, however, such as Baker University, Brothers College, University of Chattanooga, Cornell College, DePauw University, Evansville College, Kansas Wesleyan University, MacMurray College, Oklahoma City University, Ozark Wesleyan College, College of the Pacific, College of Puget Sound, and Simpson College, have recently erected classroom or science buildings of excellent design.

AESTHETIC EFFECT OF CAMPUS AND BUILDINGS

A college or university has an obligation to maintain a standard of dignity in the construction of its academic plant which is not demanded ordinarily of public high schools or elementary schools. One of the important contributions of the physical plant to the educational program is the aesthetic effect it creates.

There are few of the colleges of this group which are free from criticism from the standpoint of aesthetic effect. Four colleges—University of Chattanooga, Oklahoma City University, College of the Pacific, and College of Puget Sound—may be singled out as having harmonious and pleasing effects. In many of the colleges, however, there is a confusion of types of architecture, a clashing in the treatment of building materials, a failure to develop proper landscaping effects, or other deficiencies which seriously mar the general impression of unity and dignity that should pervade a college campus. Three of the institutions which have been referred to above as having an unusually pleasing campus development have had the rare opportunity of building a new plant on a new location. It must be recognized that this opportunity cannot come to many of the colleges. In an established institution the development of a harmonious building arrangement is a matter requiring considerable time. The adoption of a unified type of architecture and of a continuing campus plan, which will remain unchanged through succeeding administrations of the college, is necessary in order that the campus in its ultimate development may be both educationally and aesthetically satisfactory. Only a few of the colleges have adopted a campus plan looking toward the future development of the institution. It would be well if each of them would prepare a plan to govern, in a general way, the erection of future buildings.

VALUE OF PLANT AND EQUIPMENT

Table 25 shows the total value of plant, the value of dormitories, the value of the academic plant, the value of the academic equipment, and the value of grounds in the thirty-five colleges. In collecting the data for this table, the original costs were used as the basis of value wherever these figures were available. In the case of the buildings for which cost data were not available, appraised values were used.

This table shows a large range among these institutions in the value of the total plant. The colleges on the approved list of the Association of American Universities have, in general, more expensive plants than those not on this list.

Table 26 presents data regarding the value of the plant per student. The data of this table are obtained by dividing the valuations presented in Table 25 in each case by the annual carrying-load of students for the year in question.

This table shows that the colleges on the approved list of the Association of American Universities have, in general, a somewhat more valuable plant per student than the colleges not on this list. A large part of this difference comes on the item of value of academic buildings per student, although there are also relatively large differences on all the other items.

Table 27 presents data showing the relationship between the size of the

TABLE 25

VALUE OF PLANT AND EQUIPMENT OF THIRTY-FIVE COLLEGES†

Institution	Fiscal Year	Total Plant	Academic Buildings	Academic Equipment	Dormitories	Grounds
*Ohio Wesleyan‡......	1929–30	$2,468,942	$1,227,481	$433,815	$663,598	$144,048
*DePauw§............	1929–30	1,961,279	618,491	360,498	845,241	137,049
*Allegheny..........	1928–29	1,761,320	580,000	161,000	755,312	265,008
*Lawrence...........	1928–29	1,613,134	840,925	215,102	344,583	212,524
Baldwin-Wallace......	1929–30	1,368,188	664,180	170,909	404,259	128,840
*Pacific..............	1929–30	1,338,521	727,266	191,529	244,222	175,504
*Dickinson‡..........	1928–29	1,338,000	704,000	135,000	249,000	250,000
*Albion‡.............	1928–29	1,259,927	730,708	144,293	330,121	54,805
*Chattanooga.........	1928–29	1,155,000	418,000	112,000	25,000	600,000
Ohio Northern‡......	1929–30	1,061,212	844,084	129,128	13,000	75,000
*Illinois Wesleyan‡....	1929–30	982,630	635,100	163,200	73,800	110,530
*Mount Union‡.......	1929–30	878,531	334,499	203,350	190,427	150,255
*MacMurray.........	1929–30	869,090	397,071	132,722	242,693	96,604
*Morningside‖........	1928–29	743,459	266,781	81,269	289,989	105,420
*Cornell..............	1928–29	709,394	411,482	121,922	105,721	70,269
*Willamette‡..........	1929–30	701,432	263,568	52,864	135,000	250,000
*Hamline.............	1928–29	700,367	269,046	71,240	231,208	128,873
Iowa Wesleyan‡......	1928–29	700,000	405,000	72,250	122,750	100,000
Nebraska Wesleyan...	1929–30	688,952	401,832	172,120	....	115,000
Puget Sound‡........	1929–30	678,857	436,455	81,876	10,721	149,805
Evansville...........	1928–29	654,510	425,192	110,845	....	118,473
Southwestern.........	1929–30	621,420	430,664	71,356	87,000	32,400
Oklahoma City‡......	1928–29	609,177	459,032	85,789	....	64,356
*Baker‡.............	1929–30	600,985	383,641	155,145	14,223	47,976
Brothers.............	1929–30	574,583	449,667	71,366	29,800	23,750
*Simpson‡............	1928–29	558,941	349,792	57,499	74,750	76,900
Dakota Wesleyan.....	1928–29	535,541	318,776	64,745	103,835	48,185
West Virginia Wesleyan...............	1929–30	478,251	192,082	64,300	146,907	74,962
Kansas Wesleyan.....	1929–30	444,784	243,413	62,283	77,836	61,252
Ozark Wesleyan‡.....	1928–29	377,785	263,061	57,861	....	56,863
Union‡..............	1928–29	325,200	162,000	14,700	93,500	55,000
Central Wesleyan‡....	1928–29	293,900	136,000	47,900	60,000	50,000
McKendree‡.........	1929–30	254,900	100,500	34,400	110,000	10,000
Intermountain‡......	1929–30	232,693	80,700	29,317	109,000	13,676
Gooding.............	1929–30	146,100	62,500	6,000	67,600	10,000
Median, all colleges	....	$ 700,000	$ 405,000	$ 85,789	$105,721	$ 96,604
*Median, A.A.U. colleges.............	....	982,630	418,000	144,293	242,693	137,049
Median, non-A.A.U. colleges.........	....	550,062	360,304	68,051	72,718	59,058

* Institutions on the approved list of the Association of American Universities.
† Original costs are used where data are available.
‡ Appraisal values are used for some or all of the buildings, because costs are not available.
§ School of Music buildings are not included.
‖ Women's Residence Hall, which is owned by a holding company, is included.

TABLE 26

VALUE† OF PLANT AND EQUIPMENT PER STUDENT FOR
THIRTY-FIVE COLLEGES

Institution	Fiscal Year	Total Plant	Academic Buildings	Academic Equipment	Dormi- tories	Grounds
Brothers...............	1929–30	$8,977	$7,026	$1,115	$ 465	$ 371
Baldwin-Wallace.........	1929–30	3,034	1,473	379	896	286
*Chattanooga............	1928–29	3,032	1,097	294	66	1,575
*Allegheny..............	1928–29	2,960	975	271	1,269	445
*MacMurray.............	1929–30	2,463	1,125	376	688	274
*Dickinson‡..............	1928–29	2,455	1,292	247	457	459
Iowa Wesleyan‡.........	1928–29	2,147	1,242	222	376	307
*Lawrence..............	1928–29	2,065	1,077	275	441	272
*Pacific.................	1929–30	1,836	998	263	335	240
*Mount Union‡..........	1929–30	1,830	696	424	397	313
*Hamline...............	1928–29	1,769	679	180	584	326
*Illinois Wesleyan‡.......	1929–30	1,745	1,128	290	131	196
*Albion‡...............	1928–29	1,676	972	192	439	73
Ozark Wesleyan‡........	1928–29	1,657	1,154	254	....	249
Evansville..............	1928–29	1,649	1,072	279	....	298
Dakota Wesleyan........	1928–29	1,594	949	193	309	143
Intermountain‡.........	1929–30	1,541	535	194	721	91
Central Wesleyan‡.......	1928–29	1,539	712	251	314	262
West Virginia Wesleyan..	1929–30	1,481	595	199	455	232
Kansas Wesleyan........	1929–30	1,453	795	204	254	200
Union‡.................	1928–29	1,433	714	65	412	242
*Cornell................	1928–29	1,427	828	245	213	141
*DePauw§..............	1929–30	1,416	447	260	610	99
*Ohio Wesleyan‡.........	1929–30	1,383	687	243	372	81
*Willamette‡.............	1929–30	1,370	515	103	264	488
*Baker‡.................	1929–30	1,304	832	337	31	104
Ohio Northern‡.........	1929–30	1,183	941	144	14	84
Gooding................	1929–30	1,141	488	47	528	78
Southwestern...........	1929–30	1,106	766	127	155	58
Puget Sound‡...........	1929–30	1,102	709	133	17	243
*Morningside‖...........	1928–29	1,071	384	117	418	152
Nebraska Wesleyan......	1929–30	1,052	613	263	....	176
McKendree‡............	1929–30	1,012	399	137	436	40
*Simpson‡..............	1928–29	979	613	101	131	134
Oklahoma City‡.........	1928–29	683	515	96	....	72
Median, all colleges....	....	$1,539	$ 795	$ 243	$ 372	$ 232
*Median, A.A.U. colleges...............	....	1,745	832	260	397	240
Median, non-A.A.U. colleges...........	....	1,467	740	197	312	216

* Institutions on the approved list of the Association of American Universities.
† Original costs are used where data are available.
‡ Appraisal values are used for some or all of the buildings, because costs are not available.
§ School of Music buildings are not included.
‖ Women's Residence Hall, which is owned by a holding company, is included.

student body and the per capita investment in plant. In constructing this table, the colleges were first divided into three groups on the basis of enrolment; and then the averages of the per capita investments for the total plant and the various component parts of the plant were computed for each group.

It will be observed from Table 27 that there is an important difference in the average per capita value of total plant among the colleges of various sizes. The colleges with fewer than four hundred students have, on the average, almost 50 per cent more per student invested in plant than the colleges with over seven hundred students. The colleges with enrolments between four and seven hundred have an average investment per student in plant approximately halfway between that of the colleges that are larger and those that are smaller than the institutions of this

TABLE 27

PER CAPITA VALUE OF TOTAL PLANT, ACADEMIC BUILDINGS,
ACADEMIC EQUIPMENT, DORMITORIES, AND GROUNDS IN
COLLEGES OF VARIOUS SIZES

NUMBER OF STUDENTS ENROLLED	NUMBER OF COLLEGES	AVERAGE VALUE PER STUDENT OF THE FOLLOWING ITEMS				
		Total Plant	Academic Buildings	Academic Equipment	Dormitories	Grounds
700 and over.......	6	$1,401	$ 773	$202	$313	$113
400–699...........	17	1,796	866	244	356	330
Under 400.........	12	2,135	1,307	263	356	209

group. Inspection of the buildings and equipment of these colleges leads to the conclusion that the difference is not reflected in the quality of plants in the smaller institutions; in fact, if there is any difference on this point, the larger colleges in general seem to have better plant provisions than the smaller ones. The data unmistakably lead to the conclusion that the small college must necessarily have a larger investment per student in plant than the large institution, if the educational service of the two is to be on a par.

It will be noted that this principle of a more expensive plant in the smaller institutions holds good for two of the subdivisions of the plant but does not hold good for the other two subdivisions. The size of the enrolment is even more important in its effect upon the value per student of academic buildings than upon the value of the total plant. The small colleges (those under four hundred enrolment) have almost double the amount of investment per student in academic buildings that is found in the large colleges (those over seven hundred enrolment). To a smaller degree the same relationship holds for the item of academic equipment. The small colleges have approximately one-third more per student invested in academic equipment than the large colleges have. In each case the medium-sized group of colleges has an average investment per student between the two extremes.

Figure 11 shows graphically the relationship between the size of the enrolment and the average per capita value of academic buildings and equipment.

On the other two points, value of dormitories per student and value of grounds per student, the only consistent trend is for the large institutions (those over seven hundred enrolment) to have a smaller investment than the small colleges (those with less than four hundred enrolment). The middle group (those with enrolments from four to seven hundred) in both of these cases has an investment per student as high as, or higher

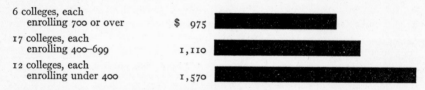

6 colleges, each
    enrolling 700 or over $ 975

17 colleges, each
    enrolling 400–699   1,110

12 colleges, each
    enrolling under 400   1,570

FIG. 11.—Average per capita value of academic buildings and academic equipment in colleges having various numbers of students enrolled.

than, that of the group of small colleges. In the case of dormitories, the explanation seems to lie in the variation in policy regarding the provision of housing accommodations for students. Some colleges tend to provide housing for larger proportions of their student bodies than other colleges, and the proportion of the enrolment accommodated in dormitories seems to be unrelated to the size of the institution. In the case of the value of grounds, the disturbing factor appears to be the unit value of acreage. A college located in a down-town district of a good-sized city (for example, the University of Chattanooga) will have a high valuation on its grounds. On the other hand, a college in a village or small city will not need a large investment to provide a very satisfactory campus.

The data regarding the value of plant per student must be interpreted with considerable caution in the case of individual institutions, owing to the fact that the basis of valuation is not the same in all of the colleges. The use of appraisal figures, which was necessitated by the absence of original cost data in some of the institutions, makes it difficult to draw any hard and fast conclusions regarding the value of the plants in individual colleges. The use of group averages, as in Table 27, to a large extent overcomes this difficulty, so far as general conditions are concerned. It seems fair to conclude that the small college must count upon a relatively large investment per student in academic buildings and equipment. The actual amounts needed for satisfactory service are certainly not less than the averages shown in Table 27.

INSURANCE

The necessity of carrying adequate protection against loss by fire needs no extended argument. A majority of the colleges studied have at some time in their history suffered serious losses of this type. Particularly in an institution with limited funds the carrying of insurance is an absolute necessity.

Four of the colleges carry insurance protection to the extent of 90 per cent or more of the value of the plant; in only seven is 80 per cent or more of the plant valuation protected by insurance. In nine of the colleges the coverage amounts to less than 50 per cent of the total value of the plant. The folly of inadequate insurance protection should be evident. There is urgent need for careful attention to this matter in many of the colleges.

Approximately half of the colleges studied carry their insurance on either the 80 per cent or the 90 per cent co-insurance plan. This plan is decidedly advantageous to the college. It provides a maximum of protection at a minimum of cost. The colleges which are carrying their insurance under some other plan would do well to investigate the savings which can be effected by the adoption of the 80 per cent or the 90 per cent co-insurance plan.

Other types of plant insurance are not uniformly carried by the colleges. Only sixteen of the thirty-five institutions carry tornado insurance, and in only ten is boiler insurance in effect. Protection against risk of loss by tornado is not expensive and should be carried by all colleges situated in areas subject to this risk. Boiler insurance is also a necessity in all cases where the college depends upon its own heating plant.

All of the colleges studied buy their insurance from local agents, this being the only method by which most of the big insurance companies deal with their clients. There is no question but that this method of purchasing insurance is costing the colleges of this group thousands of dollars every year through excessive costs for this protection. The local agent must, of course, be allowed his commission. An investigation made in 1926 by the Association of College and University Business Officers of the Eastern States showed that the losses by fire over a period of years of a group of fifty colleges and universities which co-operated in the study were only 40 per cent of the premiums paid for the same period. The conclusion drawn as a result of this investigation was that the insurance rates paid by colleges and universities were approximately $27\frac{1}{2}$ per cent higher than they should be compared with the average ratio of losses paid to premiums collected by insurance companies.

No consideration was given in the investigation noted above to the opportunities of savings in selling costs for insurance companies if a group of colleges should purchase insurance on a co-operative basis. As most insurance companies now operate, the brokerage fees, which represent a large part of their direct selling costs, average approximately 20 per cent of the premiums collected.

If the colleges of the group studied could pool their buying of insurance so as to save the brokerage fee, and so as to bring pressure to bear on insurance companies to make a proper adjustment of rates, the savings should aggregate approximately 50 per cent of the present insurance premiums paid. If co-operative purchasing of insurance does not seem feasible, this group of colleges could well consider the advisability of forming a mutual fire insurance company, thus handling their own risks on a cost basis. The possible savings by this plan would amply justify its serious consideration.

CHAPTER XII

PLANT FACILITIES AND CONDITIONS

In each of the colleges studied, a careful inspection was made of the entire physical plant. The members of the survey staff making this inspection were usually accompanied by one or more of the officers of the college, and at the time of the inspection detailed criticisms were made verbally and suggestions were given for improvement. The present report attempts to summarize, in a general way, the criticisms of conditions which were rather commonly found in this group of colleges.

CLASSROOMS

The requirements for a satisfactory classroom in elementary and secondary schools are fairly well understood by educational authorities. There has been much less study of this matter at the college level. For that reason the colleges, in designing their classroom buildings, have not had available a satisfactory set of standards by which to plan their new construction. As a result, in most of the colleges some classrooms present more or less serious deficiencies from the standpoint of educational service.

One of the important requisites of a satisfactory classroom is abundance of light. All too frequently this feature is neglected by architects, particularly if the general type of the building construction demands the use of small windows for a satisfactory exterior effect. In elementary and secondary schools it is generally understood that the light area of a classroom should be equal to not less than one-fifth of the floor area. It seems logical to suppose that this same standard should hold for college classrooms. Windows should be located on only one side of the room, and students should be seated to receive the light from the left. It is surprising to find the number of classrooms in this group of colleges in which the seating has been arranged to provide right-hand lighting. This is unsatisfactory, because, as a student writes, his eyes must focus upon material that is covered by the shadow of his hand. Light from the left avoids this difficulty and is now almost universally the rule in elementary and secondary schools.

One of the primary principles of satisfactory classroom lighting is that students should not be seated so as to face a source of light. This is very fatiguing on the eyes and undoubtedly results in educational inefficiency. In a few of the classrooms in some of the colleges of this group the seating is arranged so that students face one or more windows. Windows at the back of the room are less undesirable, but in this case the instructor must face the light, and the effect upon his vision is sometimes harmful. The only satisfactory plan is for left-hand, unilateral lighting.

The classroom seats should be comfortable and durable. A number of the classrooms of these colleges are seated with old rickety chairs upon which generations of students have carved their initials, fraternity insignia, class years, etc. In a few of the colleges seating of a modern type is employed throughout, and the desks and chairs have been well cared for.

A satisfactory blackboard is one of the requisites of a modern classroom. Formerly it was considered desirable to crowd into a classroom all of the blackboard space that could possibly be obtained. More recently, bulletin board space has come to be considered of equal importance, and there has been a tendency to make less use of the blackboard in instructional procedures. The only satisfactory material for blackboards is slate. Several of the colleges have employed substitutes for slate, but almost without exception these have proved unsatisfactory after a few years. In the long run it seems that slate is the cheapest, as well as the best, material for blackboard purposes.

The classrooms should be of ample size to accommodate the student enrolment. In the schedule of classes of the ordinary college there will be found a wide variation in the number of students enrolled. This would normally make it wise to provide some classrooms of relatively large size, a considerable number of average size, and others suitable for small groups of twelve or fifteen students. Almost never in these colleges are there found classrooms of the last-mentioned size. The classrooms seem to have been constructed on the theory prevailing in the elementary schools that all classes will be of a standard size, typically from forty to fifty students. As a result, a small class must meet in a room designed for three or four times as many students. Not only is there waste in the utilization of space from this process, but the actual instructional conditions are less congenial than would be the case if the small group had a small classroom in which to meet. It would seem desirable in future classroom-building construction to provide a rather varied schedule of room sizes in order to meet satisfactorily the needs of college classes.

LABORATORIES

The science laboratories of this group of colleges on the whole are unusually satisfactory. Almost without exception, every one of the colleges, including even the weakest ones, have an adequate amount of science equipment for the courses which are being offered. It is true that many of the colleges do not have all of the equipment which they desire or which they would need if a more extensive program of science instruction were to be undertaken, but in general it may be said that excellent judgment has been used in this group of colleges in providing the science equipment and in limiting the offerings of science courses to the fields in which adequate laboratory equipment is available.

One of the common criticisms of the laboratory rooms of colleges is the placing of desks with reference to the light. It is frequently found that desks have been so placed as to have one-half of the students face the light as they work at laboratory desks. By a simple rearrangement of the tables it is frequently possible to avoid this difficulty. This is a point which should be carefully watched in the planning of new buildings.

Perhaps the most frequent complaint found in these colleges regarding the science laboratory facilities is related to the crowded conditions which prevail. The increasing popularity of science instruction has made unusual demands upon the colleges for laboratory facilities, and the faculty members in the science departments of many of these colleges have expressed the opinion that they are badly cramped for space. In several cases this condition is due to an unfortunate arrangement of the schedule of classes and laboratory sessions. It is obvious that where it is the policy to have all laboratory work in the afternoon periods, a college will need much larger laboratory facilities than if an all-day schedule of laboratory work is maintained. It would seem advisable, before extending the space assigned to science departments, to make every endeavor to meet the situation by a rearrangement of the class and laboratory schedule.

The topic of laboratories should not be passed without commenting on the unusually excellent facilities provided in three or four of the colleges which have new science buildings. Among these may be mentioned the College of Puget Sound, the College of the Pacific, and MacMurray College. In the attention which has been paid to the minute details of planning and construction the College of Puget Sound has one of the most thoroughly satisfactory science buildings which the members of the survey staff have ever seen in a college of comparable size.

OFFICES

Two types of offices are necessary in a modern institution of higher learning. The first type is for the use of the administrative staff; the second, is for the use of faculty members.

The administrative offices in this group of institutions are generally adequate for the purposes for which they are used, and for the most part are relatively satisfactory in their layout and arrangement. A criticism applicable to a considerable number of these colleges relates to the location of the administrative offices. Ideally, the central administrative offices should be located in such a way that the casual visitor to the college will inevitably wander into the office upon first entering the campus. Several of the colleges have their administrative offices situated in out-of-the-way sections of the campus, on the second floors of buildings, or in some other location, so that it is difficult for one not familiar with the campus to find them.

One of the necessary requirements in a college administrative office layout is a centralization of the office space. In several of the colleges the administrative offices are badly decentralized, the president's office being in a different building from the dean's office, the dean and registrar being in separate buildings or on separate floors of the same building. A co-ordination of the office assignments is necessary in order to facilitate the use of records. The various personnel officers, such as the dean of men, the dean of women, and the dean of the college, should have their offices grouped around the central records office, which is usually in charge of the registrar. The president and the officer in charge of finances should be so located as to be easily accessible to each other. The same holds true of the president's office and the dean's office.

It has only been in recent years that emphasis has been given to the need for offices for faculty members. Because of this fact, in most of the older academic buildings there is an inadequate provision of office space for members of the instructional staff. A careful analysis of office facilities for faculty members was made in twenty-eight of the colleges studied. Table 28 presents data showing the percentage of faculty members of these institutions having various types of office arrangements.

This table shows that in the typical college of this group, as represented by the median, approximately one-third of the faculty members are provided with individual offices. The median situation is for slightly more than one-fourth of the instructors to be provided with offices in which two or more faculty members have their desks. This arrangement is much less satisfactory than the individual office, since students who come to confer with one faculty member interrupt the work of all who are in the same room. It is typical in this group of colleges for slightly more than one-fifth of the instructors to use classrooms for offices. This is a very uneconomical use of space, since the classroom is not available for its major use when an instructor is occupying it for an office. In several of the col-

leges, some other type of office arrangement has been made for a few faculty members, such as the use of an administrative office, a private laboratory, a cubicle in the library, etc.

TABLE 28

OFFICE FACILITIES FOR FACULTY MEMBERS IN TWENTY-EIGHT COLLEGES

INSTITUTION	PERCENTAGE OF FACULTY MEMBERS HAVING VARIOUS OFFICE ARRANGEMENTS				
	Having Individual Offices	Officing with Two or More in the Same Office	Using Classrooms for Offices	Other Arrange-ments	Without Any Office Arrange-ment
Kansas Wesleyan	82.4	11.8	....	....	5.8
Brothers..................	68.8	31.2	....	....	....
Nebraska Wesleyan.........	59.5	16.7	21.4	....	2.4
*Allegheny.................	51.3	43.5	2.6	....	2.6
*Dickinson.................	46.9	53.1	....	....	....
Oklahoma City.............	41.7	19.4	27.8	....	11.1
Intermountain.............	40.0	26.7	13.3	....	20.0
*Baker....................	39.3	21.4	39.3	....	....
Baldwin-Wallace...........	38.9	22.1	27.8	5.6	5.6
*Lawrence.................	38.8	18.4	36.7	6.1	....
*MacMurray...............	38.3	26.4	23.5	5.9	5.9
Southwestern..............	37.8	29.8	18.9	5.4	8.1
*DePauw..................	34.8	57.6	7.6	....	....
Ohio Northern.............	34.8	39.1	13.0	2.2	10.9
Puget Sound...............	34.3	40.0	11.4	5.7	8.6
*Willamette...............	33.3	33.3	21.2	9.1	3.1
West Virginia Wesleyan.....	32.0	16.0	36.0	8.0	8.0
*Illinois Wesleyan..........	29.5	17.6	50.0	2.9	....
Central Wesleyan..........	29.4	5.9	29.4	11.8	23.5
*Albion	29.0	62.0	9.0	....	....
*Mount Union.............	27.3	9.1	30.3	12.1	21.2
*Ohio Wesleyan...........	26.5	64.1	4.7	1.6	3.1
Ozark Wesleyan............	25.0	30.0	30.0	10.0	5.0
Dakota Wesleyan..........	24.0	36.0	28.0	4.0	8.0
McKendree................	23.8	9.5	47.7	9.5	9.5
Evansville................	22.2	59.3	11.1	7.4	....
*Pacific..................	20.7	56.6	17.0	1.9	3.8
Gooding..................	....	8.3	66.7	8.3	16.7
Median, all colleges......	34.7	28.3	21.3	3.5	5.3
*Median, A.A.U. colleges..	34.1	38.4	19.1	1.8	1.3
Median, non-A.A.U. col-leges................	34.7	24.4	24.6	5.5	8.1

Institutions on the approved list of the Association of American Universities.

In the median college approximately 5 per cent of the faculty members
have no office arrangement whatever. It will be noted that the percentage
of faculty members without any office arrangement varies widely among

this group of colleges. Eight colleges of the group have provided some sort of office arrangement for every faculty member, while three of the colleges have one-fifth or more of their faculty members without any office arrangement.

There is real economy in providing satisfactory office space for all members of the faculty. If an institution is to individualize its educational program, suitable rooms must be provided in which teachers and students can meet for individual or small group conferences. To employ classrooms for such purposes is an uneconomical use of space. Furthermore, the small quarters of an individual office provide a more convenient place for these student conferences. Individual offices are also necessary for study and for the research in which faculty members should engage. It would seem desirable in many of these colleges to provide additional faculty offices through some remodeling of the present space. Any new academic building which is constructed should have ample provision for instructional offices.

DORMITORIES

All but five of the institutions in this group find it necessary to provide some sort of dormitory facilities for their students. Four of the five colleges which do not have dormitories are institutions which have only recently been established or which have recently changed their location and thus have not yet had an opportunity to provide residence halls. The only old established institution of the group which does not have dormitories is Nebraska Wesleyan University. With only one exception these five institutions lacking dormitory facilities are located in large cities.

In this group of colleges the provision of dormitory facilities for women students is much more common than the provision for men students. There are only five colleges which do not have some dormitory facilities for women, but one-half of the colleges have no men's dormitories.

The types of buildings utilized for residence halls range all the way from old residences converted to dormitory uses without much remodeling up to fine new fireproof buildings constructed especially for dormitory purposes. A considerable number of the colleges have provided for expansion in their dormitory facilities by taking over buildings originally erected as residences. At the University of Chattanooga this type of building is the only one provided for dormitory purposes, and in a few other colleges a large part of the present housing accommodations are of this type.

Data were collected regarding the utilization of women's dormitories in seventeen of the colleges. Eleven of these seventeen have their women's dormitories occupied to 90 per cent or more of their capacity. Three of the colleges were, at the time of the survey visit, utilizing 50 per cent or less of their dormitory space for women. The general observation may be made that in several of these colleges more dormitory space for women is available than is needed for the present enrolment. In the case of one institution, a serious mistake has been made in constructing a large dormitory without adequate inquiry as to the needs for dormitory facilities. Although this new dormitory accommodates approximately two hundred students, during the three or four years it has been occupied there have never been more than one hundred young women housed in the building.

There seems to be a general tendency for colleges located in large cities to provide less dormitory space than is provided by colleges located in smaller communities. The fact that a large percentage of the student body of the colleges located in large cities are living at home, combined with the fact that rooming accommodations are usually more easily obtained in private homes in the large communities, makes the provision of dormitory facilities in such colleges less essential than in those located in the smaller communities.

Six or seven institutions may be singled out as having unusually excellent dormitory facilities for women. Among those which may be mentioned are Albion College, Baldwin-Wallace College, DePauw University, MacMurray College, Morningside College, Ohio Wesleyan University, and the College of the Pacific. The dormitory at MacMurray College probably is the finest of any in this group. The men's dormitories at DePauw University and the College of the Pacific are worthy of special mention.

AUDITORIUMS AND CHAPELS

Each of the colleges included in this study has made some sort of an arrangement for an auditorium or chapel. One or two of the colleges do not have satisfactory auditoriums on their own campuses but use, instead, neighboring churches.

The majority of the auditoriums in use in these colleges are rather small. Some of them do not even provide seating capacity for the entire student body; and in only a few of the colleges are the auditoriums large enough for such occasions as commencement, popular lectures, etc. Some of the colleges use their gymnasiums for the few occasions in which a relatively large seating capacity is needed. The use of the gymnasium as an auditorium is an economical method of providing for this service, but for two reasons is somewhat unsatisfactory. In the first place, it is usually necessary to interrupt the program of physical education during the time the gymnasium floor is seated for a public function. In the second place, the cost of placing and removing the chairs is considerable. Ideally, the college should have its own auditorium, and this should be large enough to provide a seating capacity considerably in excess of the number of students enrolled.

A few of the colleges may be mentioned as having unusually satisfactory auditoriums. Among these are Kansas Wesleyan University, Oklahoma City University, Illinois Wesleyan University, Ohio Northern University, the College of the Pacific, and Lawrence College. The College of Puget Sound has a small, but tastefully arranged, auditorium. The University of Chattanooga has an unusually attractive chapel; this, however, is used only for chapel purposes and is not arranged so as to serve as an auditorium. At the time of the survey Iowa Wesleyan College had almost completed the remodeling of its chapel building. With the completion of this work this college will have a very satisfactory chapel and auditorium.

GYMNASIUMS

In the typical college of this group the gymnasium is the best and newest building on the campus. In general, the gymnasiums are relatively better than such facilities as classrooms, laboratories, auditoriums, etc. On the whole, better judgment has been used in planning the gymnasiums than in almost any of the other units of these colleges. Criticisms of the gymnasiums, therefore, apply to a relatively few institutions.

In a few of the colleges the gymnasium floors are too small for a modern program of physical education. In a few cases seating capacity is inadequate, and in some instances the shower- and locker-rooms are insufficient for the present student body and the program of work attempted.

The rather general criticism may be made that gymnasium facilities for women students are decidedly inferior to those for men. Very few of the institutions have separate gymnasiums for women. Instead, the women students are allowed to use the gymnasium at hours when the class work for men students is not scheduled. In only a few of the colleges are the shower- and locker-room facilities for women students on a par with those for men.

ATHLETIC FIELDS

The recent interest in college athletics has resulted in the acquisition of rather satisfactory athletic fields by practically all of the colleges of this group. Several of the institutions have concrete stadia and have provided flood lighting for night football games. In general, the criticism may be made of the athletic fields that they have been developed almost wholly for the use of the football teams. Playing space for other games is relatively inferior. An exception might be made in the case of running tracks, however, which are usually fairly satisfactory. As in the case of gymnasiums, playing fields for women students have not been provided as satisfactorily as those for men students.

It has already been pointed out that many colleges are finding it advisable to add a golf course to their equipment for physical education. The development of such a project not only increases the amount of space needed but at the same time increases enormously the cost of upkeep. In view of the modern development in physical education, by which it is considered a function of the college to prepare students for participation in such sports as they will engage in after college days are over, it would seem that the development of facilities for golf will almost necessarily be forced upon the better colleges in this group.

MUSIC BUILDINGS

Practically all of these colleges offer some instruction in music. The advantages of a separate building for this work are numerous. This department is usually somewhat of an annoyance to the other departments unless the work is located in a separate building. Not only is there the matter of sound interference, but students are coming and going at all hours; and in general the presence of this department in an academic building is unsatisfactory. In most of the colleges the work in music is housed in a separate building. Two of the colleges—Illinois Wesleyan University and Ohio Northern University—have especially satisfactory buildings. Both of these are new, a part of the funds for their erection having been obtained through the Presser Foundation. In most of the colleges, however, the music departments are housed in old buildings which have not been especially designed for this purpose. There are peculiar needs in the matter of soundproofing and space arrangement in a music building which make it very desirable to have a building especially designed for this purpose.

INFIRMARIES

Many of the colleges have no satisfactory arrangement for the care of resident students who become ill. Those which do make such provision typically set aside one room or a suite of rooms in the dormitory, designating this space as the infirmary. A few of the colleges, such as Lawrence College, College of the Pacific, Ohio Wesleyan, and DePauw, have separate buildings for this purpose. The infirmary at the College of the Pacific is by far the best building of this type found on any college campus visited by members of the survey staff. This building, which was provided through the generosity of a friend of the college, includes almost every type of equipment needed in a modern hospital.

The colleges typically lack isolation facilities for the care of students suffering from contagious diseases. In a few cases isolation wards have been established at the dormitory. These need to have separate outside entrances and should be completely self-contained, with their own kitchens, baths, and nurses' rooms, as well as beds for patients.

A few of the colleges have made arrangements with neighboring hospitals for the care of students who are ill. In case satisfactory hospital facilities are available, such an arrangement constitutes a very satisfactory method of caring for serious cases of illness. It does not, however, obviate the need for a local infirmary under the control of the college for the care of students who are not sufficiently ill to require extensive hospitalization.

SOCIAL ROOMS

Social rooms for students in this group of colleges are typically provided in the dormitories. These are available in general only to dormitory students. Students whose homes are in the community or who live in private rooming-houses thus do not have available satisfactory facilities for social life, although in one or two institutions such rooms have been provided for students not living in dormitories. Perhaps the best example of this type of development is that which is found at the University of Chattanooga.

Relatively few of the colleges provide any sort of clubrooms for faculty members. Such facilities are becoming increasingly desirable, and colleges would do well to make some provision for them. The University of Chattanooga has recently opened a faculty club which meets this need in a very satisfactory manner.

HEATING PLANTS

There are in general three types of heating plants used in the colleges of this group: (1) the central plant which serves the whole campus; (2) separate heating plants in each building; and (3) local heating devices in the various rooms of the buildings. Willamette University is the only institution employing the last-mentioned plan, and this method is used there only in the science building, each room of which is heated separately by wood-burning stoves. In a few of the colleges a semicentral type of heating plant has been developed whereby two or more buildings are heated from a single plant located in one of the buildings. Thus, on the entire campus there may be two or three such heating plants. In general, it has been found that the central type of heating plant is more economical of fuel, more satisfactory in its operation, and cheaper in the long run than the plan of heating by means of local plants in each of the buildings.

Only a few of the colleges have provided thermostatic control for their heating systems. There are now available types of thermostatic control which are relatively inexpensive to instal and which will result in considerable saving in fuel. The thermostat can be arranged to turn the heat on and turn it off at various times in such a way as to cut down the fuel consumption during the hours in which the buildings are unoccupied. Within the past two or three years MacMurray College has added three new buildings to its plant, almost doubling its total cubature. At the same time thermostatic control was installed. The college authorities were surprised to find that the total fuel bill, even with the added cubature, has been no greater than it was before the addition of the new buildings. Albion College has also demonstrated the economies in a thermostatically-controlled heating system.

Almost every conceivable type of fuel is used in the colleges of this group. The great majority burn coal. A few are so situated that they find it advisable to burn natural gas. In two or three cases oil is used as fuel. One college relies almost wholly on wood as a fuel. In two cases heat is purchased from a local public service corporation.

FIRE HAZARDS

The lack of fireproof construction in the buildings of these colleges has already been pointed out. This lack makes it much more imperative that adequate attention be given to the elimination of fire hazards and to the provision of fire-protection equipment.

One of the most common difficulties in this group of institutions is the failure to isolate sources of fire hazard by fire walls and self-closing fire doors. Particularly where the heating plant is not constructed as a separate building, there is especial need for care in the matter of isolating this source of hazard. It is comparatively easy in the construction of buildings to provide fire walls and self-closing fire doors in such a way as to separate from the rest of the building all sources of peculiar hazard. This would also involve such provisions as an asbestos curtain for the auditorium and development of separate rooms for paint shops, waste-paper storage, etc.

A second rather common deficiency in the handling of fire hazards is the failure to provide adequate fire-protection equipment. Even in so-called "fireproof" buildings there is usually a considerable amount of combustible furniture and equipment, and fire-protection equipment is therefore necessary in all types of buildings. The most important types of fire-protection equipment are chemical extinguishers and fire hose. In several colleges incipient fires in recent years have been checked by the use of such pieces of apparatus almost as soon as they started. There is no excuse for failure to provide equipment of this sort in every college building. Hand fire extinguishers should be placed in convenient locations on every floor of every building. Points of special hazard should be provided with extra equipment. Fire hose should also be placed on each floor, with a sufficient number of outlets and an adequate length of hose to reach quickly and easily any portion of the floor in which a fire might be located.

The science laboratories need certain additional fire-protection equipment owing to the danger from explosions, acids, and the use of open-flame burners. Heavy blankets are one of the best types of fire-protection equipment for science laboratories. Modern laboratories also have overhead showers so located as to be quickly available in case the clothing of a student or instructor should become ignited.

When fire extinguishers and fire hose have been provided, it is necessary that they be inspected regularly in order that they may always be in working order. Chemical fire extinguishers of the soda-acid type should be recharged annually, and each extinguisher should bear a tag showing the date of its last recharging. This point was found to have been overlooked in a majority of the colleges studied, with the result that a large percentage of the fire extinguishers in these colleges would be unserviceable in case of need. Fire hose should also be inspected and tested at fairly frequent intervals. The hose deteriorates with age and will then burst when the water pressure is turned on. For this reason the hose should be subject to frequent inspections in order to be certain that it will always be in serviceable condition.

In several of the colleges some of the buildings are not adequately equipped with fire escapes. It must be recognized that exterior fire escapes are at best a poor substitute for an adequate number of fireproof interior stairways. A well-designed building does not need outside fire escapes if the interior stairways are of fireproof materials, are isolated from the building proper by fire doors, are adequate in number, and are conveniently located so as to be easily accessible from all parts of every floor. Most of the older buildings, however, have not been designed with this point in mind, and it is consequently necessary to depend upon exterior fire escapes.

In one college the building housing a portion of the academic work and serving as the women's dormitory was without fire escapes reaching to the third floor, although several young women were living in the rooms on this floor. This building was of Type D construction, the exterior walls being of brick, the interior of ordinary frame construction. A single non-fireproof stairway was located directly above the heating plant. There is a strong probability that a fire in this building would, almost at the outset, cut off opportunity for the escape of those sleeping on the third floor. At the suggestion of the survey staff the exterior fire escapes are being extended to the third floor of this building.

In most states the fire laws require adequate fire escapes, and these laws are rather rigidly enforced. A college can well afford, however, to go beyond the minimum requirements in an endeavor to prevent any possible disaster.

In many colleges there has been a failure to eliminate many avoidable sources of fire hazards. Janitors have been allowed to store waste paper in closets under stairways, in basement rooms not especially equipped for the purpose, and in other places which invite the starting of a fire. In several colleges paper balers have been installed in the basements of academic buildings without any especial fireproofing of the rooms. Besides waste paper, other sources of fire hazard have been found in the storage of oil mops, which are subject to spontaneous combustion, and in the storage of acids used in the science laboratories. All of these materials require special treatment in their storage. Oil mops should be kept only in metal containers. Acids should be stored preferably outside the buildings used for academic purposes. Waste paper should not be allowed to accumulate but should be disposed of as rapidly as it is collected. If it is desired to bale the paper, this work should be done in a separate building, or at least in a fireproof room; and waste paper should never be allowed to accumulate any place where it will constitute a potential source of danger from fire.

MAINTENANCE CONDITIONS

For the most part, the buildings of this group of colleges have been kept in a rather good state of repair. In only a few cases were instances of delayed maintenance noted. Delayed maintenance is always expensive and usually results in a much larger outlay in the end than would have been the case if the repairs had been made earlier. For example, in one college building the replacement of a leaky roof had been postponed until the plaster on the interior walls had been loosened, and the college was thus forced to enter upon a rather heavy repair program.

In a surprisingly large number of colleges the buildings themselves were found not to be well kept. Sweeping and dusting were poorly done, windows were not regularly washed, and there was much evidence of poor janitorial care. Almost always the use of student janitors was associated with poor building care. In none of the colleges where student labor is depended upon for janitorial work can there be said to be satisfactory service. Even with good janitorial help there is need for constant supervision if the buildings are to be kept in a satisfactory state of cleanliness.

Several of the colleges have not decorated the interiors of their buildings as frequently as desirable. This is one of the elastic items in the budget, and under pressure of limited financial resources is apt to be postponed. In one of these colleges a regular schedule of decoration has been worked out so that the program is distributed evenly through the years. Under this plan the interior of each building has a new coat of paint every four or five years; at the same time the burden in no one year is extraordinarily heavy. This college uses its regular janitorial force during the summer months for the painting of the interiors of the buildings.

There seems to be a considerable relationship between the tone of the student body and the maintenance conditions within these colleges. To a large extent students can be taught to cultivate a sense of responsibility for the college buildings and to avoid practices which deface the buildings and increase maintenance costs. In some of these institutions students carefully refrain from littering the campus with scraps of paper, candy wrappers, etc. In others, no such sense of propriety has been cultivated. In some colleges the students respect the walls and desks as if they were their own property. In others, the walls are scribbled, the desks are carved, and there is, in general, a serious disrespect shown to the property of the institution. It would seem that this field offers the possibility of a profitable cultivation on the part of the administrators of colleges. If students can be taught properly to respect the college plant, the burden of providing adequate maintenance should be considerably lightened in many of these institutions.

CHAPTER XIII

UTILIZATION OF CLASSROOM AND LABORATORY SPACE

In twenty-one of the colleges studied, an extended analysis was made of the utilization of plant space. For each of the classrooms and laboratories of the college a complete schedule of use during the semester studied was obtained, showing the periods during which the rooms were occupied and the number of students in each class occupying such rooms. A calculation was then made of the percentage of the total possible periods of the week during which each room was used. In making this calculation it was assumed that it would be possible to use each room for a maximum of forty-four periods during the week, since many colleges actually operate on the basis of a forty-four-period week. A further calculation was then made assuming that it would be theoretically possible to fill every seat in each room during each of the forty-four periods of the week. Such a degree of use would give a utilization figure of 100 per cent. While it is recognized that in practice a utilization of 100 per cent is never possible, a comparison of actual utilization with the theoretical 100 per cent affords an interesting index of actual needs for academic space.[1]

As another measure of the extent of space provisions, calculation was made of the ratio of the number of student stations to the average enrolment. A "student station" is defined as the accommodation necessary for one student during one classroom hour, e.g., one seat in a recitation room, one laboratory desk, or one chair in a lecture room. The sum of the student stations divided by the number of students enrolled yields a ratio which indicates the relative extensiveness of space provision in the various colleges.

Table 29 presents data regarding the utilization of space at the twenty-one colleges in which this study was carried on. Three measures of utilization are presented: (1) the percentage of the total possible periods used; (2) the percentage of the total possible capacity used; (3) the ratio of student stations to average enrolment.

This table shows that there is considerable variation in the twenty-one colleges with regard to the percentage of the total possible periods during

[1] For a further discussion of the measurement of space utilization see Reeves and Russell, *College Organization and Administration* (Indianapolis: Board of Education of Disciples of Christ, 1929), pp. 89–105.

which the rooms are used. It will be noted that at no institution are the rooms used on the average as much as one-half of the available time, considering the forty-four-period week as the maximum available. The median for the twenty-one institutions indicates that it is typical to use class-

TABLE 29

Use of Instructional Space at Twenty-one Colleges

Institution	Year	Percentage of Total Possible Periods Used†	Percentage of Total Possible Capacity Used†	Ratio of Student Stations to Average Enrolment
*DePauw...............	1930–31	42.8	22.9	1.5
*Morningside.............	1929–30	40.7	13.5	1.7
*Mount Union.............	1930–31	40.3	21.6	1.7
*Simpson................	1929–30	39.8	22.5	1.8
Central Wesleyan.........	1929–30	39.2	11.0	3.6
*Dickinson...............	1929–30	38.5	19.8	1.9
Dakota Wesleyan.........	1929–30	37.9	17.0	2.2
*Ohio Wesleyan..........	1930–31	37.4	‡	1.3
Oklahoma City..........	1929–30	36.7	17.5	1.7
Ohio Northern...........	1930–31	36.5	19.3	2.1
*Hamline................	1929–30	36.4	15.4	3.0
Evansville..............	1929–30	35.6	16.0	2.4
*Chattanooga...........	1929–30	35.3	15.0	2.1
*Albion.................	1929–30	32.9	18.1	2.3
Baldwin-Wallace........	1930–31	30.9	18.8	2.1
Iowa Wesleyan..........	1929–30	30.6	18.4	2.3
*Lawrence..............	1929–30	28.6	18.3	2.4
*Cornell................	1929–30	28.4	13.5	2.0
Union..................	1929–30	28.0	23.0	‡
Ozark Wesleyan.........	1929–30	27.0	12.0	3.6
*Allegheny.............	1929–30	24.4	12.7	3.0
Median, all colleges........	....	36.4	17.8	2.1
*Median, A.A.U. colleges......	....	36.9	18.1	2.0
Median, non-A.A.U. colleges....	....	35.6	17.5	2.3

* Institutions on the approved list of the Association of American Universities.
† A forty-four-period week is used as a standard.
‡ Data not available.

rooms only a little more than one-third of the possible time. This low percentage of room utilization is largely a result of the organization of the daily schedule. Most professors and most students prefer to have their classes in the forenoon. As a result, the rooms are often empty during the greater part of the afternoon. Most of the colleges still operate a five-day week and thus lose the possibility of four extra periods on Saturday morning. Some of the colleges, however, actually operate on the basis of a forty-four-period week. This seems highly advisable wherever classroom space is relatively limited.

When utilization is studied on the basis of the percentage of total possible capacity used, taking into account the size of the classrooms and the classes which occupy them, as well as the periods during which the rooms are used, it will be observed that all the institutions studied use only a small percentage of the possible capacity. No college in the group utilizes as much as one-fourth of its possible capacity; and the typical situation, as indicated by the median, is for approximately one-sixth of the maximum capacity to be utilized.

It is recognized, of course, that it would be impossible to arrange a program in such a way that every seat would be filled during every class period of every school day in the week. Classes vary in size, and it is sometimes difficult to adjust accurately the size of classes to the schedule of rooms. In designing new buildings, colleges have too frequently made the mistake of planning all rooms the same size. A brief analysis of the size of classes at any college shows that there is need for a wide variation in the size of classrooms. By assigning a small class to a small room and reserving the larger rooms for classes with large enrolments, it is possible to house the academic program satisfactorily with a much smaller amount of floor space than would otherwise be the case.

There are no data available which would indicate the maximum percentage of total capacity which a college may be expected to utilize before suffering a loss in educational efficiency. In none of the institutions studied is there any particular handicap suffered because of an inadequate amount of academic space. Although it is true that many colleges utilize space which is unsatisfactory and which should be replaced, the amount of space available is adequate in every institution. It seems fair to conclude that until a utilization of at least 25 per cent of the total possible capacity has been reached, and until classrooms are occupied on the average at least 50 per cent of the possible periods, an institution does not have any great need for additions to the academic classroom space.

The ratio of student stations to average enrolment also varies markedly among these colleges, indicating a large variation in the relative amount of space provision in this group of institutions. Two colleges have in excess of three and one-half student stations for each student enrolled, while there is another which has only 1.3 student stations for each student.

Table 30 is presented to show the relationship between the size of the college, as measured by enrolment, and the utilization of space.

This table shows that, on the average, the larger institutions tend to have their classrooms in use a slightly higher percentage of the total possible periods and to have a slightly higher percentage of total possible capacity used than is the case with the smaller colleges. On both of these points the average of the medium-sized group of colleges is between the two extremes. Although the differences in these averages are small and are probably not statistically significant, the fact that the two trends are consistent indicates a strong probability that the smaller institutions find it difficult to use their academic space as efficiently as do the larger colleges.

It will also be noted from this table that there is a relationship between the size of the college and the average number of student stations per student. The larger colleges have fewer student stations per student than the smaller institutions, and the medium-sized colleges are between these

TABLE 30

AVERAGE USE OF INSTRUCTIONAL SPACE IN COLLEGES OF VARIOUS SIZES

Number of Students	Number of Colleges	Average Percentage of Total Possible Periods Used	Average Percentage of Possible Capacity Used	Average Ratio of Student Stations to Total Enrolment
700 and over..............	6	35.8	19.2	1.88
400–699.................	9	35.0	17.0*	2.14
Under 400...............	6	33.1	16.4	2.82†

* Data available for only eight colleges.
† Data available for only five colleges.

two extremes. These data support the conclusion that the large institutions need relatively less space per student for academic purposes than the smaller colleges.

In some of the colleges studied plans are under way for additions to the academic plant. In most of these cases there should be a careful study made of utilization preceding the decision to erect additional classroom space. It is difficult to justify the use of funds for new buildings to increase the amount of space when it may be shown that present classrooms are used less than half of the available periods or that less than one-fourth of the total possible capacity is being utilized. There can, of course, be no objection to the replacement of obsolete buildings by new and up-to-date structures. Too many colleges, however, have the tendency to continue in use some of the old buildings even after new and up-to-date structures have been erected. In a few colleges it would clearly be possible, and would certainly be advisable, to discontinue the use of some of the old buildings which have outlived their educational usefulness.

CHAPTER XIV

BUILDING PROGRAMS

In every one of the colleges of this group there are unmet building needs, and the presidents of the institutions have no difficulty in outlining rather extensive additions which would be desirable in the physical plants. In almost all of the institutions, however, there are other needs, particularly for endowment, which are more pressing than the building needs.

Willamette University is perhaps the only college of the group which is in a position where building needs are relatively more important than needs for increased endowment. In the past this institution has very wisely followed the policy of diverting every possible gift to the endowment fund, and now has brought together a supporting endowment of a relatively satisfactory size. This policy has resulted, however, in a postponement of needed building construction, so that there are now a number of important additions necessary in the physical plant of the institution.

One other type of institution may be pointed out as a variation from the general rule of the precedence of endowment needs over those for new buildings. Colleges located in large cities, such as Evansville College and Oklahoma City University, can operate successfully on a relatively small endowment. When such institutions are faced by rapid increases in enrolments, it is probably wise to use funds for building purposes rather than for the development of a large endowment fund. This rule does not apply, however, until the college has accumulated an endowment of sufficient size to be assured of a permanent source for a part of its support.

In most of the confidential survey reports submitted to the colleges following the visit of the survey staff to the institutions, a building program was outlined. This was done, however, only after repeated warnings had been given regarding the precedence of endowment needs over needs for new buildings. These programs were based on the number and kind of buildings necessary in the immediate future for the reasonably satisfactory housing of the present program of service. No suggestions were made which would cover needs arising from anticipated increases in enrolment, and only unquestioned needs were included. In a few colleges, where the future life of the institution is in question, no building program was suggested, although in almost all such institutions there are rather important building needs.

A summary of the building programs suggested in this group of colleges shows that in seven institutions recommendation was made for the construction of a new classroom and administration building. In twelve colleges the construction of a new science building was recommended. The building unit needed by the largest number of colleges is the library, recommendation being made in twenty-three institutions for new library buildings. Nine of the colleges were judged to be in need of new gymnasiums. Twenty-two colleges have need of additional dormitory facilities, some institutions needing additional accommodations both for men and for women. The number of new men's dormitories needed is twenty; in fourteen cases new women's dormitories were recommended; altogether, a total of thirty-four dormitory buildings was recommended. In seven of the colleges the auditorium facilities are so deficient that this unit was recommended as a part of the new building program. Twelve colleges have need for certain relatively minor buildings, such as heating plants, music buildings, art buildings, etc.

Besides these building needs, several of the colleges have need of additional ground space for campus extensions. In nine colleges recommendation was made for the purchase of ground for additions to the campus.

A careful estimate of the cost of the new building construction needed in this group of colleges places the total requirement at approximately $20,000,000. This estimate is based upon costs during the past five years; any tendency toward a reduced building cost in future years will have a corresponding effect on the amount needed for new construction. The estimate given above is based on the presumption of the continuance of all of the colleges included in this study. Discontinuances or mergers of institutions will, of course, reduce the amount which will be needed.

The $20,000,000 estimated as needed for new construction may appear to be a staggering total, but it actually represents a rather conservative estimate of the amount needed for a reasonably satisfactory housing of the present programs of these institutions. The expenditure will naturally be spread over a few years, and it is not intended that the colleges should launch a series of campaigns to obtain this amount immediately. In planning the future financial policies of these institutions, however, these building needs should be clearly kept in mind and made a part of the fund solicitation program.

Emphasis should be given the fact that the estimate given above presumes no increases in enrolments. If increases in enrolments occur, they will tend to increase the amount of building funds needed. On the other hand, decreases in enrolments will not operate to decrease the need for any of these building facilities, with the possible exception of dormitories. The estimate given is only for new building construction and does not include the cost of needed repairs, alterations, and remodeling of old buildings.

An item which was omitted from all the building programs, but which could justifiably have been included, would have been the expense of replacing all existing non-fireproof dormitories and libraries by fireproof construction. The need for fireproofing in buildings of this type is sufficiently great to warrant the suggestion of razing all non-fireproof dormitories and libraries, in order to replace them by construction of a satisfactory type. This might be regarded as unreasonable by some presidents and boards of trustees, and consequently has not been included in the present estimate of building needs.

The $20,000,000 suggested as needed for new buildings does not differ widely from the previous history of building construction in these colleges. During the ten years since 1920, this group of colleges has expended approximately $10,000,000 on new building construction. Standards of satisfactory college building conditions are rising, and the additional expenditure during the coming years is partly necessitated by this fact. In many of the colleges the building programs have not yet caught up with the increases in enrolments following the war period, and the additional construction is needed in order to bring building facilities into line with enrolment developments.

A program of new building construction calls for unusual care and forethought on the part of the college administrator. The new buildings at the College of Puget Sound may be cited as examples of excellent educational planning. The demands of an educational plant in such matters as light, heat, ventilation, office space, blackboards, etc., are now well understood by specialists in school buildings; but all too frequently the general architect is not familiar with them. In several of the institutions included in this study serious mistakes have been made in new buildings because they were designed by architects who failed to take into account the requirements of modern educational structures. It is now possible to obtain expert criticism of college building plans from specialists in college buildings, and arrangements for this type of criticism should be made in the case of all new construction.

Another caution which needs to be observed in entering a building program is that of not proceeding with construction more rapidly than funds are available for its financing. Several of the colleges have accumulated embarrassing burdens of debt by failure to heed this principle. The temptation is often strong to proceed with the construction of a new building as soon as a sufficient amount has been pledged to cover the proposed cost. The only safe rule is to wait until the funds have been collected in cash before the construction is undertaken. Albion College is an excellent example of an institution which during recent years has consistently followed this conservative policy.

Another matter which needs to be studied before entering upon a building program is the effect of the additional buildings upon the current budget. The additional space must be heated, lighted, cleaned, and maintained in repair. This inevitably increases the budget for building operation and maintenance. The college, therefore, not only needs to have the funds with which to finance the actual building construction but also needs to have additional current funds with which to meet the increased expenditures for plant operation. Only one or two of these colleges have adopted the plan of setting aside a part of the gift for a new building as endowment for its operation and upkeep, a plan which is now followed in several of the better institutions of the country. The colleges of this group would do well to consider the adoption of such a plan as a general policy.

Finally, the warning should be repeated that endowment needs in almost all of these colleges are more important than building needs, and should have precedence in arranging the future program of financial promotion.

CHAPTER XV

LIBRARY PLANTS[1]

THE PLACE OF THE LIBRARY IN A MODERN COLLEGE

It is only in comparatively recent decades that the maintenance of a library has been recognized as a necessary function of a college. Two or three generations ago institutions of higher education, particularly those which were somewhat distantly removed from the influence of the older colleges in the East, boasted no great libraries. Such books as were available for the use of students were for the most part in the private libraries of members of the faculty, or in small collections which had been started by the literary societies of that day. Many of the college libraries of the present day trace their genesis to such collections, the small libraries of the professors or of the literary societies being transferred to the control of the institution. From time to time these collections were augmented by the gift of other materials from similar sources or by gifts from the libraries of deceased ministers. Under such circumstances the collection of books in the college library grew somewhat slowly and spasmodically, without any organized effort upon the part of the college authorities to keep the library up to date. Although the stronger and better-administered colleges began early to develop systematic plans for increasing the effectiveness of their libraries, the condition which has been described persisted in most of the weaker institutions until well into the twentieth century.

Within the last two decades certain influences which have been at work have demanded a strengthening of the library facilities. Chief among the agencies operating in this direction have been the regional standardizing associations, such as the North Central Association of Colleges and Secondary Schools and the Association of Colleges and Second-

[1] The survey staff is indebted to Professor William M. Randall, of the Graduate Library School of the University of Chicago, not only for making first-hand investigations of many of the college libraries included in this report, but also for reading and criticizing the manuscript of the chapters of this volume that deal with the libraries. At the time of the completion of this manuscript Dr. Randall had in preparation a book to be entitled *The College Library* (Chicago: American Library Association and University of Chicago Press, 1932), from data based on the visitation of a large number of educational institutions. Footnote citations will be made on occasion throughout the succeeding chapters to points upon which Dr. Randall's study supplies corroborative evidence.

ary Schools of the Southern States. State departments of education, in establishing requirements for the certification of teachers, have also had considerable effect on the provisions for library facilities. The standards set up by these agencies have stimulated the colleges to furnish better support for their libraries, to increase the size of the book collections, and to provide professionally qualified library staffs.

Under the instructional conditions which have prevailed in the past, with the dominance of the "textbook" method of teaching, the library has been a relatively unimportant adjunct of the college. The assignment of supplementary reading in the library has been looked upon by students as something of a bore, as just another chore to be performed for an over-conscientious instructor. Such conditions did not foster in students an interest in reading which carried over successfully to the years after graduation.

Much evidence is now accumulating which indicates a change in this condition. The library is coming to perform an increasingly vital function in the modern program of instruction at the college level. Certain of the newer movements in higher education which are bringing about this change in the place of the library are as follows: (1) increased registration in the social studies, departments which have always been heavy users of library materials; (2) the introduction of survey courses, cutting across the lines of several departments, and necessitating wider reading than is normally obtained by the textbook method; (3) the introduction of independent work courses, honors courses, and general reading courses, in which formal class recitation is abandoned and the student is thrown to a considerable extent upon his own resources; (4) the development of graduate study, with the offering of the Master's degree in many of the better colleges of liberal arts.

The pressure of the demands which these newer educational movements are making seems to be forcing a rapid development in the college library. The time has already passed when it can meet its obligations by providing a few supplementary reference materials. The college library of the future, if it is to serve adequately the needs of the institution, must become the center of academic activities.

LIBRARY BUILDINGS

The library plants in the group of thirty-five colleges being studied vary all the way from a single room of the ordinary classroom size to well-equipped units housed in separate buildings especially erected for library purposes. Sixteen of the colleges house their libraries in separate buildings, while in nineteen the library is located in a wing or section of a building devoted primarily to some other purpose. In only a few of the colleges having separate library buildings are the buildings used exclusively for library purposes. Such buildings typically include a few classrooms; in two or three cases the administrative offices of the college are housed in the library building; and in several colleges units such as a cafeteria, the chapel, the bookstore, etc., are located in the library building.

If these extraneous units do not interfere with the library service, and if the library itself has ample room, there can be no objection to the housing of other units in the college library. In fact, it is probably a wise policy in planning a new library building to include a larger amount of space than can be used immediately for library purposes. This extra space can be used for classrooms or other purposes until, in the normal course of expansion, the library has need of it. The difficulty with this plan is that the extra space may not be made available to the library as rapidly as the needs for expansion arise. In almost every case in this group of colleges where there are other units housed in the library building the library itself is crowded and has real need of some of the space which has been "temporarily" used for other purposes.

The growing importance of the library in the modern plan of collegiate instruction makes it necessary that this unit be located centrally upon the college campus. The ideal college plant today consists of a library surrounded by classroom and laboratory buildings, rather than a group of academic buildings with a library located on a remote corner where it is isolated from the remainder of the plant. There are only two or three of the thirty-five colleges in which the location of the library is unsatisfactory. In twenty-six of the colleges the library occupies a central location with reference to the remainder of the college plant; on account of the small size of the whole plant most of the others do not suffer any important disadvantage from the lack of a central location for the library.

The value of the book collection and the difficulty of replacing it makes advisable the housing of the library in a fireproof building. The loss of the library by fire is a real disaster to a college, and every precaution should be taken to protect the book collection against this risk. For the country as a whole, 50 per cent of the college library buildings are fireproof. The library buildings of the colleges studied average slightly better than this; but in fifteen of the thirty-five colleges the library is located in a non-fireproof building and is housed under conditions which more or less openly invite the risk of loss. Where the library is housed in a portion of a non-fireproof building used for other purposes, it is usually impossible to provide adequate protection for the book collection without an inordinate expense. The best solution is for the housing of the library in a separate building of fireproof construction. It is a serious mistake to erect a separate building for library purposes of anything other than fireproof construction. The extra cost of the fireproofing is relatively small in a building no larger than is needed for the library in the typical college, and the added security is worth many times the small extra outlay for construction. In a few of the colleges the stack space is of fireproof construction even though the remainder of the building is not. In such cases it is necessary to instal self-closing fire doors between the stacks and the reading-room.

LIBRARY READING-ROOMS

The reading-room is usually the most important unit of the library plant, so far as the amount of space occupied is concerned. The first requisite of a satisfactory reading-room is that it be of sufficient size to accommodate the student body of the college. Figures based on studies of this problem by librarians indicate that in general the reading-room should have seating provisions equal to at least one-fourth the number of students enrolled in the college.[1] Data on this point were available for thirty-two of the colleges being studied; of these, eleven have a seating capacity in their library reading-rooms equal to 25 per cent or more of the students enrolled, five have a capacity between 20 and 24 per cent of the student enrolment, eleven between 15 and 19 per cent, and five have less than 15 per cent. It is evident that, judged by the accepted standards, the criticism may be made that a large number of the colleges have an inadequate seating capacity in their library reading-rooms.

In each of the colleges specific inquiry was made of the librarian as to whether the reading-room was "crowded." A few of the colleges with seating capacity equal to one-fourth of the student enrolment indicated that at certain periods of the day the reading-room is crowded; others having an obviously inadequate seating capacity indicated that the reading-room is never crowded. It is clear that the adequacy of the reading-room is affected not only by the size of the enrolment but also by the size and utility of the book collection and the degree of use of the library by students. It speaks well for a college if the library, although having a relatively large capacity, is crowded; while the college with an inadequate

[1] Dr. Randall's book, *The College Library* (Chicago: American Library Association and University of Chicago Press, 1932), will contain statistics on this point from a large number of colleges.

reading-room capacity which does not find itself handicapped by this lack is clearly not doing what it should for its students.

Besides an adequate seating capacity, the reading-room of the library makes peculiar demands for satisfactory lighting and ventilation. The reading-room should be provided with as much natural illumination as possible, and the artificial lighting should be adequate in amount to provide a satisfactory degree of illumination at night. Overhead fixtures of the indirect or semi-direct type, plus desk lights of an approved design, should be the standard. In most of the colleges studied, the lighting of the library reading-rooms is relatively satisfactory; many do not have desk lights, however. The ventilation of the reading-rooms in these colleges is almost universally by the open-window method.

The equipment of the reading-room should consist of tables and chairs of satisfactory design, shelves for the reference collection, map and atlas cases, dictionary stands, and similar library furniture. In approximately half of the colleges studied the reading-room equipment was reasonably satisfactory. The most frequent cause of adverse criticism was the type of chairs with which the reading-rooms are furnished. A satisfactory library chair must be of sturdy construction and should be designed for comfort, so that it will not be fatiguing to students who spend long hours in the reading-room. In half of the colleges the chairs used in the library are obviously makeshift affairs, discarded from the classrooms, rickety and squeaky and uncomfortable. In about one-fourth of the colleges the reading tables are unsatisfactory.

One of the prime requisites of a satisfactory reading-room is silence, and the furniture and equipment of the room should be planned for the avoidance of all possible noise. The type of floor has much to do with the noisiness of the room. In approximately half of the colleges the floor of the library reading-room is of wood, without any covering; without exception such rooms are noisy and disturbing to the study of students. Five of the colleges have a concrete floor for the library reading-room; this is even more unsatisfactory than the wood floor. Seven of the colleges have a covering of battleship linoleum on the library floor; this is usually satisfactory from the standpoint of noise, and is reasonably durable. In three of the colleges having linoleum floors the covering was badly worn and broken, and needed replacement. The most satisfactory covering for a library floor is cork tile or rubber tile. While this is somewhat more expensive at the outset than the linoleum, it is more durable and possesses better silencing qualities. Only two of the colleges have this material on the floors of their library reading-rooms.

STACKROOMS

The stackroom is next in importance to the reading-room from the standpoint of the amount of space occupied in the library plant. The stackroom should be especially designed for this purpose, and it is not usually possible to develop satisfactory and economical stack space in a room originally designed for classroom purposes. In the majority of colleges which do not have a separate building for the library (and in a few of those that do have the separate building) the arrangement of the stacks is bad. The typical criticisms relate to the lighting, to the placing of the ranges too close together, to the height of the shelving, to the waste of cubature in rooms where the ceiling height does not correspond to the height of the shelving, and to poorly designed stairways. Approximately half of the colleges use stacks of a modern type, the remainder being either homemade wooden shelving or antiquated metal stacks. In about half of the colleges the stacks are now badly crowded and there is immediate need for extension of the stack space.

LIBRARY OFFICES AND WORKROOMS

Two of the important units of the library plant are the office of the librarian and the workroom for the staff. Data regarding these provisions were obtained from thirty of the colleges being studied. Thirteen of these have neither an office for the librarian nor a workroom, and nine others have no workroom other than the librarian's office. In the thirteen colleges having neither a library office nor a workroom the necessary technical processes of the library are carried on at the loan desk or at a table in the stacks, or in similar space which is not satisfactorily segregated from the remainder of the library. There are several reasons why a separately inclosed room is needed for the technical processes of the library. A typewriter is necessary in this work, and its use is disturbing to students who are studying in the library. The person carrying on such work as cataloguing and classifying should be reasonably free from interruptions; this is impossible if the work is done at the loan desk or in other places not properly segregated from the general part of the library. There is need both for an office for the librarian and for a workroom, and it is unfortunate if the cataloguing and classifying must be done in the librarian's office, although this is obviously better than to have no separate room whatever for this work.

OTHER LIBRARY-PLANT FACILITIES

In addition to the reading-room, stackroom, workroom, and librarian's office, there are certain other facilities necessary in a satisfactory library plant. There should be a cloakroom where students using the library may hang their wraps; this is lacking in most of the colleges included in this study. Coat racks in the reading-room are an acceptable substitute. Where there are no facilities for the care of wraps, the students must wear them into the reading-room and dispose of them on chairs and tables and in other unsatisfactory ways. There should be a separate cloak closet for the library staff. Toilet facilities should be provided for students, or should be accessible in other parts of the building in the case of libraries not housed in separate buildings. There should be a separate washroom and toilet for the library staff.

Other facilities found somewhat less frequently in the library plants of these colleges are newspaper rooms, magazine rooms, and browsing rooms. These are typically found only in the larger colleges, although a few of the smaller ones have excellent browsing rooms. Seminar rooms for individual study are not usually found in the libraries of these colleges.

CRITICISMS OF LIBRARY PLANTS

Two or three of the colleges are deserving of special mention by reason of the excellence of their library plants. All things considered, the library building at Illinois Wesleyan University is perhaps the best of any in this group of colleges. Nebraska Wesleyan University has a new library building which is well designed and unusually complete in its details. Iowa Wesleyan College has been provided with a new library building by the P.E.O. sisterhood; although this building was not completely equipped at the time of the survey visit, it gives promise of development as a very satisfactory library plant.

Perhaps the most important general criticisms of the library buildings in this group of colleges relate to the failure to make provisions for necessary expansions in the plant. Almost all of the separate library buildings have apparently been designed with the idea that they would be large enough for all time to come, and there have been provided no means of making additions to the buildings when the increased size of the student body and the book collection have made this necessary. This failure can well be understood in the older library buildings, erected before the day when this unit was so important in collegiate instruction; but a surprisingly large number of the newer buildings also exhibit this same fault. Without any exceptions, it should be the rule in constructing new library buildings to make definite plans for the expansion of the plant as rapidly as demands arise. This can be accomplished by using a unit type of construction and by actually sketching on the preliminary plans the outlines of the units to be constructed at a later date.

CHAPTER XVI

LIBRARY STAFFS

SIZE OF THE STAFF

All of the colleges included in this study have on their staffs some person or persons specifically charged with responsibility for administering the library. In four of the smaller colleges the library is in charge of a regular member of the faculty who devotes only a part of his or her time to its supervision. In every college, with one exception, the person assigned responsibility for the supervision of the library is known as the "librarian" and will be so referred to throughout this report. In the one exception there are two "assistant librarians" and no head librarian, each of the assistants giving half time to the work and being coequal in their authority. In this study they are considered as one full-time librarian.

The great majority of the librarians in this group of colleges are women, only eight of the institutions having a man in charge of the library. Almost all the full-time assistants in the libraries of these colleges are women. The great majority of the part-time student assistants employed in these libraries are women, although usually in each college there is at least one man among the group.

Figure 12 presents data regarding the number of staff members in colleges of various sizes. Part-time assistants have been counted in this tabulation at the proportionate equivalent of full time. The graph does not include data for student assistants. Brothers College is not included, since the library of this institution is administered jointly with that of Drew University. Intermountain Union College is also omitted from the tabulations because the librarianship was temporarily vacant at the time of the survey visit.

This figure shows that, on the average, the number of library staff members varies in accordance with the size of the enrolment. The colleges of the smallest-sized group average slightly less than one full-time staff member each, while those of the largest size group average five full-time staff members.

The fact that some of the comparatively large colleges are able to get along with relatively small library staffs suggests that some factor other than the number of students enrolled affects the staffing of the library. Table 31 presents data regarding the number of staff members in colleges grouped according to the number of volumes in the library. As in the case of Figure 12, part-time staff members have been equated to the full-time equivalent but student assistants have not been included.

This table shows that there is, in general, a close relationship between the number of staff members employed in the library and the size of the

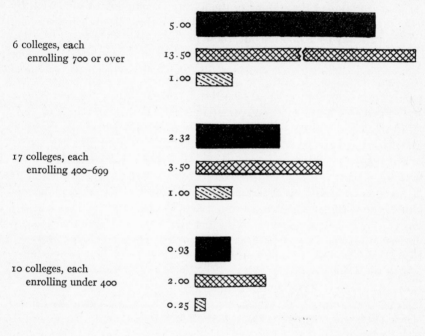

FIG. 12.—Number of staff members in the libraries of colleges having various numbers of students enrolled.

book collection. This relationship holds true not only for the average size of staff in the colleges with various numbers of volumes in the libraries but also for the colleges having the largest staff in each group and, somewhat less perfectly, for those having the smallest staff in each group. The adequacy of the staffing in these colleges varies considerably. Some of them are obviously undermanned; in none, however, does there seem to be any overstaffing. For this reason the averages shown represent something less than the desirable situation. On the whole, it is apparent that the two factors of size of enrolment and number of volumes in the library are important determinants of the number of staff members which should be employed in the typical college library.

The question of the staffing of the library is complicated somewhat by the fact that student assistants are used in all the colleges being studied. As has already been pointed out, these have not been included in the data thus far presented. Policies regarding the amount of student help employed in the library vary considerably from college to college. In one of

TABLE 31

AVERAGE NUMBER OF STAFF MEMBERS IN THE LIBRARIES OF COLLEGES
WITH BOOK COLLECTIONS OF VARIOUS SIZES

NUMBER OF VOLUMES IN THE LIBRARY	NUMBER OF COLLEGES*	NUMBER OF LIBRARY-STAFF MEMBERS, REDUCED TO FULL-TIME EQUIVALENT		
		Average	Largest	Smallest
100,000 and over..........	1	13.50	....	....
60,000–79,999.............	2	4.50	6.00	3.00
40,000–59,999.............	3	3.67	5.50	2.00
30,000–39,999.............	6	2.58	3.50	2.00
20,000–29,999.............	6	1.92	3.00	1.00
10,000–19,999.............	11	1.34	2.00	0.25
Less than 10,000..........	4	0.88	1.00	0.50

* Data are not included for Brothers College, since the library of this institution is administered jointly with that of Drew University. Intermountain Union College is also omitted from the tabulation because the librarianship was temporarily vacant at the time of the survey visit.

the smaller colleges, a student assistant is actually the librarian, although there is a faculty member who nominally bears the title. In this case the faculty member is wholly untrained in library procedures, while the student has had a modicum of practical experience in other libraries and is therefore given responsibility for the limited number of technical processes which are carried on.

The ratio of student help to full-time help varies considerably. Data on this point were not collected in all the colleges, but a few cases may be cited as typical of the variation which exists. One college with a large enrolment but a relatively small library employs only one full-time staff member in the library and uses student help to the amount of one hundred hours per week. Another college, with approximately the same number of students enrolled, and also with a relatively small book collection, has two full-time staff members and employs student help to the amount of forty hours per week. Another college, somewhat smaller in enrolment than these two colleges, but with a slightly larger book collection than either of them, has two full-time staff members in the library and uses student help to the amount of fifty hours per week. In this college the present policy represents a distinct change from that prevailing in preceding years, when only one full-time staff member was employed and there was a relatively large dependence upon student help. Two other colleges, with enrolments approximately half those of the first two institutions mentioned, each have two full-time library staff members and use approximately forty hours of student help weekly.

TRAINING OF LIBRARY STAFF

It is commonly recognized that the librarian of a college should have general training equal at least to the Bachelor's degree and should, in addition, have at least one year of professional training in library science. This standard relates to the head librarian; full-time assistants should preferably have the same minimum professional training but may have a somewhat smaller amount of academic training while working under the direction of a competent librarian. Of the thirty-four librarians included in this study,[1] only fifteen meet the standard of a Bachelor's degree plus at least one year of professional training. Ten of the librarians have had no professional training whatsoever, although four have had two years of such training in addition to the Bachelor's degree. Four of the thirty-four librarians do not have the Bachelor's degree, but eleven have general training equal to the Master's degree or higher. Two of the librarians have the Ph.D. degree.

FACULTY RANK OF THE LIBRARIAN

In only eleven of the thirty-four colleges[1] is the librarian given one of the four recognized academic ranks. Six of the librarians are given the rank of professor, two the rank of associate professor, one the rank of assistant professor, and two the rank of instructor. Some of those given the rank of professor are devoting only part time to the work of the library and hold their academic ranks by virtue of their connection with one of the instructional departments of the college.

In all but six of the colleges the librarian is considered a member of the faculty and is listed in the catalogue with the faculty. Under present-day conditions it seems that the librarian, if actually qualified, should be

[1] Data are not included for Intermountain Union College. The librarian of Drew University is considered as the librarian of Brothers College.

considered a member of the faculty in every college. A person unqualified
for a faculty rank should not be employed as librarian. Since membership
on the faculty without the assignment of an academic rank is a somewhat
anomalous status, it would seem to be entirely in order to assign an aca-

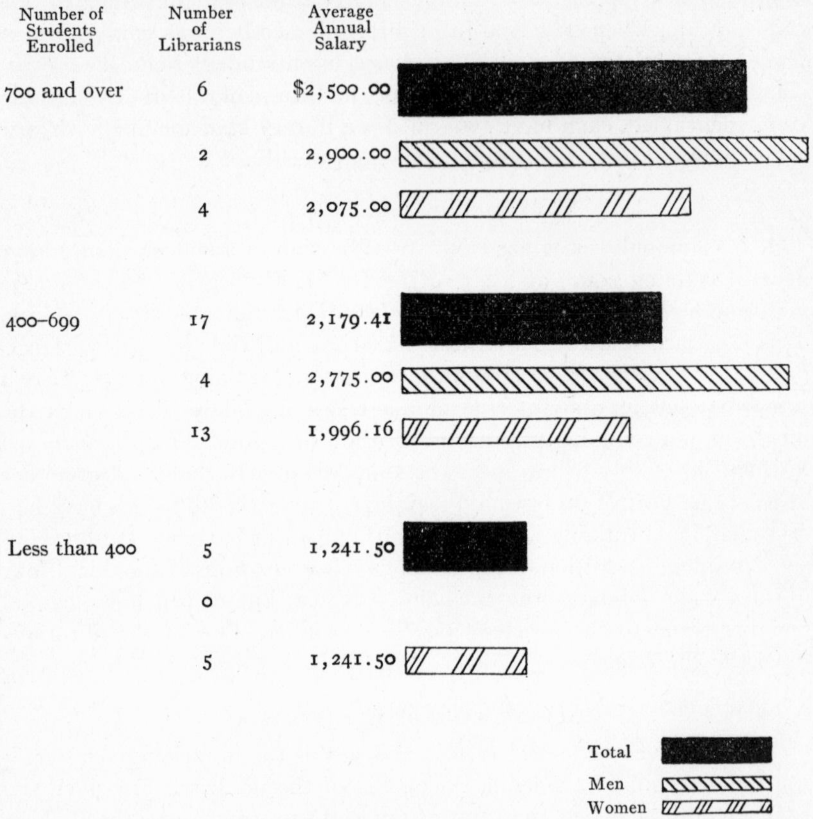

Number of Students Enrolled	Number of Librarians	Average Annual Salary	
700 and over	6	$2,500.00	
	2	2,900.00	
	4	2,075.00	
400–699	17	2,179.41	
	4	2,775.00	
	13	1,996.16	
Less than 400	5	1,241.50	
	0		
	5	1,241.50	

Total
Men
Women

FIG. 13.—Average salaries of full-time librarians in colleges having various numbers
of students enrolled.

demic rank to the librarian appropriate to his or her training and responsibilities.

SALARIES OF THE LIBRARY STAFF

Figure 13 presents data regarding the salaries of the librarians in the
group of colleges being studied. The data relate only to the salaries of the
head librarians, and only full-time librarians are considered. Four colleges
do not have full-time librarians; the librarianship was temporarily vacant

at the time of the survey visit in one college. Information is not available for two other colleges. The chart presents averages for colleges of various sizes, separate averages being presented for men and for women librarians.

This figure shows a tendency for the amount of salary paid the librarian to be related in a general way to the size of the college. In every case the group of colleges having the largest enrolments has the highest average salaries, and the group of smallest colleges has the lowest average salaries. It will also be noted that there is a general tendency for the men librarians to receive a higher salary than the women, the differential amounting to approximately 40 per cent of the salary of the women librarians.

Table 32 shows the relationship between the size of the book collection in these libraries and the salaries paid the librarians. Because of the fact

TABLE 32

SALARIES OF FULL-TIME WOMEN LIBRARIANS IN COLLEGES HAVING
BOOK COLLECTIONS OF VARIOUS SIZES

NUMBER OF VOLUMES IN THE LIBRARY	NUMBER OF COL-LEGES HAVING FULL-TIME WOM-EN LIBRARIANS*	SALARIES OF FULL-TIME WOMEN LIBRARIANS		
		Average	Largest	Smallest
60,000–79,999.............	1	$2,700.00	....	....
40,000–59,999.............	3	2,333.33	$3,000	$1,800
30,000–39,999.............	5	2,060.00	2,400	1,600
20,000–29,999.............	5	1,914.00	2,300	1,350
10,000–19,999.............	5	1,562.50	1,800	1,200
Less than 10,000...........	3	1,025.00	1,500	675

* Data are not available for two colleges.

that there are only a few men librarians and that these customarily receive a higher salary than the women librarians, this table deals only with the salaries of the women librarians.

This table shows that there is a very close relationship between the size of the library and the salary of the librarian. Although there is considerable variation in the salaries paid women librarians in each of the college groups, classified on the basis of the size of the book collection, the averages clearly show a tendency to pay higher salaries in the larger libraries than in the smaller ones. This same tendency holds true with almost uncanny precision for both the highest and the lowest salaries in each group of colleges.

Table 33 presents data regarding the relationship between the training and salaries of the women who are full-time head librarians in this group of colleges. Classification is made on the basis of both professional and general training.

This table shows a very distinct relationship between the amount of training and the average salary of women librarians. It is apparent that, for the group whose professional training is substandard, the average salary is related to the amount of general training. The amount of professional training seems also to be an important salary determinant, as indicated by the averages, except in the case of those holding the Master's degree or higher. The highest average and the highest maximum salary found in

TABLE 33

AVERAGE SALARIES OF FULL-TIME WOMEN LIBRARIANS WITH
VARIOUS AMOUNTS OF TRAINING

Amount of Training	Number of Cases	Average Salary	Highest Salary	Lowest Salary
Without Bachelor's degree and with less than one year of professional training...	4	$1,071.88	$1,500	$ 675
Holding Bachelor's degree but less than Master's and with less than one year of professional training..................	5	1,690.00	2,100	1,200
Holding Master's degree or higher and with less than one year of professional training	2	2,000.00	2,400	1,600
Holding Bachelor's degree but less than Master's and with one year or more of professional training..................	9	2,191.00	3,000	1,620
Holding Master's degree or higher and with at least one year of professional training	2	2,000.00	2,200	1,800

any of the groups shown in Table 33 are those for the librarians who have at least the Bachelor's degree but not the Master's degree and who have had at least one year of professional training.

The data relating to salaries of librarians must be interpreted with some caution, owing to the small number of cases for which comparable data are available in the present study. The findings are suggestive only and should be verified by studies including a larger number of colleges. With data from a larger number of institutions it should be possible to build a typical salary scale for librarians having various levels of training, employed in colleges of various sizes, and in charge of book collections of various sizes.

CHAPTER XVII

LIBRARY ADMINISTRATION

RESPONSIBILITY OF THE LIBRARIAN

The librarian in a modern college needs to be much more than a mere keeper of books. The person holding this office must assume a considerable measure of administrative responsibility, including the supervision of the library staff, the handling of a relatively large budget, and the oversight of an important unit of the physical plant.

In almost all of the colleges studied the librarian is classed as one of the major administrative officers and is directly responsible to the president of the institution. Typically, the librarian is appointed by the board of trustees upon the recommendation of the president and has tenure comparable to that of any other member of the administrative staff. In two or three of the colleges the librarian is not responsible directly to the president, but, instead, to a library committee of the faculty. In one case the librarian is responsible to the dean of the college rather than to the president. Any arrangement whereby the librarian is made directly responsible to a committee of the faculty seems both unwise and unnecessary. While a faculty committee may well function in an advisory capacity to the librarian, where matters of general policy are concerned, it should never be given direct authority to supervise the work of the librarian or to deal with the routine administration of the library.

DEPARTMENTAL LIBRARIES

The question of the centralization of the library administration is an important one in many of the colleges studied. In approximately one-fourth of the institutions a decentralized library administration has been set up. Under such a plan the responsibility of the librarian relates only to the central unit, and there are one or more departmental libraries not directly under the control of the librarian. The problem of handling departmental collections is difficult. There are manifest conveniences to faculty members in having the book collections relating to their special fields easily accessible. Particularly in the sciences there is need for laboratory collections which will be readily available to students for reference while working on laboratory assignments.

There are three fairly distinct plans in effect for the handling of these departmental collections. In a majority of the colleges studied there is a completely centralized library service, all books being shelved in the central library and the circulation administered from this place. In other colleges there are departmental collections which are entirely distinct from the main library, being housed in a different room or a different building (in one college some of them are housed in the main library building although the librarian has no control over them), and generally administered by the department concerned rather than the librarian of the college. Under this plan, in some colleges the departmental collection is catalogued by the librarian; in some, the assistants who manage the collection are under the control of the librarian; in other colleges the departmental collection is entirely separate and distinct from the regular library administration. A third plan represents an intermediary stage between the extremes of the first two, whereby there is a complete centralization of the library administration, but "laboratory collections" are loaned more or less permanently from the central library to departments wherever needed.

A decentralized library administration presents many disadvantages to offset the convenience which it affords to faculty members. The plan of setting up departmental libraries usually adds to the cost of administration, for there must be some supervision over these separate book collections, and attention must be given to the shelving and the circulation; this becomes disproportionately high in the small units. In the second place, the books generally cannot be as well cared for, and losses are usually greater than in the central library. In the third place, the books in a departmental collection are rarely as accessible to students as they would be when housed in a central library, despite the often-made plea for the establishment of departmental libraries "for the convenience of students." Unless an excessive amount is paid for assistance in such units, the books easily become misplaced and thus are made unavailable. Furthermore, the departmental libraries in these colleges are typically open for only a relatively few hours each day and are inaccessible to students at other times. With the exception of a comparatively small number of volumes needed by science students in connection with their laboratory work—this should be termed a "laboratory collection" rather than a departmental library— it does not appear that the setting up of departmental libraries serves the convenience of students in any important way.

It thus appears that the only important advantage in the departmental library is its convenience for faculty members. On the opposite side of the scale must be considered its extra cost, the poorer care of books, and its lack of convenience to students. The most satisfactory solution of the problem, as observed in these thirty-five colleges, is a complete centralization of the administration of the entire library service, with the policy of loaning, more or less permanently, small laboratory collections wherever needed, these to remain, however, under the central library administration. It is to be observed that such a plan is appropriate to the typical college; in larger institutions, such as a university, the departmental libraries themselves may become units of considerable size. While centralization of the library administration is advisable even in the larger organizations, the size and importance of the departmental collections invalidate many of the arguments against this plan which are valid in the typical college of liberal arts.

It may be pointed out further that, since most of the arguments against the departmental library have a bearing upon economy of management, the college which is so fortunate as to have abundant resources can neglect this phase of the matter. By employing adequate assistance, by providing duplicate copies of all books for the central library, and by keeping the departmental libraries open for the same hours that the main library is open, it is possible to overcome the disadvantages which have been pointed out in the departmental library plan. Even under such circumstances it would probably be advisable to plan for centralized administration of all the libraries, rather than to operate each as an independent unit.

ADMINISTRATION OF THE LIBRARY BUDGET[1]

Amount of the budget.—The colleges included in this study typically spend from $4\frac{1}{2}$ to 5 per cent of their educational expenditures upon the library service. There seems to be no hard and fast rule, however, as to what proportion of the educational expenditures of a college ought to be allotted to the library. Obviously the size of the total educational budget per student and the general efficiency of management will vitally affect the proportion that should go for the support of the library. The size of the enrolment also probably affects the extent of the library appropriations. Some colleges are obtaining very satisfactory library service for a percentage of the total educational budget smaller than that mentioned above, while in other institutions the use of a larger percentage than that indicated is not resulting in satisfactory library service. There is a high correlation between the total educational budget and the total library budget.

[1] For a discussion of budgetary principles, in general, as they apply to the entire institution, see chap. xlviii of this report.

The budget for the college library is usually divided into four parts: (1) books and periodicals for the various departments of the college; (2) general books and periodicals to be purchased by the librarian or the library committee; (3) salaries of the library staff; and (4) supplies and binding.

Is the appropriation for new books a departmental or a library budget?— One of the important problems of administrative policy relates to the question as to whether the allotments to the several academic departments for the purchase of new books shall be considered a part of the departmental budget or a part of the library budget. This distinction is important because of its bearing upon the treatment of departmental requests for the purchase of new books. If the budget is considered a departmental affair, then logically the department should be permitted to expend the funds allotted to it in any manner it sees fit, without any check as to the appropriateness of the books it purchases. On the other hand, if the budget is first of all a library budget, then the departmental orders come in as requests to the library, and the library administration passes on the appropriateness of the books requisitioned. This plan, furthermore, makes the librarian responsible for seeing that departments do not overspend their budgets. Under the departmental budget plan this responsibility would normally be upon the business manager of the college, rather than the librarian. Of course, under the library budget plan the librarian will depend upon the business officer of the college for the actual bookkeeping and for frequent reports as to the status of the budget allotted for the purchase of new books.

In the colleges that have been studied the plan of having the budget for new books considered as a library, rather than as a departmental, budget seems to be working more satisfactorily than the other plan. The necessity for obtaining a co-ordinated view of the library budget as a whole almost forces the construction of a centralized budget for new books, even though the various units of the budget may be administered through the several academic departments. If the plan of considering the appropriation for books as a part of the library budget is adopted, it is necessary to safeguard the integrity of the departmental allotment, and to insure the departments reasonable freedom in requisitioning books according to their needs up to the limits of the amount allotted them. A competent librarian should be expected to suggest to departments the purchase of important books that have been overlooked in departmental orders.

The foregoing discussion has presumed that the budget for new books, or at least a portion of it, will be allotted among the various academic departments. This is done in almost all of the colleges studied, although two or three follow the plan of not making any specific departmental appropriation. One of these is a small institution and has such meager resources for the purchase of new books that the problem of a departmental appropriation is relatively unimportant.

Who shall make allotments to departments for new books?—Assuming that the budget for new books will be apportioned among the departments, the question arises as to who shall make this allotment. Finally, of course, this responsibility must rest with the chief budgetary officer, who is usually the president. In one college it was found that departmental appropriations for library books were settled by the business officer. The distribution of funds in this case was so unsatisfactory as to lead to the conclusion that it is undesirable to leave this matter to the control of the business officer; the one who is in final charge of the academic policies of the institution, that is, the president, is the only officer who can be expected to carry this important responsibility.

The departments themselves should be in the best position to make the first estimate of the funds needed for the purchase of books in their respective fields. It sometimes happens that departments are not capable of performing this task satisfactorily. The college administration should be responsible for educating the less capable department heads so that they may make more intelligent requests for book budgets. To this end the librarian should advise and consult with departments regarding their library needs at the time of making the budget estimates. The requests for budget appropriations for new books should, therefore, originate with the several departments, subject to advice from the librarian. The coordination of these budget requests is a task for the chief budgetary officer; most presidents would be willing to confess their own lack of professional competence to pass upon the relative merits of the several requests, assuming, as is usually the case, that the total of the requests is larger than the expenditure which can be made from the funds available or anticipated. Under such circumstances the advice of the librarian should be sought and followed. This officer is in a peculiarly suitable position to take into account the various factors which should be considered in allotting departmental budgets for new books. In fact, it is doubtful if a satisfactory budget can be constructed without a large amount of advice from the librarian.

Criticisms of allotments of book budgets to departments.—In a large number of the colleges the distribution of the budget for new books among the various academic departments has been very poorly planned. A surprising number of colleges solve this problem by allotting the same amount, say $50 or $100, to each department. This system is defended on the grounds that it promotes peace and harmony among the departments, no department being able to prove that it has been discriminated against in the distribution of funds. A little reflection will show, however, that under this plan there is the rankest sort of discrimination against some departments; and typically it is found that under this plan several of the departments are unable to spend all their appropriations each year. Whatever departmental peace and harmony may be brought about by the flat-sum method of appropriation, this is certainly an impossible method of building a strong library collection.

In at least two colleges there are special endowments for the purchase of books in certain departments. Cornell College presents, perhaps, the extreme case in this regard, there being thirty special endowments the income of which is restricted in each case to the purchase of a particular class of books. While a permanent endowment for the support of the library is very desirable, minute restriction as to the class of books which may be purchased is usually unwise, since it tends to distort the growth of the library and makes it difficult to construct a library budget which gives a satisfactory allotment to each field of learning.

Factors that should be considered in allotting departmental book budgets.— The development of a satisfactory distribution of book funds among departments is actually a rather complicated matter. There are at least six important factors which must be taken into account in allocating funds for new books to departments.

The first of these is the enrolments of students in the classes of the department. The department with a larger enrolment will need more funds for new books, particularly for duplicate copies, than will the departments with smaller enrolments. The factor of departmental enrolment should be one of the least influential determinants of book appropriations, although in many colleges this factor is given great weight in setting up the library budget.

The second factor is the relative amount of use of library materials by the department. The departments of history, economics, and education may be mentioned as examples of those making large use of the library. Other departments, such as mathematics and ancient languages, usually do not make as liberal use of library materials as is the case with the social sciences, although this is a matter which varies from college to college. The extent of the use made of library materials is to no small degree an index of the energy and efficiency of the instructor, and a teacher who does not demand considerable work in the library from his students probably lacks something in effectiveness. As a criterion for the allocation of the book budget among departments, this relative use of library materials is a factor entirely distinct from the first one mentioned, the enrolments in the department. The only way in which it can be taken into account adequately is by the keeping of accurate circulation records by classes of books.

The third factor to be considered is the amount of new material being published in the several fields. A glance at the publishers' lists will show that in certain subjects there is an enormous volume of new material coming out, while in others the new publications are few and far between.[1] If the college library is to be kept up to date, it is necessary to buy everything of importance as rapidly as it is published. This will clearly demand much larger appropriations to some departments than to others. This third factor is usually closely associated with the second one mentioned, that is, the departments which make relatively large use of library materials are usually those in which there are large numbers of new books being published annually. This combination intensifies the need for relatively large appropriations to such departments.

The fourth factor to be taken into account is the relative cost of books per volume unit in the various fields.[2] In the sciences, for example, books are comparatively expensive per volume, while in English literature and modern foreign languages the average cost per volume is not nearly so great. Since the volume is the unit of library statistics, rather than the dollars of invested value, it follows that appropriations should be distributed so as to equalize somewhat the varying cost of books per volume.

The fifth factor to be considered in allocating the funds for the purchase of new books is the present condition of the library holdings in the several fields. If the book collection is not at present well rounded, the departments which are weak should have relatively large funds in order to build up their holdings. This is a difficult matter to deal with. Possibly the publication of the Carnegie check-lists will go far toward solving this problem, enabling colleges to measure their own collections against this standard list in order to determine what sections of the library need strengthening.

A sixth factor which must be considered in allotting funds for books to departments is the needs of instructors who are new to the institution. It

---

[1] Data on this point are presented by Dr. William M. Randall in his book *The College Library* (Chicago: American Library Association and University of Chicago Press, 1932).

[2] *Ibid.*

will usually happen that a teacher who is just joining the faculty will find that the library lacks several titles which he considers important for his classes. His predecessor has probably not considered these titles important and has used other books which the new instructor will use scarcely at all. Under such circumstances it seems wise to count definitely on making a larger appropriation for the first year of service of a new instructor than it is expected to continue during his subsequent years. This is particularly true in the case of the one-man or two-men departments which are typical of this group of colleges.

A review of these six factors which should be taken into account in allotting funds for new books to departments reveals the complexity of the problem. It is clear that no cut-and-dried formula, applicable alike to all institutions, can be expected to work satisfactorily. Two of the factors, the amount of new material coming out in the several fields, and the cost of books per volume unit in the several subjects, can well be reduced to a constant which is valid for all colleges alike. Another factor, the enrolments in the respective departments, can be reduced to statistical terms; and the keeping of adequate circulation statistics will yield valuable data on the relative use of library materials by the several departments. The last two factors discussed, the present condition of library holdings and the needs of new instructors, require individual attention in each college.

Proportion of the book budget to be expended at the discretion of the librarian.—A final question in the administration of the library budget relates to the proportion of the total budget for new books which should be allocated to departments or left in a fluid state subject to the discretion of the librarian. As has already been pointed out, one or two of the colleges put the entire budget for new books at the disposal of the librarian, making no allocation whatsoever to departments. In practically all of the colleges the librarian is given an appropriation for the purchase of general books and periodicals, i.e., those which are needed by the library but do not fall within the peculiar province of any one department. In some of the colleges the librarian is given a budget which is large enough to supplement the appropriations to departments which run short of library funds. If the college has a competent librarian, this last plan seems very desirable. Assuming the presence of a competent librarian, the ideal plan would be to place just as large a proportion of the fund as possible at the disposal of this officer.

POLICIES REGARDING GIFT COLLECTIONS

Practically all of the colleges receive more or less frequently gifts of books for the library. The majority of these gifts consist of the private libraries of deceased ministers, which usually include principally theological material of little value to a college of liberal arts. Occasionally, however, such gift collections contain items of real value and provide very welcome additions to the college library.

A few of the colleges have the unfortunate policy of accepting and shelving all such gifts. In a few cases there is a rule of the board of trustees to the effect that all gifts to the library must be accepted and shelved. Most of the colleges, however, provide that gift collections, when received, will be culled and only such items shelved as are of real use to the library. In such institutions the proffer of a gift collection is met by the polite suggestion that the library will be glad to examine the list of titles and to indicate those which it can use. Such a plan is strongly recommended as desirable if the shelves of the library are to be kept free of a useless clutter of dead wood.

ROUTINE OF ORDERING BOOKS

Orders for new books for the library typically originate in one of three ways. Books which are needed by departments will be ordered by the faculty members of the departments. Orders for general material not within the province of particular departments usually originate with the librarian or the library committee of the faculty. Since the librarian has the responsibility of keeping the book collection well rounded, it is necessary for this officer to suggest the purchase of some titles which have been overlooked by the departments in their own fields.

The order should be submitted on a stock form giving complete bibliographical information regarding the title requested. Many colleges follow the plan of having the orders submitted rather informally, leaving it to the librarian to obtain the necessary information as to exact title, publisher, price, etc. A standard order form introduces a satisfactory and business-like method of handling the book-purchase requests.

The orders for new books should be submitted by the departments directly to the librarian, who is responsible for four checks: (1) to see that the library does not already have the book on its shelves; (2) to see that the book is not already on order; (3) to see that the order is within the amount of the budget appropriation; and (4) to see that the book is actually one which the college needs. In some colleges there is a faculty committee which is assigned the responsibility of checking on all the departmental requests for new books. The wisdom of this plan is open to grave question. Faculty members usually do not have either the necessary specialized knowledge outside their own teaching fields or the necessary time to give any adequate check on the departmental requests for new books.

This is a matter which can be much more effectively handled by the librarian, whose specialized training makes possible a professional judgment regarding the desirability of the various titles suggested for purchase.

The actual placing of the order should probably be done by the business officer of the institution, although the librarian should indicate the best sources from which to buy the materials ordered. There is such a great advantage in centralizing the purchasing for the institution that it seems unwise to violate this principle in the case of orders for library books.[1] Although the formal placing of the order should be done by the business office, in practice, the matter becomes a co-operative enterprise between the purchasing agent and the librarian, the latter officer bringing to bear his specialized knowledge of sources and prices in order to obtain the best and most efficient service for the library. Sometimes it is possible to obtain better prices when books are purchased through the college bookstore.

RECORDS AND STATISTICS

There are four types of records and statistics which are commonly kept in the libraries of these thirty-five colleges: (1) the accession book; (2) the cataloguer's record; (3) the order file; and (4) circulation statistics. An accession book or some acceptable substitute is kept in practically every one of the colleges studied. In one or two colleges this was not carefully kept, and in one relatively large library it consisted of notations on loose sheets of paper. On the whole, however, this record is the one most frequently found and is the best kept of any of the four types above mentioned.

Relatively few of the colleges maintain a cataloguer's record, showing the number of books catalogued by classes. Order files are kept in a rather irregular manner in many of the institutions, and some depend only on the librarian's memory to avoid duplication in the orders. Although the necessity for an order file varies directly with the size of the institution, its keeping should be a part of every well-administered library. If orders are made on stock forms, as suggested in the preceding section, the order cards themselves can be filed and thus provide a very acceptable source of information regarding outstanding orders.

Relatively few of the colleges keep adequate records of library circulation. There are two reasons for the failure to keep these records. Most of the college libraries are understaffed, and time for keeping and compiling

[1] For a discussion of purchasing as it applies to the institution as a whole, see chap. xlvi of this report.

circulation records is lacking. Consequently, this duty is neglected in favor of more pressing responsibilities. In the second place, a considerable number of the libraries are administered on the open-shelf plan, and there is thus no opportunity for collecting statistics covering the use of books in the library. It is still possible to keep records of the out-of-library circulation under such circumstances, but such data are difficult to interpret and may actually lead to a misrepresentation of the true conditions, particularly in the case of departments which require a large use of periodicals and other non-circulating materials.

The policy with regard to the taking of inventories varies among the colleges studied. In some institutions it appears that no complete inventory of the library has ever been taken. In others, particular sections of the library are inventoried each year in such a way as to cover the entire collection in a period of four or five years. In still others a complete inventory is taken annually. The majority of the colleges have a complete inventory at least every two years.

CHARGING SYSTEM FOR BOOKS

Considerable uniformity exists among the colleges in the system of charging out books to students. Typically, books which circulate outside the library are loaned for two weeks, with a small fine for overdue books. Reserve books may be withdrawn from the library shortly before closing time and must be returned within one hour after the library opens on the following school day, with a relatively heavy fine for each hour that a book is overdue.

In most of the colleges the faculty members are given unlimited library privileges, and are allowed to withdraw books for an indefinite length of time. Several of the institutions have found it advisable to require faculty members to check in at the end of each semester or term the books which they have withdrawn. This is a very desirable procedure, as faculty members are prone to neglect the return of books which they no longer need for study. A check of the books held by faculty members at the close of each term or semester removes much of the opportunity for misunderstandings regarding books which are charged out but which the teacher claims to have returned.

CLASSIFICATION AND CATALOGUING

All the libraries of this group of colleges are classified upon one of two plans, the Dewey Decimal system, or the Library of Congress system. The former is by all odds the more commonly found, the Library of Congress scheme of classification being used in only three or four of the libraries of this group. The majority of those which are using the Dewey Decimal system have made modifications in the classification scheme to make it more suitable for the needs of a college library. This system, although originally planned for the library of Amherst College, has been developed especially to meet the needs of public libraries. Particularly after the book collection becomes large, difficulty is frequently encountered in its use in college libraries. At the time of the survey visit one college was engaged in reclassifying its entire library, changing from the Dewey plan to the Library of Congress classification.

With one exception all of the colleges maintain a public dictionary catalogue. The college which is the exception has one of the smallest libraries of any in the group and maintains only a shelf list. A few of the colleges which have public dictionary catalogues do not maintain shelf lists. Both of these types of catalogues are necessary in any well-managed library. In every case the catalogues are carried on 3×5 cards and are housed in the standard type of filing trays. In practically every college the catalogue cards are either printed (Library of Congress) or typewritten, although in several cases the catalogues contain some old handwritten cards which have not yet been replaced, and in one college the entire catalogue consists of handwritten cards. A large number of the colleges are failing to make use of the printed cards furnished by the Library of Congress. These cards are unquestionably both better and cheaper than any adequate homemade variety, and should be used exclusively for all titles for which they are available.

Practically all the colleges use either the Library of Congress subject headings or the American Library Association list. The former is recommended in all cases because it is being constantly revised and kept up to date.

On the whole, the classification and cataloguing of the libraries of this group of colleges are rather good. In no part of the work of the library is the excellence of the professional training of the staff so clearly revealed. As would be expected from the data on the training of the library staffs in these colleges, as presented in a preceding section, the classification and cataloguing in a few institutions leave much to be desired. With the acquisition of improved professional training upon the part of the library staffs, the classification and cataloguing can be expected to show corresponding improvement. Professional rules should not be followed too blindly, however. Some well-trained librarians could improve their service by giving more thought to the adapting of catalogue rules and classifications to meet the peculiar needs of a college library.

EFFORTS TO FAMILIARIZE STUDENTS WITH THE USE OF THE LIBRARY

A large percentage of the entering students are usually unfamiliar with the use of a library as large as that of the typical college in this group. Their experience has in many instances been only with small, poorly equipped high-school libraries, and they are consequently at a loss to know how to use the resources of the college library unless there is definite instruction given on this point. To a smaller extent the same is true of many older students, who are imperfectly acquainted with the library resources of their college. There is, therefore, need of some definite program of instruction in the use of the library, and a limited amount of "advertising" of the library resources is justified. A few of the efforts in this direction which have been observed will be described.

In almost all the colleges which have a Freshman Week there is some attempt made during the program to familiarize the new students with the use of the library. Typically, the class is broken into groups of twenty or thirty students, each of which spends an hour or more with the librarian, going over such matters as the general rules of the library, the locating of books in the catalogue, the finding of books on the shelves, and the methods of tracing reference material on particular topics. This is reported to be a very effective plan for introducing freshman students to the use of the library.

A second plan for familiarizing freshman students with the use of the library is to include certain units on this topic in a general freshman orientation course which is given throughout the year. Several of the colleges have such a course, and in some cases instruction in the use of the library is made an integral part of the class work.

A third plan is similar to the one just mentioned, except that the instruction in the use of the library is made a part of the regular freshman course in English composition. A considerable number of the colleges use this plan. In some cases it is used in addition to the Freshman Week program. The instruction is usually handled by allotting certain definite periods to this work, as, for example, one period each month. The assignment for the library instruction consists of a series of problems which must be looked up in the library, the list being so chosen as to cover rather completely all the various phases of library reference work. Where the freshman class is large, these assignments can be "staggered" among the various sections of English composition so that a heavy burden is not thrown on the library force at one time.

A fourth plan, one which is found in most of the well-managed libraries, is a display rack calling attention to new additions to the library holdings, or pointing out the books belonging to the library which deal with topics of timely interest. This display rack usually occupies a prominent place near the entrance of the library, where it will be readily seen by all who pass. The use of this device is, of course, aimed at the instruction not only of freshmen but of all other students as well.

The fifth plan is a dignified form of advertising, by means of news notes and bulletins in the college paper. This is being effectively used by some librarians to acquaint students with the resources of the college library.

It is a part of the responsibility of every librarian to "sell" the use of the library to students, to show them its resources and the ways in which it can contribute, not only to the furtherance of their formal education, but also to their pleasure. The ingenious librarian can devise many effective plans to these ends. In some of the colleges attractive browsing rooms have been fitted up as places for leisure reading. Plans of this sort are worthy of every encouragement.

CHAPTER XVIII

BOOK COLLECTIONS

The heart of any library is the book collection. The physical plant, the staff, and the general administrative machinery are all necessary; but there can be no good library without an adequate book collection. The standards of the North Central Association of Colleges and Secondary Schools carry the following statement regarding the library of an accredited college:

The college shall have a live, well-distributed, professionally administered library of at least 8,000 volumes exclusive of public documents, bearing specifically upon the subjects taught and with a definite annual appropriation for the purchase of new books and current periodicals. It is urged that such appropriation be at least five dollars per student registered.

TABLE 34

BOOK COLLECTIONS IN THE LIBRARIES OF COLLEGES OF VARIOUS SIZES

Number of Students Enrolled	Number of Colleges in Each Group	Average Number of Volumes in Library	Average Number of Volumes per Student	Smallest Number of Volumes in Any Library	Largest Number of Volumes in Any Library
800 and over...........	3	68,386	50	7,000	129,000
600–799...............	8	34,063	49	13,000	78,500
400–599...............	12	29,165	58	17,000	52,000
200–399...............	7	15,240	53	9,237	22,000
Under 200.............	5	10,771	80	4,855	16,000

The standards of the Association of Colleges and Secondary Schools of the Southern States require a minimum of at least 12,000 volumes in the library.

SIZE OF THE BOOK COLLECTION

Table 34 presents data regarding the number of volumes in the libraries of the thirty-five colleges studied, grouped according to the size of the institution.

It will be noted from this table that there is a very important relationship between the size of the college and the number of volumes contained in the library. The average number of volumes in the libraries for each group of colleges closely approximates a direct proportion to the enrolment. The relationship between the size of the enrolment and the average number of volumes held by the library is graphically shown in Figure 14.

The average number of volumes per student in the various groups has a very small range. This is a rather surprising finding. While it would normally be expected that the larger institutions would have somewhat larger book collections than the smaller colleges, owing to the provision of more duplicate copies, it would scarcely be predicted that the proportion would be such as to cause the number of volumes per student to remain practically a constant. The differences in the average number of volumes in the libraries of colleges of different sizes, as shown in Table 34, obviously cannot be accounted for by the presence of duplicate copies, for the number of titles of which there will be duplicate copies usually forms a relatively small proportion of the total library holdings. The data

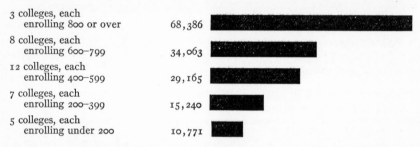

3 colleges, each
  enrolling 800 or over   68,386

8 colleges, each
  enrolling 600–799   34,063

12 colleges, each
  enrolling 400–599   29,165

7 colleges, each
  enrolling 200–399   15,240

5 colleges, each
  enrolling under 200   10,771

FIG. 14.—Average number of volumes in the libraries of colleges having various numbers of students enrolled.

therefore lead to the conclusion that the library resources of the smaller institutions are usually inferior in extent to those of the larger colleges.[1]

The standardizing associations seem to have completely overlooked this principle of relating the number of volumes in the library to the size of the enrolment, since the standard, as quoted above, refers only to a basic minimum regardless of size. One may suspect, however, that the portion of the standard which suggests an annual expenditure of five dollars per student for the purchase of new books may have indirectly influenced the relationship between the size of the library and the enrolment in these colleges.

Table 34 also presents some interesting data regarding the range in the number of volumes in the libraries of these colleges. The figures for the largest number of volumes in the library of any college in each sized group follow closely the general trend of the size of enrolments. No such relationship exists in the cases of the smallest number of volumes. The

[1] Data supporting this conclusion are presented in Dr. Randall's study, *The College Library*.

college having the smallest library in this entire group has slightly less than five thousand volumes; there are only four colleges of the thirty-five included in this study which have less than twelve thousand volumes in their libraries. There is only one college having more than one hundred thousand volumes, but there are five which have in excess of fifty thousand volumes.

ANNUAL ACCESSIONS

Table 35 presents data regarding the average number of volumes accessioned annually in the libraries of these colleges, classified according to size of enrolment. Data on this point were available in only twenty-six of the colleges. The figures are for the average annual accessions during the five-year period preceding the date of the survey visit.

TABLE 35

NUMBER OF VOLUMES ACCESSIONED ANNUALLY IN RECENT YEARS
BY THE LIBRARIES OF COLLEGES OF VARIOUS SIZES

Number of Students Enrolled	Number of Colleges for Which Data Are Available	Average Number of Library Books Accessioned Annually in Recent Years	Average Number of Books Accessioned per Student	Smallest Number of Annual Accessions	Largest Number of Annual Accessions
800 and over..........	3	2,808	2.1	1,200	5,000
600–799..............	6	1,783	2.6	500	3,451
400–599..............	8	1,258	2.5	684	2,000
200–399..............	5	694	2.3	175	1,250
Under 200.............	4	672	4.4	113	1,000

This table shows that the average number of volumes accessioned annually in the colleges of various sizes bears a close relationship to the enrolment of the institution. The average number of volumes accessioned per student is practically a constant in institutions of all sizes, with the single exception of the colleges which have fewer than two hundred students enrolled. In general, it appears that from two to two and one-half volumes per student are added annually in the libraries of these colleges.

Figure 15 illustrates graphically the direct ratio between the size of the college and the average number of books accessioned per year. The close relationship between the number of students enrolled and the number of volumes added annually to the library is to be expected in view of the standard of the accrediting associations which suggests the expenditure of five dollars per student annually for new library books.

Since a comparatively small proportion of the expenditure for new library books is used for the purchase of duplicate copies, it will be observed that the continuation of this practice of relating the number of books purchased to the size of the student body will ultimately result in the accumulation of much better library resources in the larger colleges than exist in the smaller institutions. In fact, Table 34 showed that this has already happened. It may be pointed out that the number of new books being published each year which are desirable additions to a college library is a constant for colleges of various sizes and all institutions, whether large or small, should have these titles in order to keep their collections up to date. This being the case, it will obviously be necessary for the small colleges to spend much more than five dollars annually per student in order to keep their book collections up to date in a manner

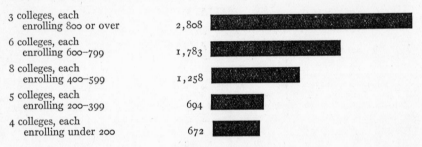

3 colleges, each
    enrolling 800 or over   2,808

6 colleges, each
    enrolling 600–799   1,783

8 colleges, each
    enrolling 400–599   1,258

5 colleges, each
    enrolling 200–399   694

4 colleges, each
    enrolling under 200   672

FIG. 15.—Average number of library books accessioned annually in recent years by colleges having various numbers of students enrolled.

comparable with the larger institutions. It seems that the standards of the accrediting associations regarding the annual expenditures per student for new library books should be graduated according to the size of the institution.

It is recognized that the variety of courses offered also bears a relationship to the size of the institution, the larger colleges typically offering a greater range of courses than the smaller institutions. The size of the book collection necessary for adequate library service will be affected considerably by the variety of course offerings in the institution. Colleges offering an extensive range of courses will need larger library resources than those with a relatively narrow range of offerings, if equally satisfactory library service is to be rendered. This relationship, however, is not proportional to the enrolment. In other words, colleges of eight hundred students do not usually offer twice as many courses as those of four hundred students. It would, therefore, not be expected that the variety of course offerings could wholly account for the differences which have been observed among colleges of various enrolments in the size of the book collections and the rate of additions to the libraries.

There is a possibility that the combination of two factors—the variety of course offerings and the provision of duplicate copies—may be sufficient to account for the variations in library facilities among colleges of different sizes. It is possible, for example, that a college of two hundred and fifty students with fifteen thousand volumes has just as effective a library unit as a college of five hundred students with thirty thousand volumes when account is taken of the fact that the latter institution typically will offer a wider range of courses and will need more duplicate copies. So far as the writers are aware, no objective study has been made to settle this point. In the absence of such data, the opinion may be expressed that the larger colleges typically have better library facilities than the smaller institutions. The number of colleges upon which this conclusion is based, however, is too small to permit a final determination of this question.[1]

Table 35 shows that there is a wide range in the number of annual accessions to the library within the groups of colleges classified by size. The largest number of annual accessions is almost in direct proportion to the enrolment, but the smallest number in each group apparently bears no relationship to the number of students enrolled. Although one college adds an average of five thousand volumes to its library annually, there are only three colleges of the group of twenty-six for which data are available that add as many as twenty-five hundred volumes, and only six that add more than two thousand volumes annually. Nine of the twenty-six colleges add fewer than one thousand volumes annually to their libraries.

POLICIES REGARDING DUPLICATE COPIES

The question of the purchase of duplicate copies for library purposes has already been raised. The colleges being studied vary widely in their policies regarding the number of duplicate copies to be purchased. A few libraries have the rather rigid rule that not more than two or three copies of any one title will be purchased. These colleges prefer to use their funds to extend the number of different titles, rather than to provide numerous duplicate copies of a smaller range of titles. At the other extreme may be cited the case of one college which, in some departments, at least, expects the library to serve as a collection of textbooks for students. In this college there are shelved from twenty to fifty or more copies of

---

[1] This conclusion is verified by Dr. Randall's study, *ibid*.

many titles; these are charged out to students for an entire semester at a time, instead of the usual two weeks, and are expected to relieve the students from the necessity of purchasing textbooks. A middle ground, on this question of the purchase of duplicate copies, is taken by many colleges which apportion the number of copies to be purchased to the size of the class which will use them. Usually one copy will be purchased for each ten or twelve students in the class. In some cases a rental library is used as the source for reference material needed by large groups of students, thus relieving the library of the necessity of purchasing a large number of duplicate copies.

The policy which is wisest to follow with regard to the provision of duplicate copies of library books seems to depend upon the circumstances within the individual college. In general, the policy of extending the range of titles, rather than the number of duplicate copies, seems sound. It may be pointed out that in some fields, particularly education, books tend to become obsolete rather rapidly. There have been observed on the shelves of several college libraries whole rows of duplicate copies of out-of-date books which will probably never again be used by any considerable group of students. These are occupying valuable shelf space and, in general, tend to clutter up the library stacks. A frequent and careful culling and a discarding of unneeded duplicates is essential in any library which follows the policy of purchasing duplicate copies in considerable number. As a rule, material of this kind has little or no salvage value, and thus the policy of purchasing duplicate copies tends to be less economical in the long run. On the other hand, the present convenience afforded students by the presence of an adequate number of copies of needed reference material may more than offset the obvious inefficiencies entailed by this policy.

PERIODICALS

Table 36 presents data regarding the number of periodicals received by the libraries of twenty-six of the colleges. Data on this point were not obtained from the other nine institutions.

This table shows that the number of periodicals received in this group of twenty-six colleges tends to be directly proportional to the number of students enrolled. The only group which is out of line with this tendency is composed of the colleges having enrolments between 600 and 799; this group has a smaller average number of periodicals than that of the next smaller-sized group. The average ratio of the number of periodicals received to the number of students enrolled tends to be relatively constant in the various-sized groups, but the colleges having enrolments of 200–

399 and of 400–599 have the highest average ratios of any of the groups, while the group with enrolments under 200 has the smallest average ratio. Since the data relate to the number of different periodicals, the question of duplicate copies is not involved, as was the case in the preceding discussion of the number of volumes in the library.

TABLE 36

NUMBER OF PERIODICALS RECEIVED BY THE LIBRARIES OF
COLLEGES OF VARIOUS SIZES

Number of Students Enrolled	Number of Colleges for Which Data Are Available	Average Number of Periodicals Received	Average Number of Periodicals Received per Student	Smallest Number of Periodicals Received	Largest Number of Periodicals Received
800 and over..........	3	384	0.28	54	849
600–799...............	5	182	0.26	86	325
400–599..............	10	197	0.38	82	298
200–399..............	5	116	0.38	70	155
Under 200.............	3	72	0.21	21	127

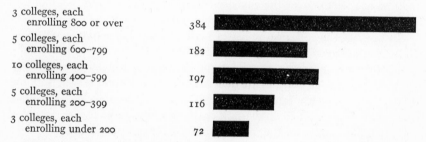

3 colleges, each
enrolling 800 or over   384

5 colleges, each
enrolling 600–799   182

10 colleges, each
enrolling 400–599   197

5 colleges, each
enrolling 200–399   116

3 colleges, each
enrolling under 200   72

FIG. 16.—Average number of periodicals received by the libraries of colleges having various numbers of students enrolled.

Figure 16 represents by means of a graph the average number of periodicals received by the libraries of colleges of various sizes. The conclusion is unmistakable that the larger colleges tend on the average to have much better collections of periodicals than the smaller colleges. The number of institutions included in this study is too small, however, to warrant the drawing of a final conclusion on this point.

Table 36 shows that there is a considerable range within the colleges of the various-sized groups in the number of periodicals taken. One college takes 849 periodicals. There is only one other college which receives more than 300 periodicals, and there are altogether only four of the twenty-six colleges included in this study which receive more than 250 periodicals. Six of these twenty-six institutions receive fewer than 100 periodicals; included among these six is a college generally recognized as one of the best in the entire group.

The data presented in Table 36 relate to the entire number of periodicals received. In each of the colleges a considerable number of publications are received free of charge. These include church papers, house organs, and periodicals of this type. The number of periodicals purchased is, therefore, somewhat less than would be indicated by the data of the table.

The majority of the colleges bind all the important periodicals which are received, but in many cases the sets are incomplete and little effort has been made to fill the gaps. A few of the colleges have followed the policy of not binding all the periodicals that deserve preservation. This is unfortunate, for materials of this kind are not readily accessible when unbound and, if used at all, are liable to become lost or misplaced. Lack of funds is the principal reason for failing to bind the standard publications. In several of the colleges it was suggested that a special gift might well be sought to cover the expenses of binding the accumulation of periodicals. This is a matter which should not be neglected.

In most of the colleges the list of periodicals includes only a very few in foreign languages, although there are two or three colleges which subscribe for an excellent list of foreign publications. Although the majority of American college libraries are deficient on this point, for satisfactory instruction in modern foreign languages and for the development of a breadth of viewpoint in students it is necessary to have in the library a considerable number of the more significant foreign magazines.

LIBRARY HOLDINGS IN SELECTED FIELDS

It must be admitted that the excellence of a library relates not only to the number of volumes it contains but also to the selection of those volumes. It would be entirely possible for a library of 25,000 carefully selected titles to be superior to one of 50,000 containing much "dead wood" and useless material.

In nine of the colleges the holdings in thirteen selected fields were checked by the sampling method. The check-lists used were obtained by taking the first 20 per cent of the titles appearing in each of these fields in the doctoral thesis of Eugene Hilton (University of California, 1929) entitled *Determination of Books for Collateral Reading Required in Basic Junior College Courses*. The library catalogues in each of the nine colleges were then checked against this list and the percentage of the total number on the list held by the library was recorded. These data are given in Table 37.

On the average, this group of nine colleges have in their libraries approximately one-half of the titles checked. Although most of the colleges are grouped rather closely around the figure of 50 per cent for their average holdings, there is one which has a notably higher percentage, and there are one or two which apparently have relatively weak collections. In al-

TABLE 37

COMPLETENESS OF THE GENERAL-REFERENCE COLLECTIONS IN THIRTEEN
FIELDS IN THE LIBRARIES OF NINE COLLEGES

FIELD	PERCENTAGE OF TITLES CHECKED WHICH WERE FOUND IN THE LIBRARY									
	Hamline	Simpson	Lawrence	Cornell	Ohio Northern	Morningside	Dickinson	Iowa Wesleyan	Intermountain	Median for All Colleges
English literature..............	83	82	91	87	93	81	96	78	89	87
United States history (general)...	82	68	81	57	76	63	48	63	62	63
History of Western Europe.......	81	68	60	61	68	62	66	54	50	62
General psychology.............	82	79	74	46	29	61	30	46	57	57
United States history (colonial)...	79	64	56	61	44	24	53	36	35	53
Economics.....................	69	56	46	47	44	47	50	47	22	47
Shakespeare...................	53	47	58	53	47	47	60	27	20	47
Political science...............	89	54	36	29	46	61	39	29	54	46
Money and banking.............	43	57	56	43	57	21	7	29	14	43
Family........................	71	36	42	29	7	36	21	50	7	36
General zoölogy................	68	68	65	16	50	32	33	32	25	33
General chemistry..............	36	39	31	25	36	15	24	29	5	29
General reading................	....	20	31	31	30	14	33	8	23	27
Average for all subjects checked	75	57	57	51	48	47	44	43	35	48

most all the colleges for which data are presented there are important weaknesses in one or more fields.

There is an interesting variation among the thirteen fields of subject matter. The subjects are arranged in Table 37 in accordance with the median percentage of holdings in the nine colleges. The field of English literature has the best representation in these libraries, no college falling below 75 per cent in this field. The two sciences which were checked fall almost at the bottom of the list; but the weakest field of all is that of general reading.

No brief is held for the validity of the particular check-list which was used in this study. It is obvious, however, that the application of such a technique will serve an important purpose in enabling colleges to study the relative needs of the various fields represented in their library holdings.

Through the courtesy of Professor William M. Randall of the Graduate Library School of the University of Chicago, data have been furnished showing the holdings of eighteen of the colleges as measured by the Carnegie check list. This check-list has been developed to guide the Carnegie Corporation in making grants to college libraries for the purchase of books. Institutions holding regional accreditation have been asked to check their library holdings against this list when making application for grants. Table 38 shows the results of this check for eighteen of the colleges studied, together with a comparison of the average for these eighteen colleges with the average for approximately two hundred colleges that have made this same check. The data of the table are expressed as the percentage of the titles on the check list held by the college library. The figures are shown not only for the entire list but separately for each of twenty-four different subjects.

It will be noted from the table that the average of these eighteen colleges for the entire list of titles exceeds the general average of holdings for the two hundred colleges. Eleven of the eighteen colleges have a larger percentage of the listed titles in their libraries than the average for the entire group of two hundred institutions. This speaks well for the general condition of the libraries in the colleges named. The general superiority of the library collections of these eighteen colleges holds throughout most of the subjects; only in the cases of English, history, and Romance languages is the average for the eighteen colleges lower than the general average, and in none of these subjects is the difference between the averages appreciably large.

The data of this table include only the accredited colleges of the group surveyed; since the general average also includes only accredited institutions, the comparison is fair. The unaccredited colleges of the group surveyed, in general, have much less satisfactory library resources than those shown for the accredited institutions.

USE OF OTHER LIBRARIES

Several of the colleges call attention to the fact that, even though their own library resources are admittedly inadequate, the students have access to other libraries in the community which supplement the shortcomings of the college library. In some instances, these are city or county libraries; other institutions are located at their state capitals and have

TABLE 38

Percentage of Titles Listed by the Carnegie Check-List in Twenty-four Subjects Held by the Library in Each of Eighteen Colleges, and Average Percentage for a Group of Approximately 200 Colleges

Institution	All Subjects Combined	Psychology	Education	Sociology and Anthropology	Religion	Physics	Philosophy	Geology
Ohio Wesleyan	38.5	59.6	61.4	57.3	57.8	44.1	41.5	51.7
DePauw	26.7	50.3	40.4	45.0	27.8	32.2	31.4	41.8
Illinois Wesleyan	26.0	45.4	40.8	43.0	29.9	46.7	37.2	47.3
Allegheny	25.6	21.0	25.5	35.1	43.9	24.3	23.0	20.9
Lawrence	25.1	40.7	35.0	30.6	29.9	22.4	37.7	25.3
Pacific	22.1	34.6	38.0	30.5	29.6	30.3	38.3	30.8
Hamline	21.8	37.6	32.6	32.1	23.7	28.9	34.3	16.9
Albion	21.5	27.8	27.6	38.9	25.8	28.9	33.0	16.5
Cornell	18.5	27.5	30.8	24.4	29.4	22.4	13.9	28.6
Mount Union	17.6	24.7	31.4	21.6	35.0	22.4	20.2	42.9
Simpson	17.1	33.3	30.9	24.2	20.8	13.2	13.0	31.9
Baker	16.2	26.2	21.2	25.5	22.9	13.2	25.8	13.2
Willamette	15.0	28.7	20.3	29.5	17.9	21.1	21.3	5.5
MacMurray	14.6	23.1	19.7	13.8	25.9	5.3	18.8	10.0
Baldwin-Wallace	12.9	26.8	36.3	29.8	8.5	29.6	11.9	16.5
Dickinson	12.7	18.5	19.7	15.5	17.1	12.5	8.7	3.3
Puget Sound	12.3	25.0	28.7	27.0	20.8	24.3	24.4	24.2
Morningside	11.9	21.6	16.4	21.2	19.0	37.5	14.1	5.5
Mean, 18 colleges surveyed	19.8	31.8	30.9	30.3	27.0	25.5	24.9	24.0
Mean, 200 colleges	16.7	29.0	24.4	22.8	20.9	19.8	19.9	16.4

TABLE 38—*Continued*

Institution	Eco-nomics	Zoölogy	Botany	History	English	Political Science	Chemis-try	Astron-omy
Ohio Wesleyan..........	38.1	34.0	43.2	32.2	37.0	54.8	37.4	41.3
DePauw................	39.4	29.9	33.1	30.8	27.3	35.7	7.8	15.9
Illinois Wesleyan........	28.8	34.4	36.0	24.4	30.0	16.1	33.9	23.2
Allegheny..............	34.7	19.9	15.8	33.4	26.3	24.5	20.4	28.3
Lawrence..............	36.1	17.8	43.9	27.8	26.4	23.2	12.2	15.9
Pacific................	27.8	21.6	21.6	16.2	23.6	26.1	27.0	21.7
Hamline...............	26.1	29.9	16.5	31.4	20.6	31.4	15.6	17.4
Albion................	31.9	37.8	33.8	23.2	21.8	25.6	15.6	12.3
Cornell................	23.6	11.2	12.2	19.2	22.5	20.1	17.8	6.5
Mount Union...........	15.4	29.4	19.4	17.6	16.5	12.3	32.2	15.9
Simpson...............	19.9	22.4	30.2	24.0	18.8	14.8	17.0	7.2
Baker.................	23.4	15.8	17.3	16.4	19.3	12.9	10.0	39.1
Willamette.............	13.8	19.9	10.1	15.9	22.8	9.7	17.4	13.0
MacMurray............	4.8	17.4	9.4	18.0	16.9	8.9	14.8	3.6
Baldwin-Wallace........	15.6	14.1	18.7	12.4	8.2	7.8	17.4	47.1
Dickinson.............	7.5	9.9	15.1	17.4	15.9	10.2	14.8	6.5
Puget Sound...........	13.3	14.6	7.9	12.6	5.5	9.6	20.9	11.6
Morningside...........	13.1	24.4	4.3	12.5	8.7	15.4	13.5	7.2
Mean, 18 colleges surveyed.............	22.9	22.5	21.6	21.4	20.5	20.0	19.2	18.5
Mean, 200 colleges...	18.5	20.0	18.1	21.5	20.6	18.9	15.9	13.3

TABLE 38—*Continued*

Institution	General	Classics	Geography	Mathematics	Physical Education and Hygiene	Music	Fine Arts	Romance Languages	German
Ohio Wesleyan....	37.0	33.9	35.2	45.0	36.0	31.7	18.8	29.7	15.9
DePauw.........	10.8	25.2	18.7	11.5	24.6	8.2	33.3	7.8	2.6
Illinois Wesleyan..	22.1	21.7	31.3	18.6	30.9	17.0	9.0	10.9	6.0
Allegheny........	22.0	35.5	19.2	36.6	7.4	6.5	14.2	18.1	16.4
Lawrence........	24.2	29.4	22.0	12.0	7.4	14.4	16.7	12.9	13.9
Pacific..........	18.1	16.0	14.8	33.2	30.9	28.7	9.1	9.3	4.3
Hamline.........	16.4	14.4	12.6	16.5	10.9	5.6	15.6	5.8	3.6
Albion..........	16.7	14.5	18.1	21.2	18.9	16.7	11.4	6.3	6.7
Cornell..........	14.2	13.1	33.0	13.2	7.4	11.4	16.1	5.2	9.2
Mount Union.....	20.2	19.5	18.1	8.1	10.3	4.4	16.1	3.1	7.2
Simpson.........	15.9	10.5	17.6	7.9	16.0	6.7	6.8	3.9	3.9
Baker...........	14.5	10.1	12.1	9.2	10.3	13.8	4.9	7.6	4.3
Willamette.......	11.7	1.4	9.3	9.1	7.4	8.2	3.1	4.6	1.9
MacMurray......	16.3	14.9	5.5	4.2	16.6	18.2	12.7	10.8	8.7
Baldwin-Wallace..	16.1	5.2	8.8	13.9	6.9	3.8	3.1	3.8	9.4
Dickinson........	13.8	14.6	6.6	6.5	5.1	3.8	12.9	4.9	2.9
Puget Sound.....	15.5	4.9	12.3	17.5	15.4	7.9	3.3	4.0	2.4
Morningside......	10.8	14.9	6.0	7.6	9.7	11.7	2.6	4.2	5.8
Mean, 18 colleges surveyed......	17.6	16.7	16.7	16.2	15.1	12.2	11.7	8.5	7.0
Mean, 200 colleges.......	17.1	15.9	14.2	12.9	11.1	11.0	10.2	10.3	7.0

available the resources of a state library; several of the colleges are located near enough to other institutions of higher learning to permit the use of their libraries by students. It seems reasonable to suppose that the presence of these other libraries would improve considerably the library resources of these colleges.

In several of the colleges an inquiry was conducted among the students to determine the extent of their use of libraries other than that of the college. In almost every instance the results were disappointing and indicated that students tend to make no considerable use of libraries other than that of the college they are attending. The factors of convenience and custom seem to be important in directing students to the use of the library of only their college.

In one or two colleges the libraries were being effectively supplemented by the outright loan of whole collections, amounting to several hundred volumes, from the city or state library. Since the loan consisted of selected titles, it supplemented in a very effective manner the college library. Where this type of co-operation exists, it can be used in an excellent way to improve the library facilities of the colleges.

It should be pointed out that the typical small city library usually does not contain much material that would be of service to college students. Unless the book collection of such a library has been deliberately planned with the needs of college students in mind, there will usually be very little of the authoritative reference material needed for college classes; instead, there will be an emphasis upon fiction, travel, and popular titles.

In view of these facts, the conclusion may be drawn that there is no substitute for an adequate college library. The only way by which the college can obtain satisfactory library facilities is to develop them in its own library under its own direction.

PART III

COLLEGE INSTRUCTIONAL FACILITIES

CHAPTER XIX

DEPARTMENTAL AND DIVISIONAL ORGANIZATIONS

DEPARTMENTS MAINTAINED

The usual type of departmental organization is found in most of the colleges studied. The number of departments maintained varies from eleven to twenty-eight with seventeen, eighteen, and sixteen as the most frequent numbers. In general, the larger colleges maintain the larger number of departments, though there are notable exceptions. Kansas Wesleyan University with fewer than three hundred liberal arts students maintains twenty departments.

The term "department" is not clearly defined in the colleges. In some institutions there are practically as many departments as members of the faculty, while in others a department represents a considerable aggregation of courses and consists of a large group of teachers. It is obvious that the smaller colleges tend to pattern after the larger ones in their departmental organization, rather than to establish an organization in keeping with their own problems and services.

The colleges show a pronounced variation in the organization of their departments of instruction. In the thirty-five colleges studied, the field of English language and literature, including public speaking, is organized under departments with fourteen different names, as follows: English, twenty-six colleges; speech, fifteen; public speaking, ten; English literature, five; English language, three; English language and literature, two; comparative literature, two; and English and expression, spoken English, English composition and rhetoric, public speaking and drama, dramatic art, English and public speaking, speech education, one each. Some of these variations in titles represent merely a different wording; most of them, however, represent real differences in the grouping of the studies in this field. In foreign languages the variation is even greater, for twenty-two different names of departments are used by these thirty-five colleges. The natural and physical sciences and mathematics are organized under twenty-one different departmental names with chemistry (thirty-one), biology (twenty-seven), mathematics (twenty-four), physics (twenty-three), and geology (ten) as the most usual. Twenty different titles are found in religion and philosophy.

Undoubtedly a large part of this variation is owing to a lack of clear principles of organization. Departments are all too frequently established to meet the idiosyncrasies of individual faculty members, rather than for any real improvement in the service to the students. It is true, of course, that some variation is justifiable on the ground of new developments and local conditions, but the utter heterogeneity displayed in the organization of subject matter into departments indicates the lack of any accepted principle as to what constitutes a satisfactory academic grouping.

Several serious objections can be made to a large number of departments in a college. Such overorganization tends to retard rather than to promote the service of the institution to its students. To correct present conditions a number of colleges have taken steps to establish divisions of instruction. Under such a plan the work usually done by the departments is grouped in a small number of major units.

The instruction offered in Brothers College has been organized under four divisions, as follows:

A. Language and Literature:
   English, French, German, Spanish, Greek and Latin languages and literature, dramatics, public speaking.
B. Philosophy, Education, and Religion:
   Philosophy, psychology, education, religion, aesthetics, college orientation, physical education, and hygiene.
C. Sciences and Mathematics:
   Chemistry, biology, physics, all other descriptive and laboratory sciences, and mathematics.
D. Social Sciences:
   Sociology, economics, history, political science, government, jurisprudence, and international law.

There is to be much flexibility in the program of Brothers College. For example, the plan contemplates that a faculty member may offer courses under more than one division.

The College of Puget Sound has adopted a divisional plan for its curriculum organization, under which arrangement five divisions are provided, as follows: (1) languages; (2) social sciences; (3) psychology, education, and philosophy; (4) science and mathematics; (5) fine arts. Each of these divisions is under the chairmanship of a well-qualified faculty member.

A divisional organization has been introduced in the College of Liberal Arts of Willamette University by grouping the subjects under four heads, as follows: (1) English and foreign languages; (2) social studies, philosophy, religion, education, physical education, and home economics; (3) science and mathematics; (4) music. The divisional organization at present is concerned primarily with student sequences; it is not as yet an administrative arrangement.

The College of the Pacific is developing the rudiments of a divisional organization. A "co-ordinating committee" has been appointed, consisting of representatives of the following fields: (1) mathematics and engineering; (2) natural science; (3) English and foreign languages; (4) social sciences; (5) education; (6) fine arts. This represents a desirable approach toward a divisional organization. In this institution there is a tendency to designate these large fields of subject matter as "schools." This terminology is apt to prove confusing in view of the common usage of the term "school" implying a curriculum leading to a separate degree.

Other colleges which have adopted the divisional plan are Albion College, DePauw University, Evansville College, and Hamline University. A few of the other colleges are discussing the divisional plan with a view to its adoption in the near future. In several instances steps in this direction are being taken by consolidating departments as an intermediate measure.

The advantages of a divisional organization are several. First, a divisional chairman may be selected who will administer the various related subjects in his division in such a way as to bring about a closer correlation of all the departments involved. Second, the curriculum offerings may be definitely reduced by the elimination of courses in various departments, which many times greatly overlap in content. Third, the divisional organization facilitates the administration of general survey courses that cut across departmental lines. Finally, a divisional organization facilitates a type of program for the student better than that now generally in vogue.

With reference to the latter point most colleges set up requirements designed to distribute some of the students' work over a wide range of studies and at the same time provide for concentration on some specific subject. To attain the latter purpose the student is generally required to select a major subject to which he devotes a large amount of attention. In following out this idea a number of colleges are now substituting a field of concentration for the major plan, on the theory that courses selected from several closely related departments can better serve the desired end than a large number of courses limited to one or two departments. For providing a well-correlated curriculum for the student, the divisional plan is a better academic organization than the department plan.

Historically, many of the present departments in colleges have been developed by dividing older departments. Other departments have been created by the addition of new subjects and new faculty members. This tendency has now gone so far in most colleges, especially the smaller ones, as to retard progress. An excessive number of departments tends to encourage overspecialization in course offerings, leads to opposition to the introduction of new subject matter, and almost always involves needless duplication in course offerings. At the same time, through useless machinery and regulations the student is bewildered in arranging a program that meets his needs.

Standardizing associations generally set eight as the minimum number of departments for a standard college. Although this number has not been scientifically determined, it may for the present be taken as suggestive. As long as this standard remains, the colleges must maintain, on paper at least, not fewer than eight departments.

The process of establishing new departments should cease in most of the colleges studied, and a strong tendency should be developed to combine closely related subjects in one department. This step could easily be taken in most of the institutions. In some cases satisfactory adjustment of the personnel of the departments may create difficult but not unsolvable problems. The combinations can usually be so arranged as to result in a greatly improved type of faculty organization from the point of view of present standards maintained by accrediting agencies.

A reduction in the number of departments through consolidation may, and in some colleges probably should, precede the establishment of a divisional organization. It may easily be an intermediate step toward a divisional plan. In fact, such a gradual adoption of a divisional plan is to be commended in view of the newness of the arrangement and the danger of producing chaotic conditions through a sudden realignment.

As the divisional organization becomes well established, it naturally follows that emphasis on departments as such becomes less and less. In fact, one of the purposes of the divisional organization is the breaking down of the sharp lines of demarcation between departments. Eventually a college with fewer than one thousand students may find it advantageous to abandon departments altogether.

The exact line-up of departments and divisions in all institutions need not by any means be the same. It should be a matter for study and decision by the administration and faculty of the college involved. Local conditions must, of course, be taken into account, and the groupings should be made in such a way as to conserve the most effective service of the faculty personnel. At the same time sound principles of academic organization should be followed.

For the administration of a division, a chairman should be selected who should be considered as an administrative officer of the college. He should be chosen by the dean and the president of the college in consultation with the faculty members of the division. The appointment to a division chairmanship should be for a term of years, probably not to exceed three, subject to reappointment. Tenure in this position should be independent of the tenure in the ordinary faculty ranks. It should not be considered a reduction in rank for a man to step out of the divisional chairmanship and to hold his teaching rank of professor or associate professor.

To the chairmen of the divisions should be delegated rather large authority in the management of their respective units. They should be the chief budgetary officers for their divisions and should have an important part in the selection of staff members. They should be largely responsible for curriculum developments within the particular field of the division.

CHAPTER XX

COURSE OFFERINGS

Table 39 presents data for each of the thirty-five colleges showing the total amount of semester-hour offerings in thirty-one different subject-matter fields. Offerings in music, art, and physical education have not been included, since much of the work in these subjects is frequently not on the credit-hour basis. These data were obtained from the catalogues of the year indicated in the table. In the case of colleges operating on the term plan, the offerings in term hours have been reduced to the equivalent in semester hours. The data of this table may be interpreted as indicating the total number of credit hours which would be taken by a student if he carried all the courses offered in the catalogue of the year mentioned. The figures indicate, in general, the breadth of the offerings in the various colleges, not only in total, but in each of the various subjects.

It is apparent from this table that the colleges differ considerably in the amount of their offerings. The college having the largest amount of course offerings has more than six times the number found in the colleges with the most limited offerings. The amount of graduate work offered is a factor which must be taken into account in studying the offerings of the various institutions. There are only a few of the colleges, however, that list any considerable number of courses open only to graduate students, so that this factor does not appreciably affect the interpretation for the majority of the institutions.

The columns showing the offerings for each of the various subjects also indicate a wide variation in practice among these colleges. These data should be of particular interest to faculty members who wish to study the offerings in their own fields.

The medians indicate that the colleges on the approved list of the Association of American Universities typically have somewhat larger offerings than those not holding national accreditation. This relationship does not hold for all of the subjects, however. The two groups of institutions have approximately the same average offerings in mathematics and journalism, and the colleges lacking national accreditation exceed the others in median offerings in home economics and education.

It is evident that a large amount of overexpansion has taken place in

TABLE 39

SEMESTER HOURS OFFERED IN VARIOUS SUBJECTS AT THIRTY-FIVE
COLLEGES ACCORDING TO CATALOGUES

Institution	Year	Total	Biology	Chemistry	Physics	Geology	Mathematics	Astronomy	Engineering	Home Economics
*Ohio Wesleyan....	1930–31	1,523	98	59	38	22	159	21	.....	45
*DePauw..........	1930–31	1,303	91	55	34	38	60	6	.....	44
*Pacific	1930–31	1,286	76	89	44	25	63	6	100	....:
Ohio Northern....	1930–31	1,034	34	61	31	....	43	3	167	.....
Oklahoma City....	1929–30	1,000	78	47	33	21	58	6	....	....
*Lawrence.........	1929–30	983	78	59	50	39	32	2	22	.....
Nebraska Wesleyan	1930–31	952	155	37	44	5	51	3	....	....
Evansville........	1929–30	946	50	76	32	10	52	.....	108	41
*Illinois Wesleyan..	1930–31	943	61	92	55	44	63	3	.....	42
Puget Sound......	1930–31	926	65	87	48	16	54	9	.....	34
*Albion...........	1930–31	910	46	88	32	6	58	10	.....	42
*Morningside......	1929–30	845	48	40	49	.....	40	.....	15	....
*Hamline..........	1929–30	844	63	58	46	3	42	....	....	6
*Baker............	1930–31	825	93	47	36	6	37	6	15	27
*Allegheny........	1929–30	824	53	64	34	24	54	8	....	....
*Simpson..........	1930–31	822	49	44	30	43	39	5	.....	45
Southwestern.....	1930–31	815	49	74	13	38	48	3	8	48
*Cornell..........	1929–30	801	32	59	35	38	41	4	32	23
*Willamette........	1930–31	799	51	34	30	16	37	6	8	26
Baldwin-Wallace..	1929–30	777	51	47	28	11	37	12	11	37
West Virginia Wesleyan...........	1931–32	748	40	62	16	20	50	....	....	41
*Mount Union.....	1930–31	712	71	59	33	25	46	10	....	....
*Chattanooga......	1929–30	664	49	32	44	.....	35	.....	6	....
Dakota Wesleyan..	1930–31	660	35	49	10	.....	27	....	....	52
Iowa Wesleyan....	1929–30	643	67	70	44	....	39	4	.....	36
Ozark Wesleyan...	1930–31	636	48	43	30	.....	40	....	....	37
*Dickinson........	1929–30	629	50	52	40	4	27	4	....	....
Kansas Wesleyan..	1930–31	628	27	44	10	.....	38	....	....	34
*MacMurray.......	1930–31	619	45	32	14	.....	27	2	.....	48
McKendree.......	1930–31	569	36	36	41	.....	38	.....	10	....
Intermountain....	1930–31	551	39	33	8	.....	51	....	....	....
Central Wesleyan..	1929–30	462	32	42	20	.....	21	....	....	....
Gooding..........	1930–31	414	25	33	10	6	29	....	....	22
Union............	1929–30	366	36	34	8	.....	27	....	....	....
Brothers..........	1930–31	249	8	20	8	.....	6	....	....	....
Median, all colleges........	....	801	49	49	33	6	40	3	0	23
*Median, A.A.U. colleges......	....	825	53	58	36	22	41	5	0	23
Median, non-A.A.U. colleges........	....	652	40	46	24	0	40	0	0	28

* Institutions on the approved list of the Association of American Universities.

TABLE 39—*Continued*

Institution	English Composition and Literature	Speech, Dramatics	Journalism	French	Spanish	Italian	German	Latin	Greek	Bible, Philosophy of Religion, and Religious Education	Education
*Ohio Wesleyan	123	89	8	68	58	22	42	52	34	145	66
*DePauw	150	58	12	55	55	....	50	73	41	102	24
*Pacific	110	50	12	58	66	....	45	38	22	56	94
Ohio Northern	51	27	6	37	26	....	22	40	16	22	126
Oklahoma City	91	19	34	42	49	14	22	24	22	49	134
*Lawrence	102	39	12	52	34	6	43	42	13	33	36
Nebraska Wesleyan	83	23	16	33	....	....	34	19	31	25	98
Evansville	62	14	4	48	....	....	14	34	18	35	168
*Illinois Wesleyan	76	40	6	40	37	12	40	57	14	44	45
Puget Sound	81	27	27	39	23	....	24	38	14	44	60
*Albion	103	41	12	46	34	12	34	20	37	24	33
*Morningside	90	32	4	46	40	6	66	60	28	51	40
*Hamline	93	35	6	36	24	....	33	36	18	45	32
*Baker	47	52	30	35	44	....	47	50	14	36	39
*Allegheny	81	20	2	68	24	18	46	44	50	31	30
*Simpson	53	24	2	32	24	....	22	36	16	28	85
Southwestern	69	35	12	24	21	....	26	6	....	46	66
*Cornell	63	31	8	44	16	....	28	35	30	31	48
*Willamette	92	34	....	40	25	....	30	52	20	16	33
Baldwin-Wallace	44	30	2	56	35	....	58	30	23	60	58
West Virginia Wesleyan	56	28	4	48	45	....	42	24	15	49	54
*Mount Union	83	12	4	38	14	....	26	48	30	38	55
*Chattanooga	47	20	2	48	44	....	28	24	18	37	39
Dakota Wesleyan	46	42	....	37	40	....	40	40	....	30	55
Iowa Wesleyan	43	27	24	34	....	....	28	33	....	23	43
Ozark Wesleyan	58	22	....	34	31	....	24	56	10	36	56
*Dickinson	62	12	....	48	18	6	42	27	34	42	21
Kansas Wesleyan	55	42	12	45	....	....	31	55	16	21	51
*MacMurray	55	29	2	46	16	....	44	38	....	35	50
McKendree	68	20	2	28	18	....	38	38	21	16	45
Intermountain	55	24	8	35	29	....	35	28	17	32	36
Central Wesleyan	27	12	6	18	20	....	36	45	19	52	38
Gooding	52	13	....	22	22	....	22	24	....	12	17
Union	57	4	....	30	....	....	....	34	....	34	43
Brothers	12	6	....	18	28	....	18	18	12	12	6
Median, all colleges	62	27	6	40	25	0	34	38	18	35	45
*Median, A.A.U. colleges	83	34	6	46	34	0	42	42	22	37	39
Median, non-A.A.U. colleges	56	24	5	35	23	0	27	34	16	33	55

* Institutions on the approved list of the Association of American Universities.

TABLE 39—Continued

Institution	Psychology	Philosophy	History	Political Science	Sociology	Economics and Business Administration	Undepartmentalized Survey Courses	Library Science	Law	Pharmacy	Agriculture	Manual Training
*Ohio Wesleyan	49	37	73	46	64	102	3					
*DePauw	44	43	90	66	40	72						
*Pacific	22	52	71	48	14	54	12	1	58			
Ohio Northern	14	12	68	28	6	26			81	87		
Oklahoma City	15	55	51	27	33	68					8	
*Lawrence	29	47	69	32	30	78		4				
Nebraska Wesleyan	25	27	57	31	20	91						44
Evansville	12	17	40	12	32	67						
*Illinois Wesleyan	12	18	42	12	31	57						
Puget Sound	24	33	42	20	40	73		4				
*Albion	9	29	44	34	31	85						
*Morningside	18	20	62	19	28	43						
*Hamline	39	30	55	40	40	64						
*Baker	28	24	27	12	24	49						
*Allegheny	13	19	66	33	9	33						
*Simpson	27	18	46	8	19	127						
Southwestern	9	21	28	23	45	100	1	2				
*Cornell	21	11	32	28	24	83		4				
*Willamette	13	17	34	33	30	46	1	1	74			
Baldwin-Wallace	9	15	38	14	28	42		1				
West Virginia Wesleyan	11	15	31	15	27	55						
*Mount Union	16	14	32	10	10	34	2	2				
*Chattanooga	9	2	38	36	14	92						
Dakota Wesleyan	13	23	35	7	10	62		7				
Iowa Wesleyan	9	6	38	15	22	38						
Ozark Wesleyan	13	17	33	18	18	12						
*Dickinson	19	12	46		12	26	1		24			
Kansas Wesleyan	9		33	6	40	58	1					
*MacMurray	25	11	38	4	8	50						
McKendree	18	20	46	10	10	10						
Intermountain	11	12	32	17	17	32						
Central Wesleyan	9		28	10	15	12						
Gooding	7	12	27		12	47						
Union	6	15	30	4		4						
Brothers	12	14	6		6	6	33					
Median, all colleges	13	17	38	17	22	54	0	0	0	0	0	0
*Median, A.A.U. colleges	21	19	46	32	24	57	0	0	0	0	0	0
Median, non-A.A.U. colleges	12	15	34	15	19	45	0	0	0	0	0	0

* Institutions on the approved list of the Association of American Universities.

the course offerings of these colleges. Dickinson College, the oldest and one of the best known of the institutions, has a total offering of only 629 semester hours. The curriculum of this college is well organized and affords an adequate range of undergraduate offerings in most fields. It is difficult to understand why so many of the other colleges have gone far beyond the limits of a conservative development of their offerings. In very few fields of subject matter should it be necessary to offer much beyond a major of work, and forty-five or fifty hours would seem to include all that needs to be offered by an undergraduate college of liberal arts in any of the subjects indicated.

To a limited extent the offerings may represent a certain amount of "padding," courses being listed which the college does not actually intend to give. This does not seem to be at all common, however. Three other causes may be suggested for the overexpansion that has occurred. The first is a desire to imitate the larger universities, offering as nearly as possible everything advertised by these large institutions with their programs of graduate work. The ambitions of individual faculty members, of departments, and of the college as a whole all co-operate to bring pressure for an increased range of offerings. The second cause for overexpansion is pressure from small groups of students who wish to follow certain special lines of interest. The intense competition for students, which many of these colleges face, leads to the adoption of almost any measure to hold those already enrolled. Rather than advise those with highly specialized interests to attend some other institution, many colleges add a course or courses in order to hold the enrolment of such students. The third cause of overexpansion is the lack of any effective machinery in the college for scrutinizing the need for proposed additions to the list of course offerings, or for eliminating unneeded courses. A careful annual culling of the courses listed in most colleges would show possibilities of many eliminations.

An overexpansion of course offerings has two unfortunate results. The first is a decrease in operating efficiency. It should be obvious that an increase in offerings, unless the enrolment of the college is increasing in a corresponding manner, is certain to result in a lower average size of class. The burden thus imposed may be carried in three different ways: the income of the college may be increased; the instructional loads of faculty members may be increased; or the number of faculty members may be increased and the average salary of teachers decreased. In most colleges the income is relatively inflexible; it therefore follows that one or the other of the two last-mentioned methods will typically be used to carry the burden of the overexpanded offerings. Neither of these methods results in improvement in the service of the institution. It thus appears that, unless funds are available for financing the expanded offerings, the college suffers a serious loss of efficiency through overexpansion in courses.

The second unfortunate result of overexpanded offerings is the effect upon the programs of the students. A large offering in any subject necessarily means the introduction of several rather highly specialized courses. At the undergraduate level the student should be concerned more with the broad foundations of knowledge than with narrow and specialized courses in any one field of study. It is educationally unwise to sacrifice this breadth of training by permitting too early specialization on the part of students. As it actually happens in practice, many students take these highly specialized courses without adequate basic training.

The colleges of this group could well afford to scrutinize carefully their programs of course offerings with a view to eliminating many of the highly specialized courses, more suitable to a graduate school than to a liberal arts college.

Table 39 indicates that the overexpansion is largely a matter pertaining to the offerings within recognized fields of study, rather than of additions of whole areas in some colleges that are not included in others. To be sure, there are some subjects represented in only a few colleges. Thus several colleges offer no work in astronomy, home economics, and Italian. Professional subjects, such as law, pharmacy, engineering, and library science, are also given in a few of the colleges. Much more important than this type of expansion is that which has taken place within the subjects commonly offered in all colleges. There is scarcely a college in the group that does not have offerings in some one or more fields that are above the median for the entire group of colleges.

The medians shown in this table should not be taken as indicating an ideal arrangement of offerings. Although an offering much above the median in any subject needs to be carefully investigated by the college, it is entirely possible that the marked tendency toward overexpansion affects the medians as well as the individual colleges. No agency has ever attempted to work out a "minimum essential" offering in the various fields of study for colleges of liberal arts. Studies of this type have been made at the secondary level, but not for colleges. It would be an excellent contribution to the administration of college curriculums for experts interested in each of the various subjects to get together and work out a typical list of offerings for colleges in their subjects.

The size of the enrolment of a college seems to have a marked effect on the amount of offerings. Data are presented in Table 40 showing the average number of semester hours of course offerings in each subject by colleges grouped according to enrolment.

TABLE 40

AVERAGE NUMBER OF SEMESTER HOURS OF CREDIT OFFERED IN VARIOUS
SUBJECTS BY COLLEGES GROUPED ACCORDING TO
SIZE OF ENROLMENT

SUBJECT	AVERAGE NUMBER OF SEMESTER HOURS OF CREDIT OFFERED BY		
	6 Colleges Having 700 or More Students	17 Colleges Having from 400 to 699 Students	12 Colleges Having Fewer than 400 Students
Total offerings all subjects.........	1,126	828	573
Sciences:			
Astronomy....................	8	5	0
Biology......................	71	62	37
Chemistry....................	62	56	45
Engineering..................	32	11	10
Geology......................	21	18	3
Home economics..............	22	20	22
Mathematics.................	68	44	35
Physics......................	36	37	20
English:			
English composition and literature	103	72	49
Journalism...................	14	8	5
Speech and dramatics..........	46	30	21
Foreign languages:			
French.......................	50	43	33
German......................	36	38	27
Greek........................	27	21	11
Italian.......................	9	2	0
Latin........................	42	38	35
Spanish......................	43	28	19
Religion, education, philosophy, and psychology:			
Bible, philosophy of religion, and religious education...........	63	29	29
Education....................	70	53	51
Philosophy...................	37	20	14
Psychology...................	27	19	11
Social studies:			
Economics and business administration......................	72	63	34
History......................	66	44	32
Political science..............	39	22	9
Sociology....................	34	23	17
Others........................	31	14	3

It is evident from this table that the larger colleges tend to have larger course offerings than the smaller ones. Expansion in the offerings of a relatively large college can take place without incurring any important inefficiency. The criticism of the overspecialization of the programs of students obtains just the same, however, even though the larger college can afford to offer a greater variety of courses than the small college.

The various subjects show interesting trends in the average offerings for colleges of various sizes. Almost all the subjects follow the trend of the total, the larger colleges having larger average offerings than the small ones. In home economics the offerings are not related to the size of enrolment, and in German and physics the relationship between amount of offerings and size of enrolment seems to be less marked than in the other subjects.

RELATIVE EMPHASIS ON VARIOUS SUBJECTS

It has already been pointed out that the colleges vary considerably in their emphasis upon the various fields of study. Table 41 presents data showing the percentage of the total offerings in various subject-matter fields. Several of the subjects listed separately in Table 39 have been grouped for presentation in Table 41.

The table brings out the relative emphasis given each field of study by the several colleges. The medians indicate that languages and literature and social studies comprise, on the average, the largest part of the offerings. There is surprisingly little difference between the medians for the two groups of colleges classified on the basis of accreditation.

It should certainly be within the province of any institution to determine its own distribution of emphasis on the various subjects. This distribution should reflect the aims and purposes of the college, as well as its general philosophy of higher education.

ALTERNATION OF COURSES

One of the plans by which a college may increase the range of its course offerings without incurring many of the disadvantages of an overexpanded program is through the alternation of courses. By this plan the more advanced courses in the various departments are offered only in alternate years, or even at three-year periods. Thus students have an opportunity to take these more advanced courses at some time during their college curriculum, and the enrolments in these courses are larger than they would be if given every year.

All but one of the colleges studied follow the plan of alternating some of their course offerings. The proportion of the total offerings that are al-

THE LIBERAL ARTS COLLEGE

TABLE 41

PERCENTAGE OF TOTAL SEMESTER HOURS OFFERED IN VARIOUS
SUBJECTS AT THIRTY-FIVE COLLEGES

Institution	Biological Sciences	Physical Sciences	Mathematics, Astronomy, Engineering	Home Economics	English, Speech, Dramatics, Journalism	Modern Languages
*Ohio Wesleyan..........	6.4	7.8	11.8	3.0	14.4	12.4
*DePauw...............	7.0	9.7	5.1	3.4	16.9	12.3
*Pacific.................	5.9	12.3	13.1	....	13.4	13.1
Ohio Northern..........	3.3	8.9	20.6	....	8.1	8.2
Oklahoma City.........	7.8	10.1	6.4	....	14.4	12.7
*Lawrence...............	7.9	15.1	5.7	....	15.6	13.7
Nebraska Wesleyan......	16.3	9.0	5.7	....	12.8	7.0
Evansville..............	5.3	12.5	16.9	4.3	8.5	6.6
*Illinois Wesleyan........	6.5	20.3	7.0	4.5	12.9	13.7
Puget Sound...........	7.0	16.3	6.8	3.7	14.6	9.3
*Albion.................	5.1	13.9	7.5	4.6	17.1	13.9
*Morningside............	5.7	10.5	6.5	....	14.9	18.7
*Hamline................	7.5	12.7	5.0	0.7	15.9	11.0
*Baker..................	11.3	10.8	7.0	3.3	15.6	15.3
*Allegheny...............	6.4	14.8	7.5	....	12.5	19.0
*Simpson................	6.0	14.2	5.4	5.5	9.6	9.5
Southwestern...........	6.0	15.3	7.2	5.9	14.2	8.7
*Cornell.................	4.0	16.5	9.6	2.9	12.7	11.0
*Willamette..............	6.4	10.0	6.4	3.3	15.7	11.9
Baldwin-Wallace........	6.6	11.1	7.7	4.8	9.8	19.2
West Virginia Wesleyan..	5.3	13.1	6.7	5.5	11.8	18.0
*Mount Union...........	10.0	16.4	7.9	....	13.9	11.0
*Chattanooga............	7.4	11.4	6.2	....	10.4	18.1
Dakota Wesleyan........	5.3	8.9	4.1	7.9	13.3	17.7
Iowa Wesleyan..........	10.4	17.7	6.7	5.6	14.6	9.6
Ozark Wesleyan.........	7.5	11.5	6.3	5.8	12.6	14.0
*Dickinson	7.9	15.3	4.9	....	11.8	18.1
Kansas Wesleyan........	4.3	8.6	6.1	5.4	17.4	12.1
*MacMurray.............	7.3	7.4	4.7	7.8	14.0	17.1
McKendree.............	6.3	13.5	8.4	....	15.8	14.8
Intermountain..........	7.1	7.4	9.3	....	15.8	18.0
Central Wesleyan........	6.9	13.4	4.5	....	9.7	16.0
Gooding................	6.0	11.8	7.0	5.3	15.7	16.0
Union..................	9.8	11.5	7.4	....	16.7	8.2
Brothers...............	3.2	11.3	2.4	....	7.2	25.7
Median, all colleges...	6.5	11.8	6.7	3.0	14.0	13.7
*Median, A.A.U. colleges..............	6.5	12.7	6.5	2.9	14.0	13.7
Median, non-A.A.U. colleges...........	6.5	11.7	6.8	4.0	13.8	13.4

* Institutions on the approved list of the Association of American Universities.

TABLE 41—*Continued*

Institution	Ancient Languages	Bible, Religious Education	Education and Psychology	Philosophy	History, Political Science, Sociology	Economics, Business Administration	Others
*Ohio Wesleyan	5.7	9.5	7.5	2.5	12.0	6.7	0.3
*DePauw	8.8	7.8	5.2	3.3	15.0	5.5	......
*Pacific	4.7	4.4	9.0	4.0	10.4	4.2	5.5
Ohio Northern	5.4	2.1	13.5	1.2	9.9	2.5	16.3
Oklahoma City	4.6	4.9	14.9	5.5	11.1	6.8	0.8
*Lawrence	5.6	3.4	6.6	4.8	13.3	7.9	0.4
Nebraska Wesleyan	5.3	2.6	12.9	2.8	11.4	9.6	4.6
Evansville	5.5	3.7	19.0	1.8	8.9	7.0	......
*Illinois Wesleyan	7.5	4.7	6.0	1.9	9.0	6.0	......
Puget Sound	5.6	4.8	9.1	3.6	11.0	7.8	0.4
*Albion	6.3	2.6	4.6	3.2	11.9	9.3	......
*Morningside	10.4	6.0	6.9	2.4	12.9	5.1	......
*Hamline	6.4	5.3	8.4	3.6	15.9	7.6	......
*Baker	7.8	4.4	8.1	2.9	7.6	5.9	......
*Allegheny	11.4	3.8	5.2	2.3	13.1	4.0	......
*Simpson	6.3	3.4	13.6	2.2	8.9	15.4	......
Southwestern	0.8	5.6	9.2	2.6	11.8	12.3	0.4
*Cornell	8.1	3.9	8.6	1.4	10.5	10.4	0.4
*Willamette	9.0	2.0	5.8	2.1	12.1	5.8	9.5
Baldwin-Wallace	6.8	7.7	8.6	1.9	10.3	5.4	0.1
West Virginia Wesleyan	5.2	6.6	8.7	2.0	9.8	7.3	......
*Mount Union	11.0	5.3	10.0	1.9	7.3	4.8	0.5
*Chattanooga	6.3	5.6	7.2	0.3	13.2	13.9	......
Dakota Wesleyan	6.1	4.5	10.3	3.5	7.9	9.4	1.1
Iowa Wesleyan	5.1	3.7	8.1	0.9	11.7	5.9	......
Ozark Wesleyan	10.4	5.7	10.8	2.7	10.8	1.9	......
*Dickinson	9.7	6.7	6.4	1.9	9.2	4.1	4.0
Kansas Wesleyan	11.3	3.3	9.6	......	12.6	9.2	0.1
*MacMurray	6.1	5.7	12.1	1.8	8.0	8.0	......
McKendree	10.4	2.8	11.1	3.5	11.6	1.8	......
Intermountain	8.2	5.8	8.5	2.2	11.9	5.8	......
Central Wesleyan	13.9	11.3	10.2	......	11.5	2.6	......
Gooding	5.8	2.9	5.8	2.9	9.4	11.4	......
Union	9.3	9.3	13.4	4.1	9.3	1.0	......
Brothers	12.1	4.8	7.2	5.6	4.8	2.4	13.3
Median, all colleges	6.4	4.8	8.6	2.4	11.0	6.0	0
*Median, A.A.U. colleges	7.5	4.7	7.2	2.3	11.9	6.0	0
Median, non-A.A.U. colleges	6.0	4.8	9.9	2.7	10.9	6.4	0

* Institutions on the approved list of the Association of American Universities.

ternated range from 4 or 5 per cent up to more than 25 per cent, the median being 11.3 per cent. The colleges on the approved list of the Association of American Universities alternate a larger proportion of their offerings than the colleges not holding national accreditation. Several of the colleges alternate courses in some departments but not in others. Consideration could well be given to a more general adoption of this plan for overcoming the inefficiencies due to a large program of offerings.

DETAILED ANALYSIS OF COURSE OFFERINGS IN A SPECIAL FIELD OF STUDY

Not only is there variation in the total amount of offerings in each subject, but the actual courses offered within each subject show a high variability among the colleges. As an illustration of the lack of agreement as to what constitutes the essential offerings, a detailed analysis has been made for the purposes of this study of the courses listed in one subject-matter field—Bible and religion.

The course offerings in Bible and religion at these thirty-five colleges present an astounding variety, both in the areas of the field which are covered and also in the nomenclature of the courses themselves. A study has been made of the types of courses offered and of the number of different titles offered under each type. Within the general field of Bible and religion there appear to be eight distinct subjects that are touched upon in one or more of these colleges, with subclasses easily distinguishable under certain of the types. These eight subjects are as follows: (1) biblical literature; (2) biblical and religious history; (3) philosophy of religion; (4) religious education; (5) psychology of religion; (6) social teachings of the Bible; (7) missions; and (8) theology.

Table 42 presents data regarding the number of different titles listed under each type and subtype, together with the number of colleges offering one or more courses of each type. In this study minor changes in the wording were not considered as constituting a different title, although such a title as "Introduction to the Literature of the Old and New Testaments" was considered as a different title from "Introduction to the Study of the English Bible." The data for the number of different titles are given in the first column of Table 42. In numerous cases the descriptions of courses bearing different titles indicate no difference in content; tabulation was accordingly made of the number of actually different courses offered in each subject. Under this method of tabulating, the two courses just cited would be counted as only one course. The data for the number of actually different courses are given in the second column of Table 42. A tabulation was also made of the number of different colleges offering one or more courses in each subject. These data are given in the third column of Table 42.

This table shows that there are a total of 260 different titles listed in the field of Bible and religion in these thirty-five colleges. Of these 260

TABLE 42

NUMBER OF DIFFERENT COURSE TITLES AND OF ACTUALLY DIFFERENT COURSES IN BIBLE AND RELIGION, CLASSIFIED BY SUBJECT, AND NUMBER OF COLLEGES OFFERING ONE OR MORE COURSES IN EACH SUBJECT

Subject	Number of Different Titles Listed	Number of Actually Different Courses	Number of Colleges Offering Work in Each Subject
Biblical and religious history	36	20	35
History of religion......	8	6	28
History of the Hebrews..	8	1	14
History of the Christian Church..............	12	7	17
Bible history...........	8	6	19
Biblical literature.........	74	37	34
Bible (general course)...	20	12	23
Old Testament.........	15	5	18
New Testament.......	19	9	19
The prophets..........	9	5	16
The gospels...........	6	5	8
Life and letters of Paul..	5	1	14
Philosophy of religion.....	48	35	34
Philosophy of religion...	16	10	23
Teachings of Jesus......	17	13	30
Modern problems of religion..............	15	12	10
Religious education.......	54	28	27
Psychology of religion.....	3	1	20
Social teachings of the Bible	13	11	15
Missions.................	18	17	9
Theology...............	14	11	9
Total..............	260	160	35

course titles, 74 are classified as biblical literature, 36 as biblical and religious history, 48 as philosophy of religion, 54 as religious education, 3 as psychology of religion, 13 as social teachings of the Bible, 18 as missions, and 14 as theology. In making this classification it was necessary in some cases to assign titles to the various classes somewhat arbitrarily. For example, under the subheading of "Teachings of Jesus," which is classified as philosophy of religion, there are a few courses which could probably be more accurately classified as biblical literature (e.g., "The Words of

Jesus") or as biblical history (e.g., "The Life and Times of Jesus"). Occasionally a course clearly falls into more than one division (e.g., "New Testament History and Literature," "History and Philosophy of Religion"). These courses, which are not numerous, have been classified according to the major emphasis given in the course as indicated by its catalogue description.

It will be noted that although there are 260 recognizably different titles listed in the field of Bible and religion at these thirty-five colleges, a careful analysis reduces the number of actually different courses to 160. In other words, 38 per cent of the variety in course titles is caused by meaningless variations in the wording. This is a condition all too common, not only in the field of Bible and religion, but in other subjects as well. Variations of this type are confusing to students and cause endless difficulty in cases of the transferring of credits.

The number of different courses which are given in the field of Bible and religion is astounding. One would be reluctant to concede that there could possibly be 160 absolutely different course units of subject matter in this field that would all be of interest and profit to undergraduate students. Obviously, there is much overlapping among these courses, and there is a distressing irregularity in defining the boundaries of the various subjects. For example, three colleges give a course in "The Gospel of John"; another gives a course in "The Gospel and Revelation of John." These courses are not coextensive, and yet they overlap considerably. Again, two colleges give a course in "The Psalms and Job," while another gives a course in "Old Testament Poems and Writings." Illustrations of this type could be multiplied. There is a great need for the teachers in this field to agree upon a common division of the subject matter, so that the units of content will be definitely allocated to specific courses and given under similar titles in all institutions. In passing, it may be remarked that a like need exists in many fields other than Bible and religion.

Criticism may be made of the number of different courses offered, not only from the standpoint of the overlapping and confusion in course titles, but also because of the excessive degree of specialization involved in the offerings of many of the colleges. Two of the categories presented in Table 42—missions and theology—have a doubtful place in an undergraduate program.[1] Certainly it would not be wise to advise an undergraduate student to specialize in "missions" to the extent of the total

[1] For an excellent treatment of what is desirable in the undergraduate curriculum in Bible and religion, see W. C. Bower, "The Teaching of Religion," in *Religion in Higher Education*, ed. M. C. Towner (Chicago: University of Chicago Press, 1931), pp. 161–74.

offerings of one or two of the colleges. The courses listed under "theology" include such titles as "pastoral theology," "homiletics," "systematic theology," etc., which clearly belong to the theological seminaries and have no place in the program of the college of liberal arts.

The lack of agreement as to what constitutes the fundamental subject matter in the field of Bible and religion is strikingly brought out by a tabulation of the number of different institutions in which each course is offered. Of the 260 different course titles, 185, or 71 per cent, are found in only one college. Seven-eighths of the titles are found in not more than two colleges. There is only one of these 260 titles that is found in as many as half of the thirty-five colleges, and there are only six titles that are common to more than one-fourth of the colleges. These six courses are: history of religion(s), Old Testament history, philosophy of religion, life and teachings of Jesus, psychology of religion, and curriculum of (in) religious education.

Some of the courses offered in the departments of Bible and religion in these colleges seem to be only remotely related to the fundamental subject matter in this field. Among those of this type may be mentioned the following: the World War, choir, discussion-group leadership, child psychology, and anthropology. The field of religious education seems to be the worst offender in this regard. The courses given in this subject frequently overlap considerably with the type of subject matter usually given in the departments of psychology and education.

The last column of Table 42 presents data regarding the number of colleges offering work in each subject. It will be observed that three of the subjects—biblical and religious history, biblical literature, and philosophy of religion—are represented by one or more courses in practically all of the thirty-five colleges. Some course or courses in religious education are given in three-fourths of the colleges, and twenty give work in the psychology of religion. Only fifteen of the colleges give courses in the social teachings of the Bible. In view of the modern emphasis on this phase of the subject, it is somewhat surprising that more of the colleges have not introduced such courses. The two subjects which were previously pointed out as of little interest in an undergraduate program—missions and theology—are represented in only nine colleges.

CHAPTER XXI

DEGREES

Table 43 lists the various Bachelor's degrees offered in thirty-four of the colleges studied, and indicates the number of institutions granting each degree. The catalogue of one of the thirty-five colleges fails to state what degree or degrees are offered. Since the data for this study were collected, this institution and one other included in the tabulations of Table 43 have become junior colleges and have ceased to offer the Bachelor's degree.

This table shows that all of the colleges for which data are available grant the Bachelor of Arts degree. In all, twenty-seven different degrees are listed as being offered in these thirty-four colleges. Ten of these degrees are in law, engineering, and pharmacy, subjects not usually represented in the liberal arts college. Besides the Bachelor of Arts, the most common degrees are the Bachelor of Music and the Bachelor of Science. The remaining degrees are granted in only a very few of the colleges. Since the visit of the survey staff some of the colleges have reduced the number of their degrees. The three engineering degrees appearing at the end of Table 43 have been discontinued.

The number of different degrees offered in each institution varies from one to ten. There are three colleges that offer only one degree, nine that offer two degrees, fourteen that offer three degrees, three that offer four degrees, two that offer five, one that offers seven, one that offers eight, and one that offers ten degrees.

The offering of a multiplicity of degrees is an evidence of an unsatisfactory academic organization. Some of the colleges have been encouraged to add to the number of their degrees by the example of the larger universities. It is inconsistent with the purpose of the liberal arts college, however, to provide the highly specialized type of courses usually given in the larger universities for the separate degrees. These degrees represent emphasis upon vocational and professional specialization rather than liberal culture. It should not be understood that the curriculums for the degrees as actually set up in these colleges are always too highly specialized to harmonize with the liberal arts motive. The point is that any subject worthy of being given in a liberal arts college should be worthy of the liberal arts degree.

The condition of multiplicity of specialized degrees has been very largely the result of the inflexibility of the requirements for the traditional

TABLE 43

BACCALAUREATE DEGREES OFFERED AT THIRTY-FOUR COLLEGES

Degrees	Number of Colleges Granting Each Degree
Bachelor of Arts.....................................	34
Bachelor of Arts in Business Administration............	1
Bachelor of Science..................................	17
Bachelor of Science in Business Administration..........	5
Bachelor of Science in Education......................	3
Bachelor of Science in Home Economics................	2
Bachelor of Science in Religious Education.............	1
Bachelor of Science in Art Education..................	1
Bachelor of Science in Physical Education..............	1
Bachelor of Science in Nursing.......................	1
Bachelor of Science in Chemical Engineering............	1
Bachelor of Science in Civil Engineering................	1
Bachelor of Science in Electrical Engineering...........	1
Bachelor of Science in Mechanical Engineering..........	1
Bachelor of Science in Pharmacy......................	1
Bachelor of Philosophy...............................	2
Bachelor of Education................................	1
Bachelor of Business Administration....................	1
Bachelor of Commercial Science.......................	1
Bachelor of Music...................................	21
Bachelor of Music Education..........................	2
Bachelor of School Music.............................	4
Bachelor of Fine Arts................................	2
Bachelor of Laws....................................	2
Civil Engineer.......................................	1
Electrical Engineer...................................	1
Mechanical Engineer.................................	1

liberal arts degrees. As new subjects have been forced into the college curriculum by the changing needs of a dynamic social system, the guardians of the traditional cultural subjects, almost always in the majority on college faculties, have been very loath to accept the newcomers on an equal academic status. A few generations ago science was fighting just such a battle against the then "Levites of culture," the classicists. Science was accepted and became a part of the defensive force against the invasion, somewhat later, of the social studies. These in turn have finally been accepted as a legitimate part of cultural education. All of these increments to the accepted body of learning have resulted in modifications of the requirements for the liberal arts degrees.

At present, the battle is raging on two fronts, and two different types of subjects are clamoring for recognition by the liberal arts college. Both of these situations are the result of rather fundamental changes in the social structure.

One of the comparatively recent social changes is the great increase in the number of people with a fairly large amount of leisure. This has afforded an opportunitiy for the development of aesthetic taste, and has brought about a demand for types of education for the worthy use of leisure; as a result, the fine arts have come into new prominence in the educational system. But academicians of the old school hold up their hands in horror at the thought that education in music, painting, sculpture, dramatics, etc., can possibly be accepted on the same footing as the time-honored Latin and Greek or mathematics or the somewhat more recently accepted sciences and social studies. The social pressure on the college for the introduction of the study of the fine arts is too great to withstand; young people will and must have facilities for this sort of training at the time they are attending college. The inflexibility of the guardians of the traditional culture has forced a compromise between the curriculum organization and the irresistible force of a social movement. As a result, the college is permitted to give these subjects, but a separate degree is provided to preserve the sacred Bachelor of Arts from contamination.

A second social change affecting liberal arts education is the increased demand for college-trained recruits in certain vocations. This is noticeably felt in school teaching, business, and home economics, and to a less extent exists in journalism, nursing, and some other subjects. As an effect of this social change, pressure has been brought to bear upon the college to provide a limited amount of professional and technical training for those who are planning to enter vocations in which this is necessary. For the most part, this pressure has been confined to callings in which the amount of professional training needed is relatively small compared to the amount of training taken in purely liberal arts subjects. Education for vocations such as law, medicine, and engineering, in which the technical and professional subjects comprise the great bulk of the training, has generally been provided for in other types of institutions.

There is evidence that history is repeating itself, and that the defenders of the academic purity of the liberal arts degrees are giving way before the social pressure for the recognition of the fine arts and a limited amount of professional training. In most of the colleges of the group studied some work in music and the fine arts is accepted toward the liberal arts degree, although, as a rule, a high degree of specialization in this subject does not lead to the Bachelor of Arts. All the colleges accept courses in education toward their regular degrees, but again the high degree of specialization usually found in the curriculum for the training of elementary or kindergarten-primary teachers typically culminates in a different degree.

There can be little doubt but that ultimately some of the subjects now discriminated against in some colleges will prove their academic worthiness. For the present, the plan of offering a separate degree for these subjects, as followed by some of the colleges, seems to be an unfortunate compromise. It would be better to limit the program strictly to the subjects that the faculty is willing to accept toward the liberal arts degree. As long as the college maintains general culture as its prime purpose, subjects and curriculums inconsistent with this purpose should not be offered. All that are offered should be accepted toward the standard degree.

The offering of a multiplicity of degrees may be questioned from an entirely different point of view. The Bachelor of Arts or the Bachelor of Science degrees from a college holding regional accreditation commands equal respect with similar degrees from the largest and strongest institutions in the country. The same cannot be said for the other specialized degrees. The Bachelor of Music given by a college having only a meager equipment for this work and lacking accreditation by the National Association of Schools of Music cannot begin to compare in value with this degree as given by the large conservatories and schools of music. The Bachelor of Science in Business Administration or the Bachelor of Business Administration given by the small college cannot possibly be the equivalent, so far as technical proficiency is concerned, of these same degrees as given by university schools of commerce. The same conclusion may be drawn regarding all of the specialized degrees, such as the Bachelor of Science in Education, in Home Economics, in Religious Education, etc. The colleges of this group would do well to limit their offering of degrees to those which will command respect, the limited amount of technical or professional work necessary for certain vocations being accepted without question toward the regular liberal arts degrees.

Some question may even be raised as to the necessity for two liberal arts degrees, the Bachelor of Arts and the Bachelor of Science. As a general rule, the only difference between the requirements for these two degrees is in the subject or field of concentration. In some instances the language requirement is somewhat more lenient for the Bachelor of Science than for the Bachelor of Arts. The presence of these two degrees is a vestige of the struggle over the introduction of science. The science people, at first forbidden the use of the Bachelor of Arts, tended to glorify their own separate degree. In some cases, particularly for students intending to go on into medicine, the Bachelor of Science is now the generally preferred degree. For the most part, however, the distinction between these two degrees now serves no useful academic purpose.

In some colleges having a well-developed conservatory of music there may be justification for the continuation of the degree of Bachelor of Music. This degree should represent a specialization sufficient to prepare students for a professional career in music. The giving of the degree should certainly be limited to those institutions holding membership with the National Association of Schools of Music. The presence of this highly specialized curriculum should be recognized as a departure from the single purpose of liberal arts education. It may be justified, however, on the grounds of service to a constituency in exactly the same manner as the existence of certain other professional schools, such as law, engineering, pharmacy, etc., maintained in conjunction with some of the liberal arts colleges.

It must be recognized that most of the colleges of this group dare not depart far in setting up their degrees from the general practice of the stronger institutions of their region. In most parts of the country a college will not endanger its academic respectability today by granting only the one degree, the Bachelor of Arts, for the completion of all its curriculums, accepting toward this degree a limited amount of professional work in such subjects as education, nursing, etc., and also an amount of fine arts equivalent to the usual requirements for a major. In areas where the Bachelor of Science is still customarily differentiated from the Bachelor of Arts, both degrees may well be given. It would appear that, at the most, the colleges of this group need give no more than three degrees, the Bachelor of Arts, the Bachelor of Science, and the Bachelor of Music. The majority should give only the one degree, the Bachelor of Arts.

REQUIREMENTS FOR THE BACHELOR'S DEGREE

There are four types of requirements for Bachelor's degrees commonly established by the colleges of this group. These requirements relate to

(1) the total amount of work, (2) the concentration of studies, (3) the distribution of studies, and (4) the quality of the work done.

The total amount of work required for the degree is typically expressed in terms of credits. The colleges differ little in their credit requirements for degrees. The actual amounts required vary from 120 to 128 semester hours, equivalent to full-time work on the part of a student for four years. The small variation shown is accounted for by the differences in the method of counting credit for physical education. There is almost absolute uniformity in the general requirement of 120 semester hours (or 180 term hours) exclusive of physical education. This condition of uniformity is in sharp contrast with the high degree of variation found in the colleges of this group on most of the other points studied. In this instance the uniformity is the result of pressure from the standardizing agencies of the country.

The credit-hour as a measure of educational advancement has recently been called into question. A few of the colleges, in setting up their degree requirements, are experimenting with the attainment of general proficiency as a standard in substitution for that of the accumulation of a certain number of course credits. Thus far this substitution has taken place only in the specific requirements of certain subjects, such as foreign languages and English composition, although there is some promise that ultimately the whole credit system, as an index of progression toward a degree, may be abandoned.

The second type of requirement for a degree, the presentation of a concentration of study in one subject or field, is usually accomplished by the system of majors and minors. All the colleges of this group with one exception, Gooding College, require a major for graduation. Gooding College has not yet accumulated sufficient resources to permit the offering of as much as a major of work in any considerable number of subjects; as a result, the students are graduated without having met any requirement for concentration.

The other colleges not only require a major but most of them also require one minor, and a few require two minors. The development of the divisional organization has frequently accompanied the introduction of a plan for a field of concentration to replace the usual requirement of a major. The distinction between the major and the field of concentration lies in the fact that the major is usually limited to courses in a single department (occasionally a small amount of credit is accepted from a closely related department), while the field of concentration cuts across depart mental boundaries, choosing the subjects most closely related to the general field of interest of the student.

In several colleges the requirements for the major or the field of concentration relate only to the subjects taken in the upper two years; in others, the entire four-year program is considered. The former plan is newer and in many respects preferable to the latter. The major purpose of the first two years should be the completion of the student's general education; the last two years should be devoted to the process of specialization. To make the graduation requirements for concentration depend partially upon work taken in the first two years is to encourage a too early specialization.

As would be expected from the diversity of plans for securing concentration, the requirements for a major or field of concentration in this group of colleges vary considerably. The range is from eighteen hours to thirty-six hours, with twenty-four as the number most frequently indicated. Not only is there a range among the institutions, but within some of the colleges the amount varies for the different departments.

The third type of requirement, a distribution of studies, is typically obtained by two plans: (1) setting up a minimum amount of credit which must be presented from each of several subjects or fields of study; (2) a limitation upon the total amount of credit that will be accepted in any one subject. Two requirements for distribution are nearly always set up in terms of the specific subject to be taken. These are English composition and physical education. These may be looked upon, not as a distribution requirement, but as tool subjects or necessary skills. They are typically set up, however, along with the other distribution requirements. Several of the colleges include not only English composition but some English literature in their requirements. The English composition requirement is generally a three-hour course for the entire freshman year. Physical education is usually required for two years, but some colleges require only one year. Meetings are usually for one hour twice a week, the time being devoted to gymnastic and recreational exercises.

Besides these two specific subject requirements, there are typically four groups of studies from which the student must present a minimum amount of credit. These groups are foreign language, mathematics and science, social studies, and philosophy and religion. The requirement in the last-mentioned group frequently is limited to the single subject of Bible, although several colleges permit students to choose between Bible courses and courses in philosophy.

The amount of foreign language required for graduation varies because of the general policies regarding this requirement and the differences in the practice of accepting language taken in high school toward meeting the requirement. All the colleges but one, Kansas Wesleyan, require some language for graduation; Kansas Wesleyan has grouped foreign language with education, and students can satisfy the requirement of this group by taking education instead of foreign language. In a few of the colleges the entire foreign language requirement can be met by the presentation of high-school language, but the typical requirement of those institutions that take high-school language into account is at least six semester hours of language taken in college, regardless of the amount taken in high school.

The typical amount specified as a total requirement is the equivalent of two years of college language, a degree of advancement that usually represents a reading knowledge. Some of the colleges go beyond this amount and require two languages. The requirements at Mount Union and Brothers College are perhaps the most extreme. Mount Union requires one year of Latin or one year of Greek, in addition to high-school Latin, and at least two years of modern foreign language. The modern language requirements can be met by high-school language. Brothers College requires all students to have an acquaintance with at least one ancient language. Students presenting three high-school units of Latin or Greek for admission are not required to continue the study of ancient language, but are advised to do so. In addition, the college requires for graduation a reading knowledge of two modern foreign languages, or a command of one modern foreign language. These requirements are not based upon course credits but upon demonstrated proficiency.

The requirements in mathematics and natural science vary considerably. Typically, no account is taken of high-school studies in setting up this requirement, although a few colleges allow excess credits in mathematics over and above the minimum entrance requirement to be used toward the credits needed in this field. The amount required varies from as little as six hours up to sixteen or eighteen hours. Perhaps the most common arrangement consists of a required course in mathematics plus a choice of one year of any laboratory science.

The requirements in the social sciences are typically smaller in amount and present a broader opportunity for choice than is the case with the foreign language or the mathematics and science requirements. A few of the colleges have no requirement for any social science toward the degree. The amount most commonly indicated is six hours, and twelve hours is the largest amount required by any college of the group.

The requirement in the general field of philosophy and Bible and religion is, as has already been indicated, limited by many colleges to a choice from courses in the Bible department. In many cases the actual course itself is specified. Only one college has no requirement in this field, although in three or four cases this field is bracketed with the social studies in arranging the plan of distribution. The requirements in philosophy and religion range from two to fourteen hours in the colleges that have such a requirement.

The limitation on the total amount of work that may be presented in one subject varies considerably, and is not found in all colleges. This limit usually is in the neighborhood of forty-five semester hours.

The fourth type of a degree requirement is that relating to the quality of work done. All the colleges issue marks or grades to indicate the quality of work done by students in courses. A very common plan provides a certain number of "points" for each grade. If the grades are set up in a five-point scale, A, B, C, D, and E, the highest grade, A, may be given three points; B, two points; C, one point; D, the lowest passing grade, no points; and E, failure, no points, or a negative point. Under this arrangement the graduation requirement typically specifies the presentation of credit "points" equal to the number of credits. This means that the student must maintain an average somewhat above passing in order to graduate. Gooding College has an even more stringent regulation than this, requiring that two-thirds of the work presented for the degree must be of grade B or better. In practice, this rule has not worked well, and consideration is being given to its abandonment.

Central Wesleyan College follows the plan of scaling the amount of credit in accordance with the grade earned. Thus, in a three-credit course a student earning the highest grade, which carries 20 per cent additional credit, will have the amount recorded as 3.6 credits. One receiving the second highest grade, carrying 10 per cent additional credit, receives 3.3 credits. One receiving a grade of "inferior" suffers a 10 per cent reduction in credit, and has the amount recorded as 2.7 credits.

Several of the colleges have the plan of granting degrees with "honors." The requirements for graduation honors are typically set up in terms of the average grade points per credit. Students attaining honors have this fact inscribed on their diplomas.

CHAPTER XXII

CURRICULUMS IN THE FINE ARTS

GENERAL PURPOSES OF INSTRUCTION IN THE FINE ARTS

Among the recent developments in higher education is the increasing importance attached to education in the fine arts. These arts are more and more regarded as disciplines highly desirable in the cultural development of the individual and of society.[1] The recognition of their importance is attested by the facilities which institutions of higher learning are providing for education in this field.

Three types of students are interested in the fine arts; consequently there are three important forms of education in these arts: (*a*) education of the professional artist, such as the professional musician (composer, performer, teacher), the painter, the sculptor, the designer, the illustrator, and the teacher of art; (*b*) education of the amateur, who does not need to use his training in a professional way but who desires it for his own culture and enjoyment; (*c*) education of the lover of art to heighten his understanding and appreciation. All these types of fine arts education demand attention, and they may well have a place in any institution of higher learning that attempts to serve students with a variety of interests. The first-mentioned type of education in the fine arts is desired by a relatively small number of students. Obviously, the number of colleges which should offer much of the first type of art education should be limited to those which are well recognized both in academic and artistic circles and are staffed with very competent teachers.

The second type of fine arts education should reach a much larger number of students than the first. The majority of these students are engaged principally in other departments of the institution and study music or art as a minor subject. Some of these students, however, desire a college education; but their principal interest is in music or art. For them a major in music or art should be provided.

The third type of fine arts education should reach a very large number of students. For it no technical training and prerequisites are necessary, and only a relatively short time need be devoted to it.

---

[1] For an interesting discussion of this point of view see Harold L. Butler, "The Fine Arts: Music, Art, and Architecture," in *Higher Education in America*, ed. R. A. Kent (Boston: Ginn & Co., 1930), pp. 243–61.

MUSIC

The thirty-five colleges included in the study present an interesting cross-section of musical education in the colleges of the country. All but one of them—Brothers College—offer some music. In Dickinson College the offering is limited to one course in the history and appreciation of music; Union College has no department of music, although it offers a few theoretical and practical courses, for which a limited amount of credit is given. All of the other thirty-two colleges offer fairly well-developed programs of instruction in music.

Purposes of music instruction.—The expressed purposes of the music instruction offered by the colleges illustrate a variety of aims. Seventeen state their purposes. Several of these statements are representative of the group. At Albion College the aim is

to develop in the student an intelligent and appreciative attitude toward music; to train capable teachers, performers, church organists, and choir leaders who shall be inspired to be of social service after graduation in the communities where they live.

The University of Chattanooga, through its Department of Music, aims to provide such facilities

as will enable the student not only to develop his own talent, but also to learn to appreciate music, to become familiar with the development of music, and to participate in its cultural benefits and values.

The courses of the Music Department at Ohio Wesleyan University are designed to serve both as a background for later professional training and as cultural courses for the general students.

All of these statements emphasize the general rather than the professional values of music education.

Several colleges that have schools or conservatories of music also state their aims. The Baldwin-Wallace Conservatory

aims to develop musicians in a broad and thorough way in order that they may be prepared to meet the demands made upon professional musicians today.

The purpose of the School of Music of Dakota Wesleyan University is somewhat broader—

to give its students a complete education in the science and art of music, and to prepare them for professional careers, both as artists and teachers; also to maintain a musical atmosphere in the University life and to cultivate a taste for good music.

The School of Music of Nebraska Wesleyan University has as its object

to afford all students a thorough, symmetrical, and comprehensive education in music.

The aim of the College of Music of Kansas Wesleyan University is

to produce not alone performers but musicians of culture and educational background; to equip young men and women for professional work in the studio, the school, the church, and the concert platform; to train teachers who know their subject and who know how to present this material according to modern psychological methods.

One of the longer statements is made by Illinois Wesleyan University, as follows:

The School of Music proposes to teach those who wish to make a serious study of music and to teach this art in the fullest and highest sense, so that its students may become men and women of highest ideals and usefulness as artists and teachers of attainment. There is also that ever increasing class who recognize that a knowledge of music and musical literature is a vital part of a liberal education; and, being conscious of this fact, it is the aim of the School of Music not to develop those professionally interested in music only, but to be of vital value in the life of every student in the University.

These statements show that the schools or conservatories of music generally place the emphasis on the professional training of musicians, although not omitting the objective of general cultural education in this subject.

Course offerings in music.—The total number of semester hours of instruction offered in music, not including applied music, varies from 117 at the College of the Pacific to four at Dickinson College, excluding Brothers College and Union College, which have no departments of music. Table 44 shows the number of hours of credit offered in each of three types of work—theory, teaching of music, and music appreciation—together with the fields in which majors in music are offered.

Instruction in the teaching of music may be had in twenty-seven of the colleges, and twenty-three of them offer courses in music appreciation. The most frequently offered majors in applied music curriculums are in voice and piano, though most of the colleges also offer majors in school music, organ, and violin. Five of them offer majors in violoncello and one— the College of Puget Sound—a major in band.

Organization of the instruction in music.—The offerings in music are variously organized, as follows: (1) in conservatories of music, twelve colleges; (2) in schools of music, seven colleges; (3) in departments of music, five colleges; (4) in divisions of fine arts, three colleges; (5) in a college of music, one college; (6) in a school of fine arts, one college; (7) in a division of music, one college; (8) in a department of fine arts, one college; (9) in a college without a department, two colleges. Obviously, the work in music

TABLE 44

NUMBER OF HOURS OF CREDIT OFFERED IN MUSIC, NOT INCLUDING APPLIED
MUSIC, AND THE MAJORS IN APPLIED MUSIC IN
THIRTY-THREE† COLLEGES

COLLEGE	SEMESTER HOURS IN MUSIC NOT INCLUDING APPLIED MUSIC			MAJORS OFFERED IN APPLIED MUSIC					
	Theory, Chorus, Band, and Orchestra	Teaching of Music	Appreciation	Voice	Piano	Violin	Organ	School Music	Others
*Albion..........	36	14	2	X	X	X	X	X	......
*Allegheny.......	18	......	2	......	......	......	......	......	......
*Baker..........	54	22	2	X	X	X	......	X	X
Baldwin-Wallace.	35	10	2	X	X	X	X	X	
Central Wesleyan	25	......	......	X	X	X	X	......	
*Chattanooga....	14	3	2	X	X	......	X	......	
*Cornell.........	26	......	2	X	X	X	X	X	
Dakota Wesleyan	46	16	4	X	X	X	......		
*DePauw........	60	36	4	X	X	X	X	X	X
*Dickinson.......	......	......	4	......	......	......			
Evansville.......	15	8	2	......	......	......			
Gooding........	34	4	2	......	......	......			
*Hamline........	28	6	......						
*Illinois Wesleyan.	22	......	4	X	X	X	X	X	
Intermountain...	18	7	4	......	......	......			
Iowa Wesleyan..	38	10	......	X	X	X	X	......	X
Kansas Wesleyan	52	28	2	X	X	X	X	X	......
*Lawrence.......	66	61	......	X	X	X	X	X	X
McKendree.....	41	8	4	X	X	......	X		
*MacMurray.....	46	24	......	X	X	X	X	X	
*Morningside.....	36	28	......	X	X	X	X	X	X
*Mount Union....	34	......	4	X	X	X	......		X
Nebraska Wesley-an............	38	12	......	X	X	X	X	X	
Ohio Northern...	52	27	......	X	X	X	X	X	
*Ohio Wesleyan...	68	8	6	X	X	X	X	X	X
Oklahoma City..	40	30	4	X	X	X	......	X	
Ozark Wesleyan..	29	4	......	X	X	X	......		
*Pacific..........	90	16	1	X	X	......	X	X	X
Puget Sound....	40	2	4	X	X	X	X	X	X
*Simpson........	38	8	2	X	X	X	X	X	
Southwestern....	47	14	4	X	X	X	X	X	
West Virginia Wesleyan.....	43	13	2	X	X	X	X	X	
*Willamette......	28	12	......	X	X	X	......	X	

* Institutions on the approved list of the Association of American Universities.
† Brothers College and Union College offer no courses in music.

is most commonly provided through a major division rather than a department of the college. In several cases the conservatories or schools of music have only a loose connection with the college rather than a well-integrated relationship. It is significant, however, that in eleven of the colleges the instruction in music is organized in departments or divisions of the college of liberal arts.

From the point of view of training the professional musician, the conservatory or school of music has some advantages; but from the point of view of music as a phase of a liberal arts education, there are advantages in having the organization controlled by the faculty which controls the instruction in the liberal arts. Evidence collected in the course of the study indicates unmistakably that a number of the conservatories and schools of music found in these colleges would be more effective if they were reorganized as departments or divisions of the colleges of liberal arts. This step should probably be taken in all the conservatories and schools which have not been, or cannot soon be, accredited by the National Association of Schools of Music. The only colleges of the group whose schools or conservatories of music at the time of the study held membership in the National Association of Schools of Music are: Baldwin-Wallace College (Conservatory of Music); Illinois Wesleyan University (School of Music); MacMurray College (Illinois Conservatory of Music); College of the Pacific (Conservatory of Music); and Southwestern College (School of Fine Arts).

Credit for music toward liberal arts degrees.—Practically all of the colleges which offer music permit a limited amount of credit in music to be counted as elective in fulfilling the requirements for the degree in arts and sciences. The amounts which may be so used vary from four semester hours at Dickinson College to thirty semester hours at Baker University. In most instances half or more of the credit in music used toward the degree in arts and sciences must be in theory courses.

The students who pursue the liberal arts curriculums in twenty-one of the colleges studied may take music as a major. Table 45 lists these colleges, and indicates for each the number of hours constituting a major in music and the number of hours which may be in applied music. These data were compiled from the college catalogues; in a few cases the catalogues did not provide the information on these points.

Usually the major in music consists of a combination of theory and applied music, but in four colleges it appears that the whole major must be in theory courses. All of these twenty-one colleges and a few others offer minors in music for students in liberal arts curriculums. These arrangements indicate a progressive attitude toward education in music as an important part of a liberal arts education, and they show a commendable desire on the part of the colleges to serve their clientèle in an up-to-date way. Several other colleges might well give thought to this tendency and make education in music serve groups that are not now reached.

TABLE 45

COLLEGES OFFERING A MAJOR IN MUSIC TOWARD THE BACHELOR'S DE-
GREE IN THE COLLEGE OF LIBERAL ARTS, AND THE NUMBER OF
HOURS IN MUSIC CONSTITUTING THE MAJOR

Colleges Offering a Major in Music toward the Bachelor's Degree in the College of Liberal Arts	Number of Semester Hours of Music Consti- tuting the Major	Number of Hours Which May Be in Applied Music
Albion............................	45	16
Baker............................	24	0
Chattanooga.......................	26	*
Cornell...........................	26	10
Dakota Wesleyan...................	33	0
Hamline..........................	36	12
Intermountain.....................	30	12
Iowa Wesleyan....................	24	12
Kansas Wesleyan..................	24	12
Lawrence.........................	24	10
MacMurray.......................	24	*
Morningside......................	20	0
Mount Union.....................	24	4
Ohio Northern....................	30	10
Ohio Wesleyan....................	24	16
Oklahoma City....................	20	8
Pacific...........................	44	*
Puget Sound......................	*	*
Simpson..........................	20	0
Southwestern.....................	30	10
Willamette.......................	25	9

* Catalogue gives no information.

Degrees in music.—Twelve of the colleges grant no professional degrees in music, while the other twenty-three grant six different degrees, as follows: Bachelor of Music, twenty-one colleges; Bachelor of Music Education, two colleges; Bachelor of School Music, four colleges; Bachelor of Fine Arts (in music), two colleges; Bachelor of Science in Education, one college; Master of Music, two colleges.

The degree Master of Music is somewhat unusual, but two of the colleges are now offering it. At the College of the Pacific this degree may be granted, upon the completion of one year's work in residence, to students who have received their baccalaureate diploma from a music school holding membership in the National Association of Schools of Music. At present the degree is offered only with applied music as the major subject and composition as a secondary subject, or with composition as a major subject. DePauw University began with the year 1931–32 to offer a course leading to the degree of Master of Music. The course of study includes three fields, one of which the student elects as a major. The three fields are advanced theory and composition, advanced musical history and research, and advanced problems in the teaching of music in public schools.

Unsolved problems.—The information presented affords convincing proof of the large place which music holds in the colleges studied. In offering this training a number of problems are evident. The need of further work on the objectives is apparent. Entire agreement has not been reached as to the administration of music training in the colleges. Furthermore, just what should be offered in music and what should be the place of music in a liberal arts education are by no means settled. Nevertheless, there is evidence that the colleges are awaking to the needs and possibilities of education in music as an integral part of liberal arts education.

ART

The graphic arts and sculpture occupy a less favorable position in the colleges studied than does music, as only twenty-three of the institutions offer this instruction. The subject is taught in nineteen colleges by departments of art while in three institutions —MacMurray College, Nebraska Wesleyan University, and Oklahoma City University—it is taught in "schools." Evansville College states that it does not maintain a regularly organized department of art, but two courses are offered in this field for students in education.

Several purposes are stated by the colleges for their offerings in art. Albion College has arranged its work to meet the needs of three classes of students: "First, those who desire to study art for its cultural value; second, those who wish to begin professional art study while pursuing a college course; third, those who intend to become teachers of art." At Ohio Wesleyan University the emphasis is, to a large extent, on professional study, the courses being intended for two groups of students: "(1) Students preparing to enter the professional fields as artists, teachers, architects, interior decorators, designers, illustrators, or the related professions [and] (2) students desiring a knowledge of the fine arts for the purposes of general culture." The courses in art at Oklahoma City University are intended for students who desire to prepare for some branch of art as a profession, and for other students who realize that some knowledge of the fine arts is a necessary part of a general education. The College of the Pacific has arranged its courses in the Art Department to meet the needs of four classes of students: "first, those who desire to study art for its cultural value; second, those who wish to begin professional art study while pursuing a college course; third, those who desire training in graphic expression for its practical use; fourth, those intending to become teachers of art." These various purposes recur throughout the statements of aims made by several other colleges. In Nebraska Wesleyan University the art work is planned primarily for students expecting to take degrees in art.

Table 46 lists the twenty-three colleges that offer work in fine arts, and shows for each the number of semester hours offered both in studio courses and in courses of other types. This table also indicates which colleges accept a major in art toward the liberal arts degree and also the professional degrees offered. The data have been compiled from the latest available catalogues of these colleges.

This table shows that several of the colleges provide rather extensive offerings in art. Oklahoma City University leads in this respect, with 157 semester hours. Other colleges which have made rather large provision in the field are the College of the Pacific (71 semester hours), College of Puget Sound (64 semester hours), Albion College (62 semester hours), Ohio Wesleyan University (54 semester hours), and Nebraska Wesleyan University (46 semester hours).

The offering of a major in art for students who pursue a curriculum in liberal arts seems to be confined to eight of the colleges. Several others provide a minor in art for liberal arts students. Clearly, art does not receive the same recognition as music in the colleges studied. A number of the institutions might well give more attention to education in art, particularly with a view to including it in a cultural education rather than with the view of training the professional artist.

DRAMATIC ART

Dramatic art receives attention in almost all of the colleges included in the study. In fact, apparently only three—Brothers College, Dickinson College, and Union College—offer no practical work in this subject.

This instruction has several purposes. The University of Chattanooga states that it

is planned to meet the needs of several classes of students; those who expect to teach English and consequently will be called upon to direct school plays; those who wish to prepare themselves to take part in or to direct club or church plays;

those who are interested in the theater from the acting or production standpoint, and those who wish a general familiarity with drama and dramatists.

The courses in dramatics at Southwestern College are arranged for three
types of students: first, those desiring platform proficiency and material
for teaching dramatics; second, those desiring the personal training and

TABLE 46

OFFERINGS IN ART IN TWENTY-THREE COLLEGES

COLLEGES	SEMESTER HOURS IN ART		MAJOR FOR THE DEGREE IN LIBERAL ARTS	PROFESSIONAL DEGREE IN ART
	Studio Courses	Other Courses		
Albion.............	54	8	Yes	....
Allegheny.........	....	14	....	....
Baker.............	12	8	....	....
Baldwin-Wallace....	....	2	....	....
Central Wesleyan..	9	2	....	Diploma
Chattanooga......	*	*	....	....
Cornell...........	11	25	Yes	....
DePauw...........	22	13	....	....
Evansville........	....	4	....	....
Gooding..........	*	*	....	....
Hamline..........	9	6	....	....
Illinois Wesleyan..	16	20	....	....
Intermountain.....	....	2	....	....
Kansas Wesleyan..	19	13	....	....
Lawrence..........	....	30	Yes	....
MacMurray.......	....	19	Yes	B.S. in Art Education
Nebraska Wesleyan	20	26	....	B.F.A. in Art
Ohio Wesleyan....	46	8	Yes	Diploma
Oklahoma City....	137	20	Yes	B.F.A. (Painting or Design)
Pacific............	54	17	Yes	....
Puget Sound......	58	6	Yes	....
Southwestern......	26	....	....	....
West Virginia Wesleyan...........	*	*	....	Diploma

* Amount of credit not stated in catalogue.

experience which will fit them for supervising dramatics in the public
high schools; and, third, those with intense professional interest and
marked ability in the drama.

Usually the instruction in dramatics is an adjunct to the work in public
speaking. In fact, twenty-five of the colleges include it in departments of
speech, public speaking, or English. However, two colleges—Lawrence
College and Morningside College—have departments of dramatics; and
Oklahoma City University has a School of Dramatic Art. At Southwest-

ern College the work in dramatics is offered in the School of Fine Arts, and at Nebraska Wesleyan University it forms a part of the service of the School of Expression.

The totals of offerings in dramatics range from two hours at Central Wesleyan College and Evansville College to thirty-nine hours at Ohio Wesleyan University. Oklahoma City University, with thirty-eight hours, is the only other institution offering more than sixteen hours in dramatic art. Eleven other colleges each offer more than ten semester hours of credit in the subject. The median offering for the thirty-two colleges is eight semester hours. The most generally used course titles are play production, play directing, and stage craft. Three colleges—McKendree, Ohio Northern, and Oklahoma City—offer courses in play writing; while Dakota Wesleyan and the College of Puget Sound offer courses entitled "creative dramatics."

The provision for instruction in practical dramatics in these colleges is another evidence of effort to use for educational purposes whatever materials help to stimulate the intellectual growth of the individual and promote the general social welfare.

ATTITUDE OF THE COLLEGES TOWARD THE FINE ARTS

The facts stated above indicate that the colleges studied have taken a friendly attitude toward the fine arts. Although in a number of instances the emphasis is on professional training, most of the colleges realize the importance of the fine arts in a program of liberal education. The future will in all probability see greater attention to this line of study.

CHAPTER XXIII

TEACHER-TRAINING

REASONS FOR TEACHER-TRAINING

Among the recent additions to the curriculums of liberal arts colleges are the professional courses in teacher-training. The causes for this addition are not hard to find. The enormous development of elementary and secondary education has created a demand for many teachers. These positions must be filled by persons who are trained to do the work of teaching in a creditable manner.

Accrediting agencies are more and more demanding that recognized secondary schools have teachers with at least a specified minimum of professional courses in education. Graduates from such high schools have preferential status in the admission lists of the better colleges and universities. This condition sets a requirement of professionally trained teachers which no high school can afford to ignore. Since the graduate of a college is not eligible for the better high-school teaching positions without having had the required amount of education courses, the liberal arts colleges have been forced to incorporate in their curriculums this form of training, although it has not in all cases been a welcome addition.

The reports made to the survey staff show that all of the thirty-five colleges included in the study are now conducting teacher-training work. In some colleges it is fairly well done; in others it might be greatly improved. The attitude toward it varies from whole-hearted enthusiasm to lukewarm tolerance.

FIELDS FOR WHICH TEACHERS ARE TRAINED

Some of the colleges limit their efforts in teacher-training to a very few fields, such as elementary schools, high schools, etc.; others have more elaborate plans calling for the training of teachers for practically every field of teaching. Thus, Willamette University trains only high-school teachers of the more or less usual subjects. Evansville College, Oklahoma City University, and the College of the Pacific each offer preparation for educational service in ten different fields. The majority of the colleges center their efforts in teacher-training on preparation for work in the high schools. Table 47 shows the number of colleges offering training for each field of teaching.

Approximately half of the colleges definitely prepare for teaching in the intermediate and primary grades. It is probably well that the number is no larger, since in many of the colleges the expense involved in providing satisfactory equipment would hardly constitute a wise investment.

SUBJECTS IN WHICH SPECIFIC TRAINING IS OFFERED

The colleges which attempt to train junior or senior high school teachers were asked to state the subjects for which they trained teachers. The

TABLE 47

NUMBER OF COLLEGES OFFERING TEACHER-TRAINING FOR
EACH TEACHING FIELD

Fields	Number of Institutions
Senior high school	35
Junior high school	31
Intermediate grades	18
High-school principal	16
Rural (one room)	13
Primary grades	13
Elementary-school principal	8
Supervisor	7
Superintendent	7
College	5
Kindergarten	4
Director of religious education	3

data show that the average number of subjects for which specific training is offered is eighteen. The range, omitting Brothers College, is from ten subjects at Illinois Wesleyan University to twenty-five subjects at Simpson College.

The colleges offer teacher-training in twenty-nine different subjects. Table 48 lists the subjects in which teachers are trained and the number of these colleges offering training in each.

Twelve of the subjects are listed in thirty or more colleges. Special training is offered for the most part in those subjects which have been in the college curriculum for a long time. Thus, Latin is mentioned as a subject for which teachers are trained by thirty-four colleges. The demand for teachers of Latin is probably decreasing; yet almost all of these four-year colleges continue to train for teaching this subject. The reports seem to indicate that the training of teachers in these colleges is based on the subjects offered and required for graduation rather than on a definitely planned program of teacher-training. This plan may have some advantages from the point of view of the liberal arts college, but it probably

TABLE 48

NUMBER OF COLLEGES OFFERING TEACHER-TRAINING
IN SPECIFIC SUBJECTS

Subjects	Number of Institutions
Latin	34
English	33
Chemistry	33
French	32
Mathematics	31
German	31
History	31
Biology	31
Botany	31
Physics	31
Civics	30
Zoölogy	30
Music	29
Economics	28
Sociology	28
Spanish	24
Physical education	24
Physiology	23
General science	22
Art	20
Physical geography	18
Home economics (not Smith-Hughes)	16
Commercial subjects	11
Home economics (Smith-Hughes)	3
Industrial arts (not Smith-Hughes)	1
Agriculture	1
Speech	1
Business administration	1

will not produce instructors well trained for the subjects they will later teach.

As would be expected, teacher-training in the vocational subjects is, with two or three exceptions, not a prominent feature of the colleges studied. Liberal arts colleges are not usually prepared to train vocational teachers. However, the fact that eleven of the institutions prepare teachers for commercial subjects shows that the colleges are feeling the demand for some training of vocational teachers.

STATE REQUIREMENTS IN TEACHER-TRAINING

The teacher-training programs of practically all of the colleges are greatly influenced by the state requirements for teachers' certificates. Table 49 lists the various ways in which the programs are influenced by state requirements and shows the number of colleges affected by each.

TABLE 49
NUMBER OF COLLEGES INFLUENCED BY VARIOUS STATE CERTIFICATION REQUIREMENTS

Requirements	Number of Institutions
State specifies total hours in education courses for teaching certificate....	33
State specifies education courses which must be completed for certificate..	29
State specifies total hours in each academic field for a certificate valid for high-school teaching in that field..................................	21
State requires the maintenance of practice-teaching facilities............	20
State inspects the teacher-training facilities generally and makes recommendations for changes which must be made if approval is continued...	17
State must approve qualifications of instructors giving education courses..	16
State prescribes separate curriculums for various types of teaching......	15
State specifies the minimum number of academic subjects in which preparation must be made for high-school certificates.......................	12
State specifies the combinations of academic subjects which may be offered for a high-school teaching certificate...............................	9

It is now rather usual for certification agencies to require a certain amount of work in education, a part of which is definitely prescribed. In addition, there is usually a prescription of content subject matter, particularly for high-school teachers. Most of the colleges have taken these requirements into account in setting up their curriculums, but a few have assumed an attitude either of negligence or of superiority in meeting the state prescriptions, much to the embarrassment of students who are faced with two sets of requirements which in some cases are not compatible.

REQUIREMENTS IN PROFESSIONAL COURSES

Most of the colleges studied offer a major in education, but thirty state definitely that students are not encouraged to major in that subject.

In twenty-eight colleges reporting on the proportion of those preparing to teach that are majoring in education, the range is from none to 100 per cent, with an average of 28 per cent. Seven colleges report no majors in education.

TABLE 50

COURSES IN EDUCATION REQUIRED OF STUDENTS PREPAR-
ING FOR TEACHING AT THIRTY-FIVE COLLEGES

Courses	Number of Colleges Requiring
Educational psychology	27
Practice teaching	17
General psychology	14
Methods	12
Principles of education	10
History of education	7
Secondary methods	7
Special methods	6
Principles of secondary education	5
Principles of teaching	4
Educational measurements	4
Secondary education	3
School management	3
High-school administration	3
School administration	3
Introduction to education	3
Principles of elementary education	3
Elementary-school organization and administration	2
Philosophy of education	2
Measurements	1
School organization and management	1
Primary methods	1
Child psychology	1
School law	1
Curriculum-making	1
Technique	1
Modern education	1
Mental tests	1

Table 50 lists the courses required in education for students preparing to teach, and the number of colleges requiring each course.

Only five courses are required by eight or more colleges, with educational psychology occupying the leading rôle. In fact, this is the only subject on which there is almost common agreement among these institutions. If, however, the special methods, secondary methods, technique, and similar subjects are noted, it is apparent that methods play no small part in the teacher-training. Practice teaching is required of those preparing to teach in almost half of the colleges. This is a sign of increasing definiteness in teacher-training in the colleges.

SPECIAL METHODS COURSES

Although the number of colleges requiring the students to pursue special methods courses is small, such courses are offered in all the institutions studied. Table 51 shows for each college the number of subjects in which special methods courses are given and the department responsible for giving this work.

In most institutions the number of fields in which special methods courses are offered is not as large as it should be. No college can, with propriety, state that it prepares teachers in a subject for high-school teaching if it does not offer a special methods course in the subject.

In some colleges there has been much discussion as to who should teach the special methods courses. One idea is that they are courses in education and should be taught by the department of education to assure the proper point of view and purpose. Another idea is that these courses should be taught by the subject-matter departments of the college, in which are found teachers of scholarly training in the content to be taught. It is held that unless these courses are taught by those well schooled in the content, they have no solid foundation. In the colleges studied, the most common practice is to have the special methods courses taught by the subject-matter departments, twenty-six colleges reporting this arrangement. Six colleges report that the courses are taught in the education department, while three report that the courses are taught co-operatively by the education and subject-matter departments.

An arrangement which works satisfactorily in several teacher-training institutions is to have the critic teachers teach the special methods courses. In this way the practice teaching and the methods harmonize and reinforce each other. Where competent critic teachers are available, this plan has decided advantages. In those cases the critic teachers should be included in the faculty of the college and given the rank which their training and experience merit. Service of this kind can usually be secured for a very reasonable figure.

PRACTICE TEACHING

Although only seventeen of the colleges of this group require, or strongly recommend, practice teaching of those preparing to teach, all except four colleges make provision for it. Three methods are employed for this type

TABLE 51

NUMBER OF SUBJECTS IN WHICH SPECIAL METHODS COURSES
ARE GIVEN AND THE DEPARTMENT OFFERING THEM

Institution	Number of Subjects	Department Giving
*Albion......................	10	Subject matter
*Allegheny..................	6	Subject matter
*Baker......................	5	Education
Baldwin-Wallace............	9	Subject matter
Brothers...................	1	Subject matter
Central Wesleyan...........	4	Education
*Chattanooga...............	2	Subject matter
*Cornell...................	8	Subject matter
Dakota Wesleyan...........	8	Subject matter
*DePauw...................	All	Subject matter
*Dickinson..................	3	Subject matter
Evansville..................	5	Education
Gooding....................	3	Subject matter
*Hamline...................	7	Combination†
*Illinois Wesleyan...........	6	Subject matter
Intermountain..............	7	Subject matter
Iowa Wesleyan.............	4	Subject matter
Kansas Wesleyan...........	6	Subject matter
*Lawrence..................	11	Subject matter
McKendree.................	5	Subject matter
*MacMurray................	10	Subject matter
*Morningside...............	3	Subject matter
*Mount Union..............	7	Subject matter
Nebraska Wesleyan.........	9	Combination†
Ohio Northern.............	8	Subject matter
*Ohio Wesleyan.............	10	Education
Oklahoma City.............	11	Subject matter
Ozark Wesleyan............	10	Subject matter
*Pacific....................	11	Combination†
Puget Sound...............	4	Subject matter
*Simpson...................	6	Subject matter
Southwestern...............	2	Subject matter
Union......................	2	Education
West Virginia Wesleyan......	All	Education
*Willamette.................	17	Subject matter
Average................	7	....

* Institutions on the approved list of the Association of American Universities.
† Courses taught co-operatively by the education and the subject-matter departments.

of training. The first is for the institution to maintain a practice school on the campus under full control of the college. Another is for the institution to co-operate with the public school of the community with complete direction of cadets in the hands of the college. The third plan is one of co-operation between the institution and the public school with limited direction of the cadets in the hands of the college. Table 52 shows the number of institutions employing each plan.

TABLE 52

METHODS USED TO PROVIDE PRACTICE-TEACHING FACILITIES
IN THIRTY COLLEGES

Method	Number Using
Maintains practice facilities through co-operation with the public-school system of the community but with complete direction of cadets in hands of the institution..	14
Maintains practice facilities through co-operation with the public-school system of the community but with limited direction of cadets in hands of the institution...	12
Combination of the first plan with one of the other two methods........	3
Maintains practice school on the campus under full control of the institution..	1

Four colleges reported the use of a practice school on the campus under the complete direction of the institution, but in only one college did this plan provide service for all of its prospective teachers. To a very great extent the colleges are relying on the public-school system for their practice-teaching facilities.

In providing for a co-operative plan for practice teaching, one very pertinent problem relates to the selection of the supervising or critic teachers. Of the thirty-four colleges which reported on this question, only one has entire control of the selection of critic teachers; in twenty-one the critic teachers are selected jointly by the public schools and the college; in five the entire responsibility for the selection is in the hands of the public schools; seven colleges have no critic teachers.

Another question is: Who pays the supervising teachers when practice teaching is done in the public schools? On this point there seems to be no general policy. Twenty of the twenty-seven colleges having critic teachers pay for this service. Table 53 summarizes the data regarding the methods of selecting and the arrangement for paying the critic teachers.

Thirty of the colleges reported on the prerequisites which are "rigidly enforced" for practice teaching. These are summarized in Table 54.

Two colleges require no prerequisites; the other demands are scattered over a number of requirements. Again psychology, both educational and

TABLE 53

RELATION BETWEEN THE SELECTING AGENT AND THE ONE PAY-
ING THE CRITIC TEACHERS IN THIRTY-FOUR COLLEGES

Relationship	Number Using
Institution selects and institution pays..................	1
Public-school system selects and public school pays......	1
Joint selection and public school pays..................	6
Joint selection and joint pay..........................	15
Public-school selection and joint pay...................	4
No critic teachers....................................	7

TABLE 54

SPECIFIC PREREQUISITES REQUIRED FOR PRACTICE
TEACHING IN THIRTY COLLEGES

Prerequisites	Number Requiring
Course requirements:	
Educational psychology...........................	10
General psychology...............................	9
Methods...	7
Special methods in subject to be taught.............	5
Principles of education............................	5
Introduction to teaching..........................	3
Child psychology.................................	2
Principles of secondary education...................	2
Technique and observation.........................	2
History of education..............................	1
Organization and administration...................	1
Elementary education.............................	1
Other requirements:	
Academic rank:	
Senior..	7
Junior..	3
Sophomore....................................	4
Specified number of hours in education..............	6
Specific academic grade requirements...............	3
Teaching-field grade requirements..................	3
Specific hour requirement.........................	3
Recommendation by department of specialization.....	1
No prerequisites required..........................	2

general, takes the lead. Methods also ranks very high in the prerequisites. A certain academic rank is a prerequisite in fourteen colleges.

Practice teaching is unquestionably the most important unit in the teacher-training program, and the quality of the provision for this work vitally conditions the excellence of the entire teacher-training program. Relatively few of the colleges studied have a satisfactory arrangement for this service. The occupational distribution of the graduates of these colleges indicates that teacher-training concerns the largest single group of students. If the colleges are going to train teachers, they must do it well. Improvement in facilities for practice teaching is most urgently needed at many of these colleges.

THE PLACEMENT AND FOLLOW-UP OF TEACHERS

At the present time institutions which train teachers for any kind of vocational work generally maintain some form of placement bureau. Some colleges merely list the names and qualifications of their students and make this list available to employers, while others definitely seek positions for their graduates.

Various agencies handle this work, such as the department in which the student is enrolled, a committee, a secretary or someone designated for that purpose, the extension department, or the alumni association. In the colleges studied, the placement of teachers is handled by a committee in four cases; by the head of the department of education, or a professor of education, in sixteen cases; and by the dean, registrar, or a secretary in ten cases. Twenty-five colleges report the results of this work as satisfactory; two report it as only partially so; and three report it as unsatisfactory.

Another phase of student service which the college is coming more and more to give is the keeping in touch with the graduates of the teacher-training courses to estimate their success in service. There are three reasons why the institution should do this. One of the best indications of the success of the work of a school is the degree to which its graduates succeed. The life of any school depends on the success it has in training its students for their specific places in life. In the second place, to know wherein graduates are failing enables the school to modify its curriculum or methods in such a way as to reduce these failures to a minimum. A third reason why graduates should be followed up in service is to discover those teachers who have achieved outstanding success in their work and to recommend them for promotion to better positions. The service also may well operate to assist graduates to avoid places where they have little opportunity to make good. Twenty-two of the institutions studied report such service; it is probable that many others will institute it before long.

CONCLUSION

The facts presented show that the colleges of this group have made important provision for training teachers, especially in a few fields. This provision is closely related to the requirements for teachers' certificates; as those requirements increase, the colleges must seek to adapt their work to meet the new conditions. A study of the facts convinces one that most of these colleges still have much improvement to make before their teacher-training reaches a high standard. Barely to meet certification requirements is not a sufficient goal. A college should strive for excellence in its teacher-training as well as in all its other work; anything else is unworthy of an institution that desires to serve its students well. If teacher-training is to be done, it should not be a makeshift; it should have the sympathetic interest and co-operation of the whole college. Unless the attitude of the college is right, the highest success will not attend the efforts put forth by those immediately in charge of the work.

CHAPTER XXIV

CURRICULUMS IN OTHER SPECIAL FIELDS

HOME ECONOMICS

Education in home economics may serve two purposes. Large numbers of women who do not desire to specialize in this field are nevertheless interested in it because it will sooner or later enter into their lives in an important way as they become homemakers. A great variety of problems relating to the family budget, nutrition, home decoration, child care, etc., take on new meaning and importance when they are studied in a scientific way.

Another group of women, a relatively smaller number, wish to become teachers of home economics, dietitians, managers of tea rooms, etc.; and they should have access to courses in home economics for professional purposes. With this group of students the liberal arts colleges are not usually greatly concerned, because the technical schools make better provision for them than the small, independent college of liberal arts can generally afford.

Home economics as a widely adopted subject of study in higher education is a comparatively new development. Only recently have the scientific materials for teaching purposes been developed and the subject placed on a basis which appeals to students of college grade. Even now, the value and proper position of home economics in higher education, particularly in the liberal arts college, are by many college administrators and students neither understood nor appreciated. Consequently, it is not unusual to find rather progressive coeducational colleges without any facilities for instruction in home economics, while in other colleges that have made provision for it the work languishes and sometimes is eventually abandoned.

Of the colleges studied, twenty offer home economics during the academic year. Central Wesleyan College offers home economics during the summer session only. A few of the colleges are giving the Smith-Hughes program for the training of teachers of home economics.

Nine of the colleges state the purposes of their work in home economics. Of these, eight definitely include the training of home economics teachers as a purpose, and five others make mention of training for institutional work and for other professional lines. Seven colleges specify homemaking

238

as an objective in this work; one specifies general knowledge; and two specify cultural purposes. Only two colleges mention the purpose of laying a basis for graduate study in this field. MacMurray College includes, among its purposes in home economics, the training of the individual "to live in society as a useful citizen"; and it states that the courses in home economics "together with all subjects correlated therewith are designed to emphasize the civic, moral and economic responsibility of the individual home to the community and instruct in the right care of human life in the home." A somewhat similar purpose is found at Willamette University, the aim of whose Department of Home Economics is "to provide courses which will give students a working knowledge of the problems of the home and the community, and a realization of woman's responsibilities as a homemaker and a citizen." It is stated by DePauw University that the training in home economics "should give intelligent homemakers not only the technical and practical phases of home making, but also a fine sense of family relationships and a rather definite philosophy of home life."

The range of course offerings in home economics in the twenty colleges teaching this subject is from six to fifty-two semester hours, with a median of thirty-nine semester hours (see Table 39). Most of the colleges teaching home economics offer enough for a major. Hamline University, which has no Department of Home Economics, offers two courses—one on child welfare in the Department of Sociology, and one on food analysis in the Department of Chemistry, which are considered as being in this general field. The two lines of work having the largest offerings in these colleges are foods and clothing.

There are a number of problems connected with the home economics work of the colleges. First, the departments for the most part emphasize vocational purposes, particularly the training of teachers. Most of the students enrolled in home economics courses are pursuing them for vocational purposes and, except in a very small number of colleges, few students take home economics as elective work. As a result, enrolments are low and the courses become very expensive per unit of student credit. This is a serious weakness from the point of view of the liberal arts college. It shows that the institutions have not yet realized the part home economics should have in a general education. Second, with few exceptions the laboratories for home economics are entirely inadequate. In fact, not a few of them would fail to measure up to the home economics laboratories now found in well-equipped high schools. Under such conditions the home economics work is not apt to attract any great amount of favorable attention from students.

Serious question should be raised regarding the offering in these colleges of a program for the training of Smith-Hughes teachers of home economics. The curriculum for Smith-Hughes training is rather highly specialized and demands a comparatively large amount of technical training. The demand for Smith-Hughes teachers in most states is very limited, and the state institutions are usually equipped to provide all the teachers of this type that are necessary. The small four-year college cannot provide equipment for the teaching of the highly specialized courses that compares favorably with that of the larger institutions. When this work is given in the small college for small groups of students, it is extremely expensive. Finally, the whole spirit of this program is completely at variance with the liberal arts idea of general culture. In view of all these facts, it would seem wise for these colleges to abandon the attempt to give Smith-Hughes training in home economics.

In general, it may be said that a few of the colleges are fairly successful with their home economics; but, for the most part, this instruction has not yet found a place in the colleges on a plane that makes it a worth-while subject for students interested principally in a cultural education.

BUSINESS ADMINISTRATION

The phenomenal development of education in commerce and business administration is reflected in this group of thirty-five colleges. Thirty-four of these institutions offer one or more courses in this type of work, other than economics, though, to be sure, not nearly all of them offer complete curriculums in commerce and business administration.

Several of the colleges have definitely stated the aims of their work in this field. The purpose of the Department of Economics and Business Administration at Illinois Wesleyan University is

to give students a well-rounded training in the principles underlying general business, with some specialization, as well as a background for practical living and appreciation of the higher ideals of life.

At Hamline University the curriculum outlined in business administration

is recommended to those students who wish to combine a cultural training with considerable training for business such as will materially shorten their apprenticeship in the business world.

The curriculum at Ohio Northern University has been planned

to meet the needs of students who expect to do graduate work in the field of economics or business administration as well as those who intend to enter industry after graduation from college.

At Southwestern College the courses are designed to serve three classes of students:

First, those students who desire a general preparation for a business career; secondly, those preparing for graduate work in economics or business; finally, all students who desire practical and cultural courses in economics and business.

By far the most detailed and careful statement of aims is that of De-Pauw University, which is stated as follows:

The department of economics offers courses with the following aims: (a) that the important discoveries and advances in the upper levels of economic science may, through the process of education, find their way to the lower levels of education, and more fully pervade and influence the thinking of greater masses of people; (b) that students may understand the economic life about them; (c) that students may develop themselves in such a way that they may more intelligently make important decisions in matters affected with an economic interest; (d) that some students get an adequate knowledge of economics and lead group thinking in economic matters; (e) that educated leaders may engage in a higher degree of economic statesmanship when directing civic and national affairs.

The University of Chattanooga has arranged a special curriculum for the completion of which the degree of Bachelor of Business Administration is conferred. Its aims are stated as follows:

The purpose of the course of study leading to the degree . . . . is to provide college training especially adapted to the needs of students preparing for business. This preparation for practical business life includes, as a cultural basis for the general business training, a study of those subjects regularly required in a liberal arts course. In other words, the course does not aim to give that type of training for business offered by the private business colleges, but rather to make possible an adequate general preparation for business *in addition to* a two-year study of basic liberal arts courses.

This field of interest has been rather well provided for in a majority of the colleges included in the study. Twelve offer 40 or more semester hours of credit in commerce and administration, not including courses in economics and labor problems, as follows: Ohio Wesleyan University, 83; University of Chattanooga, 71; DePauw University, 62; College of Puget Sound, 60; Lawrence College, 60; Southwestern College, 59; Oklahoma City University, 58; Nebraska Wesleyan University, 57; Simpson College, 56; West Virginia Wesleyan College, 49; Cornell College, 47; Baker University, 42. Nine other colleges offer from 30 to 39 credit hours, while twelve offer less than 30 credit hours.

A line of study which is in some respects closely related to business administration is secretarial training. For women, secretarial training is especially attractive. During normal times it offers good vocational opportunities, and for the colleges it provides an outlet for their graduates, now that the opportunities to place graduates in teaching positions are decreasing.

Eight of the colleges provide courses in secretarial training. All too frequently these courses are on a two-year basis and are pursued by freshmen and sophomores. The work of a capable secretary involves a broad

TABLE 55

Courses in Commerce and Business Administration and the Average Number of Semester Hours Offered in Each Type of Work in Thirty-four Colleges

Courses	Number of Colleges Offering the Course	Mean Number of Semester Hours Offered in the Colleges Giving Such Courses
Money and banking............	30	3.7
Accounting....................	28	10.8
Business law..................	24	4.5
Marketing.....................	23	3.0
Business organization..........	23	4.1
Business finance...............	21	4.7
Public finance.................	20	2.9
Transportation................	20	3.1
Problems......................	18	4.4
Advertising and selling.........	17	4.7
Advanced theory..............	13	3.6
Statistics.....................	12	3.0
International trade.............	12	2.7
Insurance.....................	10	3.4
Risk, cycles, and forecasts......	9	3.6
Secretarial work...............	8	13.2
Public utilities.................	4	3.0

training, such as a full college course gives, in addition to certain technical accomplishments. For this reason the colleges offering secretarial training should make every effort to strengthen it and place it on a four-year basis.

Table 55 presents a classification of the courses offered in commerce and business administration, together with the number of colleges offering work in each field and the average number of semester hours offered in each field.

The offerings in commerce and business have been placed under seventeen groups, as shown in the table. Ten fields of work are well represented, money and banking and accounting being in the lead from the point of view of the number of colleges offering these courses. In the average number of hours offered, other than in secretarial work, accounting takes the lead. This is due to the fact that a considerable amount of study in this subject is necessary for the attainment of proficiency.

Nine of the colleges studied have devised curriculums in business administration, which in most cases consist of curriculums in liberal arts with a major in business administration. Special degrees are conferred for the completion of these curriculums, as follows: Bachelor of Commercial Science, Kansas Wesleyan University; Bachelor of Business Administration, University of Chattanooga; Bachelor of Science in Business Administration, Evansville College, MacMurray College, Nebraska Wesleyan University, Ohio Northern University, and Simpson College; Bachelor of Arts in Business Administration, College of Puget Sound.

It would seem apparent that the work in commerce and business administration is adequate for the needs of the colleges. One of the tasks with which colleges offering this work are confronted is to prevent these practical courses from destroying the idea of a liberal arts education. For these colleges to organize the business administration courses on a professional basis seems beyond their province if they wish to remain fundamentally liberal arts colleges. However, to include such work as an important part of a liberal arts education should, if it is properly managed, bring added strength to the liberal arts colleges and provide them unusually fine opportunities to render a much needed social service as well as to minister to the practical needs of their students.

CHAPTER XXV

PROFESSIONAL AND PREPROFESSIONAL CURRICULUMS

PROFESSIONAL STUDY

Although the colleges of this group are all essentially colleges of liberal arts, several of them offer professional curriculums. The four fields represented are pharmacy, law, engineering, and nursing.

Pharmacy.—The only education in pharmacy in the colleges is given at Ohio Northern University. The College of Pharmacy of that institution, established in 1885, is a fully accredited member of the American Association of Colleges of Pharmacy. Only high-school graduates are admitted to the two curriculums offered, one of which includes three years of study and leads to the degree of Pharmaceutical Graduate, and the other covers four years of work and leads to the degree of Bachelor of Science in Pharmacy. The enrolment in the College of Pharmacy at the time of the survey visit (October, 1930) was 137.

Law.—Training in law is offered in four of these colleges. Ohio Northern University maintains a College of Law with an enrolment of fifty students (October, 1930). A three-year curriculum, based on two years of college work and leading to the degree of Bachelor of Laws, is offered. The college is not accredited by the Association of American Law Schools or the American Bar Association.

Willamette University also maintains a College of Law. This law school has a unique advantage in its proximity to the Supreme Court of Oregon. It offers the usual three-year curriculum, based on two years of college work, and the degree of Bachelor of Laws. The College of Law is not accredited by the Association of American Law Schools or the American Bar Association.

At the time of the survey visit the College of the Pacific maintained a Department of Law which offered fifty-eight semester hours of course work. This work has recently been discontinued.

Dickinson College has an affiliated School of Law, but this institution is not directly connected with the college. The college has a Department of Law which offers a total of twenty-four semester hours of course work. Students looking forward to entering the School of Law are allowed to carry, as a part of the college course, three hours a week of law throughout the junior year and six hours throughout the senior year. By judicious election and a little extra work good students may save one year in their subsequent course in the School of Law.

Engineering.—The only college studied that maintains a College of Engineering is Ohio Northern University. Training is offered in four fields of engineering: chemical, mechanical, electrical, and civil. The enrolments in these various curriculums at the time of the survey visit were 29, 40, 65, and 82, respectively. All of the curriculums are four years in length.

At the time it was surveyed, Evansville College maintained a College of Engineering offering several four-year curriculums. Since that time the four-year program has been abandoned. Under an arrangement entered into with Purdue University, the college now offers two-year curriculums in chemical, civil, electrical, and mechanical engineering. Students who complete any of these curriculums with satisfactory grades may enter Purdue University with junior standing. Those who desire to enter other engineering schools are able to plan their work to cover, in general, the work of the first two years. For these curriculums the college offers thirty-one semester hours of work in engineering. Evansville College is fortunate in having made this excellent arrangement with a strong school of engineering.

The College of the Pacific has no school or college of engineering, but it offers a major in engineering for the degree of Bachelor of Arts. For this purpose a well-organized curriculum has been devised, which includes a liberal amount of mathematics, physics, chemistry, and engineering. An interesting feature in the engineering offerings are three courses in aeronautics with a total of ten and one-half semester hours of credit.

The only other college of the group which lists any considerable amount of work in engineering is Cornell College. It offers forty-three semester hours of introductory work, which includes such courses as surveying, applied mechanics, roads and pavements, hydraulics, electricity and magnetism, and sanitary engineering. These courses are apparently designed for students who will later pursue further specialized study in a professional school.

Nursing.—Seven of the colleges studied have made some arrangement for including nurses' training as a part of the college course for students who desire such work. Young women who have completed ninety-five semester hours of academic work at DePauw University with 120 credit points, including certain prescribed courses and twenty hours of a major, may transfer to the Nurses Training School in Indianapolis and receive the Bachelor of Arts degree after completing the professional nurses' course. Illinois Wesleyan University has an arrangement with a neighboring hospital whereby students may pursue a five-year combined college and professional course leading to the degree of Bachelor of Science and the Graduate Nurses' Diploma. The curriculum for nurses at Kansas Wesleyan University consists of two years of work. MacMurray College has an arrangement with a hospital in its vicinity to offer a combined arts-nursing curriculum. Nebraska Wesleyan University offers a two-year preprofessional curriculum in nursing, and grants the degree of Bachelor of Science upon graduation from a training course in either of two affiliated hospitals. Students at Ohio Wesleyan University who have completed ninety-four semester hours of credit with the grade of at least B and have met all the regular group requirements are granted leave of absence for the senior year and given the degree of Bachelor of Arts on completing the course of nursing in the White Cross Hospital School for Nurses. The College of Puget Sound has entered into an agreement with the Tacoma General Hospital whereby a student may take a five-year course in nursing—three years at the college and two years at the hospital—and receive the degree of Bachelor of Science and a Certificate of Nursing.

Although these plans look well on paper, very little evidence has been found to indicate that they attract more than an occasional student in any of the colleges. Nursing education is not yet generally on a plane which demands a college foundation, though it is undoubtedly true that nurses with advanced general education have a greater opportunity of securing the administrative positions in hospitals and clinics than have nurses not so well educated.

PREPROFESSIONAL CURRICULUMS

It has become rather usual for colleges of liberal arts to devise more or less definite curriculums for students who wish, either before or after graduation from college, to pursue training for a profession. In several fields of professional study a part of the preprofessional training is prescribed either by national professional organizations or by the professional schools themselves. Such is the case in medicine and dentistry and, to some extent, in law. To provide the proper guidance for students many colleges have found it well to lay down plans for them to follow, both in the interest of meeting the requirements of the professional schools and for the purpose of affording a broad training for the student. The planning of these curriculums is a duty which colleges should not neglect.

All too frequently the curriculums printed are little more than an effort to combine the requirements of the professional schools with the college requirements for a degree. Such a basis for preprofessional curriculums is a doubtful one. A curriculum designed to prepare for professional study might well neglect the college requirements and aim directly at enlarging the experience of the student in those things which will be most useful to him as a citizen and as a broad-minded practitioner of his profession, as

TABLE 56

PREPROFESSIONAL CURRICULUMS PROVIDED IN TWENTY-ONE COLLEGES

COLLEGE	MEDICINE Years			DENTISTRY Years			LAW Years			ENGINEERING Years			THEOLOGY Years
	2	3	4	1	2	3	2	3	4	2	3	4	4
Albion		×					×	×			×		
Allegheny	×											×	
Baker			×								×		
Baldwin-Wallace			×									×	
Chattanooga	×	×						×					
Dakota Wesleyan		×				×	×			×			
DePauw		×											
Evansville	×									×			
Gooding	×						×			×			
Hamline		×	×				×			×			×
Illinois Wesleyan			×				×			×			×
Kansas Wesleyan	×						×			×			
McKendree	×									×			
Morningside	×												
Nebraska Wesleyan	×		×	×	×		×		×		×	×	×
Ohio Northern	×				×		×			×			×
Oklahoma City	×	×					×	×		×			
Puget Sound		×			×					×	×		×
Southwestern	×		×				×			×	×		×
West Virginia Wesleyan	×									×			
Willamette			×										

well as laying the definite academic basis for the more advanced scientific study.

Twenty-one of the colleges studied publish preprofessional curriculums in their catalogues. The other fourteen make only general statements or neglect preprofessional curriculums altogether. A number of the colleges outline more than one preprofessional curriculum in some of the fields. Table 56 lists the colleges that publish preprofessional curriculums and indicates the fields in which they are provided and the length of each.

The greatest variety is apparent in these curriculums. In three of the colleges such preprofessional curriculums as are offered are four years in length, that is, they consist of a regular college course which includes the subjects presumably of special value to the professional student. The medical schools all require at least two years of preprofessional work for admission; a few definitely require more. Twelve of the colleges have preprofessional curriculums in medicine on the two-year basis. In dentistry the usual requirement is one year of preprofessional study in college; but all except one of the predental curriculums in the colleges studied are on a two- or three-year basis. In law and engineering the preprofessional curriculums are two, three, or four years in length. Since schools of theology now generally require college graduation as an entrance requirement, the pretheological curriculums are all four years in length.

The preprofessional curriculums at Albion College are all on a three-year basis. In reality these curriculums consist of the first three years of combined literary-professional curriculums which are given in collaboration with several outstanding universities, the student taking the first three years of his work at Albion College and receiving his degree of Bachelor of Arts from the college on the completion of one year in the professional school. Albion College has discovered that this arrangement tends to hold for the junior year many students who would otherwise transfer at the end of the sophomore year.

Combined literary-professional curriculums are offered by at least sixteen more of the colleges studied. These curriculums usually require the completion of three years of work at the college, which in most cases must include the required courses for the degree. The college degree is awarded at the completion of one year in the professional school. Southwestern College awards the degree to the student in medicine when he has completed his second year of work. Nebraska Wesleyan University requires that only two years of the combined curriculums in medicine and dentistry be completed before the student leaves for the professional school, and it awards the degree to the student when he has completed two years in medicine or dentistry.

Apparently there is a considerable difference of opinion among the colleges studied on the value of definitely arranged preprofessional and combined curriculums. A number of the institutions have planned such curriculums and published them for the guidance of their students. Other colleges, however, make no pretense at this type of advice to the student except as he counsels with the administrative authorities.

CHAPTER XXVI

GRADUATE WORK

THE PURPOSE OF GRADUATE WORK

The main purposes of graduate work have heretofore been the advancement of knowledge through research and the training of research scholars, professional men, and teachers. These purposes imply highly specialized work which tends to be somewhat narrow and limited in scope. Recently a combination of factors has been stimulating work beyond graduation for purposes other than those mentioned above. This has resulted in the addition by some colleges of what might properly be called a fifth year of study rather than a year of graduate work, although the Master's degree is granted for its completion. This work is specialized and usually includes a small amount of original investigation, but its primary purpose is the more or less thorough mastery of a field of study rather than the mastery of research techniques. Although the distinction between this work and true graduate study is recognized, throughout this discussion for the sake of brevity this advanced training given to students holding the Bachelor's degree will be referred to as "graduate work."

It is the latter type of advanced study which is more and more finding a place in the strong liberal arts colleges of the country. At least three, and probably other, factors are producing a demand for it. First, the standards of teaching in the public schools, more especially in the high schools, are constantly being raised. Many of the stronger city school systems and a few states are already demanding high-school teachers with one year of training beyond the Bachelor's degree, and other states are likely to do so in the near future. Second, with the increasing complexity of civilization and the increased wealth and leisure, there are numerous students who are not satisfied with a four-year college course. The specialization in the upper college years tends to stimulate students to further study. Third, since an increasing percentage of the population is graduating from college, it becomes more and more necessary that those who wish to rise above their fellows have advanced training. These factors are producing an enlarged demand for training beyond the Bachelor's degree, with the result that progressive colleges with adequate funds are developing this work and offering the Master's degree.

GRADUATE WORK IN THE COLLEGES

Eighteen of the thirty-five colleges included in this study enrolled students who had already received the Bachelor's degree. Table 57 presents data showing the number of such students enrolled in each, the number of colleges offering the Master's degree, and the number of Master's degrees conferred during the academic year preceding the survey visit.

TABLE 57

Enrolments of Graduate Students in Eighteen Colleges, Number of These Colleges Offering Master's Degree, and Number of Master's Degrees Awarded by Each during Year Preceding Survey Visit

Institution	Number of Graduate Students Enrolled	Is Master's Degree Offered?	Number of Master's Degrees Awarded during Academic Year
*Pacific............	94	Yes	19
*Ohio Wesleyan......	40	Yes	9
*Willamette.........	13	Yes	....
*Allegheny..........	7	No	....
Nebraska Wesleyan.	6	Yes	....
Southwestern.......	6	No	....
West Virginia Wesleyan............	6	Yes	....
*Albion.............	5	No	....
*Lawrence..........	5	Yes	2
Puget Sound........	5	Yes	....
Central Wesleyan...	4	No	....
*Cornell............	3	Yes	....
*Baker.............	2	Yes	....
Evansville.........	2	No	2
*Hamline...........	2	Yes	....
Baldwin-Wallace....	1	No	....
*DePauw...........	1	Yes	....
*Simpson...........	1	No	....

* Institutions on the approved list of the Association of American Universities.

It will be noted from this table that, although eighteen colleges enrolled postgraduate students, only eleven offer the Master's degree. It is thus evident that many of the so-called "graduate" students were carrying only another year of undergraduate work. Only four of these colleges had granted a Master's degree during the academic year preceding the date of the survey visit. All but two of the eleven colleges which offer the Master's degree are among the largest of the group studied. Three of the colleges offering the Master's degree are not on the approved list of the Association of American Universities.

The two colleges which are doing the greatest amount of graduate work are the College of the Pacific and Ohio Wesleyan University. The teacher-training requirements of the state of California have forced the development of an extensive graduate program in liberal arts in the California institution. Considering its financial limitations, the college is succeeding admirably with this advanced work.

Ohio Wesleyan University has stimulated graduate study by offering fellowships, which require service for half-time and permit study during the rest of the time. For the year 1930–31 there were twenty-one of these fellowships. The graduate work at Ohio Wesleyan is on a very satisfactory basis, and the institution is well equipped for a graduate program in most fields.

With a few notable exceptions the colleges of the group being studied are not sufficiently equipped at present to give good graduate work. Most of them have wisely not tried to develop this type of service, choosing rather to improve their undergraduate offerings before extending their programs to include an expensive development of graduate work. To do graduate work in a satisfactory manner requires extensive libraries, well-equipped laboratories, and faculty members of high scholastic attainment. A number of these colleges, however, will soon be faced with a demand for graduate work, and those which are reasonably well financed and on a sure foundation should prepare to meet the demand.

REQUIREMENTS FOR THE MASTER'S DEGREE

All of the eleven colleges offering the Master's degree require the Bachelor's degree for admission to candidacy. In five of them—DePauw University, Lawrence College, Nebraska Wesleyan University, the College of the Pacific, and the College of Puget Sound—the stated or clearly implied requirement includes also an undergraduate major or practically the equivalent in the major subject of graduate study.

The requirement just stated implies a fair degree of specialization. This is carried further in six of the colleges—Baker University, Hamline University, Nebraska Wesleyan University, College of the Pacific, West Virginia Wesleyan University, and Willamette University—in which the student pursues a major and one or more related minors in his graduate study. At Cornell College the student takes his graduate work chiefly in one department, with a "possible minor" in a related department. De-Pauw University states that, unless for special reasons allowed by the graduate committee, the student's course of study "must not be chosen from one department alone, and must be so selected as to form a consistent whole." At Lawrence College not less than two-thirds of the time must be devoted to a major subject, and not more than one-third of the time *may* be given to an allied minor subject. Ohio Wesleyan University states that the program of graduate study "may include work in one or more departments or fields of study, provided not less than one-half is devoted to a major subject, and the whole shows a consistent plan pursued with a definite purpose." The College of Puget Sound sets as a minimum requirement a total of forty-four hours of combined undergraduate and graduate credit in the field of major interest, which must in all cases include at least twenty hours of graduate credit. Where it is possible under these conditions, a minor *may* be taken in a subject related to the major interest.

A reading knowledge of French or German is required of candidates for the Master's degree in Lawrence College, Nebraska Wesleyan University, and Willamette University. Both Baker University and DePauw University require a reading knowledge of one modern foreign language, preferably French or German. Hamline University requires a reading knowledge of a foreign language, ancient or modern, the language to be determined in conference with the major department, unless the graduate committee excuses the candidate from the requirement. Language requirements are not stated by Cornell College, Ohio Wesleyan University, the College of the Pacific, the College of Puget Sound, and West Virginia Wesleyan College.

A final oral examination constitutes a stated part of the requirement for the Master's degree in seven of the colleges. At Ohio Wesleyan University a final examination on all or a specified part of the work *may* be required at the discretion of the departments concerned. Hamline University requires a final written and oral examination, the latter being held after the thesis has been accepted. The examination at Lawrence College is on the candidate's preliminary training and his major subject, while at Willamette University the candidate must "pass a searching oral examination upon his preliminary training and his entire graduate course." The oral examination at the College of Puget Sound is on the field of specialization and the thesis.

A thesis requirement is general in all these colleges. At Baker University the thesis receives credit for not more than six semester hours, and at Lawrence College for not less than six hours, while at Nebraska Wesleyan University it may count for as many as fifteen semester hours. The College of the Pacific allows four "units" for the thesis, and the College of Puget Sound and Willamette University each allows from four to six semester hours for it. The candidate is required to present from one to three copies of the thesis in its final form.

Only a few of the eleven colleges granting the Master's degree offer work which is stated as "for graduates only." DePauw University offers three courses in education which are "open only to graduate students or experienced teachers, with the consent of the instructor." It also offers a reading course in history, which is open only to students who are enrolled as candidates for the Master's degree. The requirement at Hamline University includes the completion of twenty-four semester hours of work "of a graduate character" in residence at the university, but no strictly graduate courses are listed. Senior college courses offered, as partial fulfilment of this requirement, "must be supplemented to equal that of strictly graduate grade and character."

The most extensive provision for graduate courses is made at the College of the Pacific, which lists forty courses as being primarily for graduates. Ten of these courses are in education and psychology, six are in English, four are in physics, and four are in mathematics. In this college it is possible, in several departments, for a graduate student to arrange a program consisting principally of graduate courses.

The lack of courses with enrolments limited to graduates indicates that almost all of the work for the Master's degree in these colleges is undergraduate in character. Quite clearly, a Master's degree granted under such conditions represents a "fifth year" of college work rather than a year of strictly graduate study. Nevertheless, there is reason to believe that in at least several colleges this work is fairly well done, especially in those few larger colleges which have extensive course offerings, good libraries, and strong faculties. Here, however, is a weakness which should receive attention. If the work for the Master's degree is to afford the student the opportunity he should have, it should include a goodly amount of work, probably at least one-half of the amount he takes, which is clearly above the undergraduate level with reference to its degree of difficulty, the advancement of the students enrolled, and the methods of work. To fall below this standard is not affording a satisfactory opportunity to the student who already has a Bachelor's degree.

GRADUATE DEGREES IN MUSIC

Two of the colleges—DePauw University (1931–32) and the College of the Pacific—offer the degree of Master of Music. At DePauw University the prerequisite is the degree of Bachelor of Music earned in some accredited institution, with such grades in undergraduate work in music as give evidence of the candidate's ability to carry advanced courses with distinction. The requirements for the Master's degree in music include a thesis in the form of an original composition in large form, or an extended critical essay on some phase of musical knowledge. At the College of the Pacific the prerequisite is a baccalaureate diploma from a music school holding membership in the National Association of Schools of Music. An original thesis is required with a major in applied music or public-school music, and a symphonic poem of at least fifteen minutes' duration for full orchestra constitutes one of the requirements for a major in composition.

THE INSTITUTE OF PAPER CHEMISTRY AT LAWRENCE COLLEGE

A unique type of graduate work is provided at Lawrence College through the Institute of Paper Chemistry, a graduate school affiliated with the college. The Institute has its own board of trustees—leading executives in the pulp and paper industry. The purpose of the Institute is the training of technical workers in the field of paper chemistry and technology. Inasmuch as the Institute was not included in the survey, it will not be discussed further.

GRADUATE WORK AND THE FUTURE

As has been pointed out earlier in this chapter, certain social and economic factors seem to make inevitable a demand for graduate work in the stronger colleges. Coupled with these is the development of the public junior college, which in all probability will soon begin to result in diminishing freshman and sophomore classes in some of the four-year colleges. In the colleges in which this occurs the one hope for survival will probably be the development of an additional year of advanced work on a basis that will make a strong appeal to graduate students.

Although the offering of graduate work in a strong college is highly desirable from several points of view, it should not be undertaken until the undergraduate program commands satisfactory recognition. Certainly a college not accredited by the Association of American Universities should delay the offering of a graduate program until such accreditation has been attained. Adequate library facilities in the fields of graduate study should be available, especially if graduate study is to include a reasonable amount of original investigation. Such a library should be well supplied not only with books but also with bound periodicals, pamphlets, official reports, and similar fundamental source materials. If graduate work is to be undertaken in science, well-equipped laboratories should be available for it. Finally, creditable graduate work demands a scholarly faculty, men and women of high scholastic attainment and imbued with the ideals of graduate study. Until an institution can afford to meet these standards and, at the same time, do high class undergraduate work, it should proceed very slowly in offering the Master's degree.

CHAPTER XXVII

THE COLLEGE CATALOGUE

THE PURPOSE OF THE COLLEGE CATALOGUE

The need for a study of the particular problems involved in the preparation and publication of college catalogues became apparent early in the program of survey. The catalogue of a college is one of the most important sources of information for a study of the college. In the surveys upon which this volume is based the catalogues were much used, and the survey staff was consequently impressed with the strong and the weak features of those publications.

The college catalogue serves several useful purposes: First, it brings to the public, especially to parents and prospective students, information which they use as a basis for deciding whether they shall patronize the college. Many students arrive at decisions to attend particular colleges on the basis of information secured from reading this official publication. This purpose of the catalogue has certain definite implications. It should present in a dignified, clear, and honest manner the opportunities and advantages offered by the institution. Accuracy should certainly characterize the publications of a college which aspires to develop this quality in its students. Furthermore, the fact that catalogues are circulated among high-school graduates who are interested in selecting the colleges they will attend should cause the institution to strive for the utmost simplicity and clearness in arrangement and statement.

Another element of the general public to whom the catalogue represents the college is the prospective donor. A poorly constructed catalogue, printed and bound in an unattractive way, creates no favorable impression on one who is searching for a worthy institution upon which he may bestow his wealth, nor will a catalogue full of inaccurate or undignified statements help the cause of the college under such circumstances.

A second purpose of the college catalogue is to give to other colleges information which they need, especially in allowing credit to transfer students. For such use it is highly desirable that standardized and comparable terms be employed. Clear and adequate statements regarding courses, credits, and requirements are necessary to serve this useful purpose.

A third purpose of the college catalogue is to serve as a book of reference within the institution. Administrators, faculty members, and students use it constantly as a manual of advice, rules, and requirements. Through this medium confusion is overcome and orderly procedure is established. In some respects this use of the catalogue is the most important of all. Graduation requirements, sequences and curriculums, course descriptions, etc., provide the facts that both students and faculty must have if they are to work together in harmony. Anyone who has had anything to do with administering a college has often been made aware of the great amount of misinformation which students gather from advisers, faculty members, fellow-students, and others, all of which leads into difficulties. Clear and complete catalogue statements help students to follow proper directions.

Finally, the catalogue serves as a contract between the institution and the student, this status having been upheld by court decisions. It is therefore very important that all statements be clear and complete, and worded with utmost accuracy. A student can legally hold the college to the execution of every promise made in the catalogue.

SIZE OF THE CATALOGUE

The college catalogues exhibit great variety in their sizes. Table 58, which follows, shows for thirty-five colleges the total number of pages and the number of pages devoted to each principal division of the catalogues.

This table shows a wide range, both in the number of pages in the catalogue and in the distribution of the pages among the various divisions. The size of the college in part determines the number of pages for items such as faculty, lists of students, and, to a certain extent, the courses of instruction, assuming that the larger college has the greater offering.

Table 59 presents a distribution of the page sizes of the catalogues of thirty-five colleges.

This table shows an utter lack of uniformity in page size. Nine of the colleges use a page 151×228 millimeters, approximately 6×9 inches; four use a page 135×195 millimeters, approximately $5\frac{5}{16} \times 7\frac{11}{16}$ inches; and three use a page 146×220 millimeters, approximately $5\frac{3}{4} \times 8\frac{1}{4}$ inches. The remaining institutions, constituting half the total number, each use a page size like that of none of the others. Although the physical size of the catalogue is a minor matter, this is a factor in the ease with which the volume is handled. A thick volume bound with wire staples is very inconvenient. A catalogue with larger pages, perhaps 6×9 inches, is preferable to a catalogue with pages $4\frac{1}{4} \times 7\frac{3}{4}$ inches, especially if it contains more

TABLE 58

NUMBER OF PAGES IN CATALOGUES OF THIRTY-FIVE COLLEGES

INSTITUTION	TOTAL NUMBER OF PAGES	NUMBER OF PAGES DEVOTED TO					
		Faculty	Administration of Curriculum	Courses of Instruction	General Information	Statistics, Lists of Students, Graduates	Miscellaneous
*Ohio Wesleyan	372	34	20	127	52	102	37
Ohio Northern	232	10	44	103	18	41	16
*DePauw	218	20	12	100	26	44	16
Puget Sound	210	12	37	82	22	38	19
Oklahoma City	196	10	16	94	32	32	12
Nebraska Wesleyan	192	17	30	58	30	28	29
*Simpson	190	12	9	98	20	40	11
*Illinois Wesleyan	160	9	10	70	32	24	15
*Albion	152	7	12	72	25	27	9
Baldwin-Wallace	146	9	20	74	14	18	11
*Morningside	146	8	7	69	27	25	40
Evansville	144	5	39	49	9	22	20
Southwestern	143	14	22	47	21	36	3
*Mount Union	140	8	12	42	33	29	16
*Lawrence	136	8	10	57	18	30	13
*Hamline	128	7	31	41	23	14	2
*MacMurray	128	5	7	74	21	10	11
*Pacific	128	12	10	53	12	4	37
*Willamette	128	4	19	54	24	15	12
*Allegheny	126	5	13	31	21	25 .	31
West Virginia Wesleyan	126	6	8	56	30	16	10
*Baker	120	6	5	66	14	16	10
Iowa Wesleyan	118	7	11	53	10	19	18
*Chattanooga	114	8	21	43	8	10	24
*Cornell	104	6	10	42	26	12	8
Kansas Wesleyan	102	8	6	54	13	13	8
Central Wesleyan	96	6	10	37	18	13	12
McKendree	94	6	10	45	6	14	13
Dakota Wesleyan	80	4	8	35	15	9	9
Ozark Wesleyan	78	6	6	30	14	8	14
*Dickinson	76	5	6	20	20	16	9
Union	76	4	7	28	16	14	7
Brothers	64	3	16	15	15	1	14
Intermountain	64	3	8	18	16	7	12
Gooding	46	4	4	9	12	6	11
Median, all colleges	128	7	10	53	20	16	12
*Median, A.A.U. colleges	128	8	10	57	23	24	13
Median, non-A.A.U. colleges	110	6	11	48	16	15	12

* Institutions on the approved list of the Association of American Universities.

than 64 pages, the amount designated by printers as a "book." Besides ease in handling, there are other obvious advantages in the larger pages, such as a more attractive appearance, the amount of space available on a page for the arrangement of units such as a curriculum, and the ease in locating items.

TABLE 59

DISTRIBUTION OF SIZES OF CATALOGUES OF
THIRTY-FIVE COLLEGES

Size of Catalogue Page in Millimeters	Number of Colleges Having Catalogues of Each Size
125×189	1
130×189	1
130×192	1
133×189	1
133×194	1
133×197	1
134×192	1
135×195	4
136×191	1
138×203	1
141×210	1
144×203	1
145×215	1
145×218	1
146×204	1
146×220	3
147×223	1
149×215	1
149×222	1
151×228	9
152×222	1
154×231	1

ANALYSIS OF FEATURES INCLUDED IN THE CATALOGUES

A check list or score card of the items included in the college catalogues was devised for use in this study.[1] In using this check list, the catalogue of each of the thirty-five colleges was studied with reference to each item, and scored as either lacking the feature, having it but in an unsatisfactory form, or having it in good form. Table 60 presents the outline of the check list, together with the number of college catalogues given each of the three ratings on each item.

[1] This check list was developed under the direction of the survey staff by Mr. Christian Miller, now assistant registrar at the College of Puget Sound.

TABLE 60

An Analytical Rating of the Catalogues of Thirty-five Colleges

Features	Number of Catalogues with the Feature		
	Absent	Included but Poor	Included and Good
I. Introduction:			
1. Table of contents..................	23	3	9
2. Calendar, general and academic......	....	7	28
3. Map or chart of campus............	32	1	2
II. The corporation:			
1. Officers of board of trustees.........	2	....	33
2. Trustees:			
a) Date of first appointment........	30	....	5
b) Ending date of terms............	2	....	33
c) Electorate.....................	22	3	10
d) Occupations....................	33	....	2
e) Addresses......................	2	27	6
f) Committee assignments..........	8	3	24
3. Official visitors, if any.............	23	1	11
III. The administrative staff:			
1. All officers named..................	2	5	28
2. Training...........................	11	10	14
3. Professional experience.............	33	1	1
4. Date of local appointment..........	34	1	....
IV. The instructional staff:			
1. Degrees held.......................	....	1	34
2. Rank and department...............	....	3	32
3. Educational institutions attended.....	4	....	31
4. Professional experience.............	26	2	7
5. Date of local appointment..........	22	1	12
6. Committee appointments............	8	2	25
V. General information:			
1. General objectives of the college......	13	10	12
2. Historical statement...............	3	7	25
3. Accreditation......................	18	7	10
4. Location and transportation..........	2	11	22
5. Buildings and equipment............	....	6	29
6. Amount of endowment..............	25	2	8
7. Publications.......................	13	6	16
8. Number of volumes in library........	7	....	28
9. Student organizations and activities...	....	4	31
10. Religious activities..................	2	12	21
11. Discipline.........................	3	9	23
12. Student aid........................	....	6	29
13. Alumni organization and activities....	25	2	8
14. Housing and boarding facilities.......	....	10	25
15. Fees..............................	....	10	25
16. Placement service for graduates.......	21	5	9
VI. Administration of the curriculum:			
1. Admission requirements.............	....	1	34
2. Registration procedure.............	5	8	22

TABLE 60—*Continued*

FEATURES	Number of Catalogues with the Feature		
	Absent	Included but Poor	Included and Good
VI. Administration of the curriculum:—*Cont.*			
3. Class relations and credits............	2	10	23
4. Graduation requirements................	....	4	31
5. Suggested curriculums:			
a) Toward its own specific degrees....	8	17	10
b) Prevocational....................	14	6	15
c) Vocational......................	14	9	12
VII. Courses of instruction:			
1. Departmental or divisional objectives..	25	6	4
2. Explanation of terms and codes.......	6	13	16
3. Numbering scheme for courses:			
a) Simplicity.....................	1	9	25
b) Clearness......................	5	16	14
4. Sequence requirements..............	2	12	21
5. Course statements:			
a) Arrangement...................	....	11	24
b) Definiteness...................	1	14	20
c) Completeness of description......	1	17	17
d) Avoidance of repetition...........	....	14	21
e) Statement of prerequisites........	1	8	26
f) Year offered, in case of alternation..	7	5	23
VIII. Catalogue of students:			
1. Degrees awarded..................	5	1	29
2. Prizes and honors.................	16	4	15
3. Enrolments and distribution.........	....	6	29
4. Summary.......................	2	7	26
IX. Index:			
1. Adequacy.......................	6	6	23
2. Reliability......................	6	3	26
X. Size and form of catalogue:			
1. Convenience for library shelving......	....	7	28
2. Economical mailing costs............	....	4	31
3. Economical in production costs.......	....	5	30
XI. Literary qualities:			
1. Organization....................	....	18	17
2. Style..........................	....	9	26
3. Vocabulary.....................	....	6	29
XII. Accuracy of statements:			
1. Facts of general information.........	....	6	29
2. Courses offered..................	....	6	29
3. Implications....................	....	7	28
4. Date of catalogue................	....	6	29
XIII. Use of educational terms:			
1. Standard with other colleges........	....	7	28
2. Comparability...................	....	8	27
XIV. General arrangement and impression:			
1. Quality of paper.................	....	1	34
2. Type, set-up, binding..............	....	12	23
3. Use of appropriate pictures..........	20	5	10

Reference to Table 60 shows that a table of contents is not considered essential by twenty-three of the thirty-five colleges. The twelve colleges providing tables of contents include some but not nearly all of the larger institutions. A table of contents is not so essential in a small catalogue as in a large one. A good index may well serve for the smaller catalogue, but the additional expenditure for a table of contents is a good investment for institutions having large catalogues.

Academic calendars of varying degrees of completeness are included in all the catalogues. Some catalogues include a general calendar; others do not. The general calendar may serve a useful purpose on occasion, but its inclusion is by no means to be regarded as essential. Two of the institutions include maps of the campus, and one includes a map of the city showing the site of the college.

Some facts regarding the composition of the board of trustees are stated in nearly all the catalogues, but these facts are meager in a number of cases. The addresses and occupations of the trustees are useful facts for the public, since they show in a general way the type of board which controls the institution. The addresses of the trustees are given in thirty-three of the catalogues, but only six give them in sufficient detail to facilitate correspondence directly with them. The small number of catalogues giving the names of official visitors may indicate either that their names were omitted or that there are no visitors in those colleges. Although the board of visitors is frequently an uninfluential group, the names of the visitors should be published, particularly if they are outstanding educators or members of a religious group.

Several catalogues contain illustrations of interesting scenery near the colleges, and one catalogue contains pictures of the president and several faculty members. Such illustrations are rather unusual for a college catalogue, and tend to give it the aspect of an advertising circular. It is difficult to justify the expenditure of funds for them. Good pictures of the college buildings may well form a part of the catalogue. One college publishes pictures in its catalogue that give an entirely misleading conception of the type of scenery to be found in the neighborhood of the institution.

Two of the colleges omit a list of the administrative staff, and the data on this point in five other catalogues are very meager. The training and professional experience of the administrators are conspicuously absent in nearly all the catalogues. In view of the responsibility for educational leadership which devolves on the college administrators, the public is well within its rights in asking for a statement of the qualifications of these officials, upon whom to a large degree depends the character of the education afforded by the college. These statements should be presented for all those administrative officers whose work in any way enters into the educational policies of the institution.

Aside from the students, the faculty in some respects is the most important part of a college. For that reason a college catalogue should give accurate and complete information on this point. All the catalogues of the thirty-five colleges studied list the degrees and ranks of the faculty members; but in certain other respects, notably professional experience, the statements are frequently deficient. Both the educational institutions attended and the professional experience of the faculty members add to the breadth and effectiveness of the instructor; and in the interest of a proper representation to the public these items should be given. The date when degrees were received is an important matter which is all too frequently missing in the catalogues. Occasionally a catalogue contains information regarding faculty members which represents an undignified boasting. That a faculty member is listed in "Who's Who in American Education" is no particular credit to him, nor does any special distinction rest upon one because he has joined the National Society of College Teachers of Education, the National Education Association, or other similar organizations. Reference to them can scarcely be regarded as in good taste in describing members of the faculty. The date of local appointment reveals to the discriminating reader of the catalogue something as to the permanence and stability of the faculty.

Under the head of "General Information" a wide disparity is noted. The extreme variance in the statements of institutional aims is noteworthy. A number of the historical statements are open to the criticism that they use much space to eulogize the meager beginnings and fail to give the facts which would show the recent progress of the college.

Surely the accreditation of a college should be made known to the public. Only ten catalogues give fair and proper statements on this point, and in seven catalogues the statements are evasive or misleading. For example, the Association of American Colleges does not accredit colleges, although several institutions list their membership in this association under the heading of "accreditation." In the interest of truth and fair dealing, statements on accreditation should not misrepresent the college, even in minor details.

Rather flowery descriptive phrases are used in several instances in describing the location. In other instances, information on location and transportation facilities is inadequate.

The catalogues describe the buildings more or less fully. Those marked poor on this point were so judged either because of an unjustified use of superlatives or because the descriptions neglected some of the essential facilities related to the work offered.

The amount of endowment is given in only ten catalogues. This is an important item of information, showing the ability of the college to finance its program, provided the endowment produces a sizable revenue. In some ways a better indication of the financial excellence of the college than the endowment is the total income available for educational purposes.

One other item of general information, the housing and boarding facilities, deserves a clear statement. Much waste of time and useless correspondence may be avoided if the description of these facilities gives a frank and detailed statement of the accommodations available, how they may be secured, the cost, how they may be reserved, and what equipment must be furnished by the student.

Practically all the catalogues contain information on the administration of the curriculum, but not even in these important matters do all the catalogues measure up to a high standard. Admission and graduation requirements are generally well stated, but suggested curriculums are either not clearly set forth or are not given in sufficient number. Evidently there is disagreement on the value of clearly stated curriculums. There is scarcely a more helpful device for students than the model schedule set up for four years. Suggested curriculums are especially valuable in colleges that do not have a well-organized personnel staff which can give a great deal of study to the program of each individual student. Model programs, carefully worked out by the more able members of the faculty, will tend to contain fewer errors than the programs worked up quickly at the time of registration. In the prevocational and vocational fields the proportion of the institutions presenting suggested curriculums is rather small.

The courses of instruction are usually considered the principal part of the catalogue. More pages are devoted to this feature than to any other part of the catalogue. A study of the principal items falling under this head shows that only four catalogues—those of DePauw University, Illinois Wesleyan University, Ohio Northern University, and Simpson College—are fairly consistent in stating departmental or divisional aims. Other catalogues state the aims for some departments but not for others, while some catalogues omit such statements entirely. The evidence is clear that considerable improvement could be made in practically all of the catalogues on at least a number of points relating to the statements of courses of instruction.

Many of these publications are subject to criticism because of their lack of literary quality. Poor organization characterizes eighteen catalogues. In these it is often necessary to look in several places in the catalogue for information which should be brought into one unit. Several colleges have needless duplication in their published lists of students, the complete roster being printed in two or more places under different classifications. The style and vocabulary used sometimes indicate that different writers have a hand in producing the catalogue. Where this is the case, some expert in English should be given the responsibility of editing the whole manuscript. In fact, it would not be out of place to give the name of the editor in some position in the catalogue where it will be noticed. It should be the duty of the editor to study the catalogue carefully with a view to its improvement, to compare it with other college catalogues, and to collect information all year for the catalogue.

An exasperating item in several catalogues is the date. It is sometimes difficult to determine the year for which the catalogue is intended. To avoid this difficulty the exact date of publication should appear in a conspicuous position on the cover, and the list of course offerings should clearly indicate the academic year to which they apply.

Some catalogues are rated poor on the accuracy of statements of course offerings because they list a much larger number of courses than could possibly be given by the staff of the institution. Implications which the reader of the catalogue is permitted to receive and which are not justified by the facts constitute another type of inaccuracy which should be overcome.

The facts presented show clearly that, although some of the college catalogues of the institutions studied are excellent in many respects, there is much room for improvement in all of them, more in some than in others. The catalogues should be carefully prepared with a view to the variety of uses made of them. They should be attractive and help to create a favorable impression of the college, but they should be absolutely accurate to the most minute detail. There should be no opportunity for readers to gain false impressions of the institution through its catalogue. All of this suggests the need for careful editing and fine workmanship in printing and binding. After a good catalogue has been evolved—it is really an evolution over a long period of time—its publication should not be much more expensive than the publication of a discreditable document.

CHAPTER XXVIII

PROBLEMS OF CURRICULUM IMPROVEMENT

PLACEMENT OF STUDENTS IN CLASSES

Rules and regulations providing for the segregation of classes at various levels.—It is a rather common assumption among educationists that class instruction will be most efficient when given in groups that are homogeneous with respect to such factors as intelligence, scholastic level of attainment, general background, etc. In some cases this idea has led to the sectioning of students on the basis of psychological tests or other more or less reliable measures. Usually, however, college faculties are content with the type of homogeneity attained when students are enrolled in courses primarily designed for their respective class levels. Lack of homogeneity on this point is illustrated by the enrolment of a freshman student in a course intended for seniors, or the enrolment of a senior in a freshman course.

A number of colleges have organized their work in upper and lower divisions (junior and senior college) on the assumption that there are important differences between upper- and lower-classmen as to their educational attainments and their academic outlook. Whether organized with two distinct levels (junior and senior college divisions), or with the traditional four classes, there are few colleges today which do not insist upon their students doing a large amount of work in their last two years in a field of major interest or concentration in a manner somewhat akin to the methods of study used in graduate schools. Such being the case, it might be supposed that all colleges would make strong efforts to see that their students enrol only in those courses in which all persons are at least of the same division if not of the same class level.

The means employed to secure homogeneous course enrolments are extensive in variety. Many colleges use distinctive systems of numbering courses to indicate definitely the intended class level of the courses. Some colleges state clearly in their announcements the classes from which students are eligible to enrol in each of the various courses. Several institutions provide fixed schedules for freshmen and some permit very few elections in the sophomore year. A number of colleges, however, offer courses which they state are open to any student in the college.

With such a divergence of attitudes it is to be expected that the students are relatively homogeneously grouped in some colleges, while in others they are not. Up to the present very few actual studies have been made which throw light upon this problem.

The statistics of placement.—In this study a special technique has been employed to investigate the problem of placement. It is assumed that the true level at which a class is taught is determined more by the type of students actually enrolled in the course than by the catalogue statement. Thus, a course in which the students are predominantly freshmen is rated as a freshman course. The modal class of enrolment[1] is considered the index of the actual level of the course. A careful analysis of the enrolments of the thirty-five colleges of this group gives the results shown in Table 61.

It will be noted that the median percentage of students enrolled in courses at their own class level is but 66.9, while there is a range from 55.8 at Central Wesleyan College to 81.7 at MacMurray College. Apparently the number of students enrolled in the college has very little, if any, effect on the homogeneity of placement of students in classes.

Some rather striking facts are revealed by the first column of the table, which shows for each college the percentage of course enrolments of upper-division students in lower-division classes. This runs as high as 61 per cent at Ozark Wesleyan College. Since the survey visit was made, the institution has decided to limit its work to that of a junior college. The above percentage indicates that it was practically a junior college at the time it was studied. The median, 35 per cent, shows that it is a common practice in these institutions to permit students of the upper classes to take courses with the lower classes. This practice is less marked in the institutions on the approved list of the Association of American Universities than in the institutions not holding this type of accreditation.

The number of students in the lower division enrolled in upper-division courses, is comparatively small in these colleges. The highest percentage is 16.5 at Cornell College, and the lowest is 1.3 at Kansas Wesleyan University.

While it may be assumed that it is not a serious matter for a student to be but one year in advance of or behind his class in the courses he is taking, a difference of two years is significant. The table shows that the amount of course enrolments two years in advance of class levels is almost

---

[1] The modal class is the class having the largest number of registrants. Thus a course enrolling two freshmen, fourteen sophomores, nine juniors, and six seniors would be denominated a sophomore course. In practice it seems to make little difference whether the mean, the median, or the mode is used as an index of the level of the class registrations.

TABLE 61
PLACEMENT OF STUDENTS AT THIRTY-FIVE COLLEGES AS DETERMINED BY MODAL CLASS OF ENROLMENT

INSTITUTION	YEAR	PERCENTAGE OF COURSE ENROLMENTS OF		PERCENTAGE OF TOTAL COURSE ENROLMENTS		PERCENTAGE OF STUDENTS ENROLLED IN COURSES AT THEIR OWN CLASS LEVELS
		Upper-Division Students in Lower-Division Classes	Lower-Division Students in Upper-Division Classes	Two Years in Advance of Their Respective Class Levels	Two Years behind Their Respective Class Levels	
*MacMurray	1930–31	19.7	2.8	1.2	3.8	81.7
*Dickinson	1929–30	16.3	2.3	0.4	2.2	76.6
Evansville	1929–30	45.1	4.3	1.1	4.5	75.8
McKendree	1930–31	32.6	5.6	0.4	5.6	75.1
*Lawrence	1929–30	26.2	6.3	1.6	4.0	73.6
*DePauw	1930–31	36.1	4.5	1.3	5.8	71.8
Ohio Northern	1930–31	28.9	6.8	1.8	7.0	71.7
*Simpson	1929–30	41.0	3.8	1.5	6.7	71.6
Union	1929–30	39.1	8.6	1.1	3.8	71.4
Baldwin-Wallace	1930–31	33.3	7.2	1.5	6.3	69.1
Brothers	1930–31	51.1	5.3	1.0	1.0	68.8
Dakota Wesleyan	1929–30	30.9	6.7	3.0	5.9	68.5
Kansas Wesleyan	1930–31	35.0	1.3	0.7	6.9	68.2
*Allegheny	1929–30	19.4	9.5	2.0	2.9	67.5
*Illinois Wesleyan	1930–31	41.1	6.2	2.5	6.9	67.3
*Baker	1930–31	27.3	3.6	1.4	6.5	67.2
Puget Sound	1930–31	40.7	3.9	1.0	7.3	67.0
*Albion	1929–30	24.1	9.5	2.2	4.9	66.9
Southwestern	1930–31	30.7	3.2	2.5	7.4	66.4
*Pacific	1930–31	17.3	4.9	1.4	5.5	66.2
Nebraska Wesleyan	1930–31	37.6	4.3	1.1	8.6	66.0
*Willamette	1930–31	25.0	5.0	1.6	7.4	65.9
*Ohio Wesleyan	1930–31	34.1	6.2	1.0	8.0	65.0
*Mount Union	1930–31	38.4	7.7	2.5	7.4	64.7
*Cornell	1929–30	23.5	16.5	6.5	2.7	64.7
Iowa Wesleyan	1929–30	35.8	8.5	1.4	6.2	64.5
Ozark Wesleyan	1929–30	61.0	3.3	0.3	8.8	64.3
Intermountain	1930–31	29.7	12.5	4.3	10.3	63.3
*Morningside	1929–30	42.3	5.8	1.0	6.6	63.0
Gooding	1930–31	42.2	6.2	3.6	9.3	62.8
*Hamline	1929–30	35.3	8.2	2.6	9.1	62.0
Oklahoma City	1929–30	56.6	3.7	0.7	10.2	61.9
*Chattanooga	1929–30	38.6	8.5	1.9	10.7	60.4
West Virginia Wesleyan	1930–31	37.8	11.1	2.2	11.4	57.0
Central Wesleyan	1929–30	34.4	9.6	2.9	9.5	55.8
Median, all colleges		35.0	6.2	1.5	6.7	66.9
*Median, A.A.U. colleges		27.3	6.2	1.6	6.5	66.9
Median, non-A.A.U. colleges		36.7	5.9	1.3	7.2	66.7

* Institutions on the approved list of the Association of American Universities.

negligible. However, the percentage of students who are two years behind their class levels is larger.

To be sure, a certain amount of inco-ordination of class standing and course enrolment is inevitable in a college. A student may fail in a required course but pass enough work to raise his class standing. Eventually, he may repeat the required course and in that instance his class standing and his course enrolment do not correspond. Not infrequently a student's course of study is so arranged that he is forced to take a required subject when he has higher class standing than the majority of the students enrolled for that particular course. Furthermore, the elective system under varying limitations rightly permits students to study subjects in which they are especially interested. These considerations suggest that an exact co-ordination between course enrolment and class standing is neither possible nor desirable.

Efforts to promote good placement.—A study of the catalogues of the colleges surveyed shows that eleven of them have a definite rule stating that a senior, and in some instances a junior, who pursues a course designed for freshmen will be given only a part, in some cases only half, of the credit usually given for the completion of the course. Seven colleges require students to take thirty-six or more semester hours of upper-division work, but not all of them specify just when it must be taken. Other colleges have no such specific rules regarding the taking of courses, although many have distinctive numbering schemes or statements of class levels of courses or other prerequisites.

Table 62 presents the averages on three measures of placement for the colleges having each type of rule for the promotion of good placement. Eleven of the colleges follow the plan of giving upper-classmen only partial credit for lower-class courses; seven follow the plan of requiring a definite amount of upper-class work for graduation; and seventeen have no rule for securing homogeneity in class groups other than the numbering system used for courses. The number of cases studied is admittedly much too small to furnish scientific proof of the best way to secure good placement, but the differences revealed by the grouping seem to be significant.

On the basis of the criteria employed, the colleges using either the first or the second plan shown in the table have better placement than the colleges using the third plan. This is probably due to their special rules, but that cannot be positively asserted. The number of cases is too small to warrant extensive generalization. Furthermore, there are other factors which may greatly influence the placement of students, such as the administration of educational counsel, the types of curriculums offered, and the amount of work prescribed either directly or through well-articulated programs for students. The technique, however, affords an interesting analysis of the degree to which homogeneity in instructional groups is secured in these colleges.

ARTICULATION OF HIGH-SCHOOL AND COLLEGE PROGRAMS

One of the problems confronting a college in setting up its program of studies, particularly its requirements for degrees, is the relation of that program to the work which the student has had in his previous education. Obviously the student's program in high school and college should have more or less continuity, and effort should be made to prevent useless over-

TABLE 62

PLACEMENT OF STUDENTS IN CLASSES FOR THIRTY-FIVE COLLEGES, GROUPED ACCORDING TO TYPE OF REGULATION USED TO PROMOTE GOOD PLACEMENT

TYPE OF RULE USED TO PROMOTE GOOD PLACEMENT	AVERAGE PERCENTAGE OF		
	Total Course Enrolments of Upper-Division Students in Lower-Division Classes	Total Course Enrolments Two Years behind Their Respective Levels	Total Course Enrolments by Students in Classes at Their Own Levels
Upper-classmen given only partial credit for lower-class courses..................	32.1	6.1	71.3
Thirty-six or more hours of upper-class course work required for graduation.....	32.6	6.9	67.0
No rule other than a numbering system for courses	35.6	7.5	64.4

lapping and duplication. The problem is complicated by the fact that secondary and higher education have typically been given in separate institutions under different control, and by the further fact that these two levels of education have served student clientèles differing considerably each from the other. Furthermore, the college program must be arranged to meet the needs of individual students of varying interests and with different academic backgrounds.

There is now a growing tendency in the construction of college curriculums to attempt some definite form of articulation with the high-school programs of the students. Educators have been calling attention to the waste in allowing, or requiring, college students to carry courses whose content is essentially the same as studies they have already completed in high school. The curriculum followed by the individual student from the high school through the institution of higher learning is more and more coming to be considered as a unified whole. Such a policy requires that the college requirements in the case of each student be adjusted to take into account the subjects carried in high school. In general, these adjustments take three forms: (1) relief from certain college subjects required for graduation, when these subjects have been carried in high school, or when a satisfactory achievement in these lines is exhibited; (2) assignment to class sections on the basis of previous knowledge of the subject; (3) offering of survey courses of the "repair" type to fill in the student's deficiencies in certain essential lines or subjects.

The first of these forms of articulation is frequently found in several of the more commonly required subjects, especially foreign language. Of the thirty-five colleges studied, twenty-eight report a definite adjustment in the language requirements for graduation with the degree of Bachelor of Arts, the amount of college credit in language required depending upon the amount of language credit the student presents at entrance.

Several colleges go so far as to excuse students entirely from the study of foreign language in college provided they present a certain amount of entrance credit in that subject. Thus, Cornell College states that a student who has had two or more years of one language in a secondary school and successfully passes the reading knowledge test in a foreign language will have no further language requirements. At Evansville College, Hamline University, Iowa Wesleyan College, Simpson College, and Union College, students who present credits for four years in one foreign language in the secondary school are excused from all further requirements in that subject. In Oklahoma City University a student entering with three units in a language has satisfied the language requirement for graduation, while at Southwestern College he is excused from further language requirements if he presents two units at admission. Mount Union College requires for graduation with the Bachelor of Arts degree at least two years' work in a modern language, in addition to work in ancient language. Two units completed in high school satisfy the modern-language requirement, but there is no such release from ancient language. At Willamette University the student may satisfy the language requirement for graduation by demonstrating through an examination his ability to read a foreign language.

The adjustment of the foreign-language requirement at Brothers College is rather unusual. The college requires of the student an acquaintance with at least one ancient language. Students who offer three units of preparatory-school Latin or Greek for admission are not required to continue the study of an ancient language in the college. Students who enter the college without ancient language must take two years of Latin or Greek or pass a satisfactory written examination in one of them before they can be admitted to upper-class standing. In addition to the ancient-language requirement, Brothers College demands that students have a reading knowledge of two modern languages, or a command of one modern language, but no course requirements are made, proficiency being tested by examination. Thus, a student might possibly secure sufficient training in high school to satisfy the modern-language requirement for graduation at Brothers College.

Although the excusing of students from graduation requirements for the degree of Bachelor of Arts is more common in foreign languages than in other subjects, a number of the colleges do make allowances in other studies. Ohio Wesleyan University requires twelve semester hours of study in history and social sciences, but relieves the student of three hours provided on admission he offers two units of history. The student's work in this field must include, *either in high school or college*, a full-year course in medieval and modern history. Likewise, in mathematics and science this institution requires twelve hours for graduation, but relieves the student of three hours, provided on admission he presents two units of science. The student's work in science must be so arranged that he shall have *in the combined high-school and college curriculum* at least an elementary course in each of two specified laboratory sciences. Willamette University also makes adjustments in several subjects. The graduation requirement in medieval-modern or English history or economic history is met by a high-school course in medieval and modern or world history. The requirement in mathematics is also fulfilled by a unit of advanced mathematics offered for entrance. Twelve hours (or two years) are required in laboratory science, but half of the requirement may be met by high-school work. Similar arrangements are made by the College of the Pacific, in English literature; by Evansville College, in laboratory science; by the College of Puget Sound, in science; and by Southwestern College, in history and science.

Four of the colleges have special arrangements in English. At the University of Chattanooga, a freshman with an excellent high-school record in English who makes a high grade on the English tests of Freshman Week may be excused from freshman English and transferred to the sophomore composition course. At Evansville College, students who demonstrate high achievement in English as shown by tests are excused from the work of the first semester in composition. Hamline University also excuses students from freshman composition on a proficiency basis. Students at

Lawrence College who do superior work in the first semester of freshman composition are excused from further required work in the subject.

Two survey courses, one in "Modern Civilization" and the other in "Introduction to the Sciences," are required of under-classmen at Hamline University. Students may be exempted from portions of both of these courses on examination given by the instructor.

The second type of articulation—the assignment of students to different sections or courses on the basis of previous knowledge —is widely, but not universally, practiced by the colleges studied. Two elementary courses in chemistry, one for students who have studied chemistry in high school and one for students who have had no work in chemistry, are offered by Albion College, Central Wesleyan College, Iowa Wesleyan College, Lawrence College, Ohio Northern University, and Ozark Wesleyan College. Baker University, Lawrence College, and Ohio Northern University make similar provision in physics, and Albion College does likewise in biology. Several colleges, among which are Albion College, Baker University, College of the Pacific, Illinois Wesleyan University, Kansas Wesleyan University, McKendree College, Southwestern College, and the University of Chattanooga, offer two courses in college algebra, one for students who have had one unit of algebra and one for students who have had one and a half units of algebra. In English a somewhat similar plan is in vogue in several colleges. Thus, Oklahoma City University gives a placement test to the students enrolling in freshman English, and assigns students to classes "where they can make the most progress." Willamette University, by means of qualifying examinations, divides the freshman English students into three groups. The reports made by the colleges indicate that a fairly large number use placement tests to sectionize the students for some of their freshman courses.

The third type of articulation of the student's college program with his high-school program—the offering of survey courses of the repair type— is rather common in English but not in other subjects. Fourteen of the colleges report some arrangement whereby students markedly deficient in the fundamentals of English grammar or composition are required to take a course covering those essentials, usually without college credit.

A number of the colleges are making genuine efforts to articulate the student's college program with his high-school study, though most of these efforts have not proceeded as far as they might go with advantage to both the student and the college. Some of the devices employed in the larger colleges do not lend themselves so easily to use in the smaller institutions, but every college can do something to prevent, or at least reduce, overlapping in the student's work.

RECENT EFFORTS AT CURRICULUM IMPROVEMENT

The efforts of the colleges to articulate their programs with the work of the secondary schools represent one type of commendable effort to improve the college curriculum. In several other ways improvements have been made during the past few years in a number of colleges. A few colleges report practically no recent curriculum changes.

Survey courses.—A number of colleges report survey courses in several fields. These are introductory courses which cut across departmental lines, and are designed to orient the student in a large field of knowledge. Such courses are offered in the social sciences at Brothers College, Cornell College, Hamline University, Illinois Wesleyan University, Ohio Wesleyan University, and Oklahoma City University. Another field in which survey courses are found is natural science, Brothers College, Cornell College, and Hamline University reporting survey courses in this field. Cornell College reports survey, or orientation, courses in religion and ethics for upper-classmen.

The University of Chattanooga offers a course in comparative literature which is intended to survey the field of literature as revealed in the great literary masterpieces of the world. This institution reports an unsuccessful trial with several other survey courses.

The institution which has gone farther than any other in the development of survey courses is Brothers College. For lower-classmen the college has designed four survey courses: literature, science, economics and sociology, and the Bible. All students in the lower division are required to take these courses. Four other elective survey courses have also been designed—philosophy and psychology for lower-classmen, and Christianity and art for upper-classmen.

Separation of junior and senior college classes.—Nearly all of the colleges of this group give some attention to separating the work of the lower classes from that of the upper classes, although, as has already been shown, these plans are not always successful in providing homogeneous instructional groups. This division into junior and senior college levels is made on the assumption that the work of the lower classes is largely secondary in character and is for the most part prescribed, while the work of the upper classes is rather highly specialized. Brothers College has carried this idea further than any other college studied. That institution will admit students to the upper-class unit, after June, 1932, only after they have passed the upper-class admission comprehensive examinations. Most of the colleges studied make no real attempt to divide the students into an upper and a lower division. However, it is true that, in general, most of the work of the first two years of the college curriculum is prescribed, and the work of the last two years is largely elective within certain major and minor requirements or fields of concentration.

Methods of securing concentration.—Thirty of the colleges studied employ the major and one or two minors as a means of securing concentration in the student's work. Southwestern College and Iowa Wesleyan College use only the major for this purpose. Gooding College has no requirement for securing concentration. Brothers College and Hamline University have adopted the idea of a field of concentration as a means of unifying the advanced work of the student. The College of the Pacific has also begun a limited use of the field of concentration.

Honors courses.—One of the newer and most promising innovations in the colleges studied is their provision for honors, or independent work, courses. Courses of this type imply independent work on the part of the student with the advice of a member of the faculty. The student is excused from class attendance in an honors course and pursues his study individually under proper direction. In several colleges he is required to pass a comprehensive examination before he can graduate. In a number of the institutions the amount of work a student may pursue under this plan is limited, while in other colleges the student may take practically all of his upper-class work in this way. In a number of the colleges studied honors courses are available only in a few departments, while in other colleges work of this character may be had in all departments.

Honors courses are offered at Albion College, Baldwin-Wallace College, Brothers College, the University of Chattanooga, Cornell College, Dickinson College, Gooding College, Illinois Wesleyan University, Iowa Wesleyan College, Lawrence College, Morningside College, Nebraska Wesleyan University, Ohio Wesleyan University, the College of Puget Sound, and Willamette University—a total of fifteen colleges. Honors courses in practically all of these colleges may be pursued only by students who have attained a superior scholarship rating and have been approved by the faculty.

Attitude of the colleges.—These efforts at curriculum improvement show that a number of the colleges studied are experimenting with new ideas. A few colleges apparently are satisfied with their work, or find themselves unable for various reasons to adopt new ways. The general conservativeness of a few faculties militates against any important changes.

CHAPTER XXIX

SIZE OF CLASSES AND FACULTY SERVICE LOADS

SIZE OF CLASSES

An important index of the efficiency of the academic organization in a college is obtained by an analysis of the size of classes, particularly with reference to the number and proportion of exceptionally small classes that are maintained. Table 63 presents data for thirty-five colleges, showing for each the average size of class, the percentage of small classes, and the percentage of large classes. The average size of class is given both in terms of the median and the arithmetic mean.[1] The proportion of small classes is shown both as the percentage with fewer than five students enrolled and as the percentage with fewer than ten students.

There is a wide range in this group of colleges in the average size of classes, in the percentage of small classes, and in the percentage of large classes. Some of the strongest colleges in the group have an average size of class more than double that of other colleges. The percentage of small classes shows an even larger variation. All things considered, Dickinson College probably has the most economically organized instructional program of any of the thirty-five institutions. It is interesting to note that the colleges on the approved list of the Association of American Universities have a larger median size of classes, a smaller median percentage of small classes, and a larger median percentage of large classes than the institutions which do not hold national accreditation. Many college executives have assumed that small classes are a great advantage in instructional procedures. The data of this table are directly in conflict with this point of view; in so far as type of accreditation held is an index of educational excellence, it appears that the better institutions tend to have a larger average size of class, fewer small classes, and more large classes than the colleges not holding the highest recognition.

Table 64 presents data showing the relationship between the total number of students enrolled and factors relating to the size of class in this group of colleges.

[1] The "median" means the mid-point in the distribution of the size of classes, and is interpreted as meaning that half the classes are larger than this figure and half are smaller. The "arithmetic mean," frequently designated as the "average," is obtained by adding the enrolments in all classes and dividing by the number of classes.

TABLE 63

SIZE OF CLASSES AT THIRTY-FIVE COLLEGES

INSTITUTION	YEAR	MEDIAN SIZE OF CLASSES	MEAN SIZE OF CLASSES	PERCENTAGE OF ALL CLASSES		
				With Fewer than Five Students	With Fewer than Ten Students	With Thirty or More Students
*Mount Union	1930–31	21.0	19.8	14.9	26.3	22.7
*Dickinson	1929–30	20.9	19.7	2.8	8.6	8.5
*Ohio Wesleyan	1930–31	20.5	24.4	8.9	21.9	28.0
*DePauw	1930–31	20.3	21.9	6.2	19.8	19.5
*Albion	1929–30	18.8	20.4	15.4	29.1	21.8
Ohio Northern	1930–31	18.3	20.5	10.3	28.6	21.4
*Chattanooga	1929–30	18.3	19.2	15.5	29.1	20.6
*Simpson	1929–30	18.3	19.0	9.3	22.8	15.4
West Virginia Wesleyan	1930–31	17.7	18.7	7.7	30.0	21.4
*Allegheny	1929–30	17.5	21.4	5.3	20.9	18.5
Oklahoma City	1929–30	17.3	20.6	1.4	20.0	21.4
Southwestern	1930–31	17.2	19.9	9.6	29.0	18.0
*Illinois Wesleyan	1930–31	16.8	18.7	9.0	28.0	18.5
*Lawrence	1929–30	16.5	18.1	13.7	26.3	13.0
*Cornell	1929–30	16.1	18.3	19.6	37.7	18.1
*Morningside	1929–30	15.8	18.1	10.9	31.7	12.2
Iowa Wesleyan	1929–30	15.2	15.3	13.3	33.7	8.2
*Willamette	1930–31	15.1	18.8	17.3	35.2	17.2
Evansville	1929–30	14.7	17.0	16.9	36.8	16.0
McKendree	1930–31	14.5	17.8	5.7	30.2	13.0
*Baker	1930–31	14.5	17.2	20.9	33.6	11.8
Baldwin-Wallace	1930–31	13.9	16.8	16.2	36.8	16.1
Dakota Wesleyan	1929–30	13.9	14.5	15.4	36.9	1.5
*MacMurray	1930–31	13.6	16.6	13.3	33.6	7.7
*Hamline	1929–30	13.5	19.8	14.0	40.2	18.7
Puget Sound	1930–31	13.0	17.1	15.2	39.3	16.4
Union	1929–30	12.7	17.8	16.2	35.1	18.9
Nebraska Wesleyan	1930–31	12.7	15.8	18.4	41.3	13.6
Kansas Wesleyan	1930–31	12.5	15.1	18.2	41.4	12.2
Gooding	1930–31	10.6	13.2	12.5	47.5	5.0
*Pacific	1930–31	10.5	15.4	21.1	48.3	13.0
Ozark Wesleyan	1929–30	10.5	12.8	22.4	46.3	7.5
Intermountain	1930–31	9.0	11.2	22.4	56.9	1.7
Central Wesleyan	1929–30	8.6	11.1	31.2	57.8	6.1
Brothers	1930–31	7.1	10.3	43.3	59.5	2.7
Median, all colleges		15.1	18.1	14.9	33.6	16.0
*Median, A.A.U. colleges		16.8	19.0	13.7	29.1	18.1
Median, non-A.A.U. colleges		13.5	16.3	15.8	36.9	13.3

* Institutions on the approved list of the Association of American Universities.

This table indicates that the enrolment of a college tends to have a marked effect on the distribution of class size. The large colleges tend to have a larger average size of class, a smaller percentage of small classes, and a larger percentage of large classes than is the case in the smaller institutions. This relationship is shown graphically in Figure 17. It is clear

TABLE 64

AVERAGE SIZE OF CLASS FOR COLLEGES HAVING VARIOUS
NUMBERS OF STUDENTS ENROLLED

NUMBER OF STUDENTS ENROLLED	NUMBER OF COLLEGES	AVERAGE OF MEDIAN SIZE OF CLASSES	AVERAGE OF MEAN SIZE OF CLASSES	AVERAGE PERCENTAGE OF ALL CLASSES WITH		
				Fewer than Five Students	Fewer than Ten Students	Thirty or More Students
700 and over..............	6	18.6	20.9	9.3	24.3	22.5
400 to 699...............	17	15.8	18.3	13.7	31.9	15.7
Less than 400............	12	12.3	14.6	18.8	42.7	9.5

that the opportunities for providing instructional groups of relatively large size are better when the total enrolment is large than when it is small.

6 colleges, each
enrolling 700 or over   18.6

17 colleges, each
enrolling 400–699   15.8

12 colleges, each
enrolling under 400   12.3

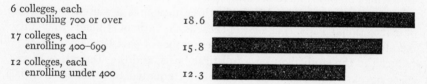

FIG. 17.—Average of median size of classes in groups of colleges with various numbers of students enrolled.

Recent educational experimentation has thrown some doubt upon the supposed advantages of instruction in small class groups.[1] This experimentation, while not proving conclusively that students learn better in large classes than in small ones, has at least shifted the burden of the proof to those who would contend that the achievement of students is improved by reducing the size of class sections. As a result of these studies several of the colleges are planning for the introduction of a policy looking toward the creation of more classes of relatively large size. A few of the institutions studied are definitely planning to take this step as an experiment,

[1] Earl Hudelson, *Class Size at the College Level* (Minneapolis: University of Minnesota Press, 1928), p. 270.

in order to test scientifically under their own local conditions the relative merits of instruction in small and large classes.

The standardizing associations have long looked with disfavor on large classes. The standard of the North Central Association of Colleges and Secondary Schools[1] reads as follows: "Classes (exclusive of lectures) of more than thirty students should be interpreted as endangering educational efficiency." During recent years the Association has not enforced this standard rigidly, however, and in view of the results of recently published studies it appears probable that even greater leniency on this matter will be shown in the future.[2]

Regardless of one's opinions respecting the merits of instruction in large classes, there can be no question regarding the financial inefficiency of instruction in groups as small as four students or even in groups with fewer than ten students. A sound curricular organization for the college may necessitate some small classes, but these should be held to the very minimum permitted by a satisfactory educational service to students. The reduction in the number of small classes presents one of the most important opportunities for economy in the organization of the colleges studied.

SERVICE LOADS OF FACULTY

Various methods have been proposed for measuring the service loads of faculty members.[3] In this study three measures are used as indexes of instructional loads. The first of these is the ratio of students to faculty members. In computing this ratio the number of part-time instructors is reduced to the equivalent on a full-time basis, and the students who are carrying part-time schedules are similarly equated to a full-time basis.

The second measure used is the average number of credit-hours taught by faculty members per week—an index of loads which is employed most generally by standardizing agencies and by college administrators in making out term schedules. This index is based upon the assumption that the teaching of one credit-hour requires a standard amount of time in preparation, of energy in conducting the class hour, and of effort in reading papers and measuring results, irrespective of the subject taught, the methods employed, or the size of class.

The third index of teaching load used is the average number of student-

---

[1] *North Central Association Quarterly*, VI, No. 1, 36.

[2] The standard was abolished by the North Central Association in March, 1932.

[3] For illustrations of the use of various measuring devices for service loads, see Reeves and Russell, *College Organization and Administration* (Indianapolis: Board of Education, Disciples of Christ, 1929), pp. 165–82.

credit-hours per instructor. A student-credit-hour is defined as one student under instruction for a given period of time for which he receives one semester hour of credit. Thus, a class of twenty students in a course for which three hours of credit are given would impose a load of sixty student-credit-hours on the instructor. This measure makes no allowances for variations in the length of the period of instruction, a two-hour or three-hour laboratory period for which one hour of credit is granted being considered equal in load to a one-hour period of lecture or recitation.

There are numerous other factors which affect the teaching load of a faculty member, such as the number of separate preparations which are to be made for class instruction, the methods employed, the subjects taught, and the training and ability of the instructor. No attempt is made to measure the effect of these factors upon load, since the purpose of the study is not to measure the loads of individual instructors but of faculties as a whole. For the latter purpose it is thought that a combination of the three indexes used affords a reasonably satisfactory measure.

Table 65 presents data regarding the service loads of faculty members at thirty-five colleges, in terms of the three measures discussed. The figures relate to the loads being carried during the semester or term in which the study was made. The data for these institutions are further summarized in Table 66 with the colleges grouped on the basis of enrolment.

It will be observed that there is a wide range in the ratio of full-time students to full-time faculty members among the thirty-five institutions represented in Table 65. The small ratio at Brothers College is due to the fact that this is a new institution and has not reached the level of enrolments for which the staffing has been planned. The institution with the highest student-faculty ratio (Oklahoma City University) is also a special case. The unusually high ratio at this institution is made necessary by a shortage of funds for the support of the program. The factors which contribute to the high ratio of students to faculty members at Oklahoma City University are: first, an unusually heavy schedule of teaching hours for faculty members; second, a relatively high average number of student-credit-hours per instructor; third, a rather low average credit-hour load carried by full-time students. Both Brothers College and Oklahoma City University are omitted from Table 66.

It will be noted that the two extremes in ratios of students to faculty members, as shown by Table 65, are occupied by institutions which are not on the approved list of the Association of American Universities. The median institution of the seventeen on the approved list of the Association of American Universities has a slightly higher student-faculty ratio

TABLE 65

SERVICE LOADS OF FACULTY AT THIRTY-FIVE COLLEGES

Institution	Year	Number of Faculty Members Equated to Full-Time Basis	Number of Students Equated to Full-Time Basis	Average Number of Student-Credit-Hours per Full-Time Instructor	Average Number of Credit-Hours Taught per Full-Time Instructor	Number of Full-Time Students per Full-Time Faculty Member
Oklahoma City..........	1929–30	27.4	839	359	17.7	30.6
*Mount Union...........	1930–31	27.5	528	329	15.1	19.2
*Albion................	1929–30	42.2	752	309	14.7	17.8
Puget Sound............	1930–31	38.0	658	301	15.1	17.3
Ohio Northern..........	1930–31	46.6	799	288	15.3	17.1
*Allegheny.............	1929–30	39.9	641	266	12.9	16.1
*Chattanooga...........	1929–30	27.1	437	292	15.2	16.1
*Dickinson.............	1929–30	36.0	570	263	14.7	15.8
*DePauw...............	1930–31	91.3	1,442	292	13.3	15.8
*Illinois Wesleyan........	1930–31	34.8	543	262	14.5	15.6
West Virginia Wesleyan..	1930–31	22.8	354	281	15.6	15.5
Baldwin-Wallace........	1930–31	27.4	423	264	14.2	15.4
Dakota Wesleyan........	1929–30	20.7	310	243	15.9	15.0
*Lawrence..............	1929–30	52.1	782	221	12.9	15.0
*Simpson...............	1929–30	42.3	621	275	14.2	14.7
Kansas Wesleyan........	1930–31	18.2	267	247	17.1	14.7
*Willamette.............	1930–31	38.0	557	292	16.2	14.7
Southwestern...........	1930–31	36.1	531	293	14.4	14.7
*Baker.................	1930–31	29.3	422	238	14.6	14.4
Union.................	1929–30	9.9	143	264	16.1	14.4
*Ohio Wesleyan..........	1930–31	128.9	1,831	274	11.4	14.2
*Cornell................	1929–30	40.5	546	268	14.2	13.5
Nebraska Wesleyan......	1930–31	44.8	573	224	13.4	13.0
Intermountain..........	1930–31	12.4	162	165	15.6	13.0
*Hamline...............	1929–30	34.9	435	280	14.3	12.5
McKendree.............	1930–31	20.9	261	210	12.6	12.5
Evansville.............	1929–30	26.0	324	199	14.8	12.4
*Morningside...........	1929–30	48.8	599	248	14.6	12.3
*MacMurray...........	1930–31	37.1	425	207	13.8	11.5
*Pacific................	1930–31	59.3	673	194	11.9	11.4
Iowa Wesleyan..........	1929–30	27.0	305	242	16.0	11.3
Gooding...............	1930–31	10.2	114	173	15.3	11.2
Ozark Wesleyan........	1929–30	20.3	199	162	13.3	9.8
Central Wesleyan........	1929–30	16.5	135	165	16.0	8.2
Brothers...............	1930–31	11.2	64	86	9.6	5.7
Median, all colleges...	....	34.8	528	263	14.6	14.7
*Median, A.A.U. colleges...............	....	39.9	570	268	14.3	14.7
Median, non-A.A.U. colleges............	....	21.9	308	243	15.3	13.7

* Institutions on the approved list of the Association of American Universities.

than the median institution of the eighteen colleges not holding national accreditation. It should be noted that several very good institutions have student-faculty ratios in excess of 15 to 1. Two colleges of higher standing (Mount Union and Albion) have full-time faculty ratios of 19.2 to 1 and 17.8 to 1, respectively.

The ratio of students to faculty members is affected by the enrolment of an institution. Table 66 shows that a positive correlation exists between institutional enrolments and ratios of full-time students to full-time faculty members. The average ratios range from over 15 to 1 in institutions with enrolments of six hundred and over to approximately 11 to 1 in institutions with enrolments under two hundred.

TABLE 66

AVERAGE SERVICE LOADS OF FACULTIES IN COLLEGES*
HAVING VARIOUS ENROLMENTS

Enrolment	Number of Institutions	Average Number of Student-Credit-Hours per Full-Time Instructor	Average Number of Credit-Hours Taught per Full-Time Instructor	Average Number of Full-Time Students per Full-Time Faculty Member
800 and over..............	2	283	12.4	15.0
600–799.................	8	270	14.6	15.3
400–599.................	12	266	14.6	14.6
200–399.................	6	243	15.8	13.6
Less than 200............	5	165	15.6	11.2

* Brothers College and Oklahoma City University are omitted from this tabulation.

In a four-year college of liberal arts with a relatively small budget for faculty salaries, a student-faculty ratio such as that of Mount Union College or Albion College is probably preferable to a lower ratio, unless the institution has a very small enrolment. Most institutions in the past have not organized their faculties on this principle; in fact, the suggestion of a larger student-faculty ratio for institutions with limited financial resources has been promulgated only recently. Studies of class size have thrown considerable doubt upon the supposed advantages of small classes for instructional purposes and are affecting the existing ideas regarding desirable ratios of students to instructors. In the light of these studies many authorities in the field of college education are now advising a higher student-faculty ratio in colleges with limited funds. It is conceded that, if ample funds are available, a low student-faculty ratio may be, and probably is, preferable to a high ratio. Where only limited funds are available for faculty salaries, however, it appears desirable to pay higher salaries to fewer instructors rather than lower salaries to a larger teaching staff.

A calculation may be made from the data of Table 65 of the number of faculty members who could be dispensed with in this group of thirty-five colleges, provided it were possible to organize all of them as economically as Mount Union College and Albion College. On the basis of a student-faculty ratio of 19.2 to 1, the services of approximately three hundred instructors could be dispensed with in this group of thirty-five colleges, assuming that the total number of students remains constant. On the basis of a student-faculty ratio of 17.8 to 1, the instructional staffs could be reduced by two hundred and twenty members. From two points of view the maintenance of smaller teaching staffs would be advantageous in institutions of limited funds. In the first place, the operating budget would be more easily balanced; in the second place, salaries for the staff members who are retained could be made more attractive, ultimately resulting in improvement in the general quality of the teaching staff.

There are several conditioning factors which affect the ratio of students to faculty. Among these factors is that of the size of the college, which has already been mentioned. In an institution with fewer than five hundred students it is usually difficult to arrange an adequate program with a relatively high ratio of students to faculty. The second conditioning factor is the general trend in enrolments. Colleges in which enrolments are increasing can plan their staffing more economically than colleges in which enrolments are decreasing. With a decreasing student body it is usually difficult to make satisfactory adjustments of the teaching staff rapidly enough to maintain an economical ratio of students to faculty.

The suggestion which is made for increasing the student-faculty ratio should not be construed to mean that instructors should carry heavier teaching schedules. The readjustment should be brought about by an increase in the student-credit-hour loads taught, rather than by an increase in the average number of hours of teaching. This suggestion means essentially that in a college with a stable enrolment there will be a reduction in the number of small classes accompanying the reduction in the size of the teaching staff.

The standards of regional accrediting associations suggest that teaching schedules in excess of sixteen credit-hours per week will be interpreted as endangering educational efficiency. It will be noted from Table 65 that four of the thirty-five colleges have average teaching loads in excess of sixteen credit-hours per week, and that two others average sixteen credit-hours per week. In all but three of the colleges (MacMurray College,

McKendree College, and College of the Pacific) one or more members of the faculty were at the time of the survey visit carrying heavier schedules of teaching hours than is permitted by the accepted standards.

It will be noted from Table 65 that several of the stronger colleges in this group have average teaching schedules of approximately thirteen hours per week or less. This is a commendable tendency. It has already been pointed out that in practically all of the colleges large numbers of small classes are maintained. The elimination of classes which are in demand by only a few students and which are not essential to the curriculum of the college should result in an opportunity to reduce the teaching schedules carried by instructors, even though the ratio of the number of students to the number of faculty members be increased. The time of faculty members thus released may well serve the college much more effectively if directed toward scholarly productivity and better teaching in the other classes than, as spent at present, in the giving of instruction to very small class groups.

Table 66 shows that the number of credit-hours taught tends to be greater in the small institutions than in the larger ones, even though the ratios of students to faculty members are much smaller in the former than in the latter.

The average number of student-credit-hours per full-time instructor shows a rather wide range. Four of the colleges shown in Table 65 have an average in excess of three hundred student-credit-hours per instructor; six (excluding Brothers College) have an average below two hundred.

In many of the non-laboratory subjects a teacher might well be expected to carry three hundred and fifty student-credit-hours per week without being overburdened, if the program is organized so that the instructor is not called upon to teach a number of small classes. It is obvious from Table 65 that the average teaching load in terms of student-credit-hours at many of these institutions could be markedly increased. An increase in the student-faculty ratio would operate to increase the average student-credit-load of instructors. As previously pointed out, however, this need not be accompanied by an increase in the number of credit-hours taught, provided there is a corresponding reduction in the number of small classes.

Throughout this discussion attention has been called to the effect of the size of enrolments upon teaching loads. These effects may be summarized from Table 66 as follows: The larger institutions tend to have a larger number of student-credit-hours, a smaller number of credit-hours per instructor, and a higher student-faculty ratio than the smaller colleges;

the smaller institutions, on the other hand, tend to have a relatively light average student-credit-hour load and a low student-faculty ratio, but the teachers carry rather heavy teaching schedules in terms of credit-hours. The comparisons all bring out forcefully the advantages enjoyed by the larger institutions. The shorter teaching schedule in terms of credit-hours, accompanied by a reasonably high student-credit-hour load, means that the time of the instructors is partially free from routine classroom teaching, with consequent opportunity for better preparation for the courses taught, for personal conferences with students, and for productive scholarship. The higher student-faculty ratio has made possible the release of funds for the payment of larger faculty salaries. The data lead to the conclusion that colleges of small enrolment have unquestionable handicaps owing to the difficulty of a satisfactory and economical assignment of teaching loads.

CHAPTER XXX

FACULTY SALARIES

AVERAGE FACULTY SALARIES BY RANKS

One of the most important indexes of the quality of the program offered by an educational institution is the average salary paid faculty members. Table 67 shows for the thirty-five colleges studied the average salaries received by full-time members of the teaching staffs, classified by rank. In making these computations all persons who did not give full-time service to the institution were excluded. The salaries of deans and other administrative officers (except the presidents) were figured in at the academic rank held.

The table shows a variation of more than 2 to 1 in the average salaries at all ranks among the thirty-five colleges. It is important to note that the median of the average salaries for the seventeen colleges on the approved list of the Association of American Universities is $384 above the corresponding median for the group of eighteen institutions which do not hold national accreditation. There is evidence from these data of a fairly close relationship between the holding of satisfactory accreditation and the average salary of faculty members. It will be noted that only two colleges which are not on the approved list of the Association of American Universities (Brothers College and Baldwin-Wallace College) have average salaries in excess of the median of the colleges approved by the Association of American Universities.[1] Three of the seventeen colleges on the approved list of the Association have average salaries below the median for the colleges not holding national accreditation.

The variation in the salary at the rank of professor is more pronounced than that for all ranks combined. The range between the lowest and the highest average for professors is 1 to 3. At this rank there is a difference of $653 between the median for colleges on the approved list of the Association of American Universities and the median for the colleges not holding this accreditation. Only two of the seventeen colleges on the Association's list have average salaries for professors below the median of the eighteen colleges not holding national accreditation. Only two colleges not on the

[1] Baldwin-Wallace College has been placed on the approved list of the Association of American Universities since these data were compiled.

285

TABLE 67

AVERAGE SALARIES RECEIVED BY FULL-TIME MEMBERS OF THE
TEACHING STAFFS OF THIRTY-FIVE COLLEGES

Institution	Year	All Ranks	Professor	Associate Professor	Assistant Professor	Instructor
*DePauw................	1930–31	$3,205	$4,070	$3,310	$2,668	$2,178
*Dickinson..............	1929–30	3,180	3,797	2,832	....	2,469
*Mount Union...........	1930–31	3,092	3,400	2,675	2,225	3,000
*Allegheny..............	1929–30	3,078	4,300	2,867	2,580	2,050
Brothers................	1930–31	3,067	4,877	3,800	2,700	1,500
*Lawrence..............	1929–30	3,060	3,696	2,975	2,536	2,000
Baldwin-Wallace........	1930–31	2,956	3,518	2,683	2,200	1,761
*Hamline...............	1929–30	2,936	3,310	3,080	....	1,933
*Ohio Wesleyan..........	1930–31	2,855	4,024	3,118	2,470	1,919
*Albion.................	1929–30	2,812	3,295	3,200	2,533	2,160
*Chattanooga...........	1929–30	2,778	3,492	2,700	2,650	1,500
Oklahoma City..........	1929–30	2,744	2,912	2,400	2,120	2,000
*Pacific................	1930–31	2,738	3,176	2,750	2,508	2,223
West Virginia Wesleyan..	1930–31	2,695	2,705	....	2,500	....
*Willamette.............	1930–31	2,588	2,905	....	2,211	1,600
Evansville.............	1929–30	2,580	3,054	2,500	2,360	1,909
Ohio Northern..........	1930–31	2,558	2,697	....	2,520	1,907
*Illinois Wesleyan........	1929–30	2,541	2,894	....	2,321	1,900
*Cornell................	1929–30	2,538	2,976	....	2,200	1,883
*Baker.................	1930–31	2,500	2,657	....	2,088	....
Puget Sound............	1930–31	2,477	2,728	2,792	1,867	1,560
Kansas Wesleyan........	1930–31	2,429	2,429	....	....	....
Dakota Wesleyan........	1929–30	2,394	2,621	....	2,033	1,780
Southwestern...........	1930–31	2,393	2,662	2,150	2,200	1,470
Nebraska Wesleyan......	1930–31	2,329	2,800	....	2,000	1,575
Union.................	1929–30	2,322	2,425	....	....	1,500
McKendree.............	1930–31	2,203	2,404	....	1,933	1,500
*Morningside...........	1929–30	2,158	2,855	....	2,100	1,717
*MacMurray............	1930–31	2,139	2,447	2,000	2,050	1,891
*Simpson...............	1929–30	2,130	2,476	2,000	1,744	1,670
Iowa Wesleyan..........	1929–30	2,091	2,276	1,950	1,800	1,233
Intermountain..........	1930–31	2,038	2,256	....	1,683	1,700
Ozark Wesleyan........	1929–30	2,015	2,015	....	....	....
Central Wesleyan........	1929–30	1,835	1,835	....	....	....
Gooding................	1930–31	1,588	1,618	....	....	1,375
Median,† all colleges..	....	$2,541	$2,855	$2,750	$2,206	$1,832
*Median,† A.A.U. colleges...............	....	2,778	3,295	2,850	2,321	1,926
Median,† non-A.A.U. colleges...............	....	2,394	2,642	2,500	2,120	1,568

* Institutions on the approved list of the Association of American Universities.
† Medians are based on the institutions in which the respective ranks are represented.

approved list have average salaries for professors above the median of those on the list.

Only nineteen of the institutions studied use the rank of associate professor for any full-time faculty member, and in most of these institutions the number of faculty members holding this title is relatively small. Consequently, the averages are somewhat less reliable than those for the rank of professor. The median for salaries paid associate professors in those colleges on the approved list of the Association of American Universities is $350 above that for the group of colleges not holding this type of accreditation.

Seven of the thirty-five colleges do not make use of the rank of assistant professor for any full-time faculty member. As in the case of associate professors, the number holding this rank is usually relatively small and consequently the averages are not especially reliable. It will be noted from the group median that there is a difference of $201 in favor of the colleges on the approved list of the Association of American Universities.

All but five of the colleges use the rank of instructor for some full-time members of the teaching staffs. In the average salaries of instructors there is a difference in the medians of $358 in favor of the colleges on the approved list of the Association of American Universities. If three or four of the exceptional cases be excluded, the range of the average salary paid instructors is much lower than that at any of the other ranks. It may be pointed out that in several of the colleges the average salaries at this rank are lower than are those ordinarily paid to well-trained high-school teachers, and probably do not permit the standard of living ordinarily expected of college teachers.

Attention may be called to the varying degrees of differentiation in average salaries among the different ranks. There is a notable difference among the institutions with respect to the ratios of average salaries of professors to average salaries of instructors. In one institution (Brothers College) this ratio is more than 3.2 to 1. In another institution (MacMurray College) the ratio is slightly less than 1.3 to 1. The colleges on the approved list of the Association of American Universities make a somewhat larger differentiation, as indicated by the median, than the colleges which are not on the approved list.

A careful study of this problem leads to the conclusion that a fairly high differentiation is advisable. Although the salaries at the lowest ranks must not fall below a satisfactory minimum, the fact that there are on the faculty some positions with a relatively high remuneration provides a stimulation to the younger members of the teaching staff, and should result in attracting and holding capable instructors.

RELATION BETWEEN SIZE OF INSTITUTION AND AVERAGE
FACULTY SALARY

Table 68 shows the average salaries of faculty members of thirty-four colleges, grouped according to the size of the institution. Data for Brothers College are not included in this table, since that institution was not yet a four-year college at the time the data were assembled; and for this and other reasons previously mentioned this college is not typical of the smaller institutions.

TABLE 68

AVERAGE SALARIES OF FACULTY MEMBERS OF THIRTY-FOUR COLLEGES,
GROUPED ACCORDING TO THE SIZE OF THE INSTITUTION

| ENROLMENT | NUMBER OF INSTITUTIONS | AVERAGE SALARIES AT THE MEDIAN INSTITUTION FOR | | | |
		All Ranks	Professor	Associate and Assistant Professor	Instructor
800 and over...........	3	$2,855	$4,024	$2,654	$2,000
600–799...............	8	2,648	3,035	2,520	1,454
400–599...............	12	2,563	2,941	2,200	1,760
200–399...............	7	2,412	2,525	1,983	1,780
Less than 200..........	4	2,015	2,015	1,683	1,500

The relationship between average faculty salaries for all ranks combined and the size of the college is shown graphically in Figure 18.

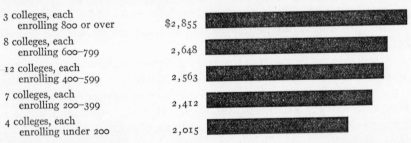

3 colleges, each enrolling 800 or over	$2,855
8 colleges, each enrolling 600–799	2,648
12 colleges, each enrolling 400–599	2,563
7 colleges, each enrolling 200–399	2,412
4 colleges, each enrolling under 200	2,015

FIG. 18.—Average faculty salaries, all ranks combined, for colleges grouped according to size of enrolment.

An examination of Table 68 shows that there is a direct relationship between salaries paid and institutional enrolments. The average salary paid to faculty members of all ranks combined is 42 per cent greater in colleges with enrolments of eight hundred and over than that in colleges with enrolments under two hundred. The average salary for staff members holding the rank of full professor is 100 per cent greater for the former group than for the latter group. In the colleges with enrolments of eight hundred and over, the average salary paid to associate and assistant professors exceeds by 58 per cent, and the average for instructors exceeds by 33 per cent, the respective averages paid to faculty members of similar rank in institutions with enrolments under two hundred.

MAXIMUM AND MINIMUM INSTRUCTIONAL SALARIES

Table 69 shows the distribution of maximum instructional salaries of full-time teachers at the various ranks in thirty-five colleges. By "maximum" instructional salary is meant the highest annual salary (nine months) paid any teacher of the college at the rank indicated.

TABLE 69

DISTRIBUTION OF MAXIMUM INSTRUCTIONAL SALARIES OF FULL-TIME TEACHERS AT THE VARIOUS RANKS IN THIRTY-FIVE COLLEGES

MAXIMUM SALARY FOR ACADEMIC YEAR OF NINE MONTHS	NUMBER OF INSTITUTIONS WITH MAXIMUM SALARIES AS INDICATED AT THE VARIOUS RANKS			
	Professor	Associate Professor	Assistant Professor	Instructor
$6,000 and above..............	2	....	....	....
5,000–$5,999................	4	....	....	....
4,000– 4,999................	10	3	....	....
3,500– 3,999................	6	2	1	1
3,000– 3,499................	7	4	2	3
2,500– 2,999................	4	6	15	5
2,000– 2,499................	2	4	8	14
1,500– 1,999................	....	....	2	6
Below $1,500.................	....	....	....	1
Total....................	35	19*	28†	30‡
Median salary§...........	$3,600	$2,850	$2,500	$2,100

* Sixteen colleges have no full-time teachers at this rank.
† Seven colleges have no full-time teachers at this rank.
‡ Five colleges have no full-time teachers at this rank.
§ Calculated from an ungrouped distribution.

This table is read as follows: At two of the colleges the maximum salary for the rank of professor is $6,000 or above; at four colleges the maximum salary at the rank of professor is between $5,000 and $5,999, etc. The table shows that in these colleges the median situation for maximum salaries of professors is $3,600; for associate professors, $2,850; for assistant professors, $2,500; and for instructors, $2,100. This means that half of the colleges pay some member of their faculty holding the rank of professor $3,600 or more, etc.

Table 70 shows the distribution of minimum instructional salaries of full-time teachers at the various ranks in these colleges. By "minimum" instructional salary is meant the lowest annual salary (nine months) paid any teacher of the college at the rank indicated.

This table is read as follows: There are two colleges which do not pay anyone holding the rank of professor less than $4,000; there are five colleges whose minimum salaries for the rank of professor fall in the range of $3,000–$3,499, etc. The medians indicate that half of the colleges have

TABLE 70

DISTRIBUTION OF MINIMUM INSTRUCTIONAL SALARIES OF FULL-TIME
TEACHERS AT THE VARIOUS RANKS IN THIRTY-FIVE COLLEGES

MINIMUM SALARY FOR ACADEMIC YEAR OF NINE MONTHS	NUMBER OF INSTITUTIONS WITH MINIMUM SALARIES INDICATED AT VARIOUS RANKS			
	Professor	Associate Professor	Assistant Professor	Instructor
$4,000 or above..............	2	....	....	....
3,500–$3,999.................	....	1	....	....
3,000– 3,499...............	5	2	....	1
2,500– 2,999...............	5	7	2	....
2,000– 2,499...............	13	8	12	1
1,500– 1,999...............	7	1	11	16
Less than $1,500.............	3	....	3	12
Total....................	35	19*	28†	30‡
Median salary§...........	$2,150	$2,550	$2,000	$1,500

* Sixteen institutions have no full-time teachers at this rank.
† Seven institutions have no full-time teachers at this rank.
‡ Five colleges have no full-time teachers at this rank.
§ Calculated from an ungrouped distribution.

some full-time member of their faculty holding the rank of professor who receives a salary of $2,150 or less. It is interesting to note that the median of the minimum salaries at the rank of associate professor is $400 above that at the rank of professor. This is brought about by the fact that the rank of associate professor is used principally in those institutions which have a somewhat higher general salary scale. Attention may again be called to the fact that the minimum salaries for the rank of instructor are relatively low. Half of the colleges using this title have some members of their teaching staffs at this rank who receive $1,500 or less. As has previously been pointed out, this is an inadequate compensation for college faculty members, even though they hold the lowest academic rank.

OUTSIDE EARNINGS OF FACULTY MEMBERS

In making this study, information was sought from the faculty members of each college regarding their outside earnings. These included all remuneration received from the college itself for other than the regular nine months teaching, such as extension work, summer-session teaching, etc. It also included work done outside the college for which compensation was received. Table 71 presents data regarding the supplementary income and total income received by full-time faculty members of the thirty-five colleges studied.

It will be observed from this table that in the median institution one-half of the faculty members received some additional remuneration beyond their annual nine months' salary. The percentage of the faculty receiving outside remuneration is smaller, on the average, for the colleges on the approved list of the Association of American Universities than for the group of institutions which do not hold this type of accreditation. It will be noted, however, that the average outside earnings of those who do outside work is larger in the colleges on this approved list than in the other institutions. In general, the consideration of the outside earnings does not make any marked difference in the ranking of the colleges according to total salary.

ADEQUACY OF FACULTY SALARIES

Life insurance carried as an index of adequacy of salaries.—In an endeavor to evaluate the salaries paid in the various institutions, information was sought from faculty members regarding the amount of life insurance carried. It was considered by the survey staff that these data might prove to be a valid index of the relative adequacy of salaries, on the assumption that life insurance represents opportunity for savings. Table 72 presents data concerning the average amount of life insurance carried by the faculty members of thirty-five colleges.

It will be observed that there is a remarkable range in the average amount of life insurance carried. Statistical calculations show that there is a coefficient of correlation (Pearson) of $+.80\pm.04$ between the average salary of faculty members and the average amount of life insurance carried. The correlation indicates a rather close relationship between average salary and amount of life insurance carried. The data indicate that the differences which exist in the average salary at the various institutions tend to be reflected in the ability of the faculty to make savings.

Local variations in cost of living.—Some of the colleges where faculty salaries are relatively low are located in regions where living costs, par-

TABLE 71

SUPPLEMENTARY INCOME AND TOTAL INCOME RECEIVED BY FULL-TIME
FACULTY MEMBERS OF THIRTY-FIVE COLLEGES

Institution	Year	Percentage of Faculty Receiving Additional Remuneration	Average Earnings of Faculty Members Doing Outside Work	Average Outside Earnings of Entire Faculty	Sum of Average Salary and Average Outside Earnings of Entire Faculty
Brothers...............	1930–31	57	$ 733	$419	$3,486
*Dickinson.............	1929–30	61	362	221	3,401
*Mount Union..........	1930–31	46	624	288	3,380
Baldwin-Wallace.......	1930–31	53	772	412	3,368
*Pacific................	1930–31	45	536	244	3,359
*DePauw..............	1930–31	35	439	153	3,358
*Allegheny............	1929–30	36	689	248	3,326
Oklahoma City........	1929–30	81	645	516	3,260
*Lawrence.............	1929–30	43	474	210	3,238
*Hamline..............	1929–30	48	400	192	3,128
*Baker.................	1930–31	37	1,707	626	3,121
*Albion................	1929–30	47	472	205	3,020
*Ohio Wesleyan........	1930–31	40	410	163	3,018
Evansville............	1929–30	71	597	424	3,004
West Virginia Wesleyan.	1930–31	79	386	306	3,001
*Chattanooga..........	1929–30	33	666	220	2,998
*Willamette............	1930–31	55	592	323	2,911
Southwestern..........	1930–31	58	861	495	2,888
*Illinois Wesleyan......	1930–31	63	476	299	2,840
Ohio Northern........	1930–31	60	378	227	2,785
*Cornell...............	1929–30	50	377	189	2,727
Puget Sound..........	1930–31	60	322	194	2,671
Nebraska Wesleyan.....	1930–31	53	617	330	2,659
Kansas Wesleyan......	1930–31	39	346	135	2,564
Dakota Wesleyan......	1929–30	50	331	166	2,560
McKendree...........	1930–31	62	454	281	2,484
*Morningside..........	1929–30	46	432	199	2,357
Union...............	1929–30	10	50	5	2,327
*Simpson.............	1929–30	38	316	120	2,250
*MacMurray...........	1930–31	26	388	102	2,241
Ozark Wesleyan.......	1929–30	50	330	165	2,180
Intermountain........	1930–31	33	377	126	2,166
Iowa Wesleyan.......	1929–30	20	290	58	2,149
Central Wesleyan.....	1929–30	78	354	275	2,110
Gooding..............	1930–31	25	540	135	1,723
Median, all colleges..	....	50	$ 439	$220	$2,888
*Median, A.A.U. colleges.............	....	45	472	210	3,020
Median, non-A.A.U. colleges..........	....	55	382	251	2,612

* Institutions on the approved list of the Association of American Universities.

TABLE 72

AVERAGE AMOUNTS OF INSURANCE CARRIED BY MEMBERS OF THE
TEACHING STAFFS OF THIRTY-FIVE COLLEGES

Institution	Year	Average Salary of Faculty Members	Average Amount of Insurance Carried
*DePauw.................	1930–31	$3,205	$9,998
*Lawrence...............	1929–30	3,060	9,255
Evansville..............	1929–30	2,580	7,846
*Chattanooga............	1929–30	2,778	7,739
*Dickinson..............	1929–30	3,180	7,727
*Hamline...............	1929–30	2,936	7,450
Southwestern...........	1930–31	2,393	7,233
*Albion.................	1929–30	2,812	7,291
*Allegheny..............	1929–30	3,078	7,165
*Mount Union...........	1930–31	3,092	6,949
*Pacific.................	1930–31	2,738	6,787
*Ohio Wesleyan..........	1930–31	2,855	6,704
*Cornell................	1929–30	2,538	6,500
Brothers...............	1930–31	3,067	6,467
West Virginia Wesleyan....	1930–31	2,695	6,379
Baldwin-Wallace.........	1930–31	2,956	6,198
*Illinois Wesleyan.........	1930–31	2,541	6,195
Puget Sound............	1930–31	2,477	5,998
Ohio Northern..........	1930–31	2,558	5,938
Kansas Wesleyan........	1930–31	2,429	5,676
Dakota Wesleyan........	1929–30	2,394	5,479
Oklahoma City..........	1929–30	2,744	5,222
*Simpson................	1929–30	2,130	5,108
*Baker..................	1930–31	2,500	5,020
Nebraska Wesleyan.......	1930–31	2,329	5,002
Ozark Wesleyan..........	1929–30	2,015	4,925
*Morningside............	1929–30	2,158	4,848
*Willamette.............	1930–31	2,588	4,615
Central Wesleyan........	1929–30	1,835	4,333
McKendree..............	1930–31	2,203	3,830
*MacMurray.............	1930–31	2,139	3,605
Union..................	1929–30	2,322	2,778
Iowa Wesleyan..........	1929–30	2,091	2,500
Intermountain...........	1930–31	2,038	2,453
Gooding................	1930–31	1,588	1,958
Median, all colleges.....	....	$2,541	$5,998
*Median, A.A.U. colleges	....	2,778	6,787
Median, non-A.A.U. colleges...............	....	2,394	5,351

* Institutions on the approved list of the Association of American Universities.

ticularly house rent, are not as high as in the larger cities. The presidents of some of these colleges have suggested that they are able to employ well-qualified faculty members at much lower rates than some of the other institutions. The validity of this contention is open to serious question. If living costs are low in the communities where the colleges which have relatively low salaries are located, this condition should be reflected in an ability on the part of faculty members to make savings in life insurance. The data presented above show that this is not the case. A study of the living costs of public-school teachers, recently completed for selected communities in New York State by Dr. Harry,[1] shows a correlation of $+.48$ between the population of a city and the index of the cost of living for its teachers. This study tends to substantiate the idea that the smaller communities have an advantage due to lower living costs. The range in living costs, however, is undoubtedly much smaller than the range in average faculty salaries, as shown in Table 67. This indicates that a large part of the variation in salary of faculty members cannot be accounted for by differences in the cost of living.

Effect of current trends in living costs on faculty salaries.—The decade just passed has witnessed a large increase in the average annual salary paid faculty members. The survey staff has not collected specific data on this point from each of the institutions; but, in several cases where the trend of salaries was investigated, the increases amounted to as much as 50 per cent over the base of a decade ago. During the year 1930–31 the survey staff encountered considerable questioning in several colleges as to the advisability of maintaining present salary scales, in view of the decreasing cost of living. At the same time colleges were finding their sources of income curtailed, and in many cases real embarrassment was being suffered because of a shortage of income. The natural suggestion of the business men on many boards of trustees was for a reduction in faculty salaries. In some cases a reduction in average faculty salaries was actually being accomplished by replacing professors at the higher salaries, who left the institutions in the normal course of the faculty turnover, by others at lower salaries. In some of the colleges the budgets constructed for 1931–32 contemplated actual decreases for the salaries of faculty members.

NEED FOR INCREASED SALARIES

At this stage of the economic cycle it is very difficult to forecast the effect of living costs on professional incomes. The writers are, in gen-

[1] David P. Harry, *Cost of Living of Teachers in the State of New York* (New York: Bureau of Publications, Teachers College, Columbia University, 1928), p. 178.

eral, in sympathy with the idea that faculty salaries should reflect changes in the cost of living. There is little question, however, but that the average salaries paid in all but a few of the institutions at the time these data were collected were insufficient to attract and hold in college teaching an adequate number of the kind of persons most needed for this work. In almost every college there is need for strengthening the faculty. In general, this can be accomplished only by making available larger funds for the payment of faculty salaries.

The recommendations made for general improvement in the faculty salary scale should not be construed to imply that there should be blanket increases to all members of the teaching staff as additional funds become available. As has already been stated, it is probable that the great majority of faculty members in these institutions are being paid all that their services would command in a competitive market. Instead of adding to the salaries of such instructors, the funds available for salary increases should be used for three purposes: first, to provide adequate remuneration for those faculty members who are now underpaid; second, to bring to the faculty, by way of replacement, capable teachers who cannot be attracted by the salary scale now in effect; third, to reward those capable members of the faculty who are improving their training and their teaching ability.

SOURCES OF FUNDS FOR NEEDED SALARY INCREASES

The question may well be raised as to the sources from which funds may be obtained for the needed increases in salaries. Two possible sources will be discussed briefly.

It has been pointed out in the preceding section that many of the colleges are now overstaffed and are maintaining student-faculty ratios markedly below that at which effective service can be rendered. To a considerable extent the funds needed for improvement in the average salary of faculty members could be obtained by a reorganization of staffing within the college itself. For example, taking the median situation of a student-faculty ratio of 14.7 to 1, and an average faculty salary of $2,541, it would be possible by increasing the student-faculty ratio to that of Mount Union College (19.2 to 1) to pay an average faculty salary in excess of $3,300. This would be a larger average than is now paid by any institution in the group. This calculation, of course, assumes that the amount available for faculty salaries per student will remain constant in the process of readjusting the student-faculty ratio.

There is no question in the minds of the writers but that most of the colleges would be better off with a faculty worthy of an average salary of $3,300 and with a student-faculty ratio of 19.2 to 1 than they now are in the typical situation of a student-faculty ratio of less than 15 to 1 and an average salary of approximately $2,500. As has previously been pointed out, this readjustment could be brought about by decreasing the number of small classes and thus increasing the student-credit-hour load carried by instructors. Under no circumstances should adjustments in the student-faculty ratio operate to increase the teaching schedules of instructors.

In spite of the opportunities in most of the colleges for a more economical staffing, it will not be possible for these institutions to obtain from this source all the funds necessary for an improved faculty salary scale. The only avenue left open by which salaries may be improved is to increase the supporting revenue of the college. Ultimately the best source is probably an increased endowment fund, although in many institutions a portion of the necessary revenue may be obtained from increased student fees and from current gifts for educational purposes.

CHAPTER XXXI

FACULTY ORGANIZATION

SELECTING A TEACHING STAFF IN TERMS OF A FACULTY ORGANIZATION

The most important academic duty confronting the chief administrative officer of an educational institution is the building of a strong and able faculty. This task has two somewhat distinct phases, the first relating to the individual faculty member, the second having to do with the faculty as a whole. The former phase of faculty selection concerns such questions as the training, the personal qualifications, and the salary requirements of the individual to whom a teaching position is being tendered. The latter phase, having to do with the faculty as a group, involves such questions as the number of faculty members to be employed, the proportion of this number to be given each academic rank, the general scale of faculty salaries, and the organization of a group that will work well as a unit.

A college president rarely has the opportunity of building a faculty *de novo*. Almost always there is a teaching staff already in existence, a going concern which can only gradually be reshaped and modified in its gross structure as opportunity is afforded by the normal turnover and replacement of the individual members. Quite naturally it then follows that the attention of most college presidents is largely centered on those aspects of faculty selection which concern the individual members of the group. Replacements are made one at a time; and such matters as the suitability of the training of the candidate for the specific position to be filled, his personal qualifications, and the salary at which he is willing to accept the position loom large in the immediate foreground. Such questions as the general policy with respect to number of faculty members to be employed and the proportion to be given each academic rank are likely to be pushed into the background when an individual is being selected for the faculty, and yet such an occasion is the only time when direct action toward a modification of the existing organization is easily possible.

In general, the administrative officers of the colleges studied, within the limits of the resources at their command, have exercised good judgment in their selection of individual faculty members. There is much evidence, however, which indicates a grave lack of attention in many colleges to the larger problem of building the teaching staff as a whole. As in most of the colleges of the country no conscious attempt seems to have been made to organize the faculty according to any model, with the result that the existing plan of organization is frequently inefficient and unsatisfactory. The problem of the number of staff members who should be given the rank of professor, associate or assistant professor, or instructor is important, since the policy maintained with respect to faculty promotions is closely related to the most effective use of the funds available for salary expenditures.

DISADVANTAGES OF TOO LARGE A PROPORTION
OF FACULTY AT THE HIGHEST RANK

One of the most frequently noted defects in faculty organization is the tendency to give the higher academic ranks to too large a proportion of the teaching staff. Some of the objections to this practice, especially as it concerns the rank of professor, may be briefly stated.

In the first place, a faculty organization with too large a proportion of staff members at the higher ranks is almost always accompanied by the development of a relatively large number of departments. In a small institution where a majority of the professors are also heads of departments, staff members tend to become dissatisfied unless the professorial rank is accompanied by departmental headship. Under such pressure the administration frequently increases the number of departments, merely to create a headship for a newly advanced professor. Some institutions with from four hundred to six hundred students enrolled have been found to have as many as eighteen or twenty different departments, a larger number than is necessary for an institution of this size. The increase in number of departments is often accompanied by an increase in the curricular offerings of the institution, which in turn results in an increase in the number of small classes.

A second objection to an organization with too large a proportion of the faculty holding the rank of professor is that it is symptomatic of a policy of advancing staff members in title as a reward for long service, rather than on a basis of merit. Particularly in an institution where funds are limited, promotions in rank may be granted in lieu of salary increases, without regard to the resources of the institution. This policy is fundamentally unsound.

A third objection to having too large a proportion of the faculty holding the rank of professor is that it practically makes impossible a satisfactory recognition for the few outstanding faculty members of exceptional ability and training who deserve such recognition. Not only is the professorial rank cheapened, but there is usually a shortage of funds with which to pay high salaries to these exceptionally well-qualified men. The large proportion of staff members at the higher ranks results in the bringing down of all salaries to approximately the same low level, with no opportunity to exceed this average by any considerable amount. In consequence, the institution tends to lose its best faculty members to competing institutions which have adopted the policy of paying attractive salaries to outstanding men.

FACULTY ORGANIZATION IN THE COLLEGES STUDIED

Table 73 shows the faculty organization by ranks for thirty-five colleges.

It will be observed from this table that there is a wide variation in the percentage of the faculty who are given the highest academic rank. In two of the institutions[1] all members of the faculty are given the rank of professor. In two other colleges not more than one-fourth of the faculty members are given the highest academic rank. Fourteen of the colleges make no use whatever of the rank of associate professor; five do not use the rank of assistant professor; and five do not use the rank of instructor. There could well be a wider use of the titles of associate professor and assistant professor. These titles can suitably be employed for faculty members who do not hold the Doctor's degree but have had two years or more of graduate work, as well as for those who have doctorates.

As has already been stated, it is usually considered preferable to assign a relatively small percentage of the faculty to the highest academic rank. It will be noted from the medians shown in Table 73 that, in general, the colleges on the approved list of the Association of American Universities are somewhat more conservative on this point than the institutions not holding this type of accreditation.

The size of the institution conditions markedly the opportunities for a desirable faculty organization. In general, the institutions with a low percentage at the highest academic rank are those which have a relatively large faculty. The coefficient of correlation (Pearson) between these two factors is $-.53 \pm .08$. In the small institution it is customary to give all department heads the rank of professor. With the maintenance of a large number of departments it thus becomes necessary to assign a large percentage of faculty members to the highest academic rank. Improvement in this situation can best be brought about by an academic reorganization decreasing the number of separate departments. This point has already been discussed in chapter xix.

[1] These have become junior colleges since the visit of the survey staff.

TABLE 73

Faculty Organization by Ranks for Thirty-five Colleges

Institution	Year	Number of Faculty Members†	Percentage of Faculty Members Holding Each Rank				
			Professor	Associate Professor	Assistant Professor	Instructor	Assistant
*Ohio Wesleyan..	1930–31	151	23	15	26	22	14
*Pacific.........	1930–31	73	25	14	34	27	......
*Allegheny......	1929–30	42	33	7	29	31	......
*Hamline.......	1929–30	44	34	9	9	43	5
Puget Sound....	1930–31	42	36	16	24	24	......
*Morningside....	1929–30	50	36	......	10	50	4
Brothers.......	1930–31	16	38	7	12	31	12
*DePauw.......	1930–31	92	40	11	20	28	1
*MacMurray....	1930–31	39	41	3	8	48	......
Evansville......	1929–30	28	43	7	18	29	3
*Chattanooga....	1929–30	30	43	10	7	40	......
Oklahoma City.	1929–30	47	44	13	11	30	2
*Dickinson......	1929–30	36	44	28	......	25	3
*Albion.........	1929–30	48	45	2	13	40	......
*Lawrence......	1929–30	57	47	11	14	23	5
Dakota Wesleyan...........	1930–31	29	49	3	3	45	......
Nebraska Wesleyan........	1930–31	46	50	......	9	41	......
*Illinois Wesleyan...........	1930–31	35	52	......	34	14	......
*Mount Union...	1930–31	32	53	19	16	12	......
Baldwin-Wallace	1930–31	36	54	17	6	17	6
*Simpson.......	1929–30	43	56	2	30	12	......
Intermountain..	1930–31	16	56	......	19	19	6
Gooding.......	1930–31	12	58	......	......	42	......
*Cornell........	1929–30	42	60	......	7	33	......
Iowa Wesleyan.	1929–30	27	60	7	7	26	......
*Willamette.....	1930–31	43	61	2	21	16	......
Southwestern...	1930–31	40	65	7	3	25	......
Ohio Northern..	1930–31	48	67	......	14	19	......
McKendree.....	1930–31	22	67	......	14	19	......
*Baker..........	1930–31	31	68	......	29	......	3
Union.........	1929–30	11	73	......	......	27	......
West Virginia Wesleyan....	1930–31	26	92	......	8	......	......
Kansas Wesleyan...........	1930–31	18	94	......	6	......	......
Ozark Wesleyan.	1929–30	21	100	......	......	......	......
Central Wesleyan...........	1929–30	17	100	......	......	......	......
Median, all colleges...	....	36	52	3	11	25	0
*Median, A.A.U. colleges......	....	43	44	7	16	27	0
Median, non-A.A.U. colleges......	....	27	59	0	8	22	0

* Institutions on the approved list of the Association of American Universities.
† Based on the number of different persons in the entire faculty.

It is evident from Table 73 that there is no model for the development of either departments or colleges. Tables 74, 75, 76, and 77 present suggested organizations of teaching staffs for colleges of various sizes and with various amounts of funds available for the payment of instructional salaries. The first of these tables is built on the assumption that there will be available only $120 per student for instructional salaries; the second assumes $150 per student for this purpose; the third, $180 per student; and the fourth, $225 per student for faculty salaries. In each table two types of faculty organization, one desirable, the other undesirable, are shown for each size of institution. In general, the situations listed as undesirable with reference to salaries paid, percentage of staff members at the higher ranks, and ratio of students to teachers represent conditions which actually exist in some of the colleges included in this group, as may be observed from an examination of Tables 65, 67, and 73. For each type of institution the total budget allowance for faculty salaries has been kept at the same figure for both the desirable and the undesirable types of organization.

These tables are read as follows, taking as an example Table 77 which assumes a budget for instructional salaries equivalent to $225 per student: A college with an enrolment of one hundred students would, under these conditions, have a total instructional salary budget of $22,500. A desirable type of organization for such a college would be to have eight teachers, all with the rank of professor, making the ratio of students to faculty members 12 to 1, and permitting an average salary for professors of $2,812. An undesirable type of organization for such a college would be to have ten teachers, all with the rank of professor, making the ratio of students to faculty members 10 to 1, and permitting an average salary for professors of only $2,250. A college of two hundred students would, under these conditions, have a total instructional salary budget of $45,000. A desirable staffing for such a college would be to have fourteen teachers, providing a student-faculty ratio of 14 to 1. A desirable organization of this faculty would be to have eight professors with an average salary of $4,000, two associate or assistant professors with an average salary of $2,500, and four instructors with an average salary of $2,000. An undesirable type of faculty organization for such a college would be to have twenty teachers, providing a student-faculty ratio of 10 to 1, with fourteen professors at an average salary of $2,643, four associate or assistant professors at an average salary of $2,200, and two instructors at an average salary of $1,600. The data for colleges of different sizes, and for the vary-

TABLE 74

FACULTY ORGANIZATIONS FOR COLLEGES WITH FUNDS ADEQUATE TO PERMIT AN
EXPENDITURE OF $120 PER STUDENT FOR INSTRUCTIONAL SALARIES

NUMBER OF TUDENTS	AMOUNT AVAILABLE FOR INSTRUCTIONAL SALARIES	TYPE OF ORGANIZATION	NUMBER OF TEACHERS	STUDENTS PER TEACHER	PROFESSORS		ASSOCIATE AND ASSISTANT PROFESSORS		INSTRUCTORS	
					Number	Average Salary	Number	Average Salary	Number	Average Salary
100......	$ 12,000	Desirable	6	17	6	$2,000	....	....	....	......
		Undesirable	8	12	8	1,500	....	....	....	......
200......	24,000	Desirable	10	20	8	2,600	....	....	2	$1,600
		Undesirable	15	13	11	1,654	2	$1,500	2	1,400
300......	36,000	Desirable	15	20	8	2,887	2	2,200	5	1,700
		Undesirable	21	14	13	1,815	4	1,600	4	1,500
500......	60,000	Desirable	22	23	8	4,050	4	2,400	10	1,800
		Undesirable	33	15	20	1,925	7	1,700	6	1,600
750......	90,000	Desirable	31	24	8	4,875	10	2,500	13	2,000
		Undesirable	47	16	28	2,057	10	1,800	9	1,600
1,000.....	120,000	Desirable	40	25	10	5,300	14	2,500	16	2,000
		Undesirable	60	17	36	2,194	13	1,800	11	1,600
2,000.....	240,000	Desirable	80	25	20	5,300	28	2,500	32	2,000
		Undesirable	120	17	72	2,194	26	1,800	22	1,600

TABLE 75

FACULTY ORGANIZATIONS FOR COLLEGES WITH FUNDS ADEQUATE TO PERMIT AN
EXPENDITURE OF $150 PER STUDENT FOR INSTRUCTIONAL SALARIES

NUMBER OF STUDENTS	AMOUNT AVAILABLE FOR INSTRUCTIONAL SALARIES	TYPE OF ORGANIZATION	NUMBER OF TEACHERS	STUDENTS PER TEACHER	PROFESSORS		ASSOCIATE AND ASSISTANT PROFESSORS		INSTRUCTORS	
					Number	Average Salary	Number	Average Salary	Number	Average Salary
100......	$ 15,000	Desirable	7	14	7	$2,143	....	....	....	......
		Undesirable	10	10	10	1,500	....	....	....	......
200......	30,000	Desirable	13	15	8	2,625	....	....	5	$1,800
		Undesirable	19	11	13	1,631	4	$1,500	2	1,400
300......	45,000	Desirable	16	19	8	3,475	3	2,400	5	2,000
		Undesirable	23	13	18	2,067	3	1,600	2	1,500
500......	75,000	Desirable	24	21	8	4,475	8	2,900	8	2,000
		Undesirable	38	13	24	2,125	8	1,800	6	1,600
750......	105,000	Desirable	36	21	9	4,444	11	3,000	16	2,000
		Undesirable	54	14	32	2,037	12	1,900	10	1,700
1,000.....	150,000	Desirable	46	22	13	5,308	15	3,000	18	2,000
		Undesirable	72	14	43	2,163	16	2,100	13	1,800
2,000.....	300,000	Desirable	92	22	26	5,308	30	3,000	36	2,000
		Undesirable	144	14	86	2,163	32	2,100	26	1,800

TABLE 76

FACULTY ORGANIZATIONS FOR COLLEGES WITH FUNDS ADEQUATE TO PERMIT AN EXPENDITURE OF $180 PER STUDENT FOR INSTRUCTIONAL SALARIES

Number of Students	Amount Available for Instructional Salaries	Type of Organization	Number of Teachers	Students per Teacher	Professors		Associate and Assistant Professors		Instructors	
					Number	Average Salary	Number	Average Salary	Number	Average Salary
100	$ 18,000	Desirable	8	12	8	$2,250	......	......	......	......
		Undesirable	10	10	10	1,800	......	......	......	......
200	36,000	Desirable	13	15	8	3,125	2	$2,500	3	$2,000
		Undesirable	19	11	13	1,969	4	1,800	2	1,600
300	54,000	Desirable	18	17	8	3,625	5	3,000	5	2,000
		Undesirable	25	12	18	2,311	4	1,900	3	1,600
500	90,000	Desirable	28	18	10	4,500	9	3,000	9	2,000
		Undesirable	42	12	24	2,317	10	2,000	8	1,800
750	135,000	Desirable	42	18	14	4,643	14	3,000	14	2,000
		Undesirable	62	12	33	2,364	16	2,100	13	1,800
1,000	180,000	Desirable	55	18	18	4,889	18	3,000	19	2,000
		Undesirable	84	12	40	2,340	24	2,100	20	1,800
2,000	360,000	Desirable	110	18	36	4,889	36	3,000	38	2,000
		Undesirable	168	12	80	2,340	48	2,100	40	1,800

TABLE 77

FACULTY ORGANIZATIONS FOR COLLEGES WITH FUNDS ADEQUATE TO PERMIT AN EXPENDITURE OF $225 PER STUDENT FOR INSTRUCTIONAL SALARIES

Number of Students	Amount Available for Instructional Salaries	Type of Organization	Number of Teachers	Students per Teacher	Professors		Associate and Assistant Professors		Instructors	
					Number	Average Salary	Number	Average Salary	Number	Average Salary
100	$ 22,500	Desirable	8	12	8	$2,812	......	......	......	......
		Undesirable	10	10	10	2,250	......	......	......	......
200	45,000	Desirable	14	14	8	4,000	2	$2,500	4	$2,000
		Undesirable	20	10	14	2,357	4	2,200	2	1,600
300	67,500	Desirable	20	15	8	4,875	6	2,750	6	2,000
		Undesirable	25	12	18	2,956	4	2,300	3	1,700
500	112,500	Desirable	33	15	11	5,227	11	3,000	11	2,000
		Undesirable	42	12	24	3,004	10	2,600	8	1,800
750	168,750	Desirable	50	15	16	5,234	17	3,000	17	2,000
		Undesirable	62	12	33	3,144	16	2,600	13	1,800
1,000	225,000	Desirable	66	15	22	5,227	22	3,000	22	2,000
		Undesirable	84	12	40	3,165	24	2,600	20	1,800
2,000	450,000	Desirable	132	15	44	5,227	44	3,000	44	2,000
		Undesirable	168	12	80	3,165	48	2,600	40	1,800

ing amounts of instructional salary expenditure per student, are read similarly.

It should be noted that for institutions with enrolments of one hundred students and salary budgets of $18,000 or more a staff of eight members with the rank of full professor is recommended. Such a staff will meet the requirements of standardizing associations. Institutions with salary budgets smaller than $18,000 would not be able to meet such requirements because of their financial limitations. For such institutions it seems desirable to have a smaller staff, in order that higher salaries may be paid. In all cases where institutions have enrolments of two hundred or more, it is recommended that at least eight staff members with the rank of professor be employed, in order that standards may be met.

In general, the desirable plans of organization call for fewer staff members than the undesirable plans; as a result, the institutions with desirable organizations have somewhat larger ratios of students to teachers and smaller percentages of staff members holding the higher ranks. One consequence of this situation is that the average salaries received by those who hold the higher ranks are much larger at such institutions than at the institutions with undesirable organizations.

In the case of the plans of organization recommended as desirable, it is not assumed that all staff members holding the same rank in an institution will receive equal salaries. For example, the salaries paid professors at an institution with one thousand students enrolled and an instructional salary budget of $225 per student may range from $3,500 or $4,000 to $6,500 or $7,000. Salary variations of a similar nature may exist among the staff members of all ranks.

The objection may be raised that a salary of $2,000 is not adequate for instructors. Possibly this is true in localities where the cost of living is unusually high. It may be that some institutions will find it advisable to pay an average salary of $2,200 or more to instructors. In most teaching fields, however, $2,000 will secure the services of a young instructor with training at least equivalent to that required for a Master's degree. In some communities for some types of teaching this same salary will secure the services of instructors with a considerable amount of training in addition to that required for a Master's degree. Scholastically an instructor with a Master's degree is as far in advance of junior college students as an instructor with a Doctor's degree is in advance of senior college students.

Appointments to instructorships should always be temporary. Only the most capable instructors should be promoted to assistant professorships, and later to associate professorships or to professorships. Such promotions should be made only when vacancies occur at the higher ranks or when additional funds available for salaries permit increases in the number of staff members employed at the higher ranks. Promotion from instructorships to higher ranks should be based upon merit and ability, not upon length of service. Even in the event of a vacancy, it should not be thought necessary to fill the position by promotion unless the man already in the institution is at least as well qualified as anyone who could be obtained from any other source.

At an institution of five hundred students it may not be possible to promote to higher ranks more than five or six of the instructors within a period of from five to ten years. Under such circumstances it appears probable that a number of instructors would seek promotion at other institutions, while others would leave the profession of college teaching. This is as it should be. Only the most capable instructors should be induced to remain in the profession by being awarded college professorships.

Several beneficial results might be expected to follow the adoption of the plans of organization listed as desirable: (1) The relatively high salaries paid to staff members of professorial rank would make possible the employment of a number of superior teachers. It is believed that superior teachers can teach relatively large classes more effectively than mediocre or poor teachers can teach small classes. (2) These relatively high salaries would be an incentive for capable instructors to remain in the institution and prepare themselves to do more effective work. (3) The less capable instructors would either leave the profession of college teaching or leave the institution to accept employment where the prospects for promotion might appear to be greater. Probably what would actually happen would be that they would receive their promotions at institutions having faculty organizations of undesirable type. Higher education would be benefited if the less capable instructors should enter some line of work other than teaching; whether they leave the profession or join the staff of another college, the institution from which they go will be benefited.

The plan outlined above calls for larger classes. It also includes a period of apprenticeship for staff members. At the end of this period of temporary employment, instructors may be either promoted or dropped; or they may be retained at low salaries, if they wish to remain, provided their teaching is satisfactory though not excellent.

In general, there are two essential factors in the building of a well-organized faculty. First, there must be in the mind of the chief administrative officer a clearly defined pattern of the desirable organization which constitutes the goal toward which he is working. In the second place, every opportunity afforded for the selection of new faculty members must be made a step toward the realization of the ultimate organization. By such measures the existing faculty organization can gradually be re-shaped without anything savoring of a drastic revolution.

CHAPTER XXXII

FACULTY TENURE, RETIREMENT, AND PROTECTION PROVISIONS

FACULTY TENURE

It is generally recognized that it is impossible to build a strong college if the annual turnover in the teaching staff is too large. For the satisfactory development of policies and the maintenance of uniform quality of instruction, it is desirable that there be a rather high degree of permanence in the teaching staff. On the other hand, long tenure is not always an unmixed blessing. Where salaries are low and the training of faculty in general is substandard, the institution will doubtless profit by a relatively high rate of annual turnover. For that reason tenure data must be interpreted with considerable caution.

Table 78 presents data regarding the average annual faculty turnover, by academic ranks, at thirty-five colleges. These data are the averages for the five-year period immediately preceding the survey visit. Figures are based upon the number of faculty members not returning for the work of the following year. Faculty members on leaves of absence are not considered as turnover unless they fail to return to the institution upon the completion of their leave.

It will be observed from this table that there is a wide variation in the rates of turnover among these thirty-five institutions. Perhaps the most significant item of data is the rate of turnover at the rank of professor. At this rank the colleges which are not on the approved list of the Association of American Universities have a median rate of turnover almost double that of the colleges which are on this approved list. The differences in the rate of turnover at the other ranks are not so pronounced between the two groups of colleges. As a matter of fact, the turnover of instructors in the colleges on the approved list of the Association of American Universities averages slightly higher than that for the entire group of institutions.

A high rate of turnover is generally the result of an inadequate faculty salary scale. In many cases, however, other factors are also important. A change of administration in the college frequently tends to result in a somewhat higher rate of turnover during the process of adjustment to new standards and new policies. An effort to improve the standing of a college

TABLE 78

AVERAGE ANNUAL FACULTY TURNOVER BY RANKS AT THIRTY-FIVE
COLLEGES, 1925–29, INCLUSIVE

INSTITUTION	PERCENTAGE OF ANNUAL TURNOVER FOR FIVE-YEAR PERIOD			
	Professors	Associate Professors	Assistant Professors	Instructors
Brothers†	0	0	0	21.1
*Allegheny	0	0	29.6	34.7
*Dickinson	1.4	12.9	‡	25.8
Baldwin-Wallace	2.5	0	0	16.0
*Pacific	3.2	10.5	8.6	20.0
*Morningside	3.6	‡	10.7	11.7
*Mount Union	5.6	5.6	10.0	12.5
*Ohio Wesleyan	6.9	10.8	12.9	25.5
*Lawrence	7.0	20.8	25.0	30.0
*DePauw	7.5	4.7	8.4	29.8
*Albion	8.0	20.0	31.3	35.4
*Cornell	8.8	‡	14.8	29.1
*MacMurray	9.1	0	11.1	26.7
Central Wesleyan	10.6	‡	‡	‡
*Chattanooga	10.9	8.3	27.3	29.6
Nebraska Wesleyan	11.0	0	17.2	11.9
McKendree	11.7	‡	20.0	23.5
Ohio Northern	12.3	‡	17.1	38.5
*Willamette	13.0	0	10.3	8.0
Puget Sound	13.6	14.3	20.0	32.3
Oklahoma City	14.0	25.0	2.8	14.8
Southwestern	14.4	15.4	25.9	26.8
*Simpson	14.6	0	29.0	60.0
Evansville	15.0	0	48.2	19.2
Ozark Wesleyan	15.4	‡	33.3	0
Intermountain	15.6	‡	60.0	66.7
*Baker	16.7	‡	32.1	33.3
*Hamline	16.8	15.4	25.0	45.8
West Virginia Wesleyan	17.5	27.3	‡	‡
Dakota Wesleyan	18.8	37.5	18.2	35.3
Kansas Wesleyan	20.8	‡	57.1	‡
Iowa Wesleyan	21.6	7.1	20.0	24.2
*Illinois Wesleyan	22.7	‡	16.9	23.8
Gooding	29.0	‡	‡	35.9
Union	37.5	‡	‡	81.8
Median, all colleges	12.3	8.3	19.1	26.8
*Median, A.A.U. colleges	8.0	8.3	15.9	29.1
Median, non-A.A.U. colleges	14.7	10.7	20.0	24.2

* Institutions on the approved list of the Association of American Universities.
† Two-year period only.
‡ No faculty members at this rank.

sometimes results temporarily in an unusually high rate of turnover. On the other hand, it cannot be argued that a low rate of turnover always indicates satisfactory conditions. It will be observed that some of the colleges with a relatively low rate of turnover also have a low salary scale and a faculty which is not particularly outstanding.

The optimum turnover is difficult to determine. It should manifestly be related to the salary scale, the training of faculty, and the general qualifications of faculty members. A turnover as large as that in the median institution of the seventeen colleges on the approved list of the Association of American Universities probably should not be interpreted as an unhealthy sign.

RETIREMENT AND PROTECTION PROVISIONS

The need for retirement provisions.—For some time, educators have been agreed that the development of a strong teaching staff is greatly facilitated by adequate provisions for retirement. Most of the more progressive cities and states have organized retirement plans for their public-school teachers. Several years ago the inauguration of the Carnegie pension plan for college and university teachers seemed in a fair way to provide for the instructional staffs of the member institutions. The withdrawal of this plan, however, has in many colleges not been followed by any similar provision for adequate retiring allowances.

It should not be necessary to present arguments in favor of adequate retirement provisions for the staff members of colleges. From a selfish point of view, the institution needs this type of protection in order to make unnecessary the retention in active service of faculty members who have passed their days of greatest usefulness. Such instructors have usually rendered long and faithful service to the college, and humane considerations prevent their being summarily dismissed when old age begins to lessen their effectiveness. If there are no retirement provisions, such teachers may be retained in service, the students paying the price in terms of inferior instruction, and the faculty members concerned also making their contributions by using up more rapidly than necessary the small remaining store of their vitality. The promotion of competent junior members of the faculty is also unduly delayed by the absence of retirement provisions.

One of the most desirable features of a satisfactory retirement plan is the morale which it develops in a faculty. With the greater sense of security due to the consciousness that their later years will not be without reasonable provision against want, there should be greater stability, more effective service during the active years, and undoubtedly more years of usefulness in a faculty than can be expected if less adequate retirement provisions obtain.

Essential features of a satisfactory retirement plan.—A satisfactory retirement plan for a college faculty should provide for the following seven features:

1. There should be compulsory participation in the plan by all faculty members above a certain academic level. The level selected should probably be that which is associated with permanent or long-term tenure. In other words, every faculty member whom the institution appoints with the idea that his services are to continue should be included in the retirement plan.

2. Contributions to the retirement plan should be co-operative. Part should be paid by the college and part by the faculty member concerned. Experience in the administration of pension systems for public-school teachers shows the wisdom of such a plan. The fact that faculty members have a stake in the plan tends to build up confidence and to improve the care with which the fund is managed.

3. The retirement allowances must be of sufficient size to provide a satisfactory standard of living at the time of retirement. Since faculty members at this age normally have no dependents other than a wife, the retiring allowances can well be considerably smaller than the salary which has been paid during the years of active service. Under many pension plans the maximum paid for a retiring allowance is 50 per cent of the salary at the time of the retirement. Under some well-managed plans the amount of retiring allowance is contingent upon the age of retirement and the number of years of service which have been given to the institution.

4. The plan should provide adequate protection for the widows of faculty members as well as for faculty members themselves.

5. Retirement should be automatic and compulsory at a certain specified age, except by special action of the board of trustees. Employment after the specified retiring age should be on an annual basis and should not be permitted to continue in any case more than a short time (probably five years) beyond the specified retiring age.

6. The age of retirement should be fixed so as to protect the institution from having to retain the services of senile teachers. It seems preferable to fix the retirement age under present-day conditions at sixty-five.

7. There must be an adequate arrangement for a fund from which retiring allowances may be paid. A plan cannot be judged satisfactory if it contemplates the payment of the necessary retiring allowances out of the current funds of the college. The pension fund should be so arranged that retirements will be based entirely upon educational considerations and will not have to be postponed because funds are not available for the payment of the necessary pensions.

Methods of arranging for a retirement fund.—Three suggestions for the arrangement of a pension fund may be mentioned: The first is a special endowment fund from which pensions may be paid. While this has the advantage of relieving the current budget, it has the inherent difficulty of not being flexible enough to adjust easily to the needs for pensions. In other words, if the number of faculty members drawing retirement pay increases, there is no way by which the endowment income can be correspondingly increased to provide the necessary pension payments.

A second suggestion is for a college-administered pension reserve. The institution could set aside each year from its current funds an amount, calculated on an actuarial basis, such that all retirements could be cared for. There are two difficulties in this plan: In the first place, the base of the risk in any one college is too small to provide a satisfactory actuarial basis for accumulating the pension reserve. One or two faculty members who happen to live longer than the expected average might seriously embarrass this arrangement. The second difficulty with the college-administered pension reserve is the temptation which is ever present to dip into this fund when the college becomes financially hard pressed. Such an action would of course jeopardize the safety of the fund, and the effects of many years of careful planning could easily be nullified within a short time by ill-considered action of the board of trustees.

The third plan suggested is for an arrangement with an insurance company dealing in annuities of this type. An annual contribution from the college and from the faculty members concerned could be used to purchase annuities in such a way as to guarantee payments of specified size at the retiring age. This plan is the most feasible for the smaller colleges. The Teachers' Insurance and Annuity Association of America, an organization whose "overhead" is financed by an endowment of Carnegie funds, seems to be the best agency through which to arrange retiring allowances for staff members. The purpose of this organization, as stated in its charter, is as follows:

. . . . to provide insurance and annuities for teachers and other persons employed by colleges, by universities, or by institutions engaged primarily in educational or research work; to offer policies of a character best adapted to the needs of such persons on terms as advantageous to its policy-holders as shall be practicable; and to conduct its business without profit to the corporation or to its stockholders.

Retirement provisions in the colleges studied.—Only eleven of the thirty-five colleges had in effect any retirement provision at the time of the survey visit. It is interesting to note that ten of these eleven colleges are on the approved list of the Association of American Universities. Only one of the eighteen colleges not on the approved list of the Association has any arrangements for a retirement plan.

The retirement plans which are in effect present varying degrees of effectiveness. Only eight of the colleges have anything which approaches a satisfactory retirement plan, and only two or three fully meet the standards which have been set up in the preceding paragraphs.

The number of faculty members now drawing retirement pay is surprisingly small. In the entire group of thirty-five institutions with a total teaching staff of almost fourteen hundred, there are only twenty-six persons drawing any retirement pay. Two of these are former presidents and one is a former librarian. In nineteen of the colleges there is no one drawing retirement pay. In each of eleven colleges one person is drawing retirement pay; there is one college with two, one college with three, one college with five, and one college with six persons drawing retirement pay. During the years since 1924–25, up to the time of the survey visit, a total of only nineteen faculty members in these thirty-five colleges were retired with a pension. It is difficult to explain these facts in any other way than that faculty members have been kept on the job of teaching longer than they should have been in some cases, and that in other cases they have been dismissed inhumanly without any retiring allowance.

The amount of retirement pay now drawn is surprisingly small. One institution has five faculty members drawing average retirement pay in excess of $3,000 each. There is only one other case in which a former faculty member (actually a former president) draws retirement pay in excess of $3,000 annually. The next highest case is one of $2,000 and the next is one of $1,500. There are three cases of retirement allowances within the range of $1,000–$1,200, and the remaining are all below $600.

One or two of the colleges which pay pensions from current funds use the ministerial retirement scale for faculty members. The amount provided by this scale is pitiably small. Since several of the faculty members in some of the colleges are ministers and are entitled to retirement pay from their Annual Conference, the college does not consider itself under obligation for other retirement provisions.

It is the judgment of the writers that, with the exception of one or two institutions, adequate retirement provisions are among the most important needs in this group of colleges. In general, retirement provisions are more urgently needed and will go farther toward making needed faculty improvement than increases in faculty salaries.

Age distribution of faculty members.—Table 79 presents data regarding the age distribution of faculty members in thirty-five colleges.

TABLE 79

PERCENTAGE OF FACULTY MEMBERS WITHIN EACH AGE GROUP
AT THIRTY-FIVE COLLEGES

INSTITUTION	YEAR	NUM-BER OF MEM-BERS RE-PORT-ING	PERCENTAGE OF FACULTY AT EACH AGE						
			20–29	30–39	40–49	50–59	60–64	65–69	70 and Over
Ozark Wesleyan.......	1929–30	20	20	35	35	10	.....	.....	.....
Evansville.............	1929–30	27	18	41	30	11	.....	.....	.....
Intermountain.........	1930–31	15	20	33	33	14	.....	.....	.....
Gooding..............	1930–31	12	25	25	33	17	.....	.....	.....
*Hamline.............	1929–30	42	22	31	36	8	.....	.....	3
*Illinois Wesleyan.......	1930–31	35	17	52	17	11	.....	.....	3
Oklahoma City........	1929–30	36	28	22	30	17	.....	.....	3
Dakota Wesleyan......	1929–30	24	38	38	8	12	4	.....	.....
*Chattanooga..........	1929–30	27	31	26	35	4	.....	4	.....
Iowa Wesleyan........	1929–30	26	25	22	21	28	.....	4	.....
*DePauw..............	1930–31	92	34	32	18	12	2	1	1
West Virginia Wesleyan.	1930–31	24	12	25	38	21	.....	.....	4
*Ohio Wesleyan.........	1930–31	129	29	28	27	11	4	1	.....
*Dickinson.............	1929–30	32	19	38	25	12	6	.....	.....
*Albion...............	1929–30	45	16	42	27	9	4	2	.....
Brothers.............	1930–31	16	25	38	25	6	6	.....	.....
Kansas Wesleyan......	1930–31	18	6	44	17	27	6	.....	.....
*Baker...............	1930–31	30	20	23	34	17	3	3	.....
*Pacific...............	1930–31	55	16	40	24	13	2	2	3
Ohio Northern.........	1930–31	47	17	28	36	11	8	.....	.....
*MacMurray...........	1930–31	38	21	32	21	18	5	3	.....
Southwestern..........	1930–31	40	17	45	10	20	5	3	.....
*Simpson..............	1929–30	43	24	24	34	10	5	.....	3
Baldwin-Wallace.......	1930–31	36	14	35	31	11	9	.....	.....
Puget Sound..........	1930–31	35	28	17	40	6	3	3	3
*Allegheny.............	1929–30	39	34	28	18	10	10	.....	.....
Nebraska Wesleyan....	1930–31	42	21	21	21	26	8	3	.....
*Lawrence.............	1929–30	52	15	40	27	6	6	6	.....
*Morningside...........	1929–30	47	27	20	19	21	2	9	2
*Mount Union..........	1930–31	34	12	35	26	12	12	.....	3
McKendree...........	1930–31	19	16	21	37	10	16	.....	.....
*Willamette............	1930–31	33	15	37	18	12	12	6	.....
Union................	1929–30	11	27	.....	27	28	.....	9	9
*Cornell...............	1929–30	39	33	21	17	10	11	5	3
Central Wesleyan......	1929–30	17	29	29	6	12	18	.....	6
Median, all colleges..	....	35	21	31	27	12	4	0	0
*Median, A.A.U. colleges.............	....	24	21	32	25	11	4	2	0
Median, non-A.A.U. colleges..........	....	39	21	29	30	13	4	0	0

* Institutions on the approved list of the Association of American Universities.

In this table the institutions are arranged in order of the percentage of faculty members sixty years of age, or above. It will be observed that thirteen of the colleges have one or more faculty members at age seventy or above, and that twenty-three have some faculty members at age sixty-five or above. In general, however, the percentage of faculty members above the age of sixty is surprisingly low. There does not seem to be any significant difference in the typical situation on this point between the colleges on the approved list of the Association of American Universities and the colleges which do not hold this type of accreditation. The data of this table reinforce the conclusion already stated to the effect that there is urgent need for a satisfactory retirement plan in most of the colleges studied.

Group life insurance.—There has recently been a considerable amount of attention given to group insurance plans for faculty members. The insurance companies have been active in promoting this type of protection. From the standpoint of the faculty member the purchase of group insurance is highly desirable, since the protection is provided at a very low cost. In some colleges arrangements have been made for the institution to pay the cost of the group insurance. Only four of the thirty-five colleges had a group insurance plan in effect at the time of the survey visit, although several others were seriously considering the adoption of such a plan.

It should be borne in mind that group insurance does not take the place of a retirement system. There is still a need for an annuity arrangement, even though a group insurance plan is provided. Arrangements can be made for a combined annuity and insurance policy which operates in such a way that, as the annuity builds up, the amount of insurance protection decreases, the total protection remaining approximately constant during all the years of the instructor's service.

CHAPTER XXXIII

TRAINING AND SCHOLARLY PRODUCTIVITY OF FACULTY MEMBERS

TRAINING OF FACULTY MEMBERS

Standards for training of faculty.—The regional standardizing associations have adopted definite requirements regarding the training of college faculty members. The standards of the North Central Association of Colleges and Secondary Schools, which are typical of those of the other regional accrediting associations, are as follows:

The minimum scholastic requirements of all teachers shall be graduation from a college belonging to this association, or the equivalent. The training of the members of the faculty of professorial rank shall include at least two years of study in their respective fields of teaching in a recognized graduate school, presumably including the Master's degree. For heads of departments, training should be equivalent to that required for the Ph.D. degree or should represent corresponding professional or technological training. The teacher's success is to be determined by the efficiency of his teaching as well as his research work. The college should be judged in large part by the ratio which the number of persons of professorial rank with sound training, scholarly achievement and successful experience as teachers, bears to the total number of the teaching staff.

Amount of training of faculty members of the colleges studied.—Table 80 presents data from thirty-five colleges regarding the percentage of faculty members who have various amounts of graduate training.

The institutions in this table are arranged according to the percentage of staff members who have the Doctor's degree or equivalent training. It will be observed that there is a wide variation on this point. One institution has no faculty members with training equivalent to the Doctor's degree. In four institutions one-half or more of the faculty members have this amount of training. The colleges which are on the approved list of the Association of American Universities are markedly superior to the other colleges on this point.

Perhaps a more valid index of the actual status of the faculty is the percentage with two or more years of graduate work.[1] On this point the range is also large and the superiority of the colleges on the approved list

[1] This figure can be obtained by adding the figures in columns three and four of the table.

TABLE 80

YEARS OF TRAINING OF FACULTY MEMBERS HOLDING THE RANK OF
INSTRUCTOR OR ABOVE AT THIRTY-FIVE COLLEGES

INSTITUTION	YEAR	NUMBER OF FACULTY MEMBERS REPORTING	PERCENTAGE HAVING VARIOUS AMOUNTS OF GRADUATE TRAINING				
			Doctor's Degree or Equivalent	Two Years Graduate Work, Less than Three	One Year Graduate Work, Less than Two	Some Graduate Work, Less than One Year	No Graduate Work
Brothers.............	1930–31	14	79	7	7	7	0
*Dickinson............	1929–30	31	65	6	16	13	0
*Lawrence............	1929–30	52	50	15	23	8	4
Union...............	1929–30	10	50	0	30	0	20
*Ohio Wesleyan........	1930–31	128	46	12	22	6	14
*Allegheny............	1929–30	38	45	18	29	0	8
*Chattanooga..........	1929–30	27	45	7	22	11	15
McKendree...........	1930–31	21	43	14	14	19	10
*Illinois Wesleyan......	1930–31	35	43	9	34	5	9
*Cornell..............	1929–30	35	42	12	17	17	12
West Virginia Wesleyan	1930–31	24	42	4	38	4	12
*DePauw.............	1930–31	91	41	16	31	7	5
*Hamline.............	1929–30	40	40	13	27	5	15
Puget Sound..........	1930–31	35	40	9	20	17	14
*Albion...............	1929–30	45	40	4	45	7	4
*MacMurray..........	1930–31	38	37	18	14	18	13
*Willamette...........	1930–31	33	37	15	24	12	12
Evansville............	1929–30	25	36	20	24	4	16
*Simpson.............	1929–30	37	33	11	35	5	16
*Mount Union.........	1930–31	34	32	18	32	15	3
Iowa Wesleyan.......	1929–30	26	31	15	23	8	23
*Pacific..............	1930–31	55	31	13	43	11	2
Nebraska Wesleyan...	1930–31	43	30	30	21	7	12
*Baker...............	1930–31	30	30	3	50	10	7
Baldwin-Wallace......	1930–31	33	27	24	31	6	12
*Morningside..........	1929–30	44	27	7	37	11	18
Southwestern.........	1930–31	40	25	20	28	17	10
Kansas Wesleyan.....	1930–31	18	22	39	22	11	6
Ohio Northern........	1930–31	40	18	20	43	12	7
Dakota Wesleyan.....	1929–30	25	12	12	36	12	28
Central Wesleyan.....	1929–30	18	11	22	28	11	28
Oklahoma City........	1929–30	36	11	17	36	8	28
Intermountain........	1930–31	15	7	33	20	33	7
Ozark Wesleyan.......	1929–30	18	6	16	50	22	6
Gooding.............	1930–31	12	0	25	34	25	16
Median, all colleges.	....	34	37	15	28	11	12
*Median, A.A.U. colleges............	....	38	40	12	29	10	11
Median, non-A.A.U. colleges.........	....	25	27	19	28	12	12

* Institutions on the approved list of the Association of American Universities.

of the Association of American Universities is less marked. In fact, some of these colleges holding the highest accreditation have a remarkably small percentage of their faculty with the training ordinarily considered necessary for the holding of professorial rank. The percentage of faculty members with no graduate training is surprisingly large in some colleges.

Only ten of the colleges have any faculty members who fail to meet the minimum requirement of the completion of a standard four-year college course. In five of these colleges there is only one teacher without a Bachelor's degree; in four there are two such teachers; and in one college three teachers fail to meet the minimum requirement. Almost without exception, these teachers are in special departments, such as art or music.

Table 81 presents an analysis of the faculty training in terms of ranks held. In making this analysis the faculty members in each institution are grouped according to the ranks held and are judged on the basis of the recognized standards of training for each rank, i.e., Ph.D. or the equivalent for department heads, two years of graduate work for professorial rank (professor, associate professor, or assistant professor), and Bachelor's degree as a minimum for all faculty members. Although the published standards of accrediting associations make no exceptions to these standards, in general practice it is recognized as not feasible to insist upon a Ph.D. or its equivalent for the headships of special departments such as music, art, elocution, physical education, etc. Some departure from a 100 per cent situation in meeting the training standards is therefore to be expected.

It will be observed that the colleges vary widely in the percentage of the entire faculty who meet the training standards for the respective ranks held. At no institution is there anything approaching 100 per cent of the faculty who meet these standards. In one college there is not a single faculty member who meets the training standard for the rank held. The data reflect the great opportunity which exists for improvement in the faculties of these colleges, and reinforces the need which has been previously pointed out for larger funds for instructional salaries, so that capable faculty members whose training is now substandard may be encouraged to take further graduate work, and others who show no desire for improvement may be replaced.

There is a marked difference, with regard to the percentage of faculty members meeting the standards of training, between the colleges on the approved list of the Association of American Universities and those which are not on this list. It will be observed that the first ten institutions at the top of the table are all on the approved list of the Association of Amer-

TABLE 81

PERCENTAGE OF FACULTY MEMBERS OF RANK OF INSTRUCTOR OR ABOVE AT THIRTY-FIVE COLLEGES WHO MEET THE RECOMMENDED STANDARDS OF THEIR RESPECTIVE REGIONAL ACCREDITING ASSOCIATIONS

Institution	Year	Number of Faculty Members Reporting	Percentage of Entire Faculty Meeting Standards for Rank	Percentage of Heads of Departments Having Doctor's Degree or Equivalent	Percentage of Those of Professorial Rank (Other than Department Heads) Having at Least Two Years of Graduate Training	Percentage of Those Holding the Rank of Instructor Having Bachelor's Degree from Standard College
*Dickinson	1929–30	31	84	87	63	100
*Allegheny	1929–30	38	84	79	73	100
*Lawrence	1929–30	52	83	76	76	100
*Hamline	1929–30	40	80	73	56	100
Brothers	1930–31	14	79	75	100	100
*MacMurray	1930–31	38	79	69	67	89
*Albion	1929–30	45	78	68	56	100
*Chattanooga	1929–30	27	78	71	0	100
*Morningside	1929–30	44	77	69	29	100
*Ohio Wesleyan	1930–31	128	77	86	63	100
*DePauw	1930–31	91	75	60	68	100
Union	1929–30	10	70	63	....	100
Nebraska Wesleyan	1930–31	43	70	50	100	86
*Cornell	1929–30	35	69	59	60	100
Evansville	1929–30	25	68	54	67	100
*Simpson	1929–30	37	67	65	17	100
*Willamette	1930–31	33	64	60	58	83
*Illinois Wesleyan	1930–31	35	63	71	38	100
McKendree	1930–31	21	62	64	0	80
Iowa Wesleyan	1929–30	26	62	44	75	100
Baldwin-Wallace	1930–31	33	61	47	43	100
Puget Sound	1930–31	35	57	58	40	83
*Mount Union	1930–31	34	53	53	47	100
Dakota Wesleyan	1929–30	25	52	23	33	100
*Pacific	1930–31	55	51	44	38	100
Southwestern	1930–31	40	50	39	36	100
West Virginia Wesleyan	1930–31	24	46	50	38	....
Ohio Northern	1930–31	40	40	12	44	100
Oklahoma City	1929–30	36	36	27	21	86
*Baker	1930–31	30	30	50	0	....
Kansas Wesleyan	1930–31	18	28	25	50	....
Intermountain	1930–31	15	20	9	0	100
Central Wesleyan	1929–30	18	17	17	17	....
Ozark Wesleyan	1929–30	18	6	7	0	....
Gooding	1930–31	12	0	0	....	....
Median,† all colleges	....	34	63	58	47	100
*Median,† A.A.U. colleges	....	38	77	69	56	100
Median,† non-A.A.U. colleges	....	25	51	42	41	100

* Institutions on the approved list of the Association of American Universities.
† Medians are based on the institutions in which the respective ranks are represented.

ican Universities. On the other hand, a few of the colleges holding this type of accreditation have a surprisingly small percentage of faculty members meeting the standards of training.

To a considerable extent, the showing made in Table 81 is related to the organization of the faculty by ranks. It was previously suggested that it is desirable to maintain a relatively small percentage of the faculty at the highest academic rank. The departmental organization also affects the showing based upon the standards of training. For many of the institutions, a reduction in the number of departments and a conservative assignment of the higher academic ranks would do much to improve the showing of faculty training as presented in Table 81, without in any way changing the personnel of the teaching staffs. A reduction in the size of teaching staffs through an increase in the student-faculty ratio, as suggested in a preceding chapter, could also be utilized to improve the general average of training of the faculty, provided, of course, that the reductions occur among the less able and less thoroughly trained members of the teaching staff.

Recency of training.—In connection with the surveys in each of the colleges, data were gathered regarding the recency of the training of faculty members. One of the most stimulating experiences for a faculty member is the opportunity to take additional graduate work in the field of his specialization. An instructor who fails to avail himself of opportunities to maintain rather close contact with the development of his field of study by means of attendance at recognized graduate schools is probably rendering something less than the service his college has a right to expect.

Table 82 presents data regarding the percentage of faculty members of thirty-five colleges who have had some training within the past ten years. The analysis is presented both by ranks and by levels of training.

This table is read as follows, using for illustration the data shown on the second line: At Dakota Wesleyan, where twenty-five faculty members reported on the dates of their training, 96 per cent of the entire teaching staff has had some training during the past ten years; 94 per cent of the department heads and professors, and 100 per cent of those holding the rank of instructor and assistant have had training during the past ten years; all (100 per cent) of those with two or more years of graduate training, and all (100 per cent) of those with some graduate training but less than two years, have had some training during the past ten years; 86 per cent of those without any graduate training have had some training during the past ten years.

In every college at least half of the faculty members have had some

TABLE 82

PERCENTAGE OF FACULTY MEMBERS OF THIRTY-FIVE COLLEGES WHO
HAVE HAD SOME TRAINING WITHIN THE LAST TEN YEARS

INSTITUTION	NUMBER OF FACULTY MEMBERS REPORTING	PERCENTAGE OF FACULTY MEMBERS OF EACH CLASSIFICATION				
		Entire Faculty	Department Heads and Others of Professorial Rank	Instructors and Assistants	Those with Two or More Years of Graduate Training	Those with Some Graduate Training but Less than Two Years	Those with No Graduate Training
Ozark Wesleyan........	18	100	100	100	100	100	100
Dakota Wesleyan......	25	96	94	100	100	100	86
Brothers..............	14	93	100	80	100	50	....
Intermountain.........	15	93	92	100	100	78	100
Ohio Northern.........	40	90	88	100	80	100	33
Union................	10	90	87	100	100	67	100
Kansas Wesleyan......	18	89	89	....	91	100	....
*Illinois Wesleyan.......	35	89	87	100	84	100	67
*MacMurray...........	38	87	90	84	95	85	60
*Albion................	45	87	82	94	94	87	50
Oklahoma City........	36	86	83	100	100	87	80
Puget Sound...........	35	86	83	100	82	85	100
*Willamette............	33	85	85	83	82	100	67
*Baker.................	30	83	83	....	67	90	100
Gooding..............	12	83	83	....	100	83	67
*Allegheny.............	38	82	72	100	75	91	100
*Simpson..............	37	81	83	50	87	93	33
Nebraska Wesleyan....	43	81	81	80	83	80	50
Southwestern..........	40	80	75	100	72	94	60
*Pacific................	55	78	78	80	63	77	89
*Ohio Wesleyan.........	128	77	70	94	69	94	72
Evansville.............	25	77	68	100	71	87	75
*DePauw..............	91	76	68	96	69	86	80
West Virginia Wesleyan.	24	75	75	....	73	80	67
*Hamline..............	40	75	67	87	73	79	75
*Cornell...............	35	74	70	87	83	92	75
Baldwin-Wallace.......	33	74	69	91	68	92	50
*Lawrence.............	52	73	63	100	65	94	50
McKendree............	21	71	76	50	83	50	67
*Morningside...........	44	70	61	78	63	75	67
*Dickinson.............	31	69	61	89	64	78	100
*Chattanooga...........	27	67	56	89	57	78	75
*Mount Union..........	34	65	66	50	71	62	....
Iowa Wesleyan........	26	62	65	50	67	62	50
Central Wesleyan......	18	53	53	....	100	100	67
Median,† all colleges	34	81	78	91	82	87	67
*Median,† A.A.U. colleges.............	38	77	70	88	71	87	72
Median,† non-A.A.U. colleges.......:....	25	85	83	100	87	86	67

* Institutions on the approved list of the Association of American Universities.
† Medians based on number of colleges having faculty members of each classification.

training within the past ten years. The medians indicate that from three-fourths to four-fifths of the faculty members normally may be expected to have had some training within the latest ten-year period. As would be expected, those holding the departmental headships and professorial rank tend to have had less recent training than those holding the ranks of instructor and assistant. A smaller percentage of those with two or more years of advanced training have attended graduate schools during the past ten years than of those with some graduate training but less than two years. It is somewhat surprising, however, to note the relatively large percentage of those having no graduate training who have taken no steps to improve their educational status during the past ten years.

It will be noted that the institutions on the approved list of the Association of American Universities tend to have on their staffs smaller percentages of members who have had training during the past ten years than the percentages for institutions not approved by this Association. This may be due to the fact, which has previously been pointed out, that the staffs of the approved institutions tend to be better trained than the staffs of those institutions which are not on the approved list. With the pressure which standardizing agencies are bringing to bear upon colleges to increase the training of their staffs, it is to be expected that faculty members with limited graduate training would have been encouraged to attend higher institutions to increase their training.

Encouragement given to further training.—To keep abreast of general developments in education, as well as within one's own field of specialization while doing full-time teaching, requires energy beyond that of many faculty members. It, therefore, becomes increasingly necessary that teachers of all ranks keep professionally up to date. One of the best methods of doing this is to return to outstanding graduate schools for study at intervals not too infrequent. It must be recognized, also, that there are many methods for keeping abreast of developments in one's field of study other than attendance at graduate schools. Travel, research, and reading are all valuable for this purpose.

Several of the colleges have introduced plans for encouraging faculty members to continue their training. Among the devices employed to this end may be mentioned sabbatic leaves for study, the basing of increases in salary on the condition that additional study be taken within certain periods, and the payment of direct bonuses for additional training. Sabbatic leaves should be allowed only when a definite program of professional and personal improvement is planned by the faculty member concerned. A desirable arrangement is to allow faculty members an entire year on half-pay or one semester on full pay after seven years of teaching service, or one semester on half-pay after four years. This is a very desirable investment for any college in which the turnover in teaching is not too high.

CONTRIBUTIONS TO PUBLISHED LITERATURE

One of the best indexes of the intellectual vitality of the members of a teaching staff is found in the contributions they are making to the advancement of the field of study in which they are interested. It is not to be expected that the amount of writing and research carried on by staff members at undergraduate colleges will be equal to that carried on by staff members of the graduate schools of universities. Many excellent teachers do not contribute extensively to journals in their fields. Live teachers, however, are constantly finding things which they wish to contribute. A faculty which is intellectually vigorous is stimulating to a student body.

In this study information was sought from faculty members by means of a personally administered inquiry blank regarding the contributions to published literature made during the preceding five-year period. Table 83 presents a compilation of these data.

It will be observed that the institutions vary markedly in the average number of contributions to published literature per staff member, and in the percentage of staff members making contributions. On this latter point the colleges on the approved list of the Association of American Universities show a marked superiority over those not holding this type of accreditation. In the average number of contributions per staff member, however, there is not a large difference in the medians for the two groups of colleges.

It was not possible within the limitation of time and funds available to make an exhaustive analysis of the quality of these contributions. It is manifestly unfair to give the same weight to a scholarly book as to a short article. Since the table reflects only averages and totals, this factor is to a considerable extent smoothed out for colleges as units. It should also be recognized that the contributions of some faculty members are not given adequate recognition in this table. For example, no account is taken of paintings by members of the art department, musical compositions by members of the music department, and unpublished speeches by other members of the faculty.

Admitting the defects of this measure, it, nevertheless, forms an interesting index of the quality of teaching staffs. There is apparent a marked relationship between the average salary of faculty members and the percentage who are making contributions to published literature. The coefficient of correlation (Pearson) between these two factors is $+.49 \pm .09$.

TABLE 83

Contributions to Published Literature by Members of the Faculties of
Thirty-five Colleges over a Five-Year Period Prior to the
Year of the Survey of the Institution

Institution	Year	Number of Staff Members Reporting	Average Number of Contributions per Staff Member	Percentage of Staff Members Making Contributions
Brothers.................	1930–31	14	2.7	57
*DePauw.................	1930–31	92	1.7	54
Baldwin-Wallace..........	1930–31	37	1.5	51
Gooding.................	1930–31	12	0.5	50
*Ohio Wesleyan...........	1930–31	128	3.4	49
*Lawrence................	1929–30	53	2.0	49
Evansville...............	1929–30	27	1.6	44
*Mount Union.............	1930–31	34	1.3	44
*Dickinson...............	1929–30	32	1.2	44
*Hamline.................	1929–30	42	1.4	43
*Baker...................	1930–31	30	1.3	43
*Albion..................	1929–30	45	1.6	42
*Allegheny...............	1929–30	39	1.1	41
*Illinois Wesleyan.........	1930–31	35	2.2	40
*Cornell.................	1929–30	40	1.3	40
Union...................	1929–30	10	0.5	40
Puget Sound.............	1930–31	35	0.6	34
Nebraska Wesleyan.......	1930–31	41	1.4	32
*Pacific..................	1930–31	55	1.4	31
Iowa Wesleyan..........	1929–30	26	1.1	31
*Willamette..............	1930–31	33	0.7	30
*Morningside.............	1929–30	47	0.6	30
Southwestern............	1930–31	40	0.6	30
McKendree..............	1930–31	21	1.2	29
*Chattanooga.............	1929–30	27	1.0	26
Ohio Northern...........	1930–31	47	0.4	26
*Simpson.................	1929–30	38	0.4	26
Dakota Wesleyan.........	1929–30	25	2.2	24
*MacMurray..............	1930–31	38	1.3	24
Kansas Wesleyan.........	1930–31	18	1.9	22
West Virginia Wesleyan...	1930–31	24	1.4	21
Oklahoma City...........	1929–30	19	0.5	19
Intermountain............	1930–31	15	0.6	13
Central Wesleyan.........	1929–30	18	0.1	11
Ozark Wesleyan..........	1929–30	20	0.8	5
Median, all colleges....	....	34	1.3	32
*Median, A.A.U. colleges................	....	39	1.3	41
Median, non-A.A.U. colleges................	....	23	1.0	30

* Institutions on the approved list of the Association of American Universities.

CHAPTER XXXIV

THE IMPROVEMENT OF INSTRUCTION

In the various colleges visited, a number of valuable procedures are being employed for the improvement of instruction. These procedures are summarized for discussion under the following headings: (1) measures used to increase student initiative and responsibility and to provide for individual differences; (2) suggestions from alumni and students; (3) administrative measures introduced to improve instruction; (4) efforts to measure more accurately the results of instruction; (5) uses made of intelligence tests; (6) classification of students into ability groups; (7) diagnosis, remedial instruction, and educational guidance of students. A statement of the most important procedures under each of these headings follow.

MEASURES USED TO INCREASE STUDENT INITIATIVE AND RESPONSIBILITY AND TO PROVIDE FOR INDIVIDUAL DIFFERENCES

Table 84 presents in summary form the methods employed by the institutions included in this study to increase student initiative and re-

TABLE 84

MEASURES USED AT THIRTY-FIVE INSTITUTIONS TO INCREASE STUDENT INITIATIVE AND RESPONSIBILITY AND TO PROVIDE FOR INDIVIDUAL DIFFERENCES

Method Employed	Number of Institutions Employing Method
Honors program and independent work courses	22
Requirement that students do general reading	17
Special plans to motivate students' work	16
Preceptorial or tutorial instruction	8
Provision for the junior year abroad	2
A comprehensive examination which is not related to an honors program or to an independent work course	1

sponsibility and to provide for individual differences, and the number of institutions employing each method.

Various forms of honors programs and independent study plans are found in the twenty-two institutions employing this method. Students are usually admitted to these courses upon the basis of a high scholastic record, of high standing in intelligence and achievement tests, or upon the basis of both scholastic record and intelligence test scores. Attendance at class lectures and discussions is frequently optional with the student. The quality of the work done is usually judged by the character of written reports submitted by the student and by comprehensive examinations in the fields covered. In some institutions a fixed amount of credit is allowed for courses pursued on the honors plan, while in others credit is allowed upon a sliding scale according to the amount and quality of the work done.

A number of colleges are providing courses in which students of initiative and ability may carry on independent study and research under the guidance of an instructor. These courses usually take the form of a general project which is agreed upon by the student and his instructor. In some colleges the credit values of the courses are fixed; in others they vary according to the amount and quality of work done. This type of individual instruction is very similar to the work done in honors courses. In a second type of individual instruction some or all of the usual class work is abolished, and students in given courses hold individual conferences regularly with their respective instructors.

The requirement that students do some general reading from a selected list of books and periodicals not directly related to course work is in some institutions a part of an honors program, while in others it is not related to honors work. In one college an entire week each semester is allowed for general reading. In the other institutions the time given to general reading is distributed throughout the year. In some colleges this requirement applies to seniors, or juniors and seniors only; while at others it applies to students of all classes. A good example of what may be done along this line is found at Hamline University. Here senior college students before graduation are expected, in addition to the other usual requirements, to be conversant with at least ten books selected from a list prepared by members of the faculty. No formal discussions or examinations are held in connection with this reading; but, instead, faculty members act as advisers or conferees to small groups of students with whom they meet several times during the year for informal discussion. The plan is highly commended by those who are most intimately concerned with its administration.

Special plans to motivate students' work include a co-operative plan of work and study, the granting of scholarships and prizes, exemption from examinations for students receiving high grades, and freedom from the requirement of class attendance for the better students.

The co-operative plan of work and study is well illustrated by the developments in the Departments of Engineering and Education at Evansville College. This arrangement is an adaptation of the "Cincinnati Plan," under which students attend courses for a period of time and then engage in practical work for the same length of time. Essential factors in successfully operating the co-operative plan are: (1) teamwork among students, so that two students may alternate between course work and practical jobs; (2) an organization of class schedules which will enable students who are in residence only half time to pursue courses without a break in their continuity; (3) satisfactory permanent connections with professional, business, and industrial organizations to provide employment for students; (4) ample personnel service at the college to supervise the student and co-ordinate effectively his college work and his practical employment. By carrying on this program on a twelve-month basis, students at Evansville College may complete their requirements for a degree in five years.[1]

In all of the institutions which make provision for preceptorial or tutorial instruction, admission to work of this type is limited to a relatively small number of students. Likewise, in the institutions making provision for the junior year abroad, only a few students benefit by the arrangement. Only one college provides for a comprehensive examination that is not related to an honors program or to an independent work course, and this institution requires all seniors to take this examination.

At each of a number of colleges several of the methods listed in Table 84 are employed in combination. Brief descriptions will be presented of the methods employed at seven of these institutions.

At Albion College students are awarded honors for high records in scholarship, three classes of honors being conferred at graduation. General honors are also announced at each commencement time for those seniors who have done superior work for the year just finished. Department honors are given to juniors whose grades meet certain standards and who do certain additional work in connection with one or more courses, and to seniors for additional work of not less than a three-hour course for one semester. Prizes and scholarships are presented also for high intellectual achievement. Two honor societies annually elect to membership such students as meet their standards of scholastic achievement.

At Willamette University honors programs and independent work courses have been introduced in several fields. General reading courses have also been announced. There are a few courses of the preceptorial

---

[1] The co-operative plan in engineering at Evansville College has been discontinued since the visit of the survey staff.

type, though their number is not large. An interesting course entitled "The Machine Age" is arranged for 1931–32 and thereafter at the senior-class level. It is planned that several members of the faculty and select seniors will participate in the course, which is of the orientation type. Its purpose is to interpret in some degree the present-day American life in its industrial, educational, social, and religious aspects.

At Nebraska Wesleyan University honors courses for the motivation of students of superior ability have been developed. General reading courses are also offered. Outside examiners are brought in for the honors courses.

At Ohio Wesleyan University honors courses are offered by the Departments of English and History to students of special ability and initiative. Students who pursue these courses are relieved of some of the requirements of undergraduate courses, but they are held to higher-than-average standards in the quality and quantity of the work done. In English, honors work is laid down by semesters covering the junior and senior years. In history, the honors course is intended for students who desire to pursue a special interest in some limited phase of the subject.

At Lawrence College two specific provisions are made to develop student initiative and responsibility. Certain departments provide tutorial instruction, a system under which the student works independently but with the guidance of an instructor. Juniors having an average grade of 85 or above, with the permission of the departments offering the privilege, may elect to study on a tutorial basis in the department selected for the major. Eighteen of the twenty-four hours required for the major must be in addition to tutorial work. The plan of tutorial instruction has elicited favorable comment from both students and faculty members. At this institution students are further motivated to do a high quality of work by the prospect of scholarships and prizes for those who show superior ability, and by the award of department and general honors in scholarship at commencement.

At Dickinson College four measures designed to develop student initiative and responsibility are employed. First, honors courses and independent work courses are offered in a number of departments. Second, arrangements are made from time to time for some students to spend one year abroad in travel and study. Third, special attention is given to all students who rank high in their work. After the first semester of each year a formal dinner is given to "A" students; the dinner is attended by faculty members and their wives; and usually an outside speaker of prominence gives an address. Fourth, a number of advanced courses in certain departments are restricted in enrolment to students whose average for the preceding semester is at least 80 per cent. These classes have small enrolments, and the instructors give personal guidance through conferences.

At Brothers College honors courses are available for junior and senior students who have shown outstanding ability for study in a particular field. The amount of work which may be taken in this way is limited to four hours each semester. At the end of each year the candidate must pass an examination upon the whole of his honors work for the year, and final honors are awarded upon the basis of comprehensive examinations given at the end of the senior year by the department concerned. Students are further motivated through honors in general scholarship. Seniors with high scholastic standing will be graduated *cum laude*, *magna cum laude*, or *summa cum laude*.

SUGGESTIONS FROM ALUMNI AND STUDENTS

Fourteen of the thirty-five institutions have attempted from time to time to improve methods of teaching by utilizing the judgments of alumni and students. These judgments are usually secured either by means of confidential conferences or through a questionnaire. Sometimes the data secured are of such a character that they may be presented to the faculty as a whole or to the instructors in a given department. Sometimes, however, the data are of such a nature that they must be kept confidential and must be made the basis of personal conference between the administrative officer and individual faculty members. Brief descriptions will be presented of the types of studies made at eight institutions.

At Hamline University the alumni graduating during the years 1925–28, inclusive, were asked to report their reactions to various methods used by the instructors while they were students. The suggestions received were written up in an impersonal way and reported to the instructional and administrative staff.

At Albion College a number of faculty members have asked their students to fill out a questionnaire in the form of a rating scale analyzing the teaching from the student point of view. The rating scales used were particularly well suited to elicit from students pertinent criticisms of the teaching techniques employed in the course. In this way the faculty members received useful suggestions upon the basis of which they modified their procedures. These rating scales were used only on the initiative of the individual instructor, and the results were not made available to anyone but the teacher concerned.

A study was also made at Albion College of the reactions of seniors to the teaching of different members of the faculty. Ratings were also made by the seniors on the ease of getting high marks in various subjects and on the values of the courses taken. After the data were collected, the faculty members were provided with a summary of the findings, the reports of individual students being retained as confidential information.

During recent years the president of Dickinson College has asked the members of each senior class to fill out a confidential questionnaire asking for suggestions relating to the improvement of instruction. Frankness in the statements of students is secured by promising that the questionnaires will be destroyed after having been read by the president. The members of the faculty concerned are given a digest of the replies received. This plan is reported to be of distinct advantage in raising the quality of instruction.

At Cornell College several members of the faculty are making regular use of student evaluations and criticisms for improvement of instruction and are using definite, objective devices for eliminating weaknesses in their courses.

At Lawrence College student opinion of instruction was studied by an organization of senior women. Each faculty member was shown his own rating, and a composite for the institution was furnished the administration. A somewhat similar method has been used by two luncheon groups —one composed of presidents of fraternities and the other of sorority presidents—which meet with the president of the college and other administrative officers. These meetings have served as a general clearing house for student opinion on instructional matters as well as other affairs of the college.

At Morningside College the opinions of alumni and students are being utilized as a means of improving the quality of instruction. From time to time the president discusses with groups of alumni who are enrolled in graduate schools the type of instruction which Morningside College provides. The information secured in this way is kept confidential by the president but is used by him for the purpose of improving the quality of instruction in the college. Each year the president also discusses confidentially with the members of the senior class the work being done at Morningside, and criticism is invited. Moreover, an attempt is made to cultivate a feeling on the part of students that any criticism which they may see fit to give will be welcomed.

The president of Willamette University recently conducted an inquiry among the seniors regarding the teaching of the various faculty members.

The plan for the inquiry was worked out co-operatively by the administration and faculty, with the understanding that each teacher was to be shown a summary of the tabulations on his own teaching. The inquiry blank, which was confidential, afforded an opportunity for diagnostic analysis of the defects of teaching techniques.

From time to time the president of Simpson College has sought the opinion of students concerning the effectiveness of the instruction which they receive. Each year he holds confidential conferences with outstanding members of the senior class. These seniors are asked to give their judgments concerning the quality of instruction and to make any suggestions for its improvement which they may care to make. Occasionally the president seeks similar information from recent graduates. Upon the basis of information secured through these conferences with students and alumni, the president discusses with members of the faculty the methods of teaching employed. In these discussions an attempt is made to point out some possible weaknesses of methods used as revealed by the criticisms made by students and recent alumni.

The most uniformly satisfactory method of utilizing student opinion concerning the effectiveness of instruction appears to be the plan by which individual faculty members ask the members of their classes to give them a confidential rating upon a number of points related to the quality of their teaching. The Purdue Rating Scale has been used at a number of colleges as a means of obtaining student judgments. In most instances teachers who have employed rating scales such as the Purdue Scale state that the results have been helpful to them in pointing out means whereby they might improve their teaching.

ADMINISTRATIVE MEASURES INTRODUCED TO IMPROVE INSTRUCTION

Table 85 presents a summary of the administrative measures which a number of institutions are employing in an effort to improve instruction.

The methods employed most frequently by the administrations of the several colleges to encourage faculty members in service to improve their training are sabbatical leave on full salary or part salary, leave of absence for further study, and promises of promotion following a period of study. An increasing number of colleges are requiring either teaching experience or professional training in education, or both, for all new appointees. The presidents of a number of the institutions included in this study have encouraged the discussion of instructional problems by occasionally bringing in speakers from the faculties of one or another of the larger universities which provide training for college teachers. At other institutions the faculties meet at regular intervals for such discussions. Frequently faculty meetings are held for the purpose of receiving reports by committees that have made studies of special problems, and for the discussion of such reports. It is interesting to note that twelve of the thirty-five institutions provide for the supervision of instruction. In most instances such supervision takes the form of class visitation by presidents, deans, or department heads.

At Albion College regular monthly faculty meetings are held for the discussion of problems relating to classroom teaching. The programs that are planned by the committee on improvement of instruction consist of

TABLE 85

ADMINISTRATIVE MEASURES INTRODUCED TO
IMPROVE INSTRUCTION

Method Employed	Number of Institutions Employing Method
Encouraging faculty members to improve their training..	29
Requirement of teaching experience for new appointees to the faculty..	25
Discussion of instructional problems in lectures, forums, and faculty committees............................	25
Requirement of professional training in education for new appointees to the faculty...........................	12
Appointment of faculty committee to study instructional problems...	12
Supervision of instruction...........................	12
Other methods......................................	6
No method employed................................	2

papers and reports which are assigned to various faculty members, with discussions by other faculty members.

The administration of Dickinson College makes teaching experience a definite requirement in employing faculty members. In addition, all faculty members are encouraged to improve their training by carrying on graduate work. Arrangements are also made, from time to time, to have instructional problems presented to the faculty; and forums are held in which such problems are discussed. Heads of departments are made responsible for supervising the instruction given by newly appointed members of the faculty in their respective departments.

At DePauw University there is a definite requirement of one year of graduate work and one year of teaching experience for all candidates for instructorships. Further training and longer periods of experience are demanded for positions of higher rank. Instructional problems are studied and discussed in forums, faculty committees, and administrative staff meetings.

The administration of Cornell College makes teaching experience a definite requirement in employing a new faculty member. It also requires that new appointees shall have had some courses of training in education as a part of their preparation. All faculty members are encouraged to improve their training by carrying on graduate work. Instructional problems are discussed in forums and in lectures, and a faculty committee has been appointed to suggest methods for the improvement of instruction. One method of improving instruction is peculiar to this institution. It has been designated by the president as "pre-college-year" faculty conference. Immediately preceding the opening of the college each fall, a two-day conference of all faculty members is held at a summer camp near the institution. Various members of the faculty prepare papers on topics such as: "What kind of student does Cornell have at present?" "What results do we expect to achieve in our students?" "What constitutes good teaching?" "How can a teacher improve his teaching?" Following the presentation of each paper a discussion is held, led by some other member of the faculty.

At Hamline University specific attempts have been made to improve the quality of instruction by the following means: (1) Teaching experience is a requirement in the employment of new faculty members. The present administration is seeking to secure the services of those who have had two or three years, and in some cases five years, of experience in their chosen fields. (2) Instructors are encouraged constantly to continue their studies. (3) Every faculty member of professorial rank has at least one opportunity to attend, during the year, a state or national professional meeting with expenses paid. Some of the faculty members attend several such meetings during a single year. (4) A committee on instruction is maintained for the purpose of investigating problems. There are occasional reports from this committee on new methods and problems. Faculty meetings are often held for the consideration of reports and for such discussions as may arise. (5) The teaching of faculty members of the lower ranks is supervised through the co-operation of the older members of the staff. (6) Continuous study of instructional problems is being carried on by a committee which has charge of the survey courses. All of these measures indicate a progressive and aggressive effort on the part of the administration in co-operation with the faculty to improve the quality of instruction.

At Oklahoma City University the administrative officers report that various measures are employed for the improvement of instruction. The following are among the more important of those listed: (1) Definite requirements are made regarding the training and teaching experience of new faculty members. To be eligible for appointment to the faculty of Oklahoma City University the applicant is expected to have an advanced degree and one or more years of successful teaching experience. (2) Although courses in education are not set up as a definite prerequisite for appointment to the faculty, they are considered desirable. (3) Faculty members are encouraged to improve their training. (4) There is some discussion of instructional problems in faculty groups. (5) A faculty committee devotes time to a study of the improvement of instruction. (6) There is some supervision of instruction.

At Willamette University a faculty forum is held monthly for consideration of professional topics. The meetings are reported to be of considerable value. A program of instructional supervision is in charge of the dean, who is also professor of education. Classes are visited as a part of this work, and each visit is followed by a friendly and constructive conference regarding the points observed in the teaching. The dean's office obtains a number of reports regarding the work of each class. For example, each instructor is asked to list the objectives of his course, the textbook used, the outline followed, etc. At the end of the semester each instructor is asked to furnish copies of the examination questions used in his courses, with comments as to the relation between the questions and the stated objectives of the course. Other reports cover such matters as the specific plans followed by each instructor for the improvement of his own teaching. The program in this regard at Willamette is unusually thorough.

In Union College specific attempts have been made to maintain and improve the quality of instruction by the following means: (1) A requirement of teaching experience is enforced in the employment of new faculty members. (2) Newly employed faculty members are required to have had some training in courses in education. (3) Instructional problems are discussed in faculty meetings. (4) Classes are visited by the president of the institution with a view to giving some supervision and direction of instruction.

Various administrative measures are employed at Simpson College for the improvement of instruction. The most important of these are as follows: (1) Teachers are encouraged to continue their training by attendance at summer school or by occasional leaves of absence. (2) Instructors are advised to include courses in education in their program of graduate studies. (3) Heads of departments are urged to visit classes of new instructors in their respective departments with a view to supervising their work and to giving specific directions for the improvement of their instruction.

At Nebraska Wesleyan University lecturers are brought in from time to time to discuss, before the faculty group, some of the problems relating to the improvement of instruction. An analysis of these efforts to improve instruction has recently been issued by the University in mimeographed form. A standing committee of the faculty arranges programs for monthly meetings of a professional character, at which instructional problems are discussed by faculty members and by visiting professors from other institutions. Faculty members are given encouragement to improve their training. Several of the teachers in Nebraska Wesleyan University are keeping in touch with advanced courses in their fields at the University of Nebraska.

EFFORTS TO MEASURE MORE ACCURATELY THE RESULTS OF INSTRUCTION

Of the thirty-five institutions included in this study, twenty-five report that efforts are being made to improve the methods employed in measuring educational achievement. The general feeling of dissatisfaction with the marking system currently used in colleges is fully justified, and numerous experiments and studies are being carried on among the colleges to find a more reliable measure of achievement. The general trend of these experiments and studies has been in two directions: First, efforts are being made to have grades given by instructors distributed on a percentile basis conforming to the curve of normal frequency. To this end, reports of the distributions of grades given by all members of a faculty and by each individual instructor are being made each semester in a number of colleges. Second, objective tests are being employed as a more accurate measurement of achievement.

The method employed at Dickinson College to bring about greater uniformity in grades awarded among the members of the faculty is illustrative of the methods employed at a number of institutions. Each semester an analysis is made of all the grades given by each teacher. The average of the grades given by an instructor in a given section is compared with the average of the grades given by all instructors to students who are in the section. The difference between the two averages shows the instructor how much above or below his fellow-instructors he is marking students in each subject. This plan is reported to have resulted in a marked improvement in the attitude of instructors toward grading and has materially reduced the divergence in the grades given by various members of the faculty.

Seven of the institutions report that objective achievement tests are used to some extent in all or nearly all of the departments. In twenty-one institutions some use of such tests is made in a number of departments. One college reports use in two departments only, and one reports use in only one department. Five of the institutions failed to provide information with reference to the use of such tests. At thirteen colleges these tests were initiated by individual instructors; at five colleges the administration suggested their introduction; at twelve colleges the introduction of these tests was at the suggestion of the administration in some departments and on the initiative of individual instructors in other departments. The use of objective tests to supplement the essay and discussion type of test seems most promising at present, but it is still comparatively undeveloped. Frequently, faculty members need to be guided in their use of the new-type examinations, so that they may be certain of covering basic understandings as well as testing factual knowledge. In the present stage of the development of objective tests, few authorities would advocate restricting all examinations and tests to those which are objective in character.

A few colleges are also introducing the comprehensive examination which is given a student at the time of his completion of a whole field of study. This type of examination is valuable in that it tends to divert the emphasis from the passing of specific courses to the mastery of a subject or field.

USES MADE OF INTELLIGENCE TESTS

Thirty-four of the thirty-five institutions included in this study report that intelligence tests are given to some or to all students. Such tests are given to all students at six institutions, to freshmen only at twenty-three institutions, and to special departmental groups, such as education or psychology, at six institutions. Table 86 presents data showing the uses made of the results of intelligence tests at twenty-five institutions which reported one or more uses.

CLASSIFICATION OF STUDENTS INTO ABILITY GROUPS

Twenty-six of the thirty-five institutions report that students in some classes have been classified into ability groups for instructional purposes. Classification of students into class sections on the basis of ability is utilized most frequently in English classes. Twenty-one of the twenty-six institutions classify freshman English students into sections on the basis of ability. Classification on an ability basis is made in the sciences at five institutions, in foreign languages at four institutions, in mathematics at three institutions, and in the social sciences at one institution.

TABLE 86

Uses Made of the Results of Intelligence
Tests at Twenty-five Institutions

Use Made of Test Results	Number of Institutions
In determining the amount of academic work students may carry	16
In determining probation for low scholarship	16
In determining dismissal for low scholarship	15
In advising students in the selection of their academic work	14
In dealing with disciplinary (deportment) cases	13
In sectioning students according to capacity	13
In making recommendations for scholarships	13
For purposes of vocational guidance	12
In guiding students into positions of leadership	12
In determining the amount of work for self-support	10
As a partial basis for admission	8
In recommending for positions or for entrance to senior college	6
In encouraging bright students to undertake senior college work	5
For purposes of student-training	2
In employing students for clerical help	1
In granting permission to participate in extra-curriculum activities	1
For purposes of student motivation	1

As a basis of classification into ability groups, twelve institutions use scores on standardized aptitude or placement tests; five use the results of non-standardized tests, examinations, and themes; two use marks received in course work; three use a combination of marks and intelligence test scores; one uses intelligence test scores alone; and one a combination of intelligence test scores, scores on non-standardized subject-matter tests, and marks received in course work. Two of the twenty-six institutions fail to report the basis of the classification of students into ability groups. Fifteen of the twenty-six institutions report favorably with reference to the value of classifying students into sections on the basis of ability; nine report a division of opinion among faculty members with reference to the value of such classification; and two report that little has been obtained from such grouping of students.

DIAGNOSIS, REMEDIAL INSTRUCTION, AND EDUCATIONAL GUIDANCE OF STUDENTS

Diagnostic and remedial procedures as a means of understanding and correcting the educational and social maladjustments of students are still unrefined in some institutions of higher learning and are entirely unknown in others. In answer to the question, "Is the institution making any special effort to diagnose the difficulties of failing or potentially failing students, and to provide remedial instruction?" twenty-four institutions answer "Yes," four answer "No," and seven fail to provide an answer.

At Albion College each student in his freshman year is placed under the guidance of a professor, who holds frequent interviews with him and carefully registers the results of these interviews for future use. These notes are kept on file in the office of the dean. Reports of unsatisfactory work are acted upon by the dean and the scholarship committee, who secure their information from a variety of sources. Students who have difficulties in particular subjects are given tutorial assistance several hours each week by senior students specializing in that particular subject.

At Cornell College a careful study has been made of the causes of failure among students based upon: (1) living conditions; (2) group membership; (3) extra-curriculum activities; (4) self-support while in college; (5) intelligence ratings. The results of this study are used in advising students who are low in their standings.

An interesting schedule for "student diagnosis" is used at Nebraska Wesleyan University. Five grades of quality are described with respect to each of the following traits: attitude, initiative, study technique, scholarship, and individual improvement. The exact qualities under each of the five grades for each trait are rather carefully outlined. Special efforts are made to diagnose the difficulties of failing and potentially failing students. Every six weeks all teachers report the names of students who are making the lowest passing grade or are failing. These are referred to the dean of men, who diagnoses their cases by personal interview. Students are then referred to their respective academic deans for further interview. The "problem students" are studied with particular reference to application, reading ability, organizing ability, intelligence, and the relationship of high-school to college training. Supervised study periods have also been introduced. Remedial work in reading is carried on by the teacher-training division of the institution.

There are vast fields to be explored in attempts to determine why students fail, to what extent they are handicapped by deficiencies in knowledge of fundamental subjects, or what personality difficulties may interfere with their scholastic progress. Diagnosis of this type is a phase of personnel service which demands a sympathetic interest in student problems and a carefully controlled laboratory technique. The method most commonly relied upon has been the personal interview, although more objective and impersonal procedures are being employed experimentally and give promise of having considerable value. Reading tests are being used to determine the rate and comprehension of reading; general intelligence tests and special interest tests are being employed in certain cases; study habits are being observed; peculiarities of thinking are being analyzed; and personal prejudices and complexes are being investigated. Such diagnoses demand special training and experience. They should be made through an educational clinic comparable to the medical clinic. The analogy may be carried even farther by saying that diagnosis must precede treatment, and the nature of the prescription will be determined by the findings of the diagnosis. There are important possibilities in this field which are not generally being utilized by institutions of higher education.

CHAPTER XXXV

SUMMER SESSIONS

INSTITUTIONS MAINTAINING SUMMER SESSIONS

Twenty-seven of the thirty-five colleges included in this study maintain summer sessions. In the great majority of those maintaining a summer session, the work is given in a single term corresponding in length to either one-sixth or one-fourth of a regular academic (nine-month) year. In seven of the colleges the work during the summer is given in two terms, equivalent to one-third of a regular academic year.

The maintenance of a summer session is much less common among the colleges of this group which do hold accreditation with the Association of American Universities than it is with the colleges which do not have this type of recognition. Of the eight colleges which do not maintain a summer session, seven are on the approved list of the Association of American Universities. The group maintaining summer sessions includes only ten colleges on the approved list of the Association of American Universities, but seventeen of the eighteen colleges not holding accreditation from this association give summer work.

REASONS FOR MAINTAINING SUMMER SESSIONS

Each of the colleges was asked to indicate the reason or reasons for maintaining the summer session. All but two of the group of twenty-seven indicate as one of the reasons the desire to serve a large group of students who demand summer-session work. One-third of the colleges indicate as a reason the desire to put the work of the institution on an all-year-round basis. One-third indicate that the summer session is maintained because of the pressure brought by a considerable number of faculty members for summer-session employment. Fifteen colleges indicate that they operate a summer session in order to meet the competition of other schools, by which students might be drawn away. Only one college indicates that the summer session is maintained in the hope of producing a financial profit.

In criticism of these reasons for maintaining summer sessions, it may be pointed out that two of those given—namely, the desire to put the work of the institution on an all-year-round basis, and the effort to meet the needs of a large group of students—are thoroughly legitimate. Interestingly enough, however, some of the colleges which indicate the second of

339

these reasons have very small enrolments in their summer sessions, so that the student group to be served is not numerically as important as the authorities of the college apparently believe.

It is probable that a penetrating analysis would have led more than one-third of the colleges to indicate that the summer session is maintained for the purpose of adding to the salaries of faculty members. The colleges which do not operate a summer session tend to be those with the higher average faculty salaries, only one of the group of eight which do not have a summer session being below the median of the entire group of thirty-five with respect to average faculty salaries. If the colleges are divided into two groups on the basis of maintaining or not maintaining a summer session, the median of the average regular-year faculty salaries for those not having a summer session is $420 above the corresponding median for those which have a summer session. It therefore seems fair to conclude that in a relatively large number of cases the summer session is maintained partly to help faculty members eke out an unsatisfactory annual salary.

ADMINISTRATION OF SUMMER SESSIONS

The administration of the summer session is typically not in the hands of the president of the college, there being only two colleges, both of them relatively small, in which the president himself carries this responsibility. The reason for the delegation of the management of the summer session is a historical one. The summer session originated in a semi-official manner. Groups of faculty members associated themselves for the purpose of giving instruction during the summer, and the only official recognition given by the institution was the permission to use the plant facilities and the acceptance of the credits earned toward the degrees of the institution. This semi-official body of teachers usually appointed one of their own group to look after the advertising, the collection of fees, the recording of credits, the registration of students, and other administrative matters pertaining to the session. Later the summer session was taken over officially by the college and recognized as an integral part of the work of the institution, but there was a desire not to add the administration of this unit as an extra burden on the shoulders of the president. Consequently, the previous custom of assigning this responsibility to a director of the summer session was continued. Thus, it is typical in American colleges to find the administration of the summer session not directly in charge of the president of the institution, but delegated to some other person who is known as the "director of the summer session."

In the group of twenty-seven colleges included in this study, the summer-session director is the dean of the college in twelve cases, and in nine cases is the head of the department of education. Three of the deans, however, are also heads of their respective education departments. (They are not included among the nine heads of departments of education mentioned above.) A conclusion may therefore be drawn to the effect that the direction of the summer session is assigned with equal frequency either to the dean or to the professor of education. There are only three cases in this group in which some member of the faculty, other than the dean or the professor of education, serves as summer-session director. In addition to these three cases, the vice-president directs the summer session in one college, and, as previously noted, in two colleges the president himself holds this responsibility.

The designation of the professor of education as the director of the summer session also has a historical explanation. The stimulus for the giving of summer work arose principally with groups of public-school teachers who found this time of the year their only opportunity for further training. Since the program of the summer session was designed primarily to serve this group of students, it was only natural that the professor of education should be asked to assist in such matters as the determination of the courses to be offered, the dates which would be most convenient for the prospective student group, the probable number of registrants that could be expected, etc. If the professor of education had administrative ability, he was very likely to be named as the director of the summer session. The naming of the dean of the college as summer-session director represents a step away from the quasi-official character of the session toward its recognition as an integral part of the year's work, with a consequent need for a close integration of its administration with that of the regular year.

The director of the summer session in this group of colleges is usually given a small extra compensation for this work. In a few of the colleges the person directing the summer session is on a straight twelve-month salary, and the direction of the session is included as a part of his regular duties. The amounts paid as extra compensation for directing the summer sessions of these colleges range from $50 to $500. Six of the directors receive $300 or more, and seven receive $100 or less. In two cases the amount paid is not a flat sum, but is based on a percentage of the regular annual salary of the director.

ENROLMENTS, TEACHING LOADS, AND SIZE OF CLASSES IN SUMMER SESSIONS

Table 87 presents statistical data for the summer sessions of twenty-seven colleges, showing the number of students enrolled, the teaching loads of the faculty members, and the size of classes.

THE LIBERAL ARTS COLLEGE

It will be noted that a majority of these colleges have only a small number of students enrolled in their summer sessions, the median enrolment being only slightly in excess of one hundred students. In general, the col-

TABLE 87

TOTAL STUDENT ENROLMENTS, TEACHING LOADS OF FACULTY MEMBERS, AND SIZE OF CLASSES IN THE SUMMER SESSIONS OF TWENTY-SEVEN COLLEGES

Name of College	Year of Data	Number of Students Enrolled in Summer Session	Number of Students per Faculty Member	Percentage of Instructors Teaching More than Sixteen Hours per Week	Median Size of Classes	Percentage of Classes with Fewer than Five Students
Ohio Northern..........	1930	430	15.4	46.4	10.2	34.1
Central Wesleyan........	1929	304	13.2	21.7	6.6	27.2
*Pacific.................	1930	263	13.2	....	14.5	16.1
Evansville.............	1929	239	14.1	52.9	14.2	12.8
*Morningside...........	1929	223	18.6	41.6	8.5	40.9
West Virginia Wesleyan..	1930	211	13.2	12.5	12.2	8.7
Southwestern...........	1930	199†	16.6	8.3	7.0	47.2
Nebraska Wesleyan......	1930	198†	10.3	5.2	15.7	8.9
*Simpson...............	1929	191	14.7	53.8	11.3	24.4
Union.................	1929	186	20.7	88.9	24.0	....
Puget Sound...........	1930	174	9.7	44.4	7.1	42.6
Oklahoma City.........	1929	163†	8.3	80.0	15.4	....
*Mount Union..........	1930	116	9.7	75.0	7.3	43.2
Kansas Wesleyan........	1930	115	19.2	100.0	20.5	....
Iowa Wesleyan..........	1929	115	8.8	38.4	10.5	25.0
*DePauw...............	1930	101	7.8	61.5	8.1	40.6
*Chattanooga............	1929	96	8.7	100.0	‡	‡
McKendree.............	1930	93	11.6	100.0	8.9	33.3
Baldwin-Wallace........	1930	84	12.0	57.1	8.5	30.0
*Allegheny.............	1929	78†	5.6	21.4	10.2	23.4
Ozark Wesleyan........	1929	73†	8.2	100.0	16.3	....
*Baker.................	1930	69†	8.6	....	5.0	50.0
*Cornell................	1929	61†	11.2	81.8	9.8	16.7
Intermountain..........	1930	55	9.2	66.7	4.0	87.2
*Willamette.............	1930	47	5.2	22.2	6.5	47.1
Gooding...............	1930	17	4.3	100.0	4.0	90.9
Dakota Wesleyan........	1929	‡	‡	72.7	6.8	43.5
Median, all colleges...	....	116	10.8	53.8	9.4	28.6
*Median, A.A.U. colleges...............	....	99	9.2	47.7	8.5	40.6
Median, non-A.A.U. colleges...........	....	169	11.8	57.1	10.2	27.2

* Institutions on the approved list of the Association of American Universities.

† Average enrolment of two terms.

‡ Data not available.

leges which are not on the approved list of the Association of American Universities tend to have larger enrolments than those which hold satisfactory accreditation. If the colleges which do not maintain a summer session are included in the distribution (the enrolments being counted as zero), the median enrolment for the colleges on the approved list of the Association of American Universities becomes 47, as contrasted with 139 for the colleges not holding this type of accreditation. This situation is in sharp contrast with the data for enrolments for the regular year. It has previously been shown (see Table 7) that the colleges of this group holding accreditation from the Association of American Universities tend to be those with the larger student bodies during the regular year. In the summer session it seems that this condition is exactly reversed.

It will be noted from Table 87 that the ratios of students to faculty are relatively low, and the teaching loads in terms of hours taught per week tend to be high. A ratio of students to faculty as low as the median shown in this table represents a very uneconomical instructional organization. The standards of the regional accrediting agencies suggest that "teaching schedules . . . . exceeding sixteen recitation hours or their equivalent per week, per instructor, will be interpreted as endangering educational efficiency"; but it is typical in these summer sessions to find at least half of the faculty members teaching more than this number of hours. On this point the colleges with lower accreditation status are greater offenders than those on the approved list of the Association of American Universities.

As would be expected from the low ratios of students to faculty members, the average size of classes tends to be very small, far below that which would be demanded by an economical organization during the regular year. The percentage of small classes is also very high.

The data of this table lead to the conclusion that in the majority of these colleges the maintenance of a summer session results in a very uneconomical organization. Enrolments of students are small, resulting in an inordinate number of small classes and in a low ratio of students to faculty members. In order to overcome the handicap of the small enrolment, the instructors are called upon to teach very heavy schedules. These conditions lead to a grave question as to the academic equivalence of the summer-session work with that of the regular year.

FACULTY SALARIES IN SUMMER SESSIONS

Various policies are followed in these summer sessions with respect to the payment of faculty salaries. In eight of the colleges the amount of remuneration is contingent entirely upon the amount of fees collected. In four other institutions a portion of the compensation is distributed on this basis, the remainder being determined on some other basis. Thus, in a total of twelve of the twenty-seven colleges the amount of compensation received by teachers is related directly to the amount of fees collected from students. Seven of the colleges pay their summer-session teachers a flat rate which is the same for all, regardless of the rank held or the salary received during the academic year. Five colleges pay a fixed amount according to the rank held, and three pay a fixed percentage of the regular yearly salary.

It is surprising to find in so many of the colleges the policy of relating faculty salaries to the amount of fees collected. This is a direct inheritance from the early informal organization of the summer session, before it was recognized as a regular and creditable part of the year's work. None of these colleges would, for a moment, think of making the regular-year salaries of their faculty members dependent upon the amount of fees collected; and there is no reason to suppose that this policy is any more satisfactory during the summer session than during the regular year. The temptation to lower entrance standards and to "soften" the work in the interests of obtaining a larger enrolment can best be obviated by making the payment for summer-session teaching entirely unrelated to the number of students or the amount of fees collected.

Perhaps the best method of setting summer-session salaries is the payment of a fixed percentage of the salary received in the regular year. To pay all teachers a flat sum, regardless of rank or annual salary, is apt to result in a relatively inferior summer-session faculty, since the lower-salaried members will be glad to stay while the more capable will tend to accept summer-session positions at other institutions having a more satisfactory salary policy. To a less extent, the fixing of salaries at a flat rate on the basis of rank held is unsatisfactory, and operates in much the same manner as the policy of a flat rate for all regardless of rank or salary. These policies are not usually followed during the regular year, and it is difficult to see how the flat-rate plan can be more acceptable during the summer than during the other nine months. The fixing of summer-session salaries at a given percentage of the regular-year salary overcomes these difficulties.

FINANCING THE SUMMER SESSIONS

The policies followed with respect to the financing of the summer session vary among this group of colleges. There are only three which expect that a subsidy will be needed from some source other than student fees in order to pay faculty salaries. Five of the colleges expect that student fee collections will cover all faculty salary payments but will leave nothing for the other expenses of the summer session. Four colleges expect that student fee collections not only will cover all faculty salary payments but will also cover a portion of the other expenses incident to the session. Twelve colleges expect student fees to cover all expenses of the summer session, including administration, salaries, plant operation, and all similar costs. Three of the colleges expect student fees not only to cover all costs but actually to leave a surplus which can be used during the regular year.

The actual financial outcomes of the most recent summer sessions are, in general, somewhat less favorable than the policies listed above would indicate. Six of the twenty-seven colleges failed to collect enough in student fees to pay the salaries of the faculty; four received enough from fees to pay salaries but nothing more; four others received enough to pay salaries and a portion of the other expenses; ten received enough to pay all directly chargeable expenses; and three produced a surplus above all expenses.

If the maintenance of a summer session is justified from an educational standpoint, there is no fundamental reason why student fees should be expected to bear the entire cost of this session any more than that of the regular year. In other words, if the summer session serves a legitimate educational purpose, it would seem to be thoroughly justifiable to subsidize it from such funds as endowment income, church gifts, etc., in exactly the same way as the work of the regular year is supported. Thus, by implication, the fact that so many of these summer sessions are managed on a self-supporting financial policy tends to raise the question of their true educational service. The further fact that such a large percentage of these summer sessions are self-supporting only because of excessive teaching loads carried by faculty members and because of unsatisfactory arrangements for the fixing of salaries also tends to raise a real question regarding the educational service of these sessions.

PROBABLE DISCONTINUANCE OF MANY SUMMER SESSIONS

A few of the colleges are giving serious consideration to the wisdom of discontinuing their summer sessions; and in one or two cases since the visit of the survey staff, the decision has been reached to discontinue the summer work. The maintenance of a session for small student groups is uneconomical. Question may be raised regarding the standards maintained in these summer sessions, judging by the teaching loads carried by faculty members, the policies followed in the financing of the summer session, and the methods used in fixing faculty salaries. Students have abundant opportunity to take summer work at the larger universities where this session is considered as a part of the regular academic year. Under such circumstances the continuation of the summer sessions in most of these colleges is of questionable wisdom. It is interesting to note that, in general, the strongest colleges of the group being studied do not maintain a summer session. The great majority of the summer students attending the colleges of the group studied are enrolled in those of relatively inferior accreditation status.

It must be recognized that there are certain valid arguments for the maintenance of the summer sessions of these colleges. In some cases they are justified as recruiting devices; students who enrol first during the summer occassionally come back to take their degrees from the college. There is also the consideration that if no summer session is maintained, the plant will be standing idle and the percentage of annual utilization lowered. Perhaps the most potent argument of all is the need felt by faculty members for supplementing their annual salaries.

On the other hand, some of the administrators of these colleges have pointed out that the maintenance of a summer session is in reality a process of undercutting the work of the regular year. If students are encouraged to attend summer sessions, their time in college is shortened, and, from a financial viewpoint, the college suffers a loss of income from fees. Perhaps more important is the effect on faculty members who teach in the summer session and are thereby deprived (or deprive themselves) of the opportunity for travel and study which would increase their effectiveness during the regular year. The valuable time of faculty members is frittered away on relatively small groups of students in most of these summer sessions.

The final answer to the question of the continuance of the summer session seems to lie in the number of students enrolled. Colleges which have a reasonably large student body during the summer are undoubtedly justified in continuing this work; those with only a small enrolment are clearly not rendering an important educational service by the maintenance of a summer session.

CHAPTER XXXVI

EXTENSION ACTIVITIES

ARRANGEMENTS FOR EXTENSION WORK

Seventeen of the thirty-five colleges included in this study engage in some form of teaching by extension. There are two principal types of extension work—class teaching and correspondence study—the former being much the commoner in this group of colleges. The extension-class teaching may be divided into two kinds, one arranged primarily for service to the local community, the other reaching out into communities at some distance from the seat of the college.

Only seven of the seventeen colleges offering work by extension have a formally organized division for the administration of this work. In the other colleges the arrangements for the giving of extension courses are in the hands of the dean or the president, and the arrangements are typically rather informal. In the seven colleges having a regularly organized extension division there is no common pattern of organization. There is a director of extension in four colleges (in one case this is the dean); in one college the department of education manages the extension work; in another there is a faculty committee which controls the work; and in another the regular administrative officers constitute the controlling staff for the extension division work.

TYPES OF EXTENSION ACTIVITIES

Seven of the colleges included in this study give fairly heavy programs of extension-class teaching in their respective local communities. From the standpoint of number of classes and student enrolments, the program at the College of Puget Sound is the most important of any in the group. At this institution the extension work is given in evening classes, the program being considered an integral part of the work of the college. Work along very similar lines has been developed at Oklahoma City University, the evening classes being organized as a regular part of the class schedule and carried as a part of the regular load of instructors. Evansville College also has a rather extensive development of extension-class teaching. This institution not only gives a considerable number of classes in the city of Evansville but also offers classes in several other centers in its region. Morningside College gives several classes by extension, most of them being offered in the down-town section of Sioux City. The University of Chattanooga is developing an evening school somewhat similar to that at the College of Puget Sound.

It will be noted that all five of the colleges which have been mentioned are located in fairly large-sized cities and have developed the extension work in an effort to meet the needs of their local communities. Other colleges which give a considerable amount of extension work in their local cities are West Virginia Wesleyan College and Southwestern College. Baldwin-Wallace College, Intermountain Union College, and Dickinson College offer a small amount of extension-class teaching, usually not more than one or two classes a year.

The programs of extension-class teaching outside the local community are relatively limited. Only two institutions—Evansville College and Union College—offer as many as six classes annually at centers away from the seat of the college. McKendree College and Ohio Northern University offer a few such classes; and Dickinson College, Ozark Wesleyan College, College of the Pacific, and West Virginia Wesleyan College have each offered one or two such classes a year.

The other form of extension work—correspondence study—is offered in only four colleges. In one of these, Dakota Wesleyan University, students are permitted only in rare cases to take a course by correspondence, and no courses are regularly given by this method. Oklahoma City University has the largest development of correspondence study of any of these colleges. Sixteen instructors are engaged in offering work by correspondence in this institution, and an extensive program of work is advertised. Ozark Wesleyan College offers a considerable amount of correspondence study, approximately 30 per cent of its teaching staff being engaged in this work. Nebraska Wesleyan University has a relatively limited program of work by correspondence study; only four instructors are giving such courses, and the only students permitted to register are those who for some good reason are unable to attend the campus classes.

PURPOSES OF EXTENSION WORK

Although it seems clear that a college located in a large population center needs to develop work of this type in order to serve the needs of the community, it would seem advisable for colleges with limited resources and not located in a large city to proceed rather slowly in this development. The strongest colleges of this group have not attempted to develop extension work, a fact that should, in itself, be an adequate warning to the weaker colleges.

The development of correspondence-study courses by any of these colleges, or the development of extension-class teaching by those in relatively small communities, is entirely unjustified from the standpoint of rendering a needed service. Particularly in the field of correspondence study prospective students have an excellent opportunity to choose courses from many of the large and well-equipped universities of the country. In most regions the state universities have well-organized extension divisions, which look after the needs for extension-class teaching. It would therefore seem unnecessary for colleges located in small communities to develop any work by extension.

In some cases it appears that extension work has been developed by these colleges in order to compete with the state-supported institutions. At the time of the survey visit one college was considering the introduction of extension-class teaching because the state university was proposing to start an extension class in the local city. While the college is justified in an attempt to render service to its local community, this does not demand any large development of extension work, and the pushing forward of such a program merely to meet the competition of another institution should be beneath the dignity of a soundly administered college.

One justification for the giving of extension work is that the program serves as a device for student recruiting. Persons who are enrolled in extension classes sometimes become interested in the work of the college and go on for a degree. This argument seems to have more weight in the case of classes conducted away from the local center than in the case of those given on the campus or in the local city. None of the colleges that give several classes in other centers has collected data regarding the effectiveness of this service as a recruiting device, although sporadic cases are pointed out of students who have been attracted in this manner.

CRITICISM OF THE EXTENSION WORK IN THE COLLEGES STUDIED

The great bulk of the extension work in this group of colleges is being done by institutions with relatively inferior accredited status. There are only four colleges in the entire group offering extension-class teaching which are on the approved list of the Association of American Universities, and not one of those offering correspondence study holds the highest accreditation. Two of the four fully accredited colleges that offer extension-class teaching do only a very small amount of such work, not more than one or two classes a year. The other two are located in large cities and have developed the work out of a sense of responsibility to their local communities.

There are two important criticisms of the extension work as given by these colleges. The first relates to the quality of the work itself. It is very difficult to maintain extension-class teaching on a parity with campus work unless extraordinary resources are available, particularly in the matter of library books and reference materials. In the second place, the work absorbs a large amount of the time and energy of faculty members which could better be devoted to the main business of the college—campus teaching. The work in extension is quite generally taken on as an extra burden and is given on the margins of the instructor's time. Travel by faculty members to and from distant centers, or even a down-town center in the same city, becomes an important item in the additional instructional burden.

The only satisfactory basis for the organization of extension work is to consider such teaching as a part of the regular load of the instructor. Under this plan the teachers who give extension classes have their campus loads correspondingly lightened, and a single salary covers the remuneration for the standard load of all types of teaching. The College of Puget Sound and Oklahoma City University are the only institutions of this group with an extensive program of such work which have an arrangement whereby extension (or evening-school) teaching is considered as a part of the regular load.

The arrangements for the remuneration to faculty members for extension-class and correspondence teaching in this group of colleges are generally very unsatisfactory. In all except two or three of these colleges the instructors who give extension work are paid partly or wholly on the basis of the fees collected from their students. This basis of payment was long ago discarded as unsatisfactory in the regular college year; there is no reason to think that it is any more satisfactory in extension work than in the work of the regular year. The tendencies for instructors to admit students to courses for which they are not qualified, and to lower the grade of work in order to become "popular" and thus build up a basis for a later course in the same community, can best be obviated by making the remuneration of the instructor wholly unrelated to the number of students enrolled in his courses.

It seems entirely probable that pressure from faculty members for extra remuneration has been an important influence in setting up extension work in many of these colleges, although definite evidence on this point has not been collected. The opportunity offered faculty members to add a little to their insufficient salaries has unquestionably been influential in leading many of these colleges to undertake an extension program, and the "bait" of extra pay has led many instructors to sanction practices that would not be tolerated in the regular work of a well-administered college.

All the circumstances surrounding the giving of extension programs by these colleges lead to a grave question regarding the advisability of continuing this service. Except in the case of colleges located in good-sized cities, no important or unique service is usually rendered. The work constitutes a severe drain upon the time and energy of staff members, and there is considerable doubt concerning the academic quality of the work in many instances. While the colleges located in cities may well be encouraged to render a necessary community service, expansion of the program to include class teaching outside the local city or to provide correspondence study should be looked upon with disfavor. It seems probable that an insistence upon satisfactory standards in the giving of extension work, including teaching-load adjustments such as to make this work a part of the normal load, and the abandonment of the fee basis for the payment of extension teachers, would almost automatically result in the elimination of the greater part of the extension activities carried on by this group of colleges.

PART IV

THE STUDENT PERSONNEL OF COLLEGES

CHAPTER XXXVII

THE INDUCTION OF STUDENTS

Institutions of higher education in America have recently been giving increased attention to students as individuals. This movement, which is concerned with students both before and after their admission, parallels the trend of increasing enrolments in colleges and universities. An effort has been made in this study to determine the extent to which the colleges visited are providing an effective personnel service for their students. Five primary sources of information regarding problems of student personnel administration are employed in this study: (1) interviews with a number of representative individual students in each of the colleges visited; (2) interviews with faculty members, administrative officers, and the persons charged with responsibility for the administration of the personnel service; (3) an analysis of records and statistical data regarding students that were made available by the officers of the various colleges; (4) a confidential inquiry form filled out by students under the direct supervision of members of the survey staff; and (5) a questionnaire inquiry among the alumni of certain schools.

The student inquiry form was administered in a general assembly in the absence of faculty members and administrative officers. Students were assured by the member of the survey staff who had charge of the assembly that replies would be treated confidentially and only averages and totals for the group would be reported. Unusual care was taken in the administration of the inquiry to make certain that each student understood clearly the meaning of all of the questions asked. It was particularly gratifying to note the fulness of the co-operation given by the students and the seriousness with which they responded. In ten colleges in which these inquiry forms were administered, returns were received from 76.5 per cent of the men students and 85.8 per cent of the women students. A statistical analysis of the returns shows that they are typical of the various student bodies represented. Data from the inquiry form are used in several chapters of this report. Wherever the "student questionnaire" is referred to, it should be understood as meaning the inquiry form just described.

The alumni questionnaire was used in only seven colleges. The percentage of returns was uniformly low, and there was no method of estimating the degree of selection in the replies; for these reasons the alumni inquiry was not used in a larger number of institutions. In each case where the alumni questionnaire was used, the blanks were mailed out by the college with a covering letter, signed by the president, explaining the purpose of the study. Self-addressed prepaid envelopes were inclosed, and the alumni were instructed to mail the blanks back directly to the office of the survey staff in Chicago. Throughout the succeeding chapters this inquiry will be referred to as the "alumni questionnaire."

RECRUITING OF STUDENTS

Administrative organization.—Detailed information regarding the administrative organization for recruiting students was secured from thirty-

TABLE 88

Officers Responsible for Recruiting Students in Thirty-five Colleges

Officer	Number of Institutions Reporting Each Officer
President	24
A committee	10
Dean of the college	5
Registrar	3
Special officer	2
Alumni secretary	2
Dean of men	1
Business manager	1
No organized recruiting	2

five institutions. Table 88 shows the officers reported to be responsible for administering recruiting procedures.

From the data of this table it appears that the president is personally responsible for administering recruiting procedures in twenty-four institutions. In ten there is a faculty or administrative committee on recruiting. Eight of these committees operate in co-operation with the president, and two operate independently. The dean of the college is reported to be responsible for recruiting in five colleges. In only two of these, according to the original data, is he solely responsible for this activity; in the other three he shares the responsibility with the president. The registrar administers recruiting wholly in one college and in co-operation with the president in two others. Two institutions employ special recruiting officers, but in both instances they co-operate with the president as chief director of recruiting. In one college an alumni secretary administers recruiting activities independently; in another, under the direction of the president. One dean of men, responsible to the president, organizes recruiting; while one business manager is the chief administrator of this procedure.

Procedures employed.—The recruiting procedures employed in these institutions are shown in Table 89.

These data show that the predominant method of recruiting is the use of circulars and form letters. Direct correspondence with individual students is almost as commonly employed. Personal solicitation by administrative officers, faculty members, students, or special solicitors, while found frequently, is less common than the direct-mail procedure. In two institutions local ministers actively aid in soliciting students.

TABLE 89

PROCEDURES EMPLOYED IN RECRUITING STUDENTS IN
THIRTY-FIVE COLLEGES

Procedure	Number of Institutions Reporting Each Procedure
Circulars and form letters	15
Direct correspondence	14
Solicitation by administrative officers	9
Solicitation by faculty members	9
Special solicitors employed during vacation	7
Paid solicitors during the school year	4
Solicitation by unpaid students	2
Solicitation by local ministers	2
Radio broadcasting	1

An evaluation of recruiting procedures.—An effort has been made to give in two ways an estimate of the comparative value of recruiting procedures. First, administrative officers in twelve of the colleges were asked which of a number of methods of recruiting they considered most effective. Second, students in ten colleges were asked in the student questionnaire to indicate the factors which influenced them to attend the institution in which they were then enrolled.

The estimates of the administrative officers may be summarized briefly as follows: Personal solicitation of students by faculty members or administrative officers is the most effective recruiting device. Almost equally effective is the employment of special representatives by the institutions, particularly during the late winter and early spring. Only one-third of those reporting attach much weight to form letters or direct correspondence. A number of them report special means of recruiting which they find particularly effective, such as special scholarships, co-operation of ministers, alumni groups in local communities, students enrolled in the institution, and special days for entertaining high-school seniors on the college campus.

The factors which students enrolled in ten colleges report as influencing them to choose the college in which they were enrolled are presented in

TABLE 90

PERCENTAGE OF STUDENTS ENROLLED IN TEN COLLEGES GIVING
VARIOUS REASONS FOR ATTENDING THE INSTITUTION
IN WHICH THEY WERE ENROLLED

Reason Given	Percentage Giving Reason
Nearness of institution to home....................	56.4
Acquaintance with other students...................	48.7
Parental wishes....................................	41.3
Influence of friends or relatives.....................	40.5
Opportunity to follow subject-matter interest.........	23.8
Offer of scholarship or financial aid..................	23.2
Church affiliations.................................	22.7
Personal interview.................................	21.5
Renown of faculty.................................	14.9
Literature from college.............................	14.2
Influence of home pastor...........................	11.5
Opportunity to join fraternity or sorority.............	5.7
Athletic success of college..........................	5.3
Address by representative of college.................	4.1
Opportunity to engage in athletics...................	3.9
Attendance at music contest........................	3.4
Attendance at an athletic meet......................	3.0
Entertainment at college social event................	2.5
Publicity given college.............................	2.3
Attendance at an oratorical contest..................	0.4

Table 90. These data were secured by asking each student to indicate in a check list included in the student questionnaire the factors which influenced his choice, and to add any items not included in the list. On an average, each student checked three different items.

Table 90 shows that the nearness of the college, acquaintance with other students, parental wishes, and influence of friends are the factors mentioned most frequently. This becomes particularly significant when compared with the data presented in Table 89, which show that circular form letters and direct correspondence are the procedures most generally employed in recruiting. The conclusion seems warranted that direct-mail recruiting is not particularly effective; further, that personal acquaintance with students, faculty, or alumni is an important factor in determining a student's decision to attend a given institution. A small percentage of the students in this group also indicate that the high grade of college work, the advantages of the small college, or low cost was a factor which affected their choice.

One of the most important factors in recruiting students should be a high quality of work given by faculty members of such outstanding reputation that alumni and present students will enthusiastically recommend the institution to their friends who contemplate entering college. Such an emphasis upon superior quality of work should make less necessary the somewhat overexpanded programs of recruiting now being maintained in certain institutions.

Where recruiting seems desirable or necessary, the most effective procedure, and at the same time the one which permits most discriminative selection of desirable students, seems to be some form of personal solicitation. The personnel available in a given institution will determine to a large degree who shall represent the institution. It seems to be a fact, however, that students enrolled in a college, if properly challenged by the high quality of work done, will be effective representatives in interesting others in the institution. Only two of the thirty-five colleges in this group have utilized this means of recruiting in an organized manner.

ADMISSION AND CLASSIFICATION OF STUDENTS

Admission requirements.—The requirements for admission to the institutions included in this study most generally include: (1) graduation from an accredited high school; (2) a prescribed total of fifteen units of high-school credit; (3) certain prescribed units, ranging in number from five to eleven. Twenty-six of the thirty-five institutions state in their announcements that graduation from high school is a requisite to admission. With four exceptions (DePauw, Hamline, Nebraska Wesleyan, and Puget Sound) these institutions require fifteen units of high-school work for entrance. DePauw University requires sixteen, while Hamline, Nebraska Wesleyan, and Puget Sound require twelve. The requirements in the last three institutions, however, are based on the work taken in the tenth, eleventh, and twelfth grades of high school. This is an up-to-date adaptation of entrance requirements to the reorganization of the secondary schools into the junior and senior high school divisions. Nine of these institutions will admit a student conditionally with less than the full number of units regularly prescribed. It is usually specified that in such cases the student will have to apply some of his college credits to make up his deficiency.

There is a wide variation among these institutions as to the number of prescribed and elective units that candidates for admission may present. The maximum number of prescribed units, eleven and one-half, is announced by Ohio Wesleyan University. Four other colleges each prescribe as many as eleven units. The minimum number of units, five, is prescribed by Cornell, Illinois Wesleyan, Kansas Wesleyan, Oklahoma City, and Union.

TABLE 91

DISTRIBUTION OF PRESCRIBED HIGH-SCHOOL COURSES REQUIRED
FOR ADMISSION TO THIRTY-FOUR COLLEGES

SUBJECTS REQUIRED	NUMBER OF INSTITUTIONS REQUIRING MINIMUM UNITS AS FOLLOWS			
	I	1½	2	3
Algebra..............................	17	1	....	....
Geometry.............................	17	....	....	....
Mathematics (courses not specified).....	....	....	9	....
English..............................	....	....	3	31
Foreign language......................	....	....	15	....
History..............................	9	....	....	....
History and social science..............	10	1	3	....
Natural science (courses not designated)..	18	....	1	....

Not only is there a wide variation as to the number of admission units actually prescribed in various institutions, but there is also a variation in what constitutes the prescribed units. A summary of the prescribed courses as announced in the catalogues of the several institutions is presented in Table 91.

This table is read as follows: Seventeen colleges prescribe a minimum of one year of algebra for admission, one prescribes one and one-half years. Likewise, seventeen prescribe one year of geometry, while nine prescribe two years of mathematics without designating the courses. It becomes apparent at once that, excepting in English and mathematics, there is very little agreement regarding courses prescribed for admission. A few colleges designate further that some elective entrance units must be restricted to specified groups of courses. These restricted electives are not included in Table 91.

Admission procedure.—Twenty-five of the thirty-five institutions included in this study require for admission the filing of a formal application blank. In approximately two-thirds of all the institutions the blank is recorded and passed upon by a registrar. In the remainder, the applicants are granted or denied admission by the dean of the college, by the president, or by a faculty committee, the latter being employed most frequently. In two or three colleges the registrar and the dean or the president share the responsibility of serving as admission officers.

Data assembled from catalogue announcements and from other sources show that fifteen of the thirty-five institutions require personal recommendations in addition to or in lieu of a formal application; nine ask for personal data; and four suggest that a personal interview is desired or required. Three institutions announce that a limit is placed upon the number of students that will be accepted, and one announces a minimum age limit for students. Five require that a health certificate accompany the application for admission; one requires a psychological examination for admission; and seven say intelligence test scores are made a partial basis of admission.

A careful analysis of the application blanks employed in these institutions shows most of them to be greatly lacking in information that will be of value, either in estimating the fitness of a student for admission or in advising him as an individual student after he has been admitted.

Most of these institutions would find it advisable to give special attention in their admission procedure to the gathering of valuable personal information which is not being secured at present. This would involve a definite centralization of responsibility for passing upon all applications; the reorganization and expansion of application blanks so as to secure valuable data; the arrangement for personal interviews whenever possible, particularly in doubtful cases; the securing of personal recommendations from individuals of competent judgment; and the giving of psychological examinations and of subject-matter tests, at least in special cases, preferably to all candidates for admission. The more personal the selection of students for admission can be made, the less will it be necessary to maintain formally prescribed requirements for admission. Moreover, the procedure of admission is less likely to be purely mechanical and routinized.

Classification of entering students.—The emphasis placed upon individual differences in elementary and secondary education in recent years has served to call attention to the same factor at the college level. No matter how carefully the admission of students is administered, there still remains the fact that freshmen differ in ability, in previous preparation, and in special aptitudes and interests. It becomes necessary, therefore, that some plan of classification of students for instruction be employed whereby each one may work most advantageously. To this end college and university administrators are employing various means of grouping students.

A number of the colleges studied have taken progressive steps in the classification of entering freshmen. As evidence of this fact it may be cited that in thirteen out of thirty-four institutions, general intelligence test scores are used in assigning students to sections of classes; in fourteen institutions the scores are used in selecting courses to be pursued; in sixteen they are used to determine the student's total load. Three institutions employ special-aptitude test scores, and fourteen employ placement tests in classifying students. Seven of the fourteen using placement tests are also in the group using general-intelligence test scores. Seven institutions use the previous high-school record either as a sole basis of classification or in combination with intelligence tests.

The steps which have been taken toward a more scientific method of classifying students for purposes of instruction are worthy of commendation. It must be noted, however, that less than 50 per cent of the institutions studied employ even one of various available methods in classifying students and that a much smaller percentage employ a combination of two or more methods. The conclusion is inevitable, therefore, that, taken as a whole, the colleges of this group can, and should, improve their methods of classification. They should have available for this purpose the previous high-school record of each student in each course pursued, the results of general-intelligence tests, the results of special-aptitude and placement tests, and ratings as to study habits and scholastic ability given by high-school instructors or administrators. The judicious use of several or all of these forms of information will make possible groupings of students for instruction that will be of advantage to students and will make for greater efficiency in instruction.

ORIENTATION OF FRESHMEN

Freshman Week.—The general recognition among these institutions of the need for some form of freshman orientation is indicated by the fact that approximately 85 per cent of them maintain a Freshman Week program. These programs vary in length from two days to five or six days. Some consist of little more than registration and a few special lectures. Others are very complete, providing for registration, psychological examinations and placement tests, social and recreational activities, lectures, campus tours, and other activities.

A study of the Freshman Week programs which have been obtained from the colleges shows several distinct problems that should be taken into account by administrative officers. Among these are the following:

1. There is a tendency in some institutions to exercise too much supervision over the freshmen, thereby tending to perpetuate a type of paternalism which exists in some secondary schools. There is particular danger in giving so much attention to freshmen that they feel they are to be "carried" through college.

2. Often an effort is made to crowd too much into Freshman Week. It is impossible within the compass of a few days to complete the process of orientation. Freshmen must grow into the life and traditions of an institution.

3. Some freshman programs are so burdened with lectures that they inevitably become fatiguing.

4. The programs in some institutions are so organized that the results of psychological examinations and placement tests are not available as an aid in registering students. One or two colleges have commendably organized programs in this respect, the tests being given early in Freshman Week and scored so promptly that the results may be employed in classification, in determining student loads, and for other purposes.

5. Some programs are so organized that there is an interval of a day or more between the Freshman Week activities and the beginning of instruction. The psychological effect of such a break is undesirable and should be offset by having the Freshman Week activities merge immediately into the program of instruction.

While Freshman Week is still in an experimental stage, it has already justified its continuation; upon the basis of critical evaluation it should be adapted better to the needs of the institutions in which it is already employed. Institutions now having no provision for freshman orientation should give serious consideration to the advisability of organizing some means of orienting their freshmen more effectively.

Orientation courses.—In a small percentage of the colleges studied, Freshman Week is followed by a series of lectures for freshmen designed to serve one or more of the following aims: (1) to aid the student to fit into college life; (2) to introduce him to a method of thinking and study; (3) to aid him in understanding the major fields of knowledge; (4) to familiarize him with the whole field of vocations so as to be able to choose a vocation more intelligently. These courses are sometimes given for credit, sometimes without credit; enrolment in them is compulsory in some institutions, voluntary in others. On the whole, they represent commendable efforts to expand the program of freshman orientation.

REGISTRATION PROCEDURES

A study has been made of the registration procedures employed in various colleges. A wide variation in practice has been found, some colleges employing an almost wholly decentralized plan, others a highly centralized procedure. There is no standard practice in registration upon the basis of which the procedures found in individual institutions may be evaluated. The decentralized plan in which students are registered by various advisers in their several offices, it is claimed, provides for more informality in the conference between the student and his adviser, is free from confusion, allows more time for each conference, and enables the adviser to have the information from his files immediately at his command. On the other hand, the centralized registration is defended on the ground that it makes for uniformity in records, provides in one place counsel from various sources to students, and saves time and energy by enabling students to complete the whole transaction at one time.

There is no agreement in practice among these colleges as to the length of time after the opening of a session within which students may be admitted. Most frequently the time limit for late entrance is two weeks, but this is by no means generally accepted as a standard limit. Similarly, the time within which changes of registration may be made varies widely. In some colleges a penalty is attached if changes are made after the first few days; in others, changes are permitted without penalty for two or three weeks after the beginning of a semester.

One of two plans is usually employed regarding the issuance of class tickets. In some colleges students are given tickets admitting them to the classes for which they are registered, these tickets to be collected by the instructors. In others, the class tickets on which have been entered the names of students registered for a given course are sent directly to the instructor. It has been found, moreover, that some colleges issue the class tickets at the time of registration prior to or independently of the payment of fees; others issue the tickets only after fees have been paid.

Without attempting to formulate a standard of practice in registration, five characteristics of an efficient registration procedure may be noted.

The first requisite is simplicity. The machinery should not be so involved that the student becomes confused and embarrassed. Where the registration of a large number of students in a comparatively short time requires a rather complicated "set-up," persons who are especially adapted and trained should be stationed at every point where special directions need to be given to the registering student.

Second, registration should be marked by economy of time. This involves making time schedules and counsel available to students in advance of registration; using some system which will prevent long lines of students waiting for indefinite periods; a distribution of functions so as to avoid duplication of activities among registering officers; the provision of adequate clerical assistance so that the time of major registering officers is not consumed in routine writing of names of courses, etc., and the setting-up of the offices so that the process may be entirely completed at one time and place.

Third, adequate counsel should be available to students. As suggested above, in so far as possible, such counsel should be given in advance of actual registration. This will provide more time for planning the student's program, which may be written out in tentative form and submitted for approval on registration day. Even when programs are tentatively planned in advance, changes will have to be made, owing to full courses or a shift in the interest of the student. This will necessitate having counselors available during registration. If student programs are not planned in advance of registration, a sufficiently large number of counselors readily available to students should be present at registration.

Fourth, registration should be a unitary procedure. It should include all the successive steps from the initial signing of a registration record to making satisfactory arrangements for settlement of accounts.

Fifth, changes in registration should be few and should be allowed only for sufficient reason. With competent educational guidance, few changes will be necessary.

CHAPTER XXXVIII

THE COUNSELING OF STUDENTS

College life has become so complex in the many adjustments which it involves that students, particularly freshmen, frequently find themselves perplexed and in need of counsel. Until recently college administrators have taken little formal account of this need. The large academic mortality among college students and the many recurring problems of maladjustment found on every campus are now beginning to attract attention to the need for some provision for individual counseling. That is, a personal relationship needs to be established between individual students and faculty members or administrative officers whereby students may have the benefit of the experience of others in solving perplexing problems.

Among the outstanding problems regarding which students need counsel are the selection of courses, the formation of good study habits, overcoming special difficulties in certain courses, or the selection of a field of specialization. All of these may be broadly classified under educational problems.

A detailed analysis has been made of the administrative provisions for the educational counseling of students in the thirty-five colleges included in this study. Table 92 presents a summary of this analysis. By far the most common provision is that of having faculty members appointed to be advisers to students. Typical faculty advisory systems are as follows:

1. One or more faculty members are appointed by the administration to serve as class officers or advisers.

2. One or more faculty members are chosen by classes to serve as class advisers.

3. Faculty members are chosen by individual students. In case a student has no choice, he is assigned to a faculty member without reference to class.

4. Faculty committees are appointed to register students and to give educational counsel.

5. Faculty members who also serve as personnel officers, e.g., the dean of men or the dean of women, include educational counseling as one of their functions.

6. Both faculty advisers and class officers are appointed, the former

366

counseling students regarding their academic programs and problems, the latter registering them and serving as advisers and sponsors in social activities.

In general, the faculty advisory systems now in operation among these colleges are unsatisfactory. This is due to several factors. First, comparatively few faculty members in most colleges are adapted to counseling. Second, faculty advisers are too often chosen upon the basis of availability instead of special qualifications. Third, even the best-qualified faculty members, unless especially trained for the work, lack an understanding of the techniques which make for effective and skilful counseling.

TABLE 92

OFFICERS RESPONSIBLE FOR GIVING EDUCATIONAL
COUNSEL TO STUDENTS IN THIRTY-FIVE
COLLEGES

Officer	Number of Institutions Using Officer
Specially appointed faculty advisers	19
Dean of the college	9
Faculty members, unorganized	5
Dean of men	5
Dean of women	4
Registrar	3
President	2
Faculty committee	2
Class deans	2
Heads of departments	2
Class advisers	1
Adviser to women	1

Table 92 shows that in some institutions other officers serve as educational counselors in addition to, or in lieu of, faculty advisers. More important among these, in terms of frequency, are the dean of the college, the dean of men, and the dean of women. Several deans of colleges have been rendering excellent service as educational counselors. Quite obviously, however, in an institution of any size, the demands for counseling are too extensive and too time-consuming to be met by a single officer who has many other academic responsibilities. In several institutions the dean of men or dean of women, or both, have, likewise, been rendering excellent service as educational counselors, particularly to freshmen. Where these officers have the essential academic background and the requisite personal qualifications, they may well be employed in this capacity.

There is no system of organized counseling of students in educational matters that can be unconditionally recommended to all institutions. Each college must develop a plan adapted to its program and needs in the light of the qualified personnel available. Whatever plan may be employed, several fundamental considerations should always be kept in mind.

First of all, there should be a reasonable degree of continuity in counseling. Under the faculty-adviser system as it generally operates, students select, or are assigned to, a new adviser periodically. Generally, the new adviser has no way of knowing what counsel has previously been given and must, consequently, proceed without any means of making his service continuous with that of his predecessor. It seems desirable, therefore, that the same advisers should continue educational counsel over a period of more than a semester or a year.

Second, the procedures should be so organized that counselors make frequent contact with their advisees. This involves the keeping of office hours on the part of counselors and the employment of a system whereby periodic conferences are held with all students assigned to them. Too frequently, faculty advisers are relatively inaccessible to students and most unsystematic in their work.

Third, every adviser to students should keep a record of his conferences and should thereby build up a file of personal data regarding each student. A system of centralized offices and files appears to be preferable inasmuch as it avoids duplication of efforts on the part of clerks and makes all data available to every adviser.

Fourth, faculty members who serve as educational advisers to students should be selected upon the basis of special qualifications. While it is highly desirable to have all members of the faculty personally interested in students, educational counseling, well done, demands specialized information and the ability to see a student's point of view along with ability to aid him in thinking through his problems.

VOCATIONAL COUNSELING

A surprisingly large percentage of the students enrolled in the colleges studied face the problem of choosing a vocation. That these students need and deserve the advantage of personal counsel in making vocational decisions is certain. That most colleges are not providing adequately for vocational counseling is the inevitable conclusion from the facts found in this study.

Table 93 shows the provisions made for vocational counseling in terms of officers specifically responsible for giving such counsel.

This table shows that twelve institutions have no definite provision for counseling students regarding their choice of a vocation. Among the remaining institutions from which specific data were secured, the dean of women is mentioned most frequently as a vocational counselor. Her counseling is limited, quite naturally, to women students. The dean of men is reported less frequently as responsible for this function. A comparatively small number of institutions designate other sources of vocational counsel.

TABLE 93

OFFICERS RESPONSIBLE FOR GIVING VOCATIONAL
COUNSEL TO STUDENTS IN THIRTY-TWO
COLLEGES

Officer	Number of Institutions Employing Officer
No definite organization.....................	12
Dean of women...........................	10
Individual faculty members..................	6
Dean of men..............................	5
Dean of the college........................	3
Department of education....................	3
President.................................	2
Faculty advisers..........................	2
Department heads..........................	2
Faculty committee.........................	2
Assistant to president......................	1
Personnel officer..........................	1

Particularly noteworthy is the fact that while a comparatively large number of these colleges appoint faculty advisers to students, as was shown in Table 92, only two institutions make these advisers responsible for giving vocational counsel. The problems of educational counseling and of vocational counseling are so closely interlocked that, excepting cases involving highly technical information, the same adviser may well deal with both. If special advisers to students are to be made responsible for vocational counseling along with other advisory functions, as the preceding statement implies, then someone should be appointed to gather information regarding vocations which may be made available to advisers in a usable form.

In addition to personal conferences regarding vocations which are provided in institutions having officers designated as vocational advisers, other methods are employed in a few colleges. Some of the more significant of these methods are briefly summarized here.

Two colleges give separate courses in vocations for men and women. One institution requires the course of all sophomores and allows credit for one semester hour; the other makes enrolment in the course voluntary and gives no credit. An examination of the outlines and materials used indicates a commendable approach to the subject. The desirability of requiring such a course of all students may be open to question.

One institution provides opportunities for practical experience in certain vocational fields. For example, through a co-operative plan with the public schools of the city in which the college is located, prospective teachers participate in actual classroom work as cadets. Likewise, prospective engineers are given opportunities for real experience through part-time employment on the co-operative plan.[1] There is little doubt that actual experience is one of the most practical forms of vocational guidance that can be provided. In most institutions it may be difficult to organize work on the co-operative plan. The administration of the part-time employment of students may in some instances be made to serve this purpose.

Special lectures on vocations by alumni or others who are prominent in various fields of business or the professions are arranged in certain colleges. An inventory is first taken of student interests in various vocations; speakers are then invited to discuss with groups of students the vocations in which they have a special interest. The lectures to groups are supplemented by conferences with individual students.

A number of colleges have built up a special library dealing with vocations. The librarian has an unusual opportunity through these libraries on vocations to aid students directly by calling their attention to new books on vocations or by directing the attention of advisory officers to new accessions.

Underlying all the procedures employed in giving vocational counsel are certain general principles which should be kept in mind. The more important of these are: (1) The choice of a vocation, in the final analysis, lies with the individual student. No procedure should be employed which deprives him of this prerogative. (2) Upon the basis of individual differences in ability, aptitude, temperament, and interest, certain individuals are more successful and happy in some types of vocations than in others. (3) Vocational counseling has a twofold objective: first, to aid the individ-

[1] The co-operative work in engineering has been discontinued since the visit of the survey staff.

ual in understanding and evaluating himself as accurately as possible; second, to aid him in understanding the nature and demands of various vocations so that he may choose as intelligently as possible. (4) Tests and other instruments designed to discover aptitudes and interests should be employed to the extent warranted by their established validity and relia- bility. (5) A complete program of vocational counseling should carry through to the point at which the individual becomes effectively adjusted to the vocation of his choice.

PERSONAL COUNSELING

A number of colleges recognize the fact that college students frequently are confronted with problems very personal in character. Approximately two-thirds of the colleges report the dean of women as being responsible for giving counsel regarding personal problems. At some institutions the dean of men and the dean of the college are also reported as responsible for this type of advisory service. A few of the colleges indicate that freshman advisers or deans share this responsibility. In one institution a social director has done excellent service in assisting both men and women in making personal adjustments.

There is an implication in the reports made by various colleges regard- ing their provisions for personal counseling of students that the approach is primarily from a disciplinary standpoint. There is undoubtedly a need in many of the institutions included in this study for less emphasis upon the disciplinary approach in dealing with the personal adjustment of students and more counseling as such, whereby students may be given a broader perspective of principles underlying life and may solve their inti- mate personal problems in the light of these principles.

STUDENT AND ALUMNI EVALUATION OF COUNSELING

In an attempt to judge the effectiveness of the counseling procedures in the colleges studied, students in ten colleges were asked on a special inquiry form to evaluate the counsel they have received with respect to seven specified problems. A summary of the student judgments is pre- sented in Table 94.

This table is read as follows: Of 3,439 students who gave an opinion regarding the counsel received in making out a regular program, 49.2 per cent considered the help received satisfactory, 39.5 per cent considered it good but limited, 8.8 per cent considered it poor, and 2.5 per cent reported no assistance. It should be noted that "no assistance" may have been given various interpretations by students, and the percentages in this column may include some who sought no assistance as well as those who sought it but received none. The first four columns are, therefore, of major significance.

It is clear from this table that in the judgment of the students the counsel given is not all that might be desired. Most satisfactory, but still subject to improvement, is the help given in making out a regular program. Least satisfactory, on the other hand, is the aid given in selecting a vocation. The accuracy of these judgments is confirmed by the fact that vocational counseling is most inadequately provided for in most institutions according to data already presented. Moreover, the inadequacy

TABLE 94

EVALUATION BY STUDENTS ENROLLED IN TEN COLLEGES OF THE
EFFECTIVENESS OF COUNSEL RECEIVED REGARDING
CERTAIN PROBLEMS

PROBLEM	NUMBER REPORTING	PERCENTAGE OF STUDENTS REPORTING EACH KIND OF HELP			
		Satisfactory	Good but Limited	Poor	No Assistance
Making out regular program........	3,439	49.2	39.5	8.8	2.5
Religious problems................	3,026	41.8	28.1	10.3	19.8
Making adjustments to college life...	3,227	39.3	34.4	14.4	11.9
Financial problems................	3,191	36.0	37.7	11.1	15.2
Personal conduct.................	3,111	35.4	28.4	17.1	19.1
Determining field of concentration...	3,152	27.7	36.1	17.3	18.9
Selecting a vocation..............	3,115	22.5	29.5	20.2	27.8

of counsel received regarding personal conduct and adjustments to college life confirm the need for less emphasis upon the disciplinary approach to personal problems of students and more actual counseling as such. The estimates of help received in meeting religious problems indicate a distinct need for more and better counseling than now is available. The same is true regarding counsel given in solving financial problems.

A second approach to an evaluation of counseling procedures was made by securing the judgments of alumni of five colleges. These judgments were limited in their application to three selected problems. Table 95 presents a summary of the judgments of alumni regarding the counsel which they received while in college.

Comparison between the data of Table 95 and those of Table 94 shows that in general the alumni consider the counsel which they received less satisfactory than the students consider the counsel given them. This may indicate a shift in judgment on the part of alumni owing to a broader experience on which to base their evaluation; or it may reflect a definite improvement in the counseling procedures, since the alumni opinions represent conditions as they formerly were rather than as they now are. The most marked variation between the evaluation given by alumni and by students is that a much larger percentage of the former indicate no assistance received. This suggests the inference that there has been an improvement in the provision for counseling students.

TABLE 95

EVALUATION BY ALUMNI OF FIVE COLLEGES OF THE EFFECTIVENESS
OF COUNSEL RECEIVED AS STUDENTS

PROBLEM	NUMBER OF ALUMNI REPORTING	PERCENTAGE OF ALUMNI REPORTING EACH KIND OF HELP			
		Satisfactory	Good but Limited	Poor	No Assistance
Counsel on educational problems....	971	18.4	55.4	3.6	22.5
Counsel on vocational problems.....	967	15.8	38.1	4.1	41.8
Counsel on personal problems.......	971	21.1	44.4	2.2	32.2

The judgments of alumni, like those of students, support the demand for further improvement of the counseling procedures.

METHODS OF DEALING WITH SCHOLASTIC FAILURES

Probation and dismissal.—Most of the colleges in this study have definite rules regarding students of low scholarship. In some, these students are placed on probation for a specified period, generally one semester; in others, they are dropped without being placed on probation; in still others, they are suspended from the institution for a semester. On the whole, these colleges still treat students doing unsatisfactory work as subjects of discipline.

There is appearing a new approach to the problem of the failing student, as is shown by the fact that approximately two-thirds of the colleges are now making some efforts to diagnose and remedy the difficulties of failing and potentially failing students.

Diagnostic and remedial procedures.—The aids given to students of low standing in twenty-four colleges are briefly summarized in Table 96.

While the aids presented in Table 96 mark a commendable beginning, they indicate that very little actual remedial work is being done. Midterm reports, counsel and warning, and reports to parents, while desirable in themselves, provide no direct approach to the fundamental causes of a student's difficulty.

The first steps in any attempt to diagnose the difficulties of failing students is to gather complete and accurate data regarding each individual case. Such data should include: (1) the previous high-school record; (2) the results of general-intelligence tests and personality ratings; (3) the previous educational history and family background; (4) the results of placement tests in fundamental subjects; (5) information concerning the student's distribution of his time; (6) an analysis of the student's study

TABLE 96

SPECIAL AIDS PROVIDED FOR FAILING STUDENTS IN
TWENTY-FOUR COLLEGES

Form of Aid	Number of Colleges Giving This Aid
Dean studies and advises...................	10
Mid-term reports........................	9
Reduced schedule........................	5
Tutoring for weak students................	4
Counsel and warning.....................	4
Report to parents.......................	3
Extra special work......................	3
Change in program......................	2
How-to-study helps......................	2
Guide to written work...................	1

habits; (7) the results of special tests in reading; (8) the results of special interest and special aptitude tests; (9) reports from instructors regarding the attitude of the student and his apparent cause of failure; (10) reports from parents regarding special conditions affecting achievement; and (11) special information which may be derived from personal interviews.

The remedial procedures will vary widely according to the needs of each individual student. Among those which are likely to be more commonly employed are: (1) supervised study; (2) special instruction in how to study; (3) instruction in fundamental subjects (e.g., English or mathematics); (4) tutoring on courses being failed; (5) correction of reading difficulties; (6) homogeneous groups; (7) reduction of load; and (8) treatment by health service, including psychiatric service.

CHAPTER XXXIX

HEALTH SERVICE AND OCCUPATIONAL PLACEMENT

HEALTH SERVICE

Student health should be a matter of fundamental consideration to college administrators, both as it affects the academic progress of individual students and as it affects the welfare of the student body as a whole. The

TABLE 97

PERCENTAGE OF THIRTY-THREE COLLEGES HAVING VARIOUS
PROVISIONS FOR STUDENT HEALTH SERVICE

Provision	Number of Colleges	Percentage of All Colleges Reporting
Physician employed full time..................	1	3.0
Physician employed part time................	13	39.4
One or more nurses employed full time........	12	36.3
One or more nurses employed part time.......	3	9.0
Hospital or infirmary on campus.............	7	21.2
Hospital in community......................	19	57.5
Physical examination required annually of all students*...............................	8	24.2
Physical examination required on entrance†....	17	51.5
Vaccination required or advised‡.............	21	63.6
Inoculation for typhoid advised..............	15	45.4
Inoculation for diphtheria advised...........	14	42.4
Inoculation for scarlet fever advised..........	12	36.3
Medical fee charged........................	14	45.4
Services of psychiatrist provided.............	2	6.0

* Required of women only in one college.
† Required of women only in two colleges.
‡ Required in only one college.

data secured from the colleges studied show, however, very inadequate provision for student health service. Table 97 presents in summary a statement of the provisions which are made for such service.

This table shows that in only one of the institutions from which data were secured was a full-time physician employed, while in thirteen a physician was employed part time. Over half of these colleges make no provision for a physician whose services shall be available to students. In these latter institutions students must call a physician in the community in case of illness. Under such conditions students frequently do not receive the prompt medical attention which they should have.

Table 97 shows further that twelve of the colleges employ one or more nurses full time. In most institutions the services of the nurses are available to both men and women. In two colleges, however, the nurse's services are available to men only, while, in one other, her services are available only to women. Three of the colleges employ nurses for part time only. In these institutions the nurse is either a student taking a part-time academic program or is available on call.

A comparatively small percentage of the colleges have hospitals on their campuses. Some have fairly satisfactory infirmary arrangements either in their dormitories or in separate buildings. More than half of the colleges (57.5 per cent) have hospital facilities available in the city or community in which they are located. The remainder provide emergency hospital arrangements in case of epidemics and send students to their homes for treatment whenever possible. The infirmary at the College of the Pacific deserves special mention for its unusual completeness and general excellence.

Annual physical examinations are required in eight of the colleges. One of these colleges requires the examinations of women only. In seventeen, physical examinations are required of entering students. Here again, two colleges require these examinations of women only. One-fourth of these institutions require no physical examinations at all. The welfare of all students certainly demands that every student be given a physical examination at least annually. The information derived from these examinations will be a means of protecting the student body as a whole against contagion, will be a basis for advising students regarding physical weaknesses of which they are not aware, and will aid in determining the load of studies and employment that students may be permitted to carry.

A majority of the institutions advise vaccination against smallpox, and half or less advise inoculation for typhoid, diphtheria, or scarlet fever, respectively. In only one institution of those from which data were secured is vaccination against smallpox definitely required. A medical fee is charged in fourteen institutions.

Particularly noteworthy is the fact that only two of these colleges provide any form of psychiatric service. The type of service provided in these few institutions is limited, being usually given either by a psychiatric nurse, the professor of psychology, or someone other than a professional psychiatrist. Recent developments in the fields of mental hygiene and of clinical psychology indicate that a surprisingly large percentage of students are affected in their work by problems of mental health which can be corrected by expert service. Most colleges cannot afford to employ a full-time psychiatrist or clinical psychologist, but in many instances arrangements can be made for periodic visits of specialists in these fields to the campus for consultation; or as an alternative, special arrangements can be made for referring students to such specialists in their own offices. Under no condition should this service be given wide publicity. It should preferably be made an integral part of the health service and be referred to only as such.

The analysis of the provisions for health service presented in this report shows clearly the inadequacy of the service now being provided. The extent to which a health service program should be developed in any institution must be determined by health facilities available in the community, the percentage of students who reside in the local community, and the resources available for this service. The least that should be expected, however, is that every student shall be given a thorough physical examination each year; that the services of a physician of good standing shall be available to students when needed; that nurse's services shall be promptly available in cases of illness; that provisions shall be made for isolation and hospitalization of students who are ill; that such measures as vaccination shall be urged, at least, if not required; and that the services of a specialist shall be provided for students whose work is impaired by worries or other forms of emotional upsets.

PLACEMENT SERVICE

Part-time employment.—The problem of part-time employment of students assumes major proportions in a number of institutions. One college reports that 40 per cent of its students are employed. The problem of part-time employment demands special consideration by a college from several aspects: first, to make a proper adjustment between the academic program of the student and his employment; second, to protect the student against undesirable working conditions and hours; third, to protect employers against imposition or misinformation on the part of student employees; fourth, to prevent employers from becoming prejudiced against student employees and college men generally, owing to the inefficiency of some individual student. In the light of these facts it appears desirable in institutions in which students make their way by part-time employment for the administration to take a hand in the direction and supervision of such employment.

Definite provisions are made for some direction of part-time employment in approximately two-thirds of the colleges studied. The officers most generally in charge of the part-time employment are the dean of men, the dean of women, and the business manager. In addition, each of the following officers assumes or shares his responsibility in one or two colleges: an employment officer, the superintendent of buildings and grounds, the registrar, the admissions officer, the Y.M.C.A. secretary, the director of promotion, a faculty committee, the president, and the secretary to the president.

Placement of graduates.—The colleges studied have quite generally made provision for the placement of their graduates in teaching positions.

TABLE 98

ADMINISTRATIVE PROVISION FOR THE PLACEMENT OF GRADUATES
IN THIRTY-THREE COLLEGES

Administrative Provision	Number of Institutions Using the Provision in Placing Teachers	Number of Institutions Using the Provision for Placement in Business
Professor of education or head of department of education..........................	12	....
Bureau of appointments or placement bureau..................................	8	3
An appointment secretary...............	4	1
An appointment committee..............	3	6
President's office.........................	1	1
Alumni committee........................	....	1
Dean of administration..................	1	....
Dean and registrar.......................	1	....
Dean of college..........................	....	1
Heads of departments....................	....	2
Head of department of economics and business administration....................	....	1
No provision............................	3	17

Much less common is any administrative arrangement for the placement of graduates in various business positions. This is no doubt explained by the fact that in these institutions more of the graduates go into teaching than into any other one vocation; the need for placement service to graduates who plan to teach is therefore felt most urgently.

The various administrative provisions for placing graduates in business and teaching positions are briefly presented in Table 98.

This table shows that most institutions making any provision for the placement of graduates in the field of business either maintain a placement bureau or committee, or rely upon the heads of departments to manage the placement. A few colleges have other arrangements whereby some special office assumes this placement responsibility.

In the placement of teachers the professor or head of the department of education is most frequently responsible. In a number of these institutions the appointment committees or bureaus which handle placement in business fields also administer the placement of teachers.

An analysis of the procedures of these placement agencies, particularly with reference to teaching positions, shows that they usually secure reports of vacancies by direct correspondence with public-school administrators, although a few depend upon friends for such reports.

The average number of applications filed for teaching positions by graduates in different institutions varies widely. The total range of the averages among the colleges is from one to thirty-three, with a median of four.

Most colleges charge no fee for their placement service, although there are several exceptions. One charges 1 per cent of the candidate's salary for the first year, another charges one dollar plus a commission of 2.5 per cent of the salary for the first year. Others charge from one to five dollars without any additional commission.

Follow-up procedures.—Approximately 50 per cent of the colleges employ some method of following up their graduates after they are placed. Letters and questionnaires are employed most frequently for this purpose, although several institutions report personal visits by a placement or administrative officer for the purpose of determining the efficiency of their graduates.[1]

Evaluations and suggestions.—Quite clearly, most of the colleges studied feel a definite responsibility for the placement of their graduates, particularly those who are prepared to teach. The responsibility for the administration of placement is usually centered in a placement officer or a head of a department. In a few instances this function is distributed among the heads of various departments or among various administrative officers. The latter plan of decentralized administration is not satisfactory, as a rule, because of the duplication of effort involved, the impossibility of unifying records and credentials, and the time required to secure credentials, list vacancies, and follow up graduates who are placed. The better plan is to have placement administered through a single office in

---

[1] The follow-up service at Intermountain Union College has recently been described by Professor Ida M. Yates, and published under the title, "After Placement—What?" *School and Society*, XXXIV, No. 878 (October 24, 1931), 568–70.

charge of a competent placement secretary. This service should include placement in business as well as in teaching positions.

The placement service in these colleges to be of maximum value should be administered so as to provide: (*a*) complete information regarding vacancies and the types of candidates required; (*b*) full credentials regarding candidates; (*c*) selective recommendation of only such candidates as can, with reasonable certainty, fill the vacancy efficiently; (*d*) adequate follow-up information regarding candidates who are placed. In a word, the placement service should be of such a character that it will command the confidence of business men and educators to such a degree that they will voluntarily report their vacancies and seek their applicants from these colleges. This quality of service will make unnecessary some questionable promotion measures which a few institutions now employ in their placement work.

CHAPTER XL

EXTRA-CURRICULUM ACTIVITIES

The analysis of the extra-curriculum activities of the colleges will be approached first by a study of the way in which the students distribute their time, not only upon these extra-curriculum activities, but also upon their academic work and in remunerative employment. Following this analysis the details of the programs of extra-curriculum activities, as maintained in the colleges studied, will be discussed.

HOW STUDENTS SPEND THEIR TIME

An analysis has been made of the amount of time which students in each of the colleges devote to three distinct types of activity, viz., educational, which includes time devoted to classroom, laboratory, and

TABLE 99

AVERAGE NUMBER OF HOURS STUDENTS* SPEND PER WEEK IN STUDY, RECITATION, AND LABORATORY WORK COMBINED AT TEN COLLEGES

Institution	Freshman	Sophomore	Junior	Senior	Total
Cornell................	46	43	46	43	45
Simpson..............	44	45	43	44	44
Iowa Wesleyan.........	43	42	41	45	43
Dickinson.............	42	40	42	40	41
Morningside...........	41	40	43	39	41
Allegheny.............	40	43	41	39	41
Evansville............	37	43	43	48	41
Hamline..............	37	39	42	43	40
Chattanooga	36	37	38	39	37
Union................	35	36	38	39	36
Median............	40.5	41.0	42.0	41.5	41.0

* Students taking less than twelve credit-hours are not included.

study; extra-curriculum, which includes all activities not a part of the regular work for credit or for pay; and work for pay. The data here presented are derived from the student questionnaires.

Table 99 presents a summary of the average amount of time per week which students report that they spend in study, recitation, and laboratory work combined.

Several facts are apparent from this table. First, there is a wider range in the average number of hours per week devoted to educational activities by freshmen than by upper-class students. Second, the higher the class level, the smaller is the deviation from the median. Third, students in the junior year tend to devote more time to educational activities than do students in any one of the other three years.

A further analysis of the data available shows that the time spent in classroom, laboratory, and study (in educational activities) per credit-hour carried ranges from 2.3 to 2.8 hours for all men, and from 2.1 to 2.9 hours for all women. The median for the ten institutions is 2.5 for both

TABLE 100

AVERAGE NUMBER OF HOURS STUDENTS SPEND PER WEEK IN
EXTRA-CURRICULUM ACTIVITIES AT TEN COLLEGES

INSTITUTION	FRESHMAN		SOPHOMORE		JUNIOR		SENIOR		ENTIRE GROUP		
	M.*	W.*	M.*	W.*	M.*	W.*	M.*	W.*	M.*	W.*	T.*
Dickinson......	7.8	3.6	8.5	5.3	8.1	4.9	8.9	6.1	8.2	5.2	7.4
Iowa Wesleyan..	6.4	3.6	10.0	4.6	12.9	5.1	9.8	4.5	9.6	4.3	6.7
Hamline........	6.8	2.1	9.4	3.9	10.3	3.8	11.5	5.5	8.9	3.7	6.5
Union..........	6.1	4.1	9.6	1.9	10.1	2.3	6.0	3.0	8.9	3.2	6.2
Cornell........	6.0	3.5	6.5	4.3	8.1	6.9	7.1	5.9	6.7	4.8	5.7
Chattanooga....	3.4	2.5	7.3	3.2	8.0	5.6	8.7	4.3	6.2	3.7	5.0
Morningside....	4.6	3.7	4.4	4.6	5.6	4.4	8.3	7.5	5.3	4.7	5.0
Simpson........	4.6	3.0	6.0	3.3	7.3	4.4	6.8	6.3	5.8	3.8	4.6
Evansville......	3.8	2.3	6.3	2.4	6.9	3.7	8.6	4.5	5.7	2.9	4.5
Allegheny......	4.1	1.4	4.4	2.7	6.1	4.1	10.0	2.9	5.6	2.5	4.4
Median....	5.3	3.8	6.9	3.8	8.1	4.4	8.7	5.0	6.5	3.8	5.4

* M. means men, W. means women, and T. means total.

men and women. These data become even more significant when compared with the time which men and women in these colleges spend in extra-curriculum activities and in work for pay.

Table 100 shows the number of hours per week which students of ten colleges report that they spend in extra-curriculum activities.

This table should be read as follows: At Dickinson College the freshman men spend on an average 7.8 hours per week in extra-curriculum activities; the freshman women spend on an average 3.6 hours per week in these activities, etc.

The data show that the median number of hours for men at these institutions is almost twice as large as the median for women. The total range of the number of hours per week devoted to extra-curriculum activities by men is from 5.3 at Morningside College to 9.6 at Iowa Wesleyan

College; similarly, the range of time given by women is from 2.5 at Allegheny College to 5.2 at Dickinson College.

There is no marked agreement in the relationship between the number of hours given to extra-curriculum activities by men and the number given by women in the same institution. For example, Morningside College ranks lowest in terms of the time given by men but ranks third from the highest in the amount of time given by women. Simpson, Chattanooga, and Cornell fall nearest the median in the number of hours given by men, while Chattanooga, Hamline, and Simpson fall nearest the median in the number of hours given by women. In Chattanooga and Simpson, then, the relative amount of time given to extra-curriculum activities by men and women in comparison with that for other institutions included in this study seems to be most consistent, even though in each of these two institutions the men give considerably more time than the women.

No explanation of the facts just presented has been sought, but the tentative inference may be made that intercollegiate sports as well as campus athletics are generally adapted to the interests of men. These are more time-consuming than are the activities provided for women; consequently, men will, sometimes must, devote more time than women to extra-curriculum activities.

Moreover, there still exists on the campuses of some of these institutions a traditional attitude that women are not eligible to participate in many major campus activities, e.g., intercollegiate debates or oratorical contests. Such an attitude will inevitably weight the program of extra-curriculum activities for men.

Table 101 summarizes the average number of hours per week which students at ten institutions report that they spend in working for pay.

From this table it appears that both men and women students at Allegheny, Dickinson, and Union spend a comparatively small amount of time in work for pay. In the remaining seven institutions men spend from 9 to 15.6 hours per week in work for pay, while women spend from 2.7 to 8.8 hours in like manner. The median institution in this group is represented by men working on an average 11.3 hours per week; women, 3.1 hours per week; and men and women combined, 7.1 hours per week.

The wide variation in the average amount of time spent in gainful employment by students is probably the result of several factors: First, some institutions because of their location enrol a larger percentage of students who are in limited circumstances than do others; second, some institutions are more advantageously situated with respect to opportunities for gainful employment; third, a few institutions encourage students of limited means to enrol by providing a part-time employment office through which a definite program of employment is promoted; fourth, educational costs vary among these colleges, making it more necessary for the student of limited means to find employment at some institutions than at others.

The average number of hours spent in extra-curriculum activities and in work for pay combined, by men in the ten institutions, ranges from 9.2 to 22.7; for women the range is from 4.4 to 13.5. In the median institution men spend in extra-curriculum activities and work for pay 18.2 hours per week, while women spend 7.3 hours per week.

TABLE 101

AVERAGE NUMBER OF HOURS STUDENTS SPEND PER WEEK IN
WORK FOR PAY AT TEN COLLEGES

INSTITUTION	FRESHMAN		SOPHOMORE		JUNIOR		SENIOR		ENTIRE GROUP		
	M.	W.	M.	W.	M.	W.	M.	W.	M.	W.	T.
Morningside....	14.2	8.8	12.6	7.5	24.2	9.5	19.4	11.0	15.6	8.8	11.6
Hamline........	13.4	9.5	15.8	8.9	14.3	7.0	10.9	4.6	13.8	7.9	11.2
Simpson........	12.5	4.4	9.3	3.7	15.1	5.6	17.7	7.6	13.1	4.9	8.1
Iowa Wesleyan..	8.5	5.2	10.3	3.7	9.7	6.6	19.2	4.7	10.3	5.0	7.7
Chattanooga....	12.8	1.5	12.2	1.0	12.0	4.7	12.2	5.2	12.3	2.7	7.5
Evansville......	9.6	1.9	9.7	2.7	16.1	4.2	17.9	14.5	12.2	2.9	6.7
Cornell........	6.8	2.2	10.3	4.5	11.4	4.0	10.3	3.4	9.0	3.3	5.8
Dickinson......	4.7	0.7	5.5	1.5	5.6	0.9	4.2	1.2	5.0	1.1	3.9
Union..........	3.2	0.5	3.8	3.2	7.7	8.2	5.5	9.0	5.1	2.6	3.9
Allegheny......	2.5	2.8	3.8	1.2	5.5	1.4	3.7	1.7	3.6	1.9	2.9
Median....	9.0	2.5	10.0	3.5	11.7	5.2	11.0	4.9	11.3	3.1	7.1

NUMBER OF EXTRA-CURRICULUM ACTIVITIES MAINTAINED

Eighteen institutions were requested to provide information as to the number of activities which are found on their respective campuses. The returns show a range from twelve to fifty-five. In these totals social fraternities and sororities are counted collectively as one activity, on the assumption that students usually do not hold membership in more than one such organization. The median institution in this group is represented by twenty-three activities. A list of these activities for Lawrence College, an institution of approximately eight hundred students, which is typical of this group, is as follows: (1) Student Senate; (2) Lawrence Women's Association; (3) Freshman Commission; (4) Forensics; (5) *Ariel* staff; (6) Young Men's Christian Association; (7) Oxford Club; (8) Sunset Players; (9) Glee Club; (10) Panhellenic; (11) Interfraternity Council;

(12) Rifle Club; (13) Journalism Club; (14) English Club; (15) French Club; (16) German Club; (17) Classical Club; (18) Spanish Club; (19) History Club; (20) Chemistry Club; (21) Trinity Club; (22) Biology Club; (23) Philotechnica; (24) men's athletics (varsity and intramural); (25) Men's Athletic Club; (26) women's athletics.

This represents a very ample program of activities for an institution the size of Lawrence College. Certainly, it would be undesirable to expand such an activities program further unless an increased enrolment should demand it; it is conceivable, on the other hand, that the program might be reduced without impairing the total educational contribution made by the institution. The program presented above is well balanced, in that it provides for practical experience in dealing with problems of student citizenship, and gives opportunities for students to engage in activities in the fields of publications, religion, music, dramatics, forensics, athletics, and special departmental interests.

The extra-curriculum activities program at DePauw University is very comprehensive and well distributed for an institution having approximately fifteen hundred students. It is briefly presented as follows:

5 honorary scholarship fraternities and clubs
2 student government associations
7 intercollegiate sports
2 athletic associations
4 journalistic enterprises
4 debate clubs
22 departmental clubs
5 musical organizations
3 other student organizations
24 Greek letter fraternities

No objective data are available whereby the adequacy of such a program as this may be evaluated. The opinion of students and administrative officers at DePauw seems to be that this program is probably over-expanded.

STUDENT PARTICIPATION IN ACTIVITIES

Extent of participation.—One of the problems commonly arising with regard to extra-curriculum activities is that a few students are overloaded with positions of leadership and responsibility in numerous activities, while a large percentage of the students fail to participate sufficiently to profit educationally from the activities. An effort has been made to determine the extent of student participation in two ways: first, by having students indicate in the student questionnaire the number and type of activities in which they engage; second, by securing from administrative officers an estimate of the percentage of students who participate in six or more activities. The latter plan was followed only in the colleges in which the student questionnaire was not administered.

Table 102 shows for ten colleges the percentage of students who participate in various numbers of activities.

The data presented in Table 102 show that a very favorable condition exists at Dickinson College in that a very small percentage of the students participate in no activities and none participate in six or more. The median institutions, Morningside and Cornell, present a less favorable situa-

TABLE 102

PERCENTAGE OF STUDENTS ENGAGING IN VARIOUS NUMBERS OF
EXTRA-CURRICULUM ACTIVITIES AT TEN COLLEGES

INSTITUTION	NUMBER OF ACTIVITIES				
	0	1	2	3–5	6 or More
Dickinson..............	4	47	31	18	....
Simpson...............	6	25	27	38	4
Iowa Wesleyan.........	8	28	19	39	6
Union.................	8	40	30	22	....
Morningside...........	10	23	21	39	7
Cornell...............	10	34	25	28	3
Hamline..............	17	30	24	24	5
Evansville............	21	36	21	20	2
Chattanooga...........	22	32	23	22	1
Allegheny.............	23	35	20	21	1
Median...........	10.0	33.0	23.5	23.0	2.5

tion in that 10 per cent of the students participate in no activities, while 46 per cent at the former institution and 31 per cent at the latter participate in three or more activities. Of greater concern, however, are the situations at Evansville College, the University of Chattanooga, and Allegheny College, where more than one-fifth of the students participate in no activities. If extra-curriculum activities can be justified on educational grounds, and it seems that they can be if properly selected, distributed, and organized, then the participation of a maximum percentage of all students is desirable.

In the colleges in which the student questionnaire was not given, the estimates of administrative officers regarding the extent of student participation in activities are in general agreement with the situation shown in Table 102, although the total range between extremes is much larger.

In one institution it is estimated that all students participate in some activity; at the other extreme it is estimated that 50 per cent of the men and 60 per cent of the women engage in no activities at all. The median institution of fifteen for which percentages are given by administrative officers has 15 per cent of its men students engaged in no activities. The median institution of fourteen from which estimates are available has 12.5 per cent of its women students engaging in no activities.

The data derived from the student questionnaires and from administrative officers show, on the whole, an unsatisfactory situation in most colleges with respect to student participation in extra-curriculum activities. In most of the institutions studied too large a percentage of students participate in no activities, while a small percentage participate in too many.

The criticism just made of student participation suggests a need for two types of administrative approach: first, the employment of some form of control or limitation; second, the more general introduction of measures designed to stimulate participation on the part of those now left out or inactive. The assumption underlying these suggestions is that a well-balanced program of extra-curriculum activities can be justified upon the basis of its educational value. It follows, then, that this value should be shared as widely as possible by all students, and should not be destroyed by excessive participation on the part of any one.

Control of participation.—Specific data concerning the control of student participation in activities were secured from seventeen institutions. The agencies of control found in these institutions are summarized in Table 103.

Most of the institutions have more than one agency of control for activities. In each one there is, however, either a faculty committee, a faculty adviser, or a dean, as the chief agent of control. Various combinations of one or two of these with other agencies are found in twelve of the institutions, while in six there is a single controlling agent. In five colleges the "control" is advisory only; in five others the control is exercised through an official limitation upon participation; four colleges designate their type of control as "supervisory"; in three colleges the institution assumes complete direction of the program; in two, the authority of the college is limited to matters requiring final action; and in two institutions the only control of extra-curriculum activities is through the setting of standards.

The conclusion to be drawn from the data available concerning control of student participation in extra-curriculum activities is that adequate provision for control exists in these institutions; the power of control, generally, is not adequately exercised, and the results achieved are not satisfactory. The real problem presented is not one of arbitrary exercise of authority in the matter, but rather one which demands a more careful study of the situation on each separate campus leading to a clearer definition of the functions and procedures involved in the administration of the activities.

TABLE 103

AGENCIES CONTROLLING EXTRA-CURRICULUM
ACTIVITIES IN SEVENTEEN COLLEGES

Agency	Number of Institutions
Faculty committee	12
Faculty advisers	7
Deans	5
Student organizations	4
Scholarship committee	2
Athletic committee	1
President	1
Registrar	1
Personnel officer	1
Administration	1

Stimulating student participation.—Certain methods of stimulating students to take part in activities now employed in some institutions are worthy of special note. Among these are the following: (1) A committee of senior girls with the dean of women as chairman interviews all women students with a view to interesting them and placing them in some group activity; (2) special clubs and societies are organized for "students generally left out"; (3) all-school parties are promoted; (4) interested faculty members promote student interest in music, debating, dramatics, and publications; (5) college credit is given for work in dramatics, music, debating, and athletics; (6) a certain amount of participation in extra-curriculum activities is made a requirement for graduation; (7) "tryouts" are held for participation in most of the activities; (8) sponsors of activities present their respective interests in chapel; (9) the college paper is used for publicity of activities; (10) medals are given for forensics, and letters for participation in athletics and the choir; (11) a general presentation is made of activities during Freshman Week; (12) individuals are canvassed for membership.

CHAPTER XLI

PERSONAL PROBLEMS OF STUDENTS

TYPES OF PROBLEMS FACED BY STUDENTS

Administrative officers of institutions of higher education are recognizing the importance of giving students adequate counsel in the solution of their personal problems. With a view to determining the extent to which

TABLE 104

NUMBER AND PERCENTAGE OF 3,513 COLLEGE STUDENTS
WHO HAVE FACED VARIOUS PERSONAL PROBLEMS

Problem	Number	Percentage
Finances...................................	1,098	31.3
Choosing a vocation...........................	851	24.2
Forming acquaintances and friendships with students of the opposite sex....................	732	20.8
Forming acquaintances and friendships with students of the same sex......................	726	20.7
Fear of failure in courses.....................	658	18.7
Poor study habits............................	562	16.0
Religious questions or doubts.................	556	15.8
Difficulty or misunderstanding with instructor ...	538	15.3
Timidity.....................................	477	13.6
Worry and extreme nervousness................	440	12.5
Attitude toward life..........................	425	12.1
Homesickness................................	383	10.9
Undesirable personal habits...................	346	9.8
Personal conduct violating college rules..........	339	9.6
Attitude toward work.........................	313	8.9
How to become admitted to a club or fraternity..	291	8.3
Whether to accept a proffered date.............	281	8.0
Failure in courses............................	261	7.4
How to secure a date.........................	259	7.4
Recreation...................................	256	7.3
Overwork....................................	241	6.9
Health.......................................	221	6.3
Difficulty or misunderstanding with fellow-student	174	5.0
Family difficulties or misunderstandings.........	172	4.9
Physical handicap............................	129	3.7
How to avoid being "oversociable".............	116	3.3
Whether to invite a chaperon.................	96	2.7

there is actual need of such personal counsel, students were asked in the questionnaire to check in a given list of problems those which they faced while attending their respective institutions. They were asked further to indicate the problems concerning which they desired more help than they received. Table 104 summarizes the data concerning problems faced by students in ten institutions.

This table shows that 31.3 per cent of the 3,513 students from whom information was secured have faced the problem of finances while in college; 24.2 per cent, the problem of choosing a vocation, etc. On an average, each student checked three of the problems given in the check list. Some of the problems are so closely interrelated that they may be grouped under a few larger headings. The data given justify the conclusion that the significant personal problems faced by students in ten colleges are: (*a*) finances; (*b*) choosing a vocation; (*c*) social adjustment, including formation of friendships with the same and the opposite sex, securing and accepting "dates," misunderstandings with instructors and fellow students, family difficulties, and personal conduct; (*d*) emotional adjustment, including fear of failure, timidity, worry and nervousness, and homesickness; (*e*) scholastic adjustment, including poor study habits, failure in courses, and attitude toward work; (*f*) health, including recreation, overwork, general health, and physical handicaps; (*g*) philosophy of life, including religious questions and doubts, and attitude toward life. The number and percentage of students who have faced each of the specific problems is sufficiently large to justify any steps which administrators are taking to provide more adequate counsel to students, and to demand special attention in institutions in which no steps to provide counsel have been taken.

The urgency for the need for personal counseling is further emphasized by the data presented in Table 105, showing for nine institutions the median percentage of students who faced personal problems and desired more help than they received.

LIVING CONDITIONS OF STUDENTS

Types of living conditions.—The academic work of students is often seriously affected by the general conditions under which they live and work. To determine the types of living conditions found among the colleges of this study, students in each of ten institutions were asked to indicate in the student questionnaire the conditions under which they were living at the time the study was made and the degree to which they found their living conditions satisfactory. A summary of the conditions under which students live in ten colleges is presented in Table 106.

TABLE 105

Median Percentage of Students at Nine Institutions Who
Faced Various Personal Problems and Who Indicated
a Desire for More Help than They Received

Problem	Median Percentage
Choosing a vocation	26.9
Attitude toward life	21.8
Finance	21.6
Living conditions	18.4*
Recreation	18.2
How to secure a date	18.2
Timidity	18.2
Family difficulties or misunderstandings	17.6
Forming acquaintanceships and friendships with students of the opposite sex	17.6
Overwork	16.7
Finding work for partial self-support	16.2*
Difficulty or misunderstanding with instructor	15.6
Poor study habits	15.4
Religious questions or doubts	15.4
How to become admitted to a club or fraternity	14.4†
Attitude toward work	13.6
Personal morality	13.0
Worry and extreme nervousness	12.5
Fear of failure in courses	12.2
Health	10.0
Difficulty or misunderstanding with fellow-students	9.4
Personal conduct violating college rules	9.3
Undesirable personal habits	9.1
Forming acquaintanceships and friendships with students of your own sex	7.5
How to avoid being "oversociable"	7.1
Homesickness	6.8
Failure in courses	6.3
Whether to accept a proffered date	5.8
Whether to invite a chaperon	0.0†
Physical handicap	0.0

* Data for only two colleges.
† Data for eight colleges.

This table is read as follows: Of the 299 men in Allegheny College from whom information was received, 13 per cent live at home, 46 per cent live in dormitories, 37 per cent live in fraternities, and 4 per cent live in private rooms or under other special arrangements. Eighty-two per cent of this group report their living conditions to be satisfactory. Living under other special arrangements, as used in this table, includes a few isolated cases in certain institutions in which students live in college buildings other than dormitories, or in private rooms in which they do light housekeeping. The

TABLE 106

LIVING CONDITIONS OF STUDENTS IN TEN COLLEGES

| INSTITUTION | NUMBER REPORTING | | PERCENTAGE LIVING AS INDICATED | | | | | | | | PERCENTAGE REPORTING LIVING CONDITIONS SATISFACTORY | |
| | | | At Home | | In Dormitories | | In Fraternities or Sororities | | In Private Homes, Rooms, or Other Special Arrangements | | | |
	M.	W.	M.	W.	M.	W.	M.	W.	M.	W.	M.	W.
Allegheny.........	299	279	13	12	46	83	37	....	4	5	82	36
Chattanooga......	154	158	70	85	....	8	10	....	20	8	95	98
Cornell...........	213	254	12	12	13	56	49	26	26	5	86	87
Dickinson.........	330	127	18	37	39	61	39	....	4	2	79	75
Evansville........	102	80	75	78	....	....	....	....	26	23	92	91
Hamline..........	196	163	32	29	13	53	38	....	17	18	80	99
Iowa Wesleyan....	134	130	26	37	....	52	47	2	27	10	96	95
Morningside......	156	203	40	36	11	36	23	....	27	29	85	91
Simpson..........	210	348	22	21	1	27	31	20	46	32	100	91
Union............	63	50	33	56	62	40	....	....	5	4	78	84
All colleges combined....	1,857	1,792	29	32	20	45	32	8	19	15	86	82

total number of these cases was so few that they did not warrant separate categories.

The data of the table show that the largest percentage of students living at home is found where colleges are located in larger cities, as, for example, Chattanooga, Evansville, and Morningside. Hamline University and Union College are exceptions to this statement. The former enrols a comparatively large percentage of its students from territory outside of St. Paul; the latter has a small enrolment which makes the percentage of those coming from the immediate community and living at home comparatively high. The average percentage of women living at home is somewhat higher than that of men.

Four of the colleges in this group—Chattanooga, Evansville, Iowa Wesleyan, and Simpson—provide no dormitories for men. At Simpson College a very small percentage of the men say they live in dormitories, but these are students who render student service in the dormitories for women and are given special rooms in which to live. Evansville College is the only institution in this group having no dormitory for women, although the University of Chattanooga has only a small dormitory.

The data show further that 20 per cent of the men in the ten institutions and 45 per cent of the women live in dormitories, while 32 per cent of the men and 8 per cent of the women live in fraternity and sorority houses, respectively. In other words, of the students who do not live at home, the largest percentage of women live in dormitories and the largest percentage of men live in fraternities. The percentage of men living in dormitories is much larger, however, than the percentage of women living in sorority houses. Approximately an equal percentage of men and of women live in private rooms or under other special conditions.

Student evaluation of living conditions.—The students who gave information concerning their living conditions were also asked to indicate whether their living arrangements were satisfactory and, if not, in what respect they might be improved. The last two columns of Table 106 show the percentage of men and women in each of ten institutions who reported living conditions to be satisfactory. It is noted, first of all, that living conditions are considered most satisfactory in institutions in which the largest percentage of students live at home. This appears to be particularly true of Chattanooga and Evansville. The data indicate that conditions are the least satisfactory at Dickinson, Union, and Allegheny. The averages for men and women show that, on the whole, a slightly larger percentage of the former than of the latter consider their living conditions to be satisfactory.

The more specific and pertinent criticisms made by students pertain to dormitories. A number of the buildings are criticized as out of date, lacking in conveniences, too noisy, and lacking in "tone." In a few instances fraternities are said to be too crowded, or to be lacking in high tone and a homelike atmosphere. In institutions in which fraternities are not all that might be desired as living centers, the plan of employing housemothers might well be adopted. A pleasing character of fraternity life has generally been found in institutions in which this plan is in operation.

The supervision of living centers.—The authorities who are responsible for the supervision of residences for women in thirty-four institutions are shown in Table 107.

TABLE 107

AUTHORITIES IN CHARGE OF RESIDENCE CENTERS FOR WOMEN
IN THIRTY-FOUR COLLEGES

INSTITUTION	WOMEN IN DORMITORIES					WOMEN IN PRIVATE HOMES					
	Dean of Women	Matron	Housemother	Assistant Dean of Women	Woman Director	Dean of Women	No One	Committee of Faculty	Matron	Dean of College	Director of Residence
*Albion	X		X			X		X			
*Allegheny	X						X				
*Baker		X				X		X			
Baldwin-Wallace	X					X					
Central Wesleyan		X							X		
*Chattanooga	X	X									
*Cornell	X			X		X					
Dakota Wesleyan	X					X				X	
*DePauw					X						
*Dickinson	X										
Evansville						X					
Gooding	X					X					
*Hamline					X						X
*Illinois Wesleyan	X	X				X					
Intermountain		X				X					
Iowa Wesleyan	X					X					
Kansas Wesleyan		X				X					
*Lawrence	X					X					
McKendree		X									
*MacMurray	X					X					
*Morningside	X	X		X		X					
*Mount Union	X	X						X			
Nebraska Wesleyan						X					
Ohio Northern	X					X					
*Ohio Wesleyan	X					X					
Oklahoma City						X					
Ozark Wesleyan	X					X					
*Pacific				X			X				
Puget Sound									X		
*Simpson	X					X					
Southwestern		X				X		X			
Union		X					X				
West Virginia Wesleyan	X								X		
*Willamette	X										
Total	20	11	1	3	2	21	3	5	1	2	1

* Institutions on the approved list of the Association of American Universities.

It is apparent from this table that the dean of women is responsible for supervising dormitories for women in twenty of the thirty institutions having dormitories for women. In six instances she is assisted by a matron, housemother, or assistant dean. In seven institutions a matron alone is responsible; in two, a director of residences; and in one, an assistant dean of women. The dean of women frequently lives in the dormitories and often is the active head resident. Occasionally, however, she is assisted in administering details by a matron, or by student self-governing organizations.

The dean of women is also generally responsible for the supervision of living conditions where women occupy furnished rooms in private houses. In seventeen institutions she alone has this responsibility; in four, she shares the responsibility with a faculty committee, or the college dean. Three institutions report that no one is specifically designated to discharge this supervisory function; in the remaining colleges, the dean of the college, a faculty committee, or a director of residences is responsible.

A summary of the provisions made in twenty-nine institutions for the supervision of living conditions for men is presented in Table 108.

With respect to the supervision of dormitories, there is a wide variation in practice. In six institutions, a faculty member, sometimes married, usually living in the dormitory, is directly responsible. A hostess, housemother, woman director, or matron is responsible for supervision in eight institutions. Other arrangements include supervision by a dean of men or a preceptor, student self-government, supervision by student residents, or no supervision.

The supervision of living conditions for men who live in privately furnished rooms generally centers in the dean of the college or the dean of men. In a few institutions a faculty member or a faculty committee is responsible, while in one case a woman director and in another a Young Men's Christian Association secretary performs the supervisory function.

It is needless to say that from the data presented it is apparent that the supervision of living conditions for men is, on the whole, not so well systematized as that for women. It seems clear that better administrative organization of living centers would improve living conditions for men in most of the institutions studied.

On the whole, the most unsatisfactory situation with respect to the supervision of living centers for men pertains to fraternity houses. This conclusion and the following comments are based upon personal visits to and studies of fraternities as living centers. In some instances fraternities have almost complete autonomy in the administration of their houses; in others, faculty members serve as advisers to fraternities, usually to the

TABLE 108

AUTHORITIES IN CHARGE OF RESIDENCE CENTERS FOR MEN
IN TWENTY-NINE COLLEGES

Institution	Men's Dormitories										Men in Private Houses							
	Dean of Men	Hostess	Preceptor	Self-Government	No One	Housemother	Faculty Member	Student Resident	Woman Director	Matron	No One	Y.M.C.A. Secretary	Dean of College	Dean of Men	President	Faculty Committee	Woman Director	Faculty Member
*Allegheny		X																
*Baker																X		
Baldwin-Wallace			X	X									X					
Brothers					X													
Central Wesleyan						X							X		X			
*Cornell							X									X		
Dakota Wesleyan								X					X					
*DePauw									X								X	
*Dickinson							X	X										
Evansville														X				
Gooding	X												X					
*Hamline							X						X					
*Illinois Wesleyan													X					
Intermountain																		X
Kansas Wesleyan													X					
*Lawrence							X							X				
McKendree										X								
*Morningside	X									X								
*Mount Union							X									X		
Nebraska Wesleyan														X		X		
Ohio Northern														X				
*Ohio Wesleyan												X						
Oklahoma City														X				
*Pacific						X					X							
Puget Sound																X		
Southwestern										X				X		X		
Union							X				X							
West Virginia Wesleyan										X				X				
*Willamette														X				
Total	2	1	1	1	1	2	6	2	1	4	2	1	7	8	1	6	1	1

* Institutions on the approved list of the Association of American Universities.

ones of which they are members; in one or two institutions the dean of men has jurisdiction, either advisory or final over fraternities; also, in one or two instances housemothers who serve as hostesses and overseers are employed by fraternities. The housemother plan, in which the housemother actually serves as a hostess, as distinct from a cook or housekeeper, has given to fraternities as residences dignity and tone which have been lacking in institutions which do not have housemothers for fraternity houses.

Various plans are in effect whereby supervision is exercised over private residences in which men students rent furnished rooms. This living arrangement proves particularly difficult to oversee. Generally, where any oversight is attempted, the dean of men inspects private rooms and approves or disapproves of them as suitable for students. Householders who rent rooms to students are sometimes asked to make regular reports to a designated administrative officer, most frequently the dean of the college or the dean of men. Such reports usually refer to the study habits and living habits of students under the immediate charge of the householder. Living conditions in private, furnished rooms would be a major problem in many of these institutions except for the fact that only a comparatively small percentage of students rent rooms in private families.

VOCATIONAL INTERESTS OF STUDENTS

The data presented in Table 104 show that choosing a vocation is one of the problems frequently faced by students in the several colleges. The same students who indicated that the choice of a vocation is or has been a personal problem were asked to indicate the vocation which they had chosen. For the sake of uniformity and convenience, vocations are classified under thirteen general heads. Each of the separate divisions is further defined as to the specific vocations which it embraces. The classification of vocations used and the choices indicated by the students in ten colleges are presented in Table 109.

This table shows, first of all, that the largest percentage of vocational choices fall in the field of education, with business as second. At the other extreme only 0.6 per cent have chosen agriculture even though in some of the institutions represented a large percentage of the students come from rural communities. There appears to be a discrepancy between the data presented in this table and those of Table 104, in that only 4.5 per cent say they are indefinite as to a vocational choice while the former table showed that 24.2 per cent faced the problem of choosing a vocation. Moreover, other data show that 26.9 per cent desire more help than they have received in making a choice. This apparent discrepancy is probably due to several factors. First, some of the choices indicated are, no doubt, expressions of a desire or preference rather than final decisions. Many of these students are most likely among those who desired more help than they received in choosing a vocation. Second, some of those who actually faced the problem of choosing a vocation while in college

TABLE 109

NUMBER AND PERCENTAGE OF 3,474 STUDENTS IN TEN COLLEGES WHO INDICATED THEIR CHOICE OF VARIOUS VOCATIONS

Vocation	Number	Percentage
Educational service (teaching, coaching, library work, personnel work, physical education).....	1,409	40.6
Business (banking, business administration, secretarial service, advertising, merchandising)......	458	13.2
Medical service (medicine, surgery, dentistry, nursing)...................................	257	7.4
Engineering (aeronautical, chemical, civil, electrical, industrial, mechanical)...............	241	6.9
Law and government (legal service, politics, military service, naval service, civil service).......	239	6.9
Religious service (ministry, religious education, mission work, Y.M.C.A., Y.W.C.A.)..........	186	5.2
Journalism...............................	117	3.4
Scientific research........................	107	3.1
Music (all music not in teaching field)...........	106	3.1
Homemaking (home economics except teaching, dietetics, institutional management)...........	58	1.7
Social service............................	49	1.4
Art (painting, sculpturing, modeling, etc.)........	39	1.1
Agriculture (farming, forestry, dairying, poultry raising, landscaping).......................	22	0.6
Indefinite................................	156	4.5
Miscellaneous............................	30	0.9
Total................................	3,474	100.0

have settled the issue and therefore no longer belong to those who are still undecided.

It is noted further from the data presented concerning the choices of vocations that a comparatively small percentage of these students are preparing definitely to enter any phase of religious service. In view of the fact that the colleges represented are all denominational in type, it might be expected that many more would indicate a choice of religious service. It should be said, however, that this is not necessarily an argument for attempting to encourage more individuals to enter religious service as a life work, for it is altogether probable that the number now preparing for this profession will be adequate to supply the needs of the church for pastors and religious workers. No information was secured on this point. Much more important is the question whether those best qualified for the profession of religious service are preparing to enter it.

Particularly striking is the fact that only a small percentage of the women (the entire group was approximately equally divided between men and women) have chosen homemaking as a career. The explanation of this probably lies in two facts: First, many young women are hesitant to say that this is their choice of a career even though it may be their secret ambition. Second, in line with changing social conditions, many more do not think of a career as incompatible with homemaking and they have, therefore, merely indicated their professional interest without at the same time indicating homemaking as a co-ordinate objective.

CHAPTER XLII
STUDENT GOVERNMENT AND DISCIPLINE

An analysis has been made of reports from the administrative officers of thirty-three institutions regarding the authorities who are responsible for discipline. This analysis is summarized in Table 110.

This table shows that in most institutions the responsibility for dealing with problems of discipline is distributed among several officers. A typical situation is that in which minor matters of discipline are handled by the dean of men and the dean of women, while more serious problems are referred from these officers to a committee on administration or to a faculty committee on discipline. Numerous variations from this plan are found; in some institutions, for example, serious cases are referred directly to the president who either deals with them personally or refers them to the faculty; in others, the academic dean becomes the central disciplinary officer. In six institutions a committee on discipline from the faculty is directly responsible for the administration of discipline.

Two questions of special significance are presented by these data. First, do students share as much as they should in the administration of disciplinary problems? Conditions vary so widely among institutions that no categorical answer can be given, but an examination of Table 110 shows that the responsibility shared by students in these institutions is very limited.

Second, should the dean of men and the dean of women bear the heavy responsibility of discipline which is now theirs? The answer to this question must likewise be determined by the definition of the essential functions of these officers. If they are to share in a personal and intimate way the problems and experiences of students, then to make them responsible for the administration of discipline is inconsistent with their chief function. The better plan is to expect the dean of men and the dean of women to deal with only such disciplinary problems as they may feel are necessary in order to help individual students.

OPINIONS OF STUDENTS REGARDING DISCIPLINE

In an effort to evaluate the general situation with respect to discipline among the colleges which were studied, several types of information

TABLE 110

AUTHORITIES WHO ARE RESPONSIBLE FOR DISCIPLINE
IN THIRTY-THREE COLLEGES

Institution	President	Dean of the College	Committee of Faculty	Dean of Men	Dean of Women or Adviser to Women	Faculty	Student Committee or Senate	Joint Student-Faculty Committee	Committee of Deans	Student Court	Committee on Administration
*Albion	X	X			X	X	X				
*Allegheny			X	X	X	X	X				
*Baker	X		X								
Baldwin-Wallace		X	X		X						
Brothers		X									
Central Wesleyan		X					X				
*Cornell	X		X								
Dakota Wesleyan			X								
*DePauw				X	X				X		
*Dickinson			X			X					
Evansville										X	
Gooding	X			X	X						
*Hamline	X			X	X						
*Illinois Wesleyan			X								
Intermountain			X		X						
Iowa Wesleyan	X	X									
Kansas Wesleyan											X
*Lawrence								X			X
McKendree	X	X									
*MacMurray		X									
*Morningside				X	X						X
*Mount Union							X				
Nebraska Wesleyan											X
Ohio Northern			X	X	X						
*Ohio Wesleyan			X								X
Oklahoma City	X										
Ozark Wesleyan	X		X								
*Pacific									X		
Puget Sound			X								
*Simpson	X			X	X						
Southwestern											X
West Virginia Wesleyan		X	X								
*Willamette									X		
Total	10	8	13	7	10	3	4	1	2	1	6

* Institutions on the approved list of the Association of American Universities.

were secured, viz., student opinions of discipline, administrative provisions for disciplinary control, and opportunities for students to participate in the government of institutions.

The opinions of students regarding the discipline in ten colleges are presented in summary in Table 111.

In some institutions in which, according to the judgment of administrative officers, very wholesome conditions prevail, a large percentage of students are not satisfied with the discipline. It is significant that in eight of the ten institutions more than 20 per cent of the students consider the discipline too rigid, while in none of these institutions do as many as 5 per cent consider it too lax. In some of these institutions the students were in a state of revolt against rules prohibiting some of the

TABLE 111

STUDENTS' OPINIONS OF DISCIPLINE AT TEN COLLEGES

STUDENTS' OPINIONS OF DISCIPLINE	PERCENTAGE GIVING EACH TYPE OF JUDGMENT		
	Average for Ten Colleges	Highest for Ten Colleges	Lowest for Ten Colleges
Satisfactory..............	68.0	88.9	48.8
Too rigid.................	24.3	44.9	3.2
Too lax..................	2.0	4.9	0.4
Noncommittal............	5.7	10.4	0.8

generally accepted forms of social recreation, particularly dancing. This condition no doubt reflects the reaction of a younger generation against the conservative restraints of administrators, who either conscientiously object to certain forbidden forms of recreation or feel that a conservative constituency demands the barring of the activities. In any event, the opinions summarized in the table reflect quite directly the need for immediate and careful consideration of the modification of disciplinary rules and procedures so as to bring students and college administrators to a mutual understanding regarding the need for and the enforcement of rules. One important step in this direction is to provide opportunities for students to participate in the government of institutions.

PROVISIONS FOR STUDENTS TO PARTICIPATE IN GOVERNMENT

There is wide variation in the provisions for students to participate in various phases of the government of the student community. In a number of the colleges there is a fairly complete set-up for students to assume governmental responsibility for the affairs that concern their own social group. Generally, however, these governmental organizations do not function to their full capacity. In fact, students who lead in these organizations often feel that they are little more than figureheads.

Moreover, reports from thirty-four institutions concerning authorities who are responsible for discipline show that in only five instances is a student committtee or court included as a disciplinary agent and in only one is a joint student-faculty committee included. The inference seems justified, therefore, that either very few institutions place any direct responsibility for discipline upon students or that most administrative officers attach little real significance to student disciplinary organizations where they exist.

One of the important functions of all education, particularly on the college level, is to give students experience in all the affairs which constitute social living. Unquestionably, intelligent participation in the governmental administration of social affairs within the college will be very valuable in preparing students for most efficient social living after they leave college. The ability to assume responsibility comes from the actual discharge of responsibility. Many educational institutions are recognizing this general principle and are in every way possible attempting to provide for student participation in governmental affairs.

Some of the specific provisions whereby this may be done are briefly discussed. First, there may be co-operation between faculty and students through a joint committee. Student representatives on this committee may present various problems affecting the student body as a whole to the committee, which in turn may make recommendations to the faculty on the questions presented. The faculty may likewise submit certain questions to this committee which it in turn may decide or may submit to the students for decision.

Second, some administrators of institutions even go to the point of arranging for student representatives to be present at the meetings of the board of trustees when matters affecting students are discussed. This gives them an insight into the general attitude of the trustees and helps them to understand better the policies which may be adopted by this body.

Third, there are always some problems of government which affect the student body as a whole. Such problems may be administered through a student commission or council which is elected by popular vote and is representative of the whole student body.

Fourth, students who live in dormitories may well have delegated to them the general government of the dormitory. Various types of such government are now operating quite effectively in different institutions.

Fifth, in many institutions there are administrative problems centering in fraternities and sororities. Such problems may pertain to actual control of living conditions or to general policies regarding the activities of these organizations on a given campus. In either event they present excellent opportunities for the delegation of responsibility to interfraternity or intersorority organizations.

Sixth, it is occasionally found desirable to have separate student governing bodies responsible for matters affecting particular interests of the separate groups. The need for such organizations will be determined largely by the relative number of men and women and the type of social life and organization of students on a given campus.

Whatever plans may be adopted for student participation in government, it is to be recognized that there are always certain traditions, certain general policies affecting the welfare of an institution, and certain limitations set by the purpose for which the institution exists, which need, to some extent, to be safeguarded by general regulations. These traditions, policies, and purposes should, from time to time, be clearly interpreted to the students so that they may understand why the general regulations are made. It should further be recognized that the friendly counsel of faculty members and administrative officers, not imposed upon students, but unofficially given, will frequently be helpful in avoiding blunders in governmental action; and when judiciously given, will be welcomed by students. In fact, the effectiveness of any plan of student participation in government will be conditioned quite as much by the sympathetic and co-operative attitude of the administration as by the formal set-up of the scheme itself.

One of the difficulties inherent in the plan of student self-government is that the student groups are apt to develop an idea that their field of activity extends to the government of the college itself. In a few of the colleges where student self-government is rather highly developed, cases have arisen (or the administrative officers have been apprehensive that cases would arise) in which the student groups dictated to the authorities of the college concerning such matters as the retention or dismissal of faculty members or executive officers, the distribution of scholarship grants, etc. It should be clear that matters affecting the college as an educational institution are outside the province of student government. The faculty, administrative officers, and board of trustees are responsible for these matters, and this responsibility cannot be delegated to students.

It should be clear that "student self-government" should be limited to matters affecting the student group as a social community.

One of the colleges included in this study has adopted an interesting plan for safeguarding the welfare of the institution even though considerable responsibility is lodged in the various student groups. This college requires each student organization to obtain a formal charter from the board of trustees. The fact that the granting of a charter is surrounded by a certain amount of "red tape" and ceremony tends to discourage the formation of unneeded or useless organizations. The charters all contain a standard clause granting the trustees of the college the power to revoke the charter at their pleasure when the student group concerned is taking action contrary to the established policies of the institution, or is doing anything which might discredit the good name of the college. The president of this institution reports that the threat to revoke the charter of a student group is sufficient to prevent any ill-considered moves from being put into effect.

The three colleges of this group that are located on the West Coast all have the organization known as the Associated Students. This is a federated organization, with local units in most of the institutions of higher learning on the Pacific Coast. The amount of power delegated to the student bodies of these colleges is much larger than is typically found in institutions in other parts of the country. A measure of faculty control is exercised through the chief supervisory officer, known as the "graduate manager," who in each case is a member of the college instructional staff. The quality of student leadership in these institutions is said to be very good. All three of these colleges express themselves as being very much in sympathy with student self-government under the auspices of the Associated Students.

CHAPTER XLIII

AGENCIES PROMOTING RELIGIOUS INFLUENCE AMONG STUDENTS

ATTITUDE OF THE INSTITUTIONS

All of the thirty-five colleges included in this study are related to the Methodist Episcopal Church. Statements culled from recent issues of their bulletins and literature emphasize the fact that they are Christian in spirit and aims, although not sectarian in any narrow sense, whether in curriculum or in the general atmosphere of the college. All seek to cultivate a positive Christian character in the student and make constant efforts to maintain an environment conducive to such an end.

With but few exceptions the catalogues of each of the institutions contain emphatic statements concerning the moral and religious spirit and aspirations of the college. The few colleges which fail to include such a statement in their published aims should be urged to develop and publish a sane but specific enunciation of the school's position. It is to be regretted that a few institutions have published flowery statements of goals whose attainment is impossible if not even undesirable.

Two of the typical and more moderate catalogue statements are included to show the general attitude of the group.

Hamline University as an educational institution is founded upon the principle that religious culture is as essential as intellectual development, and that each supplements the other. To this end the University encourages the teaching and the practice of religion not only in the curriculum of the college but also on the campus through student activities.[1]

Cornell College voices its religious affiliation in the following expression.

The college was founded by Christian Pioneers and aims to apply Christian principles and methods to its work and regulations. It is under the patronage of the Methodist Episcopal Church. Although in this sense denominational, it is not sectarian in the sense of teaching the religious tenets of any particular sect. Its advantages are offered without restriction to all who wish to spend the formative years of college life in a wholesome religious atmosphere, where Christian ideals of life are emphasized, where Christ is held as the supreme revelation of God to man, and the church as the most potent institution for human betterment.[2]

[1] *Bulletin of Hamline University, 1928–29*, pp. 26–27.

[2] *Bulletin of Cornell College, 1928–29*, p. 77.

Whatever type of objective is felt to be the most appropriate in describing the religious and moral influence of the institution, the wording and implication should be positive, yet moderate. It should be such as to make possible its actually being carried into action in the daily life of the college. Every college which receives denominational patronage should carry such a statement in its catalogue.

RELIGIOUS AFFILIATIONS OF STUDENTS

Table 112 shows the percentage of students at the thirty-five colleges who are members of or express preferences for various religious denominations.

This table shows that in the typical college of this group approximately one-half of the students are affiliated with or express preference for the Methodist Episcopal Church. The median for the group of colleges on the approved list of the Association of American Universities does not differ materially from the median for the group of colleges which do not hold this accreditation, indicating that the type of accreditation held does not, of itself, have any important relationship to the percentage of students in this group of colleges which are affiliated with the supporting denomination. Both extremes in the distribution of percentages of Methodist students are represented by colleges which are on the approved list of the Association of American Universities.

The data of this table afford an opportunity to study the relationship between the size of the local community in which the college is located and the percentage of students which are affiliated with the Methodist Episcopal Church. In compiling these data, the figures of the 1930 census were used for the population of the cities in which these colleges are located. The institutions were first grouped according to the size of the population of the local community, and then the average percentage of Methodist students for each of the groups was calculated. These data are given in Figure 19. Next the colleges were grouped according to the percentage of Methodist students, and the average population of the local communities of each group was calculated. These data are presented in Figure 20. In making these tabulations, two colleges—Hamline University and Nebraska Wesleyan University—were omitted. Both of these institutions are located in fairly large cities, but the state universities of their respective states are also located in the same communities. Since these are the only colleges of the group which face this type of local competition, they have been excluded from the tabulations.

It will be noted from these two figures that there is some relationship

TABLE 112

PERCENTAGE OF STUDENTS BELONGING TO EACH CHURCH GROUP†

Institution	Year	Methodist	Other Protestant Denominations	Roman Catholic	Jewish	Others	No Affiliation Reported
*Baker...................	1929–30	81	7	......	......	......	12
*Simpson................	1929–30	76	13	......	......	4	7
Southwestern...........	1930–31	75	22	1	......	2	......
Dakota Wesleyan........	1929–30	74	18	1	......	2	5
Nebraska Wesleyan......	1930–31	74	12	......	......	3	11
Gooding................	1930–31	73	13	1	......	3	10
*Cornell................	1929–30	73	17	1	......	8	1
Iowa Wesleyan..........	1929–30	70	24	2	......	4	......
West Virginia Wesleyan..	1930–31	69	13	2	......	10	6
Brothers...............	1930–31	68	23	......	3	6	......
*Hamline...............	1929–30	65	24	......	1	5	5
McKendree.............	1930–31	64	20	2	......	13	1
Kansas Wesleyan........	1930–31	62	30	......	......	6	2
*Morningside...........	1929–30	60	26	2	3	6	3
*DePauw...............	1930–31	58	30	2	......	6	4
*Ohio Wesleyan.........	1930–31	56	24	2	......	8	10
*Albion................	1929–30	55	22	2	1	3	17
*MacMurray............	1930–31	54	37	2	1	4	2
*Illinois Wesleyan.......	1930–31	54	31	5	......	2	8
*Willamette............	1930–31	52	29	3	......	10	6
Intermountain..........	1930–31	52	34	1	......	4	9
Central Wesleyan.......	1928–29	52	11	2	......	19	16
Ozark Wesleyan.........	1928–29	51	37	......	......	4	8
*Mount Union..........	1930–31	48	29	3	2	16	2
Baldwin-Wallace........	1930–31	46	29	7	4	8	6
*Allegheny.............	1929–30	45	37	7	......	11	......
Oklahoma City.........	1929–30	44	40	5	1	3	7
Ohio Northern.........	1929–30	40	28	9	5	9	9
Union.................	1928–29	40	45	1	......	4	10
Puget Sound...........	1930–31	37	40	7	1	4	11
*Chattanooga...........	1928–29	36	39	5	3	7	10
*Dickinson.............	1929–30	36	32	8	5	10	9
Evansville.............	1929–30	35	25	6	2	18	14
*Lawrence.............	1928–29	33	49	9	1	6	2
*Pacific...............	1929–30	33	31	3	......	8	25
Median, all colleges.....	....	54	28	2	0	6	7
*Median, A.A.U. colleges	....	54	29	2	0	6	6
Median, non-A.A.U. colleges...............	....	57	25	2	0	4	8

* Institutions on the approved list of the Association of American Universities.

† Including both those who are members and those who express a preference for each church.

between the size of the local community and the percentage of Methodist students. In general, the larger the population of the local community, the smaller the percentage of Methodist students. This relationship possibly is partially responsible for the failure to find any important difference with respect to percentage of Methodist students between the colleges holding national accreditation and those without this recognition. The number of

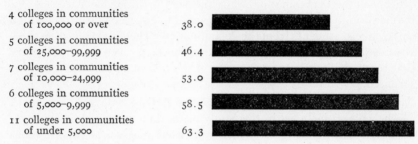

4 colleges in communities of 100,000 or over   38.0

5 colleges in communities of 25,000–99,999   46.4

7 colleges in communities of 10,000–24,999   53.0

6 colleges in communities of 5,000–9,999   58.5

11 colleges in communities of under 5,000   63.3

FIG. 19.—Average percentage of Methodist students in colleges located in communities of various sizes.

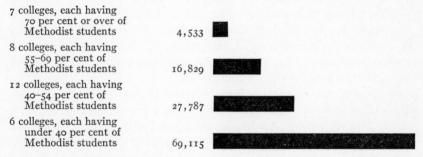

7 colleges, each having 70 per cent or over of Methodist students   4,533

8 colleges, each having 55–69 per cent of Methodist students   16,829

12 colleges, each having 40–54 per cent of Methodist students   27,787

6 colleges, each having under 40 per cent of Methodist students   69,115

FIG. 20.—Average population of local community for colleges having various percentages of Methodist students.

cases is too small to permit any further significant statistical treatment of the colleges on the basis of type of accreditation.

There appears also to be some relationship between the degree of local competition and the percentage of Methodist students in these colleges. Eleven of the colleges have strong competition from neighboring institutions; on the average 59.0 per cent of their students are Methodists. The other twenty-four colleges which are without strong local competition have on the average 53.9 per cent of their students affiliated with the Methodist Episcopal Church. It thus appears that the presence of strong local competition tends to increase the percentage of Methodist students.

One other factor should be mentioned as having an important bearing upon the percentage of students which may be expected from the supporting denomination. The relative strength of the Methodist Episcopal Church varies considerably throughout different parts of the country. A college located in a region in which the Methodist Church is not particularly strong will naturally have a relatively low percentage of students from this denomination, while another institution located in an area that is strongly Methodist may be expected to have a comparatively high percentage of students from the denomination. There does not seem to be any adequate statistical means of taking this factor into account, and for that reason its influence on the data of the preceding tables can only be surmised.

RELIGIOUS ORGANIZATIONS MAINTAINED

The colleges included in this study maintain an average of three student organizations designed primarily to exert religious and moral influences upon students. Of these, the Young Women's Christian Association is found most frequently; the Young Men's Christian Association and the Oxford Club follow in the order named. Several others are found less frequently. Among these may be mentioned the Christian Service Club, the Cosmopolitan Club, Student Volunteers, and Life Service Club. Gospel Teams are found in a number of the institutions. No attempt is made in this study to include the organizations which are maintained as part of the regular program of the work in the local churches.

Of the three major organizations the Young Women's Christian Association seems to be the most effective in a majority of the colleges. The Young Men's Christian Association seems to be, in general, much less vital in its student contacts than its sister organization. Several institutions are experimenting with a new coeducational organization to replace the ineffective men's association and the somewhat more effective women's organization. Where this is done, the new organization will require careful guidance and strong leadership in order that it may be at least as effective as the women's organization which it replaces.

A great variety of services are rendered by these bodies. Some which may be mentioned are: providing programs and talent for devotional or meditative exercises; carrying out social projects; meeting entering students and assisting them in getting located; aiding needy students; publishing handbooks; directing play and recreational activities; and maintaining social service stations. This list is not meant to be exhaustive but merely typical of the work found. In certain of the institutions some of these organizations are performing work which could better be assigned to specific administrative officers of the institution, as, for example, the placement and vocational guidance of students.

The survey staff has not attempted to evaluate objectively the quality of the influence generated by these organizations in the moral and religious lives of students. Satisfactory techniques for making such an evaluation are not now available, and some experimentation with a method for formulating a subjective judgment, carried out in one of the college surveys, did not prove successful. One of the greatest handicaps to such an evaluation is the lack of any clear definition of or agreement upon what constitutes a satisfactory religious and moral influence. In almost all the colleges the administrative officers and faculty members consider these organizations of great benefit.

CHAPEL SERVICE

Arrangements for chapel service in the colleges studied.—Chapel exercises are provided as a definite part of the program of work of every one of the thirty-five colleges. The frequency of these meetings ranges from two to five per week.

Student attendance at chapel service is compulsory in all but three of the institutions. In one other, chapel attendance is not required of all members of the senior class. Attendance is usually checked by student monitors or by office secretaries, and a record of attendance is kept by the dean, the registrar, or some other central officer.

The penalty for excessive absence found most frequently is a deduction in the number of honor or credit points earned. A few colleges deduct credits from the student's scholastic record or require additional work to be presented for graduation. Others require the preparation of special compositions, the payment of a money fine, or explanations to the discipline officer or committee. In some cases provision is made for the temporary suspension of a student who "overcuts" chapel.

One of these colleges has solved the problem of chapel attendance in an interesting manner. Credit is given for chapel in this college, and the penalty for excessive absence is forfeiture of the chapel credit. These credits are required for graduation, being known as "plus credits," i.e., in excess of the regular 120 hours. Students who fail to make their chapel credits must make up the deficiency by the substitution of other academic credits. This has proved a very effective plan for stimulating chapel attendance at the college, without involving the objectionable features of the compulsory religious service.

Ideally the chapel program should be of sufficient interest and value to students so that no artificial incentive to attendance is necessary. Practically, however, such a condition seems difficult to attain, so negative stimuli, such as punishment for non-attendance, are employed. To be effective, punishment should be appropriate and related to the offense. Some of the penalties resorted to for non-attendance at chapel clearly do not meet this test. For example, it would seem difficult to justify a fine for excessive absences. Similarly, a reduction in grade-point standing seems an inappropriate penalty. Deduction of academic credits is somewhat more suitable, if it can be assumed that chapel attendance has educational values; the "plus credit" system described in the preceding paragraph seems the most appropriate of all the methods now being utilized for the stimulation of regular attendance at chapel service.

Attitude of students and faculty.—Table 113 shows the student reactions to chapel services in seven of the colleges for which such

TABLE 113

STUDENT JUDGMENTS OF CHAPEL SERVICES AT
SEVEN COLLEGES

COLLEGE NUMBER	PERCENTAGE OF STUDENTS GIVING EACH TYPE OF JUDGMENT		
	Favorable	Unfavorable	Noncommittal
2.............	87	8	5
1.............	87	6	7
5.............	73	14	13
4.............	72	13	15
3.............	68	12	20
6.............	64	25	11
7.............	48	29	23

information was obtained. In making this study, the students were simply asked on an inquiry form, "What do you think of the chapel service?" Their replies were then classified as favorable, unfavorable, and noncommittal, with the results as given in this table.

This table shows considerable variation in the student reactions to the chapel service in the seven colleges for which comparable data are presented. The percentage of favorable responses is highest at colleges No. 2 and No. 1, while the unfavorable reactions are highest at colleges No. 7 and No. 6. College No. 2 has a very dignified and churchly religious service; at college No. 7 the depressing interior of the chapel building undoubtedly contributes to the relatively large percentage of unfavorable reactions on the part of students.

In three other colleges, data relating to student reactions to chapel services were gathered in a different manner, the students being asked to check one of five statements to indicate their attitude. The exact form of the question was as follows:

Check the statement below which expresses most nearly your estimate of the chapel service. This refers only to the chapel service proper; student assemblies and other group gatherings are *not* included.
—— Generally an attractive and helpful religious service
—— Generally enjoyable, but not especially helpful
—— Sometimes good, often boresome
—— Usually not worth the time required
—— Very poor

TABLE 114

STUDENT REACTIONS TO CHAPEL SERVICES IN
THREE COLLEGES

JUDGMENT	PERCENTAGE OF STUDENTS RESPONDING TO INQUIRY WHO GAVE EACH REACTION INDICATED, IN THE THREE COLLEGES		
	College No. 9	College No. 10	College No. 11
Generally an attractive and helpful religious service............................	52	4	10
Generally enjoyable, but not especially helpful.................................	11	8	11
Sometimes good, often boresome.........	31	77	66
Usually not worth the time required......	3	10	11
Very poor.............................	3	1	2

The results of this study in the three colleges are shown in Table 114, in terms of the percentage of the students furnishing data who indicated each of the various reactions.

This table shows that the pattern of student responses differs markedly in these three colleges. The explanation of these differences was not apparent to members of the survey staff who visited these institutions.

In nine of the colleges the opinion of faculty members was also sought regarding the effectiveness of chapel service. These data are summarized in Table 115.

A fairly strong correlation exists between the student and faculty judgments of chapel services. The colleges which have a high percentage of favorable student judgments tend to be those which also have a high percentage of favorable faculty judgments; while those which have a large proportion of unfavorable student reactions tend also to have a large proportion of unfavorable faculty reactions. This correlation tends to increase confidence in the reliability of the student judgments.

Members of the survey staff attended chapel services in almost all the institutions visited. The exercises observed could generally be classified as helpful and appropriate, but a number of adverse criticisms may also be made. Some extraneous and questionable features were included in most of the services observed. Many announcements and other details of a routine nature were observed. Such matters can better be handled through other channels, as bulletin boards, etc., and not be allowed to infringe upon time which should be given to activities which have educa-

TABLE 115

FACULTY REACTIONS TO CHAPEL SERVICES IN
NINE COLLEGES

COLLEGE NUMBER	PERCENTAGE OF THOSE RESPONDING WHO INDICATED EACH TYPE OF REACTION		
	Favorable	Unfavorable	Noncommittal
9...........	82	7	11
2...........	81	4	15
3...........	80	20	....
11...........	69	28	3
5...........	68	13	19
6...........	65	19	16
1...........	51	....	49
4...........	47	10	43
7...........	46	36	18

tional value and which are means for the cultivation of the moral and religious atmosphere of the institution.

The subconscious effect of the architectural features of the chapel is perhaps one of the most important factors contributing to the influence of the service.

THE LOCAL CHURCH

One of the agencies possessing a considerable amount of potential influence on the religious life of students is the local church. Attendance at the church services of one's own denomination is warmly encouraged in most of the colleges, and in a few institutions this is made a definite requirement for all students. In a majority of cases the local Methodist churches make special provisions for the care of college students; and there exists a general air of co-operation between the school and the pastors which is pleasant and helpful.

In a few of the colleges a special inquiry was conducted among the students in order to obtain their reaction to the program of the local church. The problem was raised in the following manner: "Give your estimate of the attractiveness of the program of the local church to young people of college age (name the local church to which you refer.)" Table 116 presents a tabulation of the replies of the Methodist students to this question, showing the percentages which were favorable, unfavorable, and noncommittal.

This table shows a fairly wide range in the percentage of students expressing a favorable opinion of the local church services in these seven colleges. The range in percentages of unfavorable opinion is considerably less, and with the exception of college No. 6, runs about the same in all of

TABLE   116

REACTIONS OF METHODIST STUDENTS TO LOCAL
CHURCH SERVICES IN SEVEN COLLEGES

College Number	Percentage Favorable	Percentage Unfavorable	Percentage Noncommittal
5.............	73	12	15
4.............	70	17	13
7.............	69	12	19
6.............	63	27	10
3.............	62	16	22
1.............	61	16	23
2.............	46	15	39

the institutions. In every case the percentage of students expressing a favorable opinion is more than twice as great as the percentage expressing an unfavorable opinion.

In three of the colleges the students were asked on a special inquiry form to express their judgments on four specific features of the local church program: the sermons, the music, the organizations for young people, and the personality of the pastor, classifying each as excellent, average, or poor. The reactions of the Methodist students in these three colleges are presented in Table 117.

It will be observed from this table that in almost every case the majority of the students classify each feature of the local church program as "average." In every case but two the proportion reacting to each feature as "excellent" is more than double the proportion classifying it as "poor."

The qualifications necessary for successful service in the pastorate of a college church are high. Not only must the minister satisfy the regular members of the congregation, but he must also be sympathetic with youth and its problems, be able to bring messages of vital import to young people of college age, and command the intellectual respect of faculty members. Although it is evident that in most cases the pastorates in the college towns are ably filled, in some cases the programs of the local church evidently fail to appeal to students. It is suggested that this is a matter which can well be given special attention by the church as a whole. The pastorates in college towns should be filled by especially capable ministers. This is particularly important if the town be small.

TABLE 117

PERCENTAGES OF METHODIST STUDENTS GIVING EACH REACTION TO
VARIOUS FEATURES OF THE LOCAL CHURCH SERVICES
IN THREE COLLEGES

COLLEGE NUMBER	SERMONS			MUSIC			ORGANIZATIONS FOR YOUNG PEOPLE			PERSONALITY OF PASTOR		
	Excellent	Average	Poor	Excellent	Average	Poor	Excellent	Average	Poor	Excellent	Average	Poor
9.......	41	57	2	30	65	5	35	57	8	63	29	8
10.......	25	69	6	40	57	3	38	53	9	33	55	12
11.......	17	58	25	25	67	8	16	56	28	35	51	14

RELIGIOUS INFLUENCE OF THE FACULTY AND
ADMINISTRATIVE STAFF

In all of the colleges studied, inquiry was made regarding the religious and moral influence of the faculty and administrative staff. The data obtained upon this point do not lend themselves to statistical treatment. It was evident, however, in every one of the colleges that specific attention is being given to the development of a satisfactory religious and moral influence on the part of the faculty and administrative staff. In only two or three of the colleges was there found anything of a negative influence, and these were local and temporary conditions that were being taken care of effectively and vigorously. Without going into details on this point, it may be categorically stated that in all the colleges there is an earnest endeavor to cultivate a satisfactory religious influence by the faculty and administration. This point is usually given considerable attention in the selection of faculty members. Wisely enough the great majority of the colleges have some faculty members who are not members of the Methodist Episcopal Church. As a rule all faculty members take an active part in the work of the local church of their choice.

CHAPTER XLIV

CURRICULUM OFFERINGS IN BIBLE AND RELIGION

All of the colleges in this group offer courses in various phases of the subjects of Bible and religion. In most of the institutions the work is concentrated in one department, although in one college there are four distinct departments dealing with this field of study. In some colleges the work in this field is combined with another subject to form a single department, the most frequent combination being with philosophy. As has been pointed out previously, a few of the colleges have introduced the divisional plan of organization. Where this has been done, the work in Bible and religion has either been set up as a separate division or has been combined with the social sciences.

Table 118 presents data for thirty-five colleges regarding the number of courses and semester hours of credit offered in the field of Bible and religion, together with the student-credit-hour load which is carried in this field.

In tabulating the course offerings, everything which related to the field of Bible and religion was so considered, whether given in this department or in some related department. For example, a course in philosophy of religion is sometimes given in the department of philosophy, a course in psychology of religion is sometimes given in the department of psychology, a course in the history of religion is sometimes given in the department of history, etc. These were all tabulated as being in the one field of Bible and religion.

It will be noted from Table 118 that there is a rather wide range in the number of courses offered in the field of Bible and religion in this group of thirty-five colleges. One institution offers forty courses, while another offers only five. There are only three colleges which offer more than twenty courses, and only six which offer fewer than ten courses. The typical institution, as indicated by the median, offers thirteen courses in this field. The medians for the colleges on the approved list of the Association of American Universities and for the colleges not on this list are identical. Considering the fact that the former group has a larger average enrolment, the data indicate a somewhat more conservative offering in this field in the colleges holding national accreditation than in those which are not so accredited. There is a close relationship between the number of

417

TABLE 118

COURSES OFFERED AND STUDENT-CREDIT-HOURS CARRIED IN BIBLE, RELIGION, RELIGIOUS EDUCATION, AND PHILOSOPHY OF RELIGION AT THIRTY-FIVE COLLEGES

INSTITUTION	Year	Total Enrolment	Number of Courses Offered in Bible and Religion	Semester Hours Offered in Bible and Religion	Percentage Semester Hours Offered in Bible and Religion Are of Total Semester Hours Offered	Percentage Student-Credit-Hours in Bible and Religion Are of Total Student-Credit-Hours Carried
Brothers................	1930–31	64	5	12	4.8	11.7
*Hamline................	1929–30	435	14	45	4.8	10.7
*Simpson................	1929–30	621	12	28	3.5	8.0
*Mount Union..........	1930–31	528	13	37	4.6	7.4
West Virginia Wesleyan..	1930–31	354	11	44	6.0	7.0
Kansas Wesleyan	1930–31	267	10	21	3.2	6.9
*Chattanooga...........	1929–30	437	14	37	5.6	6.8
Union.................	1929–30	204	10	31	8.4	6.7
Dakota Wesleyan	1929–30	347	10	30	4.6	6.5
Iowa Wesleyan	1929–30	303	17	23	3.6	6.3
Oklahoma City........	1929–30	839	17	49	4.9	5.9
*Illinois Wesleyan.......	1930–31	668	19	44	4.7	5.7
Southwestern..........	1930–31	536	17	46	5.7	5.5
Ozark Wesleyan........	1929–30	199	16	32	5.0	4.8
*Ohio Wesleyan.........	1930–31	1,821	40	145	8.9	4.7
Gooding...............	1930–31	114	6	12	2.9	4.5
*Allegheny.............	1929–30	641	9	27	3.2	4.3
*Baker.................	1930–31	422	12	36	4.1	4.0
*Willamette.............	1931–32	557	8	26	3.6	3.9
*Albion................	1929–30	752	11	27	2.8	3.6
McKendree............	1930–31	261	8	16	2.8	3.6
Central Wesleyan.......	1929–30	135	15	52	10.9	3.6
Baldwin-Wallace.......	1930–31	455	21	58	7.5	3.4
Evansville.............	1929–30	324	13	35	3.7	3.2
*Lawrence..............	1929–30	782	14	33	3.0	3.0
*Pacific................	1930–31	673	21	56	4.2	2.9
Ohio Northern.........	1930–31	799	14	26	3.0	2.9
*Dickinson.............	1929–30	570	13	42	7.0	2.9
*MacMurray............	1930–31	425	10	33	5.1	2.9
*DePauw...............	1930–31	1,442	19	105	7.9	2.8
Puget Sound...........	1930–31	658	19	44	4.7	2.8
Nebraska Wesleyan.....	1930–31	573	9	21	2.2	2.8
*Cornell................	1929–30	546	12	33	4.1	2.6
Intermountain.........	1930–31	162	15	32	5.9	2.0
*Morningside...........	1929–30	599	19	51	6.1	1.8
Median, all colleges..	....	....	13	33	4.7	4.0
*Median, A.A.U. colleges............	....	....	13	37	4.6	3.9
Median, non-A.A.U. colleges.........	....	....	13	32	4.8	4.6

* Institutions on the approved list of the Association of American Universities.

courses offered and the number of students enrolled, the coefficient of correlation (Pearson) between these two factors being $+.85\pm.03$. This indicates a marked tendency for the colleges to adjust the number of courses offered in Bible and religion to the size of the student body.

As a measure of instructional quantity, the "course" is not a constant unit. In one of the colleges (DePauw) the courses in the field of Bible and religion are typically year-courses, carrying ten semester hours of credit. In many of the colleges the typical course carries only two semester hours of credit, and there are listed numerous courses carrying only one semester hour of credit. For that reason the offerings have been expressed in Table 118, not only in terms of the number of courses, but also in terms of the number of semester hours of credit. In colleges which are organized on the term or quarter basis the offerings have been reduced to the equivalent in semester hours.

It will be noted from Table 118 that the offerings range from 12 semester hours in two colleges up to 145 in another. There are only two institutions offering more than 60 hours in this field, and six colleges offer less than 24 hours, the amount usually set as a minimum for an academic major. Thirteen of the colleges offer in excess of 36 semester hours, the amount usually set as the maximum for a major sequence. In a well-arranged program of undergraduate instruction in the field of Bible and religion it would seem unnecessary to offer more than the amount of work needed for a major, with some little elective work, the total amounting perhaps to 36 hours.[1] A more extensive program at the undergraduate level may be condemned both on the grounds of the lack of economy imposed upon the curricular organization and also upon the grounds of the undesirable degree of specialization which is afforded students before they are ready for it. This point, as it applies to the curriculum in general, has been discussed in chapter xx.

A few of the colleges are attempting to offer graduate work in the field of Bible and religion, and the extended offerings in these institutions are partially due to this fact. The wisdom of offering graduate work in this field is open to question. Clearly, the colleges should not be attempting to offer a program of theological training in preparation for the ministry, for that is the function of the theological seminaries. None of the standard seminaries of the Methodist Episcopal Church will allow excess credit in the field of Bible and religion to be transferred from a college in such a

[1] For a further discussion of this topic see W. C. Bower, "The Teaching of Religion," in *Religion in Higher Education*, ed. M. C. Towner (Chicago: University of Chicago Press, 1931), pp. 161–74.

way as to shorten the length of the seminary course. The vocational outlets for those with a Master's degree in the field of Bible and religion are at present very limited, if the ministry be excluded. In many subjects the development of graduate work is justified by the demands for increased training on the part of high-school teachers, but this point does not hold in the field of Bible and religion. In view of all these facts, it would appear desirable for the colleges, particularly those with limited funds, to proceed very cautiously with the development of graduate work in Bible and religion.

There is manifestly a close relationship between the size of the institution and the number of semester hours of credit offered in the field of Bible and religion. The coefficient of correlation (Pearson) between these two factors is $+.80 \pm .04$.

Table 118 also gives the percentage which the offerings in Bible and religion are of the total offerings of each college. These data indicate the relative weight given the subject in comparison with all the other subjects offered in each college. It will be noted that the [offerings in Bible and religion at one college comprise 10.9 per cent of the total offerings, while in another institution the proportion is only one-fifth of this amount, or 2.2 per cent of the total. The typical situation, as revealed by the median, is for 4.7 per cent of the total offerings to be in the field of Bible and religion. On this point there is little difference between the medians of the colleges on the approved list of the Association of American Universities and the colleges which do not hold this type of accreditation. In some of the colleges having a relatively low percentage of their total course offerings in the field of Bible and religion, the condition is caused not so much by a paucity of offerings in this particular field but rather by an overexpansion in other subjects, thus decreasing the relative size of the offerings, although they are in absolute terms ample for the needs of the institution. Unless there are some unusual circumstances, it would not seem necessary to have more than 5 per cent of the total course offerings in the field of Bible and religion.

Table 118 also presents data relating to the percentage which the student-credit-hours carried in the field of Bible and religion are of the total student-credit-hour load in each college. As will be observed from the table, this is quite a different matter from the course offerings in this field. The coefficient of correlation (Pearson) between the percentage which the semester-hour offerings in Bible and religion are of total offerings and the percentage of the total student-credit-hour load carried in this field is $-.01$, indicating almost no relationship between these two factors.

The percentage of the total student-credit-hour load which is carried in the field of Bible and religion is an index of the "popularity" of this department with students, or of the amount of contact between the student body and the course work in this subject. There is a wide variation on this point among the thirty-five colleges. Two have more than 10 per cent of the student-credit-hour load in the field of Bible and religion, while two others have 2 per cent or less in this field. The typical situation, as revealed by the median, is for 4 per cent of the total student-credit-hour load to be in this field. It will be noted that, on the basis of relative offerings, the course work in Bible and religion is less popular with students on the average than is work in other departments; 4.7 per cent of the total course offerings are, on the average, in this field, but only 4.0 per cent of the work taken by students is in this subject. There is some tendency for the colleges which are not on the approved list of the Association of American Universities to have a larger percentage of their student-credit-hour loads in this field than is the case with the colleges holding national accreditation; the difference, however, is not large and is probably not statistically significant.

To some extent the course elections in a field such as Bible and religion afford an index of student judgments regarding the type of instruction offered. In a church-sponsored college the teachers in Bible and religion should be at least as capable as any others in the institution. These instructors should not only be thorough scholars in their subject, able to present the material upon a high academic plane, but they should also be sympathetic with youth and its problems, particularly as these relate to the vital issues in religion. The fact that the church colleges have almost a monopoly of the instruction at the undergraduate level in these fields should mean that greater, rather than less, attention should be paid to the capabilities of those who instruct in these subjects. While the quality of instruction is not the only factor affecting the variations in the popularity of Bible and religion in these colleges, an institution in which the subject is distinctly unpopular with students would do well to see if improvement can be made in the teaching personnel.

One important condition affecting the student-credit-hour loads in this field is the amount of credit in Bible and religion required for graduation. As was pointed out in chapter xxi, all but one of the colleges require for graduation some credit in this or a related field. In a few cases it is possible to meet the requirement by courses in philosophy or ethics, without taking courses which would be specifically counted as Bible and religion. Unless the absence of the requirement is counterbalanced by an unusually popular teacher or an attractive arrangement of subject matter, colleges which do not specifically require credit in Bible and religion for graduation tend to have a relatively small percentage of their student-credit-hour loads in this field.

A second condition affecting the student-credit-hour load in this field is the placement in the curriculum of the required work in Bible and religion. In some colleges the required course is placed in the freshman or sophomore years; in others, the requirement is divided, some of it being placed in the first two years and the remainder at the senior college level; in still other colleges the requirement is not specifically placed, and thus tends to be postponed until the junior or senior years, particularly by students who are not certain that they are going to complete a four-year course. These variations in the requirement of courses in Bible and religion for graduation make impossible any absolute conclusion regarding the popularity of work in this field with students. The data of this table should afford important material for study by those colleges in which the student-credit-hour load in Bible and religion is relatively low.

Some attention may well be given to the question of whether or not there is justification for a required course in Bible and religion as a condition of graduation from the college. Involved in this problem is, of course, the more fundamental question of whether there should be any required courses whatsoever in any subject. Ideally, it would perhaps be desirable to depend upon the intrinsic appeal of the subject matter and the attractiveness of the teaching to draw interested students irrespective of formal requirements. Some question may be raised regarding the attitude with which students view the taking of a required course. But it is only fair to point out that the satisfactory covering of certain areas of human knowledge is practically a universal graduation requirement of all American colleges. It may well be argued that a required course in Bible or religion is equally as justifiable as a required course in English composition or any other subject, if the philosophy of the college considers certain specific attainments in this field on the part of students as basic to its mission and purpose. From this point of view it would seem desirable, almost necessary, for a denominational college, with the professed aim of cultivating in a distinctive manner the religious and moral life of its students, and with a constituency which supports it especially for this purpose, to make some curriculum requirements of all students in the field of Bible and religion.

It may, of course, be questioned whether it is possible to inculcate desirable attitudes and develop constructive character through the medium of academic instruction. This assumption is so basic, however, to the whole American idea of education, from the primary grades upward through almost every subject of collegiate study, that it seems out of place to doubt its application in the field of religion, at least until there has been a considerable amount of basic research indicating the contrary. A more pertinent question may be raised as to whether the courses in Bible and religion are so organized and taught as to yield the most effective results in the lives of students. This is a matter into which the present study has not inquired, just as it has not dealt with the extent to which other specific academic subjects, such as English composition, foreign languages, political science, etc., are achieving their respective objectives.

If the justifiability of a graduation requirement in Bible and religion is granted, there immediately arises the problem of the placement of this requirement in the curriculum. Shall it be a freshman requirement, shall it be distributed between the junior college and senior college levels, or shall students be free to elect it whenever they wish? The last policy is pursued in several colleges, and is justified on the grounds that there are numbers of students who take only one or two years of work before transferring to some other institution. Students who transfer to state universities or teachers colleges frequently find that they are not allowed credit for the work done in Bible and religion. It is thus argued that to force all students to take such a course, even though they are not intending to graduate from the college, works a hardship on the transfer students. This argument does not appear to have any great validity in the majority of the colleges, since the students who transfer to institutions which will not accept transfer credits in Bible and religion are relatively few. Furthermore, it may be pointed out that the college curriculum should be so organized as to meet the needs of students who intend to take four years of work, without allowing this program to be distorted in order to meet the requirements of those who intend to transfer out after one or two years.

The placing of the required course in Bible at the freshman level has the great advantage of bringing all students into contact with this important field of study. On the average, from one-third to one-half of the students who enter as freshmen do not take any further work. If the program of the first year does not include a course in Bible and religion, this large block of college students is turned out without any contact with instruction in this field. From this point of view it seems desirable to include at least one course in Bible and religion in the required work of the freshman year.

A few of the colleges have distributed the total requirements in Bible and religion so that, in addition to the course at the freshman level, there is an advanced course required at the senior college level. Such an arrangement has the advantage of reaching the students who remain in college for only two years, introducing them early in their curriculum to the field of religious study. At the same time the requirement of one course in Bible and religion in the upper two years reaches students after they have had a considerable amount of college work and have become somewhat mature in their thinking. The second course may well serve the purpose of reintegrating their philosophy of life and of reconciling conflicts which have arisen between their earlier religious concepts and the studies they have pursued in college. On the whole, this plan of a divided requirement seems to be the most effective method of arranging for desirable curricular contacts between students and the course work in Bible and religion.

CHAPTER XLV

RELIGIOUS LIFE OF STUDENTS

FACTORS INDICATED BY STUDENTS AS AFFECTING
THEIR RELIGIOUS LIFE

In ten of the colleges a special inquiry was conducted among the students, relating to the factors affecting their religious and moral life. The inquiry was phrased as follows:

In the following list check the factors, if any, which have definitely influenced
for the better your religious and moral life:

—— a) Religious organizations of students

—— b) Members of the faculty and administrative staff

—— c) Chapel services

—— d) Church attended while in this school

—— e) Courses taken in Bible and religion

——f) List any others:

Tables 119 and 120 present a tabulation of the replies in these ten colleges. The first table summarizes the responses of the Methodist students, while the second deals with those of the non-Methodist students.

A comparison of the medians of these two tables shows that in the case of each item the percentage indicating a satisfactory influence was larger for the Methodist students than for the non-Methodist. The order of importance of the five factors mentioned, as indicated by the median percentage of students checking each, is the same for both groups of students. The most important source of influence, as indicated by the median frequency with which it was checked, is the chapel service. Second in importance comes the faculty and administrative staff, while the church attended during college days is a close third (actually tied in the case of the Methodist students). The courses taken in Bible and religion are fourth in importance, and the factor checked by the smallest proportion on the average is religious organizations of students.

It will be noted that there is a marked variation in the percentage of students checking each of the factors at the several institutions. In three colleges approximately two-thirds of the Methodist students report a favorable influence from the chapel services, while in two other colleges less than one-sixth of the students are favorably influenced by the chapel services. Similar variations may be observed in almost all the factors, and

TABLE 119

FACTORS WHICH THE METHODIST STUDENTS OF TEN COLLEGES
SAY HAVE INFLUENCED FOR THE BETTER THEIR
MORAL AND RELIGIOUS LIFE

COLLEGE NUMBER	NUMBER OF METHODIST STUDENTS REPORTING	PERCENTAGE OF METHODIST STUDENTS REPORTING WHO CHECKED EACH FACTOR AS HAVING INFLUENCED FOR THE BETTER THEIR MORAL AND RELIGIOUS LIFE					
		Religious Organizations of Students	Members of the Faculty and Administrative Staff	Chapel Services	Church Attended While in College	Courses Taken in Bible and Religion	Miscellaneous
1.............	195	23	57	67	28	66	14
2.............	94	19	25	64	46	22	4
3.............	44	34	57	66	64	64	5
4.............	222	40	37	45	42	14	18
5.............	427	34	32	35	40	26	6
6.............	162	38	40	51	44	37	9
7.............	334	19	35	23	37	13	14
9.............	74	24	51	39	28	20	12
10.............	228	10	36	10	25	33	28
11.............	166	22	44	16	19	34	7
Median.....	180.5	23.5	38.5	42.0	38.5	29.5	10.5

TABLE 120

FACTORS WHICH THE NON-METHODIST STUDENTS OF TEN COLLEGES
SAY HAVE INFLUENCED FOR THE BETTER THEIR
MORAL AND RELIGIOUS LIFE

COLLEGE NUMBER	NUMBER OF NON-METHODIST STUDENTS REPORTING	PERCENTAGE OF NON-METHODIST STUDENTS REPORTING WHO CHECKED EACH FACTOR AS HAVING INFLUENCED FOR THE BETTER THEIR MORAL AND RELIGIOUS LIFE					
		Religious Organizations of Students	Members of the Faculty and Administrative Staff	Chapel Services	Church Attended While in College	Courses Taken in Bible and Religion	Miscellaneous
1.............	88	22	39	58	21	59	9
2.............	170	15	14	50	39	23	5
3.............	55	29	49	71	56	51	7
4.............	128	20	20	34	39	15	11
5.............	98	25	29	33	32	20	5
6.............	63	22	29	51	38	32	12
7.............	114	14	26	26	22	14	18
9.............	103	10	36	37	18	12	12
10.............	216	4	34	6	19	22	26
11.............	269	11	27	12	23	19	7
Median.....	108.5	17.5	29.0	35.5	27.5	21.0	10.0

among both the Methodist and the non-Methodist students. An inquiry of this type should be of value to a college in studying its own problems and in diagnosing the points at which it is failing to exert a satisfactory religious and moral influence.

ALUMNI ENTERING RELIGIOUS SERVICE

One of the measures which is usually considered important by a denomination in estimating the influence of its educational institutions is the number of the alumni who have chosen some phase of religious service as their life-work. Data on this point were available in twenty-seven of the colleges studied, and are presented in Table 121. In this study only the alumni of the last three decades are considered. The data are presented separately for each of the three ten-year periods.

This table presents the data in terms of both the number and the percentage of the graduates entering religious service as a life-work. It will be observed that the percentage of graduates going into religious service has shown a steady decrease over the three decades studied. This decrease is only relative, however, because the actual numbers are larger in the last of the three periods than in either of the two preceding ones. Remembering that there has been a steady increase in college enrolments over the period studied, it is apparent that the colleges, in general, have not been failing to provide the necessary religious leadership for the denomination. The opening up of new vocational outlets for college graduates has lessened the relative importance of religious service among the group of alumni, but even in the face of this fact a larger number of the graduates than ever before have gone into religious work during the decade just passed.

Comparison may be made between the colleges on the approved list of the Association of American Universities and those not holding this accreditation. It will be observed that the colleges on the approved list of the Association of American Universities have a considerably smaller percentage of their alumni in religious service than is the case with the colleges not holding national accreditation, as indicated by the medians for these two groups. On the other hand, the colleges holding national accreditation have a median number of alumni in religious work almost double the median of the colleges which are not on the approved list of the Association of American Universities. In other words, training for religious service holds a much larger relative place in the colleges which do not have national accreditation; but the great majority of the college alumni who have gone into religious work during the past thirty years have come from those colleges which are now on the approved list of the Association of American Universities.

TABLE 121

NUMBER AND PERCENTAGE OF ALUMNI OF TWENTY-SEVEN
COLLEGES ENTERING RELIGIOUS SERVICE

INSTITUTION	GRADUATES OF							
	1900–1909		1910–19		1920–29		Entire Group	
	Number	Percentage	Number	Percentage	Number	Percentage	Number	Percentage
Baldwin-Wallace†	51	31.5	65	23.1	61	10.8	177	17.6
Central Wesleyan	29	18.8	44	17.1	49	16.4	122	17.2
McKendree†	24	19.2	27	21.6	30	13.5	81	17.1
*Dickinson	100	19.3	77	13.3	102	12.0	279	14.3
Puget Sound†	13	27.7	32	27.1	35	8.5	80	13.9
*Ohio Wesleyan†	172	13.9	287	15.6	247	10.9	706	13.2
*Morningside	42	24.0	42	9.3	70	10.7	154	12.0
Nebraska Wesleyan†	35	14.5	71	12.4	93	11.1	199	12.0
Iowa Wesleyan	35	17.8	37	13.7	30	7.7	102	12.0
Dakota Wesleyan	13	12.8	23	11.8	36	10.4	72	11.8
Intermountain†	‡	‡	4	44.4	17	10.1	21‖	11.8‖
*Baker†	65	15.9	69	12.0	74	8.9	208	11.4
Kansas Wesleyan†	17	19.3	26	13.6	26	6.5	69	10.8
*Simpson	44	16.3	38	9.8	67	9.1	149	10.7
Southwestern†	26	24.3	58	16.7	63	5.8	147	9.6
West Virginia Wesleyan†	7	33.3	25	11.2	43	8.0	75	9.6
*Albion	47	9.3	58	9.5	70	8.3	175	8.9
*Mount Union†	27	16.8	37	11.2	39	5.6	103	8.7
*Illinois Wesleyan†	43	9.4	31	5.4	64	7.3	138	7.2
*DePauw†	76	12.3	111	9.3	115	4.8	302	7.2
Oklahoma City	3	3.0	16	19.8	34	6.0	53	7.1
*Allegheny	55	13.7	49	6.7	41	4.0	145	6.8
*Hamline	39	12.5	26	5.5	30	4.8	95	6.8
*Cornell	44	7.3	35	5.1	62	6.2	141	6.2
*Pacific†	14	8.8	18	6.9	35	5.1	67	6.0
Gooding‡	§	§	§	§	6	5.2	6‖	5.2‖
*MacMurray†	2	0.8	4	1.4	23	6.1	29	3.1
Median, all colleges	35	15.9	37	11.9	43	8.0	122	10.7
*Median, A.A.U. colleges	44	13.6	38	9.3	64	7.3	145	8.7
Median, non-A.A.U. colleges	24	19.2	27	16.7	36	8.3	81	11.9

* Institutions on the approved list of the Association of American Universities.
† Data are for the decades 1901–10, 1911–20, and 1921–30, respectively.
‡ Data not available.
§ The college did not begin operations until 1917.
‖ Based on years for which data are shown.

Considerable interest attaches to the data for the individual institutions, but space forbids any elaborate treatment of this topic. In general, the colleges follow rather closely the same general pattern as is shown by the medians. There are only two colleges, with a history covering the entire thirty-year period, which show a larger percentage of graduates entering religious service in the last decade than in the first. At the same time the actual number of alumni going into religious work in every college, with three exceptions, is larger during the most recent decade than in the decade 1900–1909. The percentages shown in this table vary considerably among the different schools. Many factors are responsible for this variation, among which may be mentioned the percentage of women students, proximity to a theological seminary, and the general traditions among the student body.

PART V
COLLEGE FINANCE

CHAPTER XLVI

BUSINESS MANAGEMENT

Efficiency in the management of business affairs is a basic necessity to the effective college. While some old and well-established institutions with relatively large resources have been able to continue a rather satisfactory existence without a well-managed business office, the younger and weaker colleges find that capable business management is one of the prime essentials of existence. The ever increasing cost of education has made it necessary to see that every dollar of the resources of an institution does its full duty in providing instructional facilities. The sharpened competition, both for students and for supporting funds, has led to a realization of the need for more effective business management than formerly obtained.

The growth of colleges in enrolments and in resources has further increased the importance and the complexity of the business management. Most of the colleges included in this study are among the largest "business" concerns in their respective communities, as indicated by total assets, total operating budget, and total employed personnel. In this study it is necessary, therefore, to examine with some care such matters as the organization for business management, the business policies which are in effect, the financial accounting, the budgetary procedure, the financial reporting, and the provisions for official audits of the financial accounts.

ORGANIZATION FOR BUSINESS MANAGEMENT

One of the important problems of the organization for business management in colleges relates to the manner in which the control descends from the board to the officer or officers charged with responsibility for the actual conduct of the business affairs. This matter was discussed in chapter x, in which the business management was viewed as a single unit of the entire administrative organization of the college. The existence of two types of organization was there pointed out, the unit type in which the president is held responsible by the board for the administration of all phases of the institution, and the multiple type in which one or more officers other than the president (usually the business officer) are responsible directly to the board for the administration of certain phases of the institution. Without repeating the advantages and disadvantages of each

433

type of control, it may be stated that, in general, the unified administrative system seems to be working more smoothly and effectively.

Under the unified plan of control it is to be expected that the president will delegate authority in business affairs to the chief financial officer, who should be given large responsibility for the conduct of the business arrangements of the college. The principal check on his authority takes place when educational as well as financial policies are involved in a single matter. In most cases in this group of colleges the business managers feel that they are in practice subordinate to the president, even though nominally co-ordinate. Most of the business managers working under the multiple type of organization confer and consult with the president on almost all matters involving a decision of any importance. Rarely do boards of trustees receive recommendations from business officers that have not previously had the approval of the respective presidents. From the standpoint both of harmony and effectiveness it is wise for the business officer to adapt himself to the program and policies of the president, even though the two officials may nominally be co-ordinate and independently responsible to the board. In only two or three of the colleges of this group is there any real question as to the ultimate responsibility of the president as the chief executive officer of all phases of the institution.

Besides this problem of the relation of the business office to the board and the president, there is the question of the centralization of the business function. Shall the business affairs be placed completely in charge of one responsible officer who shall be allowed to delegate responsibility as he sees fit, or shall these duties be scattered among a number of individuals each of whom is independently responsible to the president or board for the performance of his particular part of the business management? Practice in this group of colleges distinctly favors the former plan, there being only three or four institutions that follow the decentralized plan. It seems clear that centralization of the business function results in improved efficiency. In the average college the job is not larger than can be handled by a competent person, if suitable office help is provided. Through centralization of all business functions in the one office overlapping of duties can be eliminated, efficiency can be increased through specialization of duties, and, most important of all, the business affairs of the college can be viewed as an integrated whole rather than as a series of unrelated problems.

A third problem concerning the business organization relates to the personnel requirements of the office. It has already been shown that there is no agreement with regard to the title assigned the chief business officer.

A few of the titles commonly found are: business manager, treasurer, comptroller, business secretary, auditor, bursar, and financial secretary. The title "business manager" seems to describe most accurately the nature of this office and the functions performed. The duties of the business manager have been outlined in chapter x, in connection with the discussion of the general administrative organization of the college.

The responsibilities of the position are such as to demand unusual qualifications in the chief business officer. First of all, he must be a man of unquestioned integrity and sterling character. Since his institutional contacts are almost wholly with people of a rather high educational level, it is desirable that he be a college graduate. He must, furthermore, maintain a considerable number of contacts with outsiders—business people, salesmen, etc.—who will obtain their principal impressions of the college from him. For this reason he must have the ability to meet people well. He must be trained and experienced in purchasing. If not a qualified accountant himself, he must at least be able to direct a subordinate who will do the accounting; and he must have at a very minimum enough knowledge of accounting to interpret the usual financial reports, balance sheets, operating statements, etc. He must be a man of even temperament, able to smile in the face of abuse, and possessed of the ability to soothe the ruffled feelings of faculty members and others who are usually especially "touchy" on matters of finance. He must be a man of keen insight, firm but not dogmatic in his convictions, and broad-minded enough to alter his opinion when convinced. Finally, although the test of his effectiveness is found in the efficiency of the business office, he must be big enough to see that the college is not run for business purposes, but to educate students. He must see that his major function is to make it easy for those other officers and faculty members whose responsibility it is to give the students the best education possible within the limits of the resources the institution has at its command.

In several of the colleges the business officer is a regular member of the faculty, usually teaching one or two classes in subjects related to economics. This is an excellent plan where the business officer is suitably qualified, since it gives him desirable contacts with students and also brings to him the faculty point of view on college affairs.

The amount of assistance needed in the office of the business manager is influenced by several factors. The degree of responsibility assumed in this office for the management of endowment, the plan for the collection of pledges, the extent to which the institution engages in supplementary business activities (dormitories, dining-halls, etc.), and the amount of attention necessary for the supervision of the physical plant—these are all items which affect the burden of the business office. In a college of five hundred students with the endowment managed by a corporate trustee the business office should have one capable assistant besides the business manager. This assistant should be qualified to do the bulk of the accounting and should also be able to handle most of the stenographic work. In larger institutions, and with the addition of other responsibilities, the office staff will need to be somewhat larger.

BUSINESS POLICIES

It will be recognized that many of the commonly accepted principles of business practice are applicable to college business affairs. At the same time there are a number of conditions peculiar to the business management of an institution of higher learning. On the whole, the business affairs of this group of colleges are being skilfully and effectively managed. Detailed criticisms covering these matters have been made in a confidential report to each college. The present study discusses the points on which a considerable number of the institutions have opportunity to improve their business practices.

PURCHASING

There are three important considerations connected with the purchasing function. The first relates to the question of whether or not all purchasing shall be centralized in one officer, the alternative being a diffusion of the responsibility among several officials. The second question relates to the effectiveness of the purchasing, as revealed by the prices paid for supplies. The third has to do with the routine of purchasing, involving the system of purchase orders and requisitions.

It seems clear that purchasing should be regarded as a part of the business function. A capable business manager can usually obtain much better prices when he is given charge of all the purchasing than when a number of different officers are given this responsibility. Furthermore, unless there is a centralization of the purchasing, there is difficulty in controlling commitments, and the institution may find itself embarrassed in facing obligations for purchases which the financial officers did not know had been made, and which may exceed appropriations for the departments concerned.

It is true that some degree of specialization is advisable in purchasing various items. For example, the librarian may be better acquainted than the business manager with prices and sources for the purchase of library books. Under certain conditions it may be desirable to delegate authority to the head of the dining-hall to purchase such items as fresh vegetables and the smaller items of supplies. Canned goods, meats, and potatoes, constituting the major part of the food supply, may well be purchased by co-operation between the business office and the head of the dining-hall. It should always be possible for the business manager to have any experts on the college staff suggest the most satisfactory sources for buying materials and supplies. This arrangement does not preclude the possibility of an effective centralization of purchasing in the business office. In any event, the formal placing of all purchase orders should be routed through the business office.[1]

One of the important tests of the effectiveness of the purchasing service is the price paid for the supplies used by the institution. Judged by this standard there is opportunity for improvement in almost every one of the colleges studied. A considerable number of the business officers have no training in purchasing procedures and, hence, are unfamiliar with sources and prices. There is unquestionably an opportunity for the saving of hundreds of dollars in most of these colleges and possibly thousands of dollars in several of them through more effective purchasing. Specific assistance on this matter was given each of the colleges during the survey visit.

There is an opportunity for saving large sums of money in this group of colleges through co-operative purchasing. As matters now stand, these institutions, purchasing in relatively small quantities, compete with one another in the market and thus tend to pay higher prices than necessary. If an arrangement could be worked out whereby the purchases of these colleges could be pooled, it should be possible to obtain much better prices through the improved bargaining power of large-quantity buying.

For example, book dealers obtain much better prices from publishers than do colleges and universities. It is entirely possible that a plan for the co-operative purchase of library books might save the colleges in this group enough to enable them to obtain 20 or 25 per cent more books with their limited library appropriations. Marked savings are also possible in the purchase of athletic goods. A majority of the colleges in this group obtain the regular college discounts on athletic supplies. In many lines a margin of 40 per cent is left for the large jobber or state distributor. It is possible that through pooling the purchase of athletic supplies jobbers' prices could be obtained for the colleges, thus enabling them to save, on the average, 30 to 40 per cent of their annual expenditures for such pur-

---

[1] For a discussion of the advantages of centralization in purchasing, see Lloyd Morey, *University and College Accounting* (New York: John Wiley & Sons, 1930), pp. 69–70.

chases. Probably the largest potential savings are in the purchase of insurance. This subject has already been discussed in chapter xi. This same principle is equally applicable to a number of other lines. A group of colleges through co-operative purchasing should not only be able to save an amount equal to the selling costs of distributors but in many lines should be able to obtain distributor's prices.

A factor which militates against the most effective purchasing by individual colleges is the fact that frequently a trustee or local business man, inspired by self-interest, exerts considerable influence on the individual responsible for making purchases. The potency of this factor would be materially reduced if the prices obtainable by the colleges were even lower than those paid by local dealers.

It is recognized that the establishment of an organization of centralized purchasing would entail some additional "overhead"; but the opportunities for saving by this method of purchasing are so large as to make such expense a relatively negligible item. In fact, the saving in any one of many types of purchases would be more than enough to carry the entire overhead cost of the purchasing service. Furthermore, it might be possible to arrange for this centralized purchasing through some existing organization, such as the Board of Education, thus avoiding a large part of the additional administrative cost involved in the establishment of a separate central office for the co-operative buying.

One of the agencies developed for the assistance of college purchasing agents is the Educational Buyers Association. The members of this organization are entitled to special discounts in the purchase of a large number of items of educational equipment. The Association has a journal, the *Educational Buyer*, which is published from 6308 Cottage Grove Avenue, Chicago. This magazine is of considerable value to business officers who wish to keep in touch with sources and prices for the kinds of materials they must purchase. The institutions which are not members of the Association can well afford to avail themselves of the privilege of membership.

A third matter to be considered under the general topic of purchasing is the routine of requisitions and purchase orders. In many of the colleges studied the whole process of purchasing is very informal. Requests for materials come to the business office on scraps of paper of all shapes and sizes; frequently the request is only a verbal affair, and it may even come over the telephone. The purchase orders may be in any form, such as a letter, or a duplicate from a salesman's order pad. In other colleges there has been a rather effective systematization of the purchasing procedures. A brief description will be given of a satisfactory purchasing routine.

The heads of all departments having budget appropriations should be supplied with requisition pads to be used in making requests for supplies. There should be an iron-clad rule to the effect that purchases will be made only in response to requisitions properly filled out and signed. The requisitions that come to the business office should be uniform in style, facilitating filing and reference.

The next step in the business office should be the checking of the requisition against the balance remaining in the budget appropriation to which it is to be charged. This step prevents the overspending of budget appropriations. Following the approval of the requisition, it should go to the purchasing agent, who in the small college will probably be the business manager.

After carefully checking sources and prices, getting new quotations whenever time permits, the purchasing agent makes out the order on a specially prepared purchase order form, in at least four copies. The purchase orders should be serially numbered so that each may be properly accounted for, each of the four copies bearing the same number. The four copies of the order should be on different colored paper to avoid confusion. One copy (the original) of the purchase order should go to the vendor. Another copy should be sent to the person making the requisition, as information that the order has been placed. The other two copies should remain in the business office, one to be filed alphabetically according to the name of the vendor, the other to be filed serially according to the number of the purchase order. The requisition should have entered on it the serial number of the purchase order and should then be filed according to the department against whose budget the item is to be charged. When the goods are received, they should be checked against the purchase order to see that it has been correctly filled.

Because of other pressing duties of the president of a college, there is danger that he may become farther removed from the financial control of the institution than is desirable. It is a good plan in the small college to pass the purchase orders to the president for approval, since by this means he can keep constantly in touch with the commitments made by the institution. If it is understood that at a certain hour every afternoon the accumulated purchase orders will be sent to the president's desk, the purchasing procedure is not delayed. Some provision should be made for handling the matter in the absence of the president by having a previously designated alternate approve requisitions for him.

Two or three matters connected with the routine of purchasing deserve especial consideration. So far as possible all purchases should be made after the receipt of competitive bids. By pooling the buying for an entire year much lower prices may usually be obtained. The early summer months are generally a good time for the purchase of educational supplies, since this is the slack time for the supply houses.

Promptness in paying bills.—One of the important tests of good business management is the taking of cash discounts allowed for the prompt payment of bills. Twenty-one of the colleges of this group invariably discount all bills, seven usually do, and seven almost never take their cash discounts. The principal reason for failure to discount bills is the lack of available funds, although a few colleges indicate that discounts are sometimes overlooked.

It is difficult to figure the losses that these colleges are suffering through failure to discount bills. Very few of the colleges have their accounts set up in such a way that the amount of discount received can be figured. In the colleges which could furnish data on this point, the total cash discounts for the year ranged from $88.00 to $683.26. It seems probable that most of the colleges which are failing to discount their bills are losing several hundred dollars a year.

Shortage of cash is, of course, a very cogent reason for failing to discount bills. It is unfortunate, however, for a college to be run on such a narrow financial margin. The good name and credit of an institution in business circles is more dependent upon the prompt payment of bills than upon any other single factor. Most of the colleges of this group enjoy a very favorable credit reputation. There are a few of the institutions, however, which not only fail to take cash discounts on bills but even fail to meet their obligations when due.

In one college funds were lacking for meeting promptly the faculty salaries, and a large number of the instructors were several months in arrears on salary payments. There is nothing more disturbing to the morale of the faculty than disappointment in receiving salary payments when due. A number of the colleges of this group rightly pride themselves on their records of having never once failed to pay faculty salaries on time. Colleges which are so short of funds as to be unable to meet their obligations promptly should take immediate steps to remedy the situation, either through an increase in supporting resources or through a reduction of the program to one which can be maintained on a satisfactory basis with the resources available. It is economy for an institution to borrow money in order to pay its bills promptly. It is far better to have the debt centralized in an obligation to a local bank than to have it scattered among a large number of creditors.

Countersigning checks.—Good business practice today demands that there be at least two signatures on the checks of a business corporation. This plan has three purposes: the safeguarding of the institution against fraud, the avoidance of errors in making payments, and the acquainting of responsible officials with the current financial transactions. The countersignature safeguards against two kinds of fraud, the one external, the other internal. It is obvious that the chance of successful forgery is reduced by having two signatures on checks. It is also clear that peculation is rendered more difficult by the plan of having two responsible officers sign the checks.

For the prevention of forgery the two signatures might well be those of almost any persons connected with the college. For the prevention of peculation, for avoiding errors in payment, and for the acquainting of responsible officials with the current financial affairs of the institution it is important that the persons signing the checks be carefully chosen. It seems clear that the chief financial officer ought to be one of the persons to sign checks, since he, of all the officers of the college, should be most intimately acquainted with the necessity for the payment. Practice varies somewhat with regard to the second signature, but in the majority of cases the president is the one who countersigns the checks.

Twelve of the colleges of this group require only one signature on their checks. In every case but one the signature is that of the chief business officer, the single exception being the case of a small college in which the president attends to most of the business details, including the signing of all checks. At only six of the colleges requiring more than one signature was the president not one of those signing checks. Thus in approximately one-half of the colleges of this group the president's signature is on all checks. Two of the colleges require three signatures on their checks. A third signature does not seem necessary or advisable.

It is obvious that the purposes of the countersignature are defeated if checks are signed in advance by one of the officers. This practice is followed at a number of the institutions, but is clearly a violation of good business practice. Both the signatures should be affixed after the checks are made out, never before. In a few cases the signature of the second (and third) officers are affixed by rubber stamps. This again defeats the purpose of the countersignature, especially if the rubber stamp is in the possession of the other signing officer.

Sometimes objection is raised to the practice of having the president countersign all checks, because of the burden which this throws upon the chief executive officer. In a small college the additional burden is usually not large. A routine can well be developed so that checks will be brought to the president for countersignature at a certain time every day. The burden of this task may be considered a necessary part of the administrative work of the college, since it tends to give the president a greater familiarity with the current financial transactions. While there may not be more than one check in a hundred that the president will need to question with regard either to the amount or the purpose of the expenditure, the whole process of countersigning is an important method for safeguarding the funds of the college and for keeping the chief executive officer in close touch with its business affairs. In case of absence of the president an alternate can be provided to sign in his stead.

PROTECTION

Bonding of financial officers.—Another method of safeguarding the funds of an institution, which is closely allied to the countersignature on checks, is the bonding of all officers who have any responsibility for handling college funds. No question of the integrity of the financial officers is involved in the suggestion that they should be bonded. This is nothing more nor less than would be demanded by any well-managed business corporation. The fee for the bond should be paid out of the current funds of the institution.

The amount of the bond should be ample to protect the interests of the institution at all times. For any one officer the amount necessary will depend upon his relationship to the funds of the college. In general, it is a safe principle that the bond should be large enough to cover the largest amount which might possibly be in the officer's possession at any one time. The treasurer or business manager under the usual organization will probably carry the largest bond, with that of the others in proportion to the amount of funds they handle.

Data from the thirty-five colleges included in this study show that at six of these institutions there is no officer who is bonded. This violation of sound business principles is very unwise. No one of these colleges can afford to take any risk whatever of losing the funds intrusted to the care of its officials. The board of trustees should not hesitate to require that the president, business manager, cashier, bookkeeper, or any other official be bonded when necessary. Personal considerations should not prevent procedure against individual officers who have violated the trust placed in them.

At the majority of the colleges only one official is bonded. Two officers are bonded at Baldwin-Wallace, DePauw, Dickinson, Evansville, and

Mount Union. Lawrence and Ohio Wesleyan each bond three officers, and MacMurray and Albion bond four.

The size of the bonds vary markedly, the largest bond for any individual officer being $75,000. At twenty-nine of the thirty-five colleges the bonds are too small to furnish adequate protection to the interests of the institution. A large number of the colleges fail to bond some of the staff members who handle funds.

It is recognized that college business officers as a group are unusually trustworthy. Instances of violation of trust on the part of business officers are very rare although not entirely unknown in this group of institutions. In spite of the fact that the chances of loss are very small, the college cannot afford to assume the risk of losing an important part of its funds. The mere fact that an officer is bonded probably reduces the chances of loss and provides a valuable stimulation to honesty on the part of responsible officials.

Holdup and burglary insurance.—There are certain occasions in the year when the college has on hand a considerable amount of cash. This generally happens at the time of registration when tuition fees are collected, at the time of collecting board and room fees, and at important athletic contests. Complete protection in the form of holdup and burglary insurance should be carried to protect the college against the loss of this money. The rates for this type of insurance are not excessive, although they depend upon the section of the country in which the institution is located, the amount of local police protection, and the type of safe used.

All the colleges, without exception, should carry holdup insurance. There are a number of clauses in holdup policies that affect greatly the value of the contract, and these should be investigated carefully when the policies are taken out, in order to be certain that the institution is fully protected. The necessity for burglary insurance can be avoided if the college can make arrangements with its local bank to accept deposits after closing hours.

It is surprising to find that very few of the colleges studied carry insurance protection against loss by holdup or burglary. One of these institutions suffered a very embarrassing loss by burglary at the time of the collection of fees in the autumn of 1930. Police protection is very limited in the communities in which many of these colleges are located. No institution can afford to run the risk of loss from this source, and ample insurance protection should be carried.

Workman's compensation insurance.—The theory of workman's compensation is based on the idea that an employee injured at his task is due some remuneration for the physical disability and financial loss he incurs. All of the states in which the institutions studied are located require that some sort of provision be made by industrial firms to insure the payment of compensation to injured workmen. In many states, however, colleges or universities are not specifically required to come under the provisions of the act, since they are considered to be in a class with charitable institutions.

Regardless of legal requirements, it would scarcely seem to be in keeping with the spirit of a Christian institution to attempt to evade responsibility for injuries sustained in the line of duty by any of its employees. The taking advantage of a legal technicality to avoid such a responsibility might become most embarrassing and, in spirit, is certainly not Christian.

The financial responsibility involved in this moral liability can and should be cared for by insurance. A few states compel all employers to carry workman's compensation insurance, and in some cases this is arranged for through a state agency. Approximately one-third of the colleges studied fail to carry this type of insurance.

Public-liability insurance.—The ownership of any property used for public or semi-public purposes nearly always involves the risk of claims for accident or damage to individuals using the property, either with or without permission. This type of risk is known as public liability, and protection against it may be had by means of insurance.

Educational institutions have numerous opportunities for incurring loss from this source. For example, one of the colleges studied recently experienced a disastrous fire in its gymnasium at a time when a dramatic production was being given. Three lives were lost and several students, faculty members, and townspeople were seriously injured. Although no large claims for damage were made, the institution very properly felt obligated to compensate in some way those who had been injured, and the total payments will ultimately amount to a considerable sum. Since no public-liability insurance was carried, this entire burden fell upon the general funds of the college. If the insurance had been carried, the insurance company would have borne the expense and it is probable that those who were injured would have had a larger amount of compensation.

There are other opportunities for incurring damage claims through public liability. The responsibility of the institution for injuries to students, particularly in athletics, is an example. The courts of some states have held that the college has no responsibility in this situation; but in other states exactly the opposite has been held. Other opportunities for incurring liability are connected with the operation of science laboratories, where students may be injured by explosions or fires.

Another advantage of carrying public-liability insurance arises from the inspection given by the company carrying this risk. Even though protected by insurance the college naturally wishes to avoid every possible chance of an accident. The inspector will point out remediable hazards, which the college will want to eliminate.

Only a few of the colleges studied are carrying public-liability insurance. Good business practice demands that protection be carried against this type of risk. Some of the colleges which carry public-liability insurance are negligent in reporting accidents and injuries, particularly those happening to students. All accidents and injuries to the public and to students which occur on college property, including those sustained in laboratories as well as injuries to athletes engaged in practice or varsity contests, should be reported to the company from which public-liability insurance is purchased. This agency then assumes all of the legal liability of the institution in such cases as are reported to it, and pays claims for which the college is legally liable, at the time of the accident or at any later time. Some companies also pay the first-aid charges in the case of injuries.

Although some authorities hold that a college, because of its classification as a charitable institution, has no legal liability in the case of injuries to students, it is clear that there is a moral liability. Moreover, it is true that the moral liability cannot be evaded even though the insurance company may demonstrate that there is no legal liability. The chief protection which insurance provides a college in such cases is the avoidance of embarrassing litigation, since the company in which public-liability insurance is carried will defend the institution against any and all claims of this type.

COLLECTIONS

Collection of student fees.—The ideal plan for the collection of student fees would demand, from the standpoint of good business procedure, that all students pay all fees in advance upon the day of registration. All of these colleges, however, enrol some students on whom the enforcement of this rule would work a real hardship. In an endeavor to ease the burden imposed on worthy students of limited financial recources, many of the colleges have allowed important violations of good business practice to occur in their student-fee collections.

Arnett[1] has given a clear and forceful statement of the issues involved in the collection of student fees.

[1] Trevor Arnett, *College and University Finance* (New York: General Education Board, 1922), pp. 13–14.

Students should be required to pay all fees within the first few days of the quarter or term, or to make satisfactory arrangements for their payment. This rule, announced by most colleges, is more honored in the breach than in the observance. It should, however, be followed strictly, for its observance operates as much to the advantage of the student by training him in good business principles as it benefits the college by the prompt receipt of cash, by eliminating the expense of collection, and by avoiding bad debts. The reason most frequently given for not insisting upon prompt payment is that it might work a hardship on the poor student and might exclude him from college. Experience shows that the enforcement of the rule has not had this effect, for almost without exception a student earnestly desiring an education will in some way obtain the needed money.

The enforcement of the rule is good policy, for the student whose obligations are settled has a more wholesome attitude toward his college than one who is in its debt. If fees are not collected promptly the student is more likely to be captious and critical and offer complaints of various kinds as excuse for non-payment. Experience has shown that it is difficult to collect fees after the term has expired. A comparison between two institutions is instructive: One, a middle-western college, pursues a lenient policy; it does not insist upon prompt payment of fees, but allows its students time in which to pay their tuition, board, rent, and athletic fees, even furnishing several of these items at an immediate outlay of its own cash. It always has a large amount uncollected, a considerable proportion of which is never paid. The University of _____, in the same section, with a very much larger number of needy students, makes its collection in advance, exceptions being extremely rare, and in those cases it takes promissory notes bearing interest. No difficulty in enforcing the rule is experienced by the latter institution. Incidentally, the former teaches its students to be lax, the latter trains them to be prompt and businesslike.

The five principal defects found in the fee-collection policies are: first, the failure to investigate adequately the need of requests for delay in fee payment; second, the plan of allowing students to pay fees in instalments; third, the failure to take promissory notes as evidence of the obligations of students; fourth, the failure to insist rigidly upon the collection of all fees before the end of the semester; and fifth, the failure ever to collect some student fees.

The practices of the great majority of the institutions studied are subject to adverse criticism because of failure to investigate the need for delay in payment of fees where this is requested. In some colleges, although the catalogue definitely announces that all fees are due on registration day, the custom of delaying the payment of fees has become so deep-rooted that almost none of the students expect to pay their fees at this time.

Sound business practice demands that authority for granting delays in the payment of fees be centralized in one officer. Normally this will be the business manager of the institution, although it may be advisable to provide some agency representing the academic interests of the institution to advise with the business officer in regard to doubtful cases. In the event delays in payment of fees are allowed, the officer who is responsible for granting such requests should satisfy himself of the student's need.

One of the effective plans followed by a few of the colleges provides for a written application to be made by the student, which includes a statement of the student's proposed budget for the semester and the names of references who can testify as to his needs and worthiness. The application blank should be prepared prior to the day of registration so as to facilitate procedures in the business office. The requirement of this routine will discourage most students who do not have a real need for extension of credit and will leave only the meritorious cases for special consideration. The references given should be carefully followed up, and the extension of credit to a student should always be based upon a careful analysis of the data given in the request blank.

The policy of permitting the payment of fees on the instalment plan is an expensive one for the institution. A few of the colleges studied definitely provide for the payment of all fees in instalments, but the great majority require, at least nominally, the payment of fees for a semester in advance. It is evident that the instalment plan imposes an unusually heavy burden upon the business office. The labor involved in accounting for the fees paid is as great for each instalment as would be the case for that of the entire payment under the plan of collecting all fees in advance. Thus, instead of one "rush period" each semester or term in the business office, there will be as many as there are instalments to be collected. Furthermore, the institution is deprived of the use of the money for considerable periods of time. Under policies of investing current funds so as to produce an income, considerable revenue can be derived which is lost if fees are not collected strictly in advance.

The third criticism of fee-collection policies relates to the failure to obtain a promissory note as evidence of the student's obligation in case of a delay in fee payments. The granting of permission to a student to delay the payment of his fees should be a strictly business transaction. The institution is justified in going to some lengths to impress upon a student the formality of the procedure. One of the best methods of accomplishing this end is the requirement that a student sign a promissory note as evidence of his obligation. A considerable number of the colleges studied carry the unpaid tuition fees as open accounts. Under the plan of taking a promissory note the tuition ledger can well be dispensed with, the accounts being kept with the promissory notes as such rather than with the students. The taking of a promissory note for all unpaid fees does not improve the legal status of the unpaid accounts since the students are usually minors, but it does improve the attitude of the borrowers toward their obligations.

The fourth criticism of the plans of collecting student fees in this group of colleges relates to the failure to insist rigidly upon the collection of all fees before the close of the semester. Colleges which have investigated the matter have found that it is much more difficult to collect fees after a student has been permitted to take his final examinations and has completed the semester's work than is the case if payment of all fees is rigidly insisted upon as a condition of being allowed to take final course examinations. The student who cannot make some arrangements for obtaining the money necessary to pay his fees before the end of the semester should not be encouraged to register. There is always the possibility that loan funds, scholarships, and other types of subsidy may be drawn on to help needy but worthy students. Not only is the financial loss involved in permitting students to delay fee payments beyond the end of the semester a serious matter for the institution, but the poor business training given to students is even more serious. This point was forcefully brought out in the quotation from Arnett.

Finally, in a number of these colleges there is a relatively large amount written off the books at the close of each fiscal year for bad accounts, representing student fees which have never been collected. The loss from this source varies from nothing in a considerable number of institutions to a rather sizable amount in a few colleges. The experience of a number of these colleges indicates that it is absolutely unnecessary to incur any losses because of bad student accounts. The colleges which permit students to leave without having paid their fees are not only wronging themselves but are also inculcating unbusinesslike ideals in their students.

The great majority of requests for delays in payment of fees are not on account of necessity but rather for the convenience of borrowers. Colleges that have investigated the matter have found that many students who request delays in payment of fees actually have available enough funds to meet this obligation but seek the delay in payment in order that they may use the money for some other purpose. Not infrequently the fraternities and sororities are more successful in collecting their annual dues from such students than the colleges are in collecting tuition fees.

In some cases both the institution and the student have been embarrassed when a student, taking advantage of a lenient collection policy, has used for other purposes money given by his parents for the payment of fees.

The adoption of a rigid policy of fee collection does not mean that worthy students are to be excluded because of financial limitations. The point of this discussion is that such students should be helped in a regular way and not encouraged to obtain their education by failing to meet their just debts.

Collection of other revenues.—Under a satisfactory plan of business organization the chief business officer should be given central responsibility for the collection of all revenues belonging to the institution. In addition to the collection of student fees, considerable amounts are collected by the institution annually from such sources as admission to athletic events, plays, concerts, etc., given in the name of the college. In most of the better-managed institutions the collection of such revenues is considered a function of the business officer. In a few cases, however, the collection of these funds is delegated to students, athletic coaches, and members of the faculty. There would seem to be no question but that these collections should be considered a normal part of the business routine and made a definite responsibility of the business office. If this is not done, the way is open for the fleecing of the institution of some or all of the receipts which are due it. The auditing of funds is made more difficult, and the number of persons who should be bonded is increased by the plan of decentralizing the collection of college revenues.

In administering the collection of revenues from admission to athletic events, concerts, plays, etc., rolls of serially numbered tickets should be used. In case there are two or three rates of charges, tickets of different colors with different serial numbers should be employed. Before the sale starts a record should be made of the serial number of the first ticket on each roll. The receipts should then be checked by noting the number of the tickets which have been taken from the roll and balancing the amount with the cash on hand. This permits a complete audit of the gate receipts for every event and provides definite safeguards from loss to the institution through petty peculations.

The proceeds of these activities should become a part of the current funds of the college, and disbursements should be made in exactly the same manner as in the case of other expenditures. In a large number of cases this plan is not followed. Instead, the athletic coach is permitted to spend the gate receipts from athletic contests, the dramatic coach has charge of the expenditure of receipts from plays, and the receipts from concerts are turned over to the sponsoring department for use as it pleases. Sound business procedure demands that these funds be handled through the regular administrative channels and expended only upon proper requisition from the responsible officials.

SUPERVISING THE FINANCES OF STUDENT ORGANIZATIONS

On most college campuses there are a number of student organizations which are, for the most part, wholly outside the responsibility of the institution in so far as direct financial liability is concerned. The financial difficulties of any organization connected with the college, however, reflect on the institution as a whole, and not infrequently tradespeople and others to whom these organizations become indebted feel that the college should be held responsible for supervising their financial affairs. Because of the rapid shift in student personnel there is little opportunity to develop a continuity of financial policy in student organizations, since the officers usually hold their positions for only one year. Because of the immaturity of the students, their business policies and practices are usually somewhat unsatisfactory.

Two general policies seem to be in effect with regard to the amount of supervision exercised by the institution over the financing of student organizations such as fraternities, clubs, classes, publications, etc. Some institutions exert no supervision whatsoever over the financial transactions of these organizations, believing that the business experience obtained by the students in charge is a valuable contribution to their education. Other colleges follow policies of relatively close supervision over the accounts of these organizations, being of the opinion that by this means there is a better opportunity for giving definite business training.

An important argument in favor of some supervision is based upon the fact that the percentage of the members of these organizations who receive some business training from handling their finances is very small compared to the number of students benefiting by efficient management of the organizations. The policy of "the greatest good for the greatest number" would indicate that the finances should be well handled even though the opportunity for educating a few students in business practices is overlooked. It may be added that the handling of unaudited funds by immature students throws in their way too great a temptation for dishonesty and misappropriation. In many colleges the handling of the finances of such organizations is a rather notorious scandal among members of the student body.

Although there are good arguments both for and against the supervision of the finances of student organizations, it appears advisable for colleges to undertake at least a limited amount of supervision in these matters. Where college funds or fees collected by the college business office are turned over to student organizations for expenditure, the college has a real obligation to satisfy itself that the money is properly handled.

There is considerable advantage in centralizing the bookkeeping for all student organizations in the business office. A small charge can be made to the organizations for this work, and the whole service can be handled much more economically than if every organization tries to do its own bookkeeping. This plan also has the advantage of enabling the business office to keep close check on the financial affairs of the various organizations. Some colleges merely require reports at regular intervals from such organizations as fraternities and social clubs. In some cases the maintenance of a satisfactory financial condition is required for the continuance of the organization, and a college must necessarily have adequate data to determine the true condition of various organizations.

SELECTION AND MANAGEMENT OF STUDENT HELP

In practically all of the colleges included in this study a considerable amount of employment is given to students. In some institutions the selection of student assistants is left entirely with the person in charge of the work to be done. In others, there has been a centralization of the employment of students with an attempt to develop uniformity in rates of pay for given levels of service. The latter plan seems greatly preferable. It should be understood that the selection of persons connected with instructional activities, such as readers and laboratory assistants, should be lodged in the academic department in a manner similar to the selection of regular members of the teaching staff. The selection of students for janitorial work, stenographic work, and other similar positions can probably be best handled through a central office, although the persons in charge of the work to be done can well suggest the students whom they would like to employ. It is essential that rates of pay be fixed by some central authority, as otherwise there will be a tendency to bid up the general level of labor prices. The business office can always render valuable service by keeping adequate personnel records of employed students and by maintaining lists of students who are available for various types of employment.

One of the most common criticisms in the employment of student labor in this group of colleges relates to the failure to provide adequate supervision. Student help is notoriously inefficient. Where employment is given as a means of student aid, it appears that in many cases the funds would produce more actual educational service if the entire employment program were abandoned, a part of the funds used for this purpose being devoted to the payment of well-qualified help and the remainder being used for scholarships or other types of outright student subsidy. Other colleges claim that with adequate supervision student help can be made very effective. Again it may be pointed out that the institution is rendering an educational service of doubtful value when it inculcates in students the idea that a dollar's worth of work does not have to be done for a dollar's worth of pay. It seems fair to conclude that if the program of student aid is to include employment, provision should be made for adequate supervision of students who work for the college.

CHAPTER XLVII

FINANCIAL ACCOUNTING

REQUISITES OF A GOOD ACCOUNTING SYSTEM

The three requisites of any good accounting system are: (1) that it provide ample safeguards for funds and be easily audited; (2) that it yield very readily any type of financial information which may be sought; and (3) that it possess the quality of simplicity.

The safeguards which an effective accounting system should provide involve the establishment of procedures and the development of checks which will bring all of the detailed financial transactions into the accounts, so that theft or misappropriation of funds may be rendered difficult, if not impossible. An effective accounting system for a college should provide for a careful and detailed accounting, not only for the receipts and expenditures of the institution as a whole, but also for the various funds of the institution; for this reason a fund accounting system is desirable.

In order that an accounting system may yield satisfactory financial information, it must contain ample detail. A proper and logical classification of accounts is also necessary; and in order to facilitate the preparation of reports, the accounts should be arranged in the most effective manner. All financial transactions must be recorded in the books of account, and any offsets which bring only net results to the records ought to be avoided. A clear-cut separation should be maintained between accounts for various types of funds.

In order that the accounting system may be easily understood, it should be clear and uninvolved. No unnecessary books of account should be maintained, and irrelevant details should be eliminated. The accounting procedures should be as simple as possible, consistent with amply safeguarding the funds and providing the necessary financial information.

GENERAL CONDITIONS OF THE ACCOUNTING SYSTEMS IN THE COLLEGES STUDIED

The accounting systems of this group of colleges are, on the whole, very good. In the case of only four colleges were there defects in the financial accounting such as to warrant the recommendation that an entirely new system be installed. At the request of two institutions, the survey staff undertook the planning of a complete accounting system, although this was not included as a regular part of the survey work. Besides the four colleges in which recommendation was made for a new accounting system, there were three other institutions in which the accounting was seriously defective. In the remaining twenty-eight institutions the accounting system was considered generally satisfactory. In this respect the colleges of this group are far superior to other institutions with which the writers are familiar. It is interesting to contrast this general condition of excellence with the criticisms made of the accounting systems in the land-grant colleges as set forth in a recent survey.[1]

For many years The Board of Education of the Methodist Episcopal Church has requested an annual financial report from each of these colleges. This reporting form has always embodied the most up-to-date ideas with regard to the classification of college financial accounts. Undoubtedly the requirement of this report and the advice given by the representatives of the Board of Education have done much to insure a satisfactory accounting system in a great majority of the colleges studied.

In the past, one of the principal criticisms of all college financial accounting has been the lack of uniformity from institution to institution. A national committee has been working for the past two years on the problem of a uniform reporting system for college financial data. This committee has recently completed this portion of its task and has published a bulletin setting forth the elements of a satisfactory classification of financial accounts.[2] The committee plans to extend its work to include the formulation of an accounting system to articulate with the reporting system which has been set up. Upon the completion of this task, the colleges will be able to profit greatly by the installation of an approved and uniform type of accounting system, and items pertaining to college finance will have the same meaning all over the country. As matters now stand, it is impossible to compare the finances of any two institutions without making a detailed analysis of the actual accounts, because of the differences in the practices of classification and nomenclature.

SPECIFIC CRITICISMS OF ACCOUNTING SYSTEMS

Although the financial accounting in this group of colleges is unusually good, there are certain defects present in several of the institutions which

[1] *Survey of Land-Grant Colleges and Universities*, U.S. Department of the Interior, Office of Education, Bull. 9, I (1930), 260.

[2] *Suggested Forms for Financial Reports of Colleges and Universities* (National Committee on Standard Reports for Institutions of Higher Education; Lloyd Morey, chairman of the Committee, University of Illinois, Urbana, Illinois; first printed edition July, 1931).

should be corrected. A discussion will be given of a few of the defects which are common to a number of the institutions studied.

Failure to account properly for supplementary business activities.—There are certain college expenditures which do not constitute an actual part of the cost of the academic education of the students enrolled. Such enterprises as dormitories, dining-halls, bookstores, etc., are usually classified as supplementary business activities. It is important to know whether these activities operate at a loss or at a profit, and in order to obtain this information the accounts for the income and expenditures of these enterprises must be kept entirely separate from those for the educational activities. In approximately half of the colleges studied, the accounts for some or all of the supplementary business activities are not properly segregated from the expenditures and income for educational purposes. This failure results in a mistaken impression of the cost of education as well as an inaccurate analysis of the results of operating the supplementary business activities. In the colleges in which this error is present, it was necessary, in obtaining data for this study, to make a complete analysis of the accounts in order to discover the true costs of the various activities.

A somewhat similar error is present in twenty-five of the colleges, which fail to segregate all of the costs of supplementary business activities. The typical failure of this type is the neglect to prorate a proper share of the administrative overhead of the institution to the expenses of the supplementary business activities. It is usual in these colleges to charge the entire administrative expenses against the cost of the educational program. In a number of the institutions, however, at least half of the expenses of the business office are properly chargeable to the management of the supplementary business activities. In order to arrive at the true cost, it is therefore necessary to prorate the general overhead expenses of the college to the supplementary business activities.

The error of failing to make this allocation of overhead is found not only in the case of supplementary business activities but also in the accounting for income from endowment. In the case of colleges in which the business office has responsibility for endowment management, the cost of this service should be charged against the income from endowment rather than against the educational program of the institution.

The third failure in the accounting for supplementary business activities is the failure to separate the various enterprises from each other. In eleven of the colleges two or more of the supplementary business enterprises are carried in a single account. Under this plan it is impossible for the college authorities to determine which unit or units are responsible for the loss or profit shown. It is imperative both in the matter of adjusting rates of charges and in determining the efficiency of the management to have a separate accounting for each of the various enterprises maintained.

Lack of a budget ledger.—If the college operates under a budget plan, one of the important instruments of control is a budget ledger. Twenty-three of the colleges included in this study, although operating under a budget system, fail to have in their accounting plan a satisfactory budget ledger.

No standard form has yet been developed for a budget ledger. The requisites of this book of accounting are: (1) that one ledger sheet be used for each detailed budget item; (2) that the budget appropriation be entered at some convenient place on the ledger sheet; (3) that the sheet be so ruled as to divide it vertically into two sections. In one section should be entered the charges made against the budget appropriations. In the other section should be entered all purchases which have been made but are not invoiced. The total commitments against the budget appropriation are obtained by adding to the total charges in the first section of the ledger sheet the memoranda of purchases which have been entered in the second but not yet invoiced. This total can easily be compared with the budget appropriation; and if postings are made regularly, an absolute check on the budget is provided.

At the end of each fiscal year the budget ledger for the closing year should be put into a transfer file and a new ledger opened for the following year. The budget ledger will contain the detailed analysis of the summary income and expense accounts which are carried in the current fund division of the general ledger.

General ledger not arranged according to funds.—Owing to the fact that a college or university must account separately for such different types of funds as those for endowment, plant, and current operations, it is advisable to arrange the general ledger into at least three principal divisions, one for each of the several types of funds. Each of these divisions should be self-balancing, the sum of the debit accounts equaling the sum of the credit accounts.

The trust-fund division of the general ledger should contain two sections, one for the asset or debit accounts and one for the liability and proprietorship, or credit, accounts. The assets section should usually contain only the summary accounts for investments, the details being kept in a subsidiary investment ledger; however, if the number of investment items is small, the subsidiary ledger is not necessary. The trust-fund liabilities and proprietorship items are usually not so numerous but that they may be contained here in detail; the accounts should be grouped, however, in order to bring together items similar in nature, such as scholarships, professorships, etc. Each of these groups should be summarized on control sheets, so as to facilitate the preparation of reports.

The plant fund accounts should form a balanced division of the general ledger. Since in a small college the items are not numerous, detailed accounts may be maintained with each plant item. Any gifts received for plant purposes should be entered as plant assets, and invested so that their revenues may accrue to the benefit of plant funds until such time as they are expended.

The current-fund division of the general ledger should contain four sections, one each for current-fund assets, current-fund liabilities and proprietorship, current-fund revenue, and current-fund expense. The asset and liability sections may very well contain the detail of current-fund assets and current-fund liabilities; but the revenue and expense accounts should be only summary accounts, the details being kept in the budget ledger.

The accounting systems of twenty of the colleges studied fail to set up the accounts in the general ledger according to a fund arrangement. It will be recognized that, while this criticism relates principally to a matter of convenience in making intelligible reports, the failure to group funds properly is apt to result in confusion and possibly a misuse of funds.

Books of original entry not satisfactorily organized.—A satisfactory accounting system involves the use of at least four books of original entry. These should be the cash-receipts book, the voucher register, the check register, and the general journal. In addition to these books, a system of duplicate receipts should be maintained from which postings may be made through the cash-receipts book. A pay-roll register can well be used to advantage in connection with the general college books.

Six of the colleges fail to provide a duplicate cash-receipts system as a part of their accounting plan. Five do not include a general journal as one of the books of original entry. Four do not have a pay-roll register set up in a satisfactory form. Eight use a combination voucher register and check register. While this combination is not a violation of good accounting practice, the use of two separate books for this purpose is considered a better method.

Cash discounts not properly accounted for.—Good accounting practice requires cash discounts on bills to be entered as an item of income. Approximately half of the colleges make the mistake of deducting the discount from the face of the invoice and entering only the net payment as an expenditure. While the net result is the same no matter which method is followed, the failure to enter the cash discount as an income precludes the possibility of determining the amount of cash discounts earned during the fiscal period. As previously indicated, this is an important test of good business practice.

Revenues from students not properly accounted for.—The total credits which should be entered as revenue from students at the time of registration should be the amount which would be realized in cash, assuming that all fees are paid in cash and that no scholarships are granted or rebated fees allowed. The corresponding charges should be cash, scholarships, rebated fees, notes receivable, etc. At the end of the year liberal reserves should be set up for losses from uncollected fees, if any. Twelve of the colleges studied do not follow the practice outlined above in accounting for student fees, but enter only the net cash received. This introduces a serious error into the accounts because the item of rebated fees is not brought into the accounts at all.

Failure to account for fees as suggested also makes it impossible to make a thorough audit of the receipts from students. It should be possible for the auditor to obtain figures from the registrar regarding the number of students registered and the amount of unit fees for each. From these data the auditor should compute a figure for the total receipts from students, which should balance with that shown in the accounts of the college.

Unnecessary records kept.—It has been suggested that one of the primary qualifications of a good accounting system is simplicity. Among other things, this principle demands that no unnecessary records be kept. There are at least three types of records kept by some of these colleges which are unnecessary for an effective system of financial accounting.

The first of these is the tuition ledger. This record appears under various names such as "tuition journal," "student ledger," and "student-account ledger." It consists of an account with each student enrolled in the college. Each account is debited at the opening of each semester with the amounts of the detailed fees charged against the individual student. Credits are then entered according to the payments in cash, scholarships, loan funds, remitted fees, etc. The maintenance of this record is a rather expensive affair, and its use is practically nil.

The use of the tuition ledger probably owes its origin to the fact that students in the past have not paid their fees in cash. If fees are not paid in cash promptly on registration day, it is, of course, necessary to maintain some kind of a record indicating the obligation of the student to the institution. A strict insistence upon the payment of fees in cash by all students who are financially able eliminates almost entirely the necessity for this record. If all of the students who are granted delay in payment of fees are required to sign promissory notes, the only accounting record then needed is a note register. This eliminates entirely the need for the tuition ledger. Postings to the cash-receipts book can be made directly from the duplicate fee receipts by simply entering the total daily receipts as shown by an adding-machine tape. As suggested previously, this can always be determined and audited by computing the number of students paying each rate of fee.

There are twelve colleges in this group which still maintain student-tuition ledgers. Unquestionably, the accounting work in these colleges could be greatly reduced without any loss of efficiency through the abandonment of this record.

Another type of unnecessary accounting found in three colleges consists of duplication of pledge records, one file of pledges being arranged alphabetically, another geographically. Postings are made to both sets of records, thus materially increasing the amount of work necessary in accounting for pledges. It should be possible to keep pledge records in a single alphabetical account, with cross-reference files for any other classifications desired. The cross-reference files need not contain complete information regarding the status of each pledge.

The third type of unnecessary record found in two colleges is a purchase order register. It has already been suggested that duplication of the purchase orders can be kept in a file showing at any time the outstanding commitments of the institution. By the maintenance of a duplicate file of purchase orders there is no necessity for a purchase order register.

Failure to keep accounts in sufficient detail.—One of the very common criticisms in this group of colleges is the failure to keep adequate detail on certain types of records. In sixteen of the institutions the investments records do not give all of the details necessary for the information of the authorities of the college. In six of the institutions the accounts do not contain all of the information regarding annuities that should have been maintained. In six colleges the pledge records are subject to a similar criticism. Since the financial accounts constitute the official records of the institution, it is necessary that they contain all of the details of the records which may in any way be necessary for the effective administration of the institution.

Poor classification of accounts.—It is probable that if colleges over the country were surveyed with respect to their accounting systems, the most important and the most frequent criticism would be that the accounts with current operating income and expenses are poorly classified. The colleges of the group being studied stand out in sharp contrast with this general condition. In only four of these institutions are the accounts subject to this criticism. It has previously been pointed out that the requirement of an annual report by The Board of Education of the Methodist Episcopal Church has probably provided an effective stimulus for a satisfactory classification of accounts. The colleges of this group should be commended for their progressiveness in this matter.

It has already been pointed out that a uniform reporting system for colleges has recently been promulgated by a national committee studying this matter. It is probable that most of these colleges will wish to revise their accounting systems to conform exactly with the arrangements suggested in the report of this committee. The introduction of this uniform accounting system will mark a forward step in the financial practices of American colleges.

CHAPTER XLVIII

BUDGETARY PROCEDURE

A budget is a plan for income and expenditure covering a definite fiscal period. As a result of many years of successful use of the budget system by governmental bodies, educational institutions, and manufacturing and industrial establishments, its importance as an instrument of co-ordination and of administrative control has become axiomatic. No attempt will be made in this discussion to set up an argument in justification of the employment of budgetary procedure; but consideration will be limited to: (1) the purpose and use of the budget; (2) the method of its preparation; (3) the adoption of the budget; (4) budget execution and control.

PURPOSE OF THE BUDGET

The budget may be considered as having a twofold purpose. In the first place, it is an instrument of co-ordination by means of which all the probable and potential sources of revenue for the current support of the institution are marshaled in review in order to permit as accurate an estimate as possible of the financial contributions which may be expected from each. This is necessary in order that a program of service may be planned for which the institution will be able to pay. In the second place, the budget should not only define the limits of the program of an institution as a whole, but it should also co-ordinate the various functional units comprising the program. It is in the budget that the working philosophy of an institution is most forcefully and concisely stated, and it is by means of the budget that this philosophy may be consciously and deliberately fulfilled.

The extent of the field of service of an educational institution is almost limitless; financial support, however, is usually a definitely limiting factor. The continued existence of an educational institution is dependent on a limitation of its program of service to such activities as can be financed by the available revenues. The budget, therefore, becomes a most important instrument of administrative control in the development of the program of the institution.

METHOD OF PREPARATION

The preparation of the budget involves: (1) a careful review of the various sources of revenue, with reference to the contribution from each that may be expected within the fiscal period for application on the current expenditures involved in providing the educational program, and (2) a judicious estimate of the relative merits and needs of each functional unit in order that the available revenues may be so apportioned as best to serve the institution as a whole in the realization of its purposes and aims.

Estimates of income.—The discussion of the preparation of the income section of the budget takes precedence here because, normally, income must be received before it can be expended. College administrators, in conducting the affairs and in planning the programs of their institutions, would do well to bear this in mind. Too frequently programs are prepared with little reference to the revenues from which they must be financed. The usual result is an operating deficit and a burden of debt and interest charges which still further reduce the income available for educational purposes. Ultimately, such a procedure results in the extinction of the institution.

Probably more operating deficits are caused by too optimistic an estimate of income than by failure to keep the expenditures within the budget. The usual sources of income in the endowed denominational colleges are student fees, interest on investment, church board appropriations, local church gifts and Annual Conference grants, gifts from board of trustees and friends, profits from supplementary business activities, and financial campaigns.

Income from fees is usually the most important single factor to be considered in estimating the income of a denominational college. In all cases the estimate should be a conservative one. Usually it will be much less difficult to secure the additional instructors and instructional supplies necessary to take care of an unexpected increase in enrolment than to secure releases from contracts with instructors already employed when it is found that they are not needed.

In setting up the item of income from students, the probable attendance should be estimated as carefully as possible; and, if the institution does not have a good fee-collection system, the probable loss through uncollected items should be taken into account. In making the estimate of attendance, cognizance should be taken of the trends of enrolment in colleges in general and in the particular institution for which the estimate is being made. In addition to this factor, the economic situation, both in general and in the particular constituency from which students come, should be considered. Statistics should be available showing for years past the geographical distribution of enrolment. Data showing general enrolment trends provide valuable information.

In making the estimate of income from investments, conservatism should again be the rule. The investments should be grouped according to the type of return, whether the rate is fixed or variable. Those which produce a fixed rate of return should again be grouped according to rates produced, and a very accurate estimate of income from these should be possible. Economic conditions should again be taken into account, since defaults in interest payments are usually more numerous in periods of economic depression. Fairly liberal allowance should be made for this factor.

In estimating income from types of investment which do not produce a fixed rate of return, a careful study should be made of past experience with each item. Such investments usually are in the form of stocks, real estate, business enterprises, etc. In case of stocks, the dividend history should be studied carefully and the general economic conditions which affect income in the fields in which stocks are owned should be carefully reviewed. After all these factors are taken into account, estimates should be made very conservatively. Estimates of income from real estate owned (city property), which ordinarily will be on a lease, should include only net income after all expenses of management, operation, etc., are deducted. Income from farm real estate is usually very uncertain unless cash rental can be arranged for, and even this may not be dependable unless it is collected a year in advance. The experience of many colleges has been that more of their farms are operated at a loss than at a profit; and even if, over a period of years, the result is a net profit, this cannot be depended upon during any given year. Exceedingly conservative estimates should be made of probable income from such sources.

Appropriations from church boards have, in general, been declining for some years, and estimates of income from such sources should be made with this tendency in mind.

Income from Annual Conference grants and local church gifts depends very much upon the administration of the college and the influence which may be exerted by the president and friends of the institution. Determining factors are: the service which the institution is rendering the constituency, the aggressiveness of the administrative officers of the college, and the size and wealth of the church constituency.

The estimate of income from supplementary business activities should include only net income after all expenses are paid. Since this item may be affected by an increase or decrease in enrolment, due allowance should be made for enrolment trends in estimating income from this source.

Income for current purposes from gifts and campaigns varies widely among institutions, depending largely on the policy of the college and on its promotion machinery. Most institutions do not receive much from such sources. Exceedingly conservative estimates should be made of income from gifts and campaigns. Any budget item of income from this source should be accompanied by a carefully worked out plan which gives some assurance that the expected income will be realized.

It will be observed that a majority of the sources of income utilized by most church colleges are very uncertain; the making of a scientific appraisal of such income is one of the most difficult phases of budget preparation. Because of the uncertainties involved, only the most conservative final estimate should be employed as the basis upon which the program of the college is planned.

Estimates of expenditures.—At least six months prior to the beginning of the fiscal year, departments should be asked to submit their budget requests. A statement should be supplied each department showing its expenditures for each item for the last previous year for which complete data are available. In a parallel column should be shown appropriations for the same item for the current fiscal year. The third column should be left blank, to be filled in by the department with the amounts of its budget requests. At the time this blank is sent out, department heads should be advised as to the general administrative policy for the coming year with respect to expansions or retrenchments, both for the institution as a whole and for the particular department concerned.

The form for the individual departments should be arranged to show the needs under the headings of the budget, viz.: (1) for instructional salaries; (2) for supplies and expenses; and (3) for equipment and books. Each division should be fully itemized. Each member of the staff should be listed, together with his salary; items of supply and expense should be given in the smallest detail permitted by the accounting system; and large items of new equipment should be specifically listed. Any items representing expansions or increases over the previous year's budget should be noted as "important" or "desirable."

In submitting their budget estimates, department heads should have opportunity to confer with the president. The president should keep a record of all conferences with the dean and department heads concerning the construction of the college budget.

From the information supplied by department heads and by the other officers who have responsibility for directing expenditures, the tentative budget is drafted by the president and the business officer. It is important that the set-up of the budget conform to the chart of accounts which is used in the bookkeeping system.

In addition to the items of expenditure, the amounts of which can be ascertained with reasonable accuracy, a contingent fund should be budgeted. Because of the uncertainties in connection with the income and the unforeseen and unbudgeted needs which arise during the year, a liberal allowance should be provided, probably from 3 to 5 per cent of the total budget. The amount should depend upon the experience of the institution in connection with budget operations of previous years.

THE ADOPTION OF THE BUDGET

The detailed budget, properly balanced between income and expenditures, as proposed by the administrative officers of the college, is usually presented to a committee of the board of trustees for their careful consideration and approval. This should be done preferably before the mid-year meeting of the board. After it has been approved by this committee, and whatever changes are necessary have been agreed to by them and by the president of the college, the budget is ready for presentation to the board of trustees at their next meeting.

Because of the comparatively infrequent meetings of the board of trustees and the numerous major problems of the institution which must be brought before that body for action, the budget as presented to them should be divested of minute details and should be in summary only. If proper comparative data are supplied, this summary will serve to acquaint the board with any increases or decreases in totals and will indicate any contemplated changes in educational policy. This is the type of administrative problem which should come before the board of trustees as a whole.

The budget as adopted becomes the basis for financial control for the ensuing fiscal year. None except a balanced budget should be approved by a board of trustees unless the members of that body make definite provision to raise the money to meet the contemplated deficit.

THE FORM OF THE BUDGET

The form of the budget is determined largely by considerations involved in its presentation to the budget committee and later to the board of trustees. In order to be of most significance, the budget should present a brief history of the past, showing trends in educational policies which have resulted in present conditions. It should also present the program for the future. As a means to the accomplishment of these two purposes, the two forms shown in Figures 21 and 22 are suggested.

It will be observed that only column headings are suggested in these forms. The budget should be so arranged as to present items of income and expenditure exactly as classified in the accounting system of the college.

NAME OF COLLEGE

INCOME BUDGET FOR THE FISCAL YEAR _____

Date _____

Item	Estimated Income Last Year	Actual Income Last Year	Budget Estimated Income Current Year	Present Estimated Income Current Year	Proposed Budget Income Next Year	Increase or Decrease as Compared with Last Year

FIG. 21.—Form for the preparation of the income budget

NAME OF COLLEGE

EXPENDITURE BUDGET FOR THE FISCAL YEAR _____

Date _____

Item	Budget Appropriation Last Year	Actual Expenditure Last Year	Budget Appropriation Current Year	Present Estimate of Expenditures for Current Year	Proposed Budget for Next Year	Increase or Decrease as Compared with Last Year

FIG. 22.—Form for the preparation of the expenditure budget

Perhaps the most significant column in the budget is the one which shows increases or decreases for each item as compared with the corresponding item for last year. The presentation of a budget in this form resolves itself largely into an explanation of reasons for proposed changes. This usually will facilitate the passage of the budget and will also enlighten the board of trustees as to general trends in the policies of the institution.

It is recommended that the column heads suggested here be used not only in the detailed budget submitted to the committee but also in the summary which is presented to the entire board of trustees.

Departmental budgetary control.—When the budget has been adopted by the board of trustees, the appropriations included become available for the expenses of the several departments. The department heads receiving appropriations for supplies should be permitted, without special action by the board of trustees or the executive committee, to make requisitions and obtain supplies for their departments up to the amount of the appropriation. Thus the budget system saves a great deal of time on the part of members of the board.

In so far as the administration has confidence in the judgment of the department heads, there should be no restriction on the amounts or purposes of expenditures for instructional supplies and equipment within the limits of the budget to the particular department. For example, if Department "A" is given a budget of $500 for supplies and equipment, requisitions for such material should be passed through the business office as a matter of routine without a question as to the advisability or necessity of the expenditure, up to the limit of the budget. If due care has been exercised in the selection of department heads, this confidence in their discretion should be warranted. Close supervision and questioning of every requisition for supplies and equipment by the business office, particularly with reference to the necessity or desirability of the purchase of the particular item requisitioned, involves both a burden and a degree of judgment which the business office is ordinarily not capable of assuming. The functions of the purchasing agent should not ordinarily involve the questioning of either the quantities ordered or the specifications as to type and quality of supplies needed.

This recommendation implies that in the original setting-up of the budget, each department will be called upon fully to justify its request. That is, Department "A" will not be granted an appropriation of $500 for equipment and supplies until it has been able to convince the budget officer that this appropriation is desirable and necessary. Once this justification has been made, expenditures against the budget appropriation should be allowed on the recommendation of the department head without question from the business office.

Heads of departments receiving appropriations for furniture, supplies, and equipment should be notified monthly throughout the year as to the amount of money remaining in each subdivision of their working budgets. These reports should include not only the amount of the original appropriation and the amount remaining in the treasury at the time the report is made, but also items showing the outstanding obligations of the department at the time the report is constructed.

The business office should review carefully the monthly budget reports which are sent to the heads of departments and should keep the president informed of any apparent premature dissipation of departmental appropriations. Any check which is exercised on the department head within the limits of the budget should come from the office of the president rather than from the business office.

Freedom should be permitted in the working budget; that is, with the approval of the president, the heads of departments should be permitted to make transfers from one to another of the detailed items within their departments.

Budget revision.—The board of trustees should not look upon the budget as an absolutely iron-clad device and insist that expenditures follow exactly the pattern set out. To do so is thoroughly uneconomical. During the course of the fiscal year unforeseen conditions arise which make it necessary to revise budget estimates, and it is administrative folly not to permit such revisions when they are necessary. The board or its executive committee should therefore revise the budget periodically, probably at least twice during the fiscal year, in order to care for developments that were unforeseen at its adoption. The revision of the budget should be initiated by the president, in conference with the business office.

There are, in general, four methods of budget revision: (*a*) transfers from item to item by the addition of appropriations to items for which extra expenditure seems desirable, and the subtraction of equal amounts from items which apparently will not need their full appropriation; (*b*) transfers from the contingent fund; (*c*) additional outright appropriations, made possible by an increase in the revenue over that anticipated in the budget; (*d*) reduction of appropriations in the event of decreased income. If it is apparent that gifts are going to exceed the amounts expected from this source, it is thoroughly proper to add some of these revenues to budget items which are clearly in need of additional funds. On the other hand, if through unforeseen circumstances the income is reduced, it is proper to revise appropriations to a lower figure wherever possible.

Changes in the budget, which involve increases or transfers other than between minor subdivisions, should be made only by deliberate action of the board of trustees or its executive committee, and should form a part of the minutes of the board. No expenditure should be allowed in excess of budget appropriation until this board action has been taken, except in cases of great emergency. The board of trustees should not permit budget increases or extra budget appropriations unless increased income is available, or unless they themselves stand ready to make up the deficit, thus enabling the institution to close the year with a balanced budget.

Instruments of budgetary control.—There are three useful and important instruments of budgetary control. The first is the budget ledger, the details of which were discussed in chapter xlvii. The second is the monthly report to the heads of departments which have supply, equipment, student-labor, or book budgets. The third instrument is the monthly budget report to the president and the committee of the board of trustees responsible for the control of the budget.

The use of these instruments of budgetary control is not an absolute guarantee against operating deficits. If properly employed, however, in connection with a good accounting system, they do insure that whenever deficits occur on account of overdrafts of expenditure appropriations, it is with the full knowledge and consent of those responsible for the financial administration of the institution.

CRITICISMS OF BUDGETARY PROCEDURE IN THE COLLEGES STUDIED

All but four of the colleges included in this group ostensibly operate on the budget basis. The failure to maintain a budget should be criticized severely. Most institutions have found that the only way of avoiding deficits and of limiting the educational program to the resources available for it is through the use of a budget. Six of the colleges having a budget system failed, however, during the year preceding the survey visit to prepare a balanced budget. It should be observed that unless a balanced budget is presented to the board of trustees for approval, the institution has violated the first fundamental requisite of good budgetary procedure.

In order that the board of trustees and executive officers of an institution may form valid judgments regarding budget items, it is necessary that considerable detail be provided showing the expenditures and budget appropriation in preceding years. Twenty of the colleges fail to provide in their budget sufficient comparative detail.

In nineteen of the colleges the criticism was made that the budget is adopted too late in the year to be most effective. The budget for the ensuing year in at least tentative form should be adopted at the mid-year meeting of the board in order that plans may be made in advance for the work of the institution.

It has already been pointed out that twenty-three of the colleges fail to maintain a budget ledger in their accounting systems. These institutions necessarily do not have as adequate a control of their budget as is desirable.

In four of the colleges criticism is made because the entire board of trustees did not participate in the adoption of the budget. Perhaps none of the actions of the board is more significant in determining educational policies than the adoption of the budget. To delegate this function to a committee of the board is, therefore, unwise. The entire board should participate in the study and adoption of the budget.

More than half of the colleges fail to provide regular monthly reports for department heads regarding the status of the budget, and in six colleges such statements are not prepared for the executive officers or the board of trustees.

One of the important items connected with satisfactory budgetary control concerns the dates of the fiscal year. A considerable amount of confusion was observed in the colleges of this group with regard to the date when the fiscal year begins. The majority of the colleges of the country have adopted a fiscal year beginning on July 1, and closing on June 30. This corresponds to the academic year since, normally, the commencement is considered the closing event of the year. There may be various local reasons why other dates have been chosen, but it would be advisable for all of the colleges of this group to adopt a uniform fiscal year opening July 1 and closing June 30.

CHAPTER XLIX

FINANCIAL REPORTS AND AUDITS

REPORTS

Purposes of reports.—In order to stimulate the keenest possible interest in the college on the part of the alumni, the board of trustees and friends, and to enlist them more earnestly in its active support, both moral and financial, information should be prepared and distributed which will acquaint these interested persons with the progress which the institution is making both scholastically and financially, as well as with its hopes for the future. Furthermore, in order that adequate information may be supplied to the president and the board of trustees to assist them in the formation of wise administrative policies and enable them to judge the effectiveness of the policies under which present operations are being conducted, it is necessary that careful, detailed records be maintained and that periodic reports be prepared which will indicate how near an approach is being made to the standard set as the goal, and what progress has been made from the point of departure.

It thus appears that the two fundamental purposes of reports are, first, to supply information to potential supporters, and, second, to furnish instruments of control. The reports necessary to the accomplishment of these purposes are numerous and varied in character. In the present discussion only those which deal with the financial aspects of a college or university will be considered.

The nature, form, and frequency of reports should be determined largely by their purpose. Those which are intended to assist the persons charged with the responsibility of directing the destinies of the institution will necessarily be more detailed in nature, more technical in form, and more frequently prepared than those which are designed to create outside interest and stimulate financial and moral support. The reasons for these differences are obvious. The officers who are responsible for the development of policies for the future, and for checking the results of policies of the past and the present, must have very detailed and specific information, much of which is somewhat technical in character. If this information is to serve to best advantage, it must be presented frequently in order that undesirable tendencies may be apprehended early and checked as soon as possible. On the other hand, the majority of people are not

471

trained in accounting and statistics, and the introduction of too many details and technicalities is confusing rather than enlightening. Therefore, the reports for more general distribution should be models of simplicity and should be made as interesting and as readable as possible. At the same time they must contain accurate, authentic information if they are to inspire the confidence and enlist the support which is desired.

In many colleges the board of trustees holds meetings only annually or semiannually, owing to the large number of members and their wide geographical separation. In such cases the finances of the institution should be reviewed monthly by the executive committee in the interim between board meetings. A report of the business transacted at each meeting of the executive committee should be sent to all members of the board.

The reports which are presented to the entire board at each meeting should deal with four phases of the financial administration, as follows: first, the status and growth of the endowment funds; second, the value and growth of the plant; third, the current assets, liabilities, and operations of the institution as an educational enterprise; fourth, the status of the supplementary business activities, such as the dormitories, dining-hall, and bookstore. This whole range of information can be presented in three reports.

Comparative balance sheet.—The first report should be a balance sheet separated into five balanced divisions dealing with (1) current funds, (2) loan funds, (3) endowment and other non-expendable funds, (4) plant funds, and (5) agency funds. In each division the total debits and total credits should equal each other.[1]

A satisfactory form for this report is shown in Figure 23. It should be observed in connection with this form that four column headings have been suggested. The first column gives the status of each item as of one year ago; the second gives the position at the close of the last fiscal year; the third shows the condition at the end of the month being reported; and the fourth shows increases or decreases in each item within the past year. The fourth column will offer a more valid comparison if it shows differences between the present position and that of one year ago to date than if it compares the present position with that at the close of the fiscal year. In the current-funds section, for example, the assets and working

[1] See the report of the National Committee on Standard Reports for Institutions of Higher Education, entitled *Suggested Forms for Financial Reports of Colleges and Universities* (July, 1931), for a detailed statement of the items to be included in the balance sheet.

balance fluctuate so violently during the year that comparison of these items is relatively meaningless unless made between comparable stages or periods in different years. A comparison of the figures for October 31,

BALANCE SHEET

———— COLLEGE

Date ————

	One Year Ago to Date	As at Close of Fiscal Year	Present Situation*	Increases or Decreases
CURRENT FUNDS				
Assets				
(Detail)†				
Liabilities				
(Detail)†				
LOAN FUNDS				
Assets				
(Detail)†				
Liabilities				
(Detail)†				
ENDOWMENT AND OTHER NON-EXPENDABLE FUNDS				
Assets				
(Detail)†				
Liabilities				
(Detail)†				
PLANT FUNDS				
Assets				
(Detail)†				
Liabilities				
(Detail)†				
AGENCY FUNDS				
Assets				
(Detail)†				
Liabilities)				
(Detail)†				

* Omit this column in the case of reports made at the end of the fiscal year.

† Details should be in accordance with the recommendations of the National Committee on Standard Reports for Institutions of Higher Education.

FIG. 23.—Form suggested for balance sheet

1931, with those for June 30, 1931, would present considerable contrast; the October picture would show a much more prosperous condition because of the cash on hand from the recent collection of student fees resulting in a much larger working balance. A comparison between October 31, 1931, and October 31, 1930, would be much more significant.

The balance sheet alone, even though it be a comparative balance sheet showing growing assets, decreasing liabilities, and consequently increasing material wealth, does not signify an improved educational program, which, of course, is the purpose for which a college should exist. Nevertheless, increasing wealth in the form of a growing endowment, an improved plant, enlarged loan funds, and an enhanced working balance has a real significance which should not be overlooked.

Operating statement.—The second report recommended is a combined operating statement and summary budget report. A satisfactory form for such a report is shown in Figure 24.

The income section of this report should give the income by sources; the expense section should be arranged according to the classification of expenditures in the accounting system and should represent totals only of each class of expenditure, and not the detailed items as set up in the working draft of the budget.

This report brings out such facts as probable increases or decreases in income from student fees, endowment, gifts from members of the board of trustees, alumni, and friends; and changes in total educational salaries, administrative expenses, costs of operation of the plant, etc. When these facts are considered along with those presented in the comparative balance sheet, much is disclosed regarding trends and tendencies brought about by administrative policies which have consciously or unconsciously been operating. Trustees who have been inactive through lack of interest may be stimulated, under proper leadership and direction, to become powers for the cause of the institution.

Report of supplementary business activities.—The third report which should be rendered deals with the supplementary business activities. A balance sheet and an operating statement should be prepared at frequent intervals for each such activity. The overhead charge for services of the business office, the rental charge, and the cost of student labor which is paid in board and room should be journalized into the expense accounts at the beginning of each semester for that semester. An appropriate footnote should be included in the financial statement calling attention to the fact that these charges have been made in advance; this avoids a

OPERATING STATEMENT AND SUMMARY BUDGET REPORT
_____ COLLEGE
Date _____

Income	Total Last Year (Actual)	Total Budget Estimate This Year	Total Last Year to Date	Total This Year to Date	Balance Yet To Be Collected	Probable Increase or Decrease Compared with Budget
Student fees........						
Endowment........						
Etc.*..............						

Expenses and Working Balance	Total Last Year (Actual)	Total Budget Appropria- tion This Year	Total Last Year to Date	Total This Year to Date	Balance of Appropria- tions Yet Available	Present Estimate of Increased Need or Surplus
Administration.....						
Instruction.........						
Operation and main- tenance..........						
Etc.*						

* Items should correspond to the major divisions of the accounting system.

FIG. 24.—Form suggested for operating statement and summary budget report

series of journal entries monthly. If the statement is made in comparative form with column headings showing (1) condition one year ago to date, (2) condition at the close of the last fiscal year, and (3) situation at the present time, a close check will be provided on the operations of each enterprise. A note should be made on the statement telling how many persons are regularly being served as compared with the number one year ago, and giving the unit price as compared with that a year ago.

This report should be sent to the president of the college and the executive committee monthly, and to the whole board of trustees at least as often as it meets.

Control reports.—In addition to the reports which are intended chiefly to create interest and confidence on the part of the large board of trustees, two other types of financial report are needed by the president of a college or university and the executive committee, for control purposes. These are, first, a detailed report dealing with endowment and its investment; and, second, a budget report presenting somewhat more detail than the one recommended for general distribution.

The endowment report should present a detailed list of all endowment investments. It should also call attention to the amount of uninvested cash, with recommendations for its investment.

The budget report should be arranged in the same form as the budget, in that it should present the same detailed information with reference to each source of income and each item of expense. The income section should have column headings as follows: (1) "Total for Last Year," (2) "Budget Estimate This Year," (3) "Total Last Year to Date," (4) "Total This Year to Date," (5) "Balance Yet To Be Collected," and (6) "Probable Increase or Decrease Compared with Budget." This report should be prepared with the same detail as the budget; and, since it presents for each item the condition which existed one year ago to date (the period of last year which is comparable to the present time), it should be most enlightening, especially in view of the fact that the outcome for last year is known. This information considered in connection with changes in policies for this year and other factors which cause this year to differ from last, such as changes in tuition rates, changes in the form of investments, changes in the amount of endowment, changes in enrolment, etc., should make possible a very accurate forecast of the income for this year.

The expense section of the budget report should display in detail the information which has been presented in summary form to the whole board. It should present an exact duplicate of the budget for all departments which have supply, equipment, book, or student-labor budgets.

The salary items do not need to be reviewed, since they are fixed amounts and should progress regularly as budgeted. With this exception, the entire detail of the expense section of the budget should be reported. The column headings should be: (1) "Actual Expenditure for Last Year," (2) "Budget Appropriation for This Year," (3) "Expenditure for Last Year to Date," (4) "Actual Expenditure to Date This Year," (5) "Amount Requisitioned but Not Yet Charged," (6) "Balance Available

NAME OF COLLEGE

DETAILED BUDGET REPORT AS OF

Date ———

Expenditures	Total Last Year	Budget Appropriation This Year	Total Last Year to Date	Total Expended This Year to Date	Amount Requisitioned but Not Yet Charged	Balance Available
Ancient language:						
Salaries.........						
Supplies........						
Books..........						
Equipment......						
Art:						
Salaries.........						
Supplies........						
Books..........						
Equipment......						
Bible:						
Salaries.........						
Supplies........						
Books..........						
Equipment.....						
Etc.:						

FIG. 25.—Form suggested for detailed budget report

for Expenditure." This may be arranged in whatever form is most convenient and at the same time useful. The form shown in Figure 25 is suggested.

Departmental budget reports.—Monthly reports should be made to the heads of departments which have supply, equipment, book, or student-labor budgets, giving such information as follows: (1) budget appropriation for this year for supplies, equipment, books, student labor; (2) expenditure to date for each; (3) amount of each requisitioned, and on order but not yet charged; (4) the available balance. The available balance is that which remains after actual expenditures and requisitioned items are deducted from the appropriation. Forms should be printed for this purpose. The form shown in Figure 26 is presented to illustrate a desirable arrangement for such a report.

The labor required in the preparation of these recommended reports is by no means as great as at first it may seem to be. Since a trial balance should be taken from the books at the close of each month, giving in detail assets, liabilities, income, and expense, the task of making a balance sheet and an operating statement is comparatively small. This applies not only to the educational program of the college, but equally to the supplementary business activities.

DEPARTMENTAL BUDGET REPORT

———— College

Department_____ Date_____

Item	Budget Appropriation	Expended to Date	Requisitioned Not Yet Charged	Available Balance
Supplies.................				
Equipment...............				
Books....................				
Student help.............				
Total.................				

Fig. 26.—Suggested form for departmental budget report

The comparative data required in the balance sheet need merely be copied from reports of the previous year. This should be done in advance during the summer or at times during the year when work is a little less strenuous than at the close of the month. Thus, in connection with the balance sheet, only two columns have to be compiled monthly. The first three columns require only the time of a typist to copy. The same is true of the operating report and the budget report, and of the detailed budget report which should go monthly to the president and the executive committee.

Stenographic help is inexpensive compared with the time of a college or university president and the executive committee of the board of trustees; and the more concise and complete the reports can be made, the clearer the present picture is when viewed with past performance as a background. Intelligent judgments and decisions are much easier to make in the light of full information.

Treasurer's report.—A treasurer's report should be prepared annually for distribution among trustees, contributors, friends, and prospective donors to the college. Arnett's discussion of the treasurer's report[1] is very complete and might well serve as the pattern for such a report.

Criticisms of reporting systems.—Detailed criticisms of the reporting systems of this group of colleges have not been undertaken as a part of this study, although they were discussed in the individual reports made to the several colleges. Practically all of the colleges visited are deficient in one or more of the reporting essentials. A few of the colleges provide almost nothing in the way of financial reports. It is recognized that the number and completeness of the reports must necessarily depend upon the resources of the institution and the time which staff members have available for their preparation. No institution, however, should neglect to keep its executive officers, trustees, alumni, and friends completely and clearly informed regarding the necessary financial items.

AUDITS

An elementary rule of good business practice demands that there be each year an official audit by a disinterested public accountant. All but four of the colleges of this group follow the practice of having an annual audit. Two of the four which have not had regular audits in the past have recently arranged to make this a regular part of their business procedure.

The audit should be made by a certified public accountant, preferably one who is well acquainted with the problems of institutional accounting. In all but three of the colleges which have an audit the work is done by a certified public accountant. Two of these three use public accountants who are not certified; the other used the students in its accounting classes for the audit made the year preceding the survey.[2] This was good practice for the students, but did not result in a satisfactory audit for the college.

A good audit should furnish criticisms of the accounting plans and practices. Obviously, it is necessary for the auditor to have considerable familiarity with institutional accounting in order to make valuable criticisms. Several of the audits in this group of colleges failed to provide any criticisms of the accounting policies.

It is a good practice to rotate auditors every three or four years. This

---

[1] Trevor Arnett, *College and University Finance* (New York: General Education Board, 1922), pp. 105–70. See also *Suggested Forms for Financial Reports of Colleges and Universities* (National Committee on Standard Reports for Institutions of Higher Education; Lloyd Morey, University of Illinois, chairman; 1931).

[2] This was not the usual practice in this institution.

plan gives the benefit of a fresh point of view in criticizing the accounting. Rotation of auditors also should reduce the costs of the audit somewhat, if prices are arranged in advance.

For obvious reasons those responsible for the financial activities to be audited should have no voice in the selection of the auditor. An audit should furnish a truthful, clear-cut picture of the year's operations and the present financial position, utterly devoid of any personal bias or partiality. The auditor should not be selected either by the business officer or by the finance or investment committees of the board, but by a special committee of the board composed of persons who have been assigned no specific responsibility for financial affairs. The report of the audit should be made to this committee. Eight of the colleges studied fail to arrange for their audit by an impartial committee. In one college in which the audit was arranged for by the treasurer, the auditor had entered an item of "uninvested cash" in the endowment fund, amounting to more than $150,000. Investigation showed that this item was not uninvested cash, but consisted of endowment funds which had been loaned to current funds. The auditor's excuse for the misrepresentation was that he had been ordered to set up the item as uninvested cash by the treasurer, who employed him.

The form of the audit tables should be the same each year, so that the file of audits will permit comparative financial reports. The form of the tables and the classification may well be dictated by the administration of the college, so that the arrangement will be in the form most useful to the executive officers. The audit will be found especially useful to the treasurer in the preparation of his annual report. The rotation of auditors not infrequently results in recommendations for changes in the form of accounts and in the form of the audit. Such recommendations should not be heeded when once a satisfactory set-up is obtained, since it is more important that the audit be in comparative form from year to year than that minor adjustments be made to improve its arrangement.

The audit should be complete, in that all the financial units of the institution should be checked. Independent schools affiliated with the college, the supplementary business enterprises such as dormitories, dining-halls, and bookstore, and even the accounts of student organizations, may well be included in the audit. Three of the colleges of this group are subject to adverse criticism because the audit does not cover all the financial units. In one of these cases no audit was made of the endowment fund, certainly one of the most important units which should be included.

On the whole, the practices of this group of colleges with reference to audits are very commendable. In fourteen institutions there is no criticism whatever connected with the audit. One of the colleges, in addition to the annual audit, has arranged for a continuous audit by an outside firm of public accountants, thus insuring a check-up not only at the end of the year but at frequent intervals during the year. Annual audits by certified public accountants should certainly be continued as a part of the future policy of all these colleges.

CHAPTER L

EXPENDITURES AND ECONOMIC COSTS

CURRENT EXPENDITURES

The current expenditures of an educational institution may be grouped into two rather sharply defined divisions. The first consists of the current expenditures that are applied directly to the purpose of educating students. This group of expenditures may be termed "educational," and for purpose of analysis may be broken up into the following functions: (1) administration; (2) instruction, including instructional salaries, supplies, and the expenses of the library; (3) operation and maintenance of the plant, exclusive of that used for supplementary business activities; (4) fixed charges; (5) commencement and public occasions; (6) contributions to educational exterprises; and (7) student welfare.

The second type of current expenditure consists of items not so directly applied to the purpose of educating students. Expenditures of this type may be termed "non-educational." While of much less importance so far as the educational program is concerned, non-educational expenditures not infrequently are responsible for rather large items in the current budget of the college. This classification includes the following items: (1) scholarships and remitted fees; (2) expenses of financial promotion; (3) losses on supplementary business enterprises; (4) interest on indebtedness; (5) publicity (except the expense of the college catalogue, which is considered as an administrative charge); and (6) pensions paid from current funds (regular payments to pension funds are considered as an educational cost).

Certain types of outlays are excluded entirely from consideration in this study of costs. Among those not included are capital outlays, the payment of annuities, and funds used for the retirement of indebtedness. The expense of managing the endowment fund is not considered as a current expenditure but as a deduction from gross income on investments. The gross expenditure for such supplementary business enterprises as dormitories and dining-halls are not included, but only the net deficit, if any. The expenses of the business office have been prorated to the management of endowment and the supplementary business enterprises wherever necessary.

For the purpose of this analysis an entire reclassification was undertaken from the accounts of each of the colleges. This reclassification was made in every case by a member of the survey staff during a personal visit to the institution. Extreme care was taken to make certain of absolute uniformity in classification when analyzing the expenditures in the various colleges.

Since the collection and tabulation of these data, the National Committee on Standard Reports for Institutions of Higher Education has prepared and published suggested forms for a uniform system of financial reports for colleges and universities.[1] The classification of expenditures suggested by this committee is very similar to that used in this study, although it differs in some minor details. Because of the fact that the present set-up differs in a few details from the classification suggested by the committee, it would not be advisable for colleges which adopt the new standard reporting system to attempt to compare their costs with those presented in this volume without a re-analysis according to the classification used in this study.

Expenditures may best be compared from institution to institution by reducing them to the amount per student enrolled, thus giving comparable figures for all colleges. In making the analysis of expenditures per student for this study, the divisor used in each case is the average enrolment of full-time students for the two semesters or three terms of the regular nine-month academic year. The expenditures, used as the dividend in obtaining the unit costs, are also those of the regular academic year. Several of the colleges spend some of their funds for the subsidy of supplementary educational enterprises, such as summer sessions and extension work, which are not directly applicable to the work of the regular year. In practically every case, however, it is the policy to make these enterprises self-supporting. For that reason the net subsidy necessary from regular year funds for these projects has been considered an expenditure of the regular year in the present cost analysis. The amounts involved in all cases are small and do not materially affect the totals.

Table 122 shows the educational, non-educational, and total expenditures per student in each of thirty-four colleges. Brothers College is omitted from all the cost data presented in this and succeeding chapters because of the fact that this is a new institution and the enrolments have not yet reached the number for which facilities have been prepared.

This table shows a rather wide range in both educational and non-educational expenditures per student in the group of thirty-four colleges.

[1] *Suggested Forms for Financial Reports of Colleges and Universities* (National Committee on Standard Reports for Institutions of Higher Education; Lloyd Morey, chairman, University of Illinois, Urbana, Ill.; July, 1931).

The median educational expenditure per student for the colleges on the approved list of the Association of American Universities is somewhat

TABLE 122

EDUCATIONAL EXPENDITURES, NON-EDUCATIONAL EXPENDITURES, AND TOTAL
ANNUAL EXPENDITURES PER STUDENT IN THIRTY-FOUR COLLEGES

Institution	Fiscal Year	Educational Expenditures per Student	Non-educational Expenditures per Student	Total Annual Expenditures per Student
*Hamline	1928–29	$390.76	$102.33	$493.09
*MacMurray	1929–30	356.67	121.11	477.78
Ozark Wesleyan	1928–29	280.90	166.84	447.74
*Allegheny	1928–29	363.89	59.69	423.58
*Cornell	1928–29	340.62	74.05	414.67
Baldwin-Wallace	1929–30	365.34	43.02	408.36
*DePauw	1929–30	293.29	96.65	389.94
Evansville	1928–29	274.39	110.52	384.91
*Pacific	1929–30	339.41	42.49	381.90
*Dickinson	1928–29	326.38	34.22	360.60
West Virginia Wesleyan	1929–30	338.77	21.45	360.22
*Illinois Wesleyan	1929–30	273.49	80.99	354.48
*Ohio Wesleyan	1929–30	308.85	40.62	349.47
*Mount Union	1929–30	294.10	55.22	349.32
Kansas Wesleyan	1929–30	270.03	72.82	342.85
*Lawrence	1928–29	315.85	25.92	341.77
Intermountain	1929–30	296.65	43.34	339.99
*Chattanooga	1928–29	287.16	44.65	331.81
Iowa Wesleyan	1928–29	261.45	64.39	325.84
Nebraska Wesleyan	1929–30	290.42	30.22	320.64
Dakota Wesleyan	1929–30	257.68	45.97	303.65
Southwestern	1929–30	260.98	42.61	303.59
*Baker	1929–30	268.28	31.80	300.08
McKendree	1929–30	272.64	26.06	298.70
Gooding	1929–30	221.18	67.44	288.62
Central Wesleyan	1928–29	246.27	41.99	288.26
*Albion	1929–30	258.76	16.74	275.50
*Simpson	1928–29	207.27	52.93	260.20
*Willamette	1929–30	239.98	14.89	254.87
Ohio Northern	1929–30	214.99	34.77	249.76
*Morningside	1928–29	209.75	37.27	247.02
Oklahoma City	1928–29	152.84	65.79	218.63
Puget Sound	1929–30	190.73	17.23	207.96
Union	1928–29	188.50	12.14	200.64
Median, all colleges	....	$273.94	$ 43.18	$335.90
*Median, A.A.U. colleges	....	294.10	44.65	349.47
Median, non-A.A.U. colleges	....	261.45	43.02	303.65

* Institutions on the approved list of the Association of American Universities.

higher than that for the colleges which do not hold national accreditation. There is little difference, however, between the two groups of colleges in the median non-educational expenditure per student.

There are two possible interpretations that may be placed on educational costs—the one relating to the quality of the program, the other to the efficiency of management. For example, in a college having a relatively high cost per student it is impossible to determine, from the cost figures alone, whether the data indicate an unusually satisfactory program, with a well-qualified and well-paid faculty, a good library, good instructional equipment, etc., or, on the contrary, a wasteful administration, the increased costs being used for purposes that do not contribute to the effectiveness of the educational program. Similarly, a college having a low cost per student may be putting on a poor program, or it may be managed very efficiently, thus getting large educational returns for the funds expended. If equal efficiency in management can be assumed, the cost data then indicate variations in the quality of the program; if it can be assumed that any two institutions maintain programs equivalent in quality, then differences in costs indicate differences in efficiency of management.

Previous studies[1] have shown rather conclusively that educational costs are vitally affected by the size of the enrolment. Colleges with large enrolments can maintain a program of a given quality at a considerably lower cost per student than is possible in colleges of small enrolments. The cost data for this group of colleges must therefore be interpreted in the light of the size of the various institutions.

Figure 27 presents data showing the average educational expenditure per student in colleges of various sizes, classified according to type of accreditation.

This chart shows that the group of colleges as a whole displays the relationship between size of enrolment and per capita cost that is usually found. Classification of the institutions by type of accreditation disturbs this relationship somewhat, the largest A.A.U. colleges and the smallest non-A.A.U. colleges being out of line. The fact that most of the eleven colleges in the smallest-sized group of institutions not on the approved list of the Association of American Universities also lack even regional accreditation explains the low average cost for this group.

The interpretation of the non-educational costs per student is rather

[1] Floyd W. Reeves and John Dale Russell, *The Measurement of College Excellence*, Bulletin of the Bureau of School Service, I, No. 4 (Lexington: University of Kentucky, June, 1929), 33.

difficult owing to the variety of items which comprise this expenditure. In the case of some of the items classified as non-educational an institution should be commended for a relatively large expenditure; this is true

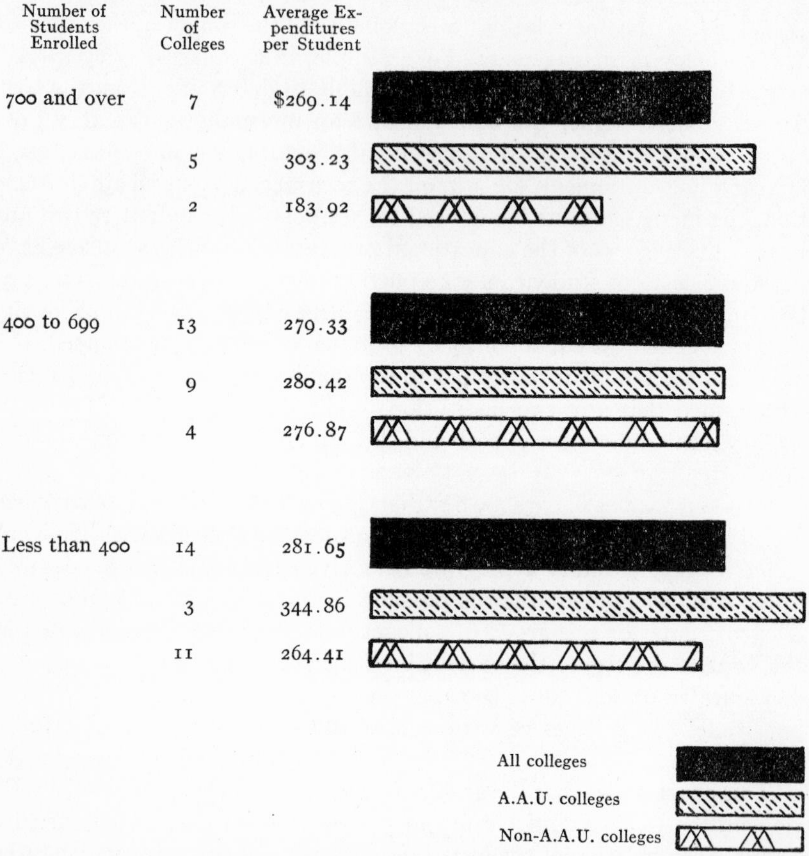

Number of Students Enrolled	Number of Colleges	Average Expenditures per Student	
700 and over	7	$269.14	
	5	303.23	
	2	183.92	
400 to 699	13	279.33	
	9	280.42	
	4	276.87	
Less than 400	14	281.65	
	3	344.86	
	11	264.41	

All colleges

A.A.U. colleges

Non-A.A.U. colleges

FIG. 27.—Educational expenditures per student in colleges of various sizes and types of accreditation.

particularly for such items as scholarships and pensions. In the case of other items in this classification, however, a large expenditure is an indication of poor business policies; this criticism applies especially to expenditure for interest payments.

Figure 28 presents data showing the average non-educational expenditure in colleges of various sizes, grouped according to the type of accreditation held.

This diagram shows that there is a close relationship between the amount of non-educational expenditure per student and the size of the enrolment, when colleges of the same accredited status are compared, the

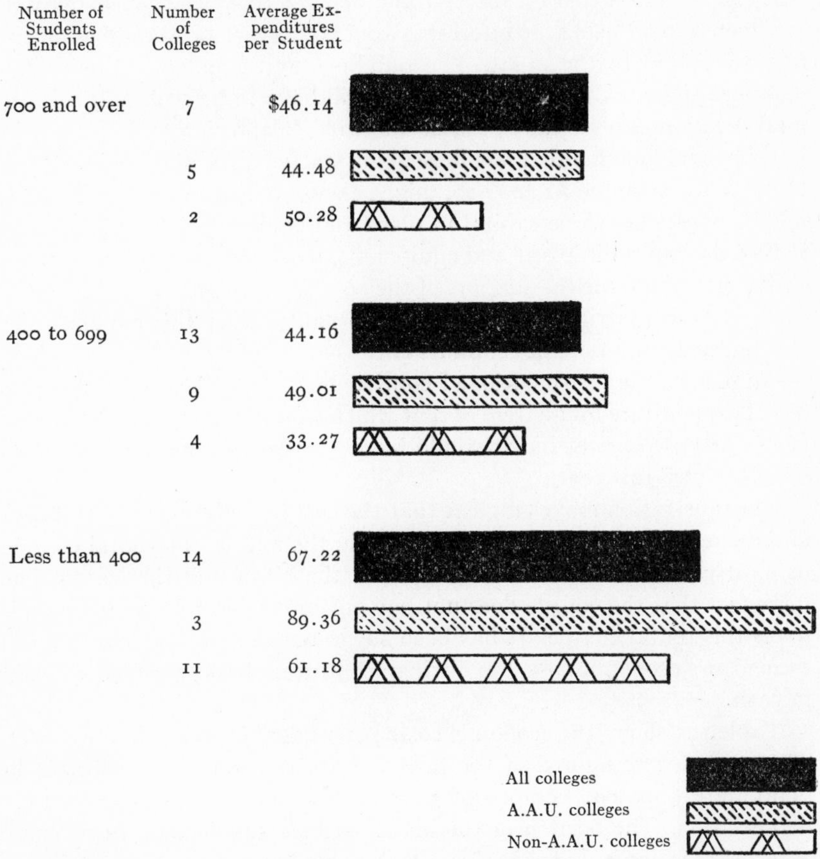

Number of Students Enrolled	Number of Colleges	Average Expenditures per Student	
700 and over	7	$46.14	
	5	44.48	
	2	50.28	
400 to 699	13	44.16	
	9	49.01	
	4	33.27	
Less than 400	14	67.22	
	3	89.36	
	11	61.18	

All colleges
A.A.U. colleges
Non-A.A.U. colleges

FIG. 28.—Non-educational expenditures per student in colleges of various sizes and types of accreditation.

larger colleges tending to have smaller expenditures per student for this purpose than the small colleges. The type of accreditation held does not seem to affect the cost for non-educational purposes.

ECONOMIC COSTS

In addition to the types of expenditures which have already been classified as educational and non-educational, there is in every college a cost of an entirely different type. As a rule, this cost does not result in an expenditure of money; but it is, nevertheless, a true cost. The college has funds invested in its physical plant and equipment. Any investment of this type entails a cost for interest and depreciation. The college may be considered to be losing the interest it would otherwise be obtaining on the funds invested in the plant. The buildings and equipment are always deteriorating, and at some future date will have to be replaced; this annual deterioration results in a cost known as "depreciation."

One could imagine that a college being started anew with a given capital sum, for example $2,000,000, might choose one of several policies. It might invest the whole capital in plant and equipment. It might invest half of the capital in plant and equipment, retaining the remainder as an endowment fund for the support of the college. It might have the opportunity to rent outright an entire college plant; under this circumstance the new institution might retain its entire capital of $2,000,000 as endowment. Under the last-mentioned contingency, the college would have a direct expenditure for an item of rent which would be lacking under either of the first two plans, but it would have a larger endowment fund from which to pay this rent.

The illustration makes it clear that the cost brought about by interest and depreciation on plant investment is in the nature of a rental charge, in most cases the institution being both the lessor and the lessee. The mere fact that the college does not pay out rent in cash in no way eliminates this rental charge. It has been suggested that this type of cost be termed an "economic cost," to distinguish it from the costs which are paid in cash.

Table 123 shows the economic costs per student in thirty-four colleges. These costs were figured at the rate of 8 per cent on the investment in plant and equipment, comprising 5 per cent for interest and 3 per cent for depreciation. The portion of the plant used for supplementary business enterprises is not included in this calculation. The basis of the calculation is the original costs of the buildings and equipment in all cases where these data could be obtained. Where these figures were not available, appraisal values were used.

Too much importance should not be attached to the figures as given in this table because of the variability in the basis of figuring the invested value of the academic plants in the various colleges. The data indicate in a rough way the relative expensiveness of the plant provisions in the various institutions. Such factors as the size of the student body, the methods of arriving at plant valuations, the quality of the space provided, etc., all condition the economic cost per student.

TABLE 123

Economic Costs per Student in Thirty-four Colleges

Institution	Fiscal Year	Economic Cost per Student
Baldwin-Wallace....................	1929–30	$252.06
*Chattanooga......................	1928–29	217.58
*Dickinson........................	1928–29	176.68
*MacMurray.......................	1929–30	166.12
*Allegheny........................	1928–29	163.70
Iowa Wesleyan....................	1928–29	152.82
*Hamline..........................	1928–29	142.14
*Pacific...........................	1929–30	139.82
*Mount Union.....................	1929–30	136.57
*Illinois Wesleyan.................	1929–30	136.36
Kansas Wesleyan..................	1929–30	117.92
Intermountain.....................	1929–30	116.07
Union............................	1928–29	115.58
*DePauw..........................	1929–30	113.12
*Lawrence........................	1928–29	110.86
Evansville........................	1928–29	107.91
West Virginia Wesleyan...........	1929–30	102.14
*Baker............................	1929–30	101.78
Central Wesleyan..................	1928–29	99.27
*Albion...........................	1929–30	98.06
Dakota Wesleyan..................	1929–30	97.85
*Cornell..........................	1928–29	96.19
*Willamette.......................	1929–30	92.28
*Ohio Wesleyan...................	1929–30	84.22
McKendree.......................	1929–30	82.31
Nebraska Wesleyan................	1929–30	79.34
*Morningside......................	1928–29	79.25
Ohio Northern....................	1929–30	77.73
Southwestern.....................	1929–30	74.75
Puget Sound......................	1929–30	73.18
Gooding..........................	1929–30	70.03
Ozark Wesleyan..................	1928–29	69.28
*Simpson..........................	1928–29	64.96
Oklahoma City...................	1928–29	18.43
Median, all colleges..............	....	$101.96
*Median, A.A.U. colleges.........	....	113.12
Median, non-A.A.U. colleges.....	....	97.85

* Institutions on the approved list of the Association of American Universities.

CHAPTER LI

EDUCATIONAL COSTS CLASSIFIED BY FUNCTION

The educational expenditures of a college may best be analyzed by classifying them according to the various functions served. For the purpose of the present study the educational activities of the colleges have been classified into seven different functions: (1) administration; (2) instruction (with the subclasses of instructional salaries, instructional supplies, and library); (3) operation and maintenance of plant; (4) fixed charges; (5) commencement and public occasions; (6) contributions to educational enterprises; (7) student welfare. A brief explanation will be given of the types of items included under each functional classification.[1]

Under administration are included all the salaries of administrative officers, with the exception of the scholastic dean or deans and the personnel deans (dean of men and dean of women). The salaries of the business office staff are prorated in such a way that the educational expenditures are not charged with the proportions of these expenses which are properly chargeable to the management of supplementary business enterprises or to the handling of invested funds. The classification of administration also includes all the salaries of the clerical staff in the administrative offices, and the office supplies, postage, telephone and telegraph, and similar office expenses. The expense of the travel of administrative officers is included. Professional service for administrative purposes, such as legal counsel, audits, surveys, etc., is charged against administration. The amounts paid as dues to educational associations are also classified as administration.

The classification of "instruction" includes three subclasses—instructional salaries, instructional supplies, and library. Under instructional salaries are put not only the payments to faculty members but also the salaries for academic administrative officers such as the dean. The expenses of the dean's office are included under instructional supplies, along with the usual items of departmental supplies and equipment. The expenditures for the library include the salaries of the staff, the outlays for new books and binding, and the supplies and equipment purchased.

---

[1] The classification here given differs somewhat from that set up by the National Committee on Standard Reports for Institutions of Higher Learning, to which reference has already been made.

The expenditures for plant operation and maintenance include the salaries of all plant workmen, the fuel, light, gas, and water, the building supplies, the repairs and replacements to the plant (not new additions or betterments), the fire insurance on the plant, and the workman's compensation insurance on plant employees.

Fixed charges include regular payments toward pension funds for faculty members, workman's compensation insurance carried on the teaching staff, and payments for sabbatic leaves.

The classification "commencement and public occasions" includes all expenditures for public lectures and entertainments, as well as the expenses of the regular commencement.

Contributions to educational enterprises include the net subsidy given to such supplementary educational activities as the summer school, extension classes,[1] and correspondence study. The amount considered as an expenditure is the excess of the gross expenditures over the gross receipts of these activities.

The classification "student welfare" includes a miscellaneous group of activities, all of which are directed toward improving the conditions under which students work. The salaries of the personnel officers (dean of men, dean of women, etc.) and the expenses of their offices are included under this category. The classification also includes the student health service, the cost of chapel and convocation programs, subsidies given student organizations, the expenses of the placement service, student entertainments, contributions to such activities as the band, glee club, debates, athletics, student publications, etc., and public lectures for the student body.

EXPENDITURES PER STUDENT FOR EACH FUNCTION
IN THE COLLEGES STUDIED

Table 124 presents data showing for thirty-four colleges the expenditure per student for each function.

This table shows considerable variation among the thirty-four colleges with regard to the expenditures per student for the various functions. It has been shown in a preceding section that the colleges on the approved list of the Association of American Universities have a higher median educational expenditure per student than the colleges not holding this type of accreditation. When the analysis is made separately by functions, the colleges on the approved list of the Association exceed those not holding

---

[1] At the College of Puget Sound the extension classes are carried as an integral part of the regular teaching load. For that reason no separation has been made in the costs of this institution on account of the extension teaching.

national accreditation in median expenditures per student for every function with the single exception of administration. The difference is rather

TABLE 124

DISTRIBUTION BY FUNCTION OF EDUCATIONAL EXPENDITURES PER
STUDENT FOR THIRTY-FOUR COLLEGES

Institution	Fiscal Year	Total Educational Expenditures	Administration	Instructional Salaries	Instructional Supplies	Library
*Hamline..............	1928–29	$390.76	$56.58	$228.07	$ 9.67	$18.50
Baldwin-Wallace.......	1929–30	365.34	39.88	224.28	17.60	14.16
*Allegheny.............	1928–29	363.89	45.79	185.04	13.09	14.72
*MacMurray...........	1929–30	356.67	55.13	233.80	8.38	14.21
*Cornell...............	1928–29	340.62	38.54	195.18	11.98	14.55
*Pacific...............	1929–30	339.41	35.37	221.39	17.41	17.64
West Virginia Wesleyan..	1929–30	338.77	47.56	198.30	14.05	14.06
*Dickinson.............	1928–29	326.38	39.16	178.65	9.15	12.88
*Lawrence.............	1928–29	315.85	29.30	195.88	8.04	16.23
*Ohio Wesleyan.........	1929–30	308.85	26.14	190.68	14.72	18.11
Intermountain.........	1929–30	296.65	62.72	180.98	5.49	6.61
*Mount Union..........	1929–30	294.10	43.94	155.05	13.27	21.61
*DePauw..............	1929–30	293.29	23.53	174.33	10.31	12.56
Nebraska Wesleyan......	1929–30	290.42	23.13	188.35	11.42	12.28
*Chattanooga..........	1928–29	287.16	54.61	172.90	8.84	11.47
Ozark Wesleyan........	1928–29	280.90	64.65	176.04	....	4.93
Evansville.............	1928–29	274.39	49.36	177.53	3.10	11.10
*Illinois Wesleyan.......	1929–30	273.49	36.84	147.14	13.13	13.93
McKendree............	1929–30	272.64	33.95	181.06	6.83	13.34
Kansas Wesleyan.......	1929–30	270.03	42.03	174.72	5.34	7.95
*Baker................	1929–30	268.28	35.50	163.71	4.96	15.17
Iowa Wesleyan.........	1928–29	261.45	40.15	147.81	15.88	9.12
Southwestern..........	1929–30	260.98	35.76	164.74	8.54	12.01
*Albion...............	1928–29	258.76	28.15	154.14	17.98	11.81
Dakota Wesleyan.......	1928–29	257.68	39.90	150.56	0.64	12.57
Central Wesleyan.......	1928–29	246.27	30.63	162.10	5.35	4.54
*Willamette............	1929–30	239.98	27.50	162.01	7.74	12.22
Gooding...............	1929–30	221.18	52.63	103.07	3.48	8.27
Ohio Northern.........	1929–30	214.99	28.94	145.73	7.03	6.09
*Morningside...........	1928–29	209.75	27.16	140.39	8.91	6.52
*Simpson..............	1928–29	207.27	20.81	121.28	11.64	7.62
Puget Sound...........	1929–30	190.60	30.19	129.57	4.18	9.03
Union................	1928–29	188.50	29.37	115.32	2.20	3.54
Oklahoma City.........	1928–29	152.84	26.65	94.46	3.47	2.85
Median, all colleges...	....	$273.94	$36.30	$173.62	$ 8.69	$12.25
*Median, A.A.U. colleges	....	294.10	35.50	174.33	10.31	14.21
Median, non-A.A.U. colleges.............	....	261.45	39.88	164.74	5.35	9.03

* Institutions on the approved list of the Association of American Universities.

TABLE 124—*Continued*

Institution	Operation and Maintenance of Plant	Fixed Charges	Commencement and Public Occasions	Contributions to Educational Enterprises	Student Welfare
*Hamline................	$49.58	$12.12	$1.54	....	$14.70
Baldwin-Wallace.......	61.09	....	1.88	....	6.45
*Allegheny.............	57.92	12.35	5.07	2.27	27.64
*MacMurray...........	32.79	0.15	0.99	....	11.22
*Cornell...............	45.77	15.09	0.65	....	18.86
*Pacific................	34.97	1.88	....	....	10.75
West Virginia Wesleyan.	41.10	....	1.88	....	21.82
*Dickinson.............	61.21	3.72	8.17	....	13.44
*Lawrence.............	39.58	7.10	1.53	3.90	14.29
*Ohio Wesleyan.........	37.28	10.47	1.04	0.14	10.27
Intermountain.........	27.51	....	0.21	....	13.13
*Mount Union..........	37.55	0.78	1.59	12.24	8.07
*DePauw	48.89	4.84	1.12	0.97	16.74
Nebraska Wesleyan....	42.61	0.31	0.47	....	11.85
*Chattanooga...........	33.34	....	1.10	3.26	1.64
Ozark Wesleyan........	28.60	....	0.63	....	6.05
Evansville.............	28.99	....	0.50	2.34	1.47
*Illinois Wesleyan.......	38.79	....	0.80	2.44	20.42
McKendree............	25.16	....	0.91	....	11.39
Kansas Wesleyan......	35.05	....	2.21	....	2.73
*Baker.................	41.29	....	1.46	1.93	4.26
Iowa Wesleyan.........	40.59	....	0.26	....	7.64
Southwestern..........	32.15	....	0.97	....	6.81
*Albion................	38.27	....	0.77	....	7.64
Dakota Wesleyan......	38.81	....	0.64	13.40	1.16
Central Wesleyan......	39.00	....	....	....	4.65
*Willamette.............	23.80	....	0.56	....	6.15
Gooding..............	38.82	....	....	....	14.91
Ohio Northern.........	23.47	0.60	0.55	....	2.58
*Morningside...........	23.65	....	....	0.78	2.34
*Simpson..............	36.70	....	....	....	9.22
Puget Sound...........	15.67	1.25	0.17	....	0.54
Union.................	32.91	....	....	5.16	....
Oklahoma City........	10.56	....	0.21	0.20	14.44
Median, all colleges..	$37.42	$ 0.00	$0.71	$0 .00	$ 8.66
*Median, A.A.U. colleges.............	38.27	0.78	1.04	0.14	10.75
Median, non-A.A.U. colleges.........	32.91	0.00	0.50	0.00	6.45

* Institutions on the approved list of the Association of American Universities.

important in the case of the functions of instructional salaries, instructional supplies, library, operation and maintenance of plant, and student welfare. In the case of a majority of these functions, costs tend to be related rather directly to the excellence of the educational program.

RELATIONSHIPS BETWEEN EXPENDITURES AND SIZE OF ENROL-
MENT AND TYPE OF ACCREDITATION

Figure 29 shows the average expenditures per student for administration in colleges of various sizes, grouped according to accreditation.

This graph shows that there is a very direct relationship between the

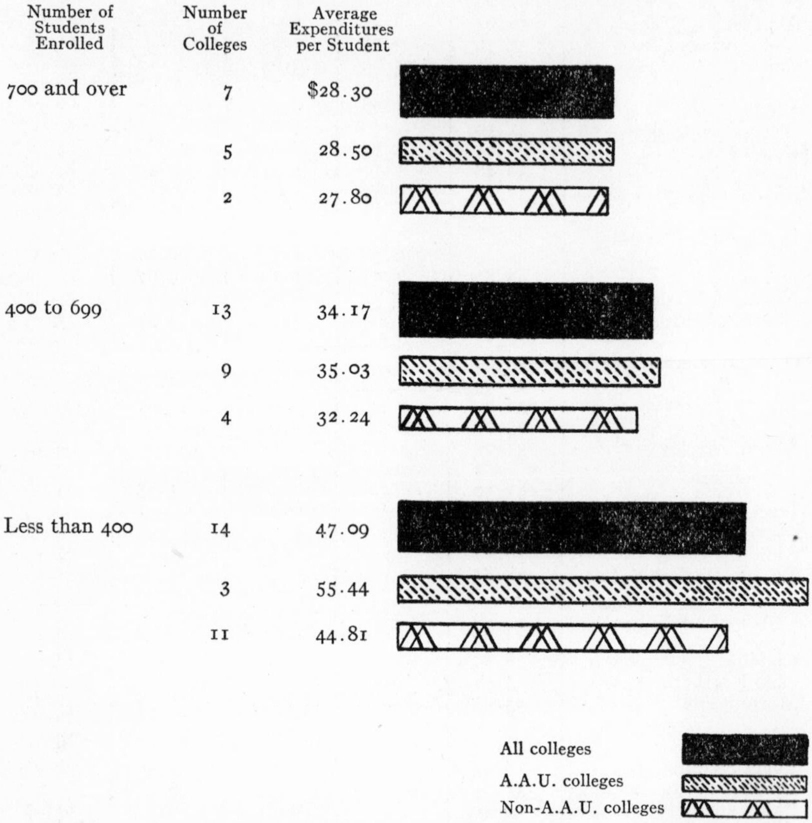

Number of Students Enrolled	Number of Colleges	Average Expenditures per Student	
700 and over	7	$28.30	
	5	28.50	
	2	27.80	
400 to 699	13	34.17	
	9	35.03	
	4	32.24	
Less than 400	14	47.09	
	3	55.44	
	11	44.81	

All colleges
A.A.U. colleges
Non-A.A.U. colleges

FIG. 29.—Average expenditures per student for administration in colleges of various
sizes and types of accreditation.

expenditures per student for administration and the size of the enrolment,
the larger institutions tending to have markedly lower costs for administration than the smaller ones. These data reflect one of the causes of inefficiency inherent in the small institution.

Figure 30 presents data showing the average per capita expenditure for
instruction (including salaries, supplies, and library) in colleges of various
sizes, grouped according to type of accreditation.

The interpretation of this diagram is rendered somewhat complicated by the fact that the small colleges have a lower average cost for instructional salaries than the groups having larger enrolments, while it would normally be expected, judging from previous studies which have been

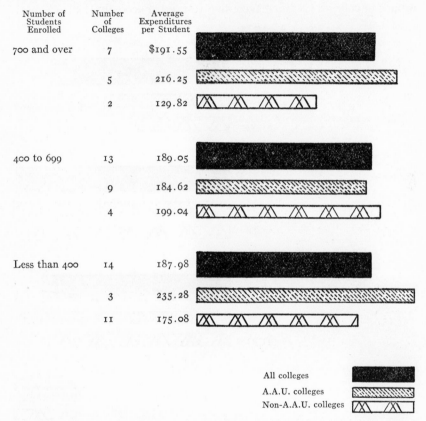

Number of Students Enrolled	Number of Colleges	Average Expenditures per Student
700 and over	7	$191.55
	5	216.25
	2	129.82
400 to 699	13	189.05
	9	184.62
	4	199.04
Less than 400	14	187.98
	3	235.28
	11	175.08

All colleges
A.A.U. colleges
Non-A.A.U. colleges

FIG. 30.—Average expenditures per student for instruction in colleges of various sizes and types of accreditation.

made, that the smallest colleges would have the highest average expenditure per student for instruction. The complicating factor in the case of Figure 30 seems to be the fact that a large proportion of institutions in the group having the smallest enrolments do not hold even regional accreditation. These institutions tend to pull down the average below what would normally be expected in colleges maintaining a minimum standard quality of program. It will be observed that for both the A.A.U. and the non-A.A.U. groups the average per capita expenditures for instruction are higher in the small institutions than in those having the larger enrolments.

Figure 31 presents data showing the relationship between expenditures for plant operation and maintenance and the size of the enrolment for groups of colleges classified according to type of accreditation.

Number of Students Enrolled	Number of Colleges	Average Expenditures per Student
700 and over	7	$33.29
	5	39.80
	2	17.02
400 to 699	13	39.86
	9	40.74
	4	37.88
Less than 400	14	35.18
	3	38.64
	11	34.23

All colleges
A.A.U. colleges
Non-A.A.U. colleges

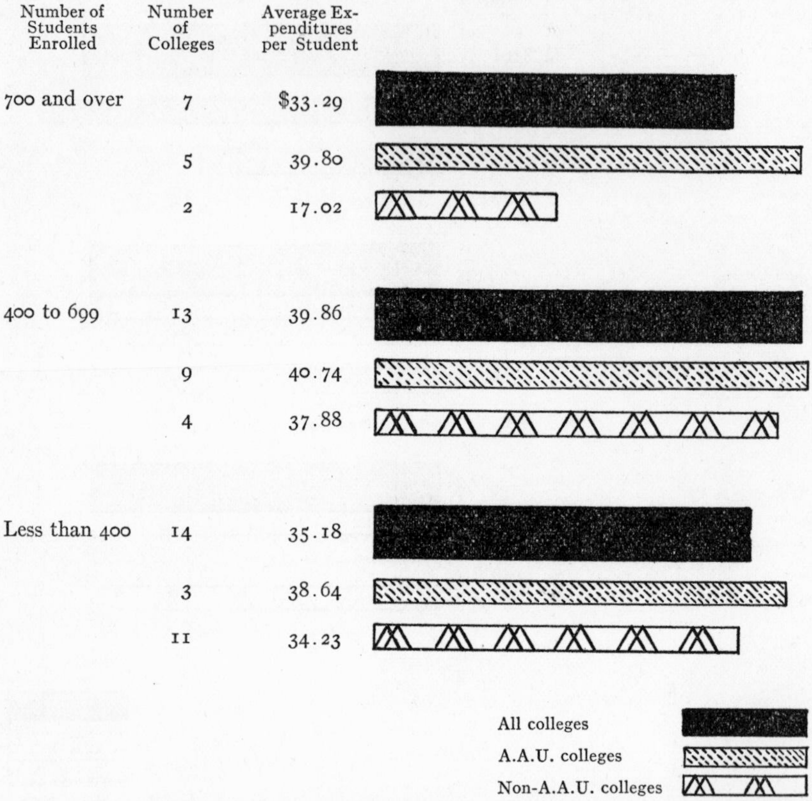

FIG. 31.—Expenditures per student for plant operation in colleges of various sizes and types of accreditation.

In this graph the interpretation is again complicated by the fact that the majority of the smaller colleges lack even regional accreditation. There appears to be no consistent relationship between the size of the institution and per capita expenditures for plant operation and maintenance.

Figure 32 shows the expenditures per student for student welfare in colleges of various sizes, grouped according to type of accreditation.

This figure shows that the larger colleges generally tend to have larger expenditures per student for student welfare than the smaller colleges have, and that a student has in general a better chance of obtaining a satisfactory amount of personnel service in a large college than in a small

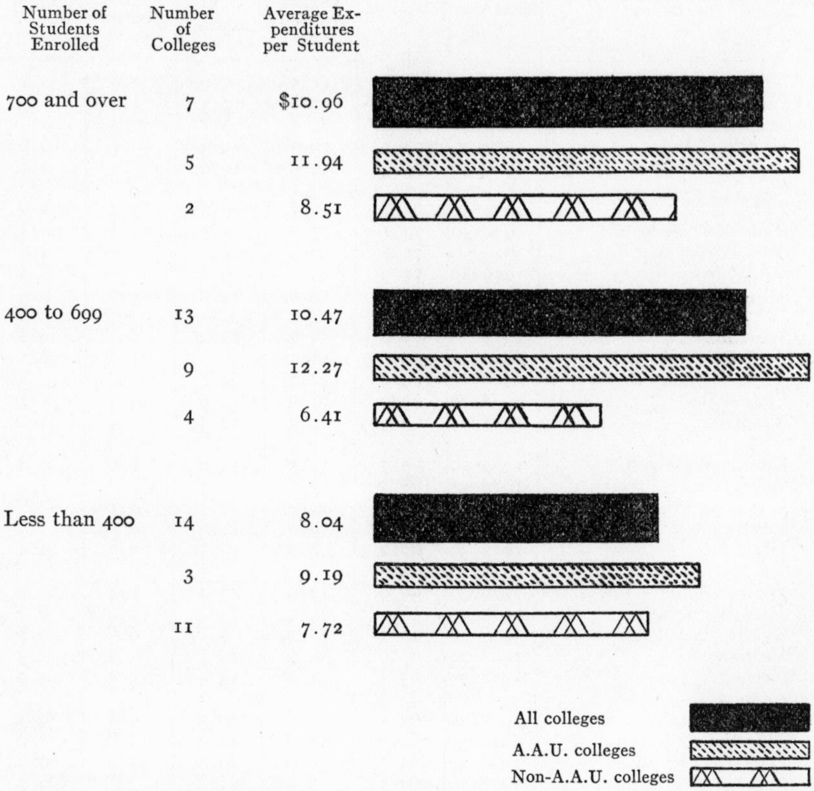

Number of Students Enrolled	Number of Colleges	Average Expenditures per Student	
700 and over	7	$10.96	
	5	11.94	
	2	8.51	
400 to 699	13	10.47	
	9	12.27	
	4	6.41	
Less than 400	14	8.04	
	3	9.19	
	11	7.72	

All colleges
A.A.U. colleges
Non-A.A.U. colleges

FIG. 32.—Expenditures per student for student welfare in colleges of various sizes and types of accreditation.

one. The counter-argument may be made that much of the real personnel service rendered in the small college is not so classified in the cost analysis, since it consists of volunteer faculty service. This may be true, but on this basis the expertness of the service may be questioned. Such items as medical and health service, vocational guidance and placement require expert handling; and expenditures for these purposes are usually fairly closely related to the quality and extensiveness of the service rendered.

TABLE 125

PERCENTAGE OF EDUCATIONAL EXPENDITURES FOR EACH
FUNCTION IN THIRTY-FOUR COLLEGES

Institution	Fiscal Year	Instruction	Administration	Operation and Maintenance of Plant	Student Welfare	Others†
*Willamette..............	1929–30	75.8	11.5	9.9	2.6	0.2
*Pacific.................	1929–30	75.5	10.4	10.3	3.2	0.6
Puget Sound............	1929–30	74.9	15.8	8.2	0.3	0.8
*Morningside............	1928–29	74.3	12.9	11.3	1.1	0.4
Ohio Northern..........	1929–30	73.9	13.5	10.9	1.2	0.5
McKendree.............	1929–30	73.8	12.5	9.2	4.2	0.3
Nebraska Wesleyan......	1929–30	73.1	7.8	14.7	4.1	0.3
*Ohio Wesleyan..........	1929–30	72.4	8.4	12.1	3.3	3.8
*MacMurray.............	1929–30	71.9	15.5	9.1	3.1	0.4
*Albion.................	1929–30	71.0	10.9	14.8	3.0	0.3
Southwestern...........	1929–30	71.0	13.7	12.3	2.6	0.4
Baldwin-Wallace........	1929–30	70.0	11.0	16.7	1.8	0.5
Central Wesleyan........	1928–29	69.9	12.4	15.8	1.9	....
Evansville..............	1928–29	69.9	17.9	10.6	0.5	1.1
*Lawrence...............	1928–29	69.7	9.3	12.5	4.5	4.0
Kansas Wesleyan........	1929–30	69.7	15.5	13.0	1.0	0.8
*Baker..................	1929–30	68.5	13.2	15.5	1.6	1.2
*Simpson................	1928–29	67.8	10.0	17.7	4.5	....
*Chattanooga............	1928–29	67.3	19.0	11.6	0.6	1.5
*DePauw................	1929–30	67.2	8.0	16.7	5.7	2.4
West Virginia Wesleyan..	1929–30	66.9	14.0	12.1	6.4	0.6
Iowa Wesleyan..........	1928–29	66.1	15.4	15.5	2.9	0.1
Oklahoma City..........	1928–29	66.0	17.3	7.0	9.5	0.2
*Hamline................	1928–29	65.6	14.5	12.7	3.7	3.5
*Cornell.................	1928–29	65.1	11.3	13.4	5.5	4.7
Intermountain..........	1929–30	65.1	21.1	9.3	4.4	0.1
*Mount Union...........	1929–30	64.6	14.9	12.8	2.7	5.0
Ozark Wesleyan.........	1928–29	64.5	23.0	10.2	2.1	0.2
Union..................	1928–29	64.3	15.5	17.5	....	2.7
*Illinois Wesleyan........	1929–30	63.7	13.5	14.2	7.4	1.2
Dakota Wesleyan........	1929–30	63.5	15.5	15.0	0.5	5.5
*Dickinson..............	1928–29	61.6	11.9	18.8	4.1	3.6
*Allegheny..............	1928–29	58.4	12.6	16.0	7.6	5.4
Gooding................	1929–30	51.9	23.8	17.6	6.7	....
Median, all colleges...	....	68.2	13.5	12.8	3.1	0.6
*Median, A.A.U. colleges................	....	67.8	11.9	12.8	3.3	1.5
Median, non-A.A.U. colleges.............	....	69.7	15.5	12.3	2.1	0.4

* Institutions on the approved list of the Association of American Universities.

† Includes fixed charges, commencement and public occasions, and contributions to educational enterprises.

PERCENTAGE DISTRIBUTION OF EXPENDITURES AMONG FUNCTIONS

It is of interest also to examine the proportions of the total educational expenditures used for the various functions in the different colleges. Table 125 presents data showing for each of the thirty-four colleges the percentage of the total educational expenditures devoted to four of the more important functions.

This table shows that the percentage of total educational expenditures devoted to the function of instruction ranges from 51.9 per cent in one college up to 75.8 in another. Only two of the colleges devote less than 60 per cent of their expenditures to instructional purposes, and two devote more than 75 per cent to this function. Two-thirds of the colleges devote from 65 to 75 per cent of their expenditures to this function. There is a somewhat similar range in the case of each of the other functions shown

TABLE 126

PERCENTAGE OF EDUCATIONAL EXPENDITURES FOR VARIOUS
FUNCTIONS IN COLLEGES OF DIFFERENT SIZES

NUMBER OF STUDENTS ENROLLED	NUMBER OF COLLEGES	AVERAGE PERCENTAGE OF TOTAL EXPENDITURES FOR EACH FUNCTION				
		Instruction	Administration	Operation and Maintenance of Plant	Student Welfare	Others
700 and over............	7	70.8	11.1	12.0	4.3	1.7
400–699................	13	68.4	12.3	14.0	3.5	1.8
Less than 400...........	14	66.5	16.8	12.8	2.7	1.2

in the table. The medians indicate that the type of accreditation held is not associated with any difference in the distribution of expenditures among the various functions.

Table 126 presents data showing the relationship between the size of the enrolment and the distribution of educational expenditures among the various functions.

This table shows that the size of the institution is associated with the percentage of total expenditures devoted to each of three functions, but that the relationship in the case of two of the functions is exactly the opposite for that of the other two. The larger colleges tend to devote a larger percentage of their educational expenditures to instruction and to student welfare than the smaller institutions, while the latter devote larger proportions to administration than the former. This table indicates that the larger institutions generally are able to put larger proportions of their funds into directly productive functions than is the case with the smaller colleges.

CHAPTER LII

TEACHING-SALARY COSTS PER STUDENT-CREDIT-HOUR

One of the valuable types of cost analysis is that of the teaching-salary expenditure per student-credit-hour. This cost unit has the advantage of being readily understood and easily calculated. Teaching-salary costs per student-credit-hour may be calculated not only for the institution as a whole but for the several departments or divisions, for courses, for individual instructors, or for different curriculums.

METHOD OF CALCULATING STUDENT-CREDIT-HOUR COSTS

The divisor unit used in obtaining this cost is the student-credit-hour, representing one student under instruction for a period of time for which one hour of credit is received. Thus a class of twenty students carrying three hours of credit produces sixty student-credit-hours. The unit may be figured either on the basis of term hours or semester hours. In the present study the semester hour has been used, and the data for the colleges which operate on the term basis have been reduced to the equivalent in semester hours.

The present study presents data on the teaching-salary costs per student-credit-hour for the various subjects taught, this being one of the more important types of comparison among institutions. In each case the data represent conditions at the institution during the semester or term of the visit of the survey staff. The student-credit-hour load of each department was first figured. The total teaching-salary[1] budget for the semester was also figured for each department. From these two items the cost for teaching salaries per student-credit-hour was calculated.

In a few cases it was necessary to do some prorating of salaries. This was true in the case of instructors teaching in more than one department, and in the case of administrative officers carrying a part-time teaching load. In allocating the salaries of instructors teaching in more than one department, the division was made on the basis of the number of credit-

---

[1] This includes only salaries specifically assigned for teaching duties. Thus, the salary of a dean, all of which is considered as an "instructional" item, is divided and only the portion specifically assignable to teaching duties is used in computing the "teaching-salary" cost.

hours taught. An instructor teaching a total of twelve credit-hours (eight credit-hours in one department and four in another) would have two-thirds of his salary charged against the first department and one-third against the second. In the case of administrative officers (other than the president) the department was charged with the fraction of time devoted to teaching, based on the presumption of a total load of fifteen hours. Thus, a dean who is teaching six credit-hours has two-fifths of his salary charged against the department in which he teaches. Where the president of a college teaches one or two classes, it was presumed that he would not be paid as a teacher a higher salary than the highest amount paid any other teacher. His department was therefore charged with the fraction of his time based on the presumption of fifteen hours of teaching, but figured from the base of the highest-salaried teacher in the college rather than from the base of the actual salary of the president.

STUDENT-CREDIT-HOUR COSTS IN THE COLLEGES STUDIED

Table 127 presents the teaching-salary costs per student-credit-hour for various subjects in thirty-four colleges.

The teaching-salary costs per student-credit-hour for all subjects combined range from $2.75 in one college to $6.95 in another. The median for the colleges on the approved list of the Association of American Universities is slightly above that for the colleges not holding this type of creditation.

In each of the subjects the range of costs is rather large. Only two subjects tend commonly to be much higher than average in costs—ancient language and home economics. The former appeals to only a few students, although most of the colleges are of the opinion that the offerings must still be maintained. Home economics appeals to only the young women, and consequently tends to have lower enrolments and higher unit costs. None of the other subjects deviate very widely from the general average for all subjects combined.

It is interesting to note that in almost every subject one or more institutions tend to have very low costs, even though the costs for this subject generally are above the average for other subjects. Thus the costs for ancient language at Dickinson and Mount Union are lower than the respective averages for all subjects at these institutions. Similarly, the cost for home economics at Gooding is below the average for all subjects at this college. On the other hand, in the case of every subject some one or more colleges will be found with a relatively high cost, even though the subject be one that is usually less expensive than the average. These

TABLE 127

TEACHING-SALARY COST PER STUDENT-CREDIT-HOUR (SEMESTER HOUR) OF
VARIOUS SUBJECTS IN THIRTY-FOUR COLLEGES

Institution	Year	All Subjects Combined	Ancient Language	Home Economics	Chemistry, Physics, and Geology	Bible and Religious Education
*Dickinson..............	1929–30	$6.95	$ 6.73	....	$8.31	$ 8.64
*Lawrence...............	1929–30	6.92	16.20	....	5.64	11.64
*Pacific.................	1930–31	6.59	42.53	....	7.78	10.63
Evansville.............	1929–30	6.40	21.43	$22.99	5.46	6.69
*Allegheny..............	1929–30	6.19	14.70	....	4.88	4.27
Ozark Wesleyan.........	1929–30	6.17	17.61	25.89	5.03	9.92
Central Wesleyan.......	1929–30	5.95	31.88	....	7.99	5.56
Nebraska Wesleyan......	1930–31	5.76	20.27	....	5.47	7.47
*Hamline................	1929–30	5.42	10.67	....	3.94	2.37
McKendree.............	1930–31	5.31	16.30	....	9.35	4.54
*Morningside............	1929–30	5.30	10.38	....	7.32	11.16
*Baker..................	1930–31	5.24	21.42	12.34	5.79	5.55
*DePauw................	1930–31	5.23	14.55	13.26	7.69	8.17
*Ohio Wesleyan..........	1930–31	5.19	9.41	7.31	6.63	5.31
Baldwin-Wallace........	1930–31	5.18	11.10	7.44	7.47	6.58
*MacMurray.............	1930–31	5.12	9.74	7.20	5.31	8.33
Dakota Wesleyan........	1929–30	4.96	14.67	5.77	7.37	5.66
*Cornell................	1929–30	4.87	16.88	7.77	5.76	7.73
*Chattanooga............	1929–30	4.80	27.50	....	5.24	4.94
Kansas Wesleyan........	1930–31	4.70	10.93	12.34	7.12	5.85
West Virginia Wesleyan..	1930–31	4.66	13.72	10.10	4.24	4.03
*Illinois Wesleyan........	1929–30	4.53	16.48	13.39	5.24	4.52
*Mount Union...........	1930–31	4.48	4.43	....	3.50	3.86
*Willamette..............	1930–31	4.46	7.75	7.95	5.49	5.96
*Albion.................	1929–30	4.36	15.25	9.55	5.97	5.15
Iowa Wesleyan..........	1929–30	4.35	8.07	13.30	4.12	4.66
Intermountain..........	1930–31	3.94	9.66	....	8.14	7.51
Southwestern...........	1930–31	3.91	21.18	3.93	5.13	10.31
Union..................	1929–30	3.89	22.22	....	5.02	2.45
*Simpson................	1929–30	3.75	7.00	6.43	5.83	2.95
Puget Sound............	1930–31	3.69	19.16	7.32	4.45	5.51
Ohio Northern..........	1930–31	3.52	13.76	....	2.15	3.77
Oklahoma City..........	1929–30	3.50	7.89	....	3.91	3.97
Gooding................	1930–31	2.75	9.62	2.68	4.49	2.78
Median,† all colleges..	....	$4.92	$14.61	$ 7.95	$5.48	$ 5.56
*Median,† A.A.U. colleges...............	....	5.19	14.55	7.95	5.76	5.55
Median,† non-A.A.U. colleges...............	....	4.66	14.67	8.77	5.13	5.56

* Institutions on the approved list of the Association of American Universities.
† Medians are based only on the colleges in which the subjects are taught.

TABLE 127—*Continued*

Institution	Mathe-matics, Astron-omy	Philoso-phy, Psychol-ogy, Education	Biology	Econom-ics, Bus. Ad., Sociology	History, Political Science	English, Speech, Dra-matics	Modern Lan-guages
*Dickinson.............	$ 4.51	$5.89	$9.80	$6.97	$6.01	$6.06	$ 5.30
*Lawrence.............	6.67	6.73	8.65	8.66	7.55	6.01	5.33
*Pacific...............	8.96	5.39	7.97	5.36	4.58	7.08	5.21
Evansville............	4.37	5.83	5.24	6.42	5.78	6.23	4.19
*Allegheny............	5.27	4.68	4.95	6.07	8.35	6.74	4.49
Ozark Wesleyan........	5.43	6.59	7.36	2.93	4.10	6.41	4.79
Central Wesleyan......	12.07	3.87	5.84	2.27	1.71	3.70	15.34
Nebraska Wesleyan....	8.84	7.35	4.49	4.26	5.00	5.79	3.25
*Hamline.............	8.08	7.49	7.35	9.28	3.40	4.68	5.85
McKendree...........	5.17	6.02	4.29	3.61	5.56	4.29	3.82
*Morningside..........	2.57	7.99	3.34	4.93	3.58	4.60	5.04
*Baker................	5.89	4.71	8.89	3.89	3.33	4.79	4.51
*DePauw..............	4.75	5.95	8.12	4.30	4.79	4.27	3.91
*Ohio Wesleyan........	7.93	6.86	4.91	3.83	4.47	4.84	4.24
Baldwin-Wallace.......	6.32	5.36	4.17	5.58	2.91	5.42	4.11
*MacMurray...........	7.77	5.04	4.69	4.59	4.49	4.54	4.10
Dakota Wesleyan......	6.98	3.47	4.68	4.60	5.36	4.36	4.46
*Cornell..............	4.81	4.42	8.98	5.44	5.87	4.31	4.03
*Chattanooga..........	7.31	5.05	7.59	5.91	3.85	3.83	3.11
Kansas Wesleyan......	5.35	4.18	4.02	5.09	3.02	3.22	4.02
West Virginia Wesleyan.	5.33	5.72	2.65	4.79	4.43	3.51	6.02
*Illinois Wesleyan......	4.99	4.33	5.19	3.75	2.92	3.74	3.97
*Mount Union..........	5.29	4.27	4.36	7.42	4.36	3.99	3.91
*Willamette............	4.29	3.06	5.38	4.05	3.87	7.19	3.06
*Albion...............	5.53	2.97	5.20	3.54	3.08	3.68	4.23
Iowa Wesleyan........	3.65	4.33	9.97	5.36	3.27	4.30	2.29
Intermountain.........	5.64	3.87	2.87	3.30	2.62	2.60	4.85
Southwestern..........	5.61	4.01	4.70	2.86	2.92	3.94	3.49
Union................	6.67	4.83	3.23	....	4.97	4.37	4.58
*Simpson..............	3.50	3.76	3.06	4.23	3.75	3.73	3.07
Puget Sound...........	5.02	5.88	3.89	2.53	2.47	2.67	3.11
Ohio Northern.........	2.49	5.60	3.27	2.64	3.80	3.59	5.57
Oklahoma City........	3.04	3.32	1.63	4.50	4.95	3.56	2.96
Gooding..............	4.22	1.68	1.36	2.45	2.08	2.61	2.34
Median,† all colleges.	$ 5.34	$4.94	$4.81	$4.50	$3.99	$4.31	$4.15
*Median,† A.A.U. col-leges.............	5.29	5.04	5.38	4.93	4.36	4.60	4.23
Median,† non-A.A.U. colleges..........	5.35	4.83	4.17	3.94	3.80	3.94	4.11

* Institutions on the approved list of the Association of American Universities.
† Medians are based only on the colleges in which the subjects are taught.

facts point to the conclusion that "expensiveness" is not a factor that is inherent in the subject itself but that the organization of the college curriculum, the popularity of instructors, and the appeal of certain types of subject matter as indicated by the choices of students have much to do with determining the cost of producing a student-credit-hour.

In none of the subjects is there a very large difference in the respective median costs for the colleges on the approved list of the Association of American Universities and for those not holding this type of accreditation. There seems to be some tendency for science to be slightly more expensive in the colleges with the higher accreditation than in the others.

The costs per student-credit-hour for all subjects combined, as shown in Table 127, differ somewhat from the instructional salary expenditures per student enrolled, as shown in Table 124, although in general an institution which has a high instructional salary expenditure per student tends also to have a high cost per student-credit-hour. The data of these two tables are not strictly comparable, for four reasons: (1) The figures of Table 127 cover only one semester of an academic year, while those in Table 124 are for the entire year. (2) The data of the two tables are not for the same year, those of Table 127 being for a year later than those of the other table. (3) Table 127 does not include data for all subjects; music, art, and physical education are omitted, as well as certain other subjects given in only a few colleges. (4) There seems to be some variation among the colleges in the average credit-hour load carried by students.

INTERPRETATIONS OF STUDENT-CREDIT-HOUR COSTS

Teaching-salary costs have the advantage of being based on a supposedly comparable unit, the student-credit-hour. Under present methods of academic bookkeeping each one of these units has the same value, since 120 of them added together are equal to a Bachelor's degree. Particularly between institutions of equal status is the comparison of these unit costs interesting.

Great caution must be used in making administrative adjustments from the basis of unit cost data. As a rule, a unit cost that is unreasonably high indicates an overstaffed department. Rarely is it true that such a condition indicates an overpaid teaching staff, although occasionally within a given college salaries may be relatively higher in some departments than in others.

Furthermore, it is perhaps a mistake to judge the worth of subjects or teachers by their credit-hour production. Some educators have recently questioned the time-honored process by which 120 hours of credit of any description add up to a college education. There is every probability that units of credit do vary enormously in educational value. Certainly, no course or subject should be eliminated from the offerings on the basis of cost alone.

One of the important uses of unit cost data is found in the preparation of the budget. Department heads should be provided with data showing the teaching-salary costs per student-credit-hour in their own departments and in other divisions of the institution. Requests for budget increases can then be viewed in the light of the entire financial situation. In general, budget increases should be used to bring up the low-cost departments. Except in extreme cases where overstaffing is apparent, little can be done to bring down the cost of expensive departments.

In some of the colleges studied, some department heads have drawn unwarranted conclusions from unit costs which they have calculated themselves. For example, if the tuition fee charged students is $210 per year, it may readily be calculated that the fee paid per credit-hour by each student carrying a yearly load of thirty credits is $7.00. A department in which the cost per student-credit-hour is only $5.00 may complain that it is not getting its full share of the budget and that it is producing a larger revenue in terms of student fees than is being returned to it in faculty salaries. A fallacy of this position lies in the fact that the college has many expenses other than faculty salaries. In the typical college approximately 60 per cent of the educational budget is spent for faculty salaries. Thus a department cannot relate its budget to the income received from its students without first taking into account its fair share of the overhead of the institution.

Most colleges have some sources of income other than student fees. The distribution of the income from these other sources to the various departments is a matter of institutional policy. The endowment income may, in practice, actually go for the subsidy of a few high-cost departments; and it is even possible that the student fees of those who enrol in the cheaper departments may be diverted to the support of the more expensive departments. Matters such as these should be covered by the general policies of the institution, and no department should feel itself aggrieved because it operates at a lower unit cost than other departments in the college. It would certainly be a serious administrative mistake to attempt to equalize departmental costs completely in any college.

CHAPTER LIII

SUPPLEMENTARY BUSINESS ENTERPRISES

KINDS OF ENTERPRISES OPERATED

Most colleges find it necessary to operate certain types of quasi-business enterprises which are somewhat indirectly connected with the educational program. Included in the list of such activities are the facilities for the housing of students, dining-halls, bookstores, etc. Any activity of this type not directly connected with the instructional program is

TABLE 128

SUPPLEMENTARY BUSINESS ACTIVITIES MAINTAINED
IN THIRTY-FIVE COLLEGES.

Type of Enterprise	Total Number of Enterprises Maintained	Number of Colleges Maintaining Each Type of Enterprise
Dormitory.............	75	30
Dining-hall or cafeteria..	44	29
Bookstore.............	20	20
Printshop.............	2	2
Social clubrooms........	1	1
Farm.................	1	1
Motion-picture show....	1	1

classified as a supplementary business enterprise. Table 128 shows the kinds of enterprises found in these thirty-five colleges, the total number of each, and the number of colleges maintaining each type of activity. The table includes only activities managed directly by the colleges. The data relate to the fiscal year immediately preceding the time of the survey visit.

This table shows that dormitories comprise a majority of the total number of enterprises maintained. There is an average of slightly more than two dormitories per college, although four of the institutions have no dormitories.[1] Considerably more than half of the dormitories are for women students, residence halls for men apparently being considered less necessary in the typical college. All but five of the institutions maintain a cafeteria or dining-hall. Slightly more than half operate a bookstore. The other types of activities are represented in only one or two colleges each.

[1] In one other college the dormitories are managed by an outside agency and hence are not included in Table 128.

In a few cases the dining and housing facilities are carried on by agencies having a semi-official relationship to the college. These have not been included in Table 128. For example, at Illinois Wesleyan University the women's dormitories and dining-hall are conducted by the Women's University Guild. The college owns the buildings, but the Guild owns the equipment and cares for all the management of these enterprises. In a few colleges cafeterias are operated by private persons in space furnished by the college.

There is a wide variation in the extent to which the different colleges engage in supplementary business activities. One college, an old and well-established institution, had maintained no such enterprise during the fiscal year immediately preceding the survey visit. Two other colleges had discontinued all their supplementary business activities during the year of the survey visit. In several cases only one small dormitory, converted from an old residence, is maintained. Other colleges maintain rather extensive dormitory systems housing the majority of their students.

There is an important field for study in the management of supplementary business enterprises. Variations in managerial effectiveness have an immediate effect upon the financial situation of the institution. The present study does not attempt to enter into any detailed criticisms of the management of such enterprises as dormitories, dining-halls, and bookstores, since attention is limited principally to the educational aspects of the institutions studied.

Because of the effect of the financial outcome of the operation of these supplementary business activities upon the resources available for the support of the educational program, this aspect of the question warrants consideration in the present study. It is clear that if the supplementary business enterprises operate at a profit, an important source of support for the educational program may be developed. On the other hand, if these supplementary activities operate at a loss, the educational budget must shoulder the burden, and the funds for such items as faculty salaries, educational supplies, etc., are reduced.

ACCOUNTING FOR THE ENTERPRISES

In accounting for supplementary business activities, most of the colleges included in this study set up the cash income and the cash expenditures, and consider the difference between these two items as the surplus (or deficit). As a rule, the colleges rather carefully allocate all direct expenditures to these activities and account for the cost of such items as heat furnished from a central plant, light, water, etc. In a few cases, however, direct charges such as those indicated had not been allocated to the enterprises in the accounts of the college, necessitating an adjustment in the data gathered for the purposes of this study.

The majority of the colleges have failed to allocate certain indirect charges to the supplementary business enterprises. The principal item of this type is the portion of the expenses of business management chargeable to these activities. If the college business office handles the financial affairs connected with the dormitory and dining-hall, including the collection of board and room fees, the purchasing of supplies, and the keeping of the financial accounts, the enterprises should be charged with the just share of the expenses of this service. In many colleges this amounts to almost one-half the entire expenses of business management. For the purpose of this study an adjustment has been made in all cases in which a portion of the expenses of business management has not been charged to the supplementary business activities.

No commercial concern would consider its profit-and-loss analysis complete without taking into account the items of interest on investment and depreciation on plant. Only one of the colleges included in this study considers such items in analyzing the results of the operation of its supplementary business activities. Interest and depreciation are very real items of cost, even if they are not paid in cash. Whether or not the college desires to consider these items in fixing rates of charges for board and room, there should at least be an analysis to show what the true results of the operation of the enterprises are; such an adjustment has been made in the data collected for this study. The rate at which the interest and depreciation charge is made was arbitrarily fixed at a total of 10 per cent of the invested value of the plant and equipment, representing 6 per cent for interest and 4 per cent for depreciation. The rate for depreciation may seem somewhat high, but it must be remembered that a large part of the investment is in equipment which deteriorates rather rapidly. The rate of 10 per cent has been recommended by some authorities as the amount which should be charged against the operation of dormitories and dining-halls. This charge is of the nature of "rent," and in this study has been called a "rental charge."

FINANCIAL OUTCOMES OF OPERATING THE ENTERPRISES

Table 129 presents data showing the outcomes of the operation of supplementary business activities in the thirty-four institutions which maintained such enterprises during the fiscal year immediately preceding the survey visit. The results are presented in three ways: (1) as shown by the books, without figuring any allocated overhead for business management unless the accounts of the college carry such a charge; (2) including all di-

TABLE 129

DISTRIBUTION OF OUTCOMES OF OPERATING SUPPLEMENTARY
BUSINESS ACTIVITIES IN THIRTY-FOUR COLLEGES

AMOUNT OF SURPLUS OR DEFICIT (DEFICITS INDICATED BY MINUS SIGN)	NUMBER OF COLLEGES HAVING EACH AMOUNT OF SURPLUS OR DEFICIT		
	According to Their Own Accounts	If All Direct Expenditures Are Included	Including Also a Rental Charge
$30,000 to $34,999.............	1	1	....
25,000 to 29,999.............	1	1	....
20,000 to 24,999.............	....	....	....
15,000 to 19,999.............	5	2	....
10,000 to 14,999.............	1	2	....
7,500 to 9,999.............	1	3	....
5,000 to 7,499.............	4	2	....
4,000 to 4,999.............	2	4	....
3,000 to 3,999.............	1	1	....
2,000 to 2,999.............	3	1	....
1,000 to 1,999.............	2	4	....
0 to 999.............	4	4	1
— 1,000 to — 1.............	5	3	3
— 2,000 to — 1,001.............	4	3	4
— 3,000 to — 2,001.............	....	2	3
— 4,000 to — 3,001.............	....	....	3
— 5,000 to — 4,001.............	....	....	1
— 7,500 to — 5,001.............	....	1	3
— 10,000 to — 7,501.............	....	....	5
— 15,000 to — 10,001.............	....	....	2
— 20,000 to — 15,001.............	....	....	3
— 25,000 to — 20,001.............	....	....	3
— 30,000 to — 25,001.............	....	....	1
— 35,000 to — 30,001.............	....	....	1
— 75,000 to — 70,001.............	....	....	1
Median*.......................	$+2,732.94	$+2,047.76	$—7,003.87

* Calculated from an ungrouped distribution.

rect and indirect assignable charges; and (3) including a rental charge of 10 per cent on the investment in plant and equipment. The data are presented in the form of a distribution table, showing the number of colleges having various amounts of surplus or deficit under each of the plans of computing the outcome.

This table shows that, according to their own bookkeeping methods, twenty-five of these colleges showed a surplus and nine showed a loss from the operations of their supplementary business activities. In each case the losses were relatively small, none being over $2,000. The surpluses tend to be much larger than the losses, approximately one-fourth of the colleges showing surpluses of $10,000 or more. The typical college, as indicated by the median, showed a surplus of $2,732.94 according to its own bookkeeping methods.

If all direct expenditures are allocated to the costs of these supplementary business activities, including a charge for the service performed in the business office, the results of operation tend to be slightly less favorable. Nine colleges show deficits; the amounts of the losses are somewhat larger than when the business office expenses are not included. The amounts of the surpluses are also slightly reduced in most institutions by this method of computing. The typical institution, as indicated by the median, shows a surplus of $2,047.76 from the operations of its supplementary business activities when a proper share of the expenses of business management are considered as a part of the cost.

The table shows that when a rental charge is included, only one of the colleges of this group shows a true surplus from the operation of its supplementary business enterprises. The deficits by this method of figuring run fairly large in many cases. The typical college, as represented by the median, fails (by $7,003.87) to make a fair rent on its investment in the plant used for supplementary business enterprises. This result is to be expected, since at a great majority of these institutions it is not a part of the policy to expect the dormitories and dining-halls to earn a rental charge.

An interesting analysis could be made of the results of operation of various types of enterprises. In several colleges the accounts are not kept in such a way as to permit an analysis of each separate activity, and for that reason data are not presented covering the surplus or deficits of various kinds of enterprises. It is apparent from the data at hand, however, that dining-halls and bookstores are much more commonly operated without a deficit than is the case with dormitories. The rental charge bears particularly heavily against the dormitory, and almost all dormitories fail to earn an amount equal to 10 per cent on the investment in plant and equipment. In the case of dining-halls and bookstores the item of rent is a comparatively small part of the total charge. The conclusion might be stated in another way by saying that it has apparently proved easier for the colleges to adjust charges for board and for items sold in bookstores to take into account the rental cost than it has been to adjust charges for dormitory rooms.

It is not within the province of this discussion to say whether or not a rental charge should be included in fixing the rates for board and room. That is a matter of institutional policy, to be decided partly in the light of the terms of the gifts which originally provided such facilities and partly in the light of the economic resources of the student body. One of these colleges has recently received a gift of funds for a new dormitory with the condition that the net "income" from its operation is to be used for scholarship purposes. Obviously, this new dormitory must be operated in such a way as to pay interest on the investment over and above all operating charges and the costs of replacing equipment, if the terms of the gift are fulfilled. Some college executives argue that one generation of students should not be required to pay for educational facilities to be used by the next generation. Those who hold this position would not attempt to accumulate a depreciation reserve for the replacement of dormitories when they are ready to be abandoned, but would expect the future generation of givers to provide the funds for replacements as rapidly as they become necessary.

Although the wisdom of including a rental charge in setting dining-hall and dormitory rates is debatable, there can be no question but that the supplementary business enterprises ought to carry the entire cost of their current operation. Most colleges nominally operate on this principle. The only alternative is to obtain subsidy from the educational funds of the college, and this is decidedly unwise. The donors who have provided the resources from which the college maintains its educational program did not give their funds for the furnishing of board and room to students at less than cost. It is usually much easier to adjust the charges for board and room to cover the full cost of providing these services than it is to obtain funds for the support of the educational program.

Rates for board and room are limited to some extent by those in competitive institutions and by the prices at which local townspeople and boarding-house keepers will provide these services. A college which cannot avoid an operating deficit in its supplementary business enterprises by charging reasonable rates for the services rendered should make a careful study of the management of these activities.

CHAPTER LIV

SOURCES OF INCOME

The nature and scope of the program which an educational institution can offer are vitally dependent upon the amount and the type of income received. For that reason, an analysis of the incomes received by the various colleges of the group being studied will be presented. This chapter will present data regarding the amount and sources of educational income in the various institutions. The following chapter will present a discussion of the possibilities of increasing the amount of income.

AMOUNT OF ANNUAL RECEIPTS

For the purposes of this study, educational income is defined as any revenue used for, or available for, educational purposes. The figures do not include receipts from borrowings, and money used for capital purposes or for addition to the endowment is also excluded. In all cases the amount shown is the net available for educational purposes. For example, the expenses of managing the endowment fund are subtracted from the income from that source; the amount received from students represents only the net amount received, excluding rebated and uncollected fees; and the amount reported as income from supplementary business activities is only the net sum available for educational purposes after the payment of all operating expenses of such activities.

Table 130 presents data showing for thirty-five colleges the total educational income received during the last fiscal year prior to the survey visit. The table also shows the educational income per student.

This table shows a fairly wide range in the amount of total educational income. Since the size of the educational task undertaken by the various institutions differs markedly, it is perhaps fairer to judge the income in relation to the number of students served. It will be noted that the range in income per student is much narrower than the range of total income.

Figure 33 shows the relationship between the total educational income and the number of members in the church constituencies of this group of colleges. This chart shows that there is a very direct relationship between the size of the church constituency and the total educational income in this group of colleges. The institutions which have a rather large supporting constituency tend strongly to be those with the larger education-

TABLE 130

TOTAL ANNUAL EDUCATIONAL INCOME AND EDUCATIONAL INCOME
PER STUDENT IN THIRTY-FIVE COLLEGES

Institution	Year of Data	Total Educational Income	Educational Income per Student
*Ohio Wesleyan............	1929–30	$617,609	$346.00
*DePauw.................	1929–30	444,517	320.95
*Lawrence................	1928–29	259,869	332.74
*Allegheny...............	1928–29	239,012	401.70
*Dickinson...............	1928–29	228,266	418.84
*Albion..................	1928–29	224,853	299.01
*Pacific.................	1929–30	217,047	297.73
Nebraska Wesleyan.......	1929–30	191,408	292.22
Evansville...............	1928–29	188,399	474.55
Ohio Northern...........	1929–30	172,815	192.66
Baldwin-Wallace..........	1929–30	171,852	390.57
Southwestern.............	1929–30	168,910	300.55
*Mount Union............	1929–30	161,702	336.88
*Cornell.................	1928–29	154,639	311.14
*Morningside.............	1928–29	153,235	220.80
*Illinois Wesleyan..........	1929–30	144,261	256.24
Oklahoma City...........	1928–29	140,057	199.25
Puget Sound.............	1929–30	136,306	221.28
*Willamette..............	1929–30	134,384	262.47
*Simpson.................	1928–29	131,593	230.46
*Hamline.................	1928–29	123,299	311.36
*Baker...................	1929–30	122,178	265.03
*MacMurray..............	1929–30	118,663	377.10
Kansas Wesleyan.........	1929–30	115,904	378.78
*Chattanooga.............	1928–29	114,999	301.83
Ozark Wesleyan..........	1928–29	113,000	463.65
Dakota Wesleyan.........	1929–30	97,937	282.23
West Virginia Wesleyan....	1929–30	91,814	284.25
Iowa Wesleyan...........	1928–29	88,129	270.33
Brothers.................	1929–30	71,930	†
McKendree...............	1929–30	61,210	242.90
Intermountain............	1929–30	51,860	343.44
Union...................	1928–29	46,444	204.59
Central Wesleyan.........	1928–29	42,741	223.77
Gooding.................	1929–30	40,246	314.42
Median, all colleges.....	....	$136,306	$299.78
*Median, A.A.U. colleges.	....	154,639	311.14
Median, non-A.A.U. colleges.................	....	105,469	284.25

* Institutions on the approved list of the Association of American Universities.

† Data regarding the income per student at Brothers College are not meaningful because enrolments at this institution have not reached the number which the college is prepared to serve.

al incomes; while the institutions having only a small constituency have, as a rule, much smaller incomes.

Figure 34, giving the relationship between educational income per student and the size of the college enrolment, shows that in general the smaller colleges have a larger educational income per student than the larger ones. This relationship is to be expected from the fact that education is comparatively more expensive in the small college than in the ones with larger enrolments.

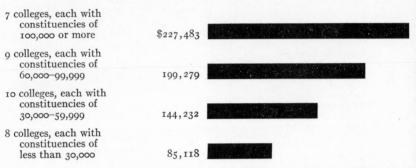

7 colleges, each with
  constituencies of
  100,000 or more $227,483

9 colleges, each with
  constituencies of
  60,000–99,999   199,279

10 colleges, each with
  constituencies of
  30,000–59,999   144,232

8 colleges, each with
  constituencies of
  less than 30,000   85,118

Fig. 33.—Average total educational income in colleges having church constituencies of various sizes.

RECEIPTS PER STUDENT FROM VARIOUS SOURCES

Table 131 presents data for thirty-four colleges showing the amount of income per student received from each source. Brothers College is omitted from this tabulation because the enrolment of this institution has not yet reached the number of students for which facilities have been prepared.

It will be noted that there are some rather striking differences in the amount received from the various sources. The colleges on the approved list of the Association of American Universities in general tend to have somewhat larger incomes per student than the colleges not holding this type of accreditation. The medians for the colleges on the approved list of the Association of American Universities exceed those of the other group in income per student from student fees, from endowment, and from supplementary business activities. The medians for the colleges not holding national accreditation exceed those of the other group in the amount of income received from local churches and Annual Conferences, from financial campaigns and miscellaneous gifts, and from The Board of Education of the Methodist Episcopal Church. It is apparent from this relationship that the unaccredited colleges are much more directly dependent upon church sources for their support than is the case with colleges holding the highest type of accreditation. Since the amount of endowment is one of the important qualifications necessary for approval by

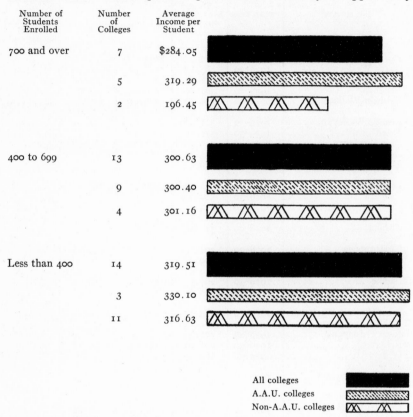

Number of Students Enrolled	Number of Colleges	Average Income per Student
700 and over	7	$284.05
	5	319.29
	2	196.45
400 to 699	13	300.63
	9	300.40
	4	301.16
Less than 400	14	319.51
	3	330.10
	11	316.63

All colleges
A.A.U. colleges
Non-A.A.U. colleges

FIG. 34.—Average educational income per student in colleges of various sizes and types of accreditation.

a standardizing association, it would naturally be expected that the amount of income from endowment would be related to the type of accreditation held. An accredited institution, furthermore, is in a position to charge higher fees than one that is unaccredited, since, according to generally accepted standards, the education which the former offers is of a somewhat superior type, entitling its students to privileges not enjoyed by the graduates of unaccredited colleges.

TABLE 131

INCOME PER STUDENT, CLASSIFIED BY SOURCE, FOR THIRTY-FOUR COLLEGES

INSTITUTION	FISCAL YEAR	TOTAL INCOME PER STUDENT	INCOME PER STUDENT FROM		
			Student Fees	Endowment and Pledges	Local Churches and Annual Conferences
Evansville.............	1928–29	$474.55	$193.73	....	....
Ozark Wesleyan........	1928–29	463.65	108.06	$ 10.85	$ 8.40
*Dickinson.............	1928–29	418.84	296.20	93.86	....
*Allegheny.............	1928–29	401.70	220.63	121.66	8.27
Baldwin-Wallace.......	1929–30	390.57	200.44	164.91	....
Kansas Wesleyan......	1929–30	378.78	156.03	17.01	35.13
*MacMurray...........	1929–30	377.10	258.06	61.27	....
*Ohio Wesleyan.........	1929–30	346.00	250.80	79.46	....
Intermountain.........	1929–30	343.44	103.51	54.05	....
*Mount Union..........	1929–30	336.88	206.08	86.43	....
*Lawrence.............	1928–29	332.74	187.71	100.88	....
*DePauw..............	1929–30	320.95	179.72	118.33	....
Gooding..............	1929–30	314.42	111.93	....	40.80
*Hamline.............	1928–29	311.36	169.25	118.15	....
*Cornell...............	1928–29	311.14	223.78	35.97	15.92
*Chattanooga...........	1928–29	301.83	154.22	142.33	....
Southwestern..........	1929–30	300.55	183.39	60.47	14.14
*Albion...............	1929–30	299.01	198.63	66.88	0.45
*Pacific...............	1929–30	297.73	232.63	13.07	....
Nebraska Wesleyan....	1929–30	292.22	171.79	59.84	27.49
West Virginia Wesleyan.	1929–30	284.25	175.38	82.82	....
Dakota Wesleyan......	1929–30	282.23	141.77	74.13	20.17
Iowa Wesleyan........	1928–29	270.33	125.89	28.97	36.90
*Baker...............	1929–30	265.03	145.63	90.12	11.49
*Willamette...........	1929–30	262.47	123.11	125.00	....
*Illinois Wesleyan.......	1929–30	256.24	178.09	43.74	2.78
McKendree...........	1929–30	242.90	120.76	63.16	33.40
*Simpson..............	1928–29	230.46	133.22	51.48	3.28
Central Wesleyan......	1928–29	223.77	87.56	31.35	7.10
Puget Sound..........	1929–30	221.28	142.48	70.43	....
*Morningside...........	1928–29	220.80	164.64	13.30	16.18
Union................	1928–29	204.59	64.28	104.54	....
Oklahoma City........	1928–29	199.25	109.00	6.69	....
Ohio Northern........	1929–30	192.66	149.58	24.19	....
Median, all colleges..	....	$299.78	$166.95	$ 62.22	$0.00
*Median, A.A.U. colleges.............	....	311.14	187.71	86.43	0.00
Median, non-A.A.U. colleges..........	....	284.25	142.48	54.05	7.10

* Institutions on the approved list of the Association of American Universities.

TABLE 131—*Continued*

INSTITUTION	Financial Campaigns and Miscellaneous Gifts	Methodist Board of Education	Surplus from Summer School	Surplus from Supplementary Business Activities	Miscellaneous
	INCOME PER STUDENT FROM				
Evansville............	$258.57	$15.11	....	$ 7.03	$ 0.11
Ozark Wesleyan........	302.27	28.51	....	....	5.56
*Dickinson.............	....	8.26	....	15.10	5.42
*Allegheny.............	9.75	7.06	....	23.41	10.92
Baldwin-Wallace.......	8.34	11.36	$0.56	....	4.96
Kansas Wesleyan......	145.38	22.88	....	0.03	2.32
*MacMurray...........	7.14	9.35	....	36.38	4.90
*Ohio Wesleyan........	9.82	5.53	....	....	0.39
Intermountain........	89.46	96.02†	....	....	0.40
*Mount Union..........	24.95	14.74	....	....	4.68
*Lawrence.............	....	5.38	....	36.85	1.92
*DePauw..............	2.51	8.34	....	9.41	2.64
Gooding..............	33.62	92.97	....	33.70	1.40
*Hamline.............	....	14.40	....	5.96	3.60
*Cornell..............	....	11.06	1.57	15.99	6.85
*Chattanooga..........	....	4.84	....	....	0.44
Southwestern.........	24.59	10.68	....	....	7.28
*Albion...............	2.69	18.85	....	0.31	11.20
*Pacific..............	28.11	12.18	....	6.69	5.05
Nebraska Wesleyan....	....	24.73	....	....	8.37
West Virginia Wesleyan.	....	20.43	2.03	1.68	1.91
Dakota Wesleyan......	14.47	18.68	....	5.56	7.45
Iowa Wesleyan........	46.03	10.42	1.95	17.96	2.21
*Baker...............	1.86	14.53	....	0.04	1.36
*Willamette...........	....	5.86	....	7.94	0.56
*Illinois Wesleyan.......	19.60	10.88	....	....	1.12
McKendree...........	....	13.89	3.91	4.17	3.61
*Simpson.............	....	28.53	3.79	10.02	0.14
Central Wesleyan......	31.67	15.70	11.61	23.31	15.47
Puget Sound..........	....	7.31	....	....	1.06
*Morningside..........	....	9.07	....	13.36	4.25
Union................	....	22.03	4.40	....	9.34
Oklahoma City........	77.76	2.79	1.00	0.94	1.07
Ohio Northern.........	5.72	4.95	....	0.09	8.13
Median, all colleges..	$ 6.43	$11.77	$0.00	$ 2.93	$ 3.61
*Median, A.A.U. colleges.............	1.86	9.35	0.00	7.94	3.60
Median, non-A.A.U. colleges..........	24.59	15.70	0.00	0.09	3.61

* Institutions on the approved list of the Association of American Universities.
† This item includes $33.11 from the Presbyterian Board of Education.

The range of income per student is large in the case of each source shown. One college obtains only $64.28 per student from student fees, while another obtains $296.20 from this source. Two colleges obtain absolutely nothing in the way of income from endowment, while another institution receives $164.91 per student from this source. More than half of the colleges receive nothing in the way of gifts from local churches or from their Annual Conferences. One college, however, receives $40.80 per student from this source, and another receives $36.90. Perhaps the most striking variation of all is found in the degree of dependence upon financial campaigns. By this is meant the campaign for gifts to be used for current support—not the receipts from campaigns for buildings, endowment, or debt liquidation. Thirteen of the colleges received no gifts for current purposes in the year for which the data were collected. In one college the supporting income from this source amounted to $302.27 per student; in another, $258.57; and in a third, $145.38.

The variation in the amount of income per student from the Board of Education is interesting, and the interpretation of the differences found in this table involves long explanation. Until 1919 the colleges received no regular appropriations from the Board of Education, every institution being supported from the public educational collection of its own Annual Conference. With the creation of a central treasury for all the benevolence funds of the Methodist Episcopal Church in 1919, it was agreed that all the collections for colleges should go through the Board of Education, and the institutions were guaranteed that no changes would be made in their individual incomes from church sources for five years. This guaranty expired in 1924; and the Board of Education, at the time the survey data were collected, had not had much opportunity for readjusting appropriations, particularly because of a steadily declining income.

The Board of Education has never formally worked out any objective basis for apportioning the funds under its control. There are two principal considerations which may enter into the problem of fund apportionment. The first has to do with the relative needs of the various institutions; the second has to do with the quantity and quality of the service rendered. Possibly, a third factor might be distinguished—the amount of income available for distribution received from the territories of the various colleges. The appropriation schedules at present followed represent varying weightings of these factors, combined with the influence of the appropriation formerly guaranteed.

The other two sources of income shown in the table, namely, surplus from summer school and surplus from supplementary business activities, represent variations in financial policies of the colleges. Most of the institutions that operate summer sessions do not expect them to pay a profit which will be available for the operating expenses of the regular year, although a few receive a small income from this source. The surplus shown from supplementary business activities in most cases does not figure a rental charge on the value of the plant and equipment used for these purposes. For that reason the income actually is a form of rent rather than a true operating surplus from the management of these activities.

Table 132 shows the relationship between the size of the institution and the amount of income from various sources.

This table shows that there is no important difference in the average income per student received from student fees in colleges of the largest

TABLE 132

INCOME PER STUDENT FROM VARIOUS SOURCES IN COLLEGES OF DIFFERENT SIZES

NUMBER OF STUDENTS	AVERAGE INCOME PER STUDENT FROM EACH SOURCE			
	Student Fees	Endowment	Board of Education	Local Churches and Annual Conferences
700 and over..............	$186.87	$58.50	$ 8.29	$ 0.06
400–699.................	183.81	78.25	12.62	7.66
Less than 400............	140.75	56.33	27.52	12.99

and medium-sized groups. Colleges with enrolments under 400 tend to have a much lower income per student from tuition fees than those of the other two groups. The medium-sized group of colleges has the largest income per student from endowment of any of the three groups. It will be noted that the appropriations from the Board of Education discriminate sharply in favor of the small institutions. The average income per student from this source in the group of small-sized colleges is over three times that in the group of large-sized colleges. The small colleges are evidently much more successful in enlisting the support for current purposes of their local churches and Annual Conferences. Very few of the large colleges obtain any income whatever from this source, but it constitutes an important source of educational income in a considerable number of the smaller colleges.

Figure 35, showing the income per student from the Board of Education in colleges having church constituencies of various sizes, indicates that there is some tendency for the income per student from the

Board of Education to be given to the colleges having small church constituencies. This tendency is not particularly pronounced, however, for the data are strongly influenced by the two colleges which receive excep-

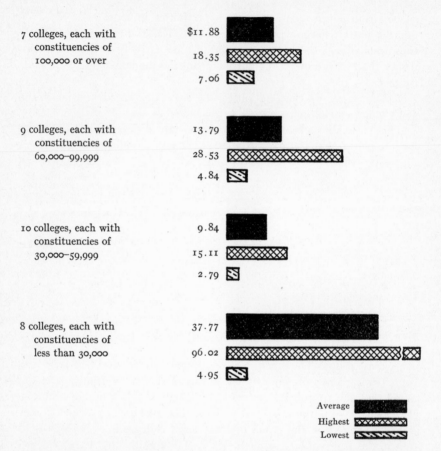

7 colleges, each with constituencies of 100,000 or over

$11.88

18.35

7.06

9 colleges, each with constituencies of 60,000–99,999

13.79

28.53

4.84

10 colleges, each with constituencies of 30,000–59,999

9.84

15.11

2.79

8 colleges, each with constituencies of less than 30,000

37.77

96.02

4.95

Average

Highest

Lowest

FIG. 35.—Income per student from Board of Education in colleges having church constituencies of various sizes.

tionally large amounts, both of which are located in territories where there are relatively few members of the supporting constituency.

Table 133 shows the relationship between the income per student from local churches and Annual Conferences and the size of the supporting constituency.

This table shows that there is an important relationship between the size of the supporting constituency and the amount of income received from local churches and Annual Conferences. In general, the colleges having relatively small constituencies obtain a larger income from local churches and Annual Conferences than is the case with colleges having larger supporting constituencies. The reason for this relationship is probably associated with the amount of endowment. Colleges which have relatively large endowments do not place much emphasis upon the receipt of gifts from churches or Annual Conferences as a means of obtaining a supporting income. The colleges which lack endowment are driven to an intensive cultivation of their church constituencies in the effort to obtain sufficient funds to continue their existence.

TABLE 133

Income per Student from Local Churches and Annual Conferences in Colleges Having Church Constituencies of Various Sizes

Number of Members in Supporting Constituency	Number of Colleges in Each Group	Number of Colleges Receiving Some Support from Local Churches and Annual Conferences	Average Amount of Income per Student from Local Churches and Annual Conferences for Entire Group of Colleges	Average Amount of Income per Student from Local Churches and Annual Conferences for Colleges Receiving Some Support from This Source
100,000 and over..........	7	3	$ 2.89	$ 6.74
60,000–99,999...........	9	3	3.73	11.18
30,000–59,999...........	10	5	11.31	22.61
Less than 30,000..........	8	5	13.95	22.32

PROPORTION OF INCOME FROM VARIOUS SOURCES

Table 134 shows, for each college, the percentage of educational income received from each source.

This table shows that it is typical for more than three-fourths of the income in these colleges to be received from two sources—students and endowment. Colleges on the approved list of the Association of American Universities tend to exceed the colleges not holding national accreditation in the proportion of income received from students and endowment, while the colleges lacking national accreditation tend to exceed the other group in the proportion received from local churches and Annual Conferences, financial campaigns and miscellaneous gifts, and the Board of Education. It was previously shown that exactly the same relationship holds for the amounts per student received from the various sources as well as for the percentages.

The colleges show a remarkable variation in the distribution of their dependence upon the various sources of support. In two institutions more

TABLE 134

SOURCES OF RECEIPTS, EXPRESSED IN PERCENTAGES, FOR THIRTY-FOUR COLLEGES

INSTITUTION	FISCAL YEAR	PERCENTAGES OF CASH RECEIPTS			
		Student Fees	Endowment and Pledges	Local Churches and Annual Conferences	Financial Campaigns and Miscellaneous Gifts
*Pacific..............	1929–30	78.1	4.4	....	9.5
Ohio Northern........	1929–30	77.6	12.5	....	3.0
*Morningside..........	1928–29	74.6	6.0	7.3	....
*Ohio Wesleyan........	1929–30	72.5	23.0	....	2.8
*Cornell..............	1928–29	71.9	11.6	5.1	....
*Dickinson............	1928–29	70.7	22.4	....	....
*Illinois Wesleyan......	1929–30	69.5	17.1	1.1	7.6
*MacMurray..........	1929–30	68.4	16.3	....	1.9
*Albion..............	1928–29	66.5	22.4	0.1	0.9
Puget Sound..........	1929–30	64.4	31.8	....	....
West Virginia Wesleyan.	1929–30	61.7	29.1	....	....
*Mount Union.........	1929–30	61.2	25.6	....	7.4
Southwestern.........	1929–30	61.0	20.1	4.7	8.2
Nebraska Wesleyan....	1929–30	58.7	20.5	9.4	....
*Simpson.............	1928–29	57.8	22.4	1.4	....
*Lawrence............	1928–29	56.4	30.3	....	....
*DePauw.............	1929–30	56.0	36.9	....	0.8
*Baker..............	1929–30	55.0	34.0	4.3	0.7
*Allegheny...........	1928–29	54.9	30.3	2.1	2.4
Oklahoma City........	1928–29	54.7	3.4	....	39.0
*Hamline............	1928–29	54.4	38.0	....	....
Baldwin-Wallace.......	1929–30	51.4	42.2	....	2.1
*Chattanooga..........	1928–29	51.0	47.2	....	....
Dakota Wesleyan......	1929–30	50.7	26.3	7.1	5.1
McKendree...........	1929–30	49.6	26.0	13.8	....
*Willamette...........	1929–30	46.9	47.6	....	....
Iowa Wesleyan........	1928–29	46.6	10.7	13.7	17.0
Kansas Wesleyan......	1929–30	41.2	4.5	9.2	38.4
Evansville............	1928–29	40.8	....	....	56.0
Central Wesleyan......	1928–29	39.1	14.0	3.2	14.2
Gooding.............	1929–30	35.6	....	13.0	10.7
Union...............	1928–29	31.4	51.1	....	....
Intermountain........	1929–30	30.2	15.7	....	26.1
Ozark Wesleyan........	1928–29	23.3	2.3	1.8	65.2
Median, all colleges...	....	55.5	22.4	0.0	2.2
*Median, A.A.U. colleges...............	....	61.2	23.0	0.0	0.7
Median, non-A.A.U. colleges..........	....	49.6	15.7	1.8	8.2

* Institutions on the approved list of the Association of American Universities.

TABLE 134—*Continued*

INSTITUTION	PERCENTAGE OF CASH RECEIPTS			
	Methodist Board of Education	Surplus from Summer School	Surplus from Supplementary Business Activities	Miscellaneous
*Pacific...................	4.1	....	2.2	1.7
Ohio Northern............	2.6	0.1	....	4.2
*Morningside.............	4.1	6.1	....	1.9
*Ohio Wesleyan...........	1.6	....	....	0.1
*Cornell.................	3.6	0.5	5.1	2.2
*Dickinson...............	2.0	....	3.6	1.3
*Illinois Wesleyan........	4.3	....	....	0.4
*MacMurray..............	2.5	....	9.6	1.3
*Albion..................	6.3	....	0.1	3.7
Puget Sound.............	3.3	....	....	0.5
West Virginia Wesleyan...	7.2	0.7	0.6	0.7
*Mount Union............	4.4	....	....	1.4
Southwestern............	3.6	....	....	2.4
Nebraska Wesleyan.......	8.5	....	....	2.9
*Simpson................	12.4	1.6	4.3	0.1
*Lawrence...............	1.6	....	11.1	0.6
*DePauw.................	2.6	....	2.9	0.8
*Baker..................	5.5	....	....	0.5
*Allegheny...............	1.8	....	5.8	2.7
Oklahoma City...........	1.4	0.5	0.5	0.5
*Hamline................	4.6	....	1.9	1.1
Baldwin-Wallace.........	2.9	0.1	....	1.3
*Chattanooga............	1.6	....	....	0.2
Dakota Wesleyan........	6.6	....	2.0	2.2
McKendree..............	5.8	1.6	1.7	1.5
*Willamette..............	2.3	....	3.0	0.2
Iowa Wesleyan...........	3.9	0.7	6.6	0.8
Kansas Wesleyan........	6.1	....	....	0.6
Evansville...............	3.2	....	....	....
Central Wesleyan........	7.0	5.2	10.4	6.9
Gooding.................	29.6	....	10.7	0.4
Union...................	10.8	2.1	....	4.6
Intermountain...........	27.9†	....	....	0.1
Ozark Wesleyan..........	6.2	....	....	1.2
Median, all colleges....	4.1	0.0	0.3	1.2
*Median, A.A.U. colleges	3.6	0.0	2.2	1.1
Median, non-A.A.U. colleges..............	6.1	0.0	0.0	1.2

* Institutions on the approved list of the Association of American Universities.

† This includes also the income from the Presbyterian Board of Christian Education.

than three-fourths of the supporting income is received from students. There are three institutions in which less than one-third of the supporting income is received from this source. There are four colleges which obtain more than 40 per cent of their income from endowment, while six obtain less than 5 per cent from this source. Three colleges obtain more than one-eighth of their income from local churches and Annual Conferences, although more than one-half of the colleges obtain nothing from this source. Two colleges obtain more than one-half of their educational income from financial campaigns and miscellaneous current gifts, although a large number of institutions obtain nothing from this source. One college obtains more than one-fourth of its supporting income from The Board of Education of the Methodist Episcopal Church, and another college

TABLE 135

PERCENTAGE OF EDUCATIONAL INCOME RECEIVED FROM VARIOUS SOURCES
IN COLLEGES OF VARIOUS SIZES

NUMBER OF STUDENTS ENROLLED	NUMBER OF COLLEGES	AVERAGE PERCENTAGE OF EDUCATIONAL INCOME FROM EACH SOURCE				
		Students	Endowment and Pledges	Board of Education	Local Churches and Annual Conferences	Other Sources
700 and over............	7	66.0	19.0	2.9	0.1	12.1
400–699................	13	61.4	25.5	4.5	2.7	5.9
Less than 400...........	14	44.6	20.1	8.8	4.4	22.1

obtains more than one-fourth of its supporting income from central church sources including the Methodist Board of Education and the Presbyterian Board of Christian Education. In five institutions the appropriations from the Board of Education constitute less than 2 per cent of the total income.

Table 135 presents data showing the percentage of educational income received from various sources in colleges of various sizes.

This table shows that the larger colleges tend to receive a larger proportion of their income from students than is the case with the smaller institutions. The trend with regard to the proportion of income which is received from endowment is somewhat confused. There seems to be a very direct relationship between the size of the institution and the proportion of income received both from the Board of Education and from the local churches and Annual Conferences, the smaller institutions tending to depend much more largely upon these sources of support than is the case with the larger institutions.

CHAPTER LV

POSSIBILITY OF INCREASING INCOME

NEED FOR INCREASED INCOME

Without a single exception the colleges of this group all have need of an increased income. The larger income is needed both for improvement in the present program and for expansions in the service of the institution.

Although a number of the colleges now maintain an educational program on a level comparing favorably with other institutions of their region, all of them could use increased income to advantage. Improvements are particularly needed in the scale of faculty salaries in order that the general quality of the teaching staff may be improved. The library service in none of these colleges is all that could be desired, and increased income is necessary for the support of this very important function. Personnel service for students is a new development which is just coming into higher education and which will demand increased funds for its support. Educational equipment in many of the colleges is in need of modernization and replacement.

The college which today is not increasing its income is almost certain to fall rapidly behind in the general forward movement in higher education. Competing institutions are everywhere improving the quality of their programs, and the college which cannot keep up the pace by constant improvements in its own program is almost certain to lose its leadership in its own territory.

It speaks well for the educational statesmanship in the institutions studied that in all of them there are visions of possible expansions of programs. In almost every case these expansions would be desirable both from the standpoint of the future of the institution and also from that of the service to the constituency. Improvements of this sort almost inevitably involve increased expenditures and can be undertaken only when additional supporting income is available or when funds are diverted from some portion of the existing program to the support of the new project.

Perhaps the greatest single need in this group of colleges can be summed up in the general idea of an increased income. Almost all of the fundamental adverse criticisms which can be made of the service of these institutions could be remedied if larger funds were available. It is important, therefore, to examine the possibilities of increasing the income of this group of colleges.

It was pointed out in a preceding chapter of this volume that there are six principal sources from which the colleges receive their incomes. These are: (1) students; (2) endowment; (3) surplus from supplementary business enterprises; (4) financial campaigns and miscellaneous gifts; (5) local churches and Annual Conferences; and (6) The Board of Education of the Methodist Episcopal Church. The possibilities of obtaining increased income from each of these sources will be briefly reviewed.

Students.—In none of the colleges studied do the fees charged students pay the entire cost of their education. This is particularly true if the economic costs comprising interest on investment and depreciation on plant are included as a part of the cost of education. Although it is the uniform practice in these colleges to grant some subsidy to all students, tuition fees being below the cost of education, there is without question in each of the colleges a very substantial group of students who could pay much higher tuitions than are now charged, and many of them could, without doubt, pay the full cost of their education.

The question has been raised as to why students who are financially able to pay the full cost of their education should have a part of this cost met by funds supposedly raised for charitable or philanthropic purposes. This has led to the suggestion that the student tuition fees might well be increased greatly, possibly up to the full cost of providing the education. Such a step would, of course, need to be accompanied by the provision of ample endowed scholarships and loan funds to care for those who are unable to pay the full cost of their education and who would be denied the privileges of higher education by the increased fees. This would require the development of a technique for determining the ability of students to pay fees. Such a plan has proved practicable and is being followed with some success in the case of medical service in certain centers.

Another factor qualifying the ability of the college to charge higher tuition fees is the amount of tuition charged in neighboring and competing institutions. It is conceivable that any large increase in fees beyond those charged in competing colleges might have the effect of reducing the number of students enrolled and thus would ultimately produce a smaller instead of a larger total income from students. It may be pointed out, on the other hand, that some institution always has to take leadership and that an increase of fees in one college would very likely be followed by corresponding increases in competing institutions within a short period.

Another factor qualifying the ability to charge fees relates to the accreditation status of the institution. A college with the highest possible accreditation is in a much better position to charge high fees than a college lacking satisfactory accreditation. This principle works both ways. If a college can charge high fees and thereby increase its income, it can frequently improve its program to a point warranting accreditation. Thus the weak college is caught in a "vicious circle," being unable, because of its inferior accreditation, to increase its fees, a step which would provide an increased income sufficient to warrant accreditation.

Of all of the sources of income, student tuition fees provide the most flexible source and the one most quickly responding to adjustment. It is for this reason that in recent years colleges have followed the policy of making rapid increases in their tuition fees. It seems highly probable that this movement will continue unless the general economic conditions are such as to make it unwise. The possibilities of maintaining greatly increased income from this source within the near future are very important in almost all of the colleges included in this study.

Endowment.—The obtaining of increased income from endowment involves two considerations: (1) the obtaining of a better rate of income on the present fund; and (2) increase in the capital amount of the funds. Present economic conditions make the satisfactory investment of the endowment fund a very difficult problem. It is probable, however, that a large number of these institutions are obtaining a lower rate of income than should be expected from their invested funds. If all the colleges could bring up the rate of income on their invested funds to a minimum of 5 per cent, the total annual revenues of the group would be increased at least a quarter of a million dollars.

Almost without exception the colleges of this group are making vigorous efforts to increase the capital amounts of their endowment fund. This is recognized as possibly second in importance only to student fees as a potential source of future increases in income. Several of the colleges have recently completed financial campaigns which will greatly improve their incomes when pledges are collected, and when the earnings from invested funds begin to be realized. From the standpoint of the long-time service of this group of institutions, increases in the capital amount of the endowment fund are of utmost importance in providing a future income of a satisfactory amount.

Surplus from supplementary business enterprises.—It has already been pointed out that several of the colleges show in their accounts a small surplus from the operation of supplementary business activities, such as dormitories, dining-halls, and bookstores, which is used for educational purposes. It has also been shown that very few enterprises of this sort actually do produce a true surplus when all the costs of their operation are included. In the case of several colleges there is a net surplus from this source after all direct and indirect outlays are subtracted from the income, but in almost no cases are these enterprises paying a profit after a rental charge for the use of the plant and equipment is made. The income shown in a preceding section as derived from this source may properly be considered a species of rent.

There is a grave question as to the advisability of using any surplus from the operation of supplementary business activities for the maintenance of the educational program. In the first place, there is need in most institutions for setting up adequate reserves to offset maintenance and depreciation charges on the parts of the plant used for dormitories, dining-halls, etc. Where this surplus is devoted to current purposes and is not set up as reserve, the institution is likely in the future to be faced by heavy charges for replacement or for losses in operation of these enterprises. Albion College is the only institution of this group that has followed the wise plan of setting up the surplus from the operation of its dormitory as a reserve against future maintenance and depreciation charges.

A second reason for not using surplus from supplementary business activities for educational purposes is related to the injustice of this method so far as the students are concerned. If a real surplus results from the operation of the dormitory or dining-hall, it is evident that rates have been set somewhat higher than necessary to cover operating costs. In the long run, this surplus is derived from students in exactly the same way as student tuition fees. In fact, most students do not discriminate sharply in their own minds between the fees paid for tuition and those paid for board and room. Thus, where a surplus results from the operation of dormitories and dining-halls, there has, essentially, been an increase in the total charges to students. This increase, however, bears only on those who avail themselves of the opportunity to use the facilities afforded by the supplementary business enterprises. Thus, the boarding students pay a proportionately higher fee than those who live at home or who make use of other residence facilities. A fair solution would be to follow the policy of charging exactly the cost of operation of supplementary business enterprises and, if additional income is needed, to obtain it from all students in the form of increased tuition charges.

Financial campaigns and miscellaneous gifts.—It has already been noted that a few of the colleges rely to a large extent upon financial campaigns and miscellaneous gifts as a source of current educational income. As at present administered in these institutions, this is a very unstable source of support. There seems to be a tendency for gifts of this type to fall off from year to year unless an increasingly intensive effort is made in the "drive" for funds.

It may be pointed out, on the other hand, that a few large colleges and universities have developed a program of current gifts as a rather satisfactory source of income. Yale University and Dartmouth College afford outstanding examples of this plan. Although the total gifts for current purposes in the institutions being studied are large, they actually form a relatively small part of the total income, and the program of the institution would not be greatly disturbed by minor fluctuations in the income from such sources.

It would seem advisable for the colleges of this group not to place any large dependence upon current gifts for future financial support. This source should not be overlooked entirely, but the continuance of the educational program should not be made as largely dependent upon this source as is the case in a few of the colleges. The amount which can be obtained from current gifts is very greatly and readily affected by changing economic conditions. Thus, at a time when the college has the greatest need for increased income, this source is likely to prove least helpful.

The one great advantage of the program of current giving is that it can be made to result in the accumulation of permanent resources where the program is well managed. A donor who has for several years given small sums annually to the college can frequently be persuaded to capitalize his gift as endowment, and thus remove the disadvantage due to the unstability of the amount of annual giving. It is an excellent plan for the college to maintain fairly intimate contact with a large number of givers. The institutions which have been successful in obtaining large gifts in recent years have in many cases found that the first gift from an important benefactor may be rather small but that, as his interest in the institution develops, he becomes increasingly generous in his giving. Thus, the financial campaign for current support affords a type of entrée to interested donors which cannot be obtained in any other manner.

Local churches and Annual Conferences.—Some of the colleges studied have been very successful in obtaining rather large amounts of supporting income from the local churches or from the Annual Conferences in which they are located. Many of the colleges, however, obtain nothing from this source.

In two or three of the colleges the authorities hold that the legislation of the church bars them from attempting to cultivate this type of support.

This opinion is based upon the idea that the appropriations from the Board of Education were intended to supersede all gifts from Annual Conferences. This opinion was widely held until the legislation was modified by the General Conference of the Church in 1928. The colleges are now free to cultivate diligently the support of their local constituencies and should be urged to do so.

It should be pointed out that income from church sources, in the form of Annual Conference grants, is unusually valuable to a weak institution because the amount can be capitalized in lieu of a part of the endowment requirements for standardization. Standardizing agencies will, in general, accept the average annual amount of receipts from such sources, capitalized at 5 per cent, as a part of the required minimum of endowment for standardization. The development of a program of current support from local churches and Annual Conferences will strengthen the attachment of donors, whether their gifts be large or small; will ultimately result in a number of large individual gifts and bequests; and will inevitably strengthen the influence of the college on its constituency.

Board of Education.—There seems to be little hope of obtaining a larger income through the appropriations of The Board of Education of the Methodist Episcopal Church. This agency, which participates in the general benevolent funds of the church, has had in recent years a constantly decreasing total for distribution. As a result, most of the institutions are suffering from decreases in the amount of income from this source. Colleges whose appropriations have been held constant in recent years have actually received increasing proportions of the total which the Board has had available for distribution. Since the survey data were collected in these colleges, the Board of Education has fixed appropriations for another fiscal year, the decrease at this time being much larger than in any preceding year. This decrease will vitally affect the programs in several of the weaker colleges.

Although it does not seem probable, from the history of the last seven years, that the group of colleges as a whole will receive any increased income from the Board of Education, there is need for some readjustments in the schedule of appropriations, which may result in an increase to certain institutions. The history of the last forty years shows that the number of institutions recognized by the Board has tended to diminish (see chap. i). The data presented in this study should provide opportunity for still further reductions in the number of institutions aided by the funds of the Board.

If the Board of Education is to continue to make distribution of funds, it would seem imperative that objective bases be established for the determination of appropriations. This has not yet been done, since the Board has not had an adequate opportunity to make a clean break with past practices. The lack of objective bases for the making of appropriations has led to many erroneous impressions among the colleges regarding the influences affecting the distribution of funds.

There are three objective bases which might well be considered by the Board of Education in determining its annual appropriations. The first is in the form of a given amount of subsidy per student in the college. If this plan were to be adopted, there would need to be a clear definition of "student enrolment" in order that the same basis of counting students might be used in all the institutions. A second plan might be in the form of a fixed amount per full-time faculty member. This plan would necessitate some definition of what constitutes full-time faculty service. Under this plan it would be possible to exclude from consideration faculty members of certain divisions, if it should happen that the church does not particularly care to subsidize the work of these divisions. It might also be desirable under this plan to limit the number of teachers to be counted to a certain ratio of students to faculty.

A third plan of distributing the fund of the Board of Education is in the form of a fixed proportion of each dollar expended for salaries. Under this plan the appropriation of the Board of Education would essentially result in larger faculty salaries, and institutions which have made efforts to provide a satisfactory salary scale for faculty members would benefit most from the appropriations.

As a general principle, it would seem wise for the Board of Education to adopt a policy of putting its funds where they will produce the largest educational results in terms of the quality of the program provided and service to the largest number of students. Perhaps especial consideration should be given to institutions so located as to serve a large group of potential students who are without other satisfactory educational opportunities. Under this principle the Board of Education would be justified in increasing its appropriation to unaccredited institutions in case this step would further their early accreditation. Institutions so situated as to serve large groups of students who lack other opportunity for attending an accredited college would be strongly supported wherever this is necessary for the maintenance of an effective program. The adoption of this policy might operate to increase the amount of aid to some of the larger and stronger institutions, and might in other cases decrease the amount provided some of the weaker and smaller colleges. While such a plan would probably meet objection in some quarters, there is no question but that the total effective educational service rendered by the denomination would be greatly increased by the following of this policy in the distribution of funds.

OTHER POSSIBLE SOURCES OF INCOME

All of the commonly employed sources of income are being utilized by some of the colleges of this group. In the preceding section it has been pointed out that many of the institutions have an opportunity to increase their income through sources which they are now utilizing. In this section two or three possibilities of new sources of income will be discussed.

Public funds.—There has recently been some discussion of the possibility of public support for the private denominational colleges, at least so far as certain phases of the work are concerned. For example, it is pointed out that in training teachers for public schools these colleges are performing a service of general value, for which they should be compensated from state or other public sources. In cases where the states have recently increased the requirements for teacher-training, an additional burden has been thrown upon the private colleges that prepare teachers; and it has been argued that this additional burden could well be met from state funds. In some states bills have been introduced in the legislature to provide state aid in private colleges for such functions as the maintenance of practice-teaching facilities.

None of the states represented in this study have provided any public funds for the support of private institutions, and in most cases there is serious objection on the part of the general public to such a procedure. It may be pointed out that public support for teacher-training in private colleges seems improbable at present because of the oversupply of teachers. In a large number of states the public institutions have adequate facilities for supplying all of the new teachers actually needed in the public-school system. For that reason there seems to be little likelihood of the appropriating of public funds for private institutions for the maintenance of teacher-training facilities in this group of colleges.

In the case of two or three of the institutions studied, there seems to be some possibility of public support on the junior college basis. This step, however, will almost necessarily be accompanied by the abandonment of the denominational connection of the institution. In the cases mentioned, the institutions are finding it very difficult to continue their operation as church colleges; and unquestionably the educational service rendered would be greatly improved by their becoming junior colleges with public support.

Interdenominational support.—A second possibility for income from sources not now commonly enjoyed is that of interdenominational support. One institution included in this study, Intermountain Union College, has operated for several years under a plan of joint support by two denominations. Another institution, Oklahoma City University, has developed a plan of joint support with the Methodist Episcopal Church, South. It has been shown throughout this volume that the size of the denominational constituency has an important effect upon many of the vital factors conditioning the success of an educational institution. Colleges located where the denominational constituency is too small to support a satisfactory program can obtain an increased constituency by development on an interdenominational basis, and may thus be provided with a supporting group of satisfactory size. In the case of some institutions, such a step would involve mergers and combinations with already existing institutions of other denominations. In other cases it would only be a matter of enlisting the support of denominational groups not having colleges of their own in the territory of the existing institution, and thereby making the college a union enterprise.

The possibilities for this type of increased support are very important. They have been overlooked by several of the colleges, which have been continuing a rather unsatisfactory existence with meager incomes largely because of an inadequate supporting constituency. While this plan will not be advantageous to old well-established institutions, it offers possibilities for some of the weaker colleges.

Investment of current funds.—One of the colleges of this group obtains a small amount of income annually from a source not cultivated in any of the other institutions. This college has made arrangements for the investment of its current funds; and although the amount received from this source is a relatively small part of the total income, it is more than sufficient to pay the entire expense of the business management in the institution concerned.

It should be clear that if a college collects in cash all of the fees which are due it and starts the academic year without any deficit or unpaid bills from the preceding fiscal period, there should be an average daily cash balance amounting to approximately one-fourth of the total annual cash income. The demands on the funds of the college come at very definite intervals, particularly at the end of the month, and can be predicted in advance. This offers the college an unusually favorable opportunity for the investment of current funds. Furthermore, the college has funds available at the very time when the normal annual business cycle results in scarcity and relatively high call-money rates, while the cash balance of the college is usually at its lowest ebb at the time when call-money rates are normally lowest. Thus, the college is in a specially favorable position for the investment of current-fund balances in short-term securities.

The difficulties in the way of receiving an income from this source relate principally to the failure to collect income when due, or to the fact that, as is the case in some of these colleges, the financial affairs are conducted on a hand-to-mouth basis, the cash balance being always very small and sometimes even a negative quantity. The experience of the one college of this group which is obtaining an income from this source offers convincing proof of the fact that the other institutions should consider the development of a plan of investing current funds for the purpose of producing an income.

CHAPTER LVI

FINANCIAL PROMOTION

The literature of higher education is singularly lacking in any well-organized discussion of the problem of fund-raising for endowed colleges. Although this is a problem common to every institution of the type of those included in this study, little of value has been written pertaining to methods and plans, and there seem to be no objective studies dealing with various types of financial promotion. As a rule, the most successful financial promotion officers work individually, using their own methods and not being especially communicative with regard to the particular plans which they find advantageous. The methods which will prove most successful in adding to the funds of colleges vary, of course, with the circumstances of the institution, the type of clientèle to which it must appeal, and its resources in terms of capable officials and board members.

TYPES OF ORGANIZATION FOR FINANCIAL PROMOTION

Four distinct types of organization for financial promotion are found in the group of colleges studied. Several of the institutions use two or more of the types in combination.

The first type is the assumption of the principal responsibility for fund-raising by the members of the board of trustees. DePauw University is a conspicuous example of an institution which has been especially successful in adding to its resources by this method. Under this type of organization the members of the board accept, as one of their primary responsibilities, the duty not only of giving funds themselves but of cultivating the interests of their friends on behalf of the institution.

A second type of organization for financial promotion places the major responsibility for this work in the office of the president of the institution. Not infrequently some members of the faculty or administrative officers give some time in assisting the president in this work. This type of organization exists to some degree in almost all of the colleges, it being considered a part of the duties of the president in almost every endowed college actively to seek funds for the institution.

A third type of organization consists of the maintenance of a special promotion office in charge of an officer devoting his full time to this work. The financial promotion officer will very frequently be assigned the title

535

of vice-president in order to give him a satisfactory standing as a representative of the institution when he approaches potential donors. In some cases the financial promotion office develops a staff of more than one full-time worker with a considerable amount of office routine, such as the maintenance of prospect lists, circularization of potential donors, and contact work for field men. Generally, the officer in charge of financial promotion is directly responsible to the president, although in a few cases organizations have been set up in which the financial promotion officer is directly responsible to the board and is independent of the president. It is obvious that the multiple type of organization which is thus created has many disadvantages. Funds must be found for objects consistent with the educational program of the college, and there is every need for a co-ordination of efforts through the chief executive officer of the institution.

The fourth type of organization for financial promotion consists of the employment of an outside agency. There are several organizations in the country which make a speciality of raising funds for charitable and philanthropic institutions. None of the colleges of this group have employed such agencies for continuous financial promotion, but they have been very largely used for the direction of fund-raising campaigns.

The outside fund-raising organizations may be divided into two distinct types. In the one, the outside agency furnishes only the executive direction of the campaign. Under this plan the organization makes a preliminary survey of the field and gives the college an estimate of the probable amount that can be received and the probable cost of the campaign. An executive officer is sent from the organization to direct the campaign for the college. All of the field work, however, is done by the friends of the institution. In the other type of organization the entire responsibility of the campaign is taken over by the outside group. The organization has its own staff of executives, field workers, and follow-up men; and the friends of the college are used only incidentally in the solicitation of funds.

From a careful study of the results of financial promotion plans in this group of colleges, it seems clear that the former type of outside organization is greatly preferable to the latter. Colleges which have used the type of organization supplying all its own field workers have, in general, had much less satisfactory after-effects from their campaigns than has been the case with the colleges employing a type of organization in which the direction comes only from the outside agency.

TYPES OF DONORS

Potential donors may be classified into three types; in many cases a given person may belong to more than one type. The first consists of individuals of comparatively limited resources who already know the college most favorably; the second consists of the alumni; and the third consists of the financially successful individuals of relatively large means. Each of these groups offers a specialized field for cultivation. Seldom will the same solicitors be successful with all groups. The small givers can probably be reached most effectively through the regular channels of the churches. The alumni can probably best be appealed to through class organizations or the alumni association. The business man with large means can best be approached by a man who can speak to him in business terms. To such an individual the institution, its work, and possibilities must be "sold." It may require an alert, far-seeing salesman to accomplish this task. In approaching the potential donor of large resources, one of the strongest arguments in favor of an institution is that it has adopted a sound financial program and that its funds are adequately safeguarded. These conditions go far toward enlisting confidence, which is the first step toward assistance.

METHODS USED IN FINANCIAL PROMOTION

There are two distinct methods used in financial promotion for colleges in general. The first consists of the quiet, persistent, and continuous program of fund-raising. The other is the spasmodic campaign. The continuous promotion program is best adapted to the organization in which promotion is under the direction of the board of trustees, the president, or a special promotion office. Occasionally the campaign method may be developed in connection with the financial promotion office of the college, but usually an outside organization is called in for the direction of the campaign.

The campaign method is much the more spectacular of the two plans. The program nearly always is initiated by the challenge of a gift from a single large donor of funds, who offers a certain sum on condition that from two to four times as much be raised from other sources within a specified time limit. Under the stimulus of this challenge a campaign organization is formed, and workers for the college comb the by-ways and hedges seeking pledges toward the goal of the campaign. As this method has operated in the past, the whole program is given a strong emotional tinge; not infrequently the propaganda goes to considerable lengths to present the institution in the most favorable light. The climax of the campaign comes as the time for the expiration of the terms of the gift approaches. It is rare, indeed, that a college is able to announce that the whole necessary amount has been pledged prior to the last few minutes before the time expires, and the stage is usually set for a striking dramatic climax. If the gift must be met by midnight on a certain date, the board of trustees is usually called for a special meeting on that day. All sorts of methods are used for working up last-minute enthusiasm. In anticipation of the probable success of the campaign, the students, faculty, and interested friends assemble during the evening in a crowd before the illuminated bulletin board on the campus. The hopes of the crowd are now raised as increased pledges are announced, now lowered as last-minute gifts seem to be falling short of the required total. A cheer greets the posting of each new gift as the dead line approaches. Finally, just as the time is about to expire, a gift is announced from an anonymous donor pledging the entire remaining amount. Uncontrollable joy immediately breaks forth as the announcement is made that the campaign has "gone over the top." Bonfires are lighted, bells are rung, fireworks shot off, and a holiday is immediately declared for the remainder of the week.

The campaign method is regarded with considerable discredit in many quarters. Not infrequently the pledges secured under the stress of emotional appeal have proved uncollectible. In the intensive effort to obtain every dollar possible toward the goal of the campaign, people who could not possibly afford gifts have been urged and almost forced to make pledges beyond their means. Students have been appealed to and, in the typical campus situation, find it very difficult to refuse a pledge for the minimum amount set by the campaign organization, although these pledges quite frequently are entirely beyond the means of the students. The campaign usually falls as a heavy burden upon the faculty and administrative staff, who are urged to give sacrificially out of their already too meager salaries in order to show their devotion and loyalty.

Several instances of very questionable practices have come to the attention of the writers in connection with the type of campaign organization that depends on its own solicitors. The customary terms upon which an outside agency of this type undertakes a financial campaign involve a stipulated payment to the organization upon the attainment of the "goal" in pledges. The organization gets its payment in cash at a time when the college has collected little or nothing from the campaign. The college is thus forced to underwrite the expenses of the campaign by borrowing funds in anticipation of future pledge collections.

Since the outside organization has no responsibility for collecting pledges, some of those taken are of an entirely unworthy type. Not infrequently pledges taken by such an organization have been repudiated. In a very few cases forgery has been claimed. One institution reports that a rather large pledge was taken during the whirlwind finish of a campaign with the stipulation that the name of the donor was not to be disclosed for two years. At the end of the period the signer of the pledge was found to be serving a long sentence in the state penitentiary. The authorities of the college had refused to accept a pledge from this person during the campaign because of his lack of financial responsibility, but the organization had foisted it upon the college under the guise of the anonymous donor.

In one case the director of the campaign organization assembled the board of trustees an hour or two before the expiration of the time for the campaign. The pledges were falling considerably short of the required total, and it seemed evident that the campaign was doomed to failure. After offering prayer, the suggestion was made by the campaign director that the trustees should "underwrite" the balance which had not yet been raised. Although all of the board members had already pledged toward the campaign all that they personally could afford, this new pledge was to be the joint obligation of the entire board. The trustees were assured by the campaign director, however, that they were not liable either personally or as a group for the payment of the amount "underwritten." The trustees acquiesced in this procedure, and the announcement was immediately made of a large anonymous gift covering the entire remaining balance. The campaign was announced as a "success," although it had actually fallen far short of the desired goal. The underwriting by the board simply meant a prolongation of the process of combing the already overworked constituency for still further pledges.

It is instances such as these, together with the increasing expensiveness of the fund-raising program and the psychological reaction to the numerous drives for funds, that have led very largely to the discreditment of this type of campaign organization. As a rule, the colleges which have used the type of campaign organization that furnishes only an executive director have not suffered any undesirable after-effects arising from high-pressure salesmanship.

The campaign method of fund-raising, although it possesses serious drawbacks, has many advantages and may sometimes be necessary. Several of the colleges have employed this method extensively and successfully in adding to their funds. There seems to be a tendency, however, to place increasing emphasis upon the other type of financial promotion—the quiet, constant, persistent effort without the ballyhoo of a campaign. Several of the colleges have recently developed financial promotion offices for the carrying-on of such a program, and in others the president or members of the board have been successful in directing fund-raising activities.

KINDS OF SUPPORT OBTAINED

At least five different types of support are obtained by the colleges of this group from their efforts at financial promotion. Perhaps the most important is that of outright gifts of cash or securities. Gifts of this sort may be for such purposes as endowment, debt liquidation, new buildings, student scholarships, and loan funds, or for current support. In a considerable number of the recent financial campaigns the gifts have been designated for omnibus objects such as "endowment, betterments, and liquidation of indebtedness." Many of the colleges receive some gifts with no stipulations whatever as to the purposes for which they are to be used.

A second form in which support is received is the pledge note. In most cases these do not bear interest, although a form of interest-bearing pledge note, known as "living endowment," has been developed by some colleges. This pledge note in effect carries with it a gift for current purposes (the interest which the donor pays on the note) as well as a capital gift for the purpose stipulated in the pledge. Pledges are, of course, of no value until collected. In one or two cases colleges have been successful in obtaining ready cash from pledge notes by securing the indorsement of the local chamber of commerce. It may be said in general, however, that most of the colleges put as much effort into the collection of pledges as was originally expended in obtaining them. A large percentage of the pledge notes are typically found uncollectible. Data were not collected on this point from all colleges; but from such data as are available, it is clear that few of the colleges have been able to collect more than 75 per cent of the pledges taken in recent years in campaigns that are now closed.

The third type of support sought in financial promotion has been gifts on the annuity basis. Under this plan the college receives cash or other securities and in return therefor pays the donor an income during his life. Although a comparatively recent development, the annuity program has proved an important method of adding to the funds of many of the institutions.

A fourth type of support which is sometimes sought in financial campaigns consists of life insurance. Friends of the college are urged to take out life insurance, naming the institution as the beneficiary. In a few colleges the custom has grown up of having each graduating class insure the life of one of its members in favor of the college, the class undertaking the payment of the necessary premiums.

One institution of the group studied has developed a unique and somewhat questionable plan for raising funds by insurance. Under this plan the donor gives the institution a fixed sum of money, say $500. The college insures his life for twice the amount of the gift, making his estate or any person whom he may designate the beneficiary. The financial officer of the college has estimated that if the $500 is invested at the usual rate of income, it will yield slightly more than enough to pay the premiums on the life insurance. The college is supposed to benefit by the difference between the yield of the fund and the amount necessary for premium payments, and by the fact that, upon the death of the insured, the capital sum becomes free for other uses by the college. It will be observed that this is essentially an annuity plan, although it is tied up with an insurance feature. The unfortunate circumstance in the particular college has been that the capital sum has not been kept invested but has been used for current purposes. Thus, the college will be faced for many years with an annual drain for premium payments, although the gift upon which the insurance was issued has already been used up.

A fifth type of support sought in many colleges is the designation of the institution as a beneficiary in the will of an interested friend. In some colleges almost the entire efforts at financial promotion are put upon the cultivation of wills. This has proved a very unsatisfactory form of financial promotion in most institutions, although it is true that several of the colleges have recently been the recipients of important legacies. There are several difficulties in concentrating too much attention upon wills as a source of financial development.

In the first place, the program must necessarily be a long-time affair; and the college, as a rule, cannot hope to realize from such designations for many years. In the second place, the friend of the college can change his will at any time and without notice. The slightest disaffection may result in the cancellation of a bequest. In some institutions of other denominations which have passed through serious internal disorders, millions of dollars, previously designated in favor of the college, have been written out of the wills of interested friends within a very short period.

The third disadvantage in the will as a type of financial promotion lies in the difficulty of collecting the bequest after the testator is dead. The decedent's relatives, both near and distant, frequently oppose the carrying-out of a bequest to an educational institution. If the will is contested in court, it is often difficult for the institution to obtain the amount which the donor had intended; and there are the usual court costs to pay. Most lawyers would unhesitatingly advise an institution to accept any reasonable compromise rather than to try to enforce a bequest when the will is contested by relatives of the decedent. Inevitably the receipt of such a bequest is delayed through court procedure and the liquidation necessary for the settlement of an estate.

Finally, the inheritance tax bears unusually heavily upon gifts of this type. Not infrequently the donor will name the educational institution as the residuary legatee, leaving the inheritance tax upon the entire estate to be taken from the residue belonging to the college. Under such circumstances there is usually a very large shrinkage in the amount actually received over that which was originally anticipated.

The foregoing discussion makes it clear that colleges should not count to any large extent upon wills for the future development of supporting resources. This does not mean that a friend of the college should not be encouraged to make a will in favor of the institution, but the various difficulties and disadvantages of this method should be pointed out. Not infrequently such a person can be persuaded to make the gift on an annuity basis during his lifetime rather than to provide it in his will. The annuity plan safeguards the interest of the giver almost as fully as if he retained actual control of the assets. At the same time, it is subject to none of the delays and disappointments which have been indicated as a factor of gifts by bequest.

NEED FOR A CHECK-UP ON THE RESULTS OF THE FINANCIAL PROMOTION OFFICE

It is especially difficult to ascertain whether a financial promotion office is producing satisfactory results. Necessarily, the effectiveness of the office can only be judged by the long-time results. It is possible, however, to employ financial officers with the understanding that they shall obtain enough free, undesignated cash as gifts to pay their own salaries and expenses. Such a clause in the contract of an officer safeguards the institution against loss in the carrying-out of the financial program. The compensation paid such officers should be commensurate with the results obtained. It is not wise, however, to make the payment on a percentage basis of the cash received, but rather to adjust the annual salary from time to time in accordance with the success of the program maintained.

Unless the results of the financial program are carefully checked, the maintenance of an extensive organization for this purpose may become an expensive luxury. In one institution of the group studied, two full-time officers were employed for fund-raising. Each of these officers received a salary of $3,600 annually and all expenses. These two officers, finding that the development of other forms of support was somewhat difficult, had concentrated almost their entire attention on the obtaining of wills drawn in favor of the college. Although the cash expenditure for salaries alone was amounting to $7,200 per year, with additional expenses making the total outlay in excess of $9,000, the actual free cash gifts received as a result of the activities of these two officers during the year preceding the survey visit was approximately $250. While it may ultimately come about that the wills obtained will add important resources to the institution, it is clear that the program in this case was not producing immediate results at all in accordance with the expense of its maintenance. Very wisely the college has decided to drop its promotion organization until a personnel can be found which can effectively cultivate other types of support.

CHAPTER LVII

INDEBTEDNESS

AMOUNTS OF INDEBTEDNESS

All but six of the thirty-five colleges were carrying some indebtedness at the time of the survey visits, and only two of the institutions in existence as long as sixty years have not had a debt at some time since 1924.

TABLE 136

DISTRIBUTION OF AMOUNT OF DEBT IN THIRTY-FIVE COLLEGES

Amount of Debt	Number of Colleges Having Each Amount of Debt
$450,001–$500,000	1
400,001– 450,000	..
350,001– 400,000	1
300,001– 350,000	2
250,001– 300,000	1
200,001– 250,000	2
150,001– 200,000	6
100,001– 150,000	2
75,001– 100,000	7
50,001– 75,000	1
25,001– 50,000	2
1– 25,000	4
None	6

Total amount of debt at time of survey	$4,355,825
Median debt,* all colleges	97,082
Median debt,* A.A.U. colleges	88,500
Median debt,* non-A.A.U. colleges	135,661

* Medians calculated from ungrouped data.

In this study the only debt considered is that owed to outside agencies. Debts consisting of interfund items within the college accounts are omitted from consideration. Table 136 shows the distribution of the amount of debt in this group of institutions.

This table shows that the total amount of outstanding indebtedness at the time of the survey visits in this group of colleges was slightly more than four and one-third million dollars. The typical amount of debt per institution, as indicated by the median, is almost $100,000. The colleges holding accreditation by the Association of American Universities had a median indebtedness approximately two-thirds as large as the median for the group of colleges not holding national accreditation.

The range in amount of indebtedness is fairly large. The college with the largest debt is carrying the greater part of the item by means of a holding company, the obligation being that of the company, and only indirectly involving the institution.

Figure 36, indicating the relationship between the amount of indebtedness and the size of the denominational constituency, shows that the institutions having constituencies in excess of 60,000 members tend, in general, to have smaller debts than the colleges with constituencies less than this figure.

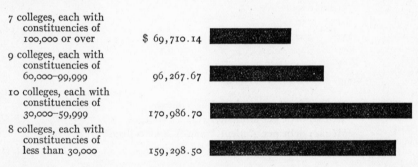

7 colleges, each with
  constituencies of
  100,000 or over $ 69,710.14

9 colleges, each with
  constituencies of
  60,000–99,999   96,267.67

10 colleges, each with
  constituencies of
  30,000–59,999   170,986.70

8 colleges, each with
  constituencies of
  less than 30,000   159,298.50

FIG. 36.—Average amount of debt in colleges having church constituencies of various sizes.

Table 137 presents a distribution of the amount of debt per student in this group of thirty-five colleges. The data of this table were obtained by dividing the total debt of each college by the number of students enrolled.

This table shows that the typical amount of debt per student, as revealed by the median, is $223.09. The colleges without national accreditation have almost three times the median debt per student that is found in the colleges on the approved list of the Association of American Universities. Although the extreme range in the amount of debt per student is large, there are only five colleges in the group which have a debt of more than $500 per student.

The amount of debt per student may be analyzed according to the size of the church constituency. Figure 37, which presents these data, shows a marked relationship between the size of the church constituency and the average amount of debt per student. The larger the constituency, the smaller the debt, and vice versa. The relationship holds equally well for the entire group of institutions, for the colleges on the approved list of the Association of American Universities, and for those not holding national accreditation. This figure reflects clearly the difficulties experienced in maintaining an educational institution with an inadequate supporting constituency.

TABLE 137

DISTRIBUTION OF AMOUNT OF DEBT PER STUDENT
IN THIRTY-FIVE COLLEGES

Amount of Debt per Student Enrolled	Number of Colleges Having Each Amount
$1,501–$2,000	1
1,001– 1,500	1
751– 1,000	..
501– 750	3
251– 500	11
101– 250	9
1– 100	4
None	6

Median debt per student,* all colleges	$223.09
Median debt per student,* A.A.U. colleges	137.15
Median debt per student,* non-A.A.U. colleges	361.00

* Medians calculated from an ungrouped distribution.

PURPOSES FOR WHICH DEBTS WERE CREATED

There are six principal items which are responsible for the creation of the debts in this group of institutions: (1) erection of academic buildings; (2) extensions of campus holdings; (3) building or improving of athletic plants; (4) construction of dormitories and dining-halls; (5) advancing funds for the conduct of financial campaigns; and (6) current operating deficits. Table 138 shows the total amount of debt for each of these purposes, the percentage of the total for each purpose, and the number of colleges which have some outstanding debt for each purpose.

This table shows that the construction of academic buildings has been responsible for the largest amount of the indebtedness of this group of colleges. The second largest amount has been the result of current operating deficits. More than half of the colleges have incurred indebtedness for academic buildings, and approximately the same number are carrying some debt because of current operating deficits. All the other items are represented by only a few colleges, and the total amount involved in each of these other items is comparatively small. A total of 57.7 per cent of the indebtedness has been incurred for plant items.

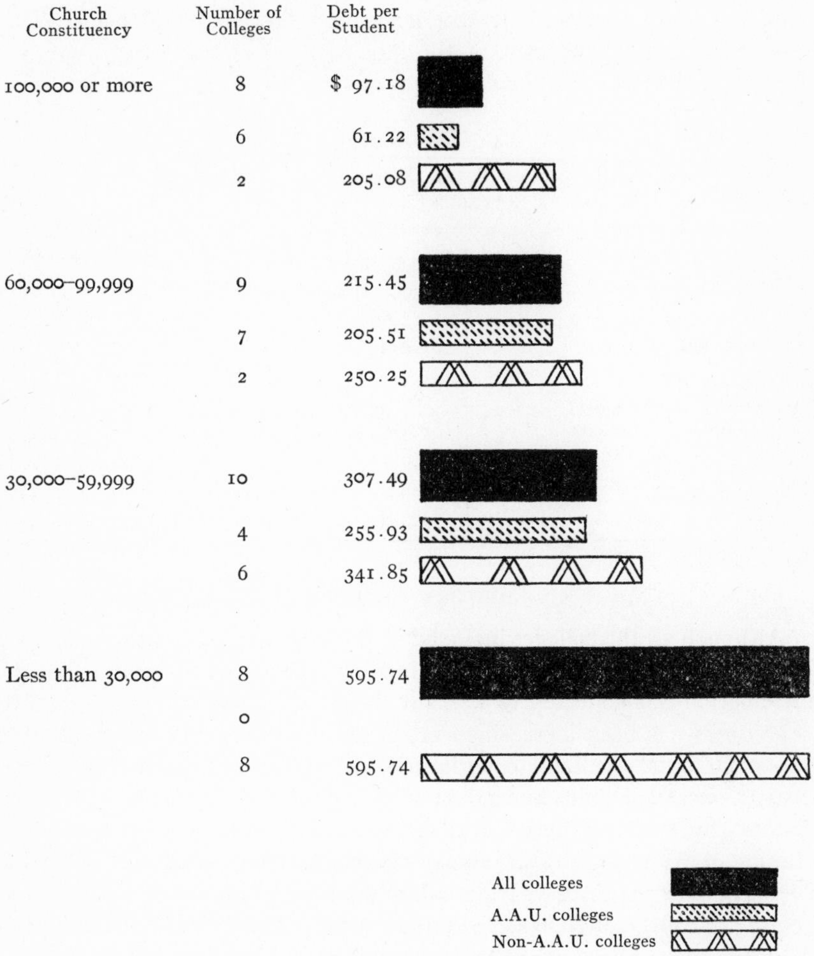

Church Constituency	Number of Colleges	Debt per Student	
100,000 or more	8	$ 97.18	
	6	61.22	
	2	205.08	
60,000–99,999	9	215.45	
	7	205.51	
	2	250.25	
30,000–59,999	10	307.49	
	4	255.93	
	6	341.85	
Less than 30,000	8	595.74	
	0		
	8	595.74	

All colleges
A.A.U. colleges
Non-A.A.U. colleges

FIG. 37.—Average amount of debt per student in colleges having various types of accreditation and church constituencies of various sizes.

The indebtedness shown as having resulted from advances made to financial campaigns will, in most cases, be liquidated when the pledges obtained are collected. In a few cases the financing of dormitories and dining-halls has been arranged in such a way that the indebtedness incurred in their erection will be retired from future earnings. None of the colleges of this group has incurred indebtedness for athletic plants with the hope of retiring the obligation through gate receipts, although several institutions of higher education in America have followed this plan in recent years. At least 85 per cent of the indebtedness of the colleges of this group constitutes a dead load without any means of self-liquidation.

TABLE 138

AMOUNT AND PROPORTION OF TOTAL DEBT CREATED FOR VARIOUS PURPOSES, AND NUMBER OF COLLEGES CARRYING DEBT OF EACH TYPE

Purposes for Which Debt Was Incurred	Total Amount of Debt for Each Purpose in Thirty-five Colleges	Percentage of Total Debt for Each Purpose	Number of Colleges Having Debt for Each Purpose
Academic plant	$1,901,650	43.7	20
Campus	65,714	1.5	3
Athletic plant	141,600	3.2	4
Dormitories, dining-halls	403,248	9.3	4
Current operating deficits	1,586,340	36.4	21
Financing campaigns	216,890	5.0	3
Miscellaneous	40,383	0.9	3
Total	$4,355,825	100.0	29

HISTORY OF DEBT

Although all the colleges included in this group could not furnish complete data regarding the history of indebtedness in recent years, enough information was collected to warrant the general conclusion that the indebtedness has been increasing very rapidly during the past five or six years. Data are available covering the period 1926–29 for twenty-three institutions, all of which had a debt at some time during this period. These twenty-three colleges increased their total debt from $2,434,081 at the beginning of the period to $3,112,494 at its close. This was a net increase of $678,413 over the three-year period, amounting to an average annual increase per college of $9,832. In sixteen of these twenty-three colleges the debt was larger in 1929 than in 1926, and only seven of these institutions had reduced their debt during the period.

Similar data were available for nineteen colleges covering a five-year period (1924–29). In this group of colleges the debt increased from $1,-719,006 in 1924 to $2,540,424 in 1929. The net increase was $821,418, an average annual increase of $8,646 per institution. In eleven of these colleges the debt was larger in 1929 than in 1924, and in eight it was smaller.

The record in the most recent years is slightly more encouraging. Data are available for fifteen colleges, permitting a comparison of the indebtedness at the close of the fiscal year in 1929 and in 1930. Eight of these colleges increased their indebtedness during the year 1929–30, while seven decreased their debt.

FORM OF DEBT

The debts of these institutions are being carried in six different forms. The first which may be mentioned is that of a holding company. It has already been stated that in one college a dormitory has been built by a holding company and that the money borrowed for the financing of this building is an obligation of the holding company. There is no doubt that at least an indirect and moral obligation also rests upon the college, and for that reason the amount has been included in this study as a debt of the college. This method of financing, however, is not common in this group of institutions, although in other American colleges it is found fairly frequently.

The second form in which the debt is being carried is that of a bond issue of the institution. Sometimes these bonds are secured by the pledge of endowment; more often the college plant or a portion thereof is the underlying security. In some cases the bonds have been very largely purchased by the friends of the institution and are not considered very seriously as pressing obligations. In other cases the bonds partake of the nature of the debentures of any commercial enterprise, are handled through a trust company or other financing corporation, and the payment of interest and retirement of principal form a definite part of the financial program of the institution.

In one case the obligations of the college have been consolidated with those of a number of other enterprises maintained by the same Annual Conference, and a bond issue floated by the Conference to fund the debts of all the participating organizations. While the bonds are the obligations of the Conference and not of the individual institutions, the assets securing the bonds are the properties owned by the organizations concerned, and the Conference looks to the institutions for the funds with which to meet interest and principal payments. The bondholders look to the good name of the Conference, however, as their primary security for the loan. This plan does not seem to be working satisfactorily in practice and is not recommended as a model for other colleges to follow.

The third form in which debts are being carried is that of mortgages on the physical property of the institution. This type of contract is the same as the ordinary commercial mortgage. In some cases the mortgage covers the entire plant; in others only a specific building or group of buildings.

The fourth form in which debts are being carried is that of promissory notes. In a considerable number of cases these notes are secured by collateral, the endowment funds being hypothecated for this purpose. In other cases the obligation is an unsecured obligation of the trustees, usually signed by the officers of the board or the executive committee.

The fifth form for the carrying of debts is in open accounts owed to those from whom equipment and supplies have been purchased. As a rule, the amount owed in this form is not large; but several of the colleges have imposed on their creditors in order to finance current deficits. Some have rather substantial amounts owed on open accounts that have been outstanding for many months or even years. This is a very unfortunate form in which to carry an indebtedness. Not only is the institution continually embarrassed by the efforts of its creditors to collect their accounts, but its credit is also impaired and the difficulty of purchasing new supplies at satisfactory prices is greatly increased. Although the college frequently avoids any direct charge for interest by carrying its debt in this form, actually the interest charge, as reflected in the loss of cash discounts and the higher prices and more unfavorable terms on future purchases, is much higher than the ordinary commercial rates of interest. A plan more satisfactory than that now employed is to borrow from a bank in order to avoid imposing on a large number of creditors.

In only one college was there found the sixth form of debt—unpaid salaries of faculty and administrative staff. To carry a debt in this form is extremely unwise, owing to the disastrous effect on faculty morale. In the one college in which this condition was found, several of the faculty members informed the survey staff that they were threatening lawsuits against the college in an endeavor to force the payment of overdue salaries. The personal credit of faculty members was being strained to the limit to carry on their necessary living expenses. A college would be justified in going to almost any extreme, even to closing, before allowing faculty salaries to go unpaid. Most of the colleges of this group rightly take pride in their long history of utmost promptness in meeting salary obligations.

IMPLICATIONS OF INDEBTEDNESS

The liquidation of indebtedness is one of the most difficult of all objects for which to raise money. Donors are not unwilling to give their funds for a new building, for student loans, or for increases in the endowment; but to give for removing indebtedness carries no real appeal to most donors, and such funds are usually secured only by strenuous efforts, and then only in relatively small amounts. It is easy to see why donors prefer to give for a purpose which looks forward instead of backward. It is probably true, also, that the mere existence of an indebtedness is mildly alarming to shrewd donors, who generally prefer to place their funds with institutions having a good record of financial management and good prospects for future stability.

The gravity of an indebtedness varies not only with its amount but also with the circumstances in which the institution is placed. A strong, well-established college, with a favorably known history, with large resources in the form of plant and endowment, serving a relatively large group of students, located in a center of population of considerable size, and with a fairly large church constituency, will probably not be unfavorably affected by an indebtedness. On the other hand, a young institution, with limited resources, not located in or near any considerable concentration of population, with a relatively small enrolment, and with a small number of members of the supporting denomination in its territory, will almost inevitably find that a debt weighs very heavily and even raises a grave question as to the ability of the college to continue its existence. It is impossible, from the data at hand, to indicate the relative importance of the various factors conditioning the gravity of a debt situation. While the ratio of the amount of debt to the resources of the institution in the form of plant and endowment are important from the standpoint of an investment analysis, it is probable that such factors as the size of the local population, the number of church members in the constituency, and the number of students enrolled are equally as important from the standpoint of future educational service.

It is also important to know the policy of the institution with regard to indebtedness. A college with excellent future prospects which has created an indebtedness because of a desire to render some type of service not adequately provided for by its present resources, and which has set up, and is following, a definite plan for the meeting of interest payments and the retirement of the principal, probably should not be criticized adversely. On the other hand, the institution in which indebtedness just seems to accumulate, increasing from year to year, with no very definite plan for systematic reduction in the debt other than the occasional "campaign," is usually on the way to early extinction. In fact, the accumulation of indebtedness is one of the important prognoses of the improbability of the future survival of an educational institution. The history of almost every college which has closed its doors is marked by an accumulating indebtedness as the first step toward the final dissolution.

Any departure from the strictly "pay-as-you-go" policy is a serious matter, and should be authorized by a board of trustees only after they have become absolutely convinced of the need for such an extreme measure. The authorities of the college should assure themselves that the emergency can be met in no other manner. At the same time that the decision is reached to incur an indebtedness, there should be formulated a plan for its liquidation. Only in the most extreme emergencies is a college justified in creating an indebtedness without being assured in advance that the plan proposed for the ultimate removal of the debt is thoroughly feasible.

CHAPTER LVIII

AMOUNTS OF PERMANENT FUNDS AND
RATES OF INCOME

The colleges of the group being studied all belong to the class of institutions generally known as endowed colleges. This means that to a greater or a less extent these institutions rely upon income from invested funds as a means of support. It therefore becomes important to examine such matters as the amounts of the trust funds, the rates of income received, the purposes for which these funds are to be used, the organization for their management, the investments of the trust-fund assets, the general policies with regard to the investment of these funds, and the history of recent increases in the funds.

AMOUNTS OF ENDOWMENT AND OTHER TRUST FUNDS

Data are presented in Table 139 showing the proprietorship side of the invested trust-fund balance sheet for each of thirty-five colleges. In this table the funds are classified as endowment, funds subject to annuity, restricted student loan funds (the income only being available for student loans), and miscellaneous. For each college the figures show the condition as of the close of the fiscal year last preceding the date of the survey visit. In practically all cases the amounts shown are the cost values of the assets owned, since this is the basis on which the college accounts are usually kept.

This table shows that the totals of the trust funds range from almost five and one-half million dollars down to less than one-seventh of a million dollars. The grand total of trust funds for the thirty-five colleges is thirty-seven and one-half million dollars. The great bulk of the trust funds (84 per cent) in these colleges is for the purposes of endowment. There is a fairly large amount of the total invested funds subject to annuity. The other types of funds form only a minor part of the total.

It is clear from the table that the colleges on the approved list of the Association of American Universities generally tend to be those with the larger amounts of trust funds. The median for the colleges of this group is more than three times that for the colleges which do not hold national accreditation.

In several of these colleges there have been important additions to the endowment funds since the close of the fiscal year for which data were collected. Three or four of the colleges have recently closed up financial campaigns that have added materially to their endowment funds. It is somewhat unfortunate that these situations cannot be reflected in the

TABLE 139

ANALYSIS OF INVESTED TRUST-FUND PROPRIETORSHIPS

Institution	Total Trust-Fund Investments	Endowment	Funds Subject to Annuity	Restricted Student Loan Funds Carried as Investments	Other Funds
*DePauw	$ 5,478,847.00	$ 5,246,817.18	$ 232,029.82	....	....
*Ohio Wesleyan	5,175,263.24	2,785,025.38	2,390,237.86	....	....
*Lawrence	1,869,920.19	1,619,921.05	200,108.51	$ 40,327.47	$ 9,563.16†
*Hamline	1,574,786.56	1,535,586.56	39,200.00	....	....
*Allegheny	1,508,033.82	1,401,879.69	18,450.50	87,703.63	....
*Albion	1,491,281.81	1,340,841.71	150,408.10	....	32.00‡
Baldwin-Wallace	1,486,262.58	1,414,542.58	71,720.00	....	....
*Mount Union	1,449,019.34	979,442.79	469,576.55	....	....
*Illinois Wesleyan	1,439,695.82	1,210,122.86	229,572.96	....	....
*Willamette	1,395,124.22	1,329,376.27	65,747.95	....	....
*Baker	1,265,889.52	961,457.82	182,384.67	19,047.03	103,000.00§
Brothers	1,050,000.00	1,050,000.00	....	....	....
*Cornell	1,034,090.01	695,303.20	332,584.20	....	6,202.35‖
Nebraska Wesleyan	1,030,854.08	950,854.08	80,000.00	....	....
*Dickinson	959,612.88	952,612.88	7,000.00	....	....
*Chattanooga	951,589.00	951,589.00	....	....	....
Puget Sound	911,617.90	781,417.90	130,200.00	....	....
*Simpson	886,987.49	720,917.95	159,722.15	6,347.39	....
*MacMurray	763,673.74	658,900.78	104,772.96	....	....
West Virginia Wesleyan	666,076.31	631,676.10	27,500.00	....	6,900.21†
*Morningside	649,683.37	599,823.37	49,860.00	....	....
Dakota Wesleyan	574,175.11	558,075.11	14,100.00	....	2,000.00**
Southwestern	553,692.35	505,514.35	48,178.00	....	....
Ozark Wesleyan	476,521.72	114,072.74	362,448.98	....	....
Ohio Northern	474,158.70	460,158.70	14,000.00	....	....
Union	426,806.00	422,006.00	4,800.00	....	....
McKendree	326,547.48	263,597.48	12,950.00	....	....
*Pacific	314,699.98	257,458.83	57,241.15	50,000.00	....
Iowa Wesleyan	306,383.01	234,418.01	71,965.00	....	....
Central Wesleyan	287,752.24	233,552.24	54,200.00	....	....
Kansas Wesleyan	167,192.36	151,592.36	15,600.00	....	....
Intermountain	151,250.42	142,024.12	500.00	....	8,726.30†
Evansville	143,530.65	110,929.29	32,601.36	....	....
Oklahoma City	142,706.69	142,706.69	....	....	....
Gooding	135,634.78	135,634.78	....	....	....
Total	$37,519,360.37	$31,549,850.11	$5,629,660.72	$203,425.52	$136,424.02
Median, all colleges	$ 886,987.49	$695,303.46	$ 54,200.00	$0.00	$0.00
*Median, A.A.U. colleges	1,395,124.22	979,442.79	150,408.10	0.00	0.00
Median, non-A.A.U. colleges	450,482.35	342,801.74	21,550.00	0.00	0.00

* Institutions on the approved list of the Association of American Universities.
† Current-fund investments.
‡ Funds carried at nominal figure.
§ Self-increasing funds.
‖ Agency funds.
** Building funds.

data of the table; the same condition would be met, however, irrespective of the closing date chosen for the receipt of such information.

RATE OF INCOME ON INVESTED FUNDS

One of the important considerations in analyzing the trust funds of colleges is the rate of income received. Unfortunately this is a difficult item on which to present accurate data. A portion of the difficulty arises from the fact that the income relates to a fiscal year, while the capital of the fund must be taken either at the beginning or at the end of the year. When the fund is increasing, as is the case in most of these colleges, the rate of income obtained by dividing the annual income by the amount of the fund at the beginning of the year is too high, while that obtained by using the data for the close of the year is too low. It would be a long and complicated process to figure accurately the true average capital of the fund, weighting each increase during the year by the length of time it was invested.

Another difficulty in figuring the rate of income on invested funds arises from the bookkeeping practices of some of the colleges. For example, in one institution losses on an item of real estate are capitalized and added to the value of the investment in the item, instead of being considered as a deduction from gross revenue. Some colleges place the management of their trust funds with a corporate trustee and count as income only the net revenue after deducting the expenses of the trustee. Others manage their funds through the college business office and make no charge against the endowment income for the expenses of management.

A third difficulty in figuring the rate of income arises from the fact that the book values of the invested trust-fund assets are almost always set up on the basis of cost. Thus a college which was fortunate in making investments in certain stocks many years ago may today be obtaining a very high rate of income on the original investment, although the rate based on present market value would be much lower. A study of income rates based upon the present market value of the trust-fund assets would be much more meaningful, but could not be made without a considerable amount of labor. Furthermore, as a test of the present management of the fund, the only sound basis would be a study of the income from the portions of the fund which have recently been invested. Certainly the present management should not be judged on the basis of the returns on investments made many years ago. These data would be very difficult to obtain.

With such reservations in mind, Table 140 is presented showing the rates of income on the invested funds in this group of colleges. Expenses of managing the fund have been deducted from the gross revenue, and only the net has been taken. An effort has been made to approximate the average capital of the fund during the year in order to compensate for increases which have occurred during the fiscal period. Information was available for only thirty-three colleges. The incomes are for the fiscal year immediately preceding the survey visit; for some of the colleges the data are for the year 1928–29, and for the others, 1929–30.

TABLE 140

RATES OF INCOME ON INVESTED FUNDS IN THIRTY-THREE COLLEGES

Rate of Income	Number of Colleges	Total Amount of Invested Funds of These Colleges
6.0 or more....................	5	$4,480,475.37
5.5–5.9......................	3	7,350,077.78
5.0–5.4......................	8	7,920,790.18
4.5–4.9......................	3	3,189,067.56
4.0–4.4......................	3	1,772,221.55
3.5–3.9......................	3	2,470,213.96
3.0–3.4......................	2	2,608,876.57
2.5–2.9......................	3	5,624,352.94
Less than 2.5.................	3	1,073,070.39

This table shows that approximately half of the colleges are obtaining an income of 5 per cent or more on their invested funds. A surprisingly large number of the colleges are obtaining very low rates of income, however. These low rates of income seem for the most part to be occasioned by unsatisfactory types of investment, particularly in farm mortgages and real estate. It must be recognized, of course, that too high a rate of income is an indication of a speculative element in the investment policy. A few of the colleges of this group are obtaining rates of income which may lead to question as to whether there is too large an element of risk in their investments.

CHAPTER LIX

ENDOWMENTS

It has already been shown that the great bulk of the invested funds of this group of colleges are classified as endowments. It is, therefore, important to examine with some care the meaning of the term "endowment," the fidelity with which the funds have been managed, the amounts of the funds, and the uses to which these funds are restricted.

DEFINITION OF ENDOWMENT

The most satisfactory definition of endowment is that given by Arnett.[1]

College endowment is a fund, the principal of which is invested and kept inviolate and only the income used for the general support of the college, or for some specific object in connection with it. The fund thus established is sacred and should not be touched or encroached upon for any object whatsoever; its income alone is available. Unless this fundamental fact is understood and respected, the endowed college is built upon an insecure foundation.

In a large number of colleges the term "endowment" has been applied loosely to include all kinds of invested funds, whether considered perpetual or only temporarily set aside for the purpose of producing an income for the support of the college. Thus, in one institution, funds which were later to be used for erecting a building were temporarily classified as endowment. In more than one institution such items as pledge notes and student loan notes are counted as endowment. The standardizing agencies have done much in recent years to inculcate a respect for the term "endowment," and many colleges have taken steps to clarify the status of their funds.

It is perfectly clear that when a donor has presented a gift to the college with the stipulation that it be considered endowment, and when the board of trustees has accepted the gift under such conditions, it would be an outright violation of trust to use the gift at any time in the future for any purpose other than that of producing an income. For a violation of such a trust the authorities of the college could probably be held both legally and morally answerable.

A somewhat different situation arises in the case of gifts, received

[1] Trevor Arnett, *College and University Finance* (New York: General Education Board, 1922), p. 24.

557

originally by the college without any stipulation by the donors as to the use to which they shall be put, which are added to the endowment by the trustees of their own free will, often without much thought as to the significance of this action. Many board members argue that since the trustees have the power to add such funds to endowment, they also have the power and the right to transfer these amounts out of endowment and put them to other uses at their pleasure. The legality of this contention seems never to have been determined by any American court.

It seems clear that in this case there is no violation of any trust imposed by the original donors, since these persons made no stipulations as to the use to which the gifts should be put. The question may be raised, however, as to whether there is not likely to be a breach of trust with subsequent donors who definitely designate their gifts for endowment purposes when these earlier undesignated gifts are transferred from endowment and used for other purposes. Givers to endowment funds are not infrequently influenced by the size of the fund to which they are giving, indicating as it does to some extent both the importance and the permanence of the enterprise they are aiding. A donor always expects his gift to add to the endowment; for the trustees to frustrate this purpose by transferring out of the endowment fund other amounts not originally designated by other donors for endowment purposes savors strongly of a violation of trust.

The principle here involved may be set forth more concretely by means of a fictitious example, which is somewhat similar to a situation found in one of the colleges studied. College A with an endowment fund of $1,-000,000 had for many years advertised this fact in its catalogues and financial promotion literature. It was known to some of the trustees that a portion of the amount labeled as endowment had originally been given the college without any restrictions whatever, having been added to the endowment fund by a deliberate action of the board. The news comes that a generous friend of the institution has made a gift of $100,000, stipulating that the amount is to be added to the endowment fund. An influential element in the college has for some time been working for the erection of a new gymnasium. The trustees are persuaded to transfer out of the endowment fund $100,000 which had not been designated by the original donor as endowment, this sum to be used now for the new gymnasium. The new gift of $100,000 is to be added to the endowment fund according to the wishes of the donor. It will be observed that after the completion of this transaction the college will still have an endowment fund of $1,000,000, just as it had before the recent gift from its generous friend; but it will also have a new gymnasium. Effectually the gift of this friend will provide the college with a new gymnasium, rather than with an increased endowment fund.

This illustration makes it clear that even though the endowment contains some funds not designated by the donors for this purpose, *when there have been subsequent gifts accepted with the restriction that they be added to the endowment fund*, a violation of trust is involved in any future transfers of any amounts whatsoever out of the endowment fund as it existed at the time of these designated gifts. Again Arnett must be referred to for a statement of sound principle.[1] " 'Once endowment, always endowment' is again the only safe, as it is the only legitimate, and the only ethical principle."

The importance of this whole matter is increased by the fact that much of the money raised in financial campaigns is designated for an omnibus object, such as "for endowments, betterments, and liquidation of debts." In order to make a good showing some colleges have added to the endowment fund a large proportion of the early pledge collections from such campaigns. The question arises as to whether the board at a later date could transfer out of the endowment such funds, using them, for example, for the liquidation of indebtedness incurred subsequent to the campaign. If such a construction is put upon the funds raised in this manner, a considerable number of these colleges have little or no true endowment in the sense of a permanent and perpetual fund. The failure to preserve inviolate all funds which have once been labeled as endowment is likely to prove disquieting to potential donors, and may ultimately be very costly to the college.

The acceptance of the principle, "once endowment, always endowment," indicates that boards of trustees should be very cautious in assigning undesignated gifts to the endowment funds. This action should be taken only after grave deliberation and after the establishment of a practical certainty that there will be no yielding to the temptation to use these funds later for other purposes.

There would be an important advantage in creating a new division of the proprietorship side of the trust-fund accounts, to be known as "Suspense Funds," or more accurately, "Funds Functioning Temporarily as Endowment." In this category could be placed all undesignated gifts until such time as the trustees are certain that they wish to add them irrevocably to the endowment fund. This classification could also include

[1] *Ibid.*, p. 47.

other types of funds which may be designated to serve as endowment for a limited number of years.

It is an interesting fact that boards of trustees hesitate much less to use endowment investments as collateral in order to borrow money for current or plant purposes than they do actually to sell endowment securities and then borrow endowment cash. They seem to have a feeling that the endowment is still intact even though a portion of it is not within their control. As a matter of fact, the two situations are identical, and both practices are to be severely condemned. It is a certainty that trustees violate their trust with the donors to an endowment fund if they use the assets for any purpose other than for investment in order to produce an income to be used in harmony with the donors' wishes. There is also some ground for the opinion that they are committing an illegal act and may be held personally accountable for such a violation of trust. It is a principle definitely accepted by all authorities on college endowments that a board of trustees has no moral right, and probably no legal right, to borrow endowment securities to use as collateral for loans, or to borrow endowment cash to use for any purpose other than that for which it was intended.

Fifteen of the thirty-five colleges had hypothecated a part of their endowment funds at the time of the visit of the survey staff. In three other colleges there was a record of hypothecation in the past, but the condition had been cleared up before the time of the survey. In five colleges endowment funds had been invested in academic buildings belonging to the college plant. In three other colleges there was a record of this type of violation of trust in preceding years, but this had been cleared up before the visit of the survey staff. Eighteen colleges of the group were, at the time of the survey visit, free from either the hypothecation of endowment or the investment of endowment funds in academic buildings of the college plant. The eighteen institutions which were free from these criticisms are as follows: Albion, Baker, Brothers, Chattanooga, Cornell, Dakota Wesleyan, DePauw, Dickinson, Intermountain, McKendree, Morningside, Oklahoma City, Nebraska Wesleyan, Pacific, Puget Sound, Simpson, West Virginia Wesleyan, and Willamette. Only fifteen of the foregoing colleges have a clear record in past years on this point.

Table 139 has already been presented to show the amount of the endowment proprietorships in each of the thirty-five colleges. The standardizing agencies, however, are unwilling to count certain types of investment as endowment. This is particularly true of investments in any part of the college plant, or of loans to other college funds. The standardizing agencies usually consider the total debt of the college as a prior claim against endowment and subtract the amount of the debt from the nominal endowment in order to get a figure representing the net endowment held by the college. Table 141 presents data showing both the gross endowment (the same figure as was shown in Table 139) and the net endowment in each of these colleges. As indicated above, the net endowment has been obtained by subtracting from the gross endowment the amount invested in college plant, the amount loaned to other college funds, and the indebtedness of the college. The table also shows the amounts of gross and net endowment per student in each of the colleges. The divisor used in obtaining the amounts per student is the average enrolment of the two semesters or three terms of the academic year preceding the date of the survey visit.

The colleges on the approved list of the Association of American Universities have a median gross endowment almost three times that of the colleges lacking national accreditation. The difference between these two groups of colleges in net endowment is even more pronounced, the ratio of the two medians being more than 5 to 1. When the data for endowment are reduced to the amount per student, the superiority of the colleges on the approved list of the Association of American Universities is still pronounced. These results are to be expected, since the amount of endowment held by a college is one of the very important factors by which it qualifies for membership in a standardizing agency.

It will be noted from the table that four of the colleges have a negative "net" endowment. In other words, when the debts of these institutions and the amounts they have invested in plant and have loaned to other college funds are subtracted from the nominal endowment, the result is a negative quantity. Thus, although these are known as endowed institutions, in the true sense they actually have no supporting endowment.

There is a wide range in the amount of both gross and net endowment per student in this group of colleges. The two extremes on both sets of figures are new institutions. The data for Brothers College, which has an endowment per student almost ten times that of any other college, are not particularly significant, since the enrolment of this new institution has not yet reached the number of students for which facilities have been prepared. Excluding this extreme, the institution having the largest gross endowment per student is Hamline University; DePauw University has

TABLE 141
ENDOWMENT FUNDS OF THIRTY-FIVE COLLEGES

Institution	Date of Information	Gross Endowment	Gross Endowment per Student	Net Endowment	Net Endowment per Student
*DePauw...............	6/30/30	$5,246,817	$ 3,788.32	$5,076,817	$ 3,665.57
*Ohio Wesleyan..........	8/31/30	2,785,025	1,560.24	2,221,174	1,244.36
*Lawrence...............	6/30/29	1,619,921	2,074.16	1,359,288	1,740.45
*Hamline...............	6/30/29	1,535,587	3,877.74	1,236,186	3,121.68
Baldwin-Wallace........	8/31/30	1,414,543	3,214.86	1,234,072	2,804.71
*Allegheny.............	6/30/29	1,401,880	2,356.10	1,175,093	1,974.95
*Albion................	6/30/30	1,340,842	1,783.03	1,320,842	1,756.44
*Willamette............	5/31/30	1,329,376	2,596.44	1,329,376	2,596.44
*Illinois Wesleyan........	6/30/30	1,210,122	2,149.42	988,172	1,755.19
Brothers...............	5/31/30	1,050,000	33,870.97	1,050,000	33,870.97
*Mount Union...........	8/31/30	979,443	2,040.51	979,443	2,040.51
*Baker..................	6/30/30	961,458	2,085.59	947,235	2,054.74
*Dickinson.............	6/30/29	952,613	1,747.91	864,113	1,583.69
*Chattanooga...........	6/30/29	951,589	2,497.61	866,589	2,274.51
Nebraska Wesleyan.....	6/31/30	950,854	1,451.69	930,573	1,420.72
Puget Sound...........	5/31/30	781,418	1,268.54	701,418	1,138.67
*Simpson...............	8/31/29	720,918	1,107.40	666,937	1,024.48
*Cornell................	8/31/29	695,303	1,399.00	595,803	1,198.80
*MacMurray............	6/30/30	658,901	1,866.57	523,819	1,483.91
West Virginia Wesleyan..	5/31/30	631,676	1,955.65	460,054	1,424.01
*Morningside†...........	5/31/29	599,823	864.30	129,465	186.55
Dakota Wesleyan.......	7/16/30	558,075	1,608.29	466,365	1,343.99
Southwestern...........	7/31/30	505,514	927.55	169,403	310.83
Ohio Northern..........	8/31/30	460,159	513.00	200,976	224.05
Union.................	5/22/29	422,006	1,859.06	397,506	1,751.13
McKendree.............	5/31/30	263,597	1,046.02	245,652	974.81
*Pacific.................	8/31/30	257,459	353.17	157,459	215.99
Iowa Wesleyan.........	6/19/29	234,418	719.07	76,818	235.64
Central Wesleyan.......	6/30/29	233,552	1,222.78	93,082	487.34
Kansas Wesleyan.......	7/31/30	151,592	495.40	−163,990	−535.92
Oklahoma City.........	8/31/29	142,707	159.99	−171,293	−192.03
Intermountain..........	6/30/30	142,024	940.56	86,156	570.57
Gooding...............	6/30/30	135,635	1,059.65	107,635	840.90
Ozark Wesleyan........	4/30/30	114,073	573.23	−265,978	−1,336.57
Evansville.............	8/31/29	110,929	279.41	−132,071	−330.15
Median, all colleges...	....	$ 695,303	$ 1,560.24	$ 595,803	$ 1,343.99
*Median, A.A.U. colleges..................	....	979,443	2,040.51	979,443	1,755.19
Median, non-A.A.U. colleges...............	....	342,802	1,052.84	185,190	705.74

* Institutions on the approved list of the Association of American Universities.

† The deductions from the gross endowment of Morningside College include the amount of $250,000 in bonds which are the obligation of a holding company. It is not thought that the standardizing associations would consider this a deductible item; the net endowment for accrediting purposes would therefore be $250,000 larger than the amount shown as net endowment in this table.

the largest net endowment per student. Baldwin-Wallace College is in third place with respect both to gross and net endowment per student. Ten of the colleges have less than $1,000 gross endowment per student, and four have less than $500. Thirteen colleges have less than $1,000 net endowment per student and ten have less than $500.

Table 142 presents data showing the relationship between the number of students enrolled and the size of the endowment funds in this group of colleges.

TABLE 142

AVERAGE ENDOWMENT AND AVERAGE ENDOWMENT PER STUDENT IN THIRTY-FOUR*
COLLEGES, GROUPED ACCORDING TO ENROLMENT

Number of Students Enrolled	Number of Colleges	Average Gross Endowment	Average Gross Endowment per Student	Average Net Endowment	Average Net Endowment per Student
700 and over......	7	$1,693,276	$1,461.70	$1,452,180	$1,236.40
400–699...........	13	961,036	1,785.33	823,931	1,545.41
Less than 400......	14	438,832	1,428.65	285,559	878.99

* Brothers College is omitted.

This table shows that there is an important relationship between the size of the endowment fund and the number of students enrolled, the

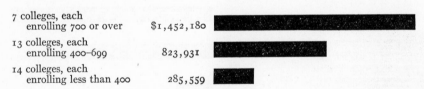

7 colleges, each
   enrolling 700 or over $1,452,180

13 colleges, each
   enrolling 400–699   823,931

14 colleges, each
   enrolling less than 400   285,559

FIG. 38.—Average net endowment in colleges grouped according to enrolment

larger colleges in terms of student enrolments generally having the larger endowment funds. The direct relationship between the average net endowment and the size of the college is illustrated graphically in Figure 38.

This direct relationship between the number of students enrolled and the amount of endowment does not hold for the data relating to amount of endowment per student. The medium-sized institutions have the largest average endowment per student, and the group having the smallest enrolments have the smallest average endowment per student.

It is of interest also to examine the relationship between the number of church members in the supporting constituency and the size of the endowment funds in this group of colleges. Table 143 presents these data.

This table shows that there is an important relationship between the size of the church constituency and both the average endowment and endowment per student. The relationship is especially marked in the case of the net endowment. The colleges with the larger constituencies

TABLE 143

AVERAGE ENDOWMENT AND AVERAGE ENDOWMENT PER STUDENT IN COLLEGES GROUPED ACCORDING TO THE SIZE OF THE CHURCH MEMBER-SHIP OF THE CONSTITUENT CONFERENCES

Number of Church Members in Constituent Conferences	Number of Colleges in Group*	Average Gross Endowment	Average Gross Endowment per Student	Average Net Endowment	Average Net Endowment per Student
100,000 or more...	7	$1,756,799	$2,430.90	$1,656,801	$2,268.66
60,000–99,999....	9	1,229,399	2,060.05	1,028,088	1,721.04
30,000–59,999....	10	492,054	961.35	311,103	630.57
10,000–29,999....	8	275,139	1,034.00	115,219	418.19

* Brothers College omitted.

tend strongly to have larger endowments and larger endowments per student than the colleges with the smaller constituencies. Figure 39 illustrates graphically for thirty-four colleges the direct relationship between

7 colleges, each with
  constituencies of
  100,000 or more $1,656,801

9 colleges, each with
  constituencies of
  60,000–99,999   1,028,088

10 colleges, each with
  constituencies of
  30,000–59,999   311,103

8 colleges, each with
  constituencies of
  10,000–29,999   115,219

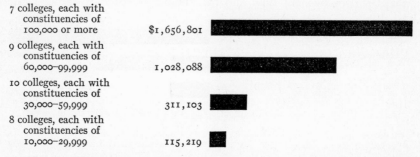

FIG. 39.—Average net endowment in colleges grouped according to the size of the church membership of the constituent Conferences.

the number of church members in the constituent church Conferences and the average net endowment.

The figure of 60,000 church members seems to be the critical point for the size of the constituency. Only one of the eighteen colleges having constituencies smaller than 60,000 has a gross endowment fund in excess of $800,000, and only three of the eighteen have net endowments of $500,-000 or more.

CLASSIFICATION OF ENDOWMENT

Endowment funds may be classified into two main types according to the use which may be made of the income. These two types are the restricted and the unrestricted funds. In each of the colleges there is a portion of the fund which is unrestricted with respect to the use of the income, i.e., the college may use the income for any purpose it sees fit. The restricted funds, however, may be used only for the specific purpose for which they were originally given, such as for scholarships, professorships, library, etc. Thus the restricted funds may be still further classified according to the specific uses which are to be made of the revenues therefrom. Table 144 presents data showing for each of the thirty-five colleges the percentage of the endowment fund which is unrestricted, and the percentages restricted for various purposes.

It has already been pointed out that one of the obligations incurred in setting up an endowment fund is that of using the income in accordance with the stipulations agreed upon at the time the various gifts were received. This table shows that in most of the colleges the great bulk of the endowment fund is unrestricted as to use of income. In all but six of the institutions, however, there is some portion of the fund which is definitely restricted to certain uses. In general, the colleges on the approved list of the Association of American Universities tend to have larger percentages of their funds restricted to special uses than is the case with the colleges not holding this type of accreditation.

The case of Cornell College is peculiar in that the unrestricted portion of the fund is a negative quantity. This institution suffered a serious loss in its endowment investments a few years ago. In accounting for this loss the entire burden was thrown upon the unrestricted portion of the fund, and the restricted parts of the fund were not written down to take their due share of the loss. The policy which was followed in this case was of doubtful wisdom. The obligations owed by the college to those who had given to the unrestricted portion of the endowment fund are in no way less than the responsibilities owed to those who had given funds for restricted purposes. Since the investments of both the restricted and unrestricted portions of the funds were consolidated, it would seem only fair to write down each fund proportionately, distributing the total loss among the several parts of the total fund. Such a procedure would have avoided the absurd condition of a negative balance in the unrestricted endowment fund.

Table 144 does not show in detail the nature of all the restrictions found in the endowment funds of the various colleges. For example, the

TABLE 144

PERCENTAGE OF TOTAL ENDOWMENT FUNDS RESTRICTED TO VARIOUS USES IN THIRTY-FIVE COLLEGES

INSTITUTION	PERCENTAGE OF TOTAL ENDOWMENT WHICH IS UNRESTRICTED	PERCENTAGE OF ENDOWMENT RESTRICTED FOR VARIOUS USES								
		Professorships and Lectureships	Scholarships and Prizes	Library	Plant	Pensions	Special Departments	Museums	President's Office	Undistributed
Brothers..........	100.0	.....	.....	.....	.....	.....	.....	.....	.....	.....
Gooding..........	100.0	.....	.....	.....	.....	.....	.....	.....	.....	.....
Iowa Wesleyan....	100.0	.....	.....	.....	.....	.....	.....	.....	.....	.....
McKendree.......	100.0	.....	.....	.....	.....	.....	.....	.....	.....	.....
Oklahoma City....	100.0	.....	.....	.....	.....	.....	.....	.....	.....	.....
Union............	100.0	.....	.....	.....	.....	.....	.....	.....	.....	.....
*Willamette........	99.1	.....	0.7	0.2	.....	.....	.....	.....	.....	.....
Puget Sound......	98.2	.....	1.8	.....	.....	.....	.....	.....	.....	.....
Ohio Northern....	97.8	.....	2.2	.....	.....	.....	.....	.....	.....	.....
Ozark Wesleyan...	97.8	.....	2.2	.....	.....	.....	.....	.....	.....	.....
Nebraska Wesleyan	97.5	.....	2.5	.....	.....	.....	.....	.....	.....	.....
*Simpson..........	97.5	.....	2.5	.....	.....	.....	.....	.....	.....	.....
Intermountain....	96.5	3.5	.....	.....	.....	.....	.....	.....	.....	.....
Southwestern.....	95.7	.....	4.2	0.1	.....	.....	.....	.....	.....	.....
*Chattanooga......	94.7	5.3	.....	.....	.....	.....	.....	.....	.....	.....
*Hamline..........	94.5	1.7	1.8	2.0	.....	.....	.....	.....	.....	.....
West Virginia Wesleyan...........	93.1	.....	6.9	.....	.....	.....	.....	.....	.....	.....
*Morningside......	91.0	.....	7.7	1.3	.....	.....	.....	.....	.....	.....
Central Wesleyan..	88.6	.....	11.2	0.2	.....	.....	.....	.....	.....	.....
Kansas Wesleyan..	88.5	.....	11.5	.....	.....	.....	.....	.....	.....	.....
Dakota Wesleyan..	87.6	7.4	3.3	1.7	.....	.....	.....	.....	.....	.....
*Allegheny........	87.5	1.1	4.6	0.9	1.4	4.5	.....	.....	.....	.....
*MacMurray.......	83.8	.....	13.8	2.4	.....	.....	.....	.....	.....	.....
*Baker............	81.0	.....	9.0	2.3	.....	.....	2.8	4.9	.....	.....
Evansville........	77.5	0.1	22.4	.....	.....	.....	.....	.....	.....	.....
Baldwin-Wallace..	77.4	.....	2.8	7.5	.....	.....	12.3	.....	.....	.....
*Albion...........	76.1	9.2	7.7	0.5	5.0	1.5	.....	.....	.....	.....
*Dickinson........	67.2	25.6	5.2	2.0	.....	.....	.....	.....	.....	.....
*Illinois Wesleyan..	62.1	4.0	23.1	10.8	.....	.....	.....	.....	.....	.....
*Lawrence.........	61.0	30.1	6.8	1.6	0.5	.....	.....	.....	.....	.....
*Pacific...........	50.7	10.5	.....	.....	.....	.....	.....	.....	38.8	.....
*Mount Union.....	45.8	46.2	6.4	1.3	0.1	.....	0.2	.....	.....	.....
*Ohio Wesleyan....	14.8	37.5	9.0	3.1	.....	.....	0.8	.....	4.0	30.8
*DePauw..........	8.6	47.5	42.8	1.1	.....	.....	.....	.....	.....	.....
*Cornell..........	−42.9	73.5	22.0	24.4	.....	22.3	0.7	.....	.....	.....
Weighted average	79.0	8.7	6.7	1.8	0.2	0.8	0.5	0.1	1.2	0.9
Median, all colleges	91.0	0.0	3.3	0.1	0.0	0.0	0.0	0.0	0.0	0.0
*Median, A.A.U. colleges	76.1	5.3	6.8	1.3	0.0	0.0	0.0	0.0	0.0	0.0
Median, non-A.A.U. colleges	97.7	0.0	2.2	0.0	0.0	0.0	0.0	0.0	0.0	0.0

* Institutions on the approved list of the Association of American Universities.

funds indicated under "professorship" are usually designated for certain specific chairs. A college may have a dozen or more distinct funds for as many professorships. In one college the endowment for library purposes consists of thirty-three separate funds, each for a very limited class of books.

There are certain disadvantages in the presence of a large number of restricted endowment funds. It will be evident, in the first place, that the accounting work is greatly increased by such funds, since there must be assurance not only that the principal of each fund is maintained inviolate but also that the income is actually used for the designated purpose. A far more important disadvantage relates to the manner in which these restrictions tie the hands of the college authorities in the making of the annual budget. The most valuable funds at such a time are those which are unrestricted as to use. It sometimes happens that restricted funds actually distort the educational program, as visioned by the college faculty and administration, through the necessity for spending certain incomes for purposes no longer consistent with the policies of the college.

The reason usually given for the presence of restricted portions of the fund is the special interest of the donors. Financial promotion agents state that it is usually easier to interest a donor in contributing to a specific object, particularly if the donor's name be attached (for example, the John Doe Professorship of Religion), than it is to interest him in such a vague and general idea as contributing to the unrestricted endowment fund of the institution.

On the other hand, it may be argued that a donor who actually has the best interests of the college at heart (rather than the creation of a memorial to his name) can readily be induced to see that unrestricted funds are more valuable to the institution than those that are restricted in use. Of course, if it comes to a question of either accepting a gift for a restricted use, or losing it altogether, the trustees will wisely choose to accept the gift, provided the purpose is consistent with the general objectives of the college. Careful guidance on the part of the financial promotion agents of the college should result in the receipt of gifts which are largely for unrestricted purposes, or which are for purposes considered as immediate goals in the program of the institution.

LIMITATIONS ON PERPETUITIES

There is now a distinct trend among philanthropists away from the establishment of perpetuities. Many of the more important benefactions which have been made in recent years in this country have stipulated that the entire principal of the gift, as well as the annual income from its investment, be expended at the discretion of the trustees. There are numerous instances in American philanthropy of the creation of perpetual trusts for an objective which later became an absurdity. It would be a conservative move for the boards of trustees of this group of colleges to adopt the policy of not creating a trust for a specific objective beyond a certain length of time, such as twenty-five years. Thus, for example, a donor who wishes to provide a professorship in a certain subject might be allowed so to designate his funds, with the understanding that after twenty-five years the board of trustees would be free to use the income for other purposes deemed wise at that time. Serious consideration should be given to the general adoption of a limitation on perpetuities for future gifts to the restricted portions of college endowment funds.

CHAPTER LX

ANNUITIES

One of the very effective methods of adding to the financial resources of an educational institution is through the cultivation of gifts on an annuity basis. Under this plan the donor receives an income from his gift as long as he lives, the college assuming the management of the fund. At the death of the annuitant the college is freed from the obligation of further annual payments and may use the capital and the income from the gift as it sees fit, within the limits originally stipulated by the donor. Annuities are sometimes taken jointly on two or more lives, the annual payment being continued after the death of the first annuitant during the lifetime of the other beneficiaries named in the original contract. Authorities generally recommend against the taking of annuities on more than two lives jointly.

All but three of the thirty-five colleges included in this study have received some gifts on an annuity basis. As was shown in Table 139, the amount of trust funds subject to annuity varies considerably among these colleges. One institution has almost two and one-half million dollars in annuity funds. The second largest fund of this type amounts to a little less than one-half million dollars. There are two colleges having in the neighborhood of one-third of a million in annuity funds, and two others have approximately one-fourth of a million dollars subject to annuity payments. Altogether twelve of the thirty-five colleges have annuity fund investments of $100,000 or more each. One college shown in Table 139 as not having any annuity investments has a small annuity obligation; the funds received from this source have been used for current purposes and thus are not entered in the table, which deals with invested trust funds.

SAFEGUARDING THE INTERESTS OF ANNUITANTS

One of the important considerations in judging the effectiveness of an annuity program is the margin of safety afforded the holders of annuity contracts. It should be clear that when a college, in return for a gift, enters into a contract to pay a stipulated income to the donor during his lifetime, the institution should have some well-considered plan for obtaining the income necessary to carry out its part of the agreement. Most colleges follow the policy of investing the gifts in income-producing securities in order to obtain the major portion of the funds necessary to discharge their obligations to the donor. Two or three of the colleges, however, have used some of their annuity gifts for current purposes or for buildings, leaving the annual payments to be met in the same manner as the other expenses of the college. This practice clearly does not afford annuitants the protection to which they are entitled.

Since most of the annuitants are well advanced in years, the college can easily maintain a reserve of ample size to discharge its obligations under its existing annuity contracts without having investments equal to its total annuity gifts, provided the rates of payment are conservative. Table 139 shows that the total of annuity investments in these thirty-five colleges is $5,629,660.72. The capital sum on which annuities are being paid totals $6,161,468.18. Thus the annuity investments provide a reserve amounting to 91.4 per cent of the capital sum originally received on the annuity basis. Considering the rates at which the annuities have been taken, this is a very satisfactory margin of safety. The difference between annuity investments and the capital sum on which annuities are being paid is accounted for principally by the practice followed by some institutions of deducting from the investment the amount paid to annuitants in excess of the earnings of the invested funds. This is a satisfactory practice, provided only that the invested reserve does not fall below the amount needed to carry the annuities on a safe actuarial basis.

Detailed investigation on this point in each of the colleges included in this study indicates that, with possibly two exceptions, each of the institutions has an ample margin of safety for the protection of its annuitants. In one of the colleges constituting an exception to the general rule, the annuity obligation is very small, entailing an annual outlay of only $60. In the other college, a relatively new institution, the entire financial program has been built around the cultivation of annuities. Assets received in return for annuity contracts have been overvalued, and the book values of the college investments have been shifted so that it is difficult to determine the true margin of safety afforded annuitants.

On the whole, the record of annuity management in these thirty-five colleges is very encouraging. The interests of the entire group of annuitants, constituting a total obligation in excess of $6,000,000, are well cared for and amply safeguarded. This record should be an encouragement to further gifts on this basis by philanthropically inclined persons who need to be assured of an income during the remainder of their lives. As a "safe" investment it would be difficult to equal the record shown by these colleges in discharging their annuity obligations.

DEVELOPMENT OF ANNUITY PROGRAMS

Some institutions could well afford to put more emphasis on the cultivation of annuity gifts. Ten of the colleges included in this study have during the past five or six years added to their resources, through the writing of annuity contracts, at the average annual rate of $61,693 each. There are seven other colleges in which annuity contracts have been written in comparatively small amount during the past few years; but half of the colleges have neglected completely this important source of financial cultivation.

Some further light is thrown upon the policies with regard to annuities in the various colleges by a study of the dates when the agreements now in effect were first entered upon. These data are given in Table 145.

TABLE 145

DATES OF ISSUE OF OUTSTANDING ANNUITIES IN THIRTY-TWO COLLEGES

Period	Amounts of Annuities at Present Outstanding Issued in Each Period	Percentages of Total Amount of Annuities at Present Outstanding Issued in Each Period	Number of Annuity Contracts Outstanding That Were Issued in Each Period	Number of Colleges Having Outstanding Contracts Written in Each Period
Since 1929*............	$ 90,418.00	1.5	35	11
1925–29................	3,445,547.92	55.9	436	28
1920–24................	1,373,415.00	22.3	169	23
1915–19................	540,210.00	8.8	91	15
1910–14................	271,032.21	4.4	42	13
1900–1909.............	171,100.00	2.7	17	8
Before 1900............	29,600.00	0.5	10	5
No information.........	240,145.05	3.9	51	14
Total..............	$6,161,468.18	100.0	851	32

* Up to the time of the survey visit in each college. The figure here given is not significant for comparative purposes, but is included in order to reconcile the total.

This table shows that considerably more than one-half of the total amount of the annuity contracts now outstanding has been written since 1925, and that approximately four-fifths of the total amount has been written since 1920. Of the eight hundred contracts concerning which data were available, six hundred and forty, or 80 per cent, have been written since 1920. All of the colleges having annuity contracts and able to provide this information have written some annuities since 1920. Caution must be used in interpreting these figures, since the annuities written in the earlier years have had more opportunity to mature than those written in the later years.

Because of the nature of the annuity contract, the college does not begin to profit from the arrangement until after the death of the annuitant. In a stable situation it would be expected that the amount of annuities maturing each year would equal the amount of new annuity contracts written. While the annuity program is in a stage of development, however, the amount of new annuities written will exceed the amount of maturities. Data collected from twenty of these colleges indicate that during the past five or six years new annuity contracts have been written at an average annual rate of $32,754.67 per institution; maturing annuities in the same colleges for the same period have averaged $5,018.91 annually per institution. It is thus evident that the annuity programs in this group of colleges are still in a stage of development and have not begun to mature in a manner at all comparable with the rate at which new contracts are being written.

AGES OF ANNUITANTS

It is interesting also to study the present ages of annuitants, since these data afford a clue as to the length of time during which the colleges must

TABLE 146

AGES OF ANNUITANTS IN THIRTY-TWO COLLEGES

Present Age of Annuitants	Average Life-Expectancy in Years*	Total Amount of Annuity Contracts at Each Age	Number of Annuity Contracts at Each Age	Number of Colleges Having Annuity Contracts at Each Age	Percentage of Total Amount of Annuity Contracts at Each Age
78 and over..........	5.7†	$ 431,765.96	150	23	7.0
73–77...............	7.7	488,176.27	104	21	7.9
68–72...............	10.1	631,709.02	123	17	10.3
63–67...............	12.9	487,925.26	117	20	7.9
58–62...............	15.9	1,720,622.26	75	16	27.9
53–57...............	19.3	549,450.00	51	13	8.9
48–52...............	22.9	94,985.80	18	7	1.6
47 and less...........	30.3‡	125,368.33	29	10	2.0
No information.......	....	1,631,465.28	184	26	26.5
Total.............	....	$6,161,468.18	851	32	100.0

* Average of male and female expectancies, according to McClintock's Table, adapted from A. W. Anthony, *Annuity Agreements for Charitable Organizations* (New York: Abbott Press & Mortimer Walling, Inc., 1927), p. 12.

† Calculated as average age 80.

‡ Calculated as average age 40.

continue the annuity payments to the present contract holders. Table 146 presents an age distribution of the annuitants for the thirty-two colleges which have annuity obligations.

This table shows that approximately one-third of the total amount of annuities for which information is available is on the lives of people sixty-eight or more years of age. The large concentration between the ages of fifty-eight and sixty-two is occasioned by one large contract amounting to more than $1,000,000. A relatively small percentage of the total is on the lives of people who are under fifty years of age. Information was not available concerning the present ages of annuitants represented by more than one-fourth of the amount of the outstanding contracts. This is an unfavorable reflection on the condition of the college records.

The column showing the life-expectancies at the various ages indicates that it will be several years before the colleges begin to realize substantial amounts of unencumbered resources from the present annuity contracts. For example, the contracts on the lives of those who are seventy-eight years or more of age total $431,765.96. According to life-expectancy figures, calculating these annuitants at an average age of eighty, it will be 5.7 years before half of these annuities mature. For the entire group of annuities, assuming that those for which information is lacking have the same average age as the others, the average life-expectancy is approximately fourteen years. In other words, it will be fourteen years before these colleges are relieved from the obligations of annuity payments on half of the total amount now in force, assuming that the group of annuitants conforms to the mortality experience of other similar groups in the past.

FINANCING ANNUITY PROGRAMS

One of the problems of an annuity program concerns the method of financing the excess of payments to annuitants over and above the earnings of the invested funds. In all but one of the colleges in this group having annuity obligations the earnings of the invested funds are less than the annual payments to the annuitants. The college constituting the one exception has only one small annuity contract, the capital amounting to $500. In half of the institutions the excess of annuity payments over earnings is less than $500 annually, but one-fourth of the colleges must provide $3,200 or more annually for this purpose. In three cases the amounts are $30,427, $20,750, and $17,812, respectively. Amounts of this size constitute a severe drain on the annual institutional budget unless some effective method is provided for furnishing the funds needed to meet the annuity payments. Five methods are now in use for the handling of this problem.

The first method, one which really avoids the problem entirely, is the refusal to accept annuity contracts at rates higher than the earnings on the invested funds. In the past, the annuity rates commonly paid by charitable organizations have been considerably higher than the usual rates of income on invested funds, particularly in the case of annuitants at the older ages. The typical rate paid in this group of colleges is one-tenth of the age of the annuitant at the time the contract is made. Since most of the colleges receive a return of 5 per cent or less on their invested funds, and since the majority of annuitants are more than fifty years of age at the time of making their contracts, it is clear that the typical rates paid will be greater than the income from investments. Recently, some authorities have advocated the policy of not accepting annuities at a rate higher than the income from investments. This plan has the advantage, not only of protecting the college against the necessity of finding other sources of income to meet this drain, but also of cultivating in the mind of the donor a keener realization of the fact that he is actually making a gift to the institution rather than a shrewd investment for himself. The difficulty with this plan arises from the fact that some competition exists among institutions for gifts of this sort, and the one that pays the highest rates is likely to be the most successful in attracting gifts on an annuity basis.

A second method of handling the problem of the excess of payments over earnings is to reinsure the annuity risks with a standard insurance company dealing in this type of contract.[1] This plan has the advantage of releasing the residue of the gift for the immediate purposes of the college, although the college loses the profit that the insurance company makes by carrying the risk. Good business ethics demands that reinsurance be carried out only with the express consent of the annuitants involved.

A third method provides for the creation of a reserve fund out of which the excess annuity payments will be made during the lifetime of the annuitant. As each annuity matures, the reserve fund will be reimbursed, and only the residue of the annuity turned over for the purposes for which it was originally designated. If desired, this residue can be retained in a self-increasing fund and allowed to build up again to the original amount of the gift before being turned over for its designated purpose. The difficulty with the reserve-fund plan is the necessity of finding an undesignated gift of sufficient size to provide for the satisfactory financing of the annuities. When once such a fund is established, it provides a very satisfactory method of handling the excess of annuity payments over and above the earnings of the invested funds.

A fourth method, one that is used by several of the colleges included in

---

[1] For a discussion of the reinsurance of annuities, see T. A. Stafford and Charles L. White, "Reinsurance of Annuities," in *Annuity Agreements—Methods and Plans of Charitable Organizations*, ed. A. W. Anthony (New York: Committee on Financial and Fiduciary Matters, 105 East Twenty-second Street, 1931), pp. 16–34.

this study, is to take the excess payments from the capital of the annuity investments. Thus each year the annuity investments are reduced by the amount of the excess payments. This plan has the advantage of relieving the current budget of the burden of these payments; but many board members and some donors object to the policy of reducing the capital amounts of funds of this type. As long as an ample margin of reserve is maintained, there can be no objection to this policy from the standpoint of safeguarding the interests of annuitants; the plan is less desirable, however, than that of providing a reserve fund from which the excess payments to annuitants are made.

The fifth method, although the least satisfactory of all, is the one used by the majority of the colleges included in this study—the payment of the excess annuity expenditures, over and above income, from the current funds of the institution. As a rule, the colleges that follow this policy do not even consider these payments as loans to the annuity funds, and the current funds are never reimbursed for the amount they have contributed to the annuity funds. In consequence, a portion of the current funds of the institution are thus every year turned into permanent funds instead of being expended for current educational purposes. It is easy to see that a plan of this kind may prove very embarrassing to a college which needs all the funds it can secure in order to balance its current budget. Even when these payments are considered as loans and eventually paid back from maturing annuities, a rapid increase in the amount of new annuity contracts throws an undue burden on the current budget. The colleges which are using this method of financing their annuity programs would do well to consider the adoption of one of the other plans outlined.

WEAKNESSES IN THE ADMINISTRATION OF ANNUITY PROGRAMS

Although the management of the annuity programs[1] in this group of colleges is, in general, very satisfactory, there are four or five defects which are sufficiently common to warrant some discussion. The first of these, and the one involving the largest number of institutions, is the failure to provide a satisfactory plan for financing the excess of annuity payments over the earnings of the invested funds. This point has already been discussed in the preceding section and needs no further elaboration here.

[1] For some excellent material on the subject of annuities, see the booklets published under the editorship of A. W. Anthony under the general title of "Wise Public Giving Series," published by the Committee on Financial and Fiduciary Matters, Federal Council of the Churches of Christ in America, 105 East Twenty-second Street, New York.

A second defect in the administration of annuity programs is the acceptance of items other than cash or readily negotiable securities in return for an annuity contract. Ten of the colleges of this group have the policy of accepting, on the annuity basis, farms, city real estate, or other forms of property that are not readily negotiable. Since it is of primary importance that the capital of the annuity funds be invested to produce as large an income as possible, the gift should be received in such a way as to permit the finance committee of the college to exercise its best judgment regarding the investment. Most college finance committees today would not deliberately purchase a farm as an investment for the permanent funds of an educational institution. The rate of income on such property is at present very low, and the college which accepts such items on an annuity basis increases unduly the amount which must be provided to meet the excess of annuity payments over and above the earnings on invested funds. Probably the only basis on which such property should be accepted in return for an annuity contract is with the condition that the actual earnings of the property, rather than a stipulated annual sum, be paid the annuitant.

An unfortunate policy, which is apt to be associated with the policy of accepting items other than cash on an annuity basis, is that of overappraising the assets offered in order to induce the donor to enter into an annuity agreement. It is clear that if a prospective donor "shops around" in seeking to place his funds on an annuity basis, the temptation may arise for some college to place a higher valuation than is warranted on the property he offers. One instance of this type was found in the group of colleges studied. This college is the only one in which there is any real question of the margin of safety afforded annuitants by the investment reserves of the institution; there is some possibility that the annuitants of this college may ultimately pay dearly for having allowed the financial promotion officer to bid up the value of the assets they offered in exchange for annuity contracts.

Another criticism of the administration of annuity programs, applicable to many of these colleges, relates to the accounting for annuities. In a surprisingly large number of the colleges complete information regarding the outstanding annuities is not available. Tables 145 and 146 show that a considerable number of the colleges could not readily furnish information regarding the dates when some of the annuities were written or the ages of some or all of the annuitants. In other colleges no record has been kept of the excess of annuity payments over the earnings of invested funds. Some institutions have failed to make a separate accounting for each annuity. Several do not follow the policy of keeping in the files of the college a duplicate copy of each annuity contract. If the annuity program is to be wisely administered, it is imperative that the accounting records of the annuities be complete and furnish all the data necessary to indicate at any time the status of each and every contract.

One defect in the administration of annuity programs, although common to many institutions, is very rare in this group of colleges. This defect is the payment of excessively high rates to annuitants. Only four of the colleges of this group could be criticized for this practice, and in no case are the rates paid sufficiently high to jeopardize seriously the position of the institution. Errors in setting annuity rates at too high a figure are typically found in the case of joint annuities, the fact having been disregarded that the life-expectancy of two persons on a joint contract is greater than that of either of the persons individually.

The administrative policy open to most serious adverse criticism—the use of annuity assets for current or plant purposes—is found in only three or four colleges. In each case the amount used was relatively small, and the invested assets of the college provided an ample margin of safety for the annuitants. Three of these colleges have used for current purposes gifts received on an annuity basis, and one has used such funds for a new building. It should be obvious that such a plan is almost certain to lead to embarrassment in balancing the current budget of the institution.

It should be emphasized that the defects that have been pointed out in the administration of annuity programs are, for the most part, confined to a few institutions and do not in any important way affect the general conclusion that the annuity programs of this group of colleges are on the whole managed in an unusually satisfactory manner.

CHAPTER LXI

ORGANIZATION FOR THE MANAGEMENT OF INVESTED FUNDS

OBLIGATIONS DEVOLVING UPON THE BOARD OF TRUSTEES

One of the most serious responsibilities imposed on a board of trustees of an endowed college and one of the most difficult duties to discharge with an acceptable degree of effectiveness is the management of invested funds. Owing to the highly technical nature of the task and the necessity for frequent attention to details, certain powers pertaining to the management of investments are normally conferred on a comparatively small group of the members of the board. The name of the committee thus created varies among the institutions, but for the purposes of this discussion the term "investment committee" will be used.

The fact that an investment committee has been established to attend to the details of investment management in no sense lessens the responsibility, legal or moral, of the entire board of trustees. Three distinct obligations devolve upon the board of trustees in the management of invested funds. The first is to keep the principal of the fund intact. This involves not only a satisfactory administration of the investments so that the securities owned do not decrease in value, but also the safeguarding of the fund from encroachments or misuse. A second obligation is to keep the fund-producing income at the highest possible rate consistent with the maintenance of a suitable degree of safety in investments. The third important obligation is to apply the income from the fund and the various portions thereof to the purposes agreed upon when the trust was created. This means that careful accounts and records must be kept both of the commitments agreed upon at the time the fund was received and also of the current income and expenditures, in order that the trustees may at all times be certain that they are carrying out the obligations which they have undertaken.

For the protection of the investment committee as well as of the board of trustees definite safeguards should be established. The scope of the authority conferred upon the committee should be clearly defined and certain general investment policies and methods of procedure should be carefully formulated. These matters should be written into the by-laws of the board.

There are three distinct types of organization for the management of invested funds in use among the colleges of this group. Each of these types is used in various combinations with the other types, so that all together there is a total of nine distinguishable forms of organization for the management of invested funds. The three types of management are: (1) the investment of funds under the direction of a committee of the board; (2) the investment of funds under the administration of some one individual, such as the treasurer of the board of trustees or the business officer of the college; and (3) the investment of funds through a corporate trustee.

In seventeen of the colleges (Brothers, Central Wesleyan, Evansville, Gooding, Illinois Wesleyan, Intermountain, Iowa Wesleyan, Kansas Wesleyan, Morningside, Mount Union, Nebraska Wesleyan, Oklahoma City, Ozark Wesleyan, Puget Sound, Southwestern, Union, and Willamette) the investment committee of the board of trustees has rather complete charge of the administration of invested funds. In several of these institutions the business officers render some assistance to the committee but the final responsibility, both technically and practically, is with the committee.

Five of the colleges (Chattanooga, DePauw, Dickinson, Ohio Northern, and Pacific) have placed the management of their endowment funds completely in the charge of corporate trustees. Even in such cases there is usually an investment committee of the board but its functions are limited to the supervision of the work of the corporate trustee.

In only three colleges (Baldwin-Wallace, Hamline, and McKendree) is the management of the invested funds intrusted to an individual who is a financial officer of the institution. In each of these three cases there is an investment committee which has a somewhat nominal supervision of the fund, the actual decisions being made by the business officer.

In the case of three colleges (Cornell, MacMurray, West Virginia Wesleyan) the responsibility for the investment of funds is shared between the investment committee of the board and the business officer of the college. This type of control is intermediary between the first type mentioned in which entire authority is vested in the committee and the third type in which the entire authority is vested in the treasurer.

Allegheny College places the management of its invested funds in a committee of the board but maintains also a custodial arrangement with a corporate trustee. In the case of two colleges (Dakota Wesleyan and Simpson) the administration of invested funds is divided according to the type of investment. A corporate trustee is engaged for the management of bondholdings, the investment committee of the board managing all other investments. In two colleges (Ohio Wesleyan and Baker) all three types of management are employed. The board of trustees has an investment committee which employs a corporate trustee, but a large degree of responsibility is retained by the chief business officer of the institution. Albion College employs a corporate trustee for the management of its fund but also has a very active investment committee of the board which supervises in considerable detail the management of the fund. Lawrence College manages its fund through a committee of the board but employs an investment counsel who advises the board with regard to its investment policies.

RATES OF INCOME IN COLLEGES HAVING VARIOUS TYPES OF FUND MANAGEMENT

An important index of the effectiveness of the various methods of managing invested funds is obtained by studying the rates of income received

TABLE 147

RATES OF INCOME ON THE INVESTED FUNDS OF COLLEGES HAVING VARIOUS TYPES OF FUND MANAGEMENT

TYPE OF MANAGEMENT	NUMBER OF COLLEGES	RATES OF INCOME*		
		Average	Highest	Lowest
Completely in charge of a corporate trustee..........................	6	5.3	6.0	4.8
Committee of the board plus an investment counsel................	1	5.3	....	....
Financial officer of the college.......	3	5.2	6.5	3.2
Committee of the board plus large assistance from the financial officer of the college......................	3	4.8	6.0	3.4
Partially in charge of a corporate trustee, remainder with committee of board..........................	5	4.1	5.1	2.6
Committee of the board in full charge.	15	3.9	6.1	0.0

* For the year 1928–29 for some institutions, and the year 1929–30 for the remainder.

by colleges having different types of management. Table 147 presents data showing the average rates and the highest and lowest rates received in each group of colleges, classified according to the type of management. Data were available regarding the rates of income for only thirty-three colleges. The classification follows in general that given in the preceding paragraphs; however, Albion College has been classified with those having management by a corporate trustee, and Allegheny College has been included with those having joint management by the committee of the board and a corporate trustee. The averages presented are the arithmetic means for the institutions, and are not weighted in accordance with the size of the invested funds.

In this table the various plans of fund management have been arranged in descending order of excellence, as judged by the rates of income received. It will be noted that the first two plans listed—namely, the placing of investments completely in charge of a corporate trustee and the management of the funds by a board committee with the advice of an investment counsel—produce not only the highest average rate, but also seem to be more successful in avoiding a low rate in any college than is the case with the other plans. The second of these plans is in effect in only one college, and therefore less reliability attaches to the data.

There are only three colleges which place their funds in charge of a financial officer of the institution; these colleges receive a fairly high average rate of income. In one of these three, however, the rate is very low, and in another it is unusually high. This latter institution obtained some unexpected income from the leasing of oil lands, and it is probable that the rate shown (6.5 per cent) will not be maintained for another year.

Caution should be observed in drawing final conclusions from the data of Table 147. It has already been pointed out that the rates of income are difficult to determine with accuracy. The number of cases in each of the categories is far too small to provide conclusive evidence. It is clear also that the length of time the colleges have been operating under the various plans should be taken into account. Most important of all is the failure to include any index of the merits of the present investment holdings; a high rate of income may possibly indicate unsafe investments rather than good management.

Although some colleges in each group obtain very satisfactory rates of income, remembering the cautions mentioned in the foregoing paragraph, it appears in general that the institutions that depend upon their board committees for the management of investments obtain lower rates of income than those using the plan of a corporate trustee. Even the employment of a corporate trustee for the partial management of the fund does not seem to produce as satisfactory results as the placing of complete responsibility in such an agent. It seems entirely probable that the income of this group of colleges could be increased considerably by a change in the methods of management of the funds on the part of those institutions which depend upon the board committee for this work.

QUALIFICATIONS OF THE INVESTMENT COMMITTEE

It should be pointed out that the great majority of these colleges are operating under an investment plan which places large dependence on a committee of the board of trustees. Knowledge and skill are required to invest endowment funds wisely. Securities which are wise investments for an individual may be unsatisfactory investments for an educational institution. Those responsible for the investment of endowment funds should have special skill and a wide knowledge of financial, economic, and political conditions. Ability of this type is not readily available. Institutions with large funds to invest find it easier to obtain expert service, since they attract to their boards of trustees, more often than the small institutions, men of large affairs. These men are accustomed to seeking the counsel of experts, and usually do seek advice from bankers and trust companies with respect to the investment of funds. Small colleges often find it exceedingly difficult to obtain financial experts as members of their boards; and when such men are available as trustees, they can seldom give a sufficient amount of their own personal attention to the institutional investments to see that they are handled most wisely.

The effectiveness with which the investments of a college are managed depends much upon the personnel of the investment committee of its board of trustees. The most satisfactory results may be expected where this committee is composed largely of men who are investment experts. Because most of such members of investment committees are very busy men and only a minimum part of their time will be at the disposal of the college, it is exceedingly important that they be relieved of petty details so that such time as is available may be devoted to passing judgment on the merits of items in the fund and to suggesting others which will be suitable for the fund. Most college business officers have plenty of details to occupy their full time and attention without attempting to handle all the questions involved in the management of investments. Very few college business officers are qualified to undertake this task, and as a result many funds are being managed with unsatisfactory results.

IMPROVEMENTS IN PLANS FOR MANAGING INVESTED FUNDS

Three possible plans of investment management are here suggested, all of which seem to promise results superior to those being secured by most institutions which do not employ some such methods. Each plan has certain advantages.

First, the services of a trust company may be employed. As previously pointed out, eleven of the thirty-five colleges of this group have some sort of arrangement with a corporate trustee either for the complete management of endowment funds or for some sort of assistance through the investment committee. Very flexible arrangements may be made with the corporate trustee. It may serve only in the capacity of custodian, in which case it provides facilities for the safekeeping of the securities. A second arrangement is that of having the trust company serve as agent, whereby, in addition to acting as custodian, it may also perform such duties as the collection of income on investments, the payment of expenses incurred in connection with investments, the maintenance of insurance on all properties securing mortgages and land contracts owned by the college, the analysis of investments and the reporting on them at intervals to the designated officers, the making of recommendations as to securities which should be sold and suggestions of others which may be purchased, the transmission of net income from investments held, and any other service which such an agent is able to render. A third possible arrangement which may be made with a trust company is that of a trusteeship. In this case the trust company actually assumes title as trustee of the endowment assets. This may facilitate the transfer of titles to properties and securities. It may also cause the trustee to assume certain other responsibilities that are not ordinarily assumed by a trust company acting as agent.

A different rate of charge is made for each of these three types of service. Many trust companies offer a discount to charitable institutions and colleges of as much as 50 per cent on the regular charges. The employment of a trust company will usually result in substantial economies, since routine services can be performed by such an organization at a lower cost than is possible if they are performed by the regular employees of the college. In addition to possible economies, usually substantial increases in income may be expected through the following of wise investment advice.

In case the services of a trust company are employed, the company should be made custodian of all securities. It might be further suggested that, as a part of the trust company's service, monthly reports be required giving in detail the status of the securities. This report might give in tabular form the cost, market value, rate of interest, current yield, yield to maturity, income collected, expenses incurred during the past month, and whatever other information the investment committee may require, as well as recommendations with respect to securities which should be sold and others which may be purchased, with reasons for such recommendations. In case the trust company purchases the securities, the banker's discount of $\frac{1}{8}$ to $\frac{1}{2}$ of 1 per cent to which it is entitled should be allowed the college, so that the trust company may have no financial advantage in mind for itself in the transaction.

There are some advantages in the employment of a trust company which does not have a bond or mortgage department of its own, and which makes all purchases for the accounts of its clients in the open market. In case a trust company which does have a bond or mortgage department is employed, it should be required to purchase securities for this client from some other financial house. This sort of arrangement is not unusual.

Another policy that should be adopted for the protection of the institution which places its investments in the hands of a corporate trustee is that of buying only seasoned securities. This prevents the trust company from loading up the account of the college with issues of new securities which it and other associated financial houses are floating.

It is desirable in selecting a trust company to secure one large enough to employ the services of an expert in economics to help guide it in its investment policies. The detailed report of the trust company together with the recommendations of the investment expert should be presented monthly at the meeting of the investment committee of the college board for its inspection and final action.

The entire invested funds of the institution, with the possible exception of the real estate, might very advantageously be consigned to a trust company for management under the direction of the investment committee of the board of trustees. Usually real estate, especially farms, can be managed best through more personal relations than are ordinarily possible with a trust company. But the more routine matters, such as clipping coupons, preparing and mailing interest notices and notices of principal maturities on mortgages and land contracts, seeing that the proper insurance is maintained on real estate which secures mortgages and contracts, etc., can be cared for more economically and effectively by a trust company than by an official such as a treasurer of a college or university.

A second alternative, which some institutions might prefer to the employment of a trust company, would be to join with a group of other colleges and universities in the formation of an investment trust which would have offices centrally located and would secure the best investment talent in the country as a finance committee to manage the organization and to review the investments at frequent intervals. Possibly several Methodist colleges might wish to form such a group for an investment trust. The possible advantages of a plan of this type are worthy of careful consideration. With perfect co-operation among the institutions, this plan would probably afford the most satisfactory arrangement for the management of investments.

A third alternative would be to join with a group of other institutions in the employment of an investment expert who would review investment holdings at frequent intervals and advise with reference to securities which should be disposed of and others which would be more desirable. This expert could also direct the general investment policy of the institution.

CHAPTER LXII

INVESTMENTS OF TRUST FUNDS

DISTRIBUTION OF INVESTMENTS AMONG VARIOUS TYPES OF SECURITIES

Table 148 presents data showing for each college the percentage of the total trust funds invested in each type of security.

It will be observed from this table that no two of these institutions follow the same policy with respect to the distribution of their investments among the various types of securities. For the entire group of colleges, real estate mortgages comprise the largest single type of investment, approximately 37 per cent of the total trust funds being invested in mortgages. The largest part of this amount is in first mortgages, although a few of the colleges have small amounts invested in second mortgages. The second largest investment item is real estate. A large part of this amount does not represent original investment, but rather an unforeseen change in the type of security, owing to the necessity of foreclosing mortgages on real estate. Almost half of the colleges have some investments in land contracts, although the total invested in this type of security is less than 1 per cent of the grand total investments. These holdings in practically every case are not original investments, but have been adopted as a means of liquidating real estate holdings.

These three forms of investment—mortgages, real estate, and land contracts—are similar in that all are based upon real estate as security. It will be noted that these three items together comprise more than three-fifths of the entire investment holdings.

The data of this table do not separate investments based on farm property from those based on city property. In several colleges farm mortgages and farm real estate comprise the bulk of the investments. Under present economic conditions these are not proving satisfactory investments for the endowment funds of colleges. Particularly unsatisfactory is the investment in farm real estate. It is extremely difficult for a college to manage farm property in such a way as to furnish a satisfactory rate of income on the invested principal. Since most of these properties have been acquired through mortgage foreclosures, it is probable that they are somewhat overvalued at present. Many of these colleges will undoubtedly experience a shrinkage in their invested funds before these frozen assets

TABLE 148

Percentage of Total Trust-Fund Investments in Each Form

Institution	Total Trust-Fund Investments	Percentage in Each Form					
		Mortgages on Real Estate	Real Estate	Land Contracts	Bonds	Stocks	Trusts Held for the Benefit of the College by Other Agencies
*DePauw	$5,478,847.00	92.1	1.3	....	1.4	0.1	....
*Ohio Wesleyan	5,175,263.24	3.0	49.9	0.2	22.5	11.4	....
*Lawrence	1,869,920.19	19.1	8.0	0.7	61.0	3.6	....
*Hamline	1,574,786.56	11.6	41.4	3.1	18.1	....	....
*Allegheny	1,508,033.82	9.7	1.3	....	63.2	13.8	....
*Albion	1,491,281.81	32.4	1.9	1.6	36.9	10.5	5.4
Baldwin-Wallace	1,486,262.58	65.3	9.8	....	5.3	8.8	8.7
*Mount Union	1,449,019.34	48.5	34.1	6.0	9.6	1.2	....
*Illinois Wesleyan	1,439,695.82	22.4	44.8	1.4	0.1	0.3	23.4
*Willamette	1,395,124.22	46.9	7.9	0.8	33.1	....	....
*Baker	1,265,889.52	76.1	8.1	13.6	0.1	....	....
Brothers	1,050,000.00	73.8	....	....	21.1	2.0	....
*Cornell	1,034,090.01	27.3	32.7	4.4	29.6	0.3	....
Nebraska Wesleyan	1,030,854.08	83.1	10.8	....	0.5	....	....
*Dickinson	959,612.88	73.7	....	....	2.3	0.1	23.9
*Chattanooga	951,589.00	90.6	1.1	....	4.9	3.4	....
Puget Sound	911,617.90	48.9	....	0.3	48.6	....	....
*Simpson	886,987.49	54.0	25.1	2.1	13.7	....	....
*MacMurray	763,673.74	26.5	36.9	....	18.4	9.8	....
West Virginia Wesleyan	666,076.31	4.9	23.3	....	62.2	6.6	....
*Morningside	649,683.37	23.1	47.5	....	26.6	0.6	....
Dakota Wesleyan	574,175.11	53.3	27.7	1.4	7.8	3.0	4.4
Southwestern	553,692.35	68.7	6.3	....	0.3	0.9	....
Ozark Wesleyan	476,521.72	1.4	93.8	....	....	4.8	....
Ohio Northern	474,158.70	15.6	....	55.1	15.6	....	....
Union	426,806.00	11.2	....	....	25.1	63.5	....
McKendree	326,547.48	33.9	23.1	....	43.0	....	....
*Pacific	314,699.98	75.5	....	....	18.4	5.6	....
Iowa Wesleyan	306,383.01	30.5	49.2	7.7	10.4	1.9	....
Central Wesleyan	287,752.24	1.4	59.7	....	27.5	1.8	....
Kansas Wesleyan	167,192.36	45.7	35.2	0.4	11.2	3.7	....
Intermountain	151,250.42	4.6	....	0.8	89.1	....	....
Evansville	143,530.65	10.7	14.4	....	54.8	....	....
Oklahoma City	142,706.69	2.1	46.1	....	0.1	16.5	35.0
Gooding	135,634.78	....	99.9	....	....	0.1	....
Weighted average	$1,071,981.73	36.8	24.0	0.9	23.9	5.4	2.9
Median, all colleges	$ 886,987.49	30.5	14.4	0.0	18.1	1.2	0.0
*Median, A.A.U. colleges	1,395,124.22	32.4	8.1	0.2	18.4	0.6	0.0
Median, non-A.A.U. colleges	450,482.35	23.1	18.8	0.0	13.4	2.0	0.0

* Institutions on the approved list of the Association of American Universities.

TABLE 148—*Continued*

INSTITUTION	PERCENTAGE IN EACH FORM						
	Collateral Loans	Leasehold	Unsecured Loans	Uninvested Cash	College Plant	Loans to Other College Funds	Miscellaneous
*DePauw	....	....	4.1	1.0	......	......	......
*Ohio Wesleyan	0.9	......	1.1	0.2	10.8	......	......
*Lawrence	1.0	......	2.2	......	4.4	......	......
*Hamline	0.6	12.7	......	......	......	10.3	2.2
*Allegheny	......	......	0.2	0.1	11.7	......	......
*Albion			......	9.1	1.4	......	0.8
Baldwin-Wallace			0.6	1.5	......		
*Mount Union			0.5	0.1	......		
*Illinois Wesleyan			3.2	0.8	0.6	1.7	1.3
*Willamette	7.4	......	......	3.8	......	0.1	
*Baker			......	1.0	1.1	......	......
Brothers			2.9	0.2	......		
*Cornell	4.8	......	0.4	0.4	......		0.1
Nebraska Wesleyan	......			1.5	......	......	4.1
*Dickinson							
*Chattanooga				......	......		......
Puget Sound				0.1	......		2.1
*Simpson			......	0.6	3.4	......	1.1
*MacMurray			1.3	2.1	......	5.0	......
West Virginia Wesleyan				......	3.0	......	
*Morningside			......	1.0	......	......	1.2
Dakota Wesleyan			......	2.4	......		
Southwestern	4.3	......	......	3.9	......	15.6	......
Ozark Wesleyan			......				
Ohio Northern	......		7.6	6.1	......		
Union			0.2	......	......		
McKendree							
*Pacific	0.5			......			
Iowa Wesleyan				0.3	......		
Central Wesleyan				2.2	......	7.2	0.2
Kansas Wesleyan			2.3	0.8	......	0.1	0.6
Intermountain			......	5.5	......		
Evansville				3.9	......	15.1	1.1
Oklahoma City				0.2	......	......	......
Gooding			......	......	......	......	......
Weighted average	0.6	0.4	0.8	1.4	1.0	1.6	0.4
Median, all colleges	0.0	0.0	0.0	0.4	0.0	0.0	0.0
*Median, A.A.U. colleges	0.0	0.0	0.0	0.4	0.0	0.0	0.0
Median, non-A.A.U. colleges	0.0	0.0	0.0	0.6	0.0	0.0	0.0

* Institutions on the approved list of the Association of American Universities.

are all liquidated. In view of the unsatisfactory rate of income on such investments, and also in view of the strong improbability of any marked increase in the values of farm lands in the near future, the colleges should be advised to liquidate their farm holdings at the earliest possible date, even though it may be necessary to absorb a substantial shrinkage in the capital of the invested funds.

Third in importance as an investment item for the whole group of colleges are bonds. These comprise almost one-fourth of the total investments of the thirty-five colleges, and all but two of the institutions have a part of their funds invested in bonds. In general, sound bonds seem to be a much more suitable type of investment for a college than either real estate or real estate mortgages. Several of the institutions, foreseeing the difficulties which have arisen with farm mortgages, wisely made plans to increase the proportion of their investments in bonds, with a corresponding decrease in mortgage investments. Some of the advantages of bonds as an investment for a college are: (1) their negotiability; (2) their marketability; (3) the readiness with which the income is collected; (4) the opportunity afforded for critical review of the soundness of the security.

The fourth largest investment item consists of stocks. This is, however, a relatively minor part of the total investment; eight of the colleges have no stocks as a part of their invested funds, and two others have less than 0.05 per cent of their total investments in this form. In many of the colleges the total value of the stocks held is an insignificant part of the total investment holdings. In many cases stocks have been received as gifts to endowment funds and have been held in the form of the original gift by the investment committee. Thus investment in stocks has not formed a deliberate part of the policy in most of these colleges. It is suggested that these institutions could well give consideration to the investment of a larger proportion of their funds in sound and well-seasoned stocks.[1] If this is done, arrangements should be made with a trust company for an investment advisory service.

The other items of investment are of minor importance so far as the total for the entire group of colleges is concerned. In a few cases there are trust funds not under the direct control of the institution, although the college receives the income. These could, of course, be classified under the other forms of investment; but most of the institutions having funds of this type have little or no information regarding the form of the investment.

[1] For a discussion of stocks as an investment for college trust funds, see Reeves and Russell, *College Organization and Administration* (Indianapolis: Board of Education, Disciples of Christ, 1929), pp. 263–64.

A considerable number of the colleges have invested small portions of their funds in collateral loans or in unsecured loans. These are usually considered much less satisfactory forms of investment than mortgages, bonds, or stocks.

Almost all the colleges have at least a small amount of uninvested cash in their trust funds. This is partially caused by the fact that investment units are larger than the amount of cash available for their purchase, and it is necessary to wait until sufficient cash accumulates to purchase the block of securities desired. Sometimes it does not prove possible to obtain desirable investments on short notice, and those in charge of the management of the fund prefer to hold the cash uninvested until they obtain a satisfactory form of investment. Occasionally the management is simply careless and fails to note forthcoming maturities or allows the uninvested cash to pile up without actively seeking an investment for it.

Two of the types of investment noted in Table 148—college plant and loans to other college funds—are considered "investments" only by courtesy, and as a sort of accounting fiction. As a matter of fact, funds so "invested" have actually ceased to be trust funds. A more straightforward method of representing such items would involve a reduction in the total of trust-fund investments, although it is wise to carry at least a memorandum of the amounts which have been diverted from their proper use, so long as there is any hope of making restitution to the trust-fund account. In most of the colleges the amounts which have been used in this manner are small; but in five colleges more than 10 per cent of the total trust funds has been diverted to this unproductive type of investment.[1]

THE PLANNING OF INVESTMENT DISTRIBUTION

It has already been pointed out that the widest possible diversity exists in this group of institutions with regard to the distribution of investments among the various types of securities. Inquiries in each of the colleges regarding the planning of investments brought out the fact that twenty-five institutions have no policy whatever governing the distribution of investments among the various types of securities. Five colleges (Baldwin-Wallace, Chattanooga, Dakota Wesleyan, DePauw, and Nebraska Wesleyan) have the policy of investing all of their funds in real estate mortgages. One other college (Southwestern) has a similar policy, except that all its investments are limited to farm mortgages. It is evident that none of these investment plans provides for a satisfactory diversification, the cardinal principle of a safe investment policy. In view of

[1] Most of the unsatisfactory investments of this type were made many years ago before principles of endowment management were well understood.

the experience of other colleges with farm mortgages, the policy of South-western College is especially unsatisfactory.

Only three colleges of this entire group (Albion, Allegheny, and Cornell) have investment policies which provide for a diversification of the funds. One other college (Lawrence) is developing a policy of this type, but information regarding it was not yet available at the time of the survey visit.

The plan of Cornell College provides for an equal division of the funds among three types of security: mortgages, real estate, and bonds. This plan cannot be considered satisfactory because of the inclusion of real estate—usually an unsatisfactory item of investment for college trust funds—and because of the exclusion of stocks.

Allegheny College has set up its investment plan in terms of the maximum percentages of the total which may be invested in each form. Investments in bonds may not exceed 90 per cent of the total, government and municipal bonds 25 per cent, foreign bonds 25 per cent, and investment trust securities 10 per cent. This plan may be criticized because of the failure to include stocks as a desirable feature of the investment policies. Government and municipal bonds are usually unsatisfactory investments for colleges, because their tax-free provision, for which a premium is paid, is of no advantage to an institution which itself enjoys freedom from taxation.

Perhaps the most satisfactory investment plan found in any of these institutions is that of Albion College, which provides a distribution of the fund approximately as follows: 30 per cent in real estate mortgages (city property); 30 per cent in bonds; 25 per cent in stocks and convertible bonds; and 15 per cent in call loans. The adoption of this plan is comparatively recent, and at the time the survey data were gathered there had not yet been sufficient time to change the form of investments to conform exactly to the distribution agreed upon. The inclusion of call loans as a feature of the investment policy provides an important element of flexibility in the plan. When the call-money rate is high, the income from this type of investment is exceptionally good; when the rate is low, it is relatively easy to decrease the investment in this type of security.

RATES OF INCOME FOR VARIOUS INVESTMENT DISTRIBUTIONS

Some light may be obtained upon the wisdom of the various plans of investment by a study of the rates of income on the invested funds. Table 149 presents data regarding the average rate and the highest and lowest rates of income received in groups of these colleges classified according to the types of investment. The rates shown are for the year 1928–29 for some of the colleges and for the year 1929–30 for the others.

TABLE 149

RATES OF INCOME ON INVESTED FUNDS IN COLLEGES HAVING VARIOUS TYPES OF INVESTMENT POLICIES

DISTRIBUTION OF INVESTMENTS AMONG VARIOUS TYPES OF SECURITIES	NUMBER OF COLLEGES	RATES OF INCOME		
		Average	Highest	Lowest
Percentage of total in real estate:				
Less than 5 per cent..................	11	5.4	6.1	4.8
5–40 per cent.......................	14	4.8	6.5	3.4
More than 40 per cent...............	8	2.4	3.5	0.0
Percentage of total in mortgages:				
Less than 5 per cent..................	6	3.1	6.0	0.0
5–35 per cent.......................	13	4.3	6.5	2.2
35–60 per cent.......................	6	4.7	5.9	3.8
More than 60 per cent...............	8	5.4	6.1	4.1
Percentage of total in bonds:				
Less than 5 per cent..................	8	4.0	6.0	0.0
5–35 per cent.......................	16	4.1	6.1	2.1
35–60 per cent.......................	5	5.2	6.5	3.7
More than 60 per cent...............	4	5.5	6.0	5.1
Percentage of total in stocks:				
No investment in stocks..............	9	4.7	6.5	3.2
Some, but less than 5 per cent.........	14	4.0	6.1	0.0
5–10 per cent.......................	4	5.5	6.0	5.0
More than 10 per cent...............	6	4.2	5.2	2.6
Percentage of total in stocks and bonds combined:				
Less than 5 per cent..................	6	3.9	5.8	0.0
5–35 per cent.......................	17	4.1	6.1	2.1
35–60 per cent.......................	4	5.3	6.5	3.7
More than 60 per cent...............	6	5.3	6.0	4.8
Combinations of real estate, mortgages, stocks and bonds:				
At least 80 per cent in mortgages, stocks and bonds, with very little real estate.	3	5.3	5.0	5.9
Principally real estate and mortgages, with very little in stocks and bonds..	5	3.9	4.9	2.8
Principally real estate and stocks and bonds, with very little in mortgages...	6	3.4	6.0	2.1
About even distribution among mortgages, real estate, and stocks and bonds...........................	5	4.2	6.5	2.2

This table is read as follows: There are eleven colleges in the group being studied which have less than 5 per cent of their total trust-fund investments in real estate. The average rate of income enjoyed by these eleven colleges is 5.4 per cent. One of these institutions obtains an income as high as 6.1 per cent, and not one of them receives less than 4.8 per cent.

The table shows clearly that real estate is an unwise investment, judging by the rate of returns received. The greater the proportion of the total investments in real estate, the lower the average rate of return. Exactly the contrary is the case with mortgages, the larger proportions of investments in this form of security yielding larger average returns than the smaller proportions. A somewhat similar situation prevails in the case of stocks and bonds when considered together. Up to the point of at least 35 per cent of the total investment in this form an increasing proportion is accompanied by increased rates of income. This general trend is clearly pronounced in the case of bonds, considered separately from stocks. The larger the proportion of investment in bonds, the larger the average rate of income.

The optimum proportion of investment in stocks, judging by the rate of income, seems to be from 5 to 10 per cent of the total amount of the fund. Since in all cases stocks form a relatively small percentage of total investments, they would not be expected to have an appreciable effect on the rate of income from the total fund. Furthermore, a large proportion of the investments in stocks represents original gifts and not the type of securities which would ordinarily be purchased for an endowment fund. Caution should therefore be observed in drawing from these data conclusions regarding the proportion of the trust funds that should be invested in stocks.

The last four lines of the table represent various combinations of investments. It is clear from these data that whenever real estate enters as an item of investment, the average rate of income suffers.

The data of Table 149 must be interpreted with some caution, owing to the small number of colleges included in the several groupings. It must be recognized that many factors affect the rate of income simultaneously; these are not separated in the table. No attempt is made in this study to analyze separately the income on the various types of securities. It was originally planned to gather this information for the study, but very few of the colleges could furnish the necessary data without an inordinate amount of extra work. In the case of each college it is therefore impossible to state exactly the cause for low rates of income. The table merely indicates clues as to the relative satisfactoriness of various investment plans.

A well-considered investment plan is absolutely essential to the effective management of a trust fund. The colleges which have adopted no plan for their investments should be urged to set up a policy toward which they will work in making future investments. While a few of these colleges are at present obtaining very satisfactory rates of income from their invested funds without having distributed their investments according to a well-thought-out plan, these are the exceptions rather than the rule. In most of these cases the satisfactory rate of income is due to exceptionally capable management or other fortunate local conditions which may not always obtain.

CONSOLIDATION OF INVESTMENTS OF VARIOUS TRUST FUNDS

There are two distinct plans followed in the investment of trust funds: (1) investment of each separate fund in a distinct group of securities which must be accounted for separately; and (2) consolidation of all securities for all trust funds, and investment of them in one group. Arguments have been advanced in favor of each method. Those which have been given in favor of the separate investment of funds are: (1) each fund may enjoy profits made through the sale of securities which are a part of the fund; (2) each fund should be entitled to the income earned on its own block of securities. The separate investment plan may be advantageous to a given fund, provided the income on the particular group of investments is especially good. It should be kept in mind that if certain funds profit at times through this plan, they are almost certain to suffer at other times, and in the long run advantages and disadvantages tend to equalize each other.

The most serious argument against the investment of funds separately is that in the case of comparatively small funds, adequate diversity of investment is difficult or even impossible of attainment. This greatly increases the danger of loss to, or even complete extinction of, certain funds, since throughout the years losses are almost certain to occur.

Another argument against separate investment of funds is that frequently a separate bank account is maintained with each fund. This plan may greatly increase the amount of uninvested cash, as it may be difficult to arrange at all times for complete investment of all funds. It is not at all unusual to find in trust funds substantial cash balances which are unproductive while awaiting investment. The multiplication of such unproductive balances may prove very wasteful.

In case of consolidation of funds for investment purposes, securities are invested with no reference as to the fund or funds concerned. Advantages claimed for this plan are: (1) consolidation simplifies the accounting for investments; (2) the income for each fund will fluctuate less over a period of years; (3) because of the possibility of greater diversity of investment, losses to each fund are much less probable and usually much less serious if they do occur; (4) the maintenance of fewer bank accounts results in more effective use of the fund; and (5) uniformity of income for all funds is probably desirable.

Sometimes gifts are accepted by the board of trustees of a college with the express stipulation that the fund shall be invested separately. Such restrictions are conditions which must be respected. The tendency among the colleges, however, is toward the consolidation plan, except in such cases as are determined otherwise by conditions of the gifts.

CHAPTER LXIII

WEAKNESSES IN INVESTMENT POLICIES

On the whole the management of the invested funds of this group of colleges is at least equal to, if not better than, the average for similar institutions the country over. In most of these institutions the boards of trustees appear to have a fairly well-defined sense of the responsibilities which devolve upon them in the administration of investments. Mistakes which have been made are largely errors of judgment, and for the most part the colleges have been following what have been conceded to be sound investment policies.

The points of weakness in the management of invested funds may be classified into five types: (1) investments in undesirable kinds of securities; (2) lack of diversification in investments; (3) administrative deficiencies in the handling of investments; (4) unsatisfactory accounting policies; and (5) neglect of common safeguards.

INVESTMENTS IN UNDESIRABLE TYPES OF SECURITIES

The investment problems of a college endowment fund differ somewhat from those of the ordinary private investor or financing corporation. Loans which may be entirely secure and a very satisfactory type of investment for the average investor may be very undesirable investments for a college.

One rule, which may be considered as a general guide in institutional investments, is that endowment funds should never be loaned to an individual, company, or association against which the college would hesitate to bring legal measures to enforce collection of principal or interest. This would preclude loans to officers, trustees, or employees of the college, or to any company in which such individuals are interested. Churches, charitable organizations, fraternal orders, or ministers of the gospel of any denomination come under the same category. The reasons for classifying the foregoing as undesirable credit risks for a college should be obvious and need no extended discussion.

Another type of undesirable investment for college endowments may be broadly designated as any part of the college plant, such as academic buildings, campus, gymnasiums, athletic fields, dormitories, laboratories, libraries, college equipment, etc. It has already been pointed out that the

595

investment of endowment funds in academic buildings is an outright violation of trust. The case regarding endowment investments in dormitories and other parts of the plant used for supplementary business enterprises rests on a slightly different basis. The first and most important objection to investments of this type is that they usually produce little or no income. A few college dormitories, especially while they are new and hence able to command high rates for services with minimum expense for repairs, are so operated that they produce some income in the form of rent; but the dormitory is rarely found which is able to produce such a return as would make it a satisfactory investment for an endowment fund over a long period of years.

A second reason why neither dormitories nor other parts of a college plant are satisfactory types of investment is that a college is in greatest need of income from endowment when income from other sources is impaired. If the attendance at a college decreases, usually income from students will also decrease, not only through a loss in tuition, but also through a decline in income from dormitories. The income from dormitories is so dependent on the prosperity of the college that it is likely to decrease at the time of the institution's greatest need. A sound principle to keep in mind is that the endowment should be so invested that it is not affected in any way by the prosperity or lack of prosperity of the college. The observance of this principle would immediately preclude the investment of endowment in any part of the college plant.

Thirteen colleges of this group now have some of their endowment funds invested in plants used for supplementary business activities, such as dormitories, cafeterias, the president's house, etc. Twelve of the colleges had, at the time of the survey visit, some outstanding loans to churches and charitable institutions. Seven of the colleges have loaned part of their endowment funds to members of their own boards of trustees. Four other institutions have been guilty of this practice in prior years but had straightened out these loans prior to the visit of the survey staff. Seven colleges have outstanding loans to faculty members or other employees of the institution. In the case of five colleges, a portion of the endowment funds is invested through or in companies in which members of the boards are financially interested.[1]

Another undesirable type of investment consists of the bonds of municipalities, school districts, the federal government, and other governmental agencies. Although these securities are very desirable investments for an

---

[1] The majority of the institutions are making vigorous efforts to liquidate investments of these types.

individual because of their tax-free features, they are undesirable for an institution which itself enjoys tax-exemption on its investments, since a special premium must necessarily be paid, in the form of a lower interest rate, for the tax-exempt feature. In seven of the colleges included in this group the by-laws definitely express a preference for such securities. This is an investment policy which fortunately does not obtain in most of the institutions and even in those in which the by-laws express such a preference the actual placing of investments has usually not followed the unwise suggestion.

Four of the colleges are open to adverse criticism because of the large uninvested balance in the endowment fund. It is clear that cash as an investment is usually not very productive. At best only a relatively low rate of deposit interest can be collected on uninvested funds. Careful management will keep the amount of uninvested cash balances at a very minimum. Adequate information regarding forthcoming maturities will suggest that new investments be ready for the cash as rapidly as old investments mature.

LACK OF DIVERSIFICATION IN INVESTMENTS

Perhaps no investment principle is more fundamental or more essential of observance for the maintenance in perpetuity of an endowment fund and in the insurance of a fair and steady rate of income over a long period of years than that of diversification. Among the more common methods of diversifying a fund are: distribution of investments among companies in a given industry; distribution of investments among industries or types of enterprises; distribution of investments among types of securities such as stocks, bonds, mortgages, etc.; distribution of investments geographically; and the provision for a fairly even distribution of maturity dates. In sixteen of the colleges of the group being studied there has been a very poor diversification of investments. Some evidence of unsatisfactory diversification was presented in Table 148.

In order to accomplish a satisfactory degree of diversity in a small fund, it is necessary to convert the assets into a comparatively large number of small units. This entails at least two disadvantages. In the first place, the effort expended in accounting for a large number of small items of principal and income is considerably greater than would be required if the fund consisted of fewer items, each of larger proportions. In the second place, very small investment units are not so readily marketable as are larger ones. But these disadvantages inherent in small investment units are of minor importance as compared with the values realized through proper diversification. This fundamental investment principle will seldom, if ever, be adequately applied except through the adoption and observance of a carefully planned investment program. The board of trustees may assist in this by the formulation of a policy with reference to the maximum amount which may be invested in the securities of one company. It would seem, for a fund of approximately $1,000,000, that $15,000 to $20,000 might be conservatively set as the maximum size of an investment unit, with the provision that occasionally the investment in the obligations of a strong, nationally known corporation might go as high as $30,-000 or $40,000. The maximum should be increased as the principal of the fund changes. The observance of this policy would insure some degree of diversification.

Examples of the dangers which arise through lack of diversity of investments are abundant. Perhaps the most conspicuous are the losses sustained within the last fifteen years by colleges and insurance companies as a result of investment in farm mortgages. Because of the general feeling that nothing has a greater degree of stability and permanence than the earth, mortgages on farm lands were a preferred type of investment for many years. Many college by-laws of fifteen or twenty years ago gave preference to farm mortgages in the state and community in which the institutions were located. In fact, some college by-laws provided that all the endowment be invested in farm mortgages. In one college of this group the by-laws still retain such a provision. As a result of this policy many colleges today are suffering serious losses in the principal of endowment as well as substantial loss of income. This is seriously interfering with their educational programs and may even be responsible in some cases for their closing. This example has been cited in order to show how suddenly and how completely the safety of an investment of a type which apparently is most secure may be seriously endangered. It should be kept in mind that regardless of how safe an investment may be at a given time, it is not wise for a college to disregard the principle of diversity and concentrate on any one type of investment.

Another instance of failure to maintain adequate diversification is brought about through the concentration of mortgage investments in one or two localities. Six of these colleges have almost their entire endowment fund in first mortgages on real estate, and in each of these six cases all the mortgage investments are concentrated in one or two localities, generally a large city near which the college is located. Anything which would affect adversely the property values in this city would have a very serious effect both on the value of the investments of the college and also on the constituency from which the student body is drawn. These two facts in combination appear to make it very undesirable to concentrate any large portion of endowment investments in mortgages on property in the immediate vicinity of the college.

In the past it has been considered advisable by many authorities to invest college endowment very largely or almost exclusively in high-grade bonds or in first mortgages on improved real estate. Arnett, writing in 1922, said:

> As a rule, common stocks should be avoided. . . . . Carefully selected first mortgage bonds and real estate first mortgages on improved farms in good localities, preferably in the same state as the college, or in contiguous states, and first mortgages on city property where the college is located, or in nearby cities, make proper investments.

Later, Arnett modified his opinion with respect to stocks as endowment investments. In March, 1927, he made the following statement:

> When the value of the dollar is appreciating, income in stated amount from bonds and mortgages becomes more valuable because of its increased purchasing power; but when the value of the dollar is depreciating, a fixed income becomes less valuable as measured in purchasing power. Investments should be selected in such proportions as to try to keep in equilibrium the two tendencies above described.[1]

A bondholder gets no increased returns if the company issuing the bonds is in a prosperous condition, but if the earnings of the company are not adequate to meet the interest payments, he often loses heavily. Some classes of common stocks, however, provide a great opportunity for profit through participation in earnings. In a recent paper Professor Irving Fisher develops the theory that common stocks are preferable to bonds as a form of investment. His conclusions follow:

> There are, then, five reasons for the now proved fact that stocks are a better investment than bonds:
> 1. The stockholder stands to win as well as to lose.
> 2. Modern dividend policy is toward steadiness.
> 3. A portion of the stockholder's earnings is reinvested for him and ultimately yields further dividends.
> 4. The unstable dollar tricks the bondholder, but any effect on the stockholder is largely neutralized.
> 5. Diversification can correct the irregularities of the stockholder's income, but not that of the bondholder. In short, the alleged safety and steadiness of bond incomes are dearly paid for.

[1] Trevor Arnett, "Handling Endowment Funds," in *Cooperation in Fiduciary Service*, ed. Alfred Williams Anthony (New York: Abbott Press & Mortimer Walling, Inc., 1927).

There appears to be little question but that a well-diversified list of investments should include some common stocks. Diversification of industries and localities is wise because there is less probability that a number of industries in several localities will be adversely affected at the same time. In the judgment of the writers, the types of investment and the proportion of each type might be as shown in the accompanying tabulation.

	Percentage
Selected bonds	35–50
Guaranteed mortgages on improved real estate	15–30
Seasoned preferred stock	5–10
Selected common stocks	20–30

ADMINISTRATIVE DEFICIENCIES

Another group of criticisms of the management of invested funds in these colleges may be broadly defined as administrative deficiencies.

Lack of critical review of investment holdings.—The commonest administrative deficiency in the management of invested funds in this group of colleges relates to the lack of a critical review of investment holdings. It is relatively easy to arrange with a trust company or other expert investment service for a review of the investment holdings at frequent intervals. By means of such a review the college may protect itself against loss or depreciation in the value of securities. One plan of watching the securities already owned, which is followed by some institutions with very satisfactory results, is to refer the list of investments to a banker, broker, or trust company for appraisal at stated times, such as once or twice each year. Advice is obtained as to the possible desirability of greater diversification, or the wisdom of disposing of certain securities. This is a type of service which all the larger investment banking-houses are glad to render. Complete reports can be made to the college on each separate security. In these reports factors which may affect the value of the security, such as callable price and date, current market, and any other weaknesses which may have developed since the last examination, will be pointed out. In view of the fact that investment advice of this sort can usually be obtained free and is of great value in safeguarding investments, it is rather surprising to find that only nine of the colleges in this group make any provision whatever for a critical review of their investment holdings.

Lack of proper restrictions in by-laws.—A second type of administrative deficiency in the management of invested funds relates to the lack of proper restrictions in the by-laws of the college. Since the by-laws constitute the codified legislation governing the institution, it seems clear that these should deal with all important restrictions imposed upon the investment committee and the board of trustees in their management of the fund. The clear formulation of such matters in the by-laws should serve to instil confidence in prospective donors, who may readily see the policies which will be followed in the handling of their gifts after the latter become the property of the institution. It seems clear that the by-laws should deal in some detail with all the more important matters affecting the management of trust funds. Approximately half of the colleges studied fail to provide any important restrictions in their by-laws covering the management of their endowment, and in relatively few of the institutions has there been set up a complete and satisfactory statement of policies regarding the investment of funds.

Failure to delimit authority of investment committee.—A third type of administrative deficiency is the delegation of complete authority for the management of funds to the investment committee, with no restrictions whatever on the amount of the fund which may be invested without a report to or authority from the board of trustees. In order to insure that the form of investments shall not be materially changed without a report to the board of trustees, some institutions have set a maximum limit on the proportion of the fund which may be reinvested without obtaining the permission of the board. A detailed report of all new investments made since the last meeting should be required at each meeting of the board. This is important since, in the final analysis, the entire board of trustees is responsible for the acts of its agent, the investment committee. For this reason, if for no other, full information dealing with changes in the form of investments should be supplied to the board of trustees at frequent intervals. In thirteen of the colleges studied the investment committee is given complete authority to make investments of any size without referring to the entire board of trustees.

Purchase of securities from corporate trustee that manages fund.—A fourth type of administrative deficiency is the policy of purchasing mortgages or other securities from the corporate trustee charged with the management of the trust fund. Four of the colleges of this group follow this unwise practice. The difficulty in this case is that the trustee cannot fairly represent two diverse interests—that of the college, which is interested in purchasing the highest possible grade of securities at the lowest possible price, and that of the seller of securities, who is interested in disposing of his most unsatisfactory holdings at the highest possible price. The difficulty which a corporate trustee will find in sitting simultaneously on both sides of the table in such a transaction renders imperative the establishment of a rule to the effect that no securities will be bought from the files of the corporate trustee in case such an arrangement is made for the management of the fund.

Loans too high a percentage of valuation.—The fifth type of administrative deficiency in the investment policies relates to the percentage of the appraised value which will be loaned upon real estate or other security. The relative proportion of the value of an item of real estate which may be borrowed through a mortgage varies somewhat, depending on the investment policy of the mortgagee. Because the minimum duration of most mortgages is three years and very frequently extensions are granted for many years beyond the original expiration date, real estate values may fluctuate violently between the date upon which a mortgage is made and the date upon which it is finally paid. For this reason a college or university should adopt a conservative policy with reference to such matters. No infallible rule can be given. Perhaps the most usual practice has been to set the maximum for such mortgages at 40–50 per cent of the value of the security offered. A maximum limit should be established by the board of trustees and should be incorporated in the by-laws. In only one of the colleges was adverse criticism made regarding excess loans on real estate as security.

Leniency in collecting interest.—A sixth type of administrative deficiency is undue leniency in the collection of mortgage interest. This condition is found in ten of the thirty-five colleges. One of the surest ways to increase the proportion of investment in real estate, particularly in farm property, is the pursuance of a lenient policy of mortgage interest collection upon such property. In none of these institutions should it be a policy to acquire additional real estate through foreclosures. Very diligent attention should therefore be given to a firm and tenacious, but tactful, policy of interest collection.

Failure to insist on reductions in principal of mortgages.—A seventh type of administrative deficiency in the management of invested funds is the failure to insist upon gradual reductions in the principal of mortgages. This condition was observed in four of the colleges studied. Many of the mortgages contained in the files of these colleges have been renewed time after time with no reduction in principal. Most investment houses today insist on gradual amortization of the principal as a condition of renewing mortgage loans. This is the only protection against a reduction in the security due to depreciation.

ACCOUNTING DIFFICULTIES

The general problems of financial accounting in colleges have been discussed in chapter xlvii. A few of the accounting problems that relate directly to the management of invested funds need to be pointed out in the present discussion. Although the financial accounting in this group of colleges is on the whole fairly good, in the case of three colleges the entire accounting for invested funds is very unsatisfactory in that it fails to yield the necessary information regarding the funds or to provide a satisfactory safeguard for the control of the various invested funds.

Pledge notes counted as endowment.—Six institutions have made the mistake of counting pledge notes as endowment. Under no circumstances should confusion arise on a point such as this. In each case the error was wholly one of accounting but, as could readily be seen, the officials and friends of the colleges might easily be misled regarding the actual amount of endowment by the inclusion of pledges which had not yet been received in cash.

In five colleges the accounting was defective because of the failure to differentiate between endowment and other trust funds. For example, in one institution funds given for a new building project had been classified in the accounts as endowment. Later, when the buildings had been erected, it was necessary to show a reduction of endowment. In another college student-loan funds of the revolving type have been counted as endowment. These are purely accounting errors, although likely to lead to serious misunderstanding on the part of those connected with the college.

Investments carried at other than cost values.—Another accounting difficulty relates to the values at which investments should be carried in the books. Most authorities on accounting recommend that inventories be carried in the accounts at cost and reported at cost. Few, if any, authorities would sanction the upward adjustment of inventory values to reflect favorable market conditions. Good accounting forbids recording a profit in the accounts until such profit is actually realized through the sale of an item at more than cost. Most institutions would never think of adjusting investment accounts to reflect declines in market quotations of securities; and conservative practice should prevent adjusting investment accounts to reflect advances in such quotations. No legitimate advantages seem to obtain through the shifting of book values of investments. An attempt to adjust book values to reflect the ever changing investment market would be hopeless because of the fact that general economic conditions, which profoundly influence the market values of securities, are in a perpetual state of flux. The plan followed by most colleges and universities, for reasons of expediency, provides for entering and carrying investments in the accounts at cost. Any pertinent explanation with reference to market values may be given in reports without actually adjusting entries in the books of account.

In fairness to the donors, gifts which are made to an institution in the form of securities should be entered in the accounts at market value as of the date of the gift. If proper market information is not available, such gifts should be conservatively appraised by, or through, the investment committee and entered in the accounts at this appraised value. Gifts, the values of which are very indefinite, may be entered in the accounts at some nominal value ($1.00) so that they may not be lost. This is very important because the books of account should present a record of each item owned in the trust funds, regardless of its size. As definite values are ascertained for such items as are being carried at nominal values, proper adjustments should be made in the accounts so as to reflect the true condition. Four of the colleges of this group fail to carry endowment securities at cost figures.

Incomplete endowment records.—Three of the institutions are subject to serious criticism because of the lack of completeness in the endowment records. Clearly, the endowment records of a college should carry all the pertinent information needed for a complete study of the whole trust-fund situation. For example, it should be possible to obtain from the records the amount of mortgage interest in arrears, the amount of mortgage principal payments in arrears, maturities of mortgages and other securities, and similar information. It should be possible, also, to analyze the income from the various types of endowment investments such as bonds, mortgages, stocks, etc.

Inadequate reports.—A large number of the institutions fail to provide adequate reports regarding the condition of the invested funds. There are, in general, two reasons for the preparation of reports regarding the trust funds of a college or university. In the first place, information should be made available to the friends and supporters of the institution to inspire and maintain their confidence. This should be accomplished through the annual treasurer's report. In the second place, information is necessary as an instrument of control for the use of the board of trustees and the committee of the board to which is delegated the responsibility for looking after the details of the management of the investments.

The reports which are prepared for purposes of control should be introduced by a summary giving totals of all trust-fund investments, giving a condensed picture of the whole investment situation, including the total investments as distributed among the various types of holdings, the relationship each bears to the whole, the rate of income on each group of items (which incidentally brings to notice the non-productive types of investment), the uninvested cash, etc. This summary report should be accompanied by an analysis of the significant facts, relationships, and trends which seem to the treasurer to be worthy of particular mention. The items

SUMMARY OF TRUST-FUND INVESTMENTS

NAME OF INSTITUTION_____Date of This Report_____

Item	Book Value	Percentage of Total	Rate of Income
Bonds (see Schedule A)......................			
Stocks (see Schedule B)......................			
First mortgages (farm) (see Schedule C)........			
First mortgages (city property) (see Schedule C)..			
Land contracts (farm) (see Schedule D)........			
Land contracts (city property) (see Schedule D)..			
Real estate (city) (see Schedule E)............			
Real estate (farms) (see Schedule E)...........			
Miscellaneous (see Schedules _____) (List).....			
Cash uninvested............................			
Total.................................			

FIG. 40.—Suggested form for summary report of trust-fund investments

in the summary schedule should be cross-referenced to supporting schedules giving complete, detailed analyses. The general form suggested for the summary report and the supporting schedules are herewith presented (Figs. 40–44). A form is also suggested for summarizing the "black list," or low-yielding trust-fund investment items (Fig. 45).

In addition to these schedules, there should be prepared and included a list of items which are of somewhat questionable soundness. This should be especially brought to the attention of the investment committee at each meeting, for its advice.

SCHEDULE A. BONDS

NAME OF INSTITUTION _____   Date of This Report _____

Issuing Corporation or Governing Unit	First Mortgage	Second Mortgage	Debenture	Source			Interest Rate	Number of Bonds Owned	Current Yield	Yield to Maturity	Date of Maturity	Income During Past Year	Total Par Value	Total Book Value	Market Value One Year Ago	Present Market Value	Grade	Marketability
				Gift	Purchase	Other												
1	2	3	4	5	6	7	8	9	10	11	12	13	14	15	16	17	18	19

FIG. 41.—Form suggested for use in tabulating bonds for purposes of investment reports

SCHEDULE B. STOCKS

NAME OF INSTITUTION_____ Date of This Report_____

ISSUING COMPANY	COMMON	PREFERRED	Gift	SOURCE Purchased	SOURCE Stock Dividend	YEAR ACQUIRED	ANNUAL RATE OF DIVIDEND	NUMBER OF SHARES OWNED	PAR OR STATED VALUE PER SHARE	INCOME FROM SALE OF RIGHTS	TOTAL PAR VALUE OR STATED VALUE IF NO PAR	TOTAL BOOK VALUE (COST)	INCOME FROM DIVIDENDS DURING PAST YEAR	UNIT MARKET VALUE	GRADE	MARKETABILITY	TOTAL APPRAISED OR MARKET VALUE
1	2	3	4	5	6	7	8	9	10	11	12	13	14	15	16	17	18

FIG. 42.—Form suggested for use in tabulating stocks for purposes of investment reports

SCHEDULE C. REAL ESTATE MORTGAGES

(Schedule D, "Land Contracts," is similar in form to Schedule C)

NAME OF INSTITUTION_____   Date of This Report_____

NAME OF DEBTOR	TYPE OF PROPERTY	HOW ACQUIRED			AP-PRAISED VALUE OF SE-CURITY	DATE MADE	DATE DUE	INTER-EST DATE DUE	INTER-EST RATE	YIELD TO MATU-RITY	TIME INTER-EST IN ARREARS	AMOUNT IN ARREARS	INCOME DURING PAST YEAR	ORIGI-NAL AMOUNT	AMOUNT OF PRINCI-PAL OUT-STAND-ING
		Pur-chase	Gift	Sale of Prop-erty											
1	2	3	4	5	6	7	8	9	10	11	12	13	14	15	16

FIG. 43.—Form suggested for use in tabulating real estate mortgages and land contracts for purposes of investment reports

SCHEDULE E. REAL ESTATE

(Other than college plant)

Name of Institution _____ Date of This Report _____

Location	Classification								Book Value	Appreciation Added	Depreciation Provided For	Date Received	Source			Gross Income During Past Year	Expenses During Past Year	Net Income During Past Year	Rate	Loss During Past Year
	Vacant Lots	Apt. Building	Residence	Hotel	Farm	Business Property	Village Property	Other					Purchase	Gift	Fore-closure					
1	2	3	4	5	6	7	8	9	10	11	12	13	14	15	16	17	18	19	20	21

FIG. 44.—Form suggested for use in tabulating real estate items for purposes of investment reports

SCHEDULE Z.   SUMMARY OF LOW-YIELDING TRUST INVESTMENTS

NAME OF INSTITUTION _____   Date of This Report _____

List Items	Class	Book Value	Probable Cash Value	Source	Total Gross Income Past Year	Deductions from Gross Earnings Past Year	Net Earnings Past Year	Rate of Net Earnings Past Year
1	2	3	4	5	6	7	8	9

FIG. 45.—Form suggested for use in tabulating low-yielding trust investments for purposes of reports

The frequency of the detailed report depends somewhat on the nature of the investments. If real estate, real estate mortgages, and land contracts predominate, it is probable that quarterly reports will suffice. If bonds and stocks become an item of any considerable size, the reports should be made monthly and carefully reviewed by the endowment committee.

NEGLECT OF COMMON SAFEGUARDS

The final type of deficiency in the management of invested funds consists of the neglect of common safeguards for the handling of the fund. All persons who have access to readily negotiable securities, such as bonds or stocks, and all persons authorized to sign checks on endowment bank accounts or to handle endowment cash in any form, should be bonded. The amount of the bond, which should be large enough to safeguard the institution against possible loss, will depend upon the arrangements for the custody of securities, the number of signatures on endowment-fund checks, the nature of the investments, the methods of collecting income from investments, etc. In fourteen of the colleges studied the bonds of officers handling endowment securities are too small to provide adequate protection to the institution.

Nine of the colleges are subject to adverse criticism because of unsatisfactory arrangements for the custody of securities. Securities should be kept in a fireproof vault, adequately insured against fire and theft. Access to readily negotiable securities should never be possible to one person alone. A copy of the by-laws, or a written statement signed by the officers of the board of trustees who are empowered to sign contracts for the college, should be filed with the official in charge of the vault, outlining the conditions under which securities may be made accessible and naming the officers who may have such access. The safekeeping official should be required to enforce these conditions rigidly.

A complete list of all the securities deposited in the safety-deposit vault should be in the custody of the college. All additions to the items originally deposited should be reported to both the treasurer and the business officer of the college. Withdrawals of securities should be possible only to those who are authorized to make such withdrawal. The safekeeping official should prepare a list of the items withdrawn, with the signatures of those making such withdrawals; copies of this list should be sent immediately to the treasurer and the business officer, and a signed copy should be kept on file by the safekeeping official. Usually a bank or trust company will be selected as custodian for the securities.

Another important matter, which falls under the category of common safeguards for the handling of the funds, relates to the method of signing endowment or trust-fund checks. If the relations of the treasurer and of the investment committee to the endowment fund are such that they are responsible for the issuance of checks conveying such funds, these checks should be signed and countersigned. Usually the treasurer should be designated to sign checks drawn against the endowment-fund bank account, and some other responsible member of the board of trustees or officer of the college should be designated to countersign. Both signer and countersigner should be bonded. Since the business officer of the college should already be bonded on account of his relation to the current funds of the college, he is frequently appointed as one of the countersigning officers. A certain flexibility should be arranged for by the provision of alternates, in case of the absence or disability of those specially designated to sign or countersign. Checks should never be signed or countersigned in advance, since this practice would introduce elements of danger equal to, or greater than, those obtaining with too few signatures. The persons appointed to sign or countersign should be officers who will have some knowledge of the business being transacted.

CHAPTER LXIV

INCREASES AND DECREASES IN TRUST-FUND INVESTMENTS

The decade just past has witnessed large increases in the amounts of trust funds held by colleges and universities. Although accurate figures for the entire United States are lacking, it seems highly probable that the total benefactions to American higher education during the last ten years have been far beyond those of any similar period since colleges were first established in this country. In studying a group of colleges it therefore becomes important to examine the rate at which additions to the endowment and other trust funds have occurred in recent years.

It has been said that in general the success of a college in attracting new supporting resources is an excellent index of the vitality of its program and of the real necessity for the service it is rendering. A judgment on this point, however, must always be qualified by taking into account the peculiar local conditions in each institution and the energy displayed by the board of trustees and other friends of the college in seeking to attract funds. Several of the colleges of this group have made extensive additions to their plants in recent years, and the great bulk of the funds which they have been able to raise has necessarily been used for buildings rather than endowments. Other institutions in recent years have directed their energies toward raising funds for debt liquidation.

It must be recognized, also, that there is the possibility of decreases in the trust funds of colleges. Such institutions are no more immune from losses on their investments than banks and other types of investing corporations.

AMOUNTS OF INCREASE AND DECREASE IN RECENT YEARS

Data are available from twenty-five colleges showing the increases and decreases in trust-fund investments over a period of years. In most of these institutions the data cover a period of four, five, or six years immediately preceding the time of the survey visit. Table 150 summarizes the situations in each of these twenty-five colleges by presenting the average annual gross increase, gross decrease, and net increase or decrease over the period for which data are available. The net change is also shown in this table as a percentage of the total fund at the end of the period used.

This table shows that the median net increase in trust funds for this group of colleges has averaged $42,249.88 annually for the last few years, the total for the group exceeding one and two-thirds millions annually. The medians indicate that the typical college on the approved list of the

TABLE 150

AVERAGE ANNUAL AMOUNT OF INCREASE AND DECREASE IN INVESTED TRUST FUNDS DURING RECENT YEARS IN TWENTY-FIVE COLLEGES

Institution	Years Covered by Data	Average Yearly Gross Increase	Average Yearly Gross Decrease	Average Yearly Net Increase (Decrease Shown by a Minus Sign)	Percentage Which Average Yearly Net Increase Is of Total Fund at Time of Survey
*Albion..................	1925–29	$ 176,452.70	$ 1,741.17	$ 174,711.53	11.7
*Dickinson...............	1925–29	110,139.63	....	110,139.63	11.5
*Mount Union............	1925–30	179,120.98	17,090.96	162,030.02	11.2
*Ohio Wesleyan...........	1925–30	611,984.79	73,539.87	538,444.92	10.4
Intermountain............	1927–30	13,441.31	....	13,441.31	8.9
Puget Sound..............	1925–29	80,268.11	912.60	79,355.51	8.7
*MacMurray..............	1925–30	84,799.29	23,499.33	61,299.96	8.0
McKendree...............	1925–30	68,775.30	43,977.41	24,797.89	7.6
Baldwin-Wallace..........	1925–30	115,606.81	5,225.00	110,381.81	7.4
*Baker....................	1925–30	89,245.49	....	89,245.49	7.1
Nebraska Wesleyan.......	1927–30	60,888.26	2,508.97	58,379.29	5.7
Dakota Wesleyan........	1925–30	33,015.28	1,616.67	31,398.61	5.5
*Illinois Wesleyan..........	1925–29	93,719.72	18,824.70	74,895.02	5.2
*DePauw.................	1925–30	317,994.73	53,839.57	264,155.16	4.8
*Simpson.................	1924–29	46,119.38	3,869.50	42,249.88	4.8
Southwestern............	1925–30	39,959.54	15,066.27	24,893.27	4.5
*Hamline.................	1924–29	83,248.54	31,855.89	51,392.65	3.3
West Virginia Wesleyan....	1925–30	39,369.23	20,726.09	18,643.14	2.8
*Lawrence................	1924–29	71,689.76	38,834.09	32,855.67	1.8
*Morningside..............	1924–28	21,795.07	19,422.40	2,372.67	0.4
Evansville................	1927–29	1,220.81	841.05	379.76	0.3
Kansas Wesleyan.........	1925–30	9,007.88	12,532.92	− 3,525.04	− 2.1
*Allegheny...............	1928–29	124,614.41	227,799.93	−103,185.52	− 6.8
*Cornell..................	1924–28	88,042.46	209,893.30	−121,850.84	−11.8
*Pacific..................	1928–30	9,101.39	75,636.40	− 66,535.01	−21.1
Total..................	....	$2,569,620.87	$899,254.09	$1,670,366.78	4.5
Median, all colleges ...	....	$80,268.11	$17,090.96	$42,249.88	5.2
*Median, A.A.U. colleges	....	89,245.49	23,499.33	61,299.96	4.8
Median, non-A.A.U. colleges............	....	39,664.39	3,866.99	24,845.58	5.6

* Institutions on the approved list of the Association of American Universities.

Association of American Universities annually adds to its invested funds more than double the amount added by the average college not holding this type of accreditation. Four of the colleges for which data are available have shown a decrease in their invested trust funds in the period studied. The net increases in the other twenty-one colleges range from less than $400 up to over $500,000. In six colleges the increases have been notably large, being in excess of $100,000 annually in each case.

The table also indicates the rate of increase (or decrease) in invested funds, based upon the total of the fund at the end of the period studied. On the average the annual increase in recent years has amounted to 5.2 per cent of the present amount of the invested trust funds. The rate of increase has been slightly larger in the colleges without national accreditation than in those on the approved list of the Association of American Universities. This is explained by the fact that the total of the trust funds averages much higher in the latter than in the former group of colleges.

On the whole, the showing of this group of colleges is very creditable. If it had been possible to obtain later data from a few of the colleges, taking into account personal gifts and campaigns that have been closed since the survey visit, the showing would have been even more favorable.

SOURCES OF INCREASES

It is interesting also to examine the sources from which the increases have accrued to the trust funds of these institutions. The data on this point are presented in Table 151.

This table shows that there have been three principal sources of increase in the trust funds of these colleges: campaigns, personal gifts, and annuity contracts. The first mentioned has contributed approximately one-third of the total of the average annual receipts; the other two principal sources have each contributed slightly more than one-fourth of the total. Two other sources, increases in value of securities sold and transfers from other college funds, have each contributed relatively minor proportions of the total increase.

It will be observed that there is marked variation among the colleges with respect to the distribution of the amounts of increase from the various sources. Ohio Wesleyan University, which has had the largest increase, has relied to a very large extent upon an annuity program. De-Pauw University, which has had the second largest increase, has received almost all of its increase from personal gifts. Mount Union College has divided its program between campaigns and annuities. Albion College has laid the major emphasis on campaigns, with a considerable amount coming also from personal gifts. Dickinson College has depended almost exclusively upon campaigns. Allegheny College has received a large amount from increases in the value of securities sold. Baldwin-Wallace College has utilized all four sources to a considerable extent. On the other hand, several of the colleges have received nothing from some sources which have produced important increases in other institutions.

Considering the fact that the years covered by these data represent a very prosperous economic period, it is somewhat surprising that such a small amount has been added to the capital of the trust funds through increases in the value of securities sold. Undoubtedly the failure to obtain increases from this source has been partially due to the relatively heavy

TABLE 151

AMOUNTS OF ANNUAL INCREASE IN INVESTED TRUST FUNDS RECEIVED FROM VARIOUS SOURCES FOR TWENTY-FIVE COLLEGES

INSTITUTION	NUMBER OF YEARS COVERED BY DATA	AVERAGE ANNUAL INCREASE FROM VARIOUS SOURCES					
		Campaigns (Including Gifts by Foundations)	Personal Gifts (Not in Campaigns)	Sale of Annuity Contracts	Increase in Value of Securities Sold	Transfers from Other College Funds	Miscellaneous
*Albion...........	5	$102,418.19	$ 44,541.33	$ 14,243.86	$ 1,955.71	$13,293.61	....
*Allegheny.......	1	....	33,158.45	....	87,955.96	3,500.00	....
*Baker..........	6	47,414.04	545.12	24,023.83	95.83	....	$ 17,166.67
Baldwin-Wallace.	6	43,751.42	15,903.99	22,535.83	33,415.57	....	....
*Cornell........	5	....	82,615.69	....	399.77	5,027.00	....
Dakota Wesleyan	6	30,040.33	1,562.29	1,266.67	145.99	....	....
*DePauw........	6	....	297,208.85	13,190.13	1,237.41	6,358.34	....
*Dickinson.......	5	82,053.51	8,228.08	....	24.60	....	19,833.44
Evansville......	3	886.89	333.92	....	....	....	....
*Hamline........	6	73,849.79	2,415.86	....	6,870.47	....	112.42
*Illinois Wesleyan	5	27,000.00	24,692.18	42,014.59	12.95	....	....
Intermountain...	4	12,095.41	....	....	95.90	....	1,250.00
Kansas Wesleyan	6	1,166.67	2,407.88	2,600.00	2,833.33	....	....
*Lawrence.......	5	17,957.74	41,846.30	....	1,439.64	8,440.40	2,005.68
McKendree.....	6	68,108.63	....	666.67	....	....	....
*MacMurray.....	6	44,555.48	19,313.07	13,195.49	7,735.25	....	....
*Morningside....	5	11,354.00	10,441.07	....	....	....	....
*Mount Union ...	5	90,675.30	8,557.13	78,840.00	642.75	....	405.80
Nebraska Wesleyan..........	4	45,622.30	12,707.07	2,050.00	508.89	....	....
*Ohio Wesleyan...	5	38,961.85	39,597.80	437,089.59	1,537.74	7,210.00	87,587.81
*Pacific..........	3	....	6,918.06	2,183.33	....	....	....
Puget Sound.....	5	57,416.71	1,928.79	18,900.00	2,022.61	....	....
*Simpson........	6	34,345.78	7,249.49	....	1,633.17	2,890.94	....
Southwestern....	6	37,456.72	765.33	529.67	....	1,175.00	32.82
West Virginia Wesleyan.....	6	27,593.01	1,000.00	166.67	5,331.10	5,278.45	....
Total.......		$894,723.77	$663,937.75	$673,496.33	$155,894.64	$53,173.74	$128,394.64
Percentage of grand total		34.8	25.8	26.2	6.1	2.1	5.0

* Institutions on the approved list of the Association of American Universities.

investments in mortgages, which ordinarily do not offer the opportunity for a profit through appreciation. The lack of competent investment advice in many of these colleges is probably also a factor affecting the amount of increase from this source.

SOURCES OF DECREASES

Table 150 showed that almost all of these colleges have experienced some decreases in their trust funds in recent years. One of the common sources of these decreases is loss in the value of securities sold. Since the increases from this source shown in Table 151 were gross figures, some counterbalancing losses would naturally be expected. In most of the colleges the gross gains from this source are considerably larger than the losses. Cornell College is an exception to this general rule, the rather large loss shown for this institution being due to an unfortunate series of investments in a single project.

Another source of decrease in trust funds has come about through the transfer of such funds to other uses. In some cases these transfers have been thoroughly legitimate, as, for example, when maturing annuities, undesignated for any particular purpose, have been used for debt retirement, new buildings, or current expenses. Colleges that follow the policy of deducting annuity payments from the principal of annuity investments must annually show a reduction in invested funds from this source. A few cases of transfer have arisen through loose use of the term "endowment," as, for example, when building funds have been classified temporarily as endowment and later used for financing new construction. Some of the transfers, which have caused decreases in trust funds, have been ethically questionable. Among such transfers may be included the hypothecation of endowment funds, the use of endowment for plant purposes, the retirement of outstanding indebtedness by the use of endowment securities, and the use of funds subject to annuity for current expenses.

NEED FOR INCREASED ENDOWMENT

Almost without exception the greatest single need in this group of colleges is for large funds for endowment purposes. While a large endowment fund does not of itself guarantee a high quality of education, necessary improvements in the programs of these colleges in almost every instance await a larger income. None of these institutions is at a point in its history where it can afford to ignore the pressing demands for additional endowment. To do so would mean virtual retrogression, for other colleges are vigorously moving forward to new goals and accumulating ever larger trust funds. The colleges of this group will do well to concentrate the greater part of their future financial efforts upon the accumulation of larger supporting resources rather than upon the erection of new buildings. Plant improvements are desirable and even necessary in many cases; but this development should not be allowed to overshadow the all-important need for larger endowment funds.

Willamette University furnishes an excellent illustration of a college which has followed the wise policy of accumulating endowment rather than spending its energies in the provision of a fine physical plant. Although data were not presented in the preceding tables showing the history of increases in the trust funds of this institution, it probably has had one of the largest relative increases of any of the colleges of this group. It is true that plant needs are now becoming relatively important at Willamette University, but it is perhaps the only institution of the group which can safely advise its friends to give their funds for building purposes rather than for endowment.

CHAPTER LXV

TUITION FEES

It has already been shown that the bulk of the revenues of this group of colleges is drawn from student fees. This fact necessitates a careful inquiry into the whole matter of the relations of students to the financing of the institutions, with regard especially to the amounts collected from students and the facilities available for furnishing financial aid to needy and worthy students.

TYPES OF FEES

In each of the colleges studied there is one academic fee (occasionally two) charged all students. This fee is known by different names, but the commonest term seems to be the "tuition" fee. The amount is usually fixed at a given sum per year, or per semester or term; in a few cases the tuition fee is fixed at a certain amount per credit-hour carried.

In addition to this general tuition fee, almost all the colleges charge a multiplicity of special fees for particular purposes. The catalogues typically contain long lists of special fees, charged for matriculation, for late registration, for change of course, for library, for graduation, etc.

Another type of special fee is related to the subjects taken. The majority of these colleges charge so-called "laboratory" fees for certain courses, particularly in science. Courses in music and art sometimes entail special fees over and above the general tuition fee. Private instruction in such subjects is nearly always given only on the basis of special fees.

Besides these academic fees, the majority of the colleges have certain fees which are used for the support of extra-curriculum activities or for semi-educational purposes. These fees are known by many different names, such as the activity fee, the student-body fee, or the semester fee. The payment of this fee is usually required of all students, the income being used for the support of publications, athletics, debate, dramatics, and other similar activities. Frequently the students are given a voice in the determination of the purposes for which the funds are to be used. Several of the colleges point out in their catalogue announcements that this fee was originally established at the request of the students. In some cases separate fees are charged for such services as health and infirmary, towel and gymnasium locker, etc. A few colleges have a mixed fee, a part being devoted to activities and semi-educational purposes and the remainder to strictly educational service, such as library, and administrative overhead.

In almost all the colleges the schedule of fees is a complex affair, covering from one to four pages of the annual catalogue. The policy of charging a multiplicity of special fees seems to be partially due to a desire to make needed advances in student charges as painlessly and unobtrusively as possible. In many of these colleges the actual amount of fees a student must pay is difficult of determination by one not accustomed to such a calculation, and there is every probability that some students before they matriculate are misled with regard to the total amount of the charges. Although the colleges have not adopted the multiplex system of fees deliberately to mislead prospective students, the authorities in many cases stated that the system could not readily be abandoned because competing institutions are using the same system; students are almost certain, according to these executives, to mistake the true situation if one college charges a number of special fees while another one charges the same total amount as a single fee. This argument is tantamount to saying that, while the college would not mislead students by the method used in publishing its fees, students would very probably be misled by similar statements made by other institutions. Thus the whole system of charging a multiplicity of special fees rests on somewhat questionable ground, so far as modern standards of ethics in advertising are concerned.

The alternative to the system of special fees, a single fee covering all the basic charges, with no extra fees for any academic purpose, other than possibly for individual lessons in such subjects as music and art, seems not only to be more straightforward and readily understood by prospective students, but is also preferable for other reasons. In the first place, the task of accounting for the single fee is very much simpler than that for the multiplex system, thus reducing labor in the business office, expediting the process of registration, and eliminating a large part of the chances for mistakes in figuring student charges.

In the second place, the single fee eliminates objectionable discrimination against any subject. It seems very unfair to ask students who happen to be interested in a subject such as science to pay extra fees in order to follow their interests. It is entirely probable that this discrimination distorts the programs of many students and reduces the effectiveness of the educational service rendered. No subject worthy of a place in a college curriculum should be discriminated against by an artificial barrier such as a special fee.

The system of charging laboratory fees for instruction in science is frequently based upon the argument of the "added cost of service." Those who take this position argue that, since the students in laboratory courses actually use up certain supplies, the imposition of a special fee is justifiable. This same argument, however, is not logically followed out in the case of other subjects. For example, under such a policy it would be appropriate to charge students in the departments of history and education special fees because of the use made of library materials. Furthermore, if "cost of service" is to be used as a basis for special fees, students should be charged more for registration in the class of a professor having a relatively high salary than for an enrolment with a low-salaried instructor. Similarly, students enrolling in large classes should be charged lower fees than those in small classes. The absurdity of the justification of these special fees on the basis of the cost of service is thus evident.

Finally, it may be shown that the subjects for which the special fees are usually charged are typically not the most expensive per unit of credit, thus breaking down completely whatever force there may be in the "cost of service" argument for the special fees.

For the reasons which have been stated the colleges of this group would do well to consider a change in the policy of charging fees, abandoning the plan of a multiplex system of special fees, and substituting a single fee payable by all students, the charge being fixed at the amount which would otherwise result from the collection of the separate fees.

HISTORY OF TUITION CHARGES

Amounts of fees charged over a twenty-year period.—Table 152 presents data showing the annual tuition fees charged at twenty colleges over a period from 1909–10 to 1929–30. The data are presented in the form of the medians and the extremes for the group of twenty colleges for each of the years indicated. The fee considered is only the general academic tuition fee charged all students. In the case of colleges where the charge is expressed as a certain amount per credit-hour, the tuition for the year is shown as the amount paid for thirty semester hours (or forty-five term hours) of credit. The data do not include student-activity fees or fees for semi-educational purposes, and all special fees have been excluded.

This table is based upon data from all the institutions which furnished information regarding the history of their fee schedules over the period of years. The table shows that the colleges on the approved list of the Association of American Universities tend to charge much higher fees than the colleges not holding this accreditation.

It will be noted that the median tuition fee has increased during the twenty-one years from $47.50 to $175.00. The median for the colleges which are now on the approved list of the Association of American Universities has increased somewhat more rapidly than the median for the colleges not holding this type of accreditation. This is possibly due to the fact that a number of these institutions have attained their accreditation during the period covered by the study. The highest fee charged by any college in the group has increased from $100.00 to $300.00, and the lowest

TABLE 152

ANNUAL TUITION FEES CHARGED AT TWENTY COLLEGES, 1909–29

Year	Median, All Colleges	Median, A.A.U. Colleges	Median, Non- A.A.U. Colleges	Highest in Any College	Lowest in Any College
1909–10	$ 47.50	$ 48.00	$ 39.00	$100.00	$28.00
1910–11	47.13	54.00	45.00	100.00	28.00
1911–12	50.50	57.00	47.50	100.00	28.00
1912–13	57.50	59.00	47.50	125.00	28.00
1913–14	60.00	60.00	45.50	125.00	40.00
1914–15	60.00	61.00	45.50	125.00	40.00
1915–16	60.00	68.62	45.00	125.00	30.00
1916–17	66.25	70.00	45.00	125.00	36.00
1917–18	70.00	75.00	45.00	125.00	36.00
1918–19	70.00	78.50	50.00	135.00	42.00
1919–20	81.13	96.00	63.50	160.00	45.00
1920–21	100.00	120.00	77.50	200.00	45.00
1921–22	114.63	120.00	90.00	200.00	45.00
1922–23	119.00	150.00	100.00	200.00	45.00
1923–24	128.38	150.00	100.00	200.00	45.00
1924–25	130.00	150.00	120.00	200.00	50.00
1925–26	140.13	150.00	131.75	200.00	50.00
1926–27	150.00	175.00	140.00	250.00	60.00
1927–28	158.25	185.00	150.00	250.00	70.00
1928–29	172.63	200.00	150.00	300.00	80.00
1929–30	175.00	200.00	152.50	300.00	90.00

fee has shown approximately the same rate of increase, from $28.00 to $90.00.

Amounts of fees in terms of dollars of constant purchasing power.— Marked changes have occurred in the purchasing power of the dollar during the period covered by this study. In order to analyze the trends of fees in terms of dollars of constant value, the data of the preceding table have been converted into equivalent dollars by the use of an index number. The index used is that developed by Paul H. Douglas in *Real Wages in the United States, 1890 to 1926.*[1] Douglas gives the index number with 1914 as the base. For the purpose of this study the index numbers have

[1] Houghton Mifflin Co., 1930.

been converted to 1928 valuations. Thus the figures given in the preceding table for 1928–29 remain the same, while figures for all other years are modified to take into account the relative purchasing power of the dollar. The index number used for each academic year is that for the calendar year in which the school term begins. Table 153 presents the data of Table 152 converted into dollars of constant purchasing power by the method above outlined.

TABLE 153

ANNUAL TUITION FEES CHARGED IN DOLLARS OF CONSTANT PURCHASING POWER FOR TWENTY COLLEGES, 1909–28

Year	Median, All Colleges	Median, A.A.U. Colleges	Median, Non-A.A.U. Colleges	Highest in Any College	Lowest in Any College
1909–10...........	$ 92.25	$ 93.22	$ 75.74	$194.22	$54.38
1910–11...........	86.53	99.14	82.62	183.59	51.41
1911–12...........	89.91	101.48	84.56	178.03	49.85
1912–13...........	101.60	104.25	83.93	220.86	49.47
1913–14...........	102.92	102.92	78.04	214.42	68.61
1914–15...........	101.44	103.13	76.93	211.33	67.63
1915–16...........	103.68	118.58	77.76	215.99	51.84
1916–17...........	104.49	110.40	70.97	197.15	56.78
1917–18...........	91.90	98.47	59.08	164.11	47.26
1918–19...........	75.46	84.62	53.90	145.53	45.28
1919–20...........	77.18	91.34	60.42	152.23	42.81
1920–21...........	82.17	98.60	63.68	164.34	36.98
1921–22...........	109.50	114.63	85.98	191.06	42.99
1922–23...........	122.12	153.93	102.62	205.24	46.18
1923–24...........	128.93	150.64	100.43	200.86	45.19
1924–25...........	130.56	150.65	120.52	200.86	50.22
1925–26...........	137.21	146.87	129.00	195.83	48.96
1926–27...........	146.27	170.64	136.51	243.78	58.51
1927–28...........	157.41	183.44	148.73	247.89	69.41
1928–29...........	172.63	200.00	150.00	300.00	80.00

This table shows that when the value of the dollar is accounted for, the true increases in tuition fees have been much less than the apparent increases shown in Table 152. With the exception of the group of colleges on the approved list of the Association of American Universities, none of the categories shows increases of as much as 100 per cent over the 1909–10 figures.

Figure 46 shows graphically the relationship between the median annual tuition fees at twenty colleges for each year from 1909–10 through 1928–29, expressed both in actual dollars and in dollars of constant purchasing power.

The general trend, as revealed by the data of Figure 46, is for the fees in 1928–29 to be slightly less than double the value of those in 1909–10. No pronounced increase in the real value of the tuition fees seems to have taken place from 1909–10 until after 1921. During the last eight or nine years covered by this study the amount charged as tuition fees, in terms of dollars of constant purchasing power, has steadily and rapidly increased.

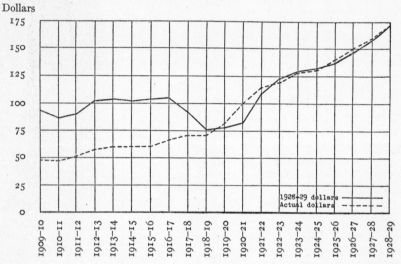

FIG. 46.—Median annual tuition fees charged at twenty colleges in actual dollars and in dollars of constant purchasing power (1928–29 base) over a period of years.

Relation of fees to wages of certain occupational groups.—An increasing fee schedule may make it increasingly difficult for certain occupational and economic groups within the total population to finance a college education for their sons and daughters. Not only may college fees increase more rapidly than the income of the population as a whole, but an increase in fees may bear particularly severely on groups whose income has lagged behind the incomes of other groups during a period of changing prices and wages. In order to explore this trend in the colleges studied, the median rates of tuition fees were analyzed in relation to the average wages of various occupational groups for each year of the period covered by the available data. Table 154 shows the percentage which the median tuition fees are of average annual earnings in certain selected occupations. For the purpose of showing trends the data are presented for each of five years, at intervals of four years.

This table is read as follows: In 1910 it required 5.9 per cent of the average annual earnings of ministers to pay the median tuition fee in this group of colleges; in 1914 the amount rose to 6.4 per cent of the average earnings of this occupational group, but dropped back again to 5.9 per cent in 1918, rising to 7.2 per cent in 1922 and to 8.2 per cent in 1926. This table shows clearly that there has been a general tendency over the period for the tuition fees to bear increasingly heavily upon all the occupational groups studied.

Data are presented in Figure 47 showing the trends for each year since 1909 in the percentage of annual earnings required to pay the median

TABLE 154

PERCENTAGES WHICH MEDIAN TUITION FEES ARE OF AVERAGE ANNUAL EARNINGS IN SELECTED OCCUPATIONS* FOR VARIOUS YEARS

Occupation	1910	1914	1918	1922	1926
Ministers..........................	5.9	6.4	5.9	7.2	8.2
Teachers...........................	9.6	11.0	10.2	10.0	11.8
Government civil service employees..	4.3	5.3	5.1	7.3	8.3
Postal employees...................	4.5	5.2	5.2	6.5	7.1
Clerical employees.................	4.1	4.8	4.2	5.8	6.5
Wage-earners in manufacturing.....	8.5	10.4	7.1	10.4	11.5
Coal miners.......................	8.5	10.9	5.7	12.3	11.3
Farm laborers.....................	14.0	17.1	11.6	23.5	25.3
All occupations excluding farm laborers........................	7.5	8.8	6.3	9.1	10.1
All occupations including farm laborers........................	8.2	9.6	6.7	9.9	10.9

* Data on earnings are from Douglas, *op. cit.*

tuition fee in this group of colleges. The figure shows the percentages both for all occupational groups combined and for all occupational groups omitting farm laborers.

This graph shows that there was a tendency prior to the beginning of the World War for fees to rise in terms of average wages. During the early period of the war fees dropped slightly in reference to wages, and during the latter part of the war, primarily owing to the very rapid increase in wages, tuition fees decreased sharply in terms of the percentage of average annual wages needed to pay such fees. Since the close of the war charges have again increased rapidly in terms of percentage of average annual wages necessary to pay the tuition fee. This situation has been brought about partly by the general decline in price levels, but more important has been the actual increase in the rates of tuition charged.

The data of this graph close with the year 1926. There is considerable evidence, however, that if data for wages were available for the years since 1926, the pronounced rise in the percentage of annual wages needed to pay tuition fees would still be continued.

Implications of recent increases in fees.—The data that have been presented show clearly a marked tendency to increase the rate of tuition charges to students in the group of colleges studied. This tendency is one which is typical of American institutions of higher learning during the

Percentage

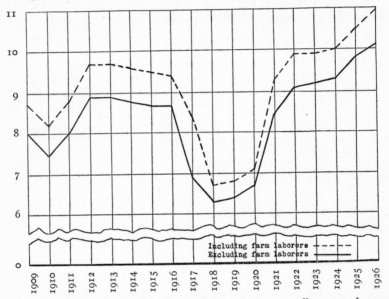

Fig. 47.—Percentages which median tuition fees in twenty colleges are of average annual earnings in all occupations, excluding and including farm laborers, for selected years.

period covered. These increases in tuition fees indicate the importance of the program of furnishing financial aid to students. Unless some method is provided for aiding worthy students of limited financial resources, the democracy of higher education is likely to be seriously affected and college training will tend to become more and more a privilege limited to the higher economic groups. It is important, therefore, to examine the provisions which the colleges have made for furnishing financial assistance to worthy students of limited resources.

One important administrative problem arising from the increases in fees concerns the rate which old students are charged after a change in the tuition. A few college executives hold that a student cannot legally be charged a higher tuition than that in effect at the time he enters. In increasing fees, these institutions make the increase applicable only to those matriculating thereafter. Most of the colleges, however, charge all students the increased fee when a new rate is established. In order to avoid controversy on this point the catalogue statement of fees should explicitly set forth the fact that the published rates apply only to the academic year covered by the catalogue.

COLLECTION OF FEES

In a preceding chapter the importance of maintaining a satisfactory fee-collection policy has been discussed from the standpoint of efficient busi-

TABLE 155

DISTRIBUTION OF AMOUNTS OF UNCOLLECTED TUITION
FEES IN THIRTY COLLEGES

Amount of Uncollected Fees	Number of Colleges
$10,001–$15,000	1
7,501– 10,000	1
5,001– 7,500	2
4,000– 5,000	..
3,001– 4,000	4
2,001– 3,000	3
1,001– 2,000	4
1– 1,000	11
None	4

Median,* all colleges.................... $1,035.62

* Calculated from an ungrouped distribution.

ness management. There is another angle to the matter of fee collections, namely, the effect which fee-collection policies have on the program of financial assistance to students. It is clear that from the standpoint of the student an uncollected fee is a form of financial assistance not greatly different from a scholarship or a remitted fee.

Table 155 presents a distribution of the amounts of uncollected tuition fees in thirty colleges for which data are available. The figures relate to the total amount of student fees uncollected at the close of the fiscal year preceding the date of the survey visit. All uncollected fees which were due in that fiscal year are included. The data, therefore, indicate the extent to which the colleges failed by the close of the fiscal year to collect the fees due during that year.

This table shows that in four of the colleges there were no uncollected fees at the close of the fiscal year. One college had more than $10,000 uncollected and three others had more than $5,000. The typical situation as indicated by the median is for slightly more than $1,000 to be outstanding at the close of the fiscal year from unpaid student tuitions for that year.

Table 156 shows the amounts of uncollected tuition fees per student enrolled for the same group of colleges. These data were obtained by dividing the total amount of uncollected student fees by the average enrolment of the two semesters (or three terms) of the academic year.

TABLE 156

DISTRIBUTION OF AMOUNTS OF UNCOLLECTED TUITION FEES
PER STUDENT ENROLLED, FOR THIRTY COLLEGES

Amounts of Uncollected Tuition Fees per Student Enrolled	Number of Colleges
$25.01–$30.00	1
20.01– 25.00	..
15.01– 20.00	3
10.01– 15.00	1
7.51– 10.00	2
5.01– 7.50	4
4.01– 5.00	3
3.01– 4.00	2
2.01– 3.00	1
1.01– 2.00	3
0.01– 1.00	6
None	4

Median,* all colleges $3.26

* Calculated from an ungrouped distribution.

This table shows that one college had outstanding tuition fees at the close of the fiscal year amounting to more than $25.00 per student enrolled. In four other institutions the amounts outstanding were more than $10.00 per student enrolled. Four colleges had no uncollected fees, and in six other institutions the amount was less than $1.00 per student. The typical situation, as indicated by the median, is for the college to have an amount equivalent to $3.26 per student enrolled outstanding in uncollected student fees at the close of the fiscal year.

Table 157 presents a distribution of the percentages of the total student fees due the college during the fiscal year that were uncollected at the end of the year for this same group of colleges. These data were obtained by dividing the total amount of uncollected tuition fees by the total amount of fees due the college.

This table shows that in one of the colleges more than 15 per cent of the total fees due the institution were uncollected at the end of the fiscal year, and in two other colleges the amounts uncollected were more than 10 per cent of the total due. As has been indicated by previous tables, four colleges collected all the fees that were due them. In a total of twelve colleges the uncollected fees were less than 1 per cent of the total tuition due.

These data indicate that there could well be a greater rigidity in the collection of student fees. In only a few of the institutions, however, is the

TABLE 157

DISTRIBUTION OF PERCENTAGES OF TOTAL STUDENT FEES
DUE THE COLLEGE DURING THE FISCAL YEAR THAT
WERE UNCOLLECTED AT THE END OF THE YEAR, FOR
THIRTY COLLEGES

Percentage of Total Fees Due the College That Were Uncollected at the End of the Fiscal Year	Number of Colleges
15.1–20.0	1
10.1–15.0	2
7.6–10.0	2
5.1– 7.5	1
4.1– 5.0	1
3.1– 4.0	5
2.1– 3.0	1
1.1– 2.0	5
0.1– 1.0	8
None	4

Median,* all colleges 1.63

* Calculated from an ungrouped distribution.

amount of uncollected fees at all large. It must be recognized also that the amounts shown in each case are practically at the maximum for the year, since the data relate to the situation at the close of the fiscal year. The data thus slightly overemphasize the effect of the uncollected fees. On the other hand, several of the colleges carry in their accounts relatively large sums of uncollected fees from previous years; these have not been considered in this study.

A few of the colleges report considerable success in collecting the past-due accounts from previous years. One institution, which has a relatively large amount of uncollected tuitions each year, insists that its actual final losses are no greater than those of most other colleges. It should be pointed out, however, that the collection of past-due student accounts entails considerable expense, and there is always a risk not only of failure to collect but of creating an unfortunate antagonism among those who are indebted to the college. Attention has been called in another connection to the fact that failure to collect fees is a very unfortunate policy because of the poor business ideals it inculcates in students.

In the case of one college the uncollected fees are considered as a loan from current funds, and are set up in the books, not as a loss due to uncollected tuitions, but as an addition to the capital amount of the college loan funds. This college has built up a rather large capital loan fund within a very few years by means of this practice. It should, of course, be clear that this plan is a mere subterfuge, since the college is actually lending funds from its own current income; this income is needed for the support of the educational program.

In some of the colleges there is a general understanding that tuition accounts will be carried until the opening of the next year, thus allowing students to apply their summer earnings on their bills for the preceding year. There is a rather rigidly enforced rule to the effect that students will not be permitted to re-register until they have paid all their obligations to the college. Under this plan many students are always one year behind in the payment of their fees; instead of saving in advance for the expenses of the college year, the student accumulates a debt to be paid from later earnings. This plan in effect results in the creation of a short-time loan fund from the current income of the college.

Three or four of the colleges studied have an ironclad rule to the effect that no student may be permitted to take the final examination in any course until all his obligations to the institution for the current term or semester are met in full. The operation of this rule seems to have had a very wholesome effect on the student body of these institutions. Not only do these colleges avoid a loss of revenue from uncollected fees, but the students are given valuable business training through the insistence upon the prompt meeting of their obligations. This plan seems preferable either to that of carrying student accounts over until the opening of the next year, or to that of considering unpaid tuitions as loans to be paid at the convenience of the student. With an adequate and properly administered system of financial aid to students the plan of requiring the payment of all fees before final examinations are taken need not work a hardship on any worthy student.

CHAPTER LXVI

ENDOWED SCHOLARSHIPS

DEFINITION OF SCHOLARSHIP

The term "scholarship" basically implies any sort of a grant given to students of special promise to encourage them to pursue an educational career. In actual practice the meaning of the term has degenerated to imply a grant, for the purpose of relieving a student from payment of tuition fees, made not only on the basis of the student's scholastic promise but for any other reason as well. Throughout this discussion the popular rather than the accurate use of the term "scholarship" is retained, the term referring in this discussion to any sort of grant by which the student is relieved of payment of tuition fees.

Two sources of funds are commonly employed for the payment of scholarship grants. A large number of the institutions have endowed funds the income of which is specifically restricted to this purpose. The other source is the current budget of the institution. In a few cases special gifts of a current nature are received to be used only for scholarships.

It is a practice in some institutions to distinguish the scholarships granted from current funds from those granted from endowment sources by calling the former "remitted fees." Actually this distinction is somewhat difficult to make, although it is an important one from the standpoint of the general theory of student aid. One of the factors making it difficult to distinguish scholarships from endowed sources from remitted fees arises from the methods used in the accounting systems of the colleges. In many cases scholarships are not properly accounted for, and it is extremely difficult to derive information from the financial records regarding the actual amount of aid furnished from each source.[1]

A second factor contributing to the difficulty of distinguishing between endowed scholarship grants and remission of fees is the fact that in the case of many of the endowed scholarships the income is insufficient to pay the entire tuition fee. In such cases the students are frequently granted as scholarships amounts larger than the actual produce of the invested fund. A grant of this sort becomes a composite, therefore, of income from

[1] For a discussion of methods of accounting for scholarships see Reeves and Russell, *College Organization and Administration* (Indianapolis: Board of Education, Disciples of Christ, 1929), p. 216.

endowed funds and income from current funds. It may be noted also that from the standpoint of students the distinction is unimportant. It is doubtless true that many recipients of scholarships never know whether their grant was from income on invested funds or from the current funds of the college. The fact that the distinction is not an important one to students has led many of the colleges to overlook its importance as a matter of institutional finance.

A few of the colleges have endowed funds which can be used either for scholarships or for loan funds as the case arises. In one institution the grant is definitely divided, one half being considered a loan and the other half a scholarship. It is important in the administration of such a fund that the student clearly understand whether he is receiving a loan or a scholarship. In its true sense a scholarship is a grant without any expectation of a financial return to the college. A student who receives a grant with such an understanding and is later asked to repay it by the institution has just cause for complaint. There should be a very definite understanding at the time of the grant as to whether or not the college will expect the student to reimburse it at a later date.

AMOUNT OF ENDOWMENT FOR SCHOLARSHIP PURPOSES

Table 158 shows the amount of endowed scholarship funds in each of the thirty-five colleges included in this study.

This table shows a very large range in the amounts of endowment held for scholarship purposes in this group of institutions. Eight of the colleges have no endowment specifically designated for scholarships. DePauw University has the largest individual endowed fund, amounting to more than two and one-quarter millions. It will be noted that the colleges on the approved list of the Association of American Universities have, on the average, much larger endowed scholarship funds than the colleges not holding this type of accreditation. The data of Table 158 are arranged in order of the size of the total endowed scholarship funds. The first twelve institutions on the list all hold accreditation by the Association of American Universities. The median endowed scholarship fund for the accredited colleges is more than five times the median for the colleges which lack national accreditation.

On the basis of the amount of endowed scholarship funds per student enrolled, the range is also very large. Again DePauw University exceeds by far all other institutions. Illinois Wesleyan University holds second place with an amount considerably in excess of the institution holding third place, which is Cornell College.

TABLE 158

AMOUNTS OF ENDOWED SCHOLARSHIP FUNDS
IN THIRTY-FIVE COLLEGES

Institution	Total Endowed Scholarship Funds	Amount of Endowed Scholarship Funds per Student Enrolled
*DePauw..................	$2,243,307.63	$1,619.72
*Illinois Wesleyan..........	279,300.00	496.09
*Ohio Wesleyan............	235,445.94	131.90
*Cornell..................	153,208.10	308.27
*Lawrence................	103,702.43	132.78
*Albion...................	99,611.10	132.46
*MacMurray...............	90,112.00	255.27
*Baker...................	86,214.54	187.02
*Allegheny................	63,802.62	107.23
*Mount Union.............	62,162.69	129.51
*Morningside..............	46,300.00	66.72
*Dickinson................	45,649.45	83.76
West Virginia Wesleyan....	43,500.00	134.67
Baldwin-Wallace...........	40,284.39	91.56
*Hamline.................	27,802.98	70.21
*Pacific...................	27,210.00	37.33
Central Wesleyan..........	26,182.37	137.08
Evansville................	24,836.47	62.56
Nebraska Wesleyan........	23,880.00	36.46
Southwestern..............	20,800.00	38.17
Dakota Wesleyan..........	18,700.00	53.89
*Simpson.................	17,884.12	27.47
Kansas Wesleyan..........	17,500.00	57.19
Puget Sound..............	14,169.15	23.00
Ohio Northern............	10,000.00	11.15
*Willamette...............	9,000.00	17.58
Ozark Wesleyan...........	2,500.00	12.56
Brothers.................	0.00	0.00
*Chattanooga..............	0.00	0.00
Gooding..................	0.00	0.00
Intermountain.............	0.00	0.00
Iowa Wesleyan............	0.00	0.00
McKendree...............	0.00	0.00
Oklahoma City............	0.00	0.00
Union...................	0.00	0.00
Median, all colleges.....	$ 24,836.47	$ 57.19
*Median, A.A.U. colleges.	63,802.62	129.51
Median, non-A.A.U. colleges................	12,084.58	17.78

* Institutions on the approved list of the Association of American Universities.

It should be noted in passing that the colleges which have no endowments specifically designated for scholarship purposes are in no way prohibited from using their general endowment funds for providing scholarships. Such a grant, however, would properly be treated as a remitted fee rather than as a specific grant from endowed scholarships. In the case

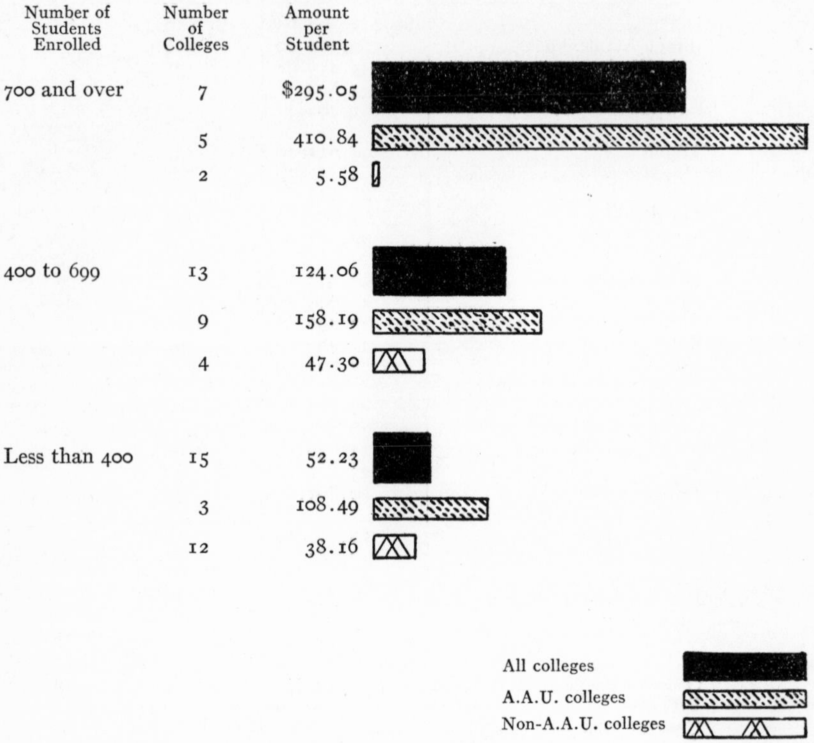

Number of Students Enrolled	Number of Colleges	Amount per Student	
700 and over	7	$295.05	
	5	410.84	
	2	5.58	
400 to 699	13	124.06	
	9	158.19	
	4	47.30	
Less than 400	15	52.23	
	3	108.49	
	12	38.16	

All colleges
A.A.U. colleges
Non-A.A.U. colleges

FIG. 48.—Average amounts of scholarship trust funds per student enrolled in colleges of various sizes and types of accreditation.

of at least one institution the records indicating the restrictions on endowment funds have been lost. Doubtless some of the endowment of this institution was originally designated for scholarship purposes, although it is not now applied in this way.

Figure 48 shows the average amounts of endowed scholarship funds per student in this group of colleges classed according to size and type of accreditation.

This graph shows that there is a very general tendency for the larger colleges to have larger amounts of endowed scholarships per student than the amounts held by the smaller institutions.[1] From this it appears that the chances for a student to obtain aid from an endowed source are considerably greater in the larger colleges than in the smaller ones.

SIZE OF SCHOLARSHIP FUNDS

The endowed scholarships are typically set up as a number of different funds. For example, the fund given by a certain donor will be designated

TABLE 159

SIZE OF INDIVIDUAL SCHOLARSHIP TRUST FUNDS

Amount of Individual Trust Fund	Number of Funds of Each Size	Percentage of Total
Less than $ 250..............	13	2.4
$ 250– 499.............	16	3.0
500– 749.............	45	8.4
750– 999.............	10	1.9
1,000– 1,249.............	300	55.7
1,250– 1,499.............	2	0.4
1,500– 1,999.............	10	1.9
2,000– 2,999.............	52	9.7
3,000– 3,999.............	11	2.0
4,000– 4,999.............	9	1.7
5,000– 5,999.............	39	7.2
6,000– 9,999.............	5	0.9
10,000– 14,999.............	9	1.7
15,000– 19,999.............	3	0.5
20,000– 24,999.............	5	0.9
25,000 and over.............	9	1.7
Total....................	538	100.0

by his name, and the income of this fund will be used for the support of one or more scholarships. Table 159 presents data showing the size of the individual scholarship trust funds. Although data were not available for all of the institutions studied, information is presented covering a total of 538 different funds.

This table shows that the individual trust funds range from relatively small amounts of less than $250 each up to a few rather large funds. More than half of the funds for which data are available amount to approximately $1,000 each. In a large number of cases these funds were received

[1] This situation is markedly influenced by the Rector Scholarship Fund at DePauw University.

in days when the tuition fees were much lower than at present. A fund of $1,000 invested at 5 per cent was sufficient to produce an income of $50 annually, which was adequate to cover the amount of a typical tuition fee. With the increases that have come about in tuition fees these trust funds are now proving seriously inadequate for providing the annual tuition payments. On the basis of a tuition charge of $200 per year, which is approximately the typical charge in the better colleges of this group, an endowed fund of $4,000, if invested at 5 per cent, is needed to provide tuition fees for one student. Since many of the colleges obtain a rate of income less than 5 per cent on their invested funds, an amount in excess of $4,000 is actually needed in many of the colleges in order to provide full tuition for one student.

Some of the larger scholarship funds are worthy of special mention. The Edward Rector Scholarship Foundation at DePauw University, amounting to $2,207,307, is the largest single fund found in any of the institutions. DePauw University has another scholarship fund of $25,000 known as the Beveridge Fund. Illinois Wesleyan University is the beneficiary of the Williams Fund. The principal of this fund is held by a Chicago bank as trustee, the annual income being distributed to the colleges designated as beneficiaries. The income received by Illinois Wesleyan University indicates that the capitalized value of its share of this fund would be $211,500. Cornell College has the King Memorial Fund of $100,000. Ohio Wesleyan University has four rather large scholarship funds—the G. Brown Fund with a capital of $23,588, the Lybrand Fund of $24,000, the Munson Fund of $20,000, the Taylor Fund of $22,312. Allegheny College has the Ballatyne Fund of $28,886. Baldwin-Wallace College has the Gamble Fund of $25,000. Mount Union College has the Shafer Fund amounting to $25,000. Lawrence College has the Philip Fund of approximately $24,000.

Another interesting example of an endowed scholarship is the Susanna Wesley Hall Fund at Albion College. This fund originated from a dormitory fund bearing the same name. The rates of charges for the dormitory service have been adjusted so as to produce each year a rental income. The accumulated income has been set up as a scholarship fund and has now reached a capital value of approximately $50,000.

It is interesting to note the geographical concentration of these larger scholarship funds. The states of Indiana, Illinois, and Ohio, with the addition of eastern Iowa, southern Michigan, and western Pennsylvania, include the territory in which almost all the scholarship funds of any large size are located in this group of colleges. At least 90 per cent of the total scholarship funds of these institutions are located in the area just described.

DESIGNATED BENEFICIARIES OF SCHOLARSHIP FUNDS

A large number of the scholarship funds are designated for the benefit of certain types of students. Table 160 shows the number of the scholarship funds that are designated for various purposes. Although data were not available from all the colleges, the table includes information concerning a total of 605 scholarship funds.

TABLE 160

NUMBER OF SCHOLARSHIP FUNDS DESIGNATED
FOR VARIOUS PURPOSES

Purpose for Which Designated	Number of Funds So Designated	Percentage of Total
Choice of donor..............	344	56.9
Religious service..............	54	8.9
Financial need only...........	48	7.9
High grades..................	45	7.4
Relatives of donor...........	15	2.5
Ministers' children...........	13	2.2
Faculty relatives.............	6	1.0
Athletes.....................	2	0.3
No preference................	70	11.6
Miscellaneous*..............	8	1.3
Total....................	605	100.0

* Premedical, music, local high-school graduates, descendants of soldiers and sailors.

This table shows that more than one-half of the funds are of the type subject to designation by the donor of the fund. Students preparing for religious service have the next largest number of funds for their benefit, and a fairly large number of funds are designated to be used only for students who are in actual financial need. There are forty-five funds designated for the benefit of students of high scholastic ability. The remainder are few in number and are devoted to various purposes. In the case of a total of seventy funds the institutions are free to use the income without any restrictions regarding the type of student which is to benefit by the scholarship.

CHAPTER LXVII

REMITTED FEES

Almost all the colleges of this group follow the practice of granting some students rebates in fees. Sometimes this plan is used as a form of student aid to those of exceptional scholastic promise in a manner exactly parallel to the granting of scholarships from endowed funds. In other cases the offer to remit a part of the tuition fees is used as a recruiting device—a type of price-cutting which is distinctly frowned upon in ethical business circles. Customarily certain occupational or social groups are automatically entitled to the remission of part or all of their fees.

MINISTERIAL REBATES

Perhaps the largest group and the one most commonly found to be entitled to this automatic reduction in fees is the ministerial class. Three subclasses may be distinguished in this group: (1) active ministers of the gospel; (2) students who intend later to enter the ministry; and (3) the sons and daughters of ministers. The great bulk of the grants of this type are of this third subclass. All but three or four of the colleges studied follow the policy of allowing a "ministerial discount."

The colleges differ somewhat in the extent to which ministers of other denominations are given the privilege of the reduced tuition fee. One college grants this privilege only to ministers and their dependents belonging to the Annual Conference by which the college is sponsored. A few other institutions allow the reduction in fee only to ministers of the Methodist Episcopal Church. A number of the colleges, however, give the ministerial discount without regard to denominational affiliation.

The colleges also differ with regard to the amount of the discount allowed ministerial classes. Active ministers are typically granted the entire amount of the tuition fee, but these cases are relatively few in number. Sons and daughters of ministers are usually granted a 50 per cent discount from the regular tuition fees. In a few colleges the amount is larger and in some it is smaller than 50 per cent. Some colleges state the amount of the remission as a flat sum rather than as a percentage of the tuition fees. Typically the ministerial discount relates only to the general fee charged all students, and does not involve a reduction in special fees, such as laboratory fees, activity fees, or fees for private music lessons. One of the largest colleges of the group goes even farther than allowing a reduction in tuition fees, and allows also a discount of 10 per cent in board-and-room charges to the dependents of clergymen.

Two reasons, other than tradition, are commonly advanced for the granting of this rebate to clergymen and their dependents. The first frequently mentioned reason is that ministers as a rule receive small salaries and would be unable to give their children a college education if the rebate were not granted. The validity of this argument is open to question. There is considerable ground for the opinion that the economic status of ministers is not greatly different from that of the average for their parishioners. Most ministers would be as able to send their sons and daughters to college as the average members of their congregations. The data presented in Table 154 indicate that ministers in general have an economic ability as high or higher than such groups as teachers, civil service employees, etc. Furthermore, the application of this rule generally would indicate that many other occupational groups, such as farm laborers and coal miners, which receive relatively low average incomes, should also benefit from the system of remitting fees. The fact that ministers generally have a cultural background somewhat higher than that of other occupational groups receiving approximately the same or lower annual income may be considered a valid argument for granting special privileges to the ministerial classes, although this practice is then seen to be somewhat counter to the ideals of American democracy.

A second reason sometimes advanced for the remission of fees to ministerial classes is that the clergymen render a service to the institution in directing prospective students toward it, and in providing in their respective communities an entrée for the representatives of the college. There is no doubt but that the ministers of the area in which the college is located do render a real service. An institution that does not have the good will of the ministers of its supporting church group usually faces many difficulties. It seems absurd, however, to make the compensation for this service dependent upon the number of children which the minister sends to the college. It may also be pointed out that the service which the local clergyman renders in directing young people to the college is actually a service to those whom he interests in the institution, and to the church and society in general, not to the institution itself. Since students commonly pay in fees much less than the cost of their instruction, no favor is shown the college by sending it additional students.

Perhaps the most cogent reason for the granting of the ministerial rebate is one not often mentioned. The clergymen to whom this privilege is accorded are very frequently the controlling element in the ecclesiastical body that sponsors the college and in some measure controls its destinies. Furthermore, these ministers are influential with the laymen of their flocks, and influence greatly the opinion which the general constituency holds regarding the institution and the generosity with which they will contribute to its support. The college needs the good will of the ministerial group and proceeds to obtain it by the somewhat indirect method of granting special reductions in fees. In order not to be too obvious, the privilege is granted to all ministers, regardless of how friendly they have been toward the college. A minister who has accepted such an emolument is, of course, not able with good grace to criticize adversely the policies of the college before either the constituency or the controlling ecclesiastical body. Viewed in this light, the ministerial rebate becomes a gentle sort of graft, a procedure that would be soundly denounced in civic affairs.

The ministerial discount is likely to violate two sound principles in the program of giving financial assistance to students. The first of these principles is that aid should be given those of greatest scholastic promise. The second is that aid should be given those who actually need the assistance. A blanket reduction in fees, applicable to all the members of a given occupational group, fails to discriminate in the selection of those who will be aided on the ground of scholastic promise. It may be true that the sons and daughters of ministers are usually good academic risks; but it does not at all follow that every person belonging to this group is of sufficient promise to warrant a special subsidy. From the standpoint of financial need it will be observed that the ministerial discount applies alike to the son of a high-salaried pastor of a city church and to the son of the pastor of a rural church who receives a relatively low salary. There are undoubtedly many cases of students availing themselves of the ministerial discount who could afford to pay the full tuition charge with less than the average amount of sacrifice.

From the standpoint of the ultimate source of the funds used to provide the ministerial discount there are two possible interpretations. This provision may be looked upon as a contribution by faculty members from their own salaries, whereby they agree to teach for slightly lower amounts in order to grant a rebate in fees to the sons and daughters of ministers. Assuming that these students could be replaced by others who would pay full fees, or that the teaching staff could be reduced proportionately if these students did not attend the college, it is evident that the amount of funds available for instructional salaries per faculty member is reduced by the granting of the ministerial rebate.

The other interpretation of the provision views it as a contribution by the other students who attend the college. In order to assist in financing the education of the sons and daughters of ministers, the college operates with a lower income per student, and is thereby obliged to offer a poorer quality of instruction than would be the case if no rebates were allowed. Thus the general fee charged all students is slightly higher than it should be for the quality of education provided when certain groups of students are granted rebates.

It thus appears that the ministerial discount is indefensible from the standpoint of the source of the funds used. In situations where there are certain endowed scholarship funds designated specifically for the benefit of the dependents of ministers, these objections do not obtain. A few colleges have such funds; but, as was shown in Table 160, the number of funds designated for the benefit of the children of clergymen is a very small part of the total number of scholarship funds. The number of funds designated for those preparing for religious service is much larger; as a result, most of the colleges rebate from current funds only a very small amount for any of the ministerial classes other than the sons and daughters of clergymen. It is evident that in this group of colleges donors have not been greatly interested in providing endowed scholarships for the benefit of the sons and daughters of ministers.

For the reasons that have been set forth the continuation of the policy of granting from current funds rebates in fees to the sons and daughters of clergymen seems unwise. Perhaps an agreement could be reached among educational institutions to abandon the whole practice of "clergy rebates." From a social standpoint it would probably be better for the denominations to add directly to the salaries of clergymen the amount needed for student fees rather than to subsidize indirectly, as by the present method. The whole question may well be raised as to whether, from an economic standpoint, clergymen are any more entitled to special favors in sending their sons and daughters to college than other classes of citizens. In other words, aid to students should be granted, not on the basis of the particular occupation followed by parents, but upon an analysis of the individual case, taking into account both financial need and scholastic promise. There should be a definite requirement relative to the maintenance of satisfactory scholastic standing on the part of recipients of scholarships.

FACULTY REBATES

Another group customarily granted an automatic rebate in tuition fees consists of the dependents of members of the faculty of the institution.

Almost without exception the colleges of this group grant rebates in fees to such students. In a few cases the faculty members themselves are the beneficiaries of this provision. The wives of members of the teaching staff are another subclass in this group, but the majority of those who benefit by the faculty rebate are the sons and daughters of faculty members.

A number of the arguments which have already been brought out in connection with the ministerial discounts apply with equal force to the faculty rebate. Although the advisability of granting faculty rebates is open to question, it is true that this practice is not open to all the criticisms made of the clergy rebate. In the first place, the granting of a rebate to a member of the instructional staff and his dependents effectually means a raise in salary to the faculty member concerned. There can be no objection to the raising of faculty salaries by the college, although there may be some objection to a contribution by the college for the purpose of raising the salaries of ministers (clergy discounts). In the second place, the college faculty is a small community in itself. The members of such a community would doubtless feel no hesitation in contributing a small amount of either time or salary for the benefit of other members of the community. The situation in this regard is distinctly different from the case of the clergy rebates, where the faculty members contribute for the benefit of those who are not intimately associated with their own community. Finally, it may be pointed out that the amount involved in faculty rebates in the average college is very small and can conceivably have no important effect on the total financial situation.

REBATES TO HONOR STUDENTS

A third type of fee rebate frequently found in this group of colleges is that to students who have been awarded honors in graduation from their local high schools. A few of the colleges automatically grant a reduction in fees to the valedictorian of any high school. Sometimes the salutatorian is also eligible for a reduction in tuition. Occasionally the provision applies to any student in the upper tenth of the high-school graduating class. In some colleges these honor scholarships are available only for the high schools of a certain area, or to the graduates of a certain restricted list of high schools.

The granting of special inducements in order to attract students of exceptional promise is an entirely worthy use of scholarship funds. The only possible criticism against the practice in the group of colleges studied is the fact that funds are not always available from which to pay the scholarships awarded. The current budget of the institution is not a satisfactory source of support for a scholarship program. It should be relatively easy in most institutions to obtain endowment in sufficient amount to meet all reasonable needs for the payment of high-school honor scholarships.

REBATES TO STUDENTS FOR NON-ACADEMIC ABILITIES

A fourth group of students receiving rebates in fees may be described as those with special abilities in certain lines other than academic. Provision of scholarships for students of this type is not common in the group of colleges studied, although several institutions rebate fees to some students of this kind. Until a few years ago it was a fairly common practice to remit the fees of students having athletic ability. This practice has been disapproved so vigorously by the proponents of amateurism in college sports as well as by educators that most of the institutions studied grant no special privileges in the way of reduced fees to athletes because of their athletic ability. One college in the group grants all the members of its debating team free tuition. Another provides free tuition to a group of students with pronounced musical ability who appear in radio programs sponsored by the college.

Rebates of the type described seem somewhat foreign to the general purpose of the scholarship award. Undue emphasis on the seeking of students because of their non-academic abilities means that the college has forsaken the purity of its purpose in the pursuit of scholarship, and has set up the additional and often rather divergent aims of success in athletics, success in debate, and success in entertaining the public over the radio.

Although the colleges typically do not now rebate fees to athletes as such, it is not uncommon to find that athletes are actually favored considerably in the granting of scholarships. An independent check on this matter was made in a number of colleges by finding the percentage of all athletes granted scholarships and comparing this with the percentage of all men students who were not athletes that received scholarships. In several colleges it was found that the proportion of athletes receiving scholarships was twice as great as the proportion of men non-athletes that were aided, even though the institution disclaimed any intention of showing special favor to athletes.

REBATES TO THOSE IN FINANCIAL NEED

A fifth group of students receiving rebates in fees are those aided solely because of their financial need. In several colleges where the endowed scholarship and loan funds are inadequate, deserving students are aided, as a last resort, by a grant from current funds in the form of a rebated fee. The motive behind such a grant is entirely worthy. It may be pointed out, however, that in such cases the college is dispensing a charity from funds which it does not possess—a procedure which is financially and socially unwise.

EFFECT OF REMITTED FEES ON CURRENT BUDGET

Throughout this discussion it has frequently been pointed out that the remission of fees is an unsatisfactory type of student aid because of the fact that the source of the funds used for this purpose is the current budget of the college. It is worth while to examine this point to see where the burden of supplying this type of aid finally falls. Clearly the most elastic item in the budget will be the one to suffer most from the reduction in income owing to rebated fees. Since the item of faculty salaries is one of the most elastic in the budget and also the largest single item, it is evident that most of the burden involved in this form of student aid will fall upon the faculty. In other words, in order to provide aid of this type the faculty members may be thought of as contributing a pro rata share of their own salaries. The matter is not usually looked at in this way, but a careful analysis makes it evident that when the current budget becomes a source of aid for students, the average faculty salary must inevitably be lower than it otherwise would be.

There is nothing to hinder a college from considering student aid as a prior claim on its endowment funds. Thus aid nominally classified as coming from the current budget may ultimately have been undesignated endowment income that was deliberately used for aiding students. One college took the step a few years ago of setting up certain scholarship funds from its undesignated endowment. In this particular case the step seems not to have been taken out of a desire to rationalize the student-aid program, but rather for the purpose of setting up memorials to former presidents of the college. It is still within the bounds of possibility for any college, however, to set up scholarships of this type from its general funds. The disadvantage of this step lies in the fact that endowments for scholarship purposes are usually much easier to obtain than funds for general undesignated purposes.

CHAPTER LXVIII

STUDENT AID IN THE FORM OF OUTRIGHT GIFTS

The two types of student aid that have been discussed in the preceding chapters, scholarships and remitted fees, are alike in that each is an outright gift to the student. The present chapter discusses the amounts of such grants, and also certain policies regarding the administration of this form of student aid.

AMOUNT OF GRANTS

Table 161 shows the total amount of student-aid grants in the form of scholarships and remitted fees, in thirty-five colleges. The table also shows the total number of such grants in thirty-two colleges, the information not having been obtained from three institutions. Owing to the difficulty of distinguishing accurately between endowed scholarships and remitted fees, the table deals with the combined amounts of aid in these two forms.

This table shows that the total amount of grants in the form of remitted fees and scholarships from endowed funds ranges from $112,723.35 at DePauw University to $125.00 at Brothers College. Every one of the colleges studied makes some grants of this type. The median amount of grants in the colleges on the approved list of the Association of American Universities is more than three times the median of the colleges not holding this type of accreditation. This difference probably reflects the difference in the amount of endowment for scholarship purposes in the two groups of colleges. The number of grants also shows a wide range.

The typical situation, as indicated by the median, is for the number of grants to be approximately one-fourth of the number of students enrolled. In the colleges on the approved list of the Association of American Universities the median indicates that it is typical for almost one-third of the students to receive aid in this form; in the colleges not holding this type of accreditation the median indicates that only one-fifth of the students receive this type of aid.

The interpretation of the data relating to the average amount of each grant is somewhat complicated by the fact that in a few cases students hold their scholarships for one semester only rather than for the entire year. Neglecting this factor, it appears that in two colleges the typical grant covers the entire fee, tuition as well as laboratory and special fees.

TABLE 161

TOTAL SCHOLARSHIPS AND REMITTED FEES IN THIRTY-FIVE COLLEGES

Institution	Amount Granted	Number of Grants	Percentage of Enrolment Granted Scholarships	Average Amount per Grant	Average Amount per Student Enrolled
*MacMurray.............,...	$ 32,397.23	152	43.1	$213.14	$91.78
*DePauw...............	112,723.35	605	43.7	186.32	81.39
*Illinois Wesleyan........	20,115.00	258	45.8	77.97	35.73
*Hamline...............	12,824.00	148	37.4	86.65	32.38
*Simpson...............	16,897.00	280	49.0	60.35	29.59
Central Wesleyan.......	5,379.25	70	36.7	76.85	28.16
*Cornell...............	12,978.00	168	33.8	77.25	26.11
*Dickinson.............	13,797.60	176	32.3	78.40	25.32
*Allegheny..............	14,757.90	†	....	†	24.80
Iowa Wesleyan........	7,815.00	134	41.1	58.32	23.97
Ozark Wesleyan........	4,941.00	80	38.1	61.76	23.53
Intermountain..........	3,247.60	81	53.6	40.09	21.51
*Ohio Wesleyan..........	36,561.65	543	30.4	67.33	20.48
Nebraska Wesleyan.....	12,549.31	230	35.1	54.56	19.16
*Mount Union..........	9,190.50	†	....	†	19.15
*Morningside...........	12,672.85	191	27.5	66.35	18.26
Gooding..............	2,226.60	42	32.8	53.01	17.39
Kansas Wesleyan.......	4,548.76	145	47.4	31.37	14.86
Baldwin-Wallace........	5,468.00	105	23.9	52.08	12.43
Dakota Wesleyan.......	4,300.50	73	21.0	58.91	12.39
Ohio Northern..........	10,683.57	117	13.0	91.31	11.91
McKendree.............	2,887.00	51	20.2	56.61	11.46
*Pacific.................	7,679.00	92	12.6	83.47	10.53
*Baker.................	4,719.87	60	13.0	78.66	10.24
Oklahoma City.........	9,051.60	120	13.5	75.43	10.15
*Albion.................	6,980.50	101	13.4	69.11	9.28
West Virginia Wesleyan..	2,696.75	38	11.8	70.97	8.35
*Chattanooga............	13,062.00	†	....	†	8.27
*Willamette.............	4,049.00	62	8.8	65.31	7.91
*Lawrence...............	5,933.50	69	12.1	85.99	7.60
Puget Sound...........	3,493.50	51	8.3	68.50	5.67
Southwestern...........	2,820.00	27	5.0	104.44	5.17
Evansville..............	1,990.43	45	11.3	44.23	5.01
Union.................	1,060.00	15	6.6	70.67	4.67
Brothers...............	125.00	1	3.2	125.00	4.03
Median, all colleges...	$ 6,980.50	97	25.7	$ 69.89	$14.86
*Median, A.A.U. colleges..............	12,978.00	160	31.4	78.19	20.48
Median, non-A.A.U. colleges...........	3,897.00	72	20.6	60.34	12.15

* Institutions on the approved list of the Association of American Universities.
† No data.

In a number of other colleges the typical grant covers one-half the tuition fees. The grants in several colleges average less than half the tuition fees.

The data for the average amount of scholarship grants per student enrolled indicate the relative extensiveness of this provision in the various colleges. It is apparent that two institutions, MacMurray College and DePauw University, are far above the others in the amount of provision made for this type of student aid. At MacMurray College the principal source of the scholarship grants is the current fund; at DePauw University the source is chiefly the endowed Rector Scholarship Fund. The colleges on the approved list of the Association of American Universities, as indicated by the median, typically have a much larger amount of grants per student enrolled than the colleges not holding this type of accreditation.

Figure 49 presents data showing the relationship between the size of the institution and the percentage of the student body granted scholarships or remitted fees.

This figure shows that in general the larger colleges aid a smaller percentage of their students by means of scholarships and remitted fees than is the case with the smaller colleges. This relationship is especially noticeable when the data are analyzed separately by the two types of accreditation. It is probable that this relationship is an indication that the small colleges use this student-aid plan as a recruiting device to a greater extent than the larger colleges do. The larger colleges evidently are able to attract a greater proportion of students from the higher economic levels than the small colleges, although the number of institutions from which data are available is too small to warrant definite conclusions.

POLICIES CONCERNING SCHOLARSHIPS AND REMITTED FEES

There are four problems that will be discussed under the general head of policies concerning scholarships and remitted fees. These are: (1) the administrative control of the granting of scholarships and remitted fees; (2) policies concerning the handling of scholarships, the beneficiaries of which are designated by the donors; (3) methods of handling endowed scholarships that do not cover full tuition; and (4) the relative importance of various factors in assigning scholarships.

Administrative control of scholarships.—Table 162 presents data showing the assignment of responsibility for administering scholarships in thirty-one colleges. The table is arranged to show not only the types of officers or committees and the number of colleges following each plan, but also the number of colleges naming each of the various administrative officers on the scholarship committee, where the control of this matter is lodged in a committee.

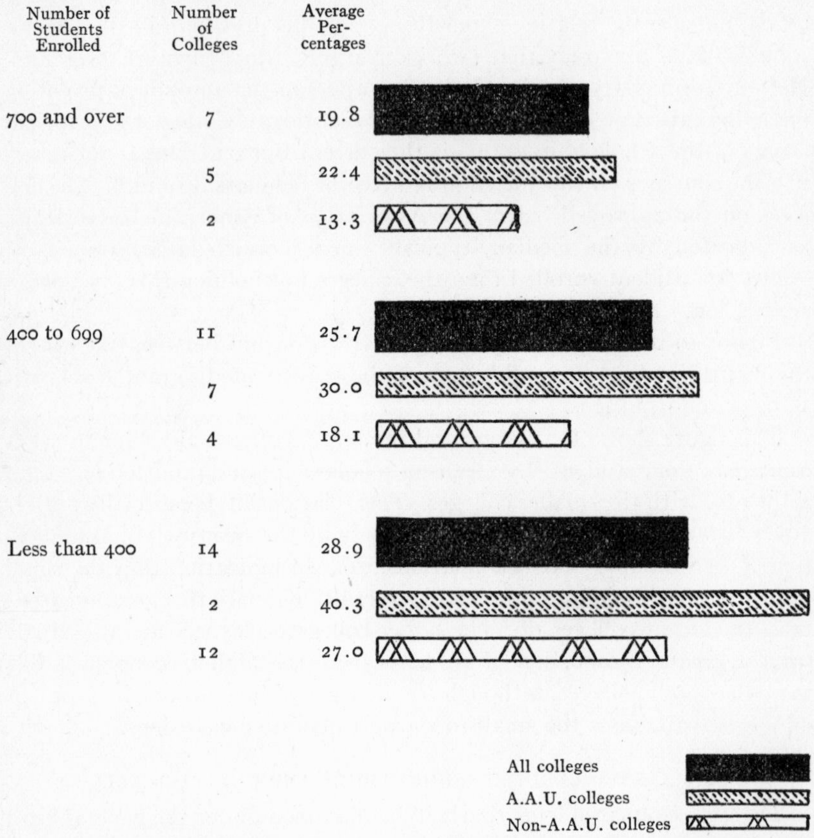

Number of Students Enrolled	Number of Colleges	Average Percentages	
700 and over	7	19.8	
	5	22.4	
	2	13.3	
400 to 699	11	25.7	
	7	30.0	
	4	18.1	
Less than 400	14	28.9	
	2	40.3	
	12	27.0	

All colleges
A.A.U. colleges
Non-A.A.U. colleges

FIG. 49.—Average percentages which total number of grants of scholarships and remitted fees are of total number of students enrolled in colleges of various sizes and types of accreditation.

Table 162 shows that the colleges of this group are almost equally divided between the plans of administering scholarships by a single administrative officer and by a committee. In a great majority of the cases where this responsibility is lodged in a single administrative officer the president is the one to whom the duty is assigned. There are two types of committees used in the administering of scholarships: the one consisting only of administrative officers, the other consisting of both administrative officers and faculty members. The former has been designated in this tabulation as a committee of administrative officers, the latter as a com-

TABLE 162

ASSIGNMENT OF RESPONSIBILITY FOR ADMINISTERING
SCHOLARSHIPS IN THIRTY-ONE COLLEGES

Person or Committee Assigned Responsibility for Administering Scholarships	Number of Colleges in Which This Person or Committee Is Given Final Responsibility	Number of Colleges in Which Various Officers Are Members of the Scholarship Committee
President..........................	12	....
Vice-president....................	1	....
Dean.............................	2	....
Committee of administrative officers	12	....
Including in its membership:		
President.........................	....	11
Vice-president....................	....	1
Dean.............................	....	6
Business officer..................	....	10
Registrar.........................	....	2
Dean of women...................	....	6
Dean of men......................	....	3
Personnel officer.................	....	1
Student secretary.................	....	2
Alumni secretary.................	....	1
Field secretary...................	....	1
Secretary to the president........	....	1
Committee of the faculty..........	4	....
Including on its membership:		
President.........................	....	3
Dean.............................	....	2
Registrar.........................	....	3
Business officer..................	....	1
Promotion officer.................	....	1
Dean of men......................	....	1
Dean of women...................	....	1
Alumni secretary.................	....	1

mittee of the faculty. The use of a committee of administrative officers is much more widespread than the use of a faculty committee.

It is interesting also to note the frequency with which various administrative officers are concerned with this problem, either as bearing sole responsibility or as members of the scholarship committee. In twenty-six of the thirty-one colleges the president is closely concerned with the granting of scholarships. The officer next most frequently mentioned is the business manager; this officer is in no case given sole responsibility, but is a member of the scholarship committee in eleven of the thirty-one colleges. The academic dean is concerned with the granting of scholarships in ten of the colleges, the dean of women in seven, and the dean of men in four. Almost all the commonly found administrative officers are concerned with scholarships in one or more colleges.

Donor-designated scholarships.—The second matter of policy that needs discussion relates to the handling of donor-designated scholarships. In former years many of the colleges granted persons giving certain specified sums of money the right to name the recipients of the scholarships based on their gifts. It was understood that the college would invest the gift as a part of the endowment, but the donor would annually name a "scholar" whose tuition was to be paid from the income on the gift. Sometimes the right to name a scholar was definitely understood to run for a term of years. Occasionally the right expired at the death of the donor, but sometimes the right was understood to be perpetual, passing on to the heirs and assigns of the original donor. In some cases the right to name the scholar was vested in a church group or other civic organization. In a few cases there was the limitation that the recipient must be a direct descendant of the donor.

The system of donor-designated scholarships has many disadvantages. In the first place, several of the colleges failed to add the funds so received to their endowment, but used the money for current purposes, thus leaving no provision for a source of income from which to meet the obligation in future years. Other colleges have lost all record of the funds given under this condition, and are unable to check the authenticity of some applications for scholarships of this type.

In the second place, the capital amount of the gift was originally set in most cases at the amount necessary to yield the then tuition fee when invested at the rate of 5 per cent. Since the gift was received, however, tuition fees have been markedly increased. Some of the gifts were received with the understanding that they were to provide "full tuition." The institution is therefore embarrassed in meeting the terms of this contract because of the markedly higher fees now charged. Typically it is necessary to take funds from the current budget for the supplementing of these scholarships. The executives of some colleges contend that the contracts bind them only to pay a fixed amount, not "full tuition," and thus are able to avoid a scholarship subsidy from the current budget. In other cases the colleges consider these scholarships to be worth only the amount of tuition charged at the time the gift was received.

A third disadvantage arises from the fact that many of the colleges are not able to invest their funds to yield 5 per cent. This again entails a subsidy from other sources in order to meet the scholarship payments on these donor-designated funds.

The most important disadvantage of scholarship funds of this type is the violation of sound principles of institutional administration involved in allowing some person not connected with the college the right to designate the beneficiaries of its scholarship funds. The college should have the sole right to select its own students, and should grant scholarships under terms which it approves and controls. The plan of having an outside agency designate the recipients of scholarships may result in the presence of some students who are undesirable members of the academic community. Failure to admit as a student one who has been designated as the beneficiary of a scholarship would be embarrassing to all concerned.

Almost without exception the authorities in the colleges concerned recognize the undesirability of scholarships of this type. Several institutions have been making vigorous efforts to remedy the mistake that was made in accepting funds under this provision. In some cases an endeavor is being made to buy back these scholarships by returning the original amount of the grant. In other cases an effort is being made to induce the donors to waive their rights of naming scholars. Other colleges are requiring each applicant for such a scholarship to present rigorous proof of his or her rights to the grant. Several of the colleges are finding that the donors in some instances are happily neglecting to exercise their rights of naming a scholar. One college is following the plan of depreciating the capital of these scholarship funds by the amount of excess payment required above the interest income to provide the full tuition fee. This is done with the understanding that when the capital of the original gift has been entirely used up, the college will have no further obligation to furnish the scholarships. The great majority of the colleges indicate that the plan of donor-designated scholarships will not be used as a fund-raising device in the future.

Scholarships not covering full tuition.—A third matter of policy which merits discussion is the method of handling scholarship funds that do not provide full tuition. More than half of the colleges have some scholarship funds, the income on which is insufficient to provide the full cost of tuition. Eight of the colleges having such funds follow the policy of supplementing the grant from current funds, so that it actually provides full tuition. Sixteen colleges give as scholarships only the actual earnings of the funds; in several cases, however, the earnings are figured at an arbitrary rate, usually 5 per cent, although the invested funds actually earn a lower rate of income. Only one college follows the policy of allowing the income to accumulate until it is large enough for a single scholarship. Under this plan the scholarship is not awarded every year, but only in those years in which the accumulated income is sufficient for full tuition fees.

Reasons for awarding scholarships.—Another matter of policy concerns the weight given various factors by the college authorities in assigning scholarships to individual students. In each of the colleges studied the chief executive officer was asked to indicate the relative importance of each of a group of factors as they operated in the assigning of scholarships. A tabulation of the replies indicates the types of students who would have the best and the poorest chance of obtaining scholarships in this group of institutions. The data indicate that children of ministers have the very best chance of all, closely followed by students ranking in the highest tenth in high-school scholarship. Active ministers are in third place, although almost equal weight is given to the factor of personality promising future community leadership. Children of faculty members are in fifth place. Other groups having markedly less chance for scholarships than those just mentioned are: (1) those who are in financial need and would otherwise go to a tax-supported institution because of free or lower tuition; (2) those preparing for the ministry; and (3) children of missionaries.

The replies indicate a curious mixture of a vocational rating with the factors of scholastic promise, personality, and financial need as bearing an important weight in the assignment of scholarships in this group of colleges.

The question may well be raised as to whether scholarships are customarily granted for educational reasons or as an administrative measure. There is some evidence throughout this chapter that in most of the colleges the handling of scholarships amounts to little more than an administrative routine, with questions of the educational implications of scholarship grants pushed far into the background. In some colleges it seems that scholarships are rather frequently used for propaganda purposes and as a recruiting device rather than primarily for the educational advantage of those who most merit them. A program of scholarship aid which fails to achieve significant educational purposes cannot be said to be successful, regardless of the number of students who may be assisted.

CHAPTER LXIX

STUDENT LOAN FUNDS[1]

A form of student aid which is increasing in popularity is the loan fund. The use of this form of aid is based upon the idea that at least a part of the value of a college course results in increased earning-power on the part of the student. On this basis the college is justified in asking the student to borrow capital as an investment toward increasing his future earning-power. The topic of student loan funds as it applies to the thirty-five colleges being studied will be discussed under six headings: (1) types of loan funds classified with respect to control of principal; (2) types of loan funds classified with respect to the manner in which the principal is used; (3) the amount of loan funds in the various colleges and the number and amounts of loans made annually; (4) the Board of Education Fund; (5) administration of student loan funds; (6) conditions under which students are granted loans.

TYPES OF LOAN FUNDS CLASSIFIED WITH RESPECT TO CONTROL OF PRINCIPAL

Broadly speaking, there are two general types of loan funds. In one the principal is owned and controlled by the college itself; in the other, an outside agency provides the funds and controls the operations of the loans. Twenty-four of the thirty-five colleges studied have some loan funds which they own and control themselves.

All the colleges of this group also have available the Student Loan Fund of The Board of Education of the Methodist Episcopal Church. This Fund is available for students who belong to the Methodist Episcopal Church, and who are attending any of the colleges recognized by the University Senate of the Church.[2] Each of the institutions is allocated annually a definite amount for loans to its students. The Board of Education co-operates with the local college authorities in the administration of the loans, but from the standpoint of the control of the principal it must be classified as an outside rather than a college fund.

[1] For a further discussion of the topic of student loan funds see L. J. Chassee, *A Study of Student Loans and Their Relation to Higher Educational Finance* (New York: Harmon Foundation, 1925), p. 92, and Reeves and Russell, *College Organization and Administration* (Indianapolis: Board of Education, Disciples of Christ, 1929), pp. 280–90.

[2] The Fund is also available, under certain rules, for Methodist students attending non-Methodist colleges and universities that hold regional or national accreditation.

Various philanthropic and civic agencies provide loan service for students. Table 163 presents a tabulation of the various sources of outside student loan funds that are utilized by the thirty-five colleges studied.

The agency most frequently mentioned as supplying outside loan funds is the Knights Templar. Twenty-one of the colleges have availed themselves of the loan facilities of this organization. Seventeen colleges report that students may obtain loans from certain civic organizations such as Rotary and Kiwanis clubs, Chambers of Commerce, etc. The other types of agencies are represented in only a few of the colleges studied. This table indicates that many, in fact most, of the colleges are neglecting an

TABLE 163

SOURCES OF OUTSIDE STUDENT LOAN FUNDS UTILIZED
BY THIRTY-FIVE COLLEGES

Agency Supplying Fund	Number of Colleges Utilizing This Source of Student Loan Funds
Civic organizations (Rotary, Kiwanis, Chamber of Commerce, etc.)	17
Knights Templar	21
Eastern Star	6
Other Masonic groups	3
P.E.O. Sisterhood	4
Alumni Association	3
State Epworth League	1
Harmon Fund	2
Other foundations	4

important method of increasing the amount of financial aid they can furnish students, since a large number have failed to avail themselves of the loan facilities afforded by the various types of organizations represented in the table. It would seem advisable for the colleges to investigate somewhat more fully the possibilities of increasing their loan service to students through greater use of these outside philanthropic and civic agencies.

TYPES OF LOAN FUNDS CLASSIFIED WITH RESPECT TO THE MANNER IN WHICH THE PRINCIPAL IS USED

Two general types of loan funds are distinguished on this basis—the one known as the restricted loan fund and the other as the revolving loan fund. The restricted loan fund is one in which the principal is kept invested in income-producing securities, only the income being used for student loans. The revolving type of student loan fund is one in which the

entire capital of the fund is loaned to students. The advantages of the revolving fund over the restricted fund have been thoroughly discussed by
Mr. Chassee.[1]

Of the twenty-four colleges included in this study that have loan funds
of their own, twelve have only the revolving type of loan funds, two have
only restricted funds, while ten have one or more funds of each type. Thus
a total of twenty-two colleges have some revolving funds, while twelve
have some restricted funds. In view of the advantages of the revolving
type of fund, it is commendable that the larger number of funds is of this
type.

One of the colleges of this group is creating a fund of a slightly different
type from either of the two previously described. This institution grants
loans to students from its current funds up to and including the full
amount of tuition fee for any given year. The college has in this manner
built up a relatively large capital fund from its current income. It is
planned as collections are made to utilize this fund as a revolving type of
student loan fund. While this policy has resulted in the building-up of a
relatively large fund, it is unfortunate that the current income of the institution, urgently needed for the support of the current educational program, has been drawn upon to provide the necessary resources.

AMOUNT OF LOAN FUNDS AND LOANS MADE DURING YEAR

Table 164 shows the capital amount of the funds for student loans belonging to each of the colleges studied, and also the amount loaned during the year, the number of grants during the year, the average amount
per grant, and the average amount per student enrolled.

This table shows that eleven of the colleges have no loan funds under
their own control. In thirteen others the loan funds are less than ten
thousand dollars. Two or three of the colleges, on the other hand, have
loan funds of rather large amounts. The typical situation as indicated by
the median is for the college to have a loan fund of approximately three
thousand dollars.

The medians indicate that the colleges on the approved list of the Association of American Universities typically have much larger loan funds
than those not holding this type of accreditation. The ratio between the
median capital amounts of the funds of the two groups of colleges is approximately 20 to 1.

The amount of loans made during the year from college funds does not
correlate closely with the amount of capital funds. One of the important

[1] *Loc. cit.*

TABLE 164

AMOUNT OF STUDENT LOAN FUNDS CONTROLLED BY THIRTY-FIVE COLLEGES

Institution	Year	Amount of Capital Funds for Student Loans at Close of Fiscal Year	Amount Loaned during Year	Number of Grants	Amount per Grant	Amount of Grant per Student Enrolled
*Allegheny..............	1928–29	$96,203.63	$ 5,326.00	42	$126.81	$ 8.95
McKendree............	1929–30	50,000.00	4,668.00	31	150.58	18.52
*Lawrence..............	1928–29	40,012.26	1,911.75	19	100.62	2.45
West Virginia Wesleyan.	1929–30	26,154.50	8,902.50	36	247.29	27.56
*Cornell................	1928–29	25,000.00	....	....	......	......
*DePauw..............	1929–30	23,390.60	16,090.00	212	75.90	11.61
*Baker.................	1929–30	19,429.53	771.50	20	38.58	1.67
Southwestern..........	1929–30	17,539.20	13,959.47	67	208.35	25.61
Ozark Wesleyan........	1929–30	15,000.00	305.00	3	101.67	1.45
*Willamette............	1929–30	14,030.00	1,854.00	23	80.61	3.62
*MacMurray...........	1929–30	11,694.74	1,974.00	20	98.70	5.59
*Simpson..............	1928–29	8,221.14	1,027.75	19	54.09	1.80
*Ohio Wesleyan........	1929–30	8,199.43	16,615.25	335	49.60	9.31
*Mount Union..........	1929–30	5,734.97	1,025.00	11	93.18	2.14
*Pacific................	1929–30	4,888.34	8,338.34	47	177.41	11.44
Nebraska Wesleyan.....	1929–30	4,231.08	2,523.95	37	68.21	3.85
*Hamline..............	1928–29	3,523.15	247.00	6	41.17	0.62
Dakota Wesleyan.......	1929–30	3,073.61	2,100.00	24	87.50	6.05
Oklahoma City........	1928–29	1,781.28	1,133.20	22	51.51	1.27
Evansville............	1928–29	1,767.90	154.50	2	77.25	0.39
Intermountain........	1929–30	475.22	944.00	23	41.04	6.25
Gooding..............	1929–30	402.50	368.00	3	122.67	2.88
Kansas Wesleyan.......	1929–30	300.00	396.78	5	79.36	1.30
Puget Sound...........	1929–30	250.00	....	.....	.....	.....
*Albion................	1929–30	0.00	....	.....	.....	.....
Baldwin-Wallace.......	1929–30	0.00	....	.....	.....	.....
Brothers..............	1929–30	0.00	....	.....	.....	.....
Central Wesleyan.......	1928–29	0.00	....	.....	.....	.....
*Chattanooga...........	1928–29	0.00	....	.....	.....	.....
*Dickinson.............	1928–29	0.00	....	.....	.....	.....
*Illinois Wesleyan.......	1929–30	0.00	....	.....	.....	.....
Iowa Wesleyan.........	1928–29	0.00	....	.....	.....	.....
*Morningside...........	1928–29	0.00	....	.....	.....	.....
Ohio Northern.........	1929–30	0.00	....	.....	.....	.....
Union.................	1928–29	0.00	....	.....	.....	.....
Median, all colleges...	....	$ 3,073.61	$ 396.78	6	$ 51.51	$ 1.45
*Median, A.A.U. colleges...............	....	8,199.43	1,025.00	19	49.60	1.80
Median, non-A.A.U. colleges...........	....	438.86	336.50	3	59.86	1.29

* Institutions on the approved list of the Association of American Universities.

reasons for the lack of correlation is the presence of some relatively large funds of restricted type. Since only the income from these funds is available for student loans, the amount of loans is necessarily much smaller than in the revolving type of fund. A few institutions report a larger amount of loans than the capital of their fund. This represents a policy of making short-term loans, the funds being repaid and reloaned during the fiscal year. In two cases there is a turnover of approximately 200 per cent in the fund during the fiscal year. The medians indicate that the colleges on the approved list of the Association of American Universities loaned approximately three times as much on the average as the colleges not holding this type of accreditation.

The average amount per grant represents a variation in policies with regard to the size of loans. It will be observed that some of the colleges tend to loan students relatively small amounts while others generally make loans that approach or even exceed the entire tuition charge. It is usually considered advisable in a well-administered loan program to provide funds in ample amount to "see the student through." It is clear that several of the colleges are not now following this policy.

The amount of student loans granted per student enrolled indicates the relative adequacy of the loan service in the various colleges. The variation on this point is fairly large; clearly, a number of the colleges do not have an adequate amount of funds.

The amount of funds which an institution needs for student loans is affected by many factors. The economic level from which students come and their general social background is a very important conditioning circumstance. The types of vocations into which students go after graduation also affects the need for student loans. The sex distribution of students seems also to have some bearing upon the necessity for loans. The relative amount which is available for student aid in other forms, particularly endowed scholarships, conditions the adequacy of the loan funds. The fact that all these institutions have available also the Student Loan Fund of the Methodist Episcopal Church must be taken into account, since this Fund operates in a manner similar to the college-controlled fund. The data for Board of Education loans are not included in Table 164.

STUDENT LOAN FUND OF THE METHODIST EPISCOPAL CHURCH

The Student Loan Fund which is administered by the Board of Education has been in operation for more than half a century. The capital is being constantly augmented by the annual Children's Day collections, and by the interest earnings from the loans that are made. In administering the Fund each of the colleges is allotted at the beginning of the year a definite sum; loans are granted students up to the full amount of this sum on the recommendation of the college.

Table 165 shows for the thirty-five colleges the total amount of student loans made in each, and the total number of students aided from this fund for three years, 1928–29, 1929–30, and 1930–31.

Brothers College is the only one of the institutions studied that did not benefit from the Student Loan Fund. The reason for this situation is that Brothers College at the time of its survey had not yet been officially recognized by the University Senate; the Board of Education cannot make loans until the institution has been accredited by this agency.

The total loans from this Fund in these thirty-five colleges have been increasing over the period studied, the increase in the latest year being particularly large. The totals indicate that the average loan per student amounts to approximately one hundred dollars.

The factors entering into the allocation of loan funds to a given institution are: (1) the costs of living and tuition at the college; (2) the amount of the Children's Day collection in the churches of the territory; (3) the number of Methodist students enrolled; (4) the number of Methodist students reported as needing aid; (5) the record of repayments by former borrowers; and (6) the general record of the loan officer of the institution in making recommendations.

The Student Loan Fund of the Methodist Episcopal Church is the largest fund of this type in America. There is abundant evidence of the success with which the Fund is being managed, and of the large service that it is rendering.

ADMINISTRATION OF LOAN FUNDS

Table 166 presents data showing the number of colleges assigning responsibility for administering the student loan funds to each of various administrative officers or committees. The data of this table relate only to the college loan fund. Although there are twenty-four institutions having this type of fund, two did not furnish information regarding the method of administering the fund.

This table shows that the administration of the student loan funds is most frequently a function of a committee. Only five of the twenty-two institutions place this duty in the hands of a single executive officer. The use of a committee of administrative officers is much commoner than the use of a committee that includes some faculty members in its membership. When the personnel of these committees is analyzed, it will be ob-

TABLE 165

LOANS FROM THE STUDENT LOAN FUND OF THE METHODIST EPISCOPAL
CHURCH AT THIRTY-FIVE COLLEGES

Institution	1928–29		1929–30		1930–31	
	Total Amount Loaned	Number of Students Aided	Total Amount Loaned	Number of Students Aided	Total Amount Loaned	Number of Students Aided
*Albion................	$ 7,115	68	$ 7,050	56	$ 8,930	76
*Allegheny.............	3,400	27	3,800	28	6,075	47
*Baker.................	6,000	86	5,920	82	7,500	90
Baldwin-Wallace.......	3,290	37	3,495	38	4,000	50
Brothers†.............	....	....	....	....	....	....
Central Wesleyan.......	2,400	18	1,800	17	400	4
*Chattanooga...........	1,625	16	2,000	13	2,250	13
*Cornell...............	7,430	71	7,500	74	8,000	82
Dakota Wesleyan.......	4,265	42	4,700	51	4,800	64
*DePauw...............	8,845	71	9,505	75	10,675	77
*Dickinson.............	8,000	55	7,830	46	8,000	57
Evansville.............	2,085	18	2,000	18	2,910	26
Gooding...............	2,350	26	2,225	24	2,250	24
*Hamline..............	5,150	35	5,500	43	6,500	54
*Illinois Wesleyan.......	4,895	46	4,805	44	4,900	49
Intermountain.........	1,615	14	1,510	14	1,815	12
Iowa Wesleyan.........	3,125	34	2,900	25	4,000	42
Kansas Wesleyan.......	3,035	31	2,950	29	3,400	35
*Lawrence.............	4,900	31	4,725	27	5,265	32
McKendree............	1,200	13	1,650	16	2,500	27
*MacMurray...........	2,450	19	2,250	16	2,775	21
*Morningside..........	8,535	85	8,500	80	8,750	88
*Mount Union..........	3,525	24	3,840	30	5,000	39
Nebraska Wesleyan......	7,900	76	8,000	93	9,000	82
Ohio Northern.........	600	6	900	7	2,255	18
*Ohio Wesleyan.........	14,980	108	13,170	97	15,095	107
Oklahoma City.........	2,015	22	2,025	23	2,505	24
Ozark Wesleyan........	1,225	12	1,500	15	1,310	18
*Pacific...............	3,375	25	3,525	27	3,500	24
Puget Sound...........	1,980	17	1,745	12	2,635	21
*Simpson...............	8,450	114	8,910	124	9,000	120
Southwestern..........	9,100	98	9,000	104	9,000	111
Union.................	50	1	300	4	980	10
West Virginia Wesleyan..	3,480	35	3,500	36	4,460	34
*Willamette.............	4,045	30	4,100	29	4,080	41
Total..............	$152,435	1,411	$153,130	1,417	$174,515	1,619

* Institutions on the approved list of the Association of American Universities.

† Brothers College had not been recognized by the University Senate at the time of the study, and hence was not eligible to participate in the Student Loan Fund.

served that the business officer of the college is the person most frequently
connected with the administration of loan funds. In four institutions this

TABLE 166

ASSIGNMENT OF RESPONSIBILITY FOR ADMINISTERING STUDENT
LOAN FUNDS IN TWENTY-TWO COLLEGES

Person or Committee Assigned Responsibility for Administering Student Loan Funds	Number of Colleges in Which This Person or Committee Is Given Final Responsibility	Number of Colleges in Which Various Officers Are Members of the Committee Which Administers Student Loans
President.....................	1	....
Business officer................	4	....
Committee of board and alumni..	1	....
Committee of administrative officers.....................	11	....
Including in its membership:		
President.....................	....	10
Business officer...............	....	9
Dean........................	....	7
Registrar....................	....	3
Member of the board........	....	1
Dean of women.............	....	1
Alumni secretary...........	....	1
Personnel officer...........	....	1
Student secretary..........	....	1
Committee of the faculty........	5	....
Including in its membership in addition to faculty members the following administrative officers:		
President.....................	....	2
Business officer...............	....	2
Dean........................	....	2
Dean of men................	....	2
Dean of women.............	....	2
Registrar....................	....	1
Y.M.C.A. secretary.........	....	1
Y.W.C.A. secretary.........	....	1
Alumni secretary...........	....	1

officer is given sole responsibility for administering the fund, in nine he
is a member of the administrative officers' committee, and in two he is a
member of the faculty committee on student loans. Thus in a total of
fifteen of the twenty-two colleges the business manager is connected with
the administration of student loans. The president is given final respon-

sibility for this matter in one college, is a member of the administrative committee handling loans in ten cases, and is a member of the faculty committee in two cases. Thus in a total of thirteen out of the twenty-two colleges the president is concerned rather intimately with the granting of student loans. The dean does not appear as an officer granted final responsibility for student loans, but in nine of the colleges he is a member of the committee handling this matter. The other administrative officers appear much less frequently as members of the student loan committee.

One case deserves special comment. In this institution the student loan fund is administered as a separate fund, the governing board consisting of selected members of the board of trustees, representatives of the alumni, and other friends of the college. Perhaps this fund should be considered as an "outside" fund although the loans are available only to the students of this institution and the fund itself bears the name of the college. The explanation of this peculiar arrangement is that the fund was originally established as a device for aiding athletes. The arrangement was called into question by the standardizing associations, and the college has now agreed that athletes will not be favored above other students in the granting of aid from this fund. Nevertheless, the original arrangement for administering the fund is still continued. It would seem advisable, as long as this is considered as a college fund, to place a somewhat more direct control of its administration in the hands of the responsible executive officers and faculty of the college.

CONDITIONS UNDER WHICH LOANS ARE GRANTED

All the colleges quite naturally consider the general character and reputation of the student as an important factor in deciding eligibility for a loan. Inquiry was made in all the colleges having their own loan funds regarding other factors which were considered in determining whether or not a student should be granted a loan. Table 167 presents a tabulation of the various requirements, showing the number of colleges indicating each.

In all but four colleges of the group the grades made by the student are considered in determining the eligibility of students for loans. In nine cases the student must be earning high grades; in four cases he must be making at least the minimum for graduation; and in six colleges the only requirement is that he be making passing grades. Six colleges require a student to be doing part-time work for self-support in order to be eligible for loans. In two of these cases a definite ratio has been established between the amount a student may borrow and his earnings. Nine of the colleges indicate that they consider the future potential earning-power of the student before granting a loan. One college insists that the student keep a personal financial account as a condition for receiving a loan. Another college makes athletic ability the paramount consideration for the granting of a loan.

TABLE 167

CONDITIONS UNDER WHICH STUDENTS ARE GRANTED LOANS
IN TWENTY-THREE COLLEGES HAVING STUDENT LOAN
FUNDS UNDER COLLEGE CONTROL

Requirements for Eligibility for a Student Loan	Number of Colleges Having Each Requirement
Maintenance of high grades	9
Maintenance of grades at least at the minimum for graduation	4
Maintenance of passing grades	6
Grades not considered in granting loans	4
Keeping of a personal financial account by the student	1
Part-time work by student for self-support	6
Definite ratio between amount a student can borrow and amount he earns	2
Future potential earning-power	9
Athletic ability	1

RELATIVE MERITS OF LOANS AND SCHOLARSHIPS
AS FORMS OF STUDENT AID

The questions as to whether the aid should be given as a scholarship or as a loan demands some attention. The decision on this point involves a fundamental analysis of the value of an education. If an institution regards the education it is giving the young people of the generation as a contribution to society, with society later to reap the rewards of the education, the natural suggestion is a scholarship for the needy student. On the other hand, if the education is viewed as an individualistic matter, of worth primarily to the individual in enabling him to earn more money and to enjoy more of the comforts of life, it is only fair to ask the individual to pay for the cost of his education; and aid to needy students naturally takes the form of a loan. Perhaps no institution follows either of these philosophies in the extreme form; but as varying emphasis is placed upon the social and the individualistic aims of higher education, just so must the emphasis be shifted between scholarships and loan funds as a method of aiding students.

It is believed that most institutions will find a place for both scholarships and loan funds. The degree to which each will be employed will vary with the aims and purposes of the institution, the type of training it gives, and the general status of its student body. Differentiation as to which students should receive each form of aid may be made along several lines. For example, students preparing for a type of life-work the advantages of which accrue mainly to society as a whole rather than to the individual, for work which is socially important yet rewarded by a relatively low salary, or for work in fields where the demand for workers exceeds the supply might well be given scholarships. On the other hand, students preparing for work which is not socially important, for work the rewards of which come to the individual in terms of high salary, or for work in fields where the supply of workers exceeds the demand should be financed by loans. A student who gives no promise of better-than-average ability should not be financed by scholarships, since his potential contribution to society is limited by his ability. On the other hand, such a student may be entirely eligible for aid in the form of a loan, provided only his ability is high enough to give some assurance that he will be able to profit by the education for which he is being financed.

Student aid, in the form of either scholarships or loan funds, is an object that has a peculiar appeal to donors. It should be possible for most of these colleges to increase materially their funds for this purpose. Considering all the circumstances, it seems probable that loan funds will be easier to obtain and will probably render a greater total educational service than scholarship funds. Most of the colleges should therefore give the principal emphasis in their student-aid program to the provision of a larger amount of loan funds.

CHAPTER LXX

STUDENT EMPLOYMENT

Although in theory the employment of students differs materially from the other forms of aid, in practice the prospect of obtaining remunerative work frequently makes it possible for a student of limited means to attempt the financing of a college year in much the same way as a scholarship or a loan. Some students, choosing to be independent of the "charity" involved in receiving a scholarship, and not wishing to undertake the obligation of repaying a loan, actually prefer remunerative employment as a means of assistance.

From the educational standpoint question has been raised as to the wisdom of allowing students to devote their energies to non-educative work at a time in life when they should be giving full time to their studies. The actual effect of part-time employment on the scholarship of students is somewhat difficult to ascertain. Although some of the very best students frequently are those engaging in outside remunerative work, it must also be recognized that these students are more actively motivated than the average. Furthermore, although a student may make a good scholastic record while earning his way through college, the question can never be settled as to what sort of a record the student would have made had he been relieved of the necessity of working. Finally, employment frequently reduces the opportunities for the most educative types of social experience, a vital part of the whole educational procedure.

Colleges located in small communities, where there is little opportunity for outside employment, frequently find it difficult to provide enough work to supply the demands of students for this type of assistance. It seems that in some instances jobs are created not so much because of need for the service as to provide students with remunerative work. In several colleges that make extensive use of student services the work could undoubtedly be done more efficiently and at lower cost by the employment of full-time persons who are not students.

In some colleges student employment is used as a recruiting device. One of the smaller institutions included in this study advertises that it will furnish sufficient employment to provide half the charges for board and room to any student who wishes to avail himself or herself of this opportunity. The officers of the college who are charged with the supervision of this student labor state that they frequently find difficulty in arranging sufficient work to keep all their employees busy.

As a rule no cash expenditure is involved in the employment of students, since there are nearly always offsetting charges for tuition, board, and room. A few of the colleges studied do not even make an accounting for the student labor used in the supplementary business enterprises, particularly the dormitories and dining-halls, where the students receive payment only in service. Failure to account for the cost of student labor makes impossible a careful analysis of the operations of these enterprises.

Table 168 presents data regarding the employment of students in thirty-five colleges.

This table shows considerable variation among the colleges in the amount expended for student employment. The institutions on the approved list of the Association of American Universities have, on the average, almost twice the expenditure for this purpose that is found in the colleges lacking national accreditation. The average amount earned per case of employment also varies widely. The colleges on the approved list of the Association of American Universities tend to distribute their employment somewhat more widely than the other colleges, the median amount per case of employment being 25 per cent higher in the latter group than in the former.

The column showing the average amount of student employment per student enrolled indicates the relative extensiveness of the program of aiding students by this method. Two colleges, both of which have small enrolments, are far above all the others on this point. The range between the two extremes is at the ratio of approximately 25 to 1. The medians indicate that the colleges lacking national accreditation generally have a more extensive system of student employment than those on the approved list of the Association of American Universities.

Figure 50 presents data showing the relationship between the size of the enrolment and the amount of student employment in the colleges of this group.

This figure shows the rather interesting fact that exactly the opposite relationship exists in the two groups of colleges between the size of the enrolment and the amount of student employment per student enrolled. In the colleges on the approved list of the Association of American Universities the larger institutions tend to have larger amounts of student employment per student than the smaller ones have, although the differences are not particularly marked. In the colleges not on the approved list the institutions with small enrolments tend to have much larger amounts of student employment per student than the colleges with large enrolments.

TABLE 168

EMPLOYMENT OF STUDENTS BY THIRTY-FIVE COLLEGES

Institution	Total Amount Expended for Student Employment	Number of Cases	Average Amount per Case of Employment	Average Amount per Student Enrolled
Brothers.....................	$ 2,516.86	19	$132.47	$81.19
Gooding.....................	9,064.10	77	117.72	70.81
*Pacific.....................	25,576.68	130	196.74	35.08
Southwestern................	17,940.12	357	50.25	32.92
McKendree.................	8,048.00	52	154.77	31.94
*Baker......................	14,187.10	80	177.34	30.78
West Virginia Wesleyan.......	9,330.00	56	166.61	28.89
Ozark Wesleyan.............	6,007.80	40	150.20	28.62
*Cornell.....................	13,699.61	160	85.62	27.56
Intermountain..............	3,878.18	27	143.63	25.68
Dakota Wesleyan............	8,681.60	41	211.75	25.02
*Hamline....................	9,665.87	72	134.25	24.41
Nebraska Wesleyan..........	14,714.00	165	89.18	22.46
*Allegheny...................	13,248.85	139	95.32	22.27
Baldwin-Wallace.............	8,997.33	71	126.72	20.45
*Mount Union................	9,242.08	91	101.56	19.25
*Albion.....................	12,463.70	125	99.71	16.57
Kansas Wesleyan............	4,953.79	88	56.29	16.19
*Lawrence...................	11,330.00	115	98.52	14.51
*Illinois Wesleyan............	8,086.21	35	231.03	14.36
Union......................	3,250.00	31	104.84	14.32
*Simpson....................	7,722.82	58	133.15	13.53
Iowa Wesleyan..............	4,345.00	37	117.43	13.33
Central Wesleyan............	2,509.40	21	119.50	13.14
*Ohio Wesleyan..............	23,198.73	393	59.03	13.00
*MacMurray.................	4,361.75	64	68.15	12.36
*Morningside................	6,990.00	41	170.49	10.07
Evansville..................	3,746.92	21	178.42	9.44
*Dickinson..................	4,959.75	67	74.03	9.10
*DePauw..................	11,866.87	121	98.07	8.57
*Chattanooga................	2,707.00	45	60.16	7.10
Oklahoma City.............	6,285.00	33	190.45	7.05
*Willamette.................	3,515.10	19	185.01	6.87
Puget Sound................	2,253.00	60	37.55	3.66
Ohio Northern..............	3,032.66	39	77.76	3.38
Median, all colleges........	$ 8,048.00	60	$117.72	$16.19
*Median, A.A.U. colleges....	9,665.87	80	99.71	14.36
Median, non-A.A.U. colleges	5,480.80	41	123.11	21.46

* Institutions on the approved list of the Association of American Universities.

There are three principal types of work in which students are engaged: (1) dormitory and dining-hall; (2) campus and janitorial; and (3) laboratory, library, and departmental assistance. It will be observed that only the last-mentioned type has any important educative possibilities; the

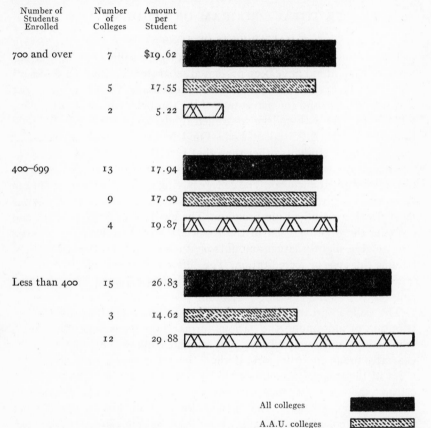

Number of Students Enrolled	Number of Colleges	Amount per Student
700 and over	7	$19.62
	5	17.55
	2	5.22
400–699	13	17.94
	9	17.09
	4	19.87
Less than 400	15	26.83
	3	14.62
	12	29.88

All colleges
A.A.U. colleges
Non-A.A.U. colleges

FIG. 50.—Amounts of student employment per student enrolled in colleges of various sizes and types of accreditation.

remainder of the work, which in most colleges includes the great majority of students who are given employment, is of relatively low grade, either entirely unskilled or semiskilled. A few of the colleges employ student help in the bookstore, and in some cases student assistants are employed in the administrative offices. The use of students for office-work may be seriously questioned, however, because of the confidential nature of the data that these helpers must handle.

CHAPTER LXXI

THE TOTAL PROGRAM OF STUDENT AID

TOTAL AMOUNTS OF STUDENT AID

In preceding chapters the amounts spent by the colleges for the various forms of student aid have been presented separately. Table 169 shows for each of thirty-five colleges the total amount of student aid in all forms per student enrolled, and the percentage of the total given in each form. This table deals only with college-controlled funds, and does not include aid from the Methodist Student Loan Fund or other outside agencies, or employment of students other than that furnished by the college.

This table shows a wide range among the colleges in the total amount of aid per student enrolled. The college having the most extensive system of student aid gives more than ten times as much as the college having the most restricted student-aid program. The medians indicate that the colleges on the approved list of the Association of American Universities tend to give slightly larger amounts of student aid than the colleges not holding this type of accreditation. The difference between the two groups, however, is not large considering the wide range among the individual colleges.

The table indicates also that there is no common pattern for the distribution of aid among the various forms. Two types of student aid—scholarships and remitted fees, and student employment—stand out as generally much more important than the other types, from the standpoint of the relative amounts of aid given in each form. Many of the colleges, however, do not distribute their aid in the manner indicated by the general average. The medians indicate an important difference between the colleges on the approved list of the Association of American Universities and those not holding this type of accreditation with regard to the distribution of student aid. The nationally accredited colleges tend to give a much larger proportion of their aid in the form of scholarships and remitted fees, and a much smaller proportion in the form of employment than is the case with the other group of colleges. The nationally accredited colleges also tend to have slightly larger percentages of aid in the form of loan funds and uncollected fees, but the differences on these items are not large enough to be statistically significant.

Some comment should be made regarding the relatively insignificant

668

TABLE 169

AMOUNT OF TOTAL STUDENT AID FROM COLLEGE SOURCES PER STUDENT ENROLLED,
AND PERCENTAGE OF TOTAL AID GIVEN IN EACH FORM,
FOR THIRTY-FIVE COLLEGES

INSTITUTION	TOTAL AMOUNT OF STUDENT AID PER STUDENT ENROLLED	PERCENTAGE OF TOTAL GIVEN IN EACH FORM			
		Scholarships and Remitted Fees	Student Employment	Loans from College Loan Funds	Uncollected Tuition Fees
*MacMurray............	$119.53	76.8	10.3	4.7	8.2
*DePauw..............	101.57	80.1	8.4	11.5	....
Brothers.............	91.10	12.9	44.6	42.5	....
Gooding.............	91.08	18.1	73.6	3.0	5.3
*Cornell..............	82.24	31.8	33.5	....	34.7
*Hamline.............	75.07	43.2	32.5	0.8	23.5
Southwestern.........	65.49	7.9	50.3	39.1	2.7
West Virginia Wesleyan.	64.80	12.9	44.6	42.5	....
McKendree...........	61.92	18.5	51.6	29.9	....
*Pacific..............	60.34	17.5	58.1	19.0	5.4
Ozark Wesleyan........	57.98	40.6	49.3	2.5	7.6
*Allegheny............	56.79	43.7	39.2	15.8	1.3
Intermountain........	53.44	39.7	47.4	11.5	1.4
*Illinois Wesleyan.......	53.33	67.0	26.9	....	6.1
*Baker................	50.47	20.3	61.0	3.3	15.4
*Simpson.............	48.68	58.6	26.8	3.6	11.0
Dakota Wesleyan......	48.19	25.7	51.9	12.6	9.8
Nebraska Wesleyan....	45.48	41.5	48.6	8.3	1.6
*Ohio Wesleyan.........	42.91	47.8	30.2	21.7	0.3
Central Wesleyan......	41.30	68.2	31.8	....	....
*Mount Union..........	40.54	47.2	47.5	5.3	....
*Dickinson.............	39.29	64.4	23.2	....	12.4
Iowa Wesleyan........	37.93	63.2	35.1	....	1.7
Union................	34.48	13.6	41.5	....	44.9
Baldwin-Wallace.......	32.88	36.6	60.3	....	3.1
Kansas Wesleyan......	32.35	25.4	27.6	2.2	44.8
*Morningside...........	31.27	58.4	....	....	41.6
*Albion...............	25.86	35.9	64.1	....	....
*Lawrence.............	24.56	30.9	59.1	10.0	....
*Willamette............	20.57	38.4	33.4	17.6	10.6
Evansville............	19.88	25.2	47.5	2.0	25.3
Oklahoma City........	18.71	54.2	37.7	6.8	1.3
*Chattanooga...........	15.37	82.8	17.2	....	....
Ohio Northern........	15.29	77.9	22.1	....	....
Puget Sound..........	11.11	51.1	32.9	....	16.0
Median, all colleges..	$ 45.48	40.6	39.2	3.3	3.1
*Median, A.A.U. colleges..............	48.68	47.2	32.5	3.6	6.1
Median, non-A.A.U. colleges..........	43.39	31.2	46.0	2.8	2.2

* Institutions on the approved list of the Association of American Universities.

part played by student loans in the program of aid in these colleges. The data of the table probably are somewhat misleading on this point, since the loans from the Student Loan Fund of the Board of Education are not included. The fact that a considerable number of the colleges have no loan funds of their own also tends to reduce the average amount of aid from this source. The table indicates, however, that in several of the colleges a considerable proportion of the aid is given in the form of student loans. The colleges studied could well afford to devote some attention to the building-up of more satisfactory resources for student loan funds, thus permitting a smaller amount of the financial assistance to be given in the form of remitted fees and uncollected tuitions. Some of the colleges have found that it is relatively easy to raise funds for student loans, this being an object that has a peculiar appeal to interested donors.

PERCENTAGE OF STUDENTS AIDED

Table 170 presents data showing for thirty-two colleges the relative extensiveness of the program of student aid in terms of the percentage which the total number of cases of aid is of the total student enrolment.

The first column of this table indicates the total number of cases of aid, obtained by adding together the number of students receiving aid in each of the four forms shown in Table 169. Since in most institutions there are many students who receive aid from more than one source, e.g., a loan and student employment or a scholarship and a loan, the table does not indicate the actual number of different individuals receiving aid. In a few of the colleges studied a check was made of the number of students receiving aid in any form in an endeavor to ascertain the amount of duplication involved. It appears from this check that approximately 20 per cent of those aided typically receive aid in more than one form. The amount of labor necessary to eliminate this duplication made it inadvisable to carry the technique farther.

Because of the duplication involved, care must be taken in interpreting the second column of Table 170. The table indicates in a rough way the relative extensiveness of the system of student aid in the various colleges, although the actual percentages shown should probably be scaled down approximately one-fifth in order to indicate more accurately the true percentage of the students being aided.

NEED FOR STUDENT AID

The need for an extensive program of student aid is conditioned by several factors. The economic level from which the students are drawn

TABLE 170

TOTAL NUMBER OF CASES OF STUDENT AID FROM ALL COLLEGE
SOURCES,† AND PERCENTAGE THAT CASES OF AID ARE OF
TOTAL STUDENT ENROLMENT, FOR THIRTY-TWO COLLEGES

Institution‡	Total Number of Cases of Student Aid	Percentage That Number of Cases of Student Aid Is of Total Enrolment
Gooding...................	132	103.1
Kansas Wesleyan............	311	101.6
*Cornell...................	464	93.4
Intermountain..............	131	86.8
*DePauw...................	938	77.3
*MacMurray................	272	77.1
Brothers...................	23	74.2
*Ohio Wesleyan.............	1,275	71.4
Southwestern...............	372	68.3
Nebraska Wesleyan..........	440	67.2
Ozark Wesleyan.............	123	61.8
*Hamline..................	227	57.3
*Illinois Wesleyan...........	319	56.7
Iowa Wesleyan..............	180	55.2
*Simpson...................	357	54.8
McKendree.................	134	53.2
*Baker.....................	223	48.4
Central Wesleyan............	91	47.6
*Dickinson.................	256	47.0
Baldwin-Wallace.............	184	41.8
West Virginia Wesleyan......	130	40.2
Dakota Wesleyan............	138	39.8
*Albion....................	226	30.1
*Morningside...............	191	27.5
*Lawrence..................	203	26.0
*Pacific....................	186	25.5
*Willamette................	125	24.4
Puget Sound...............	150	24.4
Union.....................	46	20.3
Oklahoma City.............	175	19.6
Ohio Northern.............	156	17.4
Evansville.................	68	17.1
Median, all colleges.......	185	50.8
*Median, A.A.U. colleges...	242	51.6
Median, non-A.A.U. colleges.................	136	50.4

* Institutions on the approved list of the Association of American Universities.
† Does not include loans from the Methodist Board of Education.
‡ Colleges omitted are *Chattanooga, *Allegheny, and *Mount Union.

has a very important bearing. The cost of tuition and board and room is also important. The table indicates that the type of accreditation held does not influence the extensiveness of the program of student aid, the medians being very nearly the same for the two groups classified upon the basis of membership or non-membership in the Association of American Universities. In some of the colleges it appears that the amount of competition influences markedly the amount of aid given. In these colleges the program of student aid doubtless serves, to some extent, as a recruiting device. Colleges facing competition from neighboring state-supported institutions usually rank high in the extensiveness of their student-aid program. The reason for this is obvious. There does not seem to be any relation between the size of the supporting constituency and the amount of aid given students.

TABLE 171

AVERAGE AMOUNT OF FINANCIAL ASSISTANCE TO STUDENTS PER STUDENT ENROLLED, AND AVERAGE PERCENTAGE WHICH NUMBER OF CASES OF AID IS OF NUMBER OF STUDENTS ENROLLED, FOR COLLEGES GROUPED ACCORDING TO THE POPULATION OF THE COUNTY IN WHICH LOCATED

POPULATION OF COUNTY	FINANCIAL ASSISTANCE PER STUDENT ENROLLED		PERCENTAGE OF CASES OF AID	
	Number of Colleges	Average Amount	Number of Colleges*	Average Percentage
Over 100,000.............	12	$41.97	10	40.8
40,000–100,000...........	9	47.23	8	50.8
Less than 40,000.........	14	55.87	14	60.1

* No data from three colleges.

One of the important factors affecting the extensiveness of the student-aid program is the size of the community in which the college is located. Table 171 presents data showing the relation between the size of the population of the county in which the college is located and the amount of student aid; the latter factor is shown both as an average amount per student enrolled and also as the average percentage which the number of cases of aid is of the number of students enrolled.

This table shows a general tendency for the colleges located in the larger communities to have less extensive programs of student aid than those located in communities of smaller population. The fact that a larger number of the students of colleges located in fair-sized cities can live at home while attending the institution doubtless is an important determinant of the need for financial assistance. There is usually greater opportunity for self-help in the form of outside employment in the larger communities than in the smaller ones.

PART VI
THE FUTURE OF THE COLLEGE

CHAPTER LXXII

THE FUTURE OF THE COLLEGE

The demise of the college of liberal arts has frequently been prophesied. As long ago as 1902, President Nicholas Murray Butler of Columbia University expressed the opinion that numerous factors then operating would result in the college ceasing to exist unless it abandoned the four-year program. In 1903 President David Starr Jordan of Stanford University asserted that the college would eventually disappear in effect, if not in name, the best colleges becoming universities and the others returning to their place as academies. Almost a generation has passed since these prophecies were made, but the college of liberal arts remains a vigorous and vital part of the American system of higher education. It appears, therefore, that prophecies regarding the future of such institutions are hazardous, and should be made cautiously, if at all.

The present study has analyzed in detail a mass of data relating to thirty-five typical American colleges of liberal arts. From the information presented in preceding parts of this volume it is readily apparent that the future of the college will be affected by a number of factors now at work. It is the purpose of this concluding chapter to review briefly a few of these factors and to discuss their implications for the future of the college.

Most Americans are familiar with the remarkable growth in school enrolments, particularly at the secondary and higher levels, that has occurred during the twentieth century. The colleges of liberal arts have felt the full effects of this movement and have been compelled to expand their resources rapidly in order to keep pace with the demands of students. In a few institutions a limitation has been placed upon the number of students to be admitted. The expansions in college enrolments during the past six or eight years have been much less rapid, however, than was the case during the preceding decade, and a number of colleges have recently experienced decreases in enrolments. The future trend of enrolments is affected by so many factors that it is difficult to make predictions; but obviously, any considerable change in either direction in the trend of enrolments would have important implications for the service of the college. This study shows that, in general, the colleges in the most satisfactory situation are those so located as to serve a large population group and with a supporting constituency of considerable size.

A second factor affecting the future of the college is the growth of other types of institutions of higher learning. Two that are of comparatively recent development have a distinct bearing on the case—the junior college and the teachers college. Particularly as public funds are made available for the support of these newer types of institutions, the church-related college of liberal arts finds itself faced by a new competition. In a similar category may be placed the development of strong professional schools that base their entrance requirements on something less than the traditional four years of undergraduate work. It is this competition with the junior college from below, and with the graduate and professional schools from above, accompanied by a challenge from the teachers colleges now placed upon a new academic level, that has led to many of the dire prophecies regarding the ultimate extinction of the college of liberal arts. There is every evidence that these factors will have a marked effect. Some of the weaker four-year colleges will become junior colleges; others will close. The stronger ones will add a fifth year of work and offer the Master's degree in competition with the graduate schools of universities. These are not prophecies, but simply the record of that which is actually happening today.

The development of junior colleges is symptomatic of another important trend that is vitally affecting the college of liberal arts. A line of cleavage has developed between the so-called "lower" and "upper" divisions, the freshman-sophomore and the junior-senior years, which sharply bisects the program of the college. The purposes of these two levels are increasingly differentiated, the lower division being devoted to the completion of general education, the upper to specialization. The facts that specialization is identified also with the purpose of the graduate school and that general education is a function of the secondary school increase the difficulties of the four-year college of liberal arts. The reduction of the program to the junior college basis is one solution, although probably a temporary one. Another that has been proposed is the development of a new type of liberal arts institution, basing its entrance requirements upon the completion of general education, and carrying its students through a three-year program to the completion of what is now the first year of graduate study. Undoubtedly, however, many liberal arts colleges will continue to exist in the present form as long as there are students who can afford four years of general education above the secondary-school level or who desire a program that provides only a limited degree of specialization.

Coincident with the expansions in enrolment has been the development of a number of new subjects of instruction at the college level. The student group that has been brought into the college as a result of the recent expansion differs materially from that which attended college a generation or two ago. Instead of a group that is relatively homogeneous in cultural background and in vocational outlook, there is now the widest diversity; and the interests of the new group have made demands for new subjects of instruction. At the same time, the development of science and technology has opened new areas of study. The increase of leisure time has brought new demands and new opportunities for instruction in such subjects as the fine arts and music. A few colleges have tried to withstand the pressure for the introduction of these new subjects and courses into the traditional liberal arts program. In most institutions, however, there has come a broadened conception of the meaning of cultural education, and a modification of the program to meet the demands of the new students and the new subjects. It appears highly probable that this tendency will continue.

One of the most hopeful signs for the future of the liberal arts college is the vigor with which these institutions are attacking their own problems. On every hand there is discussion and inquiry concerning the functions and services of colleges; and within the circle of those most intimately concerned, the faculty and administrative officers, there is an encouraging openmindedness and general willingness, even eagerness, to study questions of this type. The fact that a comprehensive program of survey was called for and carried out among so large a group of institutions as is represented in this study is itself testimony of the growing interest in the problems of higher education.

Many factors have combined to increase the difficulty of financing the independent college of liberal arts. The increased enrolments of students have made necessary increased supporting resources. General improvements in the programs of competing institutions have forced corresponding developments in other colleges. The extensive use of public funds for the support of junior colleges, teachers colleges, and state universities have made new demands on institutions supported from philanthropic sources. The relation that generally exists between the amount of supporting resources and the educational excellence of institutions of higher learning has made it increasingly difficult for the inadequately supported institution to survive. Although the past decade was marked by unusually large increases in the endowment funds of a great many colleges, in comparatively few institutions have these increases been able to keep pace with the new demands. There has even been a tendency for the gifts from church sources for the support of the current program to decline, and the spectacular financial campaign has proved decreasingly productive of supporting resources. The American college of liberal arts faces a real problem of financing, and on the solution of this problem depends much of the future service of the institution.

The data upon which this study is based were collected before the economic depression had begun to make itself seriously felt in this group of colleges. The developments that have taken place since the survey visits emphasize strongly the acuteness of the financial problems confronting institutions of this type. In almost all colleges and universities throughout the country, public as well as private, considerable retrenchment has been necessary; and in a few cases the reductions in income have been so drastic as to constitute a grave threat to the future of the institutions. For the most part, the situation has been faced courageously by boards of trustees, administrative officers, and faculty members. The ultimate effect of the depression will depend on its duration, its intensity, and the rapidity of the recovery. A long delay of the expected return to more prosperous times would undoubtedly mean the extinction of some American colleges.

Although the economic depression is a painful experience, there is some indication that in the long run the effects on American higher education may not be wholly bad. This is a purging time, and may actually serve as a corrective to some misdirected efforts and enterprises. Under conditions of reduced income and uncertain support, it becomes increasingly important to scrutinize critically the services rendered, to eliminate waste and duplication of effort, and to weigh values. Although the process is not always pleasant, the results may actually mean an ultimate improvement in the total program of higher education.

Too often the mere continuation of the individual institution is considered more important than the kind and amount of service rendered. The great majority of those connected with a college—the constituency, students, faculty members, administrative officers, and trustees—are so immersed in the problems of the individual institution that they fail to give thought to the program of higher education as a whole. There is need for clear vision on this point, not only on the part of a few educational leaders in the country, but by the rank and file of those who serve in colleges and universities. As a result, there should be a closer co-operation among institutions and a better integration of the entire program of liberal arts education in America.

The college of liberal arts has rendered a great service to the cause of

American culture. The potential future service that may be rendered by institutions of this type is limited principally by two general factors: (1) the financial support available; (2) the flexibility with which the college is able to adapt its program to the changing conditions of a dynamic society. The latter is the more important; the evidence is that institutions which meet important social needs are usually successful in attracting supporting resources.

INDEX

INDEX

A

Ability grouping, 335–37, 362

Absence:
—from chapel, 411
—leaves of, 321–22

Academic:
—administration, 103–7
—buildings and equipment. *See* Buildings
—dean. *See* Dean
—policies, functions of faculty in, 105
—ranks of faculty. *See* Ranks of faculty members
—records, 87

Accessibility of books in departmental libraries, 160

Accession records in libraries, 168

Accessions of library books, annual, 175–77

Accounting:
—financial, 88, 92, 95, 453–60:
  for annuities, 576–77
  for cash discounts, 440
  for investments, 593, 603–10
  for losses in endowment, 565
  for pledges, 459
  for restricted endowment, 567
  for scholarships, 631
  for supplementary business activities, 507–8
—personnel, 87

Accreditation of colleges, 19–21, 227, 259, 262

Accreditation, relation to:
—ability to charge fees, 526–27
—administrative salaries, 100
—age of faculty members, 313–14
—alumni occupations, 55, 56
—amount of:
  course offerings, 194–97
  debt, 544–46
  endowment, 561–64, 632–34
  student aid, 645–48, 668–72
  student employment, 665–67
  student loan funds available, 655–57
  trust funds, 553–54
—classification of students, 46, 47

—constituent membership, 31
—costs per student, 494–97
—costs per student-credit-hour, 501–4
—distribution of offerings in various fields, 202–3
—educational expenditures, 484–86, 494–97
—educational income, 513–18
—enrolment, 38, 39
—extension work, 348–49
—faculty organization, 299–300
—faculty retirement provisions, 311–12
—faculty salaries, 285–87
—faculty service load, 279–81
—faculty tenure, 307–9
—faculty training, 315–19
—local population, 25
—method of selecting board members, 70
—non-educational expenditures, 484–87
—number of alumni in religious service, 427–29
—number of ministers on the board, 73
—occupational distribution of alumni, 57, 58, 59, 427–29
—offerings in Bible and religion, 418–24
—outside earnings of faculty, 291–92
—percentage distribution of educational expenditures, 498–99
—percentage distribution of sources of income, 522–23
—proportion of courses alternated, 204
—publications of faculty members, 322–23
—rate of increase in endowment fund, 614–15
—rate of increase in enrolment, 42
—ratio between administrative and faculty salaries, 102–3
—recency of faculty training, 320–21
—religious affiliations of students, 407–8
—requirements for classification, 50
—residence of students, 27–29
—restrictions on endowment, 565–66
—retention of students, 53–54

683

Alumni secretary, 84, 356–57:
—functions in assigning scholarships, 649–50
—functions in assigning student loans, 660–61
Amateur standards of athletics, 108
American Association of Colleges of Pharmacy, 244
American Bar Association, 244
American Library Association, subject headings, 170
Amending by-laws, 64
Analyses of investment holdings, 600
Ancient languages:
—cost per student-credit-hour, 501–2
—department of, 164
—requirement for graduate degree, 252, 270–71
Announcements in chapel services, 414
Annual Conference (see also Constituency):
—assumption of college debts by, 549
—election of trustees by, 70
—income from, 514–18, 524, 529–30
Annuities, 459, 482, 540, 542, 553–54, 569–77, 615–16:
—for faculty retirement, 309–14
Anthony, A. W., editor, Wise Public Giving Series, 574, 575, 599
Anthropology, 183, 207
Appeals from students, board committee on, 80
Application blanks for admission, 361
Applied music, credit-hours in, 221–22
Appointment bureau. See Placement service
Appreciation of fine arts 10, 14, 217, 220
Apprenticeship period for staff members, 305
Appropriations:
—by Board of Education, v, 518, 530–32
—for new books, 162
—in budget, availability of, 467
Approved list of the Association of American Universities, 20, 21. See Accreditation
Aptitude tests, 362
Architects, training of, 223
Architecture, of college buildings, 115–16, 414

Arnett, Trevor:
—College and University Finance, 445, 479, 557, 559
—Handling Endowment Funds, 599
Art:
—buildings for, 142
—curriculums in, 223–24
—degrees in, 225
—director of, 83
—fees for, 619–21
—offerings in, 194, 224–25
—survey courses in, 273
—teacher-training in, 229
—vocational interests of students in, 398
Art Education, Bachelor of Science in, 209
Articles of incorporation, 62, 63, 65
Articulation of high-school and college programs, 215, 216, 269–72
Artists, education of, 217
Assignment of administrative duties, 88–89
Assistant professors:
—number of, 297–306
—salaries of, 285–96, 301–6
—tenure of, 307–9
Assistants:
—in office of business manager, 435–36
—student, in library, 154–55
—student, selection of, 451–52
Associate professors:
—number of, 297–306
—salaries of, 285–96, 301–6
—tenure of, 307–9
Associated students, 405
Association of American Colleges, 262
Association of American Law Schools, 244
Association of American Universities, 20, 21
Association of College and University Business Officers of the Eastern States, 121–22
Association of Colleges and Secondary Schools of the Southern States, 19, 145–46
Associations, accrediting, 19–21, 87, 145–46, 173–76, 192, 227, 259, 262, 278, 282–83, 315, 530, 557, 560–61, 661
Associations, for student government, 385
Astronomy:
—course offerings in, 195, 200, 202

E